Antarctica

Jeff Rubin

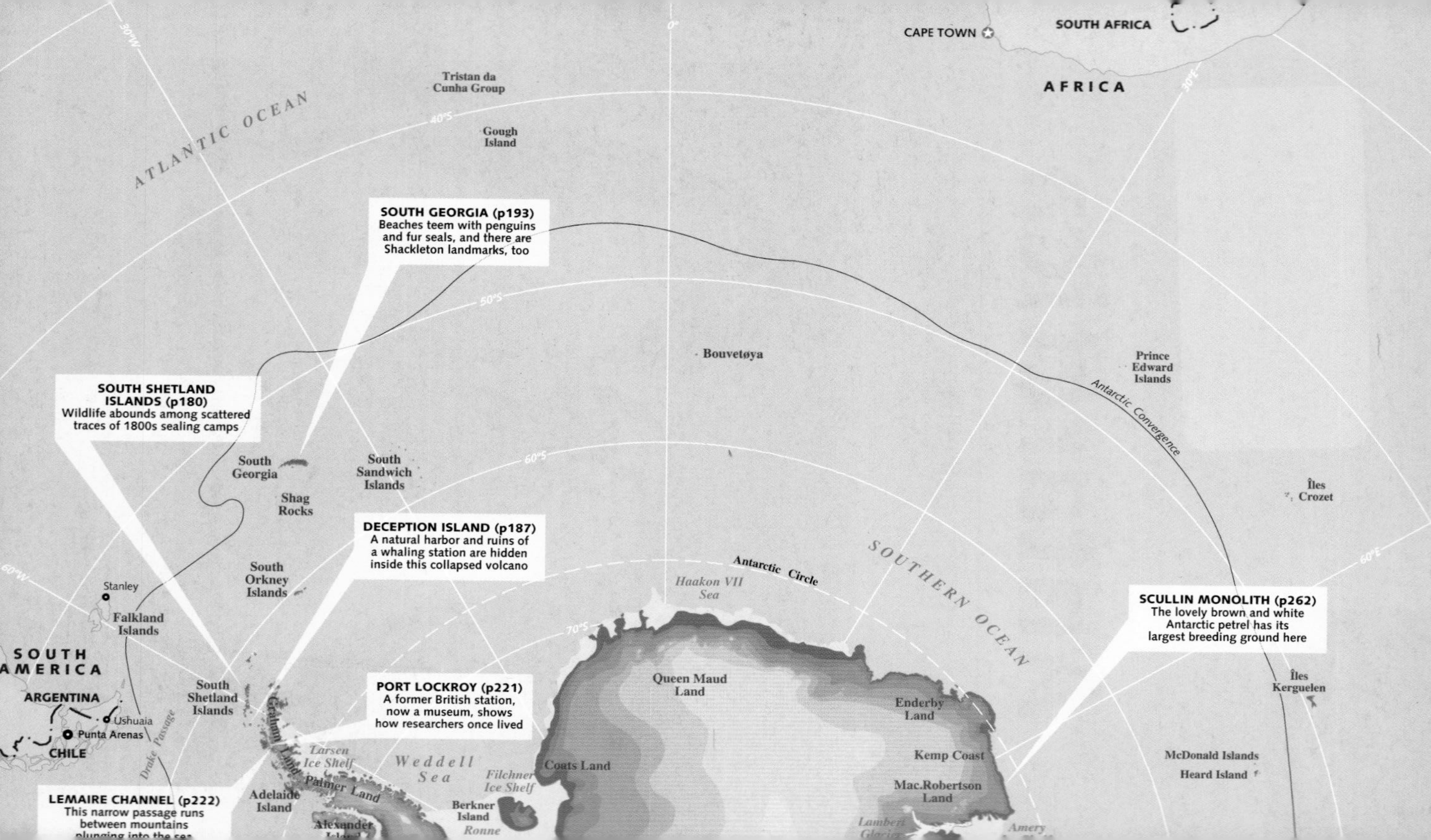
SOUTH AFRICA
CAPE TOWN
AFRICA
ATLANTIC OCEAN
Tristan da Cunha Group
Gough Island
30°W
0°
30°E
40°S
50°S
60°S
70°S
60°W
60°E
SOUTH GEORGIA (p193)
Beaches teem with penguins and fur seals, and there are Shackleton landmarks, too
SOUTH SHETLAND ISLANDS (p180)
Wildlife abounds among scattered traces of 1800s sealing camps
Bouvetøya
Prince Edward Islands
Antarctic Convergence
Îles Crozet
South Georgia
Shag Rocks
South Sandwich Islands
DECEPTION ISLAND (p187)
A natural harbor and ruins of a whaling station are hidden inside this collapsed volcano
South Orkney Islands
Stanley
Falkland Islands
SOUTH AMERICA
ARGENTINA
Ushuaia
Punta Arenas
CHILE
Drake Passage
South Shetland Islands
Antarctic Circle
Haakon VII Sea
SOUTHERN OCEAN
SCULLIN MONOLITH (p262)
The lovely brown and white Antarctic petrel has its largest breeding ground here
Îles Kerguelen
Queen Maud Land
Enderby Land
Kemp Coast
Mac.Robertson Land
McDonald Islands
Heard Island
PORT LOCKROY (p221)
A former British station, now a museum, shows how researchers once lived
Graham Land
Larsen Ice Shelf
Weddell Sea
Filchner Ice Shelf
Coats Land
Palmer Land
Adelaide Island
Berkner Island
Ronne
LEMAIRE CHANNEL (p222)
This narrow passage runs between mountains

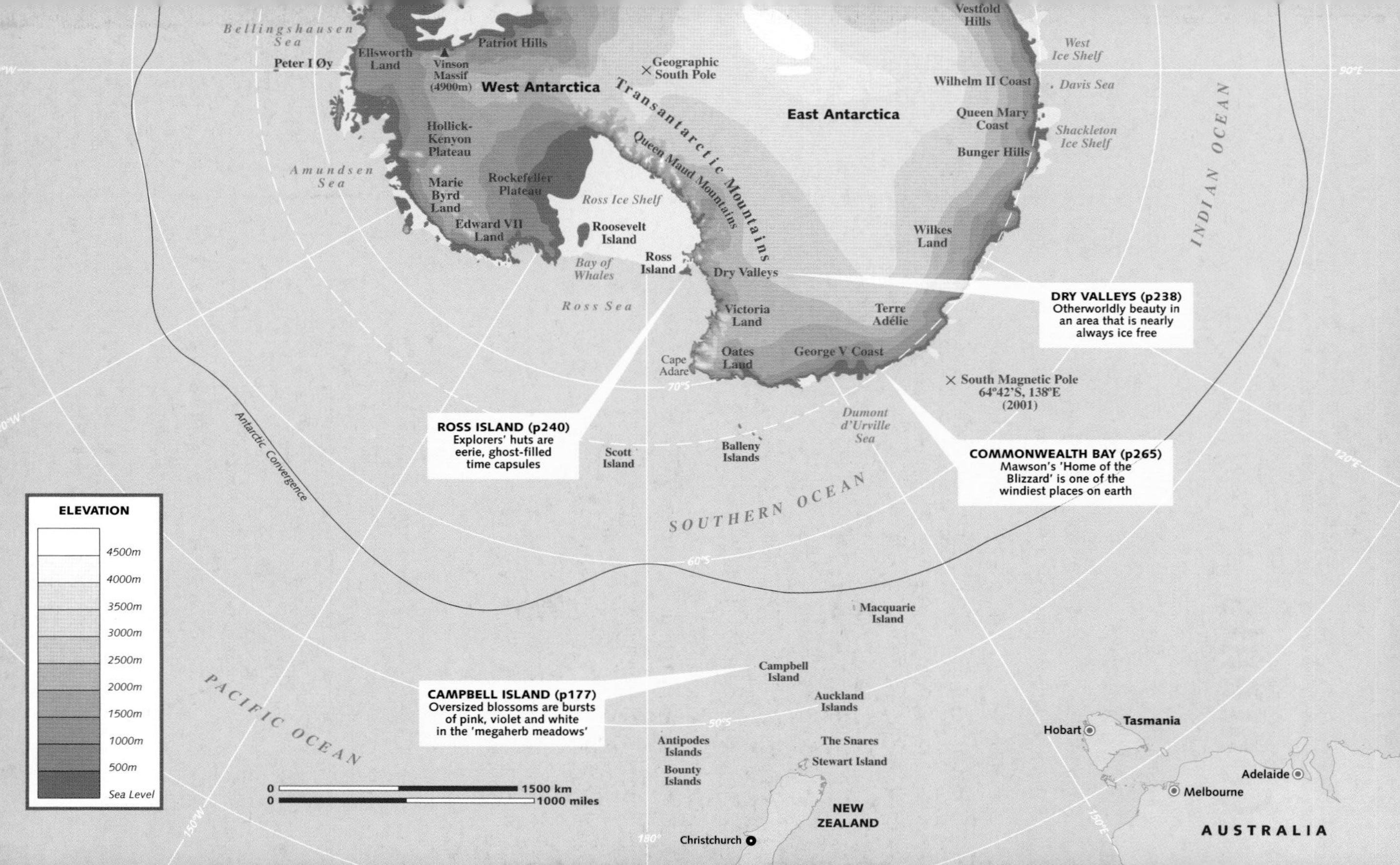

Bellingshausen Sea
Peter I Øy
Ellsworth Land
Vinson Massif (4900m)
Patriot Hills
West Antarctica
Geographic South Pole
Transantarctic Mountains
East Antarctica
Vestfold Hills
West Ice Shelf
Wilhelm II Coast
Davis Sea
Queen Mary Coast
Shackleton Ice Shelf
Bunger Hills
INDIAN OCEAN
Hollick-Kenyon Plateau
Amundsen Sea
Marie Byrd Land
Rockefeller Plateau
Edward VII Land
Queen Maud Mountains
Ross Ice Shelf
Roosevelt Island
Ross Island
Bay of Whales
Ross Sea
Dry Valleys
Wilkes Land
DRY VALLEYS (p238)
Otherworldly beauty in an area that is nearly always ice free
Victoria Land
Terre Adélie
Oates Land
George V Coast
Cape Adare
70°S
South Magnetic Pole 64°42'S, 138°E (2001)
ROSS ISLAND (p240)
Explorers' huts are eerie, ghost-filled time capsules
Antarctic Convergence
Scott Island
Balleny Islands
Dumont d'Urville Sea
COMMONWEALTH BAY (p265)
Mawson's 'Home of the Blizzard' is one of the windiest places on earth
SOUTHERN OCEAN
60°S
90°W
90°E
120°W
120°E
ELEVATION
4500m
4000m
3500m
3000m
2500m
2000m
1500m
1000m
500m
Sea Level
Macquarie Island
Campbell Island
CAMPBELL ISLAND (p177)
Oversized blossoms are bursts of pink, violet and white in the 'megaherb meadows'
Auckland Islands
50°S
PACIFIC OCEAN
Antipodes Islands
The Snares
Stewart Island
Bounty Islands
Hobart
Tasmania
Adelaide
Melbourne
0 1500 km
0 1000 miles
NEW ZEALAND
150°W
180°
Christchurch
150°E
AUSTRALIA

Contents

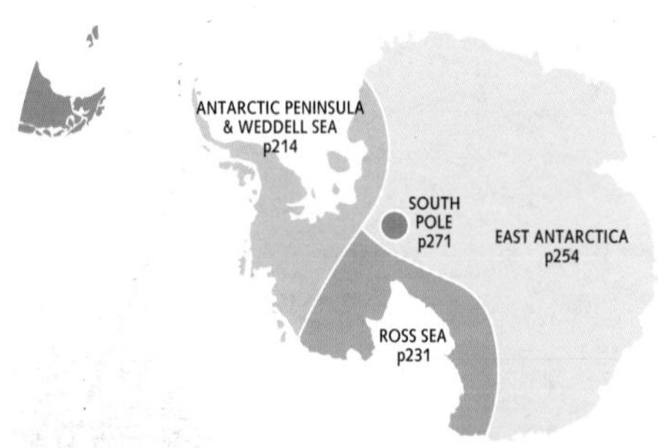

Lonely Planet books provide independent advice. Lonely Planet does not accept advertising in guidebooks, nor do we accept payment in exchange for listing or endorsing any place or business. Lonely Planet writers do not accept discounts or payments in exchange for positive coverage of any sort.

Destination Antarctica

Antarctica is one of the most beautiful places on earth – a spectacular wilderness of snow, ice and rock, teeming with wildlife. Its gigantic icebergs and ice shelves are found nowhere else; its vast mountain ranges and the enormous emptiness of the polar plateau boggle the mind. Nearly everyone who visits Antarctica says that their expectations were not only met, but greatly exceeded. Traveling to Antarctica is like visiting no other country. Indeed, many people in Antarctica commonly talk about 'when I return to the world.'

No one owns Antarctica. It's too big and too important to belong to any single nation. The international treaty governing Antarctica works so well not just because it has been carefully crafted by consensus, but also because Antarctica's real value lies not in the riches that can be extracted from it. Instead, the continent's true wealth, the world agrees, lies in the continuation of its unique status as a peaceful, free and unmilitarized land of international cooperation, scientific research and unsullied beauty.

The earth's most isolated continent, Antarctica must be earned, through either a long, often uncomfortable voyage or an expensive flight. Weather and ice – not clocks or calendars – set the schedule, and Antarctic tour companies emphasize that itineraries are always subject to the continent's changing moods.

Tourism has become Antarctica's growth industry – not mining or oil drilling, as many people once feared. Provided visits are properly managed, tourists may turn out to be one of the best assurances that this wilderness can remain (nearly) as pure as the driven snow. Let us hope!

GRANT DIXON

Wildlife

Antarctic's stark beauty and abundant wildlife is the highlight of a voyage to the continent. The vast numbers of penguins, seals and seabirds – nearly all unafraid of humans – are unmatched anywhere else in the world.

You'll never forget your first close sighting of **whales** (p105), while the flight of the endangered **wandering albatross** (p115) appears almost effortless and makes for fascinating viewing.

DAVID TIPLING

Marvel at lovely white snow petrels (p120), true creatures of the ice

Observe the massive southern elephant seal (p109): once hunted for its blubber, it now dozes peacefully in smelly wallows

KERRY LORIMER

Be patient – penguins (p110) abound in the Antarctic, and if you're very quiet and still, they may even approach you

JULIET COOMBE

Natural Wonders

Nearly all of Antarctica is a wilderness unsullied by humans, but there are some extra-special places of exceptional beauty.

The **Ross Ice Shelf** (p252) glistens in the summer sun like bright-white Carrara marble, while the otherworldly beauty and sculpted ventifacts of the **Dry Valleys** (p238) are unlike any elsewhere on earth. The **Arched Rock** (p163) at Îles Kerguelen was a landmark for centuries before its collapse.

JULIET COOMBE

Squeeze through the Lemaire Channel (p222) in your ship as spectacular reflected mountains surround you

Cruise among the icebergs of Paradise Harbor (p223), one of the Antarctic's most visited and wondrous areas

RALPH LEE HOPKINS

Enter the hidden natural harbor of Deception Island (p187) through the sea-breached wall of a volcanic crater

RALPH LEE HOPKINS

HIGHLIGHTS The Human Presence

People have made relatively little impact on Antarctica so far, but there's plenty of interest for fans of polar history and those who find cutting-edge scientific research fascinating.

Marvel at Australia's **Mawson station's wind turbines** (p261), which are both innovative and environmentally responsible. The United States' new **Amundsen-Scott South Pole station** (p278), built on jackable stilts, is Antarctica's most modern. Wander through an Antarctic 'ghost town' at one of East Antarctica's abandoned Russian bases, **Molodezhnaya** (p261) or **Leningradskaya** (p257).

KERRY LORIMER

Visit Mawson's huts (p266) at the 'Home of the Blizzard' on Commonwealth Bay; these huts endure some of the strongest winds on earth

Climb Observation Hill (p247), pausing at the cross raised to Scott and his men

SCOTT DARSNEY

Inspect the ghost-filled time capsules that are the historic huts (p233) of the Ross Sea region

SCOTT DARSNEY

Getting Started

Unless you're planning your own expedition, you'll visit Antarctica as part of a group tour, most likely on a ship. This has the advantage of combining your transportation, meals and accommodations all in the one vessel. It also means that no infrastructure has to be built ashore in Antarctica's delicate environment.

Antarctica is not as cold as you might imagine, at least not in the summer, which is the only time tourists visit. As they say, there's no bad weather, only inappropriate clothing.

WHEN TO GO

Tourists do not visit Antarctica during winter, when the pack ice extends its frozen mantle for 1000km around most of the continent. In any case, few people would pay thousands of dollars to experience the Antarctic winter's near round-the-clock darkness and extreme cold – the thermometer can plummet to -50°C. At that temperature, boiling water thrown into the air freezes instantly – and noisily – into a cloud of snow.

See Climate (p285) for more information.

The Antarctic tour season is short – about four months, with each offering its own highlights. November is early summer: the spring pack ice is breaking up, and birds – especially penguins – are courting and mating. December and January, when penguins are hatching eggs and feeding chicks, are the height of the austral summer, bringing warmer temperatures and up to 20 hours of sunlight every day. In the late summer month of February, whale-watching is best, penguin chicks are beginning to fledge and adult penguins are ashore molting.

There are other factors to consider in deciding when to travel: cruises later in the season may be less crowded, so you may not spend as much time waiting around for Zodiacs (motorized dinghies) and station tours. However, the longer you wait to go, the greater the risk that much of the wildlife will already have headed out to sea. For those wishing to see Ross Island's historic huts (p233), your best bet is to go as late in the season as possible. Even with an icebreaker, it may be impossible to penetrate the pack ice that far south earlier in the season.

DON'T LEAVE HOME WITHOUT...

- **Windproof and waterproof jacket** Much better as an outer layer than a heavy, bulky coat.
- **Knee-high waterproof boots (ie Wellingtons)** Essential for landings, when you'll be stepping into the surf and walking through penguin guano.
- **UV-filtering sunglasses** The sun reflecting off ice, snow and water makes for lots of glare.
- **Warm gloves** Fingers freeze fast.
- **Hat** Any sort will prevent rapid heat loss.
- **Double the film or digital-photo storage capacity you think you'll need** Antarctica is a photographer's dream and when the light is right, you'll be unable to stop snapping.
- **Seasickness pills** Although the ship's doctor will also have a supply.
- **Flashlight** Especially useful inside dark historic huts.
- **Patience** Antarctica's rapidly changing weather and unpredictable seas set the schedule, not calendars or clocks.

COSTS & MONEY

Antarctica is not a cheap destination to visit. It's a long way from the rest of the world, and operating tours there is an expensive business.

The heavy ship traffic sailing to Antarctica from Ushuaia (p150) sometimes makes it possible to find bargain prices if you can get to the port yourself. Since the ships are ready to sail, if they have open berths they may be willing to negotiate the fare, on the theory that making some money is better than making none at all. Be warned, however, that much of the time, Antarctic ships are fully booked – often many months in advance. Late in the season (mid-February onwards), you may be more likely to find cabin space still available.

Solo travelers pay a premium for a single cabin (1.4 times the regular fare, or more). If you're willing to have the tour company match you with another solo traveler of the same gender, you each pay the regular fare – and making a new acquaintance can add to the experience.

Most Antarctic tour brochures carefully spell out what is included in the price of the cruise. Additional costs include port taxes, and optional items such as alcohol, laundry, faxes, phone calls, email, tips, souvenirs, extra helicopter time and massages. Most ships, regardless of the country of origin, only accept US dollars for cash transactions.

TRAVEL LITERATURE

Antarctica has a vast number of books on its wildlife, exploration and science, but worthwhile travel narratives about the continent are much less common.

LIFE ABOARD A POLAR SHIP

Voyages to polar seas are different from other sorts of travel, and even seasoned 'cruisers' may need to make some adjustments. Some people find shipboard life difficult to handle at first, feeling a bit claustrophobic. This can be heightened in Antarctica, since the cruise ships may be small and relatively spartan.

It's also completely normal to feel lethargic and sluggish during the several days of sailing required to reach Antarctica. As one passenger wrote about a recent cruise: 'The time I spent in my bunk, sliding down hitting my feet on the wall, then sliding up and hitting my head, bracing with elbows and knees to prevent being dumped out during the up-pitched weightless rolling motions, was, well, interesting. It sounds bad, but it wasn't.'

Typically, a printed bulletin listing the day's planned activities is distributed the night before to let you know what's ahead. It helps to attend the educational lectures and video screenings, which are given, in part, to relieve the monotony of long ocean crossings. Enterprising passengers will find activities to occupy themselves – seabird-watching, iceberg spotting, visits to the bridge or engine room, diary writing, reading – but even these can get stale after three or four days. Don't worry: Antarctica is worth the wait.

International law requires that every ship hold a lifeboat drill within 24 hours of sailing. These drills are serious and are mandatory for all passengers. Each cabin should contain a sign or card telling which lifeboat station the occupants should use. There will also be a life vest for each person in the cabin; these are usually equipped with a whistle, reflective patches and a battery-powered beacon light, which starts flashing automatically upon contact with saltwater. The universal signal to proceed to lifeboat stations is seven short blasts on the ship's bell or horn, followed by a long blast. This signal may be repeated several times for the lifeboat drill. Since there's only one such drill held during each voyage, if you ever hear the signal a second time during your voyage, it is the *real thing*. You should go immediately to your cabin to pick up your life vest and some warm clothing and then head straight to your lifeboat station to await instructions from the crew.

The Worst Journey in the World (1922), by Apsley Cherry-Garrard, is *the* Antarctic classic. It's a highly readable account of Captain Scott's fatal expedition and the hellish midwinter manhaul to study the emperor penguins at Cape Crozier.

The Crystal Desert (1992), by David G Campbell, is beautifully written and chronicles the ecologist's three summers studying the life of the Antarctic Peninsula region. This is one of the best books about Antarctica.

South (1919), by Ernest Shackleton, tells the amazing story of his ill-fated *Endurance* expedition from the leader's perspective. Shackleton loved poetry, and this book (written with a ghost writer) has a poetry all its own.

The South Pole (1912), by Roald Amundsen, describes in surprisingly engaging prose the polar technician's triumph in reaching 90° South (even though the North Pole had been his lifelong goal).

Scott's Last Expedition (1913), by Captain Robert F Scott, is the firsthand account of the doomed *Terra Nova* expedition, taken from his diaries and published posthumously. Scott was deservedly known as a skillful writer.

Alone Across Antarctica (1997), by Børge Ousland, describes the Norwegian's startlingly fast solo crossing of the continent – the first ever. Ousland accomplished the amazing feat in only his second attempt. This book includes loads of great photos.

Let Heroes Speak: Antarctic Explorers, 1772–1922 (2000), by Michael H Rosove, is a compilation of the major early expeditions to Antarctica. Rosove wisely lets the explorers tell their own stories, quoting liberally from their published accounts.

Extra care is needed when moving about any ship, but passengers on Antarctic cruises especially should keep in mind the rule of 'one hand for the ship,' always keeping one hand free to grab a railing or other support should the ship roll suddenly. You may notice that even some berths on the ship (usually those running fore-and-aft) are equipped with airline-style seat belts for use when seas get a bit heavy. Take care not only when climbing steep ladders and stairs, but also in wide-open 'flat' areas such as the bridge, dining room or lecture hall, where a sudden slam into a chair or table could result in a broken arm or leg. Although the rolling motion of a ship on the open sea tends to be fairly regular and predictable, a vessel pushing through ice can lurch suddenly, pitching unaware passengers onto their noses. Closet and bathroom doors likewise can become dangerous swinging projectiles in high seas. You should also take care not to accidentally curl your fingers around doorjambs, as a fractured finger can result if the door closes suddenly. Decks can be slippery with rain, snow or oil, and you can easily trip on raised doorsills, stanchions and other shipboard tackle.

Cameras or video equipment should be securely stowed in the cabin. The best place to put such valuables, especially at night, is either on the floor or closet-bottom. You don't want the sound of your Leica shattering as it hits the floor after flying off your desk to be the first noise that alerts you to the onset of a sudden storm.

Antarctic tourist ships generally maintain an 'open bridge,' welcoming passengers to the navigation and steering area. The bridge will be closed during tricky navigation and whenever the pilot is aboard or the ship is in port. Etiquette demands that no food or drink be brought to the bridge, especially alcohol, and going barefoot on the bridge is also not appreciated. Keep your voice down; excessive noise interferes with communication between the navigator and helmsman. The low humming sound audible on the bridge is the ship's gyrocompass. Of course, it's always unwise to touch any equipment without being invited to do so by an officer of the watch. One further warning: sailors are a superstitious lot, and whistling anywhere on a ship is considered bad luck – seriously. Tradition says that a person whistling is calling up the wind, and that a storm will result.

Life on the Ice (2002), by Roff Smith, is an easy read and a pleasant travelogue of Smith's three trips to Antarctica, courtesy of the Australian Antarctic Division, the US government and the National Geographic Society.

Water, Ice and Stone (1995), by Bill Green, is a geochemist's personal account of his work studying the unusual lakes of Antarctica's Dry Valleys, written in a well-crafted, literary style.

The Ice: A Journey to Antarctica (1986), by Stephen J Pyne, rewards the patient reader of its dense, erudite prose – the amount of information, and the well-ordered way it's presented, is incredible.

TOP TENS

Antarctica in the Movies

Antarctica has been featured in surprisingly few movies, given its exotic nature, but the cost of actually filming there is significant. You'll have to hunt for some of these in a specialist video store.

- *South* (1998; p53)
- *Scott of the Antarctic* (1948; p42)
- *The Thing* (1982; p54)
- *With Byrd at the South Pole: The Story of Little America* (1930; p55)
- *Cry of the Penguins* (aka *Mr Forbush and the Penguins*; 1972; p31)
- *Antarctica* (1984; p49)
- *Virus* (1980; p64)
- *Hell Below Zero* (1953; p57)
- *90° South: With Scott to the Antarctic* (1933; p41)
- *Der Kongress der Pinguine* (*The Congress of the Penguins*; 1994; p47)

Natural Wonders

Antarctica itself is a gigantic natural wonder, but there are some extra special parts.

- The Lemaire Channel (p222)
- The Dry Valleys (p238)
- The Ross Ice Shelf (p252)
- Vinson Massif, Antarctica's highest peak (p66)
- The collapsed Arched Rock at Kerguelen (p163)
- Just about any iceberg (p89)
- Paradise Harbor (p223)
- Mt Erebus (p250)
- Aurora australis (southern lights; p236)
- The Lambert Glacier, the world's largest glacier (p262)

Amazing Moments

At times in Antarctica, you may feel as though you're living in an extraordinary documentary. Here are some examples of stories you may be able to tell on your return home.

- Entertaining a curious penguin chick by letting it nibble your boot
- Watching a mother minke whale and her calf surface alongside your Zodiac
- Grabbing any available support as your ship pitches through the Drake Passage
- Cruising in Zodiacs through a field of grounded bergs close enough to touch
- Seeing a blue-eyed shag regurgitate a meal to its chick
- Spotting the first iceberg (they're so big!) at dawn as you arrive on the bridge
- Inhaling your first whiff of a penguin colony
- Gazing in fascinated horror as a leopard seal devours an unlucky Adélie penguin
- Stepping out of the Zodiac into the surf on your first continental landing
- Sighting a rare blue iceberg or an even rarer bottle-green one

INTERNET RESOURCES

70 South (http://70south.com) Updated daily, this site strives to be an Antarctic news service. Includes an extensive archive of hundreds of 'Antarcticles.'

International Association of Antarctica Tour Operators (www.iaato.org) The trade association of tour companies offering trips to Antarctica. Lots of contact information, as well as tourism statistics.

Lonely Planet (www.lonelyplanet.com) Includes links to useful travel resources elsewhere on the Web.

Itineraries

CLASSIC ROUTES

THE ANTARCTIC PENINSULA

Seven to 14 days

By far the most popular Antarctic trip, this route is also an excellent introduction to Antarctica.

Starting from **Ushuaia** (p150), your ship will cross the **Drake Passage** (p149). Depending on the size of your vessel – and the weather you encounter along the way – the crossing could take as little as 1½ days, or as long as…well... Remember, everything depends on Antarctica's moods. Most likely, you'll make your first landing at one of the **South Shetland Islands** (p180) at the discretion of the expedition leader. Among the places you might visit: volcanic **Deception Island** (p187), **Livingston Island** (p186), the **Aitcho Islands** (p185), **Greenwich Island** (p186), **King George Island** (p182), or **Half Moon Island** (p186).

Next, you'll steam down to the **Antarctic Peninsula** (p216). Again, depending on the expedition leader's judgment, you may visit such places as: **Port Lockroy** (p221), the US **Palmer station** (p221), **Neko Harbor** (p223), **Paradise Harbor** (p223), or **Waterboat Point** (p224).

Homeward bound, you may be able to catch sight of **Cape Horn** (p150) off the port side.

The Antarctic Peninsula itinerary, the most popular trip and a good introduction to Antarctica and its spectacular wildlife, takes from one to two weeks.

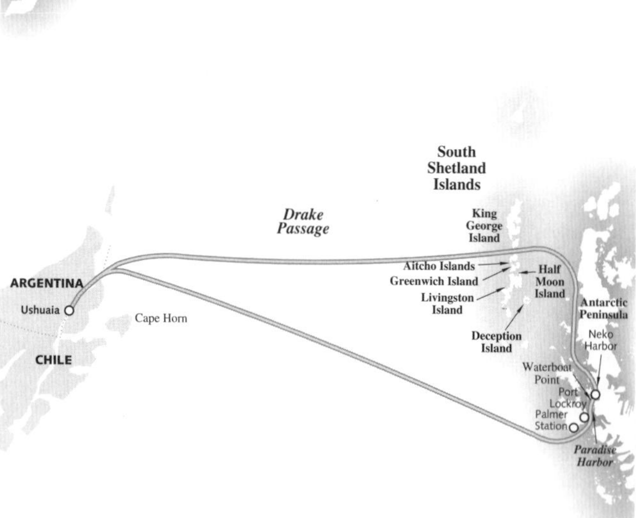

THE PENINSULA, SOUTH GEORGIA & THE FALKLANDS

14 to 20 days

This route is increasingly popular, as it combines the wildlife and scenery of the Peninsula with South Georgia's history and Shackleton connections.

Departing once again from **Ushuaia** (p150), you may either head straight to the Peninsula and then on to South Georgia (which has the advantage of following the prevailing westerly winds), or the route may be done in reverse (which means going against the westerlies – with often heavy head seas). Go with the flow: head south across the **Drake Passage** (p149), stop in the **South Shetland Islands** (p180), then visit the **Antarctic Peninsula** (p216). See p14 for more information on the Antarctic Peninsula.

After bidding goodbye to the Peninsula, head east (with following seas, which come from behind you, resulting in a faster and more comfortable trip) to the **South Orkney Islands** (p191), provided there's time and the weather cooperates.

One of your first **South Georgia** (p193) stops is likely to be **Grytviken** (p195), home to an abandoned **whaling station** (p197) and **Shackleton's grave** (p198).

For South Georgia wildlife, visit **St Andrews Bay** (p199) or **Salisbury Plain** (p199) to watch the antics of king penguins by the thousand. **Albatross Island** (p200) or **Prion Island** (p200) are also good places to gaze upon the endangered and magnificent wandering albatross. Fur seals abound on many beaches, particularly on the northwest coast.

On the way back to Ushuaia, cruise past the lonely, wave-thrashed **Shag Rocks** (p193). Then stop in at the Falklands for a visit to one of its outer islands and its engaging capital, **Stanley** (p208).

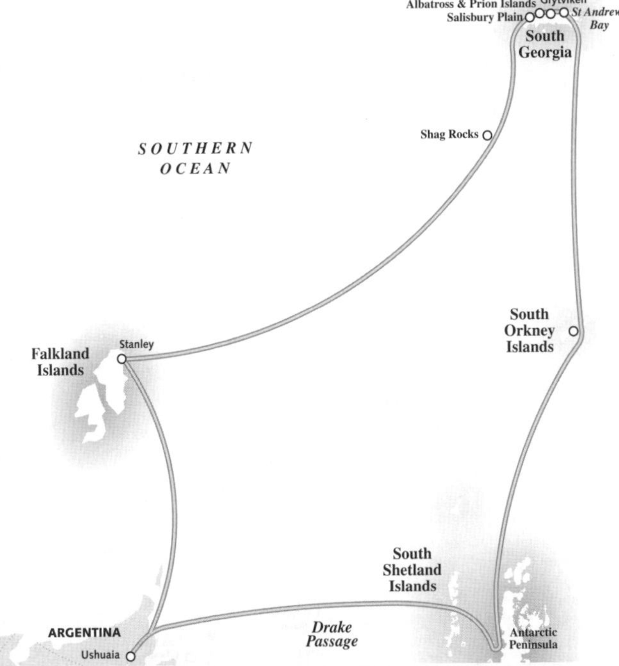

This itinerary includes the popular Peninsula region, plus the stunning mid-ocean mountains of South Georgia and the fascinating Falkland Islands. It takes from two to three weeks.

ROADS LESS TRAVELED

THE ROSS SEA

18 to 28 days

The Ross Sea is Antarctica to another degree: the cold and wind is a magnitude greater, the tabular icebergs more abundant. As the explorers' gateway to the South Pole, the region has the continent's richest historic heritage.

Starting from an Australian or New Zealand port, spend a couple of days on the **Southern Ocean** (p149) getting your sea legs and watching the abundant bird life. Depending on your route (and the unpredictable weather), you may stop at either **Macquarie Island** (p169), **Campbell Island** (p177), or the **Auckland Islands** (p174), all famous for their breeding seabirds. After a cruise past the shudder-inducing, icebound coasts of the **Balleny Islands** (p172), and a quick visit to Antarctica's first buildings at **Cape Adare** (p233), if the wind allows (not likely), turn to starboard and head south into the **Ross Sea** (p232) and the fabled shores of **Ross Island** (p240), home of the historic huts.

If you're fortunate – and the pack ice permits – you'll hit the historic hut trifecta, making landings at **Scott's Discovery Hut** (p246), Shackleton's hut at **Cape Royds** (p249) and the tragedy-pervaded hut at **Cape Evans** (p248), to which Captain Scott and his men would have returned if they had not perished on their return from the Pole.

Add a visit to one of Ross Island's human communities, the US **McMurdo station** (p240) and/or New Zealand's **Scott base** (p240) for a look at Antarctic scientific research and perhaps some shopping, and your trip is complete.

The Ross Sea itinerary includes not only the rich historic heritage of the Ross Island huts, but also scientific research stations and several of the lonely peri-Antarctic island groups. It takes from three to four weeks.

The Author

JEFF RUBIN

Coordinating Author

Jeff first visited Antarctica in 1987, when he made a three-month voyage to the continent while writing a story about Australia's Antarctic science program for *Time* magazine's Australian edition. Since then, he has returned to Antarctica many times. Jeff is the Antarctic Editor of the *Polar Times*, the official publication of the American Polar Society, and writes the magazine's 'Due South' column. He lives in Ohio with his wife Stephanie and daughters Emily and Isabel. The *New York Times* called Jeff's first edition of this book 'the only travel guide that any visitor to the region should need,' while the *Sydney Morning Herald* called it 'the first book on Antarctica destined for the suitcase, not the coffee table.'

My Favorite Trip

Since I'm interested in early Antarctic history, I always enjoy visiting South Georgia (p193) and the South Shetland Islands (p180), where early 19th-century sealers operated before there were even sketch maps of these places. Just imagining, as I can't help doing when cruising among these rocky islands, the primitive conditions in which the sealers lived – and the brutality of the slaughter that was their work – makes me appreciate the comfortable manner in which we visit Antarctica today! The wildlife in the Peninsula (p216) region is unmatched anywhere else in the Antarctic. And, of course, everywhere you go in Antarctica, there's ice, which I find fascinating and beautiful in all its myriad incarnations.

CONTRIBUTING AUTHORS

John Cooper wrote the Wildlife Guide (p105). John has undertaken ecological and physiological research on African, sub-Antarctic and Antarctic seabirds over more than 30 years at the University of Cape Town. He has chaired the Scientific Committee on Antarctic Research on the Bird Biology Subcommittee (now known as the SCAR Group of Experts on Birds) and the World Conservation Union's Antarctic Advisory Committee. He is a co-editor of *Marine Ornithology*, an international journal of seabird science and conservation, which he founded in 1976. In 1997 he initiated BirdLife International's Seabird Conservation Programme and its 'Save the Albatross Campaign,' which he led for four years. His current interests and activities center on fostering and supporting international agreements that help conserve seabirds and their habitats, especially the Agreement on the Conservation of Albatrosses and Petrels, which came into force in February 2004.

Dr Maj De Poorter is the author of the Environmental Issues chapter (p94). Dr De Poorter worked with Greenpeace as an Antarctic campaigner from 1984 to 1996. She participated in five Greenpeace expeditions (three as leader), and has personally carried out inspections on more than 35 bases throughout Antarctica checking environmental performance. Dr De Poorter has attended official meetings of the Antarctic Treaty System as an NGO observer since 1986. She is a member of the World Conservation Union's Antarctic Advisory Committee and serves as a senior advisor to the Antarctic and Southern Ocean Coalition (ASOC). She is also on New Zealand's Environmental Assessment and Review Panel – the body that advises on all environmental-impact assessments for New Zealand's Antarctic activities.

Colin Monteath wrote the Private Expeditions chapter (p65). Colin has had 26 seasons in Antarctica since 1973, including 10 years with the New Zealand Antarctic Programme. Since 1983 he has been a freelance photographer and writer, specializing in polar and mountain regions. With his wife Betty, Colin runs the Hedgehog House New Zealand photo library (www.hedgehoghouse.com). He has climbed many new routes on Antarctic peaks and has been involved in seaborne tourism since 1983.

Professor David Walton is the author of the Antarctic Science chapter (p128). Professor Walton first became interested in the Antarctic as a teenager. After achieving a first degree in botany from Edinburgh University, he began work in 1967 with the British Antarctic Survey (BAS), studying sub-Antarctic plants. He spent 20 years as a research scientist for BAS before taking on the responsibilities for its science management. He is now responsible for all BAS's information and public relations, as well as the conservation and environmental management of the UK in the Antarctic. Professor Walton also chairs the international Antarctic scientific committee that coordinates the input of science and environmental information to Antarctic Treaty Meetings, and he represents the interests of Antarctic science at these meetings. He is the author of more than 80 scientific papers, the editor of several books and the editor-in-chief of the international journal *Antarctic Science*.

Dr David Goldberg co-wrote the Health chapter (p305). Dr Goldberg completed his training in internal medicine and infectious diseases at Columbia-Presbyterian Medical Center in New York City, where he has also served as voluntary faculty. At present, he is an infectious diseases specialist in Scarsdale, New York, and the editor-in-chief of the website www.MDTravelHealth.com.

Snapshot

The biggest issue in Antarctica is the environment and its protection.

Since Antarctica has no native population, the impact on its environment is caused by people from other parts of the world – even people who have never visited Antarctica. Studies by Italian researchers at Mario Zucchelli station have found that minute particles of lead from gasoline combustion are blown to Antarctica as quickly as one month after they leave exhaust pipes in South America, Australia and New Zealand. Meanwhile, Chinese researchers have discovered pesticide residue in seabird guano at King George Island, and plastic continues to wash up on Antarctica's beaches in ever-increasing amounts.

Aside from headline-grabbing topics, such as global climate change and the ozone 'hole' (see p98 and p142, respectively), two other Antarctic stories have received prominent play in the world's media recently.

Longline fishing for Patagonian toothfish *(Dissostichus eleginoides)* has been a twofold environmental disaster. Not only are toothfish caught in enormous and unsustainable numbers, with much of the catch illegal, but albatrosses in their thousands are also caught on the steel hooks when the birds seize the bait as the lines are being thrown overboard (the euphemistic fisheries term is 'bycatch'). The birds are then dragged down hundreds of meters and drowned – an ignoble end for such magnificent fliers.

Countries such as Australia and France have declared exclusive fishing zones around the peri-Antarctic islands they administer, which means that toothfish poachers have sometimes been pursued by fishery vessels and warships intent on arresting the unauthorized ships and their crews, and seizing the vessels and their valuable cargoes. These 'low-speed' chases across thousands of kilometers of storm-wracked Southern Ocean may last for weeks as the pursuers attempt to force the poachers to a suitable port. However, for each pirate fishery vessel caught and fined, many more escape. The difficulties of patrolling such a vast, empty ocean are manifest. For unscrupulous operators, the rewards outweigh the relatively small risk of being caught: a single haul of toothfish (known in the trade as 'white gold' for its popularity among diners) can net a boat more than US$1 million.

Antarctic tourism is the other story in the news. Visitor numbers are steadily rising as more people discover Antarctica's beauty, wildlife and isolation. While governments fret over how to regulate tourism to minimize its impact (see p93 for more information on this topic), they're hindered by the fact that because no one owns Antarctica, no single country can legislate behavior there. The Antarctic Treaty works through consensus, and since Treaty parties now number 45, it can take years to arrive at agreement on simple measures such as controlling tourism.

In the meantime, Antarctic tour companies continue to police themselves, although no industry in history has ever been completely successful at that task, fraught as it is with conflicts of interest. As more ships and larger ships head south, the challenge of self-regulation will continue to grow. For Antarctica's sake, may the parties involved use their best judgment for the sake of preserving the Antarctic environment, and not just their own individual financial concerns.

FAST FACTS

Population: 5000 (summer), 1200 (winter)

Tourist arrivals: 13,571 (2002–03)

Lowest recorded temperature: -89.6°C

Highest elevation: Vinson Massif (4900.3m)

Ice-free land: <1%

Deepest ice core drilled: c 950,000 years old at its bottom

History

FORMATION OF THE CONTINENT

Around 200 million years ago, Antarctica was joined with Australia, Africa, South America, India and New Zealand in the supercontinent Gondwana. Ten million years later, Gondwana began the enormously slow process of breaking into the pieces we recognize today, and the continents, subcontinent and islands began moving into their present positions. By about 70 million years ago, the continents were becoming widely separated and what is now known as the Drake Passage opened. After making its final detachment from the Australian continent, about 40 million years ago, Antarctica settled into its present polar position and began to cool dramatically.

German naturalist Alexander von Humboldt, noticing how the shapes of the continents bordering the Atlantic fit together, was the first to suggest (c 1800) that they might once have been joined. In 1851, British botanist Joseph Hooker wrote to Charles Darwin about similarities he had noticed among plants in New Zealand, Tasmania, Îles Kerguelen and the Falkland Islands. At about the same time, French geologist Antonio Snider-Pellegrini, noticing identical fossil remains in both Europe and North America, theorized that the continents must once have been joined. He too fit two pieces of the supercontinent puzzle together, proposing the childishly simple idea that Africa's west coast once abutted South America's east coast.

In 1885 Austrian Eduard Suess was the first to propose that there had been a southern supercontinent. Suess gave it the name Gondwana, derived from the historic region in central India occupied by the Gond people where fossil strata similar to that of other widely removed continents was found – thus supporting the supercontinent theory. In 1908 American Frank Taylor suggested that mountain ranges had been formed in ancient times by the collision of drifting continents.

Antarctica: The Extraordinary History of Man's Conquest of the Frozen Continent (1990), by the editors of *Reader's Digest*, is packed with photos and fascinating narratives about the explorers. It is unquestionably the single best book on Antarctica.

German Alfred Wegener came up with the first fully articulated theory of continental drift in 1912, which envisioned a supercontinent he called Pangaea ('all lands'). For his hypothesis, Wegener quickly received much scorn from the world scientific community, mostly because no one could conceive the thought of continents being able to move.

Later scientists – mainly working in the Southern Hemisphere – followed Wegener's work, and in 1937 South African geologist Alexander Du Toit refined the idea of Pangaea to include two continents – Gondwana to the south, and another called Laurasia to the north. Australian geologist S Warren Carey found evidence that the fit between the continents was even better along the offshore continental shelves, but he believed this was explained by an expanding-earth model, in which the planet's diameter was slowly increasing.

Exploration of the sea floor in the 1950s and '60s provided new data and new ideas, leading to the theory of plate tectonics. Geologist HH Hess postulated that the sea floors are spreading away from the mid-ocean

TIMELINE

1400 Maoris from New Zealand may have visited the Auckland Islands

1497 Da Gama proves that Africa is not attached to a southern continent

ridges, thus providing the mechanism to drift the continental land masses as Wegener's theory and geologic data had suggested.

Among the fossil evidence found in Antarctica that clearly supports the supercontinent theory is a deciduous conifer *(Glossopteris)*, a fern *(Dicroidium)* and a terrestrial reptile *(Lystrosaurus)*. All of these species lived on Gondwana and their fossil remains have been found in rocks of the same age in such widely separated locales as India, South America, Australia, Africa and Antarctica. Because *Glossopteris*' seeds and *Dicroidium*'s spores could not have been blown, and *Lystrosaurus* could not have swum across the oceans that separate these continents, their fossilized remains offer certain proof that the continents were all once united.

HISTORY & EXPLORATION

THE ANCIENTS

Antarctica, unlike any other continent, was postulated to exist long before it was actually discovered. The ancient Greeks, beginning with Pythagoras in about 530 BC, believed the earth to be round, an idea Aristotle supported and refined further, suggesting that the symmetry of a sphere demanded that the earth's inhabited northern region should be balanced by an equally inhabited – or, at the very least, inhabitable – southern region. Indeed, without it, the top-heavy globe might tumble over. This idea of earthly balance gave rise to the name we give the southern continent today: Antarktos, or 'opposite Arktos,' the constellation in the northern sky. The Egyptian Ptolemy agreed that geographical equilibrium required an unknown southern continent, but he believed that the unknown land would be populated and fertile. A map he drew c AD 150 showed a large continent linking Africa and Asia.

Two factors conspired, however, against anyone actually going out to look for this mysterious undiscovered continent. First, ancient thinkers as far back as Parmenides (460 BC) believed that between the two temperate regions of the earth would be found a zone of fire and perhaps even monsters. This may have been wisdom somehow gleaned from an early traveler who had experienced a tropical summer. In any case, this torrid zone was thought to be impassable and deadly. If mortal fear was not enough to dissuade would-be discoverers, perhaps eternal damnation did the trick, for the Catholic Church found the idea of a southern continent – with its own population, and thus its own separate relationship with God – unacceptable. The idea that the Creator could possibly have made two sets of humanity was deemed heretical, and the flat-earth theory was given full backing.

'Ancient thinkers believed that between the two temperate regions of the earth would be found a zone of fire and perhaps even monsters'

That is not to say that intrepid voyagers did not push back the boundaries of their known worlds. As early as 700 BC, the Greek historian Herodotus records, a Phoenician fleet sailed from the Red Sea south along the African coast and around Cape Agulhas to the Straits of Gibraltar. This incredible voyage was not to be repeated for nearly 2000 years. In AD 650, according to Rarotongan legend, a Polynesian navigator named Ui-te-Rangiora sailed so far south that he reached a place where the sea was frozen. These voyages were neither repeated nor widely known,

1519
Magellan discovers Tierra del Fuego – and his namesake straits

1522
Elcano, completing Magellan's circumnavigation of the earth after Magellan's death, discovers Île Amsterdam

however, and it was not until late in the 15th century that further progress was made on answering the question of Antarctica.

THE EXPLORERS

The Portuguese made the first important penetrations south, beginning with a naval voyage in 1487–88 led by Bartholomeu Días de Novaes and João Infante, who sailed around the southern tip of Africa, Cape Agulhas, as far as present-day Mozambique. Their voyage opened the way for another naval expedition, led by Vasco da Gama in 1497, to discover the way around Africa to India. These expeditions proved that if there was a great southern continent, it was not attached to Africa.

Likewise, the Portuguese explorer Fernão de Magalhães (Ferdinand Magellan), leading the first circumnavigation of the globe from 1519–22, discovered and named Tierra del Fuego ('Land of Fire,' named not for the ancients' torrid regions, but for the campfires, built by the native Yahgan people, that had been spotted onshore). By sailing through the straits that now bear his name, Magellan proved that the southern land was not connected to South America, either, although it remained possible that it was attached to Tierra del Fuego.

'Antarctica was a mysterious place, thought to cover the whole Southern Ocean'

What is remarkable about these discoveries is that their makers were *disproving* rather than proving the existence of a great southern land. Antarctica was a mysterious place whose extent was originally imagined to be enormous: it was thought to cover the whole Southern Ocean and connect to the southern extremes of the known continents. Although each subsequent voyage of discovery pared off great sections of open ocean where Antarctica obviously was *not* located, few people seemed able to conceive that the continent might not exist at all; instead the belief persisted strongly that Antarctica – a greatly diminished Antarctica, to be sure – must lie just a little further south. But the Southern Ocean's terrifying storms and impenetrable pack ice conspired to keep the continent's white face shrouded from inquiring eyes for centuries more.

Terra Australis (Southern Land) – the term was first used by Flemish mapmaker Oronce Finé in 1531 – continued to exert its southerly attraction, however. Englishman Francis Drake, sailing in *Pelican* (later named *Golden Hind*), made the second circumnavigation of the globe from 1577–80. Drake discovered the passage that now is named after him, definitively proving that no great southern continent was connected to either South America or Tierra del Fuego. As the sub-Antarctic and Southern Ocean archipelagoes were found in succession (the Falklands, the South Sandwich Islands, South Georgia, Bouvetøya, Îles Kerguelen) some were initially thought to be northerly projections of *Terra Australis*, but each eventually proved merely insular. Dutchman Abel Janszoon Tasman's voyages charting parts of Tasmania and New Zealand in 1623–25, and again in 1644, also sparked hope, at first, that they might be part of the great missing continent, but these hopes, too, soon died.

Cook

Yorkshireman James Cook (1728–79), once apprenticed to a shopkeeper, was the widest-ranging explorer who ever lived. He circumnavigated the globe three times and discovered more territory than anyone else in history.

1531
Flemish mapmaker Oronce Finé is the first to use the term 'Terra Australis'

1578
Drake discovers the Drake Passage separating Tierra del Fuego and Antarctica

At the age of 40, he undertook the first of his three great voyages of discovery, and between 1768 and 1771, he found New Zealand and the whole east coast of Australia, claiming them for Britain. On his third voyage, from 1776 to 1779, he explored the Arctic coasts of North America and Siberia before being killed by natives in Hawaii in 1779. Not the least of Cook's accomplishments was his virtual defeat of scurvy among his crews, thanks to such provisions as sauerkraut and 'Mermalade of Carrots.'

Cook's Antarctic discoveries came on his second voyage, beginning in 1772 aboard HMS *Resolution* and HMS *Adventure*. Like HMS *Endeavour*, Cook's previous ship, these vessels were colliers from the north country of England. Part of Cook's genius lay in persuading the Royal Navy of the value of these ships that he had come to know in his earliest seagoing days as a deckhand on the coal run from Yorkshire to London: he knew that these shallow-drafted barques could explore close inshore without the risk of running aground. On his second voyage with the ships, Cook sailed 109,500km and penetrated further south than anyone else before. He crossed the Antarctic Circle on January 17, 1773, becoming the first person to do so, and crossed it twice again without ever sighting land, despite pushing to a record 71°10'S. On his third pass through the pack ice, Cook landed on South Georgia, which he called the Isle of Georgia, and discovered the South Sandwich Islands.

'Cook crossed the Antarctic Circle on January 17, 1773 – the first person to do so'

Despite his remarkable first circumnavigation of Antarctica – which he did without losing a single person – Cook failed to find the southern continent itself. It's almost more remarkable that he *didn't* find Antarctica, given that he managed to get so much further south than anyone before him. Cook simply had poor luck: in the longitudes where he managed to penetrate furthest south, the coast of Antarctica itself also swerved southward. Upon leaving the frozen southern seas for the last time, Cook wrote:

> Thick fogs, Snow storms, Intense Cold and every other thing that can render Navigation dangerous, one has to encounter and these difficulties are greatly heightned by the enexpressable horrid aspect of the Country, a Country doomed by Nature never once to feel the warmth of the Suns rays, but to lie for ever buried under everlasting snow and ice.

If there were any remaining doubt how Cook felt about the prospects of a still-undiscovered Antarctica, he later underscored this opinion:

> ...whoever has resolution and perseverance to clear up this point by proceeding farther than I have done, I shall not envy him the honour of discovery, but I will be bold to say that the world will not be benefited by it.

So convincing were the pessimistic sentiments recorded in his journal that Cook discouraged other explorers from seeking the great southern continent for decades afterward. But he also recorded his observations of large numbers of seals and whales in the southern waters – and others, more commercially minded than the Royal Navy, took notice.

1603
Gabriel de Castilla, aboard *Nuestra Señora de la Merced*, penetrates to approximately 64°S in the Southern Ocean south of the Drake Passage

1675
De la Roche sights South Georgia

THE EARLIEST ANTARCTIC LANDINGS *Robert Headland*

The earliest crossing of the Antarctic Circle was made during the circumnavigation of the continent by Captain James Cook on January 17, 1773, but Cook saw no land. There are uncorroborated reports of early sightings, but these are very doubtful. It's far more likely that a dirty iceberg was observed during poor weather and reported as land. The first corroborated sighting was made by a Russian expedition led by Fabian von Bellingshausen aboard *Vostok* (East), accompanied by Mikhail Lazarev aboard *Mirnyy* (Peaceful). This expedition circumnavigated Antarctica in high southern latitudes and extended some of Cook's work. On January 27, 1820, two coastal areas in Kronprinsesse Martha Kyst and Prinsesse Ragnhild Kyst were mapped at about 69°35'S, 2°23'W. These were parts of the ice shelf and, although not reported then as such, they were the first part of the mainland to be seen, as well as the first land south of the Antarctic Circle to be confirmed. Three days later, Edward Bransfield discovered Trinity Peninsula, and many US and British sealers working from the newly discovered South Shetland Islands saw, and some mapped, this part of the continent.

The South Shetlands were discovered in February 1819, and, starting the following austral summer, a large number of sealers exploited them. This began what was in effect a three-year 'gold rush,' ending with seals on the verge of extinction. There is evidence that during the 1820–21 austral summer three sealing masters working from the islands independently landed on the Antarctic Peninsula – thus becoming the first humans on the continent. They were John Davis aboard *Cecilia* from Nantucket, on February 7, 1821, and John McFarlane and Joseph Usher aboard *Dragon* and *Caraquette* respectively, both from London but working out of Valparaiso, at an unknown date. Few details are known of these landings because no fur seals were found, thus the trips were of little interest to those involved. These are the only recorded landings

The Sealers

Motivated by profit, not discovery, the sealers came from Britain, the Cape Colony (now part of South Africa), France, New South Wales (in present-day Australia), New Zealand, Tasmania and the United States.

Fur seals have two layers that make up their coats: stiff, outer 'guard hairs' to protect the body when they clamber over rocks, and a dense layer of underfur to trap insulating air bubbles and keep the skin dry. Preparing the pelts required the removal of the guard hairs, a technique that was for many decades known only by the Chinese.

Sealing was an extremely hard way of life. Gangs were typically dropped off on a promising beach and left to live and work for months at a time while the ship would continue in search of other sealing grounds. The sealers lived in tents, rude huts, or occasionally in small caves among the rocks. None offered more than a little shelter from the wind and weather.

The brutality of their work impressed even the sealers themselves. 'By having our hands daily imbued in the blood of animals,' wrote an American named William Dane Phelps in 1871, 'our natures were so changed, that acts of cruelty, which, one year previous, would have been revolting to us, we now seemed to enjoy…'

Greed was the watchword as the sealing gangs slaughtered without thought for the future of their industry. Captain James W Budington, a Connecticut sealer who worked in the Antarctic for more than 20 years, testified to the US Congress in 1892:

1739
Bouvet de Lozier finds the island that will bear his name: Bouvetøya, the most isolated island on earth

1772
Marion du Fresne discovers Îles Crozet

(their order is equivocal) from more than 60 sealing vessels from Britain and the United States that worked at the South Shetlands and searched the region for seals during that season. Just two more continental landings by sealers during the rest of the century are known, one on the Antarctic Peninsula and the other in the vicinity of Cape Adare. It is likely that several other landings were made, but because of the absence of seals they were regarded with little interest and weren't recorded. During the sealing period, about 1780 to 1892, more than 1100 sealing ships visited Antarctic regions, compared to barely 25 exploratory vessels – thus discoveries, especially of the islands, were inevitable.

An oft-cited, but spurious, claim to a first Antarctic landing dates from 1895. A Norwegian sealing and whaling exploration, led by Henrik Bull aboard *Antarctic*, commanded by Leonard Kristensen, reached Cape Adare and landed on January 24. The assistant biologist, Carsten Borchgrevink, claimed to have been the first ashore and thus to be the 'first on the Antarctic continent.' The captain also claimed to have been first and thus to be 'the first man who ever put foot on South Victoria Land.' Alexander Tunzleman (a boy recruited in Stewart Island) may, however, have preceded both: he claimed to have got off first to steady the boat for the captain to disembark. The expedition leader, Henrik Bull, indicating no precedence, stated only: 'The sensation of being the first men who had set foot on the real Antarctic mainland was both strange and pleasurable...' They dispute an empty claim – for there had been at least five earlier landings by sealers. In defense of *Antarctic*'s crew, however, earlier landings may not have been known to them.

Borchgrevink does have, however, a firm claim to fame as the leader in 1899 of the first expedition to winter on Antarctica. Traveling aboard *Southern Cross*, this expedition landed on Ridley Beach near Cape Adare and built two huts that still stand today.

Robert Headland is the archivist and curator at the Scott Polar Research Institute, Cambridge, England

> We killed everything, old and young, that we could get in gunshot of, excepting the black pups, whose skins were unmarketable, and most all of these died of starvation, having no means of sustenance, or else were killed by a sort of buzzard, when the mother seals, having been destroyed, were unable to protect them longer... The seals in all these localities have been destroyed entirely by this indiscriminate killing of old and young, male and female. If the seals in these regions had been protected and only a certain number of 'dogs' (young male seals unable to hold their positions on the beaches) allowed to be killed, these islands and coasts would be again populous with seal life. The seals would certainly not have decreased and would have produced an annual supply of skins for all times. As it is, however, seals in the Antarctic regions are practically extinct, and I have given up the business as unprofitable.

Another Connecticut sealer, George Comer of East Haddam, testified to the Congress in the same year about the enormous waste of life involved in the sealing business:

> In the first part of a season we never disturbed the rookeries we visited, always letting the seals come on shore; then we would kill them on land with clubs or rifles. During the latter part of a season the seals became very wild, and we used to shoot them in the water from boats. When we shoot them in the water, we lose certainly

1772
Kerguélen-Trémarec is the first to see Îles Kerguelen

1773
Cook crosses the Antarctic Circle, reaching 71°10'S – but never sees Antarctica

> three out of five we kill by sinking, and we also wounded a great many more. Shooting seals in the water is the most destructive method of taking them as compared with the number of skins we have to show for our work.

DID YOU KNOW?

The fur seal's rich pelt has a density of about 40,000 hairs per sq cm.

Elephant seals also were hunted for the oil that can be rendered from their blubber rather than for fur, which they lack. Elephant seals grow to massive sizes, particularly males, but the sealers found 'sea elephants,' as they called them, easy prey. 'To the skilful hunter their overthrow is but the work of a moment,' wrote one sealer on Kerguelen. 'He fearlessly approaches the animal in front, and, as it raises the left forepaw to advance upon him, with great address plunges his lance, 10ft or 12ft [3m to 3.5m] long, into its heart.'

Sealing voyages far outnumbered expeditions that could be called strictly scientific – there were about 44 times as many sealing voyages made than expeditions – and nearly a third of the sub-Antarctic and Southern Ocean islands were discovered by sealers. But sealers considered their discoveries proprietary information and kept the information to themselves (although drunken sailors in port taverns were not always able to restrain themselves from boasting about newfound sealing grounds). So it remained for kings, czars and governments to send out expeditions to explore and chart new territory, in hopes of extending their sovereignty over ever-greater empires.

Bellingshausen

Fabian von Bellingshausen (1778–1852), an Estonian who was a captain in the Russian Imperial Navy, led the first Russian circumnavigation in 1803–06. In 1819 Czar Alexander I called Bellingshausen to St Petersburg and dispatched him on a voyage of discovery into the Southern Ocean, a dream assignment for Bellingshausen, who had long admired Cook's voyages. With his flagship *Vostok* (East), a newly launched corvette with a copper-sheathed hull, and the older, sluggish *Mirnyy* (Peaceful), which constantly slowed the expedition, Bellingshausen sailed from Kronstadt, an island off St Petersburg, in July 1819. Unique to his expedition was the shipboard sauna he constructed as a hygienic measure for his crew and their clothing; heated cannonballs inside a tent on deck supplied the healthful steam for bathing and washing.

They crossed the Antarctic Circle on January 26, 1820, and the next day Bellingshausen became the first person to sight the Antarctic continent. Through a heavy curtain of falling snow, at 69°21'S, 2°14'W, he saw 'an icefield covered with small hillocks.' The trouble was, he didn't realize the importance of his discovery; he merely noted the weather conditions and his position in the ship's log before continuing. The two ships sailed eastward, pushing further south than anyone else had previously done. Eventually they tacked north to escape the oncoming winter, spending four months in the South Pacific in 1821. Turning south again, they crossed the Antarctic Circle six more times, eventually probing as far as 69°53'S, where they discovered Peter I Øy, the southernmost land known at that time. They also found a second piece of ice-free land below the Circle, which Bellingshausen called Alexander Coast after the czar. It is now known to be an island joined to the Antarctic Peninsula by an ice shelf.

1775

Cook discovers the eight most southerly of the South Sandwich Islands

1786

The first British seal hunters arrive at South Georgia after reading Cook's description of fur seals there

Returning north through the South Shetlands, Bellingshausen met the American sealer Nathaniel Brown Palmer, in the sloop *Hero*, who claimed to know well the coast that he had just explored. A legend created by Palmer's biographer, sealer Edmund Fanning, insists that Bellingshausen was so impressed by Palmer's claims of knowledge that he named the new territory after Palmer, but the meticulous Bellingshausen never noted this alleged act in his diaries or charts, and the story appears to be fantasy.

Despite Bellingshausen's discoveries – and his duplication of his hero Cook's circumnavigation of Antarctica – he returned to Russia to find that his countrymen had little interest in his voyage. It took nearly 120 years and the start of the Cold War before his accomplishments were fully appreciated – by a Soviet Union newly anxious to assert its right to authority in the Antarctic.

Weddell

Scotsman James Weddell (1787–1834), an upholsterer's son who became a Master in the Royal Navy, rejoined the merchant service in 1819 and took command of the brig *Jane* on a sealing expedition to the recently discovered South Shetlands. Although the voyage was a financial failure, he independently discovered the South Orkney Islands, which had just been sighted by American sealer Nathaniel Brown Palmer and British sealer George Powell, who were working together. In 1822 Weddell persuaded *Jane*'s owners to send him on another voyage. This time accompanied by the cutter *Beaufoy*, he sailed again from England in September. It was a hard passage for both ships, small and fragile in the enormous rollers of the Southern Ocean. The sailors' unenviable jobs were made somewhat more tolerable by their daily ration of rum: three full wineglasses per man.

'The sailors' unenviable jobs were made somewhat more tolerable by their daily ration of rum: three full wineglasses per man'

By the end of January 1823, the two vessels had reached the eastern end of the South Orkney chain, and a landing was made at Saddle Island. Weddell himself went ashore, and six skins of a new species of seal were collected; today this animal is known as the Weddell seal. But by early February, Weddell had given up on finding a harvestable population of fur seals, so he changed course southward into a sea normally covered in impenetrable ice as far north as 60°S.

Constant gales soaked the crew, but on February 16, when the 70th parallel was crossed, the weather took a turn for the better. The breeze backed to the northeast and *Jane* and *Beaufoy* began a fine run south. Well aware of the remarkable conditions he was encountering, Weddell made the following notation in his log on February 18: '*not a particle of ice of any description was to be seen.*'

By February 20, they had reached an amazing 74°15'S – a new southing record, 344km further south than Cook. But Weddell was worried. The season was getting on, and despite the open water that lay ahead to the south, he ordered a retreat. But first a gun was fired in celebration and the sea named to honor the sovereign, King George IV (the name was changed in the next century to honor Weddell's discovery). The ships' crews, disconsolate at not pursuing further progress, were no doubt cheered by the extra ration of rum allotted to them that day.

1800–02
Fanning takes 57,000 fur-seal skins from South Georgia, probably the most profitable voyage ever made to the island

1810
Hasselborough sights Macquarie Island, although sealers are likely to have visited earlier

Smith & Bransfield

Although he was once credited with being the first to sight Antarctica, it is now agreed that Edward Bransfield (c 1795–1852) was beaten to that honor by Bellingshausen by three days.

After English merchant Captain William Smith announced his discovery of the South Shetlands in 1819, the Royal Navy chartered Smith's ship, *Williams,* to survey the islands. Bransfield was put in command with Smith as pilot, and they sailed south from Valparaiso, Chile. Two months were spent charting the coastlines of what they called New South Britain; a landing was made at George Bay on King George Island to claim the group for – surprise – George IV, the British sovereign.

Continuing south, Bransfield sighted the Antarctic Peninsula on January 30, 1820, calling it Trinity Land. One of his midshipmen, quoted in the *Literary Gazette and Journal of Belle Lettres*, called it 'a prospect the most gloomy that can be imagined...the only cheer the sight afforded was in the idea that this might be the long-sought Southern Continent.' They charted the islands along it for another 20 days before being stopped by pack ice and turning north.

Palmer

'Palmer claimed that he had found the Antarctic continent, calling his discovery Palmer Land'

American sealer Nathaniel Brown Palmer (1799–1877), the son of a shipyard owner, left his home of Stonington, Connecticut at the age of 14 to go to sea. On his second sealing voyage to the South Shetlands in 1820, commanding the sloop *Hero* (which carried a complement of five, including Peter Harvey, born in Philadelphia in 1789, the first black person to reach such a high southern latitude), Palmer sailed south with a small fleet of other sealers. Upon his arrival in the South Shetlands, the need for a more secure anchorage for the five ships drove Palmer to push south ahead of the others. He dropped anchor inside the caldera of Deception Island, almost certainly the first person ever to do so. On November 16, from a high lookout at Deception, he caught sight of Trinity Island to the southeast and probably the Antarctic Peninsula beyond. The next day Palmer sailed to investigate, but due to heavy ice thought it imprudent to try to land. In later years, Palmer claimed that he had found the Antarctic continent, calling his discovery Palmer Land. But even if he did spot Antarctica on that occasion, his sighting came 10 months after Bellingshausen's (January 27) and Bransfield's (January 30) in that same year.

Nevertheless, Palmer has another clear Antarctic discovery to his credit: a year later, while commanding the sloop *James Monroe*, Palmer was searching for seals in the South Shetlands with British Captain George Powell of *Dove*. Finding no seals, they steered east, and on December 6, 1821, discovered a large island of a new group, the South Orkneys. Finding no seals, Palmer had no further interest in the island, but Powell went ashore and claimed it for the British crown, calling it Coronation Island.

Biscoe

Another Briton, John Biscoe (1794–1843), joined the Royal Navy at 18 and fought in the 1812 war against the US. Dispatched by the London firm of Enderby Brothers in July 1830, he made the third circumnavigation of

1819
Smith, blown off course while rounding Cape Horn, discovers the South Shetlands

1819
Bellingshausen discovers the three northernmost South Sandwich Islands

Antarctica, sailing in the brig *Tula*, accompanied by George Avery in the cutter *Lively*. The ships sighted what they called Enderby Land on February 24, 1831, and confirmed the discovery three days later – the first sighting of the Antarctic continent in the Indian Ocean sector. Biscoe was also struck by the ethereal beauty of the aurora australis, which, he recorded in the ship's log, 'at times (appeared) not many yards above us.' Oncoming winter forced the ships to head north to Hobart, but scurvy so ravaged *Tula*'s crew that only Biscoe, three other men and a boy were able to work. Aboard *Lively*, which had become separated from *Tula*, all but three of the crew died of scurvy or other diseases.

Sailing again with both ships in October 1831, on what after all was supposed to be a commercial voyage, Biscoe spent three months searching for whales or seals off New Zealand. Finding none, he headed south once more, and discovered Adelaide Island (which he named for the consort of King William IV) on February 16, 1832. Biscoe discovered land again (now thought to be present-day Anvers Island) on February 21, and claimed the territory for King William IV. Still seeking seals or some other valuable cargo to bring home, he was forced to sail for England after *Tula* damaged her rudder. (En route home, *Lively* was wrecked in the Falklands.) Although he returned to London in January 1833 with empty holds and one ship missing, Biscoe was fortunate to have extremely open-minded bosses. Instead of being reprimanded or fired, he received the highest award of the newly established Royal Geographical Society.

After Biscoe's return, the stretch of coast he discovered was named Graham Land, for James RG Graham, First Lord of the Admiralty. Although this was in fact a southern portion of the Antarctic Peninsula, which had already been sighted by Bransfield, Smith and Palmer, the name eventually came to be applied to the entire Antarctic Peninsula on British maps, while the name Palmer Land was used by American chartmakers. (This difference continued until 1964, when the US and the UK agreed to use the name Antarctic Peninsula for the entire northward-reaching extension of the Antarctic continent, with the northern part to be called Graham Land and the southern, Palmer Land.)

British discoveries in the Antarctic Peninsula region had not escaped the attention of the US government, however, and after nearly a decade of being urged to do so, the US Congress voted to send crews and ships south to explore the region.

'It was the most ill-prepared, the most controversial, and probably the unhappiest expedition which ever sailed the Antarctic seas'

Wilkes

By the time American Lieutenant Charles Wilkes (1798–1877) was offered command of the US Exploring Expedition in 1838, the position had already been declined by several senior officers. Perhaps they knew something Wilkes didn't, for this inauspicious beginning foretold great hardship for the expedition. In the words of polar historian Laurence P Kirwan, it was 'the most ill-prepared, the most controversial, and probably the unhappiest expedition which ever sailed the Antarctic seas.'

For a start, the six ships selected were poor choices: three of them, *Vincennes*, *Peacock* and *Porpoise*, were naval warships with gun ports that let heavy seas pour into the ships; *Sea Gull* and *Flying Fish*, former New York pilot boats, were quite odd choices for Antarctic exploration;

1819
The Spanish man-of-war *San Telmo* sinks off Livingston Island, killing 650 men – Antarctica's worst loss of life

1820
Bellingshausen sights Antarctica on January 27, becoming the first person to see the continent

and the sluggish storeship *Relief* rounded out the sorry fleet. As might be expected of an expedition planned by committee, the US Ex Ex, as the expedition became known, had a distinct lack of focus. Antarctica was to be only one area of its endeavor, and a minor one at that: Wilkes was also directed to explore the whole of the Pacific, from Chile to Australia to the northwest coast of North America. Meanwhile, a jealous Navy Department did all it could to exclude civilian scientists from the expedition, although Wilkes did manage to take with him artist Titian Ramsey Peale. One unsuccessful applicant for the position of expedition historian was American writer Nathaniel Hawthorne.

By the time the expedition sailed on August 18, 1838, a depressed Wilkes confided to his private diary that he felt 'doomed to destruction.' After sailing down the east coast of South America to Orange Harbour, near the tip of Tierra del Fuego, Wilkes divided the fleet into three parts. He directed *Peacock* and *Flying Fish* to sail southwest to try to better Cook's southing record, while *Vincennes* and *Relief* were to survey the coast of Tierra del Fuego. Placing himself aboard *Porpoise*, he set off south with *Sea Gull* to see how far he could penetrate the pack ice. The ships soon lost contact with one another, each undergoing its own trials. Gales blew out sails and tangled rigging, boats were crushed by ice, and men were injured and frozen. Wilkes himself, in the flagship, narrowly missed running aground on Elephant Island in fog. *Sea Gull* was lost with all hands off Chile. But *Peacock* and *Flying Fish* managed to cross the 70th parallel, little more than a degree away from beating Cook's record.

DID YOU KNOW?

The first photograph of an iceberg was made by Britain's *Challenger* Expedition in 1874.

Diminished by two – *Sea Gull* was lost and *Relief* had been sent home as unsuitable for ice work – the expedition reconvened in Sydney in November 1839 after surveying in the South Pacific. After a month's recuperation, the four ships sailed south again on December 26, with Wilkes commanding *Vincennes*. On board was one of the first recorded canine visitors to the Antarctic, a dog acquired in Sydney and named after that port. Again the ships were quickly separated, and in late February *Flying Fish* gave up its search for the others and returned to New Zealand alone. The other three vessels managed to rendezvous, however, and on January 16, 1840 – three days before Dumont d'Urville made his discovery – they sighted land in the region of 154°30′E, putting a boat ashore three days later to confirm it. Separating again, *Vincennes* continued west, sighting and charting discoveries until reaching the present-day Shackleton Ice Shelf, which Wilkes named Termination Land. The massive ice shelf, which today extends nearly 290km out to sea, convinced him that it was time to head home, which he did on February 21.

Having followed the Antarctic coast for nearly 2000km, Wilkes announced the discovery of an Antarctic continent upon his return to Sydney. Although he was the first to do so, his only reward upon his homecoming in New York was a court-martial. Petty jealousy from some of his officers, coupled with his harsh shipboard discipline, entangled Wilkes in a messy trial in a Naval Court of Inquiry held at the Brooklyn Navy Yard. Two long months later, all of the charges against him – save one – were dismissed. Found guilty of ordering a too-severe punishment for some thieving seamen, Wilkes was officially reprimanded by the Secretary of the Navy. The US Congress, however, handed Wilkes his bitterest defeat,

1820
Peter Harvey (a member of Palmer's crew on *Hero*) is the first black person to reach such a high southern latitude

1821
Sealer John Davis lands on the Antarctic Peninsula becoming the first human to step on the continent

authorizing publication of just 100 copies of the expedition's official report. Today, the full set of the *Narrative* is one of the rarest and most valuable polar books.

Dumont d'Urville

Long before Frenchman Jules-Sébastien-César Dumont d'Urville (1790–1842) sailed for Antarctica, he had earned for himself a footnote in history. In 1820, while surveying the eastern Mediterranean, Dumont d'Urville heard about a remarkable statue that had recently been excavated on the island of Milos. Struck by its rare beauty, he urged the French government to buy it, something the government agreed to do 'whatever it might cost.' Today, that purchase – the *Venus de Milo* – graces the Louvre in Paris, minus its arms, which were knocked off during its collection.

Cry of the Penguins (aka *Mr Forbush and the Penguins*; 1972) stars John Hurt as a blasé scientist who volunteers for Antarctic duty to impress a girlfriend, then begins to identify with the Adélie penguins he's studying.

Already a veteran of two circumnavigations (and fluent in English, German, Greek, Hebrew, Italian and Spanish), Dumont d'Urville sailed from Toulon in 1837 with *Astrolabe* and *Zélée*, which, like Bellingshausen's ships, were clad in copper for protection from the ice. Although Dumont d'Urville hoped to reach the South Magnetic Pole – magnetism was then one of science's hottest questions – his orders from King Louis Philippe were simply to proceed as far south as possible in the Weddell Sea. Indeed, the explorers were promised a bonus of 100 gold francs each if they reached 75°S and another 20 francs for each additional degree gained toward the Pole. But the ice in the Weddell Sea that season extended much further north – indeed, this is its normal configuration – and much to his frustration Dumont d'Urville was unable to penetrate anywhere near as far south as Weddell did. At the end of February he discovered (or rediscovered, since sealers had probably already landed there) Louis Philippe Land and Joinville Island at the northern tip of the Antarctic Peninsula. By this time, scurvy plagued his ships, and on the return to Tierra del Fuego a sailor died of the dreaded disease.

After a year spent making ethnological voyages in the Pacific, during which 23 men died during an outbreak of dysentery and fever, Dumont d'Urville and his crews headed south again in January 1840. On the 19th, they spotted what they felt certain was land, confirmed the next day by a clearer sighting. Unable to go ashore because of the massive ice cliffs, they sailed west before coming upon a group of islets just a few hundred meters offshore. A group was landed, a few chips of granite hacked off as proof that they had found terra firma, and the discovery claimed for France. An officer who had anticipated success brought out a bottle of Bordeaux and a toast was raised to the King.

Dumont d'Urville honored his wife by naming the newfound territory for her (he was the only one of the early explorers to honor his wife in this fashion). Terre Adélie was dedicated to 'the devoted companion who has three times consented to a painful separation in order to allow me to accomplish my plans for distant exploration.' Heading east in search of the Magnetic Pole, Dumont d'Urville's lookouts were astonished one afternoon to see an American man-of-war emerge from the fog, running before the wind straight toward them. The ship was *Porpoise*, part of Charles Wilkes' US Exploring Expedition, but thanks to a misunderstanding, the two ships did not stop to communicate. Each side later blamed

1821
Palmer and Powell jointly discover the South Orkneys, but only Powell (for Britain) makes a claim

1821
Bellingshausen discovers Peter I Øy, naming it for czar Peter the Great

ANTARCTIC MUSEUMS *Robert Headland*

With the exception of the former British base turned museum at Port Lockroy, there are no permanent museums in Antarctica. But many scientific stations maintain at least a small 'cabinet of curiosities.' The Antarctic Treaty, meanwhile, has designated 76 'historic sites and monuments.' A proportion of these mark sites of genuine international importance (although many important sites remain unmarked). Others, including statues of recent national leaders, are of dubious interest – and many have been buried by decades of snow accumulation.

The following museums display Antarctic material. Many other museums have smaller exhibits, and temporary exhibitions on Antarctica circulate frequently. For information on the Falkland Islands Museum in Stanley, see p209. For information on museums in Ushuaia, see p151.

Australia

The Queen Victoria Museum in Launceston, the Powerhouse Museum in Sydney and the Victorian National Museum in Melbourne all have small Antarctic displays. The Australian Antarctic Division headquarters in the Hobart suburb of Kingston has a large one-room museum.

Germany

The sealer *Grönland* is docked at Bremerhaven, and includes a display about her 1872 Antarctic voyage.

Japan

The icebreaker *Fuji* has a permanent exhibition on board; she is moored in Nagoya City. The Shirase Antarctic Expedition Museum, near Konoura, includes much material on the expedition of 1910–12.

New Zealand

Christchurch's International Antarctic Centre features hands-on exhibits, video presentations and the 'sights and sounds' of Antarctica. The Southland Museum in Invercargill includes an interesting

the other for raising sail and blowing past. Returning to France to great acclaim after a 38-month voyage, Dumont d'Urville and his men were rewarded by the French government with 15,000 francs to be divided by the expedition's 130 surviving members.

Ross

Scotsman James Clark Ross (1800–62), considered one of the most dashing figures of his time, had all of the advantages for Antarctic exploration that Wilkes lacked. After joining the Royal Navy at the tender age of 11, Ross went on to a career filled with Arctic discovery. Between 1818 and 1836, he spent eight winters and 15 summers in the Arctic, and in 1831, as second-in-command of a voyage led by his uncle, John Ross, he located the North Magnetic Pole. In 1839 he was asked to lead a national expedition to explore the south, and if possible, to locate the South Magnetic Pole. The contrast between his commission and Wilkes' could not have been greater. With his government firmly behind the effort, both philosophically and financially, Ross was given excellent ships, officers and provisions; the sailors on the expedition were volunteers on double pay.

1823
Weddell penetrates the sea that now bears his name, reaching a record 74°15'S

1831
Biscoe discovers Enderby Land, the first sighting of Antarctica from the Indian Ocean sector

display on New Zealand's sub-Antarctic islands. In Auckland, Kelly Tarlton's Antarctic Encounter includes a replica of Scott's Cape Evans hut, an Antarctic aquarium and displays on the history of Antarctica. The Lyttelton Museum features artifacts from James Cook's, Scott's, Shackleton's and Byrd's expeditions. The Canterbury Museum in Christchurch houses one of the world's best collections of material from early Antarctic expeditions – see the boxed text on p44.

Norway

Sandefjord and Tønsberg both have excellent whaling museums with a lot of Antarctic material (they are particularly strong on South Georgia). Oslo has three sites: the famous polar ship *Fram*, used by Amundsen; Amundsen's home 'Uranienborg;' and some additional Amundsen material in the Ski Museum.

Russia

St Petersburg is home to the Arctic and Antarctic Museum, located in a former church at Ul Marata 24A.

United Kingdom

The Scott Polar Research Institute in Cambridge, England, is a major polar center, with a public museum featuring many artifacts from the expeditions of Scott and Shackleton, as well as from more recent research activities. Scott's ship *Discovery* is moored in Dundee, Scotland.

United States

The many New England whaling and sealing museums often have Antarctic material, particularly where it refers to the early sealing industry. New York City's American Museum of Natural History includes a large but often-overlooked display on Lincoln Ellsworth.

Robert Headland is the archivist and curator at the Scott Polar Research Institute, Cambridge, England

Setting sail in September 1839 in *Erebus* and *Terror*, three-masted barques specially strengthened for ice navigation, the expedition stopped in Hobart on its way south. There, the Governor of Van Diemen's Land (Tasmania) was John Franklin, himself a veteran Arctic explorer who would later and tragically sail Arctic waters again – in the very same *Erebus* and *Terror* – before disappearing and triggering the greatest polar search in history.

In Hobart, Ross heard troubling news: both Wilkes and Dumont d'Urville were exploring the area in which he intended to search for the magnetic pole. In the same whining tone that Robert Scott would later use upon hearing that Roald Amundsen (or Ernest Shackleton, for that matter) was heading to 'his' territory, Ross expressed his unhappiness that the Americans and the French would even consider sailing into 'his' area. He did take with him a useful gift from Wilkes – a chart tracing his track and discoveries – and later used it to denounce Wilkes. Meanwhile, Ross reacted quickly, changing his plans to a more easterly longitude for the push south.

Good fortune was to be on his side, although the elements made Ross earn it. Sailing south along the 170°E meridian, he pushed through pack ice for four days, trusting that his reinforced ships would be able to go where none had gone before. On January 9, 1841, he broke through to

1839
Balleny and Freeman jointly discover islands; since Freeman disappears en route home, they soon bear Balleny's name

1840
Dumont d'Urville discovers a stretch of coast and a penguin species, and names both for his wife, Adélie

open water, becoming the first to reach what we know today as the Ross Ice Shelf. The next day, Ross sighted land, a completely unexpected development. A boat was put ashore two days later on an islet named Possession Island and the new territory claimed for Queen Victoria.

Exciting though the discovery was, Ross' goal was the South Magnetic Pole, which had been calculated to lie both north and west of his current position. To follow the coast south and eastward would appear to be the 'wrong' way to get there, but to sail west would mean following in the tracks of Wilkes and Dumont d'Urville, something equally unappealing. Ross may have been thinking of the islands and channels of the Arctic he knew so well; perhaps sailing south and eastward would reveal a passage back toward the expected pole. So he stayed his course, discovering High (now called Ross) Island, and naming its two mountains – Erebus, the steaming volcano, and Terror, its easterly sister – for his ships.

'In Ross' path was a formidable obstacle – an enormous wall of shimmering ice towering 60m above the sea'

Lying in Ross' path, however, was a formidable obstacle, one that so overwhelmed him that he called it simply 'the Victoria Barrier,' an enormous wall of shimmering ice towering 60m above the sea. It was, Ross wrote, 'a mighty and wonderful object far beyond anything we could have thought or conceived. What was beyond it we could not imagine.' But this barrier, today known as the Ross Ice Shelf, also frustrated Ross: 'We might with equal chance of success try to sail through the Cliffs of Dover, as penetrate such a mass.' The two ships, tiny by comparison, cruised along the Barrier for 450km, the sailors in awe of its unchanging face, which was oblivious to even the most gigantic wave crashing against it. After reaching a new southing record of 78°9′30″S on January 22, 1841, Ross ordered the yards braced around and headed for Hobart.

Sailing south again in November 1841, Ross this time aimed for the eastern extremity of the Barrier. New Year's Day found *Erebus* and *Terror* moored beside a large ice floe, on which the crews held 'a grand fancy ball,' complete with carved-ice thrones for the captains and a refreshment bar cut into the ice. Then, after surviving a horrifying storm among ice fragments as 'hard as floating rocks of granite' that nearly destroyed the rudders of both ships, they again reached the Barrier. It appeared to join a range of mountains, but winter's onset forced a retreat. Ross' third season was equally disappointing: trying to best Weddell's southing record in Weddell's namesake sea, Ross found conditions similar to those previously encountered by everyone but Weddell. He was forced to head home after reaching 71°30′S. The expedition reached England on September 2, 1843, after nearly 4½ years away. When Ross married later that year, his bride Anne's father set one condition: he must promise to end his exploring days, a pledge Ross made and faithfully kept – with one exception. In 1847–48 he returned to the Arctic to search for John Franklin, who had disappeared after sailing in Ross' old ships *Erebus* and *Terror* in 1845 to try to navigate the Northwest Passage.

After Ross' important discoveries, Antarctica was once again ignored by the rest of the world. Ironically, this was partly because Britain's naval resources were diverted for more than a decade in the search for some sign of Franklin's fate.

1841
Ross breaks through pack ice to penetrate the sea that will bear his name

1841
Ross reaches a new southing record of 78°9′30″S on January 22

Larsen

Norwegian Carl Anton Larsen (1860–1924) went to sea at 14, and at 25 became master of his first whaling ship. His first brush with polar fame came when he sailed in *Jason* on the same voyage that carried Fridtjof Nansen to Greenland for his famous east–west crossing in 1888. Whaling entrepreneur Christen Christiansen dispatched Larsen in *Jason* in 1892 to search for whales in the Antarctic. In 1893, having found fur and elephant seals, but no whales of any species that he could catch, Larsen returned home. He went south again independently later that year, this time with three ships: *Jason*, *Hertha* and *Castor*. The expedition explored both coasts of the northern Antarctic Peninsula, discovered Oscar II Land and made the first use of skis in Antarctica. Larsen also found petrified wood on Seymour Island. He went on to captain Otto Nordenskjöld's ship *Antarctic* in 1901 (p39), and to set up the whaling station at Grytviken on South Georgia in 1904.

Bull

Norwegian-born Henrik Johan Bull (1844–1930) traveled to Australia in 1885 and set himself up in business. Convinced that a fortune could be made by reviving the Antarctic whaling trade, but unable to convince any Australians to join him, Bull returned to Norway in 1893. There he persuaded Svend Foyn, the wealthy inventor of the exploding harpoon gun, to back an expedition to assess the Ross Sea's potential as a whaling ground. Whales in the Northern Hemisphere had been hunted to commercial extinction, and although petroleum products had to some degree replaced whale oil, baleen (whalebone) was as prized as ever for women's fashions.

Sailing from Norway in 1893 in a refitted whaling steamer, *Antarctic* (later to be used by Nordenskjöld), Bull's expedition encountered many misfortunes in its hunt for whales, of which it saw few. A £3000 profit made from sealing in Îles Kerguelen evaporated when the ship ran aground at Campbell Island. Putting in for repairs at Melbourne, the ship picked up a young Norwegian naturalist, Carsten E Borchgrevink (p37), who signed on as assistant biologist in 1894. On January 18, 1895, *Antarctic* landed on the Possession Islands, where Borchgrevink discovered lichens, the first time vegetation had been found south of the Antarctic Circle.

Six days later, a party from *Antarctic* went ashore at Cape Adare in what was claimed to be the first landing ever made on the continent outside the Peninsula. Although Borchgrevink himself asserted that he had leapt out of the landing boat as it neared the shore in order to ensure himself a place in history – and made a widely reproduced drawing showing himself in the act – two others in the landing party disagreed upon just who first placed his foot on the frozen shore, and their differences were eventually aired in the correspondence columns of *The Times* of London. In any case, the landing was only one of several disputed 'first landings' on the continent (see the boxed text on p24). Penguins, rock specimens, seaweed and more lichens were collected, and although the voyage was not commercially successful, it helped to revive interest in Antarctica. Bull himself continued sealing and whaling, and at the age of 62 was shipwrecked and marooned on Îles Crozet for two months.

1845
Sir John Franklin disappears in 1845, triggering the greatest polar search in history and diverting attention from Antarctica

1853
Heard discovers Heard Island, which is 'rediscovered' three times the next year

De Gerlache

Belgian Adrien Victor Joseph de Gerlache de Gomery (1866–1934), a lieutenant in the Royal Belgian Navy, persuaded the Brussels Geographical Society to finance a scientific expedition to Antarctica. Sailing in a refitted three-masted sealing ship (with an auxiliary engine) that he purchased in Norway and rechristened *Belgica*, de Gerlache left Antwerp in 1897 with a decidedly international crew. The Belgian Antarctic Expedition included a Romanian zoologist, a Russian meteorologist, a Polish geologist (Henryk Arctowski, for whom the Polish research base on King George Island is named) and a Norwegian who offered to join the expedition as first mate, without pay: Roald Amundsen. As the ship's surgeon, de Gerlache signed an American, Frederick A Cook, who joined *Belgica* in Rio de Janeiro.

The expedition got a late start sailing south, leaving Punta Arenas on December 14. Some now speculate that this tardy departure was a deliberate attempt by de Gerlache to ensure that *Belgica* would be beset in the ice and thus be forced to remain in the Antarctic for the winter. Others have correctly pointed out that Antarctic pack ice was known to be at its most navigable late in the summer. By early February, the expedition had discovered and mapped the strait which now bears de Gerlache's name on the western side of the Antarctic Peninsula, as well as the islands on the west side of that strait: Brabant, Liège, Anvers and Wiencke (the last named for a sailor who fell overboard and drowned). They also charted the Danco Coast of the Peninsula, along the eastern side of the strait, which was named for the ship's magnetician, who also died during the expedition.

'Midwinter darkness toyed with the men's sanity, and the lack of vitamin C made them ripe for scurvy'

Photography was first used in Antarctica on this expedition, and Cook recorded that 'as the ship steamed rapidly along, spreading out one panorama after another of a new world, the noise of the camera was as regular and successive as the tap of a stock ticker.' (Seem familiar?)

On February 15, 1898, *Belgica* crossed the Antarctic Circle, and by March 1, already deep into the heavy pack ice, she reached 71°31'S. The next day began a long imprisonment in the ice. In fact, the ship would not be freed for 377 days – and then only by enormous effort and a great deal of luck. During this, the first time anyone had wintered south of the Antarctic Circle, the expedition underwent great hardships: midwinter darkness toyed with the men's sanity, and the lack of vitamin C made them ripe for scurvy.

Frederick Cook, who had been on the North Greenland Expedition with Robert E Peary in 1891 and then returned to Greenland twice more in the next three years, is probably responsible for saving the ship. To prevent scurvy, he urged de Gerlache to set an example by eating fresh seal and penguin meat, which the men detested. He organized elaborate betting games to take the crew's minds off their desperate circumstances and encouraged them to think of things to amuse themselves. One popular event, held on Belgian King Leopold's birthday, was the 'Grand Concourse of Beautiful Women,' in which 464 illustrations of beauties 'representing all kinds of poses and dress and undress' were selected from a Paris journal and judged according to 21 characteristics, including 'rosy complexion,' 'underclothes,' 'most beautiful face' and 'sloping, alabaster shoulders.' It was the men's hope that once the expedition returned to civilization the winners would agree to appear before the committee to receive their prizes.

1850–90
Interest in Antarctica declines as seal populations struggle to recover

1895
Bull lands at Cape Adare, the first landing outside the Peninsula region

However, that they *would* return to civilization was by no means certain. By January 1899, Cook suggested that they attempt to liberate themselves by hand-sawing a canal 600m long from a polynya, or stretch of open water, back to the ship, pushing the ice pieces that they cut from the canal out into the open water. They worked like dogs for a month. When they were within 30m of the ship, a wind shift tightened the pack ice and their hard-won canal closed up within an hour. Two weeks later, the ice opened and they steamed into the polynya, only to be forced to wait another month until they could gain access to the open sea. *Belgica* finally reached Punta Arenas on March 28, 1899.

The primary achievement of the Belgian Antarctic Expedition – surviving the first Antarctic night – proved that bases could be set up on the continent itself, enabling a full-time program of exploration. That knowledge was crucial for the next phase of Antarctic discovery.

Adrien de Gerlache remained involved in Antarctic affairs. In 1903 he joined Charcot's *Français* expedition (p43), but resigned in Buenos Aires. He later launched a business venture he called 'polar safaris,' taking tourists to East Greenland and Spitsbergen, but the enterprise collapsed in its initial phase, and de Gerlache sold his ship, *Polaris*, a 300-ton barquentine, to Ernest Shackleton, who renamed it *Endurance*. De Gerlache's son, Gaston de Gerlache, joined the Belgian Antarctic Expedition of 1957–59.

Borchgrevink

Carsten Egeberg Borchgrevink (1864–1934), the son of a Norwegian father and an English mother, got his start in Antarctic exploration shipping out with Bull in *Antarctic* in 1894. His landing at Cape Adare convinced Borchgrevink that it would be possible to survive an Antarctic winter ashore, so he decided to organize his own expedition with the goal of being the first to accomplish it.

After failing to raise any money for his expedition in Australia, Borchgrevink visited Britain, where he met with rejection after rejection – until 1897, when he convinced a wealthy magazine publisher, Sir George Newnes, to sponsor the expedition to the tune of £40,000. Borchgrevink's stunning fundraising success infuriated the British exploration establishment, headed by the Royal Geographical Society, because it was preparing to mount its own voyage of Antarctic discovery. Even more galling was the fact that Borchgrevink's 'British' Antarctic Expedition of 1898–90 was British in name only; just three (two Englishmen and one Australian) of the 31 men were not Norwegians. The expedition ship *Southern Cross*, a converted Norwegian sealer equipped with powerful engines, sailed under the Union Jack only at the insistence of its magnanimous sponsor.

Southern Cross departed London on August 22, 1898, and arrived at Cape Adare on February 17, 1899. Two weeks later, after a pair of simple wooden huts were erected on Ridley Beach, which Borchgrevink named after his mother, *Southern Cross* departed to winter in New Zealand. The 10 men left behind were some of the most solitary in history, having the entire Antarctic continent to themselves.

They had plenty of canine companionship, however, for Borchgrevink had brought 90 sledge dogs with him, the first dogs ever used in Antarctic

1897
Roald Amundsen joins de Gerlache's Belgian Antarctic Expedition as a first mate – without pay

1898
De Gerlache's *Belgica*, frozen into pack ice, is the first expedition to overwinter in the Antarctic

work. The expedition also pioneered the use of kayaks for sea travel, and was the first to bring to Antarctica the Primus stove, a lightweight, portable pressure stove invented in Sweden six years before. Although the kayak never became an important mode of Antarctic transportation, the Primus stove was carried by nearly every expedition that followed Borchgrevink's, and is still in use today.

Unfortunately, the expedition marked another first – the first human death on the continent – when Norwegian zoologist Nicolai Hansen died on October 14, 1899, and was buried on the ridge above Cape Adare. Aside from Hansen's death, there were other accidents – including a nearly disastrous fire and a narrow escape from asphyxiation by coal fumes – but the expedition escaped the dietary and psychological dangers experienced by *Belgica*'s crew during their long Antarctic night. By the time the ship returned on January 28, 1900, to pick up the expedition, it had proven a critical fact: humans could survive Antarctica's fiercely cold, dark winter ashore, using a wooden hut as a base for travels along the coasts and inland toward the Pole.

Borchgrevink's expedition produced many positive results, including excellent maps of the Ross Sea area produced by the expedition's English surveyor and magnetician, William Colbeck of the Royal Navy, which would prove invaluable to later explorers. Nevertheless, Borchgrevink's return to England was all but unheralded. The exploration establishment was still embittered by his fundraising success – and absorbed by Robert F Scott's impending expedition. Not until 1930 did the Royal Geographical Society see fit to award Borchgrevink its Patron's Medal. He died in Norway four years later.

Drygalski

Erich Dagobert von Drygalski (1865–1949), a geography professor at the University of Berlin and leader of a four-year expedition to Greenland, was given command of the German South Polar Expedition in 1898. Three years later, Drygalski and 31 other men sailed from Kiel on August 11, 1901, in *Gauss*, a three-masted schooner fitted with auxiliary engines. Drygalski named the ship after German mathematician Johann Karl Friedrich Gauss, who had calculated the position of the South Magnetic Pole, the accuracy of which James Clark Ross had set out to test.

Stopping en route at Cape Town and Îles Kerguelen (where it picked up 40 dogs), the expedition sighted land on February 21, 1902, in the region of 90°E, a territory which Drygalski named Kaiser Wilhelm II Land (now called Wilhelm II Land). On the same day, the ship got caught in the ice, soon becoming, in Drygalski's words, 'a toy of the elements.'

With *Gauss* trapped in the west-drifting pack, the men settled into a routine of scientific work by day and card games, lectures, beer and music by night. With snow drifting up over the ship, its warm, humid interior was infused with a very German *gemütlichkeit*, or coziness. A sledging party journeyed 80km to the Antarctic coast, discovering along the way a low hill they named Gaussberg after their ship. On March 29, 1902, Drygalski ascended to 480m in a large, tethered hydrogen balloon and used a telephone to report his observations to the ship. This was the second use of aviation in Antarctic history, after Scott's tethered flight during

1899
Nicolai Hansen is the first human to die on the continent, on October 14

1899–1900
Borchgrevink's *Southern Cross* expedition is the first to winter on the continent

the *Discovery* expedition (p41). The men also recorded penguin sounds with an early phonograph, and undertook two more sledging trips to Gaussberg. On the last of these trips Drygalski and his companions nearly became lost in the trackless white wasteland of snow-covered sea ice.

Being beset during the winter was one thing, but when spring and then summer arrived, the men began to feel desperate, especially after sawing, drilling and even dynamiting the 5m- to 6m-thick ice did nothing to free the ship. *Gauss*' captain suggested that they toss message-filled bottles into the sea - and launch others by balloon - in hopes that a rescue party might find them. In the end, they were liberated thanks to a basic principle of physics luckily observed by Drygalski himself during a walk on the ice. He remarked that cinders from the ship's smokestack caused the ice on which they landed to melt, since the dark ashes absorbed the sun's heat. Devising an ingenious method of escape, he ordered his men to lay a trail of coal ash, supplemented by rotting food and other garbage, across the 600m of ice that separated *Gauss* from open water.

As hoped, the trick worked, and soon there was a 2m-deep channel filled with water. Two months passed, however, before the bottom of the canal cracked open, on February 8, 1903, and the ship was freed. The expedition then spent seven weeks trying to chart the Kaiser Wilhelm II coast, but constantly shifting sea ice threatened to trap *Gauss* once more, and Drygalski reluctantly ordered the ship north on March 31. After reaching Cape Town, he wired Berlin for permission to return to the Antarctic the following season. But the Kaiser, apparently disappointed that more new territory was not discovered and claimed for the Fatherland, refused the request. Despite his disappointment, Drygalski spent the next three decades writing up the expedition's reports, which occupy 20 full volumes.

Nordenskjöld

Swedish geologist Nils Otto Gustav Nordenskjöld (1869–1928) had previously led expeditions to the Yukon and Tierra del Fuego, and his uncle, the North Polar explorer Nils AE Nordenskjöld, made the first transit of the Northeast Passage around Siberia. So he was well suited for the task assigned to him in 1900: leadership of the Swedish South Polar Expedition, which would be the first to winter in the Antarctic Peninsula region.

Sailing in *Antarctic*, the stout former whaler used by Henrik Bull in 1893–95, the expedition left Gothenburg on October 16, 1901. At *Antarctic*'s helm was Captain Carl Anton Larsen, the Norwegian who had already discovered Oscar II Land during a previous expedition in 1892–94 (p35), and who would later set up Antarctica's first whaling station at Grytviken on South Georgia. By late January 1902 *Antarctic* was exploring the western side of the Peninsula, making several important geographical discoveries in the area (among them, the fact that the Orleans Strait connected with the Gerlache Strait, and not with the Weddell Sea, as had been believed) before sailing back to the tip of the Peninsula. There, they crossed between the Peninsula and off-lying Joinville Island, naming the strait for their ship, *Antarctic*.

Next the expedition attempted to penetrate south into the Weddell Sea, but its infamous ice stopped them, and instead Nordenskjöld and five men set up a winter base on Snow Hill Island, off the east coast of

DID YOU KNOW?

A female blue whale caught at Grytviken in the 1911–12 season measured just over 33.5m – the largest animal ever recorded.

1899

Borchgrevink brings 90 sledge dogs on his expedition, the first dogs ever used in Antarctic work

1902

Scott makes the first flight in Antarctica, in a tethered balloon named *Eva*

the Peninsula, in February 1902. *Antarctic*, meanwhile, sailed for the Falklands to winter there. Poor weather confined the shore party to its small hut for most of the winter, but in December Nordenskjöld was able to sledge to Seymour Island, directly north of Snow Hill, where he found some striking fossils – including the bones of a giant penguin – bolstering earlier fossil finds made by Captain Larsen on the island in 1893.

'*Antarctic* sailed around Joinville Island and headed south, soon becoming caught in the pack ice, whose relentless grip inexorably crushed it'

However, December is midsummer in Antarctica, and the men were getting distinctly anxious about their ship, which should have arrived by then. Their fears were justified, although they were not to learn why for many months. After wintering in Patagonia and South Georgia, *Antarctic* had returned south, again surveying the western side of the Peninsula. Trying unsuccessfully to cross through her namesake strait to reach the Peninsula's east coast – and the men at Snow Hill Island – *Antarctic* stopped at Hope Bay on the Peninsula's tip to drop off three men, who would try to hike the 320km to Snow Hill. The ship then sailed around Joinville Island and headed south, soon becoming caught in the pack ice, whose relentless grip inexorably crushed it. The end, on February 12, 1903, was recorded by one of the men, Carl Skottsberg:

> Now the name disappears from sight. Now the water is up to the rail, and, with a rattle, the sea and bits of ice rush in over her deck. That sound I can never forget, however long I may live...the streamer, with the name *Antarctic*, disappears in the waves. The bowsprit – the last mast-top – She is gone!

The ship sank 40km east of tiny Paulet Island, and the men sledged for 14 days to reach it.

The three men left at Hope Bay, meanwhile, found their way to Snow Hill Island blocked by open water, so they settled down to wait for *Antarctic*'s return, according to a prearranged plan. The Swedish Antarctic Expedition was now split into three groups, two living in very rough conditions, with no group aware of the others' fates. How they all managed to survive is one of the greatest examples of good fortune in Antarctic history.

The Hope Bay trio, after eking out the winter in a primitive hut and living primarily on seal meat, set out again for Snow Hill Island on September 29. By a lucky coincidence, Nordenskjöld and another man were dog-sledging north at the same time on a research journey, and on October 12, the two groups met. Nordenskjöld was so struck by the Hope Bay men's remarkable appearance – they were completely soot-blackened, and wearing odd masks they had fashioned to prevent snow blindness – that he wondered if they were from a previously unknown race of men. Nordenskjöld's companion, Ole Jonassen, considered that an unholstered revolver might be a necessary precaution in facing these disconcerting apparitions. But they quickly established the identities of their fellow expeditioners, renaming the point of their rendezvous 'Cape Well Met.'

Antarctic's crew, meanwhile, wintered on Paulet Island. They built a stone hut and killed 1100 Adélies for food before the birds left for the winter. On June 7, just before midwinter, one of the party who had been sick for weeks, Ole Wennersgaard, died. On October 31, Larsen led a group of five others in an open boat to search for the trio at Hope Bay. Finding a

1902
Colbeck discovers the tiny island that will later be renamed to commemorate Scott

1902
Scott's *Discovery* expedition makes the first dedicated attempt to reach the South Pole, but gets only to 82°16'30"S

note the three had left at their hut, Larsen decided he would have to follow by sea the route that the Hope Bay men were taking to Snow Hill Island.

Even as Larsen's group rowed their boat south, outside help was on its way to Snow Hill Island. Since nothing had been heard of the Swedish expedition, three search parties had been dispatched. Argentina sent a naval ship, *Uruguay*, to search for it in 1903. On November 8, *Uruguay*'s crew found two of the men from Snow Hill Island camped at Seymour Island, and after waking them, joined them in the short trek to Snow Hill – arriving, by incredible coincidence, only a few hours ahead of Larsen and his group. After a joyful reunion, all that was left to do (on November 11) was to pick up the remaining *Antarctic* crew members back on Paulet Island, who, ironically, had just finished collecting 6000 penguin eggs, their first surplus food supply.

Although Nordenskjöld's expedition is remembered primarily for its survival against nearly overwhelming odds, it also performed the most important research in Antarctica undertaken up to its time.

Scott's *Discovery* Expedition

Even as Nordenskjöld's men were struggling for survival, British explorer Captain Robert Falcon Scott (1868–1912) was working from a base established on Ross Island. The son of an upper-middle-class brewer, Scott had joined the Royal Navy's training ship *Britannia* as a cadet at the age of 13, and advanced through the ranks, being promoted to commander in June 1900. A month later he was named leader of the British National Antarctic Expedition, which the country's exploration establishment had been planning since the mid-1880s. Borchgrevink beat Scott's *Discovery* expedition to the punch, however, securing his large grant from Sir George Newnes in 1897 (p37).

When Scott's well-financed expedition sailed from England on August 6, 1901 in *Discovery*, a specially built wooden steam barque, it was the best-equipped scientific expedition to Antarctica to that date. After stopping in New Zealand for refitting and reprovisioning, the expedition got off to an inauspicious start when a seaman fell to his death from the top of the mainmast. By January 3, 1902, *Discovery* crossed the Antarctic Circle, and six days later stopped briefly at Cape Adare. Penetrating the Ross Sea, Scott cruised along the Ross Ice Shelf, discovering King Edward VII Land on the shelf's eastern margin. He also made the first flight in Antarctica, on February 4, 1902, in a tethered balloon called *Eva*. From a height of 240m, Scott saw the undulating surface of the Ross Ice Shelf rising toward the polar plateau. Camera-toting expedition member Ernest Shackleton went up next, making himself Antarctica's first aerial photographer.

By mid-February 1902, Scott's men had established winter quarters at Hut Point on Ross Island. Although a hut was built ashore, *Discovery*, frozen into the sea ice, served as the expedition's accommodations, with officers and crew separated into wardroom and mess deck, befitting the quasi-naval expedition that it was. The shore building was reserved for scientific work and recreation, including theatrical performances, with the 'Royal Terror Theatre.' But life in McMurdo Sound was not all research and games: in a violent snowstorm during a sledge trip, a young sailor named George Vince slipped over a precipice to his death. The winter

90° South: With Scott to the Antarctic (1933) is 'camera-artist' Herbert Ponting's tribute to his lost companions. It's deeply moving, with superb cinematography of wildlife and the expedition's daily activities, all narrated by Ponting.

1903
Bruce establishes a base on Laurie Island; eventually transferred to Argentina, it's now the longest-running weather station in Antarctica

1904
Larsen establishes Grytviken on South Georgia, beginning the Antarctic whaling era

passed fairly quietly otherwise, the group's accommodations made cheerier by another Antarctic first – electric lights (powered by a windmill). With Shackleton as editor, the expedition published Antarctica's first magazine, the monthly *South Polar Times*, as well as one issue of a more ribald alternative, the *Blizzard*, whose title page featured a figure holding a bottle, captioned 'Never mind the blizzard, I'm all right.'

With spring, the expedition's real work began. To the cheers of *Discovery*'s men, Scott set out for the South Pole on November 2, 1902, with Shackleton, scientific officer Dr Edward A Wilson, 19 dogs and five supply sledges hitched up in train formation. Despite initial optimism and a large depot of food laid by an advance party, the trio soon struck harsh reality, Antarctica style. They had never tried skiing or sled-dog driving, and their inexperience produced predictably poor results.

Scott of the Antarctic (1948) is a popular classic. This melodramatic British film perhaps not surprisingly takes a near-worshipful view of Captain Scott, played by John Mills.

Through sheer willpower, they reached 82°16′30″S on December 30 before turning back. Actually, Scott and Wilson reached that point, Shackleton having been ordered to remain at camp that morning to look after the dogs. This may or may not have been an intentional slight on the part of Scott (although certainly it was petty), but Shackleton smarted at the gesture.

For all of them, the trip home was miserable. The remaining dogs by now were nearly worthless, and soon were hitched *behind* the sledge, which the men pulled themselves. On at least one occasion, a dog was carried *on* the sledge. As dogs weakened, they were shot and fed to the others. The men, meanwhile, were also breaking down. Shackleton especially was suffering from scurvy, and suffering badly – but those accounts of the trip that say he had to be carried on the sledge are false.

Two weeks before the southern party's return home on February 3, the relief ship *Morning* had arrived in McMurdo Sound. *Morning*'s captain, William Colbeck, had been the surveyor on Borchgrevink's *Southern Cross* expedition. Colbeck and Scott, upon his return, decided that with *Discovery* still frozen into the ice, *Morning* should not wait to depart. Seeing that he would probably have to remain another winter, Scott sent home eight men, including Shackleton, who went only upon being ordered to do so. The following summer, after Scott led a sledging party in southern Victoria Land, *Morning* returned, in company with *Terra Nova*, sent by the British government. The two vessels bore a distressing order: if *Discovery* could not be freed within six weeks, it would have to be abandoned. After weeks of cutting and blasting with explosives, Scott was nearly ready to give up, but nature relented, and the ice gave way. One final blast, on February 16, 1904, released *Discovery* for the long journey home.

Bruce

Scotsman William Spiers Bruce (1867–1921), the physician son of a surgeon, joined a whaling voyage to the Antarctic from Dundee as the *Balaena*'s surgeon and naturalist in 1892. He would have joined Bull's *Antarctic* expedition in 1894–95, but was unable to reach Melbourne in time to meet the ship. Bruce also later made many trips to the Arctic. In 1901 he declined the offer of a position on Scott's expedition because he was in the midst of planning his own, the Scottish National Antarctic Expedition.

Sailing from Troon on November 2, 1902 in *Scotia*, a renamed Norwegian steam sealer with extremely elegant lines, the expedition pushed

1908
Mt Erebus is first climbed by a party from Shackleton's *Nimrod* expedition

1909
Shackleton and two companions reach record south, 88°23′S, just 180km from the Pole

south into the Weddell Sea. By 70°S, *Scotia* was beset, and after freeing herself, headed north to winter at Laurie Island in the South Orkneys. There the expedition set up a meteorological station, hand-built of stone and called Omond House, on April 1, 1903. Midwinter's Day (June 22) 1903 was celebrated with a barrel of Guinness porter, a brew made more potent by the freezing of its water, unintentionally yielding concentrated alcohol. At the end of the first season, *Scotia* sailed to Port Stanley and Buenos Aires. Bruce asked the British government to continue staffing Omond House, but his request was refused. Instead, at the invitation of the British Ambassador, the Oficina Meteorológica Argentina agreed to assume responsibility for the station. This duty, which the Argentine government maintains to the present day, makes the station (now called Orcadas) the oldest continuously operated scientific base in the Antarctic.

Pushing south again in January 1904, Bruce was able to penetrate the Weddell Sea to 74°S. There he discovered Coats Land, named for the expedition's patrons, Andrew and James Coats of Paisley, Scotland. *Scotia* followed the coast for 240km, but always the fast ice kept the ship two or three frustrating kilometers offshore, and no landing could be made. The Scottish expedition, however, could claim an important milestone: moving pictures were made in the Antarctic for the first time. There was another pioneering achievement: a remarkable series of photographs, documenting the first known use of bagpipes in the Far South, shows an emperor penguin, head thrown back and beak agape, being serenaded by a kilted piper. Although an observer noted 'only sleepy indifference,' some of the photos show that the bird was tethered by a line to prevent escape.

'Photographs show an emperor penguin, head thrown back and beak agape, being serenaded by a kilted piper'

Although Bruce later became a world authority on Spitsbergen in the Arctic, he must've retained a special love for the Antarctic; upon his death in 1921, his ashes were carried south and poured into the Southern Ocean.

Charcot

French physician Jean-Baptiste Etienne August Charcot (1867–1936) inherited 400,000 gold francs and a Fragonard painting, *Le Pacha*, from his father, a famous neurologist whose work influenced Freud. Charcot used this entire fortune to finance construction of a three-masted schooner, *Français*, and to outfit it with laboratory equipment. His original intention had been to sail north to the Arctic, but when word arrived that Nordenskjöld's expedition was missing in Antarctica, Charcot decided to go south. Meanwhile, French citizens rallied for the French Antarctic Expedition, contributing 450,000 francs.

Français sailed from Le Havre on August 15, 1903 – into immediate tragedy. Just minutes off the quay a hawser parted, striking and killing a sailor; the expedition was delayed 12 days before departing without further incident. Belgian explorer de Gerlache accompanied the expedition as far as Buenos Aires, where he told Charcot that he missed his new fiancée too much to continue. Also in Buenos Aires, the expedition learned that the Argentine ship *Uruguay* had already rescued Nordenskjöld and his men, so Charcot decided instead to investigate the west coast of the Peninsula. He deliberately chose to avoid the Ross Sea, with its potential for international rivalry, an act for which the territorial Robert Scott later called him 'the gentleman of the Pole.'

1909
The South Magnetic Pole is attained for the first time, by three members of Shackleton's *Nimrod* expedition

1911
Amundsen and four others are the first people to reach the South Pole, on December 14

By February 19, 1904, Charcot had discovered Port Lockroy on Wiencke Island. Sailing on, he decided to winter at a sheltered bay on the north coast of Booth Island, a place he named Port Charcot. The bay was so small that the explorers were able to stretch a hawser across its mouth to keep out ice that might otherwise crush their ship. Winter passed with various amusements (including reading and discussing old newspapers) and sledging expeditions to nearby islands. The peace was marred only by the death of the ship's pet pig, Toby, who ate a bucketful of fish – along with the hooks that caught them.

After the spring breakup, the expedition sailed north, running into trouble on January 15, 1903, when *Français* struck a rock. Despite attempts at plugging the hole and round-the-clock pumping, the ship continued to flood. Temporary repairs effected at Port Lockroy enabled the expedition to continue to Tierra del Fuego and Buenos Aires, where Charcot sold *Français* to the Argentine government. Then he headed home to a hero's welcome from all of France – except his wife (a granddaughter of Victor Hugo) who divorced him for desertion.

Four years later, Charcot returned to Antarctica, this time as head of an expedition sponsored by the French government, which granted him 600,000 francs. On August 15, 1908, he again sailed from Le Havre, this time in the newly built and amusingly named *Pourquoi Pas?* (Why Not?), which he had once christened his toy boats as a child. Among those aboard was Charcot's second wife, Meg, who sailed as far as Punta Arenas. (Wary of repeating his failed first marriage, Charcot had secured a prenuptial agreement from her that she would not oppose his explorations.)

A WINDOW ON THE 'HEROIC ERA' *Baden Norris*

New Zealand has been linked to Antarctica since the 1840s, when both the British explorer James Clark Ross and US Navy Lieutenant Charles Wilkes visited during their voyages to and from the continent. Today many important aspects of Antarctica's past still live in New Zealand, as part of the Antarctic collection at the Canterbury Museum in Christchurch.

In 1901 Robert F Scott used Lyttelton (the port of Christchurch) to prepare for his voyage to Antarctica. Edward Wilson, the expedition's zoologist, worked at the Canterbury Museum while preparing albatross skins and other specimens collected during the voyage over from England. The association between Scott, Wilson and the museum meant that upon *Discovery*'s return from the Antarctic many items used on the expedition were deposited with the museum. At the Canterbury Museum's Sir Robertson Stewart Hall of Antarctic Discovery, these items are still the nucleus of the collection, which now ranks as the most comprehensive assembly of relics from Antarctica's past.

Nearly every subsequent expedition – including those led by Ernest Shackleton, Scott and Richard Byrd – left artifacts with the museum; later expeditions, such as the US's Operation Deep Freeze and the British Commonwealth Trans-Antarctic Expedition, continued this tradition. The result is that the gallery covers most of the important events in recent Antarctic history.

The Hall of Antarctic Discovery opened to the public in 1977. It is divided into three sections: geology, natural history and exploration. The extensive geology gallery is arranged in order of geological age and includes numerous fossils. The natural history section includes dioramas covering the life histories of penguins, whales and seals. There are also displays about huskies, the hard-working dogs that until recently provided welcome companionship for the continent's human population.

1912
Scott and four others sledge to 90°S on January 17 – all die on the return to Ross Island

1912
A Norwegian whaling firm establishes a shore station at Deception Island

After a stop at Deception Island's whaling station, where Charcot saved a man from a hideous death by amputating his gangrenous hand, *Pourquoi Pas?* sailed on Christmas Day 1908, and continued the survey work on the western side of the Peninsula that Charcot had begun with *Français*. As on his previous voyage, unfortunately, Charcot struck a rock, damaging *Pourquoi Pas?*, which had pumps that were able to manage the water pouring in through the seam. The expedition pushed on, discovering and naming the Fallières Coast, circling Adelaide Island and proving its insularity, and discovering Marguerite Bay, naming it for Meg. Most useful for this survey work was a small, iron-prowed motorboat carried in *Pourquoi Pas?*. The ship also boasted electric lighting and a 1500-volume library.

Those amenities proved valuable during the winter of 1909, when the expedition wintered at Petermann Island, with *Pourquoi Pas?* frozen into the ice at a bay they called Port Circumcision. The group set up a shore station, with huts for meteorological, seismic, magnetic and tidal research, and passed the winter with reading, lectures, meetings of the 'Antarctic Sporting Club' and recitations from a novel being written by one of the officers.

At winter's end, they returned north to resupply the ship with coal at Deception Island – where a whaling-company diver inspected the ship's damaged hull and warned against further exploration. Charcot ignored this advice, heading south a final time. On January 11, 1910, he made his most personally treasured discovery, sighting an uncharted headland at 70°S, 76°W. This he called Charcot Land (since proven to be an island) – not after himself, but after his esteemed father. Twenty-six years later, Charcot and *Pourquoi Pas?* were again sailing in treacherous

The exploration gallery is the hall's most popular. It includes many fascinating relics, among them a dinner plate from James Clark Ross' ship *Erebus*, a medicine chest for sledge dogs and, what is perhaps the collection's single most important item, the Polar Medal awarded to Scott in 1904 – the first one ever presented.

Shackleton's expeditions are also well represented, with artifacts such as the red ensign flown from his ship *Nimrod*, tinned supplies recovered from the hut at Cape Royds, the Arroll-Johnston motor-sledge his Ross Sea party took with them on the ill-fated Imperial Trans-Antarctic Expedition of 1914–16 and a surprisingly modern-looking Primus stove taken on *James Caird* on its 1420km journey from Elephant Island to South Georgia after *Endurance* was crushed in pack ice.

Roald Amundsen, victor in the race to the South Pole, is given prime billing in a display featuring the pocketknife used to sharpen a bamboo stake that Amundsen's party drove into the ice at the Pole to proudly support the Norwegian flag.

Items from Scott's *Terra Nova* expedition include pony snowshoes, a shaft from one of the motorsledges, Wilson's microscope and a box of cigars with a typed inscription: 'For final dash, compliments of the Sol factory, Havana.' Byrd's important role in Antarctic aviation is documented by a Primus lamp from his Advance Base and a champagne bottle covered with the signatures of many of the men involved in his first flight over the Pole.

Dominating the hall are two large pieces: a Tucker Sno-Cat oversnow vehicle, one of four used by Vivian Fuchs in the first crossing of Antarctica; and a Ferguson farm tractor, one of three employed by Edmund Hillary to reach the South Pole.

Baden Norris is the Antarctic curator emeritus at the Canterbury Museum

1912–13
Six land stations, 21 factory ships and 62 catcher boats kill and process 10,760 whales

1913
Mawson returns to his base barely alive after two companions perish on a sledging trip

waters, this time off Iceland, when a gale arose and claimed captain, ship and all but one of the 43-man crew.

Shackleton's *Nimrod* Expedition

Irishman Ernest Henry Shackleton (1874–1922), second of 10 children born to a doctor and his Quaker wife, was badly stung by his breakdown on the return from Scott's furthest south in 1902. Indeed, Shackleton lived by his family motto: *Fortitudine vincimus* (By fortitude we conquer). Even as he was being sent home as an invalid by Scott, Shackleton resolved that he would one day return to Antarctica – which he did in 1908. An indefatigable worker with a charming and forceful personality, Shackleton inspired fierce loyalty and admiration from his men, who called him 'The Boss.'

There could be a bit of Antarctica just down the road from you... Check out www.antarctic-circle.org, by Robert Stephenson, which describes sites linked with The Ice but not located in Antarctica, such as museums, graves, homes, even an Irish pub – the South Pole Inn – kept by Tom Crean and associated with both Scott and Shackleton.

Following his return from *Discovery* expedition, Shackleton married and fathered the first of his three children, at the same time holding a succession of jobs: magazine journalist, secretary of the Scottish Royal Geographical Society, (unsuccessful) candidate for Parliament and, finally, PR man for a big Glasgow steelworks. The works' owner, William Beardmore, took a liking to Shackleton and agreed to sponsor an Antarctic expedition.

The British Antarctic Expedition sailed from Lyttelton, New Zealand, on New Year's Day 1908, in *Nimrod*, a three-masted sealing ship with 40 years' experience in the Arctic. To conserve coal, the ship was towed part of the 2700km to the ice edge by the steel-hulled *Koonya*. Although Shackleton had originally intended to use *Discovery*'s old base at Ross Island, Scott wrote to him describing his own plans for another Antarctic expedition and asked him to establish his shore base elsewhere, a show of territoriality that seems presumptuous today. Shackleton agreed to seek his own headquarters, but when he arrived at the Ross Ice Shelf in January 1908, he was dismayed to find that the Bay of Whales, the inlet where *Discovery* had launched its balloon just six years before, had disappeared. Evidently the great ice shelf had calved, and if so, it would be very risky to try to set up a base on top of it. But *Nimrod* was unable to push further east, due to pack ice, so Shackleton reluctantly decided to use Ross Island as his base – breaking his promise to Scott.

Unforgiving ice blocked his path to Hut Point, however, and Shackleton was compelled to build his hut at Cape Royds on Ross Island, 30km further from his goal. While he didn't bring sledge dogs, neither did Shackleton agree with Scott's romantic but misguided notion that manhauling was 'more noble and splendid' than dog-driving. Instead, Shackleton brought with him ponies from Siberia, which unfortunately were unsuited to the task. Although they managed to pull loads a considerable distance across the Ross Ice Shelf, they did not have the stamina or versatility of dogs.

With three companions – Jameson Adams, Eric Marshall and Frank Wild – Shackleton pioneered the route up to the polar plateau (which he claimed, and named, for King Edward VII) via the Beardmore Glacier, which he named for the expedition's patron. By January 9, 1909, the foursome had trudged on foot to within 180km of the Pole before being forced by dangerously dwindling supplies of food to turn and run for home. It was the hardest decision of Shackleton's life. He told his wife Emily later: 'I thought you'd rather have a live donkey than a dead lion.' Still, they had achieved a remarkable run, beating Scott's furthest south by 589km,

1915
Shackleton's *Endurance* is crushed by Weddell Sea pack ice

1916
On his fourth attempt, Shackleton rescues the men stranded on Elephant Island

discovering almost 800km of new mountain range, and showing the way to anyone who would attempt the Pole after them. They also found coal and fossils at Mt Buckley at the top of the Beardmore Glacier.

The expedition achieved other firsts as well. Six men, led by Professor TW Edgeworth David, ascended Mt Erebus for the first time, reaching the rim of the volcano's crater on March 10, 1908 after a five-day climb. While the polar party was out, three of the expedition's members – Douglas Mawson and Alistair Mackay with Professor David again leading – hiked nearly 1600km to the South Magnetic Pole, reaching it on January 16, 1909, the first time it had ever been visited. (Today the Pole is offshore in the Dumont d'Urville Sea, and Antarctic tour ships routinely sail over it.) The expedition also saw the Antarctic's first motorcar, an Arrol Johnston, tested at Cape Royds (it was no good in snow, but proved useful for transporting loads across the sea ice), and produced about 80 copies of *Aurora Australis*, the first – and only – book published in Antarctica.

Amundsen

Norwegian Roald Engelbregt Gravning Amundsen (1872–1928) was already a veteran explorer by the time he sailed in 1910 from Christiana (modern-day Oslo) on his way to what only he and a few others knew was the Antarctic. Amundsen had been with the first group to winter south of the Antarctic Circle, the *Belgica* expedition, and in 1903–06 had accomplished the first navigation of the Northwest Passage, a goal sought by mariners for centuries. He spent three winters in the Arctic, learning from the native Eskimos much about polar clothing, travel and dog-handling that would later prove invaluable.

Der Kongress der Pinguine (*The Congress of the Penguins*; 1994) is a Swiss film that stars gentoo penguins in a bizarre morality tale of alleged environmental destruction in Antarctica and South Georgia. It's definitely weird.

The Arctic had always been Amundsen's first interest, and he had long dreamed of reaching the North Pole. Indeed, he was well into planning an expedition where he would freeze his ship into the ice and drift with the current across the Pole when news reached him that American Robert E Peary claimed to have reached 90°N on April 6, 1909. Amundsen quickly – and secretly – turned his ambitions 180°.

Fram, Amundsen's aptly named ship (it means 'Forward'), which had been used by Norwegian explorer Fridtjof Nansen on his unsuccessful attempt to reach the North Pole, sailed from Norway on June 6, 1911. *Fram* had a diesel engine, allowing quick start-up (as opposed to a coal-fired steam engine), as well as a rounded hull so that it would rise up out of pressing ice floes rather than being nipped as a standard hull would. In order not to let his rival Robert Scott know of his plans, Amundsen kept quiet about his intentions – revealing them to just three members of the expedition – until he reached Madeira. There he told his stunned men, and soon after, sent his infamous telegram to Scott in Melbourne: 'Beg leave to inform you *Fram* proceeding Antarctic Amundsen.'

Amundsen did not share Shackleton's fear of a dangerously calving Ross Ice Shelf. Instead, he established his base, Framheim ('home of *Fram*'), right on the shelf at the Bay of Whales, where Scott had previously made Antarctica's first balloon flight. There, in a small prefab wooden hut, nine men spent the winter. Outside, some of the 15 identical tents served as store sheds – and some as doghouses for the expedition's 97 North Greenland dogs. From Framheim, Amundsen had the advantage

1922
Shackleton dies aboard *Quest*, moored at Grytviken on South Georgia

1928
Wilkins makes the first powered flight in Antarctica from Deception Island

of starting 100km closer to the Pole, but he also had to pioneer a route up to the polar plateau from the Ross Ice Shelf. Scott, following Shackleton's lead, could take the charted course up the Beardmore Glacier.

Setting out from Framheim on October 19, 1911, after making one false start too early in the season, Amundsen and his four companions had four sledges, each pulled by 13 Greenland dogs. Dogs and skis made the difference for them. As Norwegians, they were well trained in the use of skis, and during his years in the Arctic, Amundsen had developed excellent dog-driving skills. He also planned meticulously, took three or four backups of every critical item, and laid 10 extremely well-marked depots as far as 82°S, which together contained 3400kg of stores and food.

Antarctica: The Complete Story (2001), by David McGonigal and Lynn Woodworth, is literally a massive effort, weighing 3.6kg. It's gorgeous, with lush color photography on every page, and the wildlife and history sections are excellent.

The five men – Amundsen, Olav Bjaaland, Helmer Hanssen, Sverre Hassel and Oscar Wisting – reached the South Pole on December 14, 1911, camping for three days at what they called *Polheim*. Amundsen claimed the polar plateau for Norway, calling it King Haakon VII Land, and wrote a note to Scott in the dark green tent he left behind. Then, they turned for home.

'On January 25, at 4am,' Amundsen laconically recorded in his diary, 'we reached our good little house again, with two sledges and 11 dogs; men and animals all hale and hearty.' Despite his near-flawless success, there were those who felt Amundsen's achievement was tainted by several factors. In some ways, he had made the polar journey look *too* easy. There was also the view taken by some that Amundsen's surprise assault on the Pole had forestalled Scott, as though the British explorer had the 'right' to reach the Pole first (although Amundsen, in fact, preceded him to the Antarctic). Finally, the tragic drama of Scott's expedition was much more the stuff of legend than was Amundsen's cool triumph of technical skill.

Scott's *Terra Nova* Expedition

When Amundsen's startling cable reached him, Scott became deeply distressed, although he worked hard not to show it. He had first watched Shackleton come close to snatching what he regarded as his prize, and now a dangerous new threat had arisen.

Sailing from New Zealand on November 29, 1910, in *Terra Nova*, the old Scottish whaler that had been one of the two relief ships sent at the end of the *Discovery* expedition, Scott's British Antarctic Expedition got off to a rough start. Just three days after weighing anchor, *Terra Nova* was hit by a screaming gale that lasted 36 hours and nearly sank the ship. Arriving at Ross Island in January 1911, Scott found ice blocking the way to his old *Discovery* hut on Hut Point, so he established winter quarters at Cape Evans, named after his second-in-command, ERGR 'Teddy' Evans. As soon as the hut was built, Scott commenced an ambitious program of depot-laying. He also introduced a useful innovation to Antarctica: a telephone line was established between Cape Evans and Hut Point. Mules, ponies, motor-sledges and dogs were employed to set up supply caches, but once again, when these methods failed, the expedition resorted to the old British standby of manhauling.

The next spring, on October 24, Scott dispatched a party with two motor-sledges, and eight days later followed with a larger group of men and 10 ponies. Various teams relayed the supplies and laid depots until, on January 4, 1912, the last support party turned back. For the final push to the Pole,

1929
Byrd and three companions become the first people to fly over the South Pole

1934
Byrd, alone at his Advance Base, becomes the first person to winter in Antarctica's interior

Scott had chosen his companion on his previous furthest south, Edward Wilson, along with Lawrence Oates, Edgar Evans and Henry Bowers, who was added only the night before. (Another tactical error, since the food, tent and skis had been planned for four-man teams.)

What happened next is the most famous Antarctic story of all: the five arrived at the South Pole on January 17, 1912, to find that Amundsen had beaten them by 35 days. Nothing tells the tale better than Scott's diary itself, unless it is one of the many biographies that deconstruct what has grown to be a hoary legend. Their return home was a haunting, desperate run of barely sighted depots, slow starvation and incredible cold. A delirious Evans died on February 17. A month later, Oates was in such bad shape that he prayed not to wake upon retiring. The next morning, deeply disappointed to find himself still among the living, Oates walked out of the tent during a raging blizzard, telling his companions simply, 'I am just going outside and may be some time.' Another blizzard kept the three remaining men in their tent from March 21 onwards. Scott's last entry was dated March 29.

(In a depressing fin-de-siècle postscript to the story, Captain Scott's descendants decided to sell several artifacts from his last expedition at an auction in London in late 1999. They had been kept in a bank vault for half a century by Sir Peter Scott, Captain Scott's son (and a cofounder of the World Wildlife Fund), who died in 1989. Parts of the Primus stove on which the three last members of the polar party may have cooked their final hot meal brought £27,600. A Union Jack found with the bodies, possibly flown by the party at the Pole, sold for £25,300.)

Antarctica (1984), the story of sled dogs abandoned on a 1958 Japanese expedition, is a heartrending film. The eerie soundtrack of the same name is by *Chariots of Fire* composer Vangelis.

Despite being beaten to the Pole, Scott's last expedition accomplished a great deal of important science. (In fact, the push for research had itself contributed to the polar party's destruction, since the men dragged a sledge that carried, among other items, 16kg of geological samples.) The infamous three-man midwinter trek to Cape Crozier, which Apsley Cherry-Garrard chronicled so eloquently in *The Worst Journey in the World*, braved 24-hour darkness and temperatures as low as -59°C – so cold that the men's teeth cracked in their mouths and they were 'beginning to think of death as a friend,' as Cherry-Garrard wrote – all so that they could be the first to collect emperor penguin embryos. A separate Northern Party, led by Victor Campbell, discovered Oates Land (named for Lawrence Oates) and spent a winter of terrible privation in a snow cave at Terra Nova Bay on the western shore of the Ross Sea. And a six-man group led by geologist Griffith Taylor explored the mysterious, otherworldly Dry Valleys, which Scott had found on the *Discovery* expedition.

Shirase

Coming from a country with no tradition of exploration, Nobu Shirase (1861–1946), a lieutenant in the Japanese Army and the eldest son of a Buddhist priest, was a surprise visitor to Antarctica. Despite the Japanese public's outright scorn of his fundraising efforts, Shirase organized an Antarctic expedition in 1910. Sailing from Tokyo on December 1 in *Kainan Maru* ('Southern Pioneer'), the expedition reached Victoria Land in March 1911. Unable to land, however, it returned to winter in Sydney, where Shirase and his countrymen set up camp in the garden of a well-to-do resident of suburban Vaucluse.

1935
Ellsworth, on his third attempt, completes the first trans-Antarctic flight

1935
Norwegian Caroline Mikkelsen becomes the first woman to set foot on the continent

By mid-January 1912, *Kainan Maru* was back in the Ross Sea, this time with 29 Sakhalin sledge dogs. There it met Amundsen's expedition at the Bay of Whales on the Ross Ice Shelf. Amundsen – and Scott, too – had by this time already reached the Pole, although Shirase, of course, could not know it. Despite being far behind, Shirase and six of his men formed a 'dash patrol' and in a symbolic gesture, headed south with dogs and sledges. First, however, they had to claw their way to the top of the Ross Ice Shelf, which towered nearly 90m over the sea where *Kainan Maru* stood offshore. The patrol pushed 260km to a furthest south of 80°5'S, reached on January 28, 1912. There, Shirase claimed all the area of the Ross Ice Shelf within sight as the 'Yamato Yukihara,' or 'Yamato Snow Plain' ('Yamato' being a poetical name for Japan). This claim has never been taken seriously (even by Japan), given that Amundsen had already traveled through the area on his way south to the Pole. The expedition had to abandon a score of dogs, eerily prefiguring the dogs marooned at Syowa station 46 years later. Nevertheless, the expedition's members were welcomed as heroes when they returned to Yokohama on June 20, 1912.

Mawson

Australian geologist Douglas Mawson (1882–1958) had been asked by Robert Scott to accompany *Terra Nova*, but he declined the invitation in favor of leading his own expedition. Already a veteran of Shackleton's *Nimrod* expedition, Mawson wanted to explore new territory west of Cape Adare. With the Australian government granting over half the expedition's cost, Mawson escaped some of the financing worries that plagued other explorers.

The Australasian Antarctic Expedition (AAE) sailed from Hobart on December 2, 1911, in *Aurora*, an old sealer with years of experience in the Arctic and the relief of Shackleton's Ross Sea party to its credit. Its master was Captain John King Davis, and onboard was the first airplane taken to the Antarctic, a Vickers REP monoplane that had crashed during a test flight before the expedition even left Australia. Mawson brought the wingless aircraft with him anyway, hoping to use it as an 'air tractor,' but it failed at this task too when its engine seized while towing a heavy load.

Polar Castaways: The Ross Sea Party of Sir Ernest Shackleton, 1914–17, written by Richard McElrea and David Harrowfield and published in 2004, is based on previously unpublished interviews with survivors of the expedition.

Aurora arrived at the ice edge in January 1912, then headed west and followed the coast to new territories, which Mawson called King George V Land and claimed for the British crown. At Cape Denison on Commonwealth Bay, he set up his base, unaware that the roaring katabatics make the spot one of the windiest places on earth. He later gave it the memorable name 'the home of the blizzard.' A party of eight men, led by Frank Wild, also a veteran of Shackleton's *Nimrod* expedition, was landed at the Shackleton Ice Shelf, 2400km west of Cape Denison. Battling wind speeds that occasionally reached more than 320km/h at Commonwealth Bay, the expedition systematically explored King George V Land, as well as neighboring Terre Adélie, during the summer of 1912–13. On one of these sledging trips, the first Antarctic meteorite was found. The expedition also made the first radio contact between Antarctica and another continent, on September 25, 1912, using a wireless relay at the five-man station the expedition established on Macquarie Island.

Despite those accomplishments and the comprehensive research done by the expedition, it is remembered primarily for the ordeal that its leader

1938–39
A secret Nazi expedition is dispatched by Göring to claim territory for Germany

1946
Operation Highjump, the largest-ever Antarctic expedition, brings 4700 men to The Ice

endured on a deadly dog-sledging journey. With Belgrave Ninnis, a British soldier, and Xavier Mertz, a Swiss mountaineer and ski champion, Mawson left Cape Denison on November 10, 1912, to explore east of the expedition's base. By December 14, after crossing two heavily crevassed glaciers (later named for Mertz and Ninnis), they had reached a point 500km from their base. That afternoon, Ninnis disappeared down an apparently bottomless crevasse with his team of dogs – and most of the party's food, all of its dog food and its tent. Wrote Mawson later: 'It seemed so incredible that we half expected, on turning round, to find him standing there.'

Thus began a harrowing trek home. Battling hunger, cold, fatigue and, possibly, vitamin A poisoning from the dog livers they were forced to eat, Mawson and Mertz struggled on. After Mertz died on January 7, when they were still more than 160km out, Mawson sawed the remaining sledge in half with a pocketknife to lighten his load. By now his body was literally falling apart: hair coming out, toenails loosened and even the thick soles of his feet sloughing off. Somehow he got back to Cape Denison – only a few hours after *Aurora* had sailed away.

'Mawson's body was literally falling apart: hair coming out, toenails loosened and even the thick soles of his feet sloughing off'

Six men had remained behind at the hut, hoping against hope that the missing party might return. Although they radioed the ship, heavy seas prevented *Aurora* from reaching Cape Denison, and they were forced to spend another winter, arriving back in Australia in late February, 1914.

In 1929–31 Mawson returned to Antarctica, leading the two summer voyages of the British, Australian and New Zealand Antarctic Research Expedition (Banzare) to the west of Commonwealth Bay, where they discovered Mac.Robertson Land, named for Sir MacPherson Robertson, a benefactor of the expedition.

Filchner

With the Pole won, Bavarian army Lieutenant Wilhelm Filchner (1877–1957) decided to tackle another issue of Antarctic discovery: the question of whether the Weddell and Ross Seas were joined by a channel, as some geographers posited. Educated at the Prussian Military Academy and a veteran of a pioneering horseback journey through the Pamirs and another expedition to Tibet, Filchner hoped to cross the continent, starting from the Weddell Sea, to solve this puzzle. When he was unable to raise the large amount of money the two-ship expedition would require, he decided merely to push as far south as he could into the Weddell Sea.

Sailing from Bremerhaven on May 4, 1911 in a Norwegian ship renamed *Deutschland*, the Second German South Polar Expedition called in at Buenos Aires on the way south. There, Filchner met aboard *Fram* with Amundsen, who was on his triumphant return from the Pole. By mid-December, *Deutschland* reached the Weddell Sea pack ice. After 10 days of pushing through narrow leads, the ship penetrated to the sea's southern coast, William Bruce's Coats Land. Sailing west, Filchner reached new territory, calling it 'Prinz Regent Luitpold Land' (now Luitpold Coast). He also discovered a vast ice shelf, naming it 'Kaiser Wilhelm Barrier' for his emperor (who later insisted that it be renamed after Filchner). Filchner then tried to establish a winter base ('Stationseisberg') on the ice shelf, but these plans had to be hastily abandoned when a huge section of the shelf – carrying the expedition's nearly completed hut – calved into the sea.

1947
The first women, Edith ('Jackie') Ronne and Jennie Darlington, winter on Antarctica

1954
Australia establishes Mawson, the first permanent scientific station set up on the continent

The Antarctic winter closed in before *Deutschland* could escape to lower latitudes and the ship was beset and drifted for nine months. During this period of monotonous tedium, one crew member managed to read an entire dictionary from A to Z. The expedition was also riven by a deep divide caused by the ship's captain, Richard Vahsel, who was suffering from syphilis. He died in August 1912 during the drift and was, as Filchner later wrote, 'committed to the sea in a sack, along with a heavy weight.'

Filchner led a three-man party on a dangerous midwinter dog-sledging trip over some 65km of sea ice to the charted location of 'New South Greenland,' which American sealer Benjamin Morrell claimed to have sighted in 1823. Finding nothing but frozen ocean, Filchner proved the nonexistence of Morrell's 'discovery.' Successfully navigating back to the ship was a great feat, since the instruments were nearly destroyed by the -34°C cold – and *Deutschland* had drifted almost 65km with the current-driven pack ice.

On November 26, 1912, the decaying ice released the ship, which sailed to South Georgia and home. Back in Germany, armed with his newly won knowledge of the Weddell Sea coast, Filchner again tried to raise interest in a crossing of Antarctica, from the Weddell to the Ross Sea. But Germany's attention, on the eve of WWI, was elsewhere.

Shackleton's *Endurance* Expedition

After losing his most sought-after prize – but saving himself and his companions – on the *Nimrod* expedition, Ernest Shackleton had also set his sights on crossing Antarctica. The threat of a German expedition attempting the same journey helped Shackleton to raise funds, as nationalistic Britons sent in contributions to the 'first crossing of the last continent.' His plan was simple but ambitious: Shackleton would sail in *Endurance* to the Weddell Sea coast, establish a base, then trek across the continent via the South Pole. At the top of the Beardmore Glacier, the crossing party would be met by another group, which would have been landed at Ross Island by *Aurora*, sailing from Hobart.

The Endurance: Shackleton's Legendary Antarctic Expedition (1997), by Caroline Alexander, retells the *Endurance* story and includes most of the terrific photographs taken by expedition photographer Frank Hurley.

Even as *Endurance* prepared to sail, the firestorm ignited by the assassination of Archduke Franz Ferdinand and his wife on June 28, 1914 was engulfing Europe. Britain declared war on Germany on August 4, and Shackleton immediately offered *Endurance* and her crew for service. Winston Churchill, then First Lord of the Admiralty, wired his thanks, but the expedition was told to proceed. *Endurance* sailed from Plymouth on August 8 'to carry on our white warfare,' as Shackleton put it. After calling at Madeira, Buenos Aires and South Georgia, the expedition pushed into the Weddell Sea pack ice and soon found itself squeezing through ever-narrower leads.

By January 19, 1915, *Endurance* was caught. The events that followed have grown to legend, becoming nearly as famous as the story of Scott's last expedition. The ship, inexorably crushed by the grinding ice floes, finally sank on November 21. Shackleton and his men lived on the pack ice for five months before they sailed three small boats to Elephant Island in the South Shetlands. Since the island was uninhabited, Shackleton and five others were forced to sail another 1300km across the open sea in one of the boats, the 6.9m *James Caird* (which the ship's carpenter had decked over with spare timbers) to seek help from the whalers at South

1956
John Torbet and six others fly across Antarctica via the South Pole (Ross Island to Weddell Sea and back, without landing) on January 13

1957–58
Forty-six Antarctic stations (including one at the South Pole) operated by 12 countries contribute to the International Geophysical Year

Georgia. After 16 exhausting days at sea, they landed at South Georgia, completing one of history's greatest navigational feats.

But their landfall was at King Haakon Bay, on South Georgia's bleak, uninhabited southwest coast, and the whaling stations were on the island's northeastern side. Although no one had previously penetrated further than a kilometer or so from the coast, Shackleton had no choice but to try to cross the island. He and two of the six men who had sailed *James Caird* with him, Tom Crean and Frank Worsley, hiked for 36 straight hours over the 1800m-high mountains and crevassed glaciers to reach the whaling station at Stromness Harbour. As they neared the station, impassable ice cliffs forced them to lower themselves down an icy, 9m waterfall. Upon their arrival at the station, on May 20, 1916, their long beards, matted hair, ragged clothes – and fierce body odor, no doubt – caused the first three people they met to flee in disgust.

South (1998), Frank Hurley's film of the *Endurance* expedition, was beautifully restored by the British Film Institute. It includes very good footage of Shackleton's men and dogs working on *Endurance* and of the ship beset by pack ice.

At the home of the station manager, where they bathed and were fed and clothed, Shackleton asked, 'When was the war over?' 'The war is not over,' the manager answered. 'Millions are being killed. Europe is mad. The world is mad.' That night a whaler was dispatched to pick up the three men left behind at King Haakon Bay. After three failed rescue attempts over the next four months, Shackleton enlisted the help of *Yelcho*, a steamer lent by the Chilean government, and was finally able to pick up all 22 men stranded at Elephant Island on August 30.

Still, Shackleton's troubles were not over – the Ross Sea party had encountered its own difficulties. *Aurora* had intended to winter at Ross Island, but a blizzard blew the ship from its moorings, stranding at Cape Evans 10 men who spent a miserable winter with minimal supplies. *Aurora*, meanwhile, was beset for 10 months, finally getting free on March 14, 1916. Shackleton met the ship in New Zealand and after an extensive refitting *Aurora* was able to relieve the marooned Cape Evans party on January 10, 1917. The war, meanwhile, raged for another 22 bloody months, long enough for two of Shackleton's men to die in the fighting.

Shackleton himself lived to mount one final assault on the Antarctic, the ill-defined *Quest* expedition. Upon reaching South Georgia, he suffered a massive heart attack and died on January 5, 1922 aboard his ship, which was moored alongside at Grytviken.

Wilkins

Australian George Hubert Wilkins (1888–1958), a Balkan War combat photographer and veteran of two Antarctic expeditions including Shackleton's final voyage in *Quest*, decided in 1928 that the time was right to attempt a flight in Antarctica. He had already flown 4000km across the Arctic Ocean earlier in the year, becoming the first to cross the region by air, and now Wilkins took the same pilot (Carl Ben Eielson) and the same plane (now called *Los Angeles)* south to tackle The Ice.

With his Arctic success guaranteeing him a well-funded expedition – including a lucrative US$25,000 news-rights contract with American press baron William Randolph Hearst – Wilkins was transported on a whaling ship, *Hektoria*, which called at Deception Island. He also brought with him a backup pilot, Joe Crosson, and a second wood-framed Lockheed Vega monoplane, christened *San Francisco*. These planes were considered

1958
Fuchs' Commonwealth Trans-Antarctic Expedition is the first to cross the continent

1959
The Antarctic Treaty, reserving the continent for peace and science, is signed on December 1

revolutionary for their time, having no wires or exposed controls that offered extra wind resistance.

Wilkins had equipped the Vegas with pontoons to enable them to take off from the protected waters of Deception's Port Foster, but on test runs he encountered a uniquely Antarctic obstacle: hundreds of albatrosses, attracted to the open water created when the ship broke the harbor ice. So Wilkins and his men – aided by crews from the nearby whaling station – cleared a rough runway on shore. Rough it was: running 800m up a hill, down across ditches, up another hill, and down to the harbor. If a plane hadn't gotten up enough speed to take off by then, it would plunge into the water. On November 16, 1928, Wilkins and Eielson took off in the *Los Angeles*, flying for just 20 minutes before the weather closed in. Still, it was a useful shakedown – and it made history as the first powered flight in Antarctica.

The Thing (1982) stars an extraterrestrial that terrorizes polar research stations. This much-too-gory remake of the 1951 original (set in the Arctic) is a bona fide Antarctic movie, but feels a lot like *Alien*.

Little more than a month later, Wilkins and Eielson were ready to tackle a longer flight. Although they hoped to fly from the Peninsula to the Ross Sea, bad weather made this impractical. But on December 20, taking off again from Deception, they flew for 11 hours across the Peninsula and along its eastern side, covering 2100km and reaching as far south as 71°20'S. Eight years before, as a member of the British Imperial Expedition to Graham Land, Wilkins had been frustrated by 'the slow, blind struggles' to make progress over the difficult terrain. 'This time,' he exulted, 'I had a tremendous sensation of power and freedom – I felt liberated...for the first time in history, new land was being discovered from the air.' Important though the flight was, Wilkins was deceived by the appearance of the Peninsula from above and wrongly concluded that it must be an archipelago.

Wilkins returned to the Antarctic the next summer, making more flights and discoveries. All told, he mapped 200,000 sq km of new territory, proving beyond any doubt the efficacy of the airplane in Antarctic work. He later supported Lincoln Ellsworth (p55) with his flights over Antarctica.

Byrd

Wilkins scared American flier Richard Evelyn Byrd (1888–1957). A graduate of the US Naval Academy at Annapolis, Byrd had claimed in 1926 to be first to fly over the North Pole (the claim remains controversial to this day). In 1927 he was narrowly beaten by Charles Lindbergh in the era's greatest race: solo across the Atlantic. Soon after, he made it his goal to become the first to fly over the South Pole.

Crowned with his Arctic 'success,' Byrd raised nearly a million dollars from such eminent sponsors as Charles Lindbergh (US$1000), the National Geographic Society and the *New York Times*, which paid US$60,000 for exclusive rights and the privilege of sending its own reporter, Russell Owen, on the expedition. Byrd's United States Antarctic Expedition was the best-funded private expedition to Antarctica in history. It sailed from Hoboken, New Jersey, in August 1928, in the square-rigged *City of New York* with not one, but three separate aircraft. 'Accompanied by business managers, physicians, cameramen, dog trainers, scientists, aviators, newspapermen,' *Time* magazine wrote of the departing expedition, 'the size and diversity of its personnel suggests a circus.'

The expedition's base, 'Little America,' was established at the Bay of Whales on the Ross Ice Shelf in January 1929. Byrd quickly set up a flying

1961
Leonid I Rogozov, physician at Russia's Novolazarevskaya station, successfully removes his own appendix in an emergency operation

1965
Grytviken, South Georgia's last shore-based whaling station, closes

program with his three planes – the big aluminum Ford trimotor *Floyd Bennett*, named for his North Pole pilot who had died of pneumonia earlier in 1928; the smaller, single-engine Fairchild, *Stars and Stripes*; and a single-engine Fokker Universal named *The Virginian* for Byrd's home state.

In March the expedition suffered Antarctica's first plane crash, but luckily no one was in *The Virginian*. A five-man party had been flown south to survey the Rockefeller Mountains (named for an expedition sponsor), when a blizzard blasted them for 12 days. Although the Fokker was tied down, so furious was the wind that when the pilot made a radio call back to Little America from inside the plane, he noticed that the airspeed indicator read 140km/h. A few mornings later, the men awoke at their nearby camp to find that the plane had flown itself 800m to an inevitable crash. Byrd and the others eventually rescued the stranded party.

With winter's onset, the two remaining planes were cached in snow shelters. The men settled down to an under-snow routine of research, repair work, radio training, and recreation, which included watching some of the expedition's 75 movies, selected for their nonprovocative story lines. On August 24 the sun rose again, and preparations for the big flight began. By November, a fuel depot was set up at the foot of the Axel Heiberg Glacier (the same glacier Amundsen had used) leading up to the polar plateau, since *Floyd Bennett*'s fuel tanks couldn't carry enough to reach 90°S and back.

On November 28, an expedition field party working in the Queen Maud Mountains far to the south radioed to Little America that the weather was clear. Four men – Byrd as navigator; Bernt Balchen, chief pilot; Harold June, second pilot and radio operator; and Ashley McKinley, photo surveyor – climbed into the big Ford trimotor. Flying up the Liv Glacier, an icy on-ramp to the polar plateau, the plane was unable to climb due to the cold, thin air, forcing the men to ditch 110kg of their emergency rations. Balchen, an experienced Arctic pilot, gained a little more altitude by throwing the aircraft into a hard turn toward the towering rock face on his right and catching an updraft amid the rush of air flowing down the glacier.

With Byrd at the South Pole: The Story of Little America (1930), a record of Richard Byrd's flight to the Pole in 1929, won the Academy Award for Best Cinematography in 1930.

From there, it was simply a four-hour drone to the Pole, praying that *Floyd Bennett*'s engines would keep beating out their powerful rhythm. They did, and at 1:14am, on November 29, 1929, the plane reached the earth's southern axis. 'For a few seconds we stood over the spot where Amundsen had stood December 14, 1911, and where Scott had also stood,' Byrd wrote. 'There was nothing now to mark that scene; only a white desolation and solitude disturbed by the sound of our engines.'

Byrd returned to the US as a national hero, feted with ticker-tape parades, a promotion to rear admiral, and a special gold medal struck in his honor. He went on to lead four more Antarctic expeditions including the second USAE of 1933–35 (during which he nearly died of carbon monoxide poisoning while living alone at a tiny weather station called 'Advance Base') and the massive US Government exercise known as Operation Highjump (p57). But this was his finest hour.

Ellsworth

American Lincoln Ellsworth (1880–1951), scion of a wealthy Pennsylvania coal-mining family, had whetted his appetite for polar exploration in 1925, when he made the first flight toward the North Pole with Roald

1966
Antarctica's highest peak, Vinson Massif, is first climbed by four members of a private US expedition

1969
The first women to reach the South Pole arrive by US Navy aircraft

Amundsen. The flight failed, but he did reach the Pole in 1926, three days after Byrd claimed he did.

In 1931 Ellsworth began what would become a long and productive association with Hubert Wilkins – with the goal of crossing Antarctica by air. For the first of their four expeditions together, Ellsworth bought a Northrop Gamma monoplane, which he named *Polar Star*, and a stout Norwegian fishing vessel, named *Wyatt Earp* after his hero, the gun-slinging marshal of the Old West, whose wedding ring Ellsworth wore and whose gun and holster he carried with him everywhere. For his pilot, Ellsworth chose Bernt Balchen, chief pilot on Byrd's expedition.

The first Ellsworth Antarctic Expedition in 1933–34 ended after just one short flight from skis in the frozen-over Bay of Whales. The plane was parked overnight on an ice floe, and a massive breakup early the next morning left the aircraft dangling by its wingtips from two separate pieces of the floe. The expedition was forced to retreat north, where Ellsworth's money soon funded the plane's repair.

In late 1934 he was back in the Antarctic, with a new flight plan: the expedition would fly from Wilkins' old base at Deception Island to the Ross Sea via the Weddell Sea. But the season's first try was another disaster – an engine seized up after its heavy preserving lubricant was not drained before starting. The expedition again retreated north, to pick up a spare part that Ellsworth had flown in from the factory to a South American port. The next flight was equally frustrating: Balchen turned the plane around after little more than an hour, citing heavy weather to the south, although Ellsworth saw only a small squall. While he retained respect for Balchen, Ellsworth never hired him again.

'Suddenly I felt supremely happy for my share in the opportunity to unveil the last continent in human history'

The third try, in 1935, was lucky for Ellsworth, but only on the season's third attempt. Ellsworth's new pilot, English-born Canadian Herbert Hollick-Kenyon, made two false starts – the first aborted by a leaky fuel gauge and the second by a threatening storm. *Polar Star* finally took off from Dundee Island at the tip of the Peninsula on November 22, 1935, headed for the Bay of Whales on the Ross Ice Shelf. As the pair flew south, sighting and naming the Eternity and Sentinel Ranges, Ellsworth was overcome with the realization that his years of effort were finally paying off: 'Suddenly I felt supremely happy for my share in the opportunity to unveil the last continent in human history.'

The 3700km flight was intended to last just 14 hours, even with landings to refuel. But poor weather stretched the actual trip to two weeks, during which time the pair established four separate camps. Unfortunately, their radio went dead during that period, prompting fear that they had perished. Even on the last leg of the flight, problems plagued them: *Polar Star* ran out of fuel 25km from the Bay of Whales on the Ross Ice Shelf, and they trekked eight days to reach it. Australia, meanwhile, urged on by Douglas Mawson and John King Davis, dispatched a 'rescue' attempt, although Wilkins and *Wyatt Earp* had already made detailed plans to pick up Ellsworth and Hollick-Kenyon at the Bay of Whales after their flight. The Australians met the explorers at Byrd's former base, Little America II, where the explorers had been living comfortably for nearly a month. Heavy ice, meanwhile, slowed *Wyatt Earp*, which arrived four days later. After returning to a heroes' welcome in the US, Ellsworth made

1978
The first 'native-born' Antarctican, Emilio Marcos de Palma, is born at Argentina's Esperanza station on January 7

1979
Air New Zealand Flight 901 crashes into Mt Erebus, killing all 257 people on board

a final expedition to Antarctica with his faithful friend Hubert Wilkins in 1938, and then retired from exploration for good.

THE CONTEMPORARY ERA

Wilkins' flight was one of the last the large private expeditions made to Antarctica. WWII interrupted the plans of many explorers, although a secret Nazi expedition in 1938–39, led by Alfred Ritscher, was dispatched to Antarctica by Field Marshal Hermann Göring. Göring was interested both in claiming territory and in protecting Germany's growing whaling fleet. The expedition used seaplanes to overfly vast stretches of the ice sheet, dropping unique 1.5m darts inscribed with swastikas to establish sovereignty (claims that were never recognized).

In 1943 Britain began the permanent occupation of Antarctica, establishing Base A at Port Lockroy (p221) on Wiencke Island. After the war the cost of mounting a major expedition pushed nearly everyone but national governments out of the game.

Operations Highjump & Windmill

In 1946 the US launched Operation Highjump, the largest-ever Antarctic expedition. Officially called the US Navy Antarctic Developments Project, it was primarily a training exercise that gave US forces experience in polar operations, which would have been valuable had the Cold War, then developing with the Soviet Union, flared into an all-out Arctic fight. Highjump sent 4700 men, 33 aircraft, 13 ships and 10 Caterpillar tractors to the continent, and used helicopters and icebreakers for the first time in the Antarctic. Tens of thousands of aerial photographs were taken along nearly three-quarters of the continent's coast (although their usefulness for mapmaking was limited by a lack of ground surveys). A smaller, follow-up expedition the next year (later nicknamed 'Operation Windmill' for its extensive use of helicopters) surveyed major features sighted by Highjump.

Hell Below Zero (1953) sees an investigation among Antarctic whalers turn deadly. It's a pretty awful film – the final sword fight is performed with ice axes on an ice floe – but it includes interesting, authentic whaling footage.

ANARE

In February 1954, Phillip Garth Law and the Australian National Antarctic Research Expeditions (ANARE) set up Mawson station in East Antarctica. Named after Douglas Mawson, this was the first permanent scientific station set up on the continent, and the only one outside the Peninsula. Today, Mawson is one of Australia's three continental stations.

International Geophysical Year (IGY)

A growing interest in the earth and atmospheric sciences during the late 1940s prompted the declaration of the International Geophysical Year. The IGY, which ran from July 1, 1957, to December 31, 1958, was timed to coincide with a peak level of sunspot activity. Its objective was to study outer space and the whole earth, with 66 countries participating from locations all around the planet. But the IGY left its greatest legacy in Antarctica.

Twelve countries – Argentina, Australia, Belgium, Chile, France, Japan, New Zealand, Norway, South Africa, the UK, the US and the USSR – established more than 40 stations on the Antarctic continent and another 20 on the sub-Antarctic islands. Among these were the US base at the South Pole, created through a massive 84-flight airdrop of 725 tonnes

1983
Vostok records the lowest-ever temperature on earth: -89.6°C

1985
Scientists at Britain's Halley station discover the 'ozone hole'

THE ORIGINS OF ANARE *Dr Phillip G Law*

The Australian National Antarctic Research Expedition (ANARE) was established in 1947, partly because Douglas Mawson was urging Australia to send another expedition to Antarctica. The word 'Expedition' was later changed to the plural, 'Expeditions,' to reflect the ongoing nature of ANARE's work.

During its first season, ANARE sent naval vessel HMALST *3501* to establish bases on Heard Island (in December 1947) and on Macquarie Island (in March 1948). Meanwhile another ship, HMAS *Wyatt Earp*, which had sailed to Antarctica four times with American aviator Lincoln Ellsworth, was dispatched to find a site suitable for a permanent Australian Antarctic base. Bad ice conditions and the lateness of the season, however, prevented *Wyatt Earp* from reaching the Antarctic coast.

As leader of ANARE, I thought *Wyatt Earp* was quite unsuitable for our purposes, and in the absence of any other vessel, further efforts in Antarctic waters were not possible, so I concentrated on building up the scientific programs at our island stations. In 1952, I learned that the Lauritzen shipping line in Denmark had built a polar ship, *Kista Dan*, for work in Greenland, and I was able to interest them in chartering it to us during the Northern Hemisphere winter. I explained this to the Australian government and obtained approval to mount an expedition in 1954 to establish an Antarctic station. My book *Antarctic Odyssey* (1983) describes this in greater detail.

Aerial photographs of the Antarctic coast taken by the US' Operation Highjump helped me to select a suitable site for the station. The area appeared as a horseshoe-shaped expanse of rock attached to the fringe of the continental ice. Mawson station, established in February 1954, was built in the head of the horseshoe. The two arms of the horseshoe circled around to the entrance, where the water was deep enough to allow a ship to enter and stand with hawsers running to the shore.

It was an exciting moment for me as we raised the Australian flag over the site. I had been brought up on the stories of Scott and Shackleton and other explorers – and here I found myself

of building materials, and the Soviet Vostok station at the Geomagnetic South Pole. Many countries also operated tractor traverses across great sections of the continental interior. The British Commonwealth Trans-Antarctic Expedition, led by Vivian Fuchs, was the first to cross the continent overland (p65). The international cooperation promoted by the IGY led to the creation of the Antarctic Treaty (p290).

Women in Antarctica

Women have been largely excluded from the work done in Antarctica until relatively recently. The first woman to set foot on the continent was the Norwegian Caroline Mikkelsen, who landed at the Vestfold Hills with her husband Klarius, captain of a whaling ship, on February 20, 1935. It was to be another 40 years before women had any kind of significant presence on The Ice.

In fact, Antarctic programs operated by various national governments had an official ban on women for decades, and women were notably absent from early expeditions. This is perhaps better understood today when we recall that expeditions were often staffed by members of the military – a group that was then all-male. Still, Antarctic sexism was often justified by lame rationalizations about physical strength, sexual frustrations and even the difficulty of providing separate toilet facilities. The influence of the male expedition members' wives back home may have had something to

1987
The first ascent of Mt Minto, a 4163-high peak, is made

1989
The Argentine navy ship *Bahía Paraíso* spills 645,000L of diesel fuel and other petroleum products near Palmer station

in a similar position, on virgin territory, raising a flag and claiming the land in the name of the English sovereign.

Today, Mawson is the oldest permanently occupied station south of the Antarctic Circle. It is fascinating for me to look back and remember Mawson as it was when I first walked to the rocky area, with our airplane waiting on the frozen sea offshore. Over the years, from a fixed point in the rock area, I photographed the gradual development of the station, chronicling the steady growth of the number of buildings and the total space occupied by the station.

When the International Geophysical Year (IGY; 1957–58) was mooted, I approached the Australian government again, suggesting a second station on a rocky expanse of land known as the Vestfold Hills, where Lincoln Ellsworth had once landed. We established Davis station (550km east of Mawson) in January 1957.

At the end of the IGY, the US Antarctic Program, in order to cut back its extensive activity, decided to close its Wilkes station (1300km east of Davis). Several US scientists approached me, suggesting that because of its value as a scientific observatory, it would be fine if Australia could agree to take it over and continue its programs. I was able to persuade my government to accept this offer. For several years, Wilkes was run as a joint US–Australian station, before coming under total Australian control. About 10 years later, the station, which had deteriorated badly, was evacuated, and a new station that we built nearby – Casey – was opened.

'Hit-and-run' landings from ships were also made at numerous points along unknown coasts, while men from ANARE stations made long inland traverses. Memorable exploits include a 700km dogsled journey from Enderby Land to Mawson in 1958, a 2900km tractor-train journey from Wilkes to Vostok and back in 1962–63, and a four-man winter occupation of a camp on the Amery Ice Shelf for glaciological research in 1967.

Dr Phillip G Law was leader of ANARE from 1949 to 1966; in 1987, Australia established Law Base, named in his honor, in the Larsemann Hills

do with the policy. Indeed, many people say that the sexual tensions that build in Antarctica's isolation *are* exacerbated by mixed company.

The first women wintered on Antarctica in 1947, when Edith ('Jackie') Ronne and Jennie Darlington spent a year with their husbands on Stonington Island in the Antarctic Peninsula region during the Ronne Antarctic Research Expedition. They had planned to accompany the expedition just as far as Valparaiso, Chile. Only at the last minute did leader Finn Ronne convince his wife to stay with the expedition to help write its newspaper dispatches. Jennie Darlington, who was asked to remain as well, became pregnant during the expedition and nearly gave birth to the first native Antarctican. She later wrote *My Antarctic Honeymoon* (1957) about the expedition's trying personal relationships.

The first women to see the South Pole were two flight attendants, Patricia Hepinstall and Ruth Kelly, aboard the first commercial flight to Antarctica, a Pan Am stratocruiser that departed Christchurch and landed at McMurdo on October 15, 1957.

In 1956 Russian marine geologist Marie V Klenova worked for part of the summer at Russia's Mirnyy station, and in 1968–69, four Argentine women did hydrographic research in the Antarctic Peninsula region.

In 1969 the US finally allowed women to participate in its national Antarctic program. A four-woman group of geologists and a husband-and-wife team worked on The Ice that year, and New Zealand also sent a

1991

The Protocol on Environmental Protection to the Antarctic Treaty is adopted, designating the Antarctic as a natural reserve

1994

The last sled dogs leave Antarctica in accordance with the Protocol on Environmental Protection to the Antarctic Treaty

THE ANTARCTIC TREATY: A UNIQUE PACT FOR A UNIQUE PLACE *Andrew Jackson*

Imagine a world where there are no wars, where the environment is fully protected and where research is the priority. Antarctica is this land – one that the Antarctic Treaty parties call a natural reserve, devoted to peace and science.

A Landmark Agreement

The Antarctic Treaty is a landmark agreement through which countries active in Antarctica consult on the uses of the whole continent. The Treaty, which applies to the area south of 60°S, is surprisingly short but remarkably effective (see p290 for the full text of the Treaty). In its 14 articles, the Treaty:

- stipulates that Antarctica should forever be used exclusively for peaceful purposes and not become the scene or object of international discord
- prohibits nuclear explosions, the disposal of nuclear waste and any measures of a military nature
- guarantees freedom of science and promotes the exchange of scientists and research results
- allows on-site inspection by foreign observers to ensure the observance of the Treaty
- removes the potential for sovereignty disputes between Treaty parties.

The Treaty was negotiated by the 12 nations present in Antarctica during the International Geophysical Year (IGY; 1957–58). These nations wanted to maintain the cooperation that characterized the IGY, when science proceeded unhindered. Such cooperation was particularly important in the context of the Cold War, which was at that time causing international tensions elsewhere. Since coming into force on June 23, 1961, the Treaty has been recognized as one of the most successful international agreements ever negotiated. Problematic differences over territorial claims have been effectively set aside, and as a disarmament regime the Treaty has been outstandingly successful. Treaty parties remain firmly committed to a system still effective in protecting their essential Antarctic interests.

Membership to the Treaty continues to grow. There are (as of September 2004) 45 parties to the Treaty. Twenty-seven are Consultative Parties on the basis of either being original signatories or by conducting substantial research in Antarctica. The parties meet annually to discuss issues as diverse as scientific cooperation, environmental protection measures, management of

woman biologist to Antarctica. On November 11, 1969, the first women to reach the Pole arrived by US Navy aircraft and spent a few hours there before flying back to McMurdo; they included a reporter from a Detroit newspaper.

In 1974 American biologist Mary Alice McWhinnie, who had spent nearly a decade doing research in Antarctic seas aboard the research vessel *Eltanin*, became chief scientist at McMurdo. McWhinnie and her colleague Sister Mary Odile Cahoon, a teaching nun from Minnesota, wintered at McMurdo that year, the first women to do so. Sister Mary later said, in Barbara Land's excellent book *The New Explorers: Women in Antarctica*, that the US Navy and the National Science Foundation 'felt more comfortable having a couple of maiden aunts test the situation.' The first woman to winter at the South Pole, physician Michele Eileen Raney, was the station's lone female during the winter of 1979.

1997
Børge Ousland completes the first solo crossing of Antarctica in just 64 days

c 1997–2001
Volcanic activity at Australia's rarely visited McDonald Islands more than doubles the size of the main island

tourism and the preservation of historic sites – and they are all committed to making decisions by consensus.

Protection of the Environment

Protecting Antarctica's unique ecosystem is a major priority of the Treaty. Specific environmental measures include:

The Convention for the Conservation of Antarctic Seals (1978) provides a means to regulate commercial sealing activities, in the unlikely event that they should ever be resumed. Three species of seal are totally protected and catch limits are set for others.

The Convention for the Conservation of Antarctic Marine Living Resources (CCAMLR; 1980) was adopted in response to fears that unregulated fishing for krill, which are at the center of the Antarctic food chain, might threaten the marine ecosystem. It ensures that the Southern Ocean's living resources are treated as a single ecosystem. Measures under CCAMLR identify protected species, set catch limits, identify fishing regions, define closed seasons, regulate fishing methods and establish fisheries inspection. CCAMLR is leading the fight to protect the highly prized Patagonian toothfish, which is unique to the Southern Ocean, and which in recent years has been taken illegally in alarming numbers (see p19 for more information).

The Protocol on Environmental Protection to the Antarctic Treaty (1991) was negotiated following the failure of the Antarctic minerals convention in 1989. Also known as the Madrid Protocol, it arose out of proposals for a comprehensive regime that would guarantee protection of the environment. The Protocol comprises a number of environmental protection measures in a single, legally binding form. Among its provisions, the Protocol:

- designates Antarctica as a 'natural reserve, devoted to peace and science'
- establishes environmental principles for the conduct of all activities
- prohibits mining
- subjects all activities to prior assessment of their environmental impacts.

Annexes to the Protocol detail measures relating to environmental impact assessment, conservation of Antarctic fauna and flora, waste disposal, marine pollution and the management of protected areas.

Andrew Jackson is Manager, Antarctic and International Policy at the Australian Antarctic Division

Artist Nel Law was the first Australian woman to set foot in Antarctica, accompanying her husband Phillip Law there in 1960–61. It was another 15 years before the first Australian women were allowed to work in Antarctica, and the first Australian woman, Louise Holliday, wintered only in 1981, at Davis station. The first woman to head an Antarctic station was Australia's Diana Patterson, who was station leader at Mawson in 1989.

Other nations took longer to allow women to participate in their Antarctic programs. Japan, for instance, only sent its first two women to winter in Antarctica in 1997, while China included two women in the winterover group at Chang Cheng station for the first time in 2000.

In December 1990, Germany's Georg von Neumayer station was staffed by the first all-women group to winter in Antarctica. Eight women spent 14 months at the station, nine of them in complete isolation. The group's physician, Monica Puskeppeleit, was the station leader.

1998–99
Bill Arras and Geoff Somers make the first 'free-flying' hot-air balloon flight in Antarctica, at Patriot Hills

1999
Brazilian Amyr Klink completes the first full solo circumnavigation of Antarctica in 77 days

GOVERNMENT & POLITICS

No country holds indisputable title over any part of Antarctica, and since there are no indigenous people, it has no native government. During the years of its discovery, parts of Antarctica were being 'claimed' in the name of various queens, kings, emperors, potentates, dictators and presidents. Argentina, Australia, Chile, France, New Zealand, Norway and the United Kingdom all claim territory in Antarctica. As long as very little was going on in Antarctica, no one cared too much about these sovereignty claims. It is also important to note that many world powers – the US and Russia, for example – have made no formal territorial claims on Antarctica. But they have carefully preserved their right to do so in the future.

In the wake of the IGY, scientists and diplomats decided to codify the spirit of international cooperation developed during that 18-month period. They wrote an incredible and unprecedented document, the Antarctic Treaty, which was signed in 1959 and which has governed the continent since 1961. Although some countries, such as Malaysia, have complained that the Antarctic Treaty member nations constitute an elite 'club' and should be replaced by a United Nations–ruled Antarctica, in fact Treaty members represent about 80% of the world's population. Also, the Treaty is open to any UN member state that wishes to accede to it. Any such state performing significant scientific research in Antarctica can become a 'consultative party,' or full voting member.

DID YOU KNOW?

In 2002 a medic on HMS *Endurance* discovered a 65-hectare island (highest point: 6m) along the Antarctic Peninsula that teems with penguins and other seabirds.

Despite the Treaty's 'freezing' of territorial claims, various methods have been employed by different countries to try to reinforce their 'sovereignty' over large sections of Antarctic real estate. Chief among these have been flagpoles, plaques and even large representations of national flags painted on the sides of buildings. Conflicting claimants used to remove offending physical representations of sovereignty placed there by rivals, and pointedly, although politely, return them via diplomatic channels. Antarctic historian Robert Headland imagines that a typical scene might have involved an ambassador being called in by a rival head of state, who would have said something like 'We found this in *our* territory recently and wondered if you might like it back....'

Only a few times in Antarctic history has this careful diplomacy nearly disintegrated into 'political relations...by other means,' as Clausewitz famously euphemized war. One such incident occurred in 1952 at Hope Bay, when British expeditioners arriving to re-establish a base that had burned down earlier were greeted with a decidedly unfriendly welcome from their Argentine neighbors, who fired a machine gun over their heads. The governor of the Falkland Islands responded by dispatching two gunboats to reassert British 'sovereignty,' and the commander of the Argentine station was recalled. In 1953 Argentina and Chile got together and each built a hut on an airstrip used by Britain at Deception Island. Royal Marines arrived to oust the Argentines and Chileans from 'British territory,' and several Argentines were brought to Grytviken in South Georgia and deported to Argentina. In 1975 Britain's HMS *Shackleton* was fired on by an Argentine navy ship, which demanded that it proceed to Ushuaia, a demand *Shackleton* ignored, sailing to Stanley instead.

2000

The largest iceberg ever recorded, measuring 298km by 37km, calves from the Ross Ice Shelf

2002

American long-distance swimmer Lynne Cox swims 1.9km in 0.5°C water at Neko Harbor

TERRITORIAL CLAIMS & YEAR-ROUND STATIONS

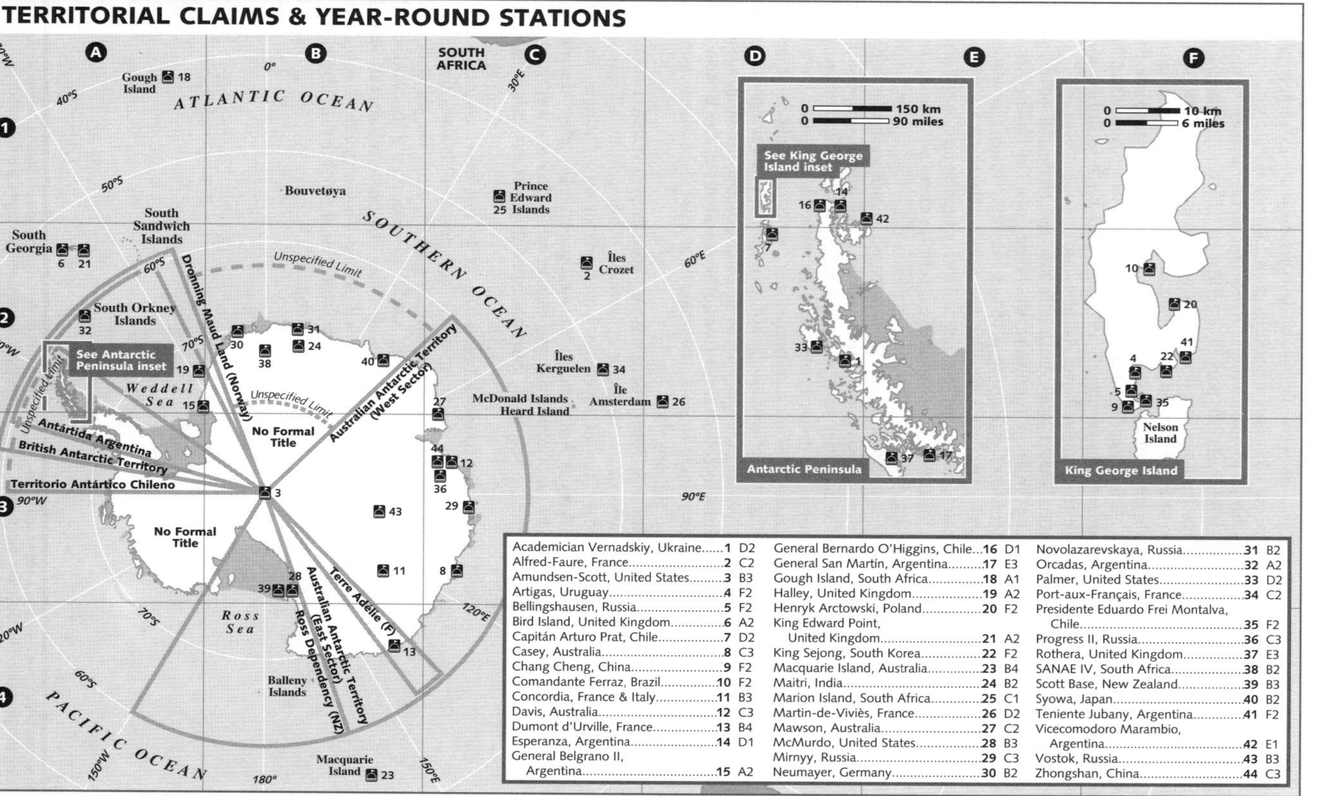
A
B
C
D
E
F
1
2
3
4
SOUTH AFRICA
Gough Island 18
ATLANTIC OCEAN
SOUTHERN OCEAN
PACIFIC OCEAN
Bouvetøya
Prince Edward Islands 25
Îles Crozet 2
Îles Kerguelen 34
Île Amsterdam 26
McDonald Islands
Heard Island
South Georgia 6 21
South Sandwich Islands
South Orkney Islands 32
See Antarctic Peninsula inset
Weddell Sea
Ross Sea
Balleny Islands
Macquarie Island 23
Unspecified Limit
Dronning Maud Land (Norway)
Australian Antarctic Territory (West Sector)
Australian Antarctic Territory (East Sector)
Ross Dependency (NZ)
Terre Adélie (F)
Antártida Argentina
British Antarctic Territory
Territorio Antártico Chileno
No Formal Title
No Formal Title
30°W
0°
30°E
60°E
90°E
120°E
150°E
180°
150°W
120°W
90°W
60°W
40°S
50°S
60°S
70°S
0 150 km
0 90 miles
See King George Island inset
Antarctic Peninsula
0 10 km
0 6 miles
Nelson Island
King George Island
Academician Vernadskiy, Ukraine......1 D2
Alfred-Faure, France......2 C2
Amundsen-Scott, United States......3 B3
Artigas, Uruguay......4 F2
Bellingshausen, Russia......5 F2
Bird Island, United Kingdom......6 A2
Capitán Arturo Prat, Chile......7 D2
Casey, Australia......8 C3
Chang Cheng, China......9 F2
Comandante Ferraz, Brazil......10 F2
Concordia, France & Italy......11 B3
Davis, Australia......12 C3
Dumont d'Urville, France......13 B4
Esperanza, Argentina......14 D1
General Belgrano II, Argentina......15 A2
General Bernardo O'Higgins, Chile...16 D1
General San Martín, Argentina......17 E3
Gough Island, South Africa......18 A1
Halley, United Kingdom......19 A2
Henryk Arctowski, Poland......20 F2
King Edward Point, United Kingdom......21 A2
King Sejong, South Korea......22 F2
Macquarie Island, Australia......23 B4
Maitri, India......24 B2
Marion Island, South Africa......25 C1
Martin-de-Viviès, France......26 D2
Mawson, Australia......27 C2
McMurdo, United States......28 B3
Mirnyy, Russia......29 C3
Neumayer, Germany......30 B2
Novolazarevskaya, Russia......31 B2
Orcadas, Argentina......32 A2
Palmer, United States......33 D2
Port-aux-Français, France......34 C2
Presidente Eduardo Frei Montalva, Chile......35 F2
Progress II, Russia......36 C3
Rothera, United Kingdom......37 E3
SANAE IV, South Africa......38 B2
Scott Base, New Zealand......39 B3
Syowa, Japan......40 B2
Teniente Jubany, Argentina......41 F2
Vicecomodoro Marambio, Argentina......42 E1
Vostok, Russia......43 B3
Zhongshan, China......44 C3

Virus (1980) is gloriously awful. After a deadly germ wipes out the earth's human population, 858 men – and eight anxious women – struggle to survive in Antarctica. The film has achieved cult status aboard Antarctic ships.

Acts of war – or even of physical destruction – are extremely rare in Antarctica. More common are subtle, even somewhat pathetic, attempts made by countries to bolster their territorial claims – usually completely ignored by their rivals. As part of its effort to 'colonize' Antarctica, for example, Argentina has frequently sent women and children to its Esperanza station at Hope Bay on the Antarctic Peninsula. One such woman, Silvia Morello de Palma, was married to Army Captain Jorge de Palma, Esperanza's station leader, and was flown to Antarctica when seven months pregnant. On January 7, 1978, she gave birth to Emilio Marcos de Palma, the first 'native-born' Antarctican.

Other methods used by governments to assert territorial 'sovereignty' include issuing Antarctic stamps, which, being prized by philatelists, offer the added benefit of generating profit at the same time. The leaders of national bases in Antarctica are often given titles reflecting a governmental or administrative role over their slice of The Ice such as justice of the peace or local administrator. Some countries go so far as to 'naturalize' foreign citizens at their Antarctic stations.

Britain levies a special tax on its citizens who work in the 'British Antarctic Territory,' which goes to the colonial government of the territory and is used for activities such as producing publications or restoring old research stations as historic sites. The territory is governed by a British Government–appointed commissioner, so its residents must endure 'taxation without representation,' something that got Britain in trouble with another of its colonies long ago! Interestingly, the commissioner makes no effort to collect taxes from other residents of the British Antarctic Territory, including the nationals of at least eight other countries that maintain stations there.

Likewise the US Government has an expediently 'flexible' view of the territorial status of its Antarctic operations. Although the US has never made a formal claim of sovereignty over any of the continent, the IRS taxes US workers at Antarctic stations at domestic US rates. Meanwhile, American laws on overtime pay and worker safety do not cover the workers because the US Supreme Court has ruled that Antarctica is a 'foreign' country.

The US has also found a practical way to put other countries at a distinct disadvantage in the Antarctic 'competition.' It bans the licensing to anyone, bar the American military, of LC-130s, the ski-equipped Hercules cargo planes that are so useful in resupplying its continental stations at McMurdo and the South Pole. The powerful aircraft would be just as useful in the Arctic as well, so the US Government considers the use of LC-130s to be a security issue, but the restriction also neatly hampers other nations' Antarctic ambitions.

2003

British scientist Kirsty Brown is killed by a leopard seal while snorkeling at Rothera station, the first-known such fatality

2004

The rebuilt Bonner Laboratory opens at Britain's Rothera station more than two years after the original was destroyed by fire

Private Expeditions

Colin Monteath

EVOLUTION OF PRIVATE EXPEDITIONS

Joseph Banks, the botanist on Captain Cook's first voyage of discovery to the southern latitudes in 1769–71, was perhaps the first to express a desire to stand at the geographic South Pole. 'O, how Glorious would it be,' Banks said, 'to set my heel upon the Pole! and turn myself 360° in a second!'

The drive to reach the South Pole rapidly grew into an obsession for a number of explorers, as the myth of the great southern continent *Terra Australis Incognita* was dispelled – or at least vastly diminished – by Cook's second voyage in 1772–75, and as the coastline of the Antarctic continent was gradually delineated by voyages throughout the 19th century.

Norwegian Roald Amundsen inspired the world when he became the first to reach the Pole in 1911. Amundsen's triumph, however, did not stifle the desire to stand briefly at 90°S. Just as the first ascent of Everest in 1953 opened the gate for a continuous stream of mountaineers trying to scale the peak, Amundsen's success spawned other attempts to reach the Pole.

A passion for the Pole runs deep in our psyche. Today it has reached fever pitch, since many of the psychological and bureaucratic barriers to Antarctica have been overcome. Traverses to the interior are now commonplace as private air transportation to the Antarctic has become routine.

Antarctica is geographically well endowed for adventure. Not only are its flat ice sheets suitable for skiing and hauling sledges, but the continent is studded with some of the world's great mountain ranges. While not as high as Andean or Himalayan peaks, Antarctic summits have an allure of their own, enhanced by remoteness and extreme cold. Antarctica will certainly be one of the most important mountaineering meccas in the 21st century.

Colin Monteath has climbed many new routes on Antarctic peaks and has been involved in seaborne tourism since 1983. For more about Mr Monteath, see p18.

The Early Days

Much of the exploration and science in Antarctica during the early 20th century would not have happened without private initiative and sponsorship under the leadership of famous figures from the heroic era such as Mawson, Scott, Shackleton and Amundsen. As far back as the 1820s, sealers such as Weddell, Smith, Bransfield and Palmer played a vital exploratory role. During the late 1920s and early '30s, wealthy private aviators such as Lincoln Ellsworth of the US and Hubert Wilkins of Australia dared to make the first long-distance flights in Antarctica. Likewise, American Richard Byrd's two expeditions in 1928 and 1933 were essentially private affairs.

More modest private expeditions on the Antarctic Peninsula in the 1930s and '40s played a significant role in piecing together Antarctica's geographical puzzle. Australian John Rymill led the British Graham Land Expedition in 1934, while American Finn Ronne led an unhappy though productive team from his base on Stonington Island in 1946; among Ronne's team were the first two women to winter in Antarctica.

For more information about early expeditions, see p22.

In the 1950s private expeditions took a backseat to the buildup for the International Geophysical Year (IGY), which ran from July 1, 1957, to December 31, 1958, and a coordinated, multinational drive established government science bases around Antarctica (and in the Arctic, too).

Commonwealth Trans-Antarctic Expedition

Inspired and led by Englishman Vivian Fuchs, the Commonwealth Trans-Antarctic Expedition was associated with the IGY. On his way to complete Shackleton's dream of crossing Antarctica from the Weddell Sea coast to the

Ross Sea, Fuchs reached the Pole with heavy tracked vehicles on January 19, 1958, after a winter at Shackleton base on the Weddell coast. With Fuchs was a dog team, the first to reach the Pole since Amundsen. Preceding his arrival at the Pole by two weeks was Edmund Hillary's team of New Zealanders, who had driven modified farm tractors to lay fuel depots from Scott Base on Ross Island, New Zealand's (NZ) newly established IGY station.

Although the expedition was both government sponsored and privately funded, it was never planned that Hillary would go past his last depot to the Pole. His action angered NZ's Ross Sea Committee, the organizers of Fuchs' support team. Perhaps this discord foreshadowed misunderstanding and distrust between government departments (which rapidly asserted their control over access to Antarctica) and strong-willed individuals with proven field experience and adventurous spirits.

First Ascents of Vinson Massif & Mt Herschel

The origins of modern Antarctic mountaineering came even later. Although Ellsworth saw the northern part of the Ellsworth Mountains during his trans-Antarctic flight in 1935, he did not see its highest peak, Vinson Massif. Remarkably, Vinson was not sighted until US Navy pilots made a reconnaissance flight in association with the IGY in 1957.

In 1966 after three years of lobbying by the American Alpine Club, the US National Science Foundation agreed to support a US mountaineering expedition, whose prime objective was reaching the summit of Vinson. The American Alpine Club team, led by Nicholas Clinch, was flown from NZ to McMurdo and on to the Sentinel Range in the Ellsworth Mountains, using a ski-equipped US Navy Hercules. After ascending Vinson on December 18, 1966, a climb of little technical consequence, the expedition went on a climbing spree of other major summits, notably Tyree (which may well be Antarctica's most difficult peak), Gardner and Shinn.

ON TOP OF THE BOTTOM OF THE WORLD *Jeff Rubin*

Antarctica's highest peak is 4900.3m Vinson Massif. The mountain is 20km long by 13km wide in the Sentinel Range and was discovered in 1958 by US Navy aircraft. It's named for Congressman Carl G Vinson of Georgia, who influenced the US government to support Antarctic exploration during the period from 1935 to 1961. Thanks to the mountaineering hajj of the 'Seven Summits' (scaling the highest peak on each continent), Vinson is also Antarctica's most climbed mountain.

On December 18, 1966, four members of a private US expedition led by Nicholas B Clinch made the first ascent. Over the next few days, the expedition also reached the summits of Antarctica's second-, third- and fourth-highest peaks, the neighboring Tyree (4845m), Gardner (4686m) and Shinn (4661m), respectively. You can read all about it in the June 1967 issue of *National Geographic*. Interestingly, this early expedition, sponsored by the American Alpine Club, received not only cooperation but also vital help from the US government in the form of the Navy, which flew the climbers through Christchurch and McMurdo. This friendly policy soon turned around 180°; the US and other governments generally no longer support private expeditions to Antarctica.

Adventure Network International (ANI) guided more than 450 climbers to Vinson's summit beginning in 1985. An ANI brochure advised, 'Technically, Vinson is not a difficult climb…However, climbers should be experienced and in good physical condition to cope with the stresses of altitude and low temperature.' The time required to reach the summit ranges from two to 14 days, varying with the weather, as well as with the climber's experience and fitness level. One successful summiteer has called Vinson 'similar in difficulty, weather and altitude' to the West Buttress of Alaska's Mt McKinley. Vinson's neighbor, Mt Tyree, only 52m lower, is regarded as the continent's most challenging peak – Clinch said that Vinson had been 'a Sunday stroll' by comparison – but dozens of other Antarctic mountains remain virgin.

In 1967 another group received valuable government assistance. The NZ Antarctic Expedition, inspired by Edmund Hillary, was flown by the US Navy from McMurdo Sound in a ski-equipped Hercules, which landed at Cape Hallett. The expedition made the first ascent of the 3300m Mt Herschel in North Victoria Land. For NZ climbers to gain US Navy support was unprecedented; it would not have happened without Hillary's influence on senior NZ government officials. Even so, the NZ team was obliged to take surveyors and geologists with them to add a veneer of respectable science.

Requests Denied

After the American Alpine Club and NZ expeditions, it was clear to US and NZ authorities that providing official support to private teams had created two awkward precedents, which were likely to increase requests for transport and backup logistics from mountaineers and adventurers worldwide.

The US government became the most obvious target for requests of support, thanks to its extensive network of fuel depots around the continent and its long-range ski-equipped Hercules aircraft and icebreaking ships. Many applicants thought they should receive assistance as a matter of right, yet they had little idea of just how stretched the Americans were in servicing a complicated science program so far from home. The cost of fuel alone became astronomical after it had been transported by sea from the US to NZ and on to McMurdo, before being flown to inland Antarctic bases. To support private expeditions with aircraft or ships, even in a meager way, would require cancellation of preplanned science programs. It also became evident that some of the aspiring expeditions simply didn't have a proven track record of expedition planning and independent travel in remote regions. The US feared that if these teams were given official support, a percentage of them would require rescue, which would divert scarce resources away from its primary mission in Antarctica, science.

The US and NZ governments drafted a joint policy on private expeditions that effectively ruled out any assistance to private teams in the future. It was much simpler to give all applicants the 'cold shoulder' and ignore the protests from the growing band of adventurers who were rapidly realizing the recreational potential of Antarctica. In 1969 a well-planned NZ team hoping to climb Mt Minto, the highest peak in North Victoria Land, was the first victim of this policy. While the US-NZ policy of noncooperation was understandable, its interpretation and application soon became overly bureaucratic and unnecessarily obstructive. Resentment toward government 'ownership' of Antarctica grew.

'Resentment toward government ownership of Antarctica grew'

Embarrassingly for US Antarctic administrators, the rug was pulled from under their own policy several times when senior American politicians insisted that their pilot friends attempting 'record-breaking' jaunts across Antarctica receive all-important refueling at McMurdo. In 1971 for example, Elgin Long, who'd already flown solo over the North Pole, flew solo in his twin-engined Piper Navaho from Chile to McMurdo, via the South Pole, to become the first person to fly solo over both poles. In 1983 pilot Brooke Knapp, whose husband was an associate of US President Ronald Reagan, received similar support at McMurdo after a flight from NZ. Knapp then flew over the Pole to South America, claiming no less than 41 aviation records during her speedy round-the-world flight.

BRITISH JOINT-SERVICES EXPEDITIONS

With the US-NZ policy in place, no private expeditions made traverses to the interior of Antarctica during the 1960s and much of the '70s. Instead, Britain allowed several 'Joint Services' expeditions to hold 'adventure training' exercises that made use of Royal Navy transport to reach remote islands, such as South Georgia. Several British teams repeated Shackleton's crossing of South Georgia, taking the same route the explorer took after his journey from Elephant Island in *James Caird* in 1916. The first crossing was under the command of Malcolm Burley in 1964. In 1970 Burley led a British military group which landed on Elephant Island and carried out survey and ornithological work. One member of the team, Chris Furse, returned to Elephant Island in 1976 with 15 others to climb its peaks and experiment with sea kayaks in the ice-choked waters. Furse, with another large military team of mountaineers, returned to the Antarctic in 1983–85 to winterover in tents and snow caves on Brabant Island, off the Peninsula.

'Kershaw flew the Otter to the South African base to help in a major rescue – an example of private adventurers helping government personnel in trouble'

MAJOR PRIVATE TRAVERSES

During the 1960s and '70s many government expeditions crisscrossed the polar plateau with large tractor trains supporting glaciological or geophysical research. By this stage Antarctica had also been well mapped and documented by aerial photography. The private traverse parties that have reached Antarctica since 1979, then, can not be called explorers. But their journeys can be seen as a valid form of recreation in their own right – tests of spirit and endurance, as well as of new equipment. As a result of their responsibilities to sponsors, these expeditions have also educated schoolchildren and the public about the need to look after the polar regions.

Transglobe Expedition

The British Transglobe Expedition of 1979–82 did what all of the polar pundits said couldn't be done: complete a crossing of Antarctica using open snowmobiles pulling sledges. Determined to circumnavigate the globe by following the Prime Meridian (0°), Ginnie and Ran Fiennes led a team to the South African side of Antarctica. They commissioned a ship to transport equipment to the continent and to pick the expedition up from Ross Island after the crossing. For resupply on the polar plateau, the expedition had a ski-equipped Twin Otter, flown by veteran polar pilot Giles Kershaw. The Transglobe team wintered on the continent's edge in a prefabricated cardboard hut before setting out for the interior the following spring. Later, when at the Pole, Kershaw flew the Otter to the South African base to help in a major rescue – an example of private adventurers helping government personnel in trouble. Despite efforts by the US, British and NZ governments to block Transglobe, Fiennes and team members Ollie Shepard and Charlie Burton completed the second crossing of Antarctica in only 67 days, reaching NZ's Scott Base in January 1981. Fiennes and Burton went on to cross the Arctic Ocean, becoming the first to reach both poles by surface means. The Transglobe Expedition proved that, given the determination and ingenuity to bring together a massive pyramid of resources a small private team could undertake a major traverse in Antarctica.

In the Footsteps of Scott

Determined to retrace Scott's 1911–12 journey to the South Pole via the Beardmore Glacier, Englishmen Robert Swan and Roger Mear and Canadian Gareth Wood set out from an overwinter base beside Scott's Cape Evans hut in October 1985. Seventy days later, they manhauled their sledges up to the US Amundsen-Scott South Pole station. They received a rather 'frosty' official reception – in tune with the poor relations the expedition had experienced with US leaders at McMurdo.

Literally moments after reaching the Pole, the team received the news that their support vessel, the trawler *Southern Quest*, had been crushed by pack ice and sunk off Beaufort Island in the Ross Sea. The expedition's aircraft, a modified Cessna 185 flown by Giles Kershaw, had already been off-loaded and was on standby near Ross Island to retrieve the trio from the Pole. US helicopters recovered the ship's crew and flew them to McMurdo, sparking heated debate on both sides. Kershaw reluctantly agreed not to fly to the Pole as long as the US didn't call the retrieval of Swan's group a 'rescue.'

Most of *Southern Quest*'s crew were flown back to NZ by US Hercules. However, a team of three stayed for a second winter at Cape Evans to look after the Cessna, with the view of removing the entire base the following summer. The Footsteps of Scott hut was eventually incorporated into Greenpeace's Cape Evans base and removed from Antarctica when the Greenpeace base closed in 1992. The three winterers were picked up at Cape Evans in the spring of 1986 by a Twin Otter again piloted by Kershaw, a remarkable 9600km roundtrip flight from Punta Arenas.

The US government charged Swan's expedition US$80,000, a small portion of the costs, for the expedition's 'rescue' from Ross Island and repatriation to NZ. Relations between governments and private expeditions had reached an all-time low.

Norwegian 90° South Expedition

The next private expedition to Antarctica was led by Norwegian glaciologist Monica Kristensen. 'Was it difficult,' she was asked, 'to be a woman and lead a group of men?' Kristensen responded that she had no experience of being anything other than a woman.

The expedition aimed to retrace Amundsen's route to the Pole using dog teams. Sailing from NZ in November 1986 with her own ship, *Aurora*, to transport dogs and equipment, she positioned the vessel near an iceberg in the Ross Sea. A Greenland Air Twin Otter then took off from southern NZ and, at the limit of its fuel, landed on the tabular berg. Refueled from *Aurora*, the plane flew to the Bay of Whales on the Ross Ice Shelf. From there, it placed depots across the Ross Ice Shelf and at the head of the Axel Heiberg Glacier, Amundsen's gateway through the Transantarctic Mountains.

Kristensen and her three male companions then drove 22 huskies all the way to the polar plateau. Slowed down by heavy glaciology gear and having missed one of the depots, the team turned back several hundred kilometers short of the Pole. Not wishing to winter on the continent, Kristensen knew the timing of her decision to turn back was crucial: she needed to arrive back early enough so that *Aurora* would not be trapped by sea ice.

In 1993 she returned to the Antarctic, this time on the Weddell Sea side, for another expedition combining science, adventure and the dream of locating Amundsen's tent buried beneath the snow. This expedition was criticized for poor glacier-travel techniques. One man died in a crevasse accident, sparking a rescue mission from US and NZ bases on Ross Island.

'The attraction of Vinson Massif and other remote peaks spurred mountaineers to overcome the barriers of aircraft logistics and government bureaucracy'

ADVENTURE NETWORK INTERNATIONAL

It is important to interrupt the chronology of overland traverses to the Pole at this point, because all expeditions after the Norwegian 90° South Expedition – since they did not wish to overwinter or outfit their own ships – have used aircraft to reach Antarctica.

Mountain climbers led the way. The attraction of Vinson Massif and other remote peaks spurred mountaineers to overcome the barriers of aircraft logistics and government bureaucracy in order to reach Antarctica's inland Ellsworth Mountains.

In 1983 American businessmen Frank Wells and Dick Bass wanted to climb Vinson in their quest to ascend the highest peak on each of the seven continents. With pilot Giles Kershaw and mountaineers Chris Bonington and Rick Ridgeway, Bass and Wells flew to Antarctica in an 'experimental' ski-equipped tri-turbo DC-3. Their climb of Vinson, only its third ascent, was the forerunner of dozens of ascents that were to take place every summer over the next decade.

The operation was risky, with no backup should the plane become grounded. In 1984 Canadian Pat Morrow – on his own Seven Summits odyssey – failed to reach Vinson with the tri-turbo after developing engine trouble. Morrow remained determined to reach Vinson. Pulling together major sponsorship and a landmark deal with the Chilean air force whereby they agreed to airdrop aircraft fuel for the expedition, Morrow, with fellow Canadian guide Martyn Williams and pilot Giles Kershaw, flew to Vinson in a ski-equipped Twin Otter in November 1985. This was the birth of Adventure Network International (ANI), which henceforth took paying passengers on other adventures in Antarctica.

By 1986 Kershaw was experimenting with a wheeled DC-4, which could be flown in a single 10-hour flight from Punta Arenas, Chile, to land on natural areas of wind-polished ice. This allowed ANI to set up a base camp at Patriot Hills, not far from the Ellsworth Mountains. With the DC-4, and eventually a DC-6, hauling clients and fuel from South America, expeditions could then be serviced from the Patriot Hills camp with two Twin Otters.

Using its own chartered ship or Quark Expedition's Russian icebreakers to position Twin Otter fuel depots on both sides of the continent, ANI gradually developed the capability to reach even the remotest locations in Antarctica safely. This allowed climbers to begin dreaming of vast new mountain playgrounds in the Transantarctic Mountains and in the Queen Maud Mountains. The mountains on the coast of Queen Maud Land were climbed in 1993 on a private Norwegian expedition led by Ivar Tollefsen. This expedition used a Russian government ship to reach Antarctica and achieved by far the hardest mountaineering yet done in Antarctica.

In 1988 ANI director Martyn Williams led a commercial expedition from the inland edge of the Ronne Ice Shelf to the South Pole. This was an especially remarkable piece of guiding, since one of the clients had never been on skis before. The expedition included the first two women to ski overland to the Pole, Tori Murden and Shirley Metz. The group flew back to Patriot Hills, now a commonplace way to end a traverse to the Pole.

Fuchs-Messner Ski Traverse

The austral summer of 1989–90 was a big season for private Antarctic expeditions, as both the third and fourth crossings of the continent took place. The third was made by Austro-Italian mountaineer Reinhold Messner, the most celebrated climber in history, and German Arved Fuchs (no relation to Vivian Fuchs). The pair teamed up to ski across Antarctica, using depots laid by ANI aircraft.

Although Messner was the first person to ascend all 14 Himalayan 8000m peaks, he had never been to the polar regions. Fuchs was a good choice of partner and navigator, since he had just returned from the North Pole. Towing heavily laden plastic sledges, they reached the South Pole on New Year's Eve, 1989. Fuchs thus achieved the distinction of skiing to both geographic poles within 12 months.

The pair continued on across the continent, striking out for Ross Island on January 3, 1990, and reaching it on February 12 – a total of 92 days since departing the Weddell Sea coast. With no resupply flight on the second half of the trip, they pared everything back to a minimum; not even radios were carried. When the wind allowed, parachutes were used to help pull the sledges. The best day with parachutes saw one degree of latitude (60 nautical miles, or about 111km) clatter under their skis.

Messner and Fuchs had arranged a pickup from the Ross Sea coast by a tourist ship scheduled to visit the region. If this rendezvous had failed, they could have elected to summon a costly ANI flight from Patriot Hills. As it turned out, the pair sailed for NZ on board an Italian government resupply vessel. Despite external political pressure not to do so, the Italians were probably pleased to assist Messner, who was almost a cult figure at home in Italy.

International Trans-Antarctic Expedition

The fourth crossing of Antarctica turned out to be a truly marathon journey, spanning seven months from July (midwinter) 1989 to March 1990. An international team of six from Japan, UK, China, the Soviet Union, France and the US, led by Jean-Louis Etienne and Will Steger, planned to drive dog teams across the continent. In preparation, the expedition made a 2400km south-to-north traverse of the Greenland ice cap.

In Antarctica, the expedition chose to traverse the longest possible axis: down the continent's spine along the Antarctic Peninsula to the South Pole, then via Vostok to Mirnyy. In all, the trek covered a punishing 6400km. Making use of seven depots laid the year before along the Peninsula by an ANI Twin Otter, the expedition sledged its way into the South Pole on December 11, 1989, after 137 days and 3187km.

Unlike the last dog team to reach the Pole in 1958 (with the Commonwealth Trans-Antarctic Expedition), which was flown out, Steger's American huskies were still only halfway through their journey: 3212km lay between them at 90°S and Mirnyy. Somewhere in between, across the 'zone of inaccessibility,' was the Soviet Vostok station and a rendezvous with supplies they couldn't afford to miss. By providing aircraft fuel at the South Pole, the Soviets made it possible for an ANI Twin Otter to bring in supplies at the crucial midpoint of the expedition, as well as to place two depots between the Pole and Vostok. After nearly losing Japanese team member Keizo Funatsu in a blizzard, the dog teams and their weary drivers finally reached Mirnyy on March 3. From NZ, Reinhold Messner sent the message: 'Congratulations on completing one of the great polar journeys of all time. Let us both now fight for a World Park Antarctica.'

'Congratulations on completing one of the great polar journeys of all time. Let us both now fight for a World Park Antarctica'

Sjur & Simen Mordre

The fifth crossing of Antarctica, in 1990–91, was carried out with efficiency and élan. The Norwegian Mordre brothers, Sjur and Simen, both expert Nordic skiers, used a dog team in their journey to the Pole from the Weddell Sea. An ANI Twin Otter then flew the dogs back to Patriot Hills while the brothers, with a photographer, skied on toward Ross Island. Pulling sledges and making use of parachutes where possible, the trio used Amundsen's route down the Axel Heiberg Glacier to the Ross Ice Shelf. They reached the coast after a 105-day crossing and were picked up on schedule by the tour ship *World Discoverer*.

Ran Fiennes & Mike Stroud

The planned sixth crossing of Antarctica didn't quite make it. Englishman Ran Fiennes returned to Antarctica in 1992, this time with Footsteps of Scott veteran and physician Mike Stroud. The pair planned to haul sledges from the Weddell to the Ross Sea coasts, with no aircraft support or prelaid depots, a 2500km journey. They made it some 2100km to the southern edge of the Ross Ice Shelf before requesting evacuation by ANI aircraft.

Erling Kagge

At the same time that Fiennes and Stroud were walking to the Pole, Norwegian skier Erling Kagge was skiing solo to the Pole. Although some of the media – inaccurately – tried to represent this as a replay of the 'race' between Amundsen and Scott, Kagge never intended to make a complete traverse. He reached the Pole with little fuss after 49 days and flew back to Patriot Hills.

American Women's Expedition

In contrast to the media attention given to Fiennes, Stroud and Kagge, the American Women's Expedition received little notice in the international press. This group, led by Ann Bancroft, successfully reached the South Pole in January 1993, starting from Patriot Hills, 10° inland from the coast. Although the expedition originally planned to cross the continent, the members decided against pushing past the Pole, due to sickness in the team. Bancroft became the first woman to travel overland to both poles, having reached the North Pole in 1986 on an expedition led by Will Steger.

Other Traverses

'Ousland covered a staggering 226km in a single parasail-assisted day during his final run to Scott base'

Other traverses to the Pole include Norwegian Liv Arnesen's solo ski trek in 1994, and the journey made by three other Norwegians (including Cato Pederson, who lost one arm and half of the other in an accident at age 14), who also skied to the Pole in 1994. Still another Norwegian, Børge Ousland, gave up an attempt at a solo crossing in 1995–96, but not before he reached the Pole, thus attaining both poles on skis, solo and without depots.

The sixth crossing of the continent was Børge Ousland's remarkable solo journey. In just 64 days, covering 2845km, he skied from Berkner Island to Ross Island. Learning valuable lessons from his previous attempt in 1995–96, and now highly disciplined in order to maintain a strict routine, Ousland didn't take a break even when he reached the South Pole, immediately heading northward toward the Axel Heiberg Glacier. Unsupported by aircraft-laid depots even at the Pole, he skied on down to the Ross Ice Shelf, covering a staggering 226km in a single parasail-assisted day during his final run to Scott base, where he arrived on January 19, 1997.

Belgians Alain Hubert and Dixie Dansercoer completed a 3500km traverse in 1997–98. They started from the coast of Queen Maud Land and 98 days later, with only one ANI resupply flight to replace a broken sledge, reached Ross Island. Their best day's travel with parasails was an astonishing 271km. Significantly, as was Ousland the year before, the Belgians were flown out of Antarctica to NZ on a US government aircraft.

Five expeditions hauled sledges to the South Pole over the 1998–99 summer, navigating their way on five different routes. After an ANI Twin Otter flight from Patriot Hills to Hercules Inlet, lone Swede Ola Skinnarmo skied 1000km to the Pole, while a French team of five led by Thierry Bol[illegible] traveled 1300km from Berkner Island to the Pole. Both teams flew out with ANI. Reaching the Blue One base camp established in Queen Maud Land by ANI-Polar Logistics and flying aboard an Ilyushin 76 aircraft from South Africa, a two-man Dutch team under Ronald Naar made it to the Pole, a distance of 2250km; the third team member was evacuated early due to injury. Also setting out from Blue One was 46-year-old solo Japanese skier Mitsuro Oba, who covered an audacious 3824km via the South Pole reaching Ellsworth Land before being pulled out by ANI.

In an unusual move by the NZ Antarctic program, a three-man Australian and NZ 'Iridium Icetrek' team (Eric Phillips, Jon Muir and Peter Hillary) received air transport and government backing to enable them to se out for the Pole from Ross Island. Their aim was to lay depots across the Ross Ice Shelf and up the Shackleton Glacier, then make a return journey to Ross Island utilizing these depots. By underestimating the severity of the polar plateau, the trio ran out of food and fuel, necessitating a US government Twin Otter to make a resupply flight. The team reached the South Pole after 83 days, returning to McMurdo on a routine US Navy flight.

MOUNTAINEERING

Australian Bicentennial Antarctic Expedition

On December 31, 1987, the eve of Australia's bicentennial year, the yacht *Alan and Vi Thistlethwayte* sailed from Sydney with a team of climbers under Greg Mortimer's leadership. They made the first ascent of Mt Minto, at 4163m the highest peak in North Victoria Land. The mountain was reached after manhauling 150km inland from Cape Hallett.

Mt Vaughan Expedition

Alaskan Norman Vaughan was a dog driver with Richard Byrd's 1928 expedition to Antarctica. In 1993 he planned to drive sled dogs across the Ross Ice Shelf and climb the 3140m virgin summit of Mt Vaughan, named after him by Byrd. His motto: 'Dream big, dare to fail.'

Vaughan's big dream was to reach the summit of 'his' mountain on December 19, 1993 – his 88th birthday. His team took the gamble of flying people, dogs and supplies from Punta Arenas to Patriot Hills in an old rented DC-6, flown by a pilot who had worked for ANI in the past. In late November, however, the plane crashed short of the ice runway at Patriot Hills in foul weather, badly injuring one of the four team members on board. Anne Kershaw, Giles' wife and director of ANI, immediately sent a Hercules aircraft from Punta Arenas to evacuate the team from Antarctica.

'His motto: dream big, dare to fail'

After daring to fail, Vaughan was back in Antarctica in 1994, this time with ANI air support and two experienced mountaineering guides, Vernon Tejas and Gordon Wiltsie. Three days short of his 89th birthday, Vaughan and his wife, Carolyn, reached the summit of their dreams.

Dry Valley Mountaineering Expedition

Until 1990 no cruise vessel had ever been into the Ross Sea twice in a single season. Now, however, it is not uncommon for tour vessels to achieve this. On its maiden voyage, the Antarctic tour ship *Frontier Spirit* (now *Bremen*) dropped off a five-man expedition at Cape Royds under the leadership of Colin Monteath. With their own helicopter to transport them across McMurdo Sound, the climbers were able to ascend several peaks in the Dry Valleys in February and March of 1991. An ascent of Mt Erebus was also made with two members of the Greenpeace Cape Evans overwinter team.

South Georgia Climbs

Climbers have reached South Georgia on expeditions by using their own yachts as bases or by gaining permission for transport aboard British military vessels. A 1984–85 NZ expedition led by Ian Turnbull to the peaks above St Andrew's Bay, although delayed by the Falklands War, successfully combined science and mountaineering. In 1989 Stephen Venables led a British expedition that also used military transport. The group made several first ascents, including Mt Carse at the island's southeastern end.

Queen Maud Land Mountaineering

In 1994 Norwegian Ivar Tollefsen led a 13-man private expedition (using Russian government sea transport) to complete the first 'big-wall' rock climb on the red granite spire Ulvetanna (Wolf's Fang). The climb involved 11 days of hard climbing with nights spent in hanging bivouacs. Tollefsen flew from the summit using a *parapente* canopy. The expedition climbed 36 peaks, including 2965m Jøkulkyrkja (Glacier Church).

The publishing of Tollefsen's book *Queen Maud Land Antarctica* in 1994 sparked interest in this remote region. In 1997–98 a division of ANI called Polar Logistics began making Hercules flights from South Africa direct to a wind-polished ice runway in Queen Maud Land called 'Blue One.' Two mountaineering groups – another Norwegian team again led by Tollefsen and a six-member US team spearheaded by Alex Lowe – reached Mt Bergersen and the Filchner Mountains with the help of an ANI Twin Otter. Another big-wall route fell to the Norwegians after a total of 17 days climbing on the stunning north face of Ronde Spire, while the Americans climbed four peaks, including a big-wall route on Rakekniven (Razor).

'The flight, on a rare windless day, lasted five minutes, covered 1.5km and reached about 100m above the ground'

AIRBORNE ADVENTURES

On November 5, 1988, ANI's Giles Kershaw acted as copilot for Australian aviator Dick Smith, flying a Twin Otter 14 hours from Hobart to Australia's Casey station. Such a flight in a Twin Otter was only possible thanks to auxiliary fuel tanks, extending its range from 1600km to 3500km. This impressive venture helped pave the way for future cooperation between private expeditions and government science programs in Antarctica.

Kershaw and Smith assisted the Australian government science program for two weeks, completing extended aerial surveys along the coastline to Davis and Mawson stations. They also made goodwill visits to Syowa, Molodezhnaya and Mirnyy stations. The aviators continued on to the South Pole on November 23, having flown from Casey to Ross Island to pick up two Greenpeace members who wanted to inspect the South Pole station. By November 29, they were back at Casey and ready for a flight to South America via Vostok, the South Pole, Patriot Hills and King George Island.

Giles Kershaw's calm and positive manner as a pilot and skillful knowledge of a Twin Otter's capability took the expedition across 41,448km of Antarctica and the Southern Ocean in the space of five weeks (171 hours of flight time). Sadly, on March 5, 1990, Kershaw died in a gyrocopter crash on the Peninsula while he was assisting a film crew on another private expedition led by Mike Hoover. Antarctica lost a great ambassador.

Ballooning

The first 'free-flying' hot-air balloon flight in Antarctica (Scott made the first tethered flight in 1902) was made during the summer of 1998–99, from the Patriot Hills camp in interior Antarctica by American Bill Arras and Englishman Geoff Somers. The flight, on a rare windless day, lasted five minutes, covered 1.5km and reached about 100m above the ground.

In the summer of 2000 a Russian-inspired expedition drove balloon-tired 'snow buggies' to the South Pole from Patriot Hills. Expedition members made a brief hot-air balloon flight, the first known at 90°S.

Skydiving over the South Pole

What began as a spectacular stunt, intended to be a routine linkup of four skydivers 2500m above the South Pole, ended less than a minute after the jumpers bailed out of an ANI Twin Otter with the deaths of three of the six participating parachutists. In only the fifth parachute jump at 90°S (the first was made in 1956 by US Air Force Sgt Richard Patton, who jumped from 500m), the three Americans, one Austrian and two Norwegians each paid ANI US$22,000 to make the jump in December

1997. Hans Rezac and Ray Miller were experienced parachutists who had already jumped at the North Pole, while Steve Mulholland was a skilled BASE (Bridges, Antennas, Spans & Earth) jumper with past Antarctic work experience. All three died instantly, having failed to deploy their chutes after aborting the four-man linkup as they hurtled toward the ice at 320km/h. Of the four, only the survivor, Michael Kearns, wore an automatic activation device (AAD), which was preset to release his chute at a safe altitude. AADs are normally used when low temperatures or hypoxia are expected to impair the judgment or physical function of the jumper, both significant factors at the South Pole, since the effective altitude at bailout was 6000m. The Norwegian pair, Trond Jacobsen and Morten Halvorsen, survived their tandem jump, the first at the South Pole.

SEABORNE ADVENTURES

As early as 1910, the British travel company Thomas Cook advertised a 50-day cruise from NZ to McMurdo Sound. It was reported that 'members of the NZ Parliament, a number of ladies and several gentlemen interested in scientific matters' were keen to endure the rigors of the Ross Sea in a wooden vessel, but the voyage never took place.

Today, tourist vessels ply Antarctic waters in large numbers every season. Some ships have carried private expeditions, dropping them off on one cruise and picking them up at a predetermined location during a later voyage. In 1994 an Australian sea-kayak expedition led by Wade Fairley spent two weeks paddling along parts of the Peninsula, having been transported by a tour ship.

In 1972 NZ physician David Lewis attempted a solo circumnavigation of Antarctica in his 10m *Ice Bird*. The yacht capsized twice on the 14-week voyage from Sydney to the US's Palmer station. After repairs and a winter's delay, Lewis sailed for Cape Town, again capsizing en route. In 1977–78, he sailed to Cape Adare in the Ross Sea on the yacht *Solo*. With five others in 1982, Lewis froze the steel yacht *Dick Smith Explorer* into an anchorage near Australia's Davis base and wintered aboard.

Australians Don and Margie McIntyre wintered in Antarctica in 1995, after being dropped off by their yacht at Commonwealth Bay. For more information about their experiences, see the boxed text on p266.

In 1983 Gerry Clark, a 56-year-old New Zealander, set off from NZ in the 10m wooden yacht *Totorore* to circumnavigate Antarctica. His three-year odyssey involved some remarkable single-handed yachting combined with adventures and ornithological work achieved with crews picked up in South America. Near Heard Island Clark's journey turned into a survival epic when *Totorore* lost its mast and rigging and he was lucky to make it to Fremantle, Western Australia.

Led by Bill Blunt, the Australian 'Project Blizzard' expedition twice visited Mawson's hut at Commonwealth Bay. The voyages, in 1984 (aboard *Dick Smith Explorer)* and 1985 (aboard *Southern Quest*), were undertaken to make an assessment of the historic hut's condition.

American Ned Gillette's four-man team *rowed* across the Drake Passage to Antarctica in March 1988. The men required 14 days to row *Sea Tomato* 1100km from Cape Horn to Nelson Island in the South Shetlands. Gillette traded *Sea Tomato* to the Chilean navy in exchange for a flight back to Punta Arenas.

The first-ever true solo winters in Antarctica both took place in 1990. Frenchman Hughes Delignières wintered on his 9m yacht *Oviri*, frozen into a bay near Pleneau Island along the Peninsula. He made winter sledging journeys south toward Marguerite Bay. Meanwhile, Brazilian Amyr Klink on *Paratii* wintered alone slightly further north at Dorian Cove on Wiencke Island; he later completed a full solo circumnavigation of Antarctica in 77 days in 1999. (Some would say that Admiral Byrd's celebrated winter alone in 1934 at Advance Base on the Ross Ice Shelf was not really a solo, since Byrd was close to assistance from other expedition members, who had to come to his rescue when he was afflicted by carbon-monoxide poisoning.)

In 1993, during a tourist voyage on the Russian icebreaker *Kapitan Khlebnikov*, a replica of Shackleton's lifeboat *James Caird* was transported to Elephant Island. Led by Trevor Potts, three Englishmen and a woman then sailed the craft, which they called *Sir Ernest Shackleton*, 1480km to South Georgia. The 'Wake of Shackleton' team did not, however, attempt to cross the island.

No yacht had ever been south of Cape Hallett until 1993, when Frenchman Jean-Louis Etienne returned, this time aboard the luxury steel yacht *Antarctica* instead of behind a dog team. The expedition made an ascent of Mt Erebus and shot footage on the Peninsula for educational TV.

'Private expeditions to Antarctica are a spirited and valuable expression of our desire to travel in a great polar wilderness'

French yachtsman Bernard Espinet circumnavigated Antarctica in the yacht *Croustet* during a two-part voyage, sailing from Wellington in April 1996 and returning 15 months later in August 1997, having cruised 29,600km around the Southern Ocean. He was accompanied on the first leg to Cape Horn and the Falklands by 23-year-old New Zealander Matt Thorpe, but Espinet completed the voyage solo via South Georgia, Kerguelen and Hobart.

A second attempt to recreate Shackleton's open-boat voyage from Elephant Island to South Georgia took place in January 1997, this time by a seven-member Irish crew led by Paddy Barry and Frank Nugent. Five of the team sailed on a replica of *James Caird* called *Tom Crean* after one of Shackleton's Irish crew members. Unlike the 'Wake of Shackleton' expedition in 1993 that set out without a support vessel, *Tom Crean* was shadowed by the yacht *Pelagic*. After capsizing repeatedly in huge waves, *Tom Crean* was abandoned and finally scuttled halfway to South Georgia and the crew taken aboard *Pelagic*. Landing in King Haakon Bay, four team members crossed South Georgia and descended to the now-derelict whaling stations on the north coast just as Shackleton's party had 81 years before. A subsequent attempt to climb the virgin Mt Roots was abandoned.

THE FUTURE

Over the last five years Antarctica has witnessed a never-ending supply of adventurers, each with their own version of 'first this' or 'unsupported that,' who have made purely recreational or fund-raising traverses to the South Pole from either Berkner Island or ANI's Patriot Hills camp. Inspirational journeys though they are to those concerned, little, if any, new ground has been broken.

Is there anything left to do? With Antarctica's stunning untraveled mountain ranges, the answer is certainly yes – but it doesn't involve sledging to the South Pole, sadly the only destination that will attract sponsorship for the costly ventures. Some of the recent mountaineering expeditions to the rock spires of the Queen Maud Mountains, after long flights from South Africa, prove that the spirit of real adventure is still very much alive. New climbs have also been achieved on South Georgia peaks after rugged yacht voyages from South America.

Private expeditions to Antarctica are a spirited and valuable expression of our desire to travel in a great polar wilderness. Today, there is no excuse for poor planning. Expedition leaders must discuss objectives and support plans with their own government's Antarctic program administrators before departure. They all have an obligation to leave Antarctica exactly as they find it: pristine. Above all, they must educate others upon their return of the dire need to treat Antarctica with the greatest respect.

The Culture

THE ANTARCTIC PSYCHE

People come to work in Antarctica from dozens of countries, and a well-developed sense of adventure is perhaps the single most common denominator found among long-termers. Workers must also be healthy to pass the physical and mental exams most countries require. Each research station, of course, has its own 'home-grown' character that relates much more to its country of origin than it does to other Antarctic stations.

LIFESTYLE

People are much more isolated in Antarctica than they are almost anywhere else on earth, save perhaps those people living on the remote mid-ocean islands, such as Tristan da Cunha.

Although it's rarely a problem for tourists, Antarctica's remoteness can be difficult for winterovers (those who spend the dark, cold winter months in Antarctica; also known as winterers) – despite the availability of email and Internet access, which has reduced the sense of isolation dramatically from the 'old days.'

One of the most difficult aspects of the winter isolation is a lack of privacy – it can be very hard to find a place to be alone for very long. Escaping one's fellow station members can be all but impossible in a place where safety requirements mean that you often cannot wander far from home without at least one companion and a radio.

Perhaps inevitably, the outside world becomes less important for people living in Antarctica. 'You lose interest in the news from up north,' one winterover says. Another adds: 'You don't care so much what's happening in the rest of the world. After all, if something happens, what can you do?'

Many people find that the Antarctic winter's cold and darkness affect their short-term memory. This common disorder, called 'polar T3 syndrome' after a thyroid hormone known as triiodothyronine (T3), also raises blood pressure and cholesterol levels.

Several mental health–coping mechanisms are common. To relieve the boredom of the polar winter, expeditioners sometimes shave their heads or pierce their ears or noses, knowing they can revert back to their 'old selves' before returning home. Occasionally whole stations indulge in a kind of collective cultism, in which a certain song or movie is replayed over and over, with station members memorizing the entire dialogue and playing particular roles. A film version of Jane Austen's *Pride and*

DID YOU KNOW?

Due to radio blackouts and a lack of flights, South Pole residents in 1963 didn't learn about US President John F Kennedy's assassination for 20 days!

MARRIED WITH PENGUINS

In February 1978, at Argentina's Esperanza station, what is believed to be the first wedding in Antarctica took place when Julia Beatriz Buonamio and First Sergeant Carlos Alberto Sugliano were married by a military chaplain.

Since then, many more have been celebrated. In 1985, the chaplain at the US McMurdo station flew to the South Pole to officiate at a wedding there – the bride carried a bouquet of fresh vegetables. On New Year's Day, 1999, another couple got married at the Pole station, with their fellow station residents standing hand in hand in a circle around them at the Ceremonial Pole. The lucky pair spent their wedding night in a heated tent. Shipboard weddings, with the captain presiding, are not unusual. On one voyage, the ship's hotel manager and a senior lecturer tied the knot, and the bride wore a hand-sewn wedding dress made from white polar fleece!

Prejudice, for example, assumed bizarre importance for winterers at one sub-Antarctic island.

Perhaps flirting with a little paranoia, winter crews at the South Pole usually screen *The Thing* (p54) right after the departure of the year's last plane out.

POPULATION

Antarctica has never had a native population. Even today, its harsh environment assures that all residents are temporary. The continent's winter population is around 1200 – about a third scientists and the rest, support personnel. In summer, the population increases about sixfold.

Tourists, who numbered 13,571 in 2002–03, come largely from the US (about 40%), Germany and the UK (each 13–15%), Australia (6%), and Japan, Canada and Switzerland (each 3%).

MEDIA

With no permanent residents, Antarctica has no homegrown media. But three websites can help you keep up-to-date on Antarctic matters (all three include extensive archives of past material).

70 South (www.70south.com) Run by Brendon Grunewald of Brussels, 70 South is updated daily with what he calls 'Antarcticles.'

The Antarctican (www.antarctican.com) An independent news service devoted to news about Antarctica, edited by veteran Australian journalist Andrew Darby.

The Antarctic Sun (www.polar.org/antsun/) Published during the summer at McMurdo station, this site includes a popular 'Around the Continent' section, as well as articles about life in Antarctica's biggest town.

WOMEN IN ANTARCTICA

Most governments operating in Antarctica banned the participation of women for decades. Although women are still in the minority at most Antarctic stations, their numbers are growing. On tourist ships, women often outnumber men. For information on women in Antarctic history, see p58.

ARTS

Literature *Fauno Cordes*

Fauno Cordes is the world's foremost authority on Antarctic fiction. Her bibliography on the subject can be found at www.antarctic-circle.org/fauno.htm.

Antarctic fiction started in 1605 with the publication of a Utopian story, *Mundes Alter et Idem* ('Another World and Yet the Same'), by Bishop Joseph Hall of England, in which a traveler to Antarctica finds it inhabited by gluttons, drunkards and eccentrics. The genre has been enriched by such celebrated writers as Samuel Taylor Coleridge, James Fenimore Cooper, Rudyard Kipling, Edgar Allan Poe and Jules Verne (in *20,000 Leagues Under the Sea)*.

Coleridge, of course, wrote the most famous polar poem, *The Rime of the Ancient Mariner* (1798), in which an Antarctic ship is cursed when a sailor kills an albatross. In Cooper's fantasy, *The Monikins* (1835), a British baronet rescues four South Polar Monikins (simian-like beings) and returns them to their home. Another novel by Cooper, *The Sea Lions* (1849), draws on his personal experience as the major owner of a whaling ship to tell the story of two rival schooners searching for a mysterious sealing ground in the Antarctic. Kipling's *The Jungle Book* (1893) includes the story of Kotick, the white seal, who visits several sub-Antarctic islands.

Poe's novella *The Narrative of Arthur Gordon Pym* (1837) has been the most influential Antarctic story. It so inspired Verne that he wrote a sequel,

Le Sphinx des Glaces, in 1897. Other authors who took up Poe's storyline were Charles Romyn Dake in *A Strange Discovery* (1899), Steven Utley and Howard Waldrop in the short story 'Black as the Pit, from Pole to Pole' (in *The Year's Finest Fantasy*, 1978), and Rudy Rucker in *The Hollow Earth* (1990). Echoing from Pym through all these works is the eerie cry *Tekeli-li*, the call of the white birds in the South Polar region. (Poe wrote another story about a whirlpool at the South Pole, the shorter and more mysterious 'MS. Found in a Bottle' of 1833.)

Antarctic fiction over the last century has tended toward adventure stories and 'thrillers.' It can be classified by themes, which have remained consistent.

The adventure story *Olga Romanoff or The Syren of the Skies* (1894), by George Griffith, envisions Îles Kerguelen as a submarine and aircraft base, while in *Mary of Marion Island* (1929), H Rider Haggard maroons Mary on the island with a young British lord.

DID YOU KNOW?

For obvious reasons, drag enjoys a long history in Antarctica, from Scott's *Discovery* expedition to Australian stations' tradition of performing bawdy versions of *Cinderella*.

Volcanic activity destroys part of Antarctica in Godfrey Sweven's *Limanora, the Island of Progress* (1903), while in the title story of Valery Brussof's *The Republic of the Southern Cross and Other Stories* (1977), an epidemic wipes out most of Antarctica's human population. A huge section of the ice cap breaks away in James Follett's *Ice* (1977), while in Richard Moran's *Cold Sea Rising* (1986), an undersea volcanic plume severs the Ross Ice Shelf and sets it adrift. Solar flares cause a surge of the ice sheet in Crawford Killian's *Icequake* (1979), and Antarctica is about to heat up after nuclear war tilts the earth's axis in David Graham's *Down to a Sunless Sea* (1981).

Captain WE Johns' *Biggles' Second Case* (1951) tracks a Nazi U-boat carrying stolen British gold near Kerguelen. Marion Morris' *The Icemen* (1988) sees a remnant group of Nazis taking over an Argentine Antarctic station. In Richard Henrick's *Ice Wolf* (1994), Nazis try to retrieve the Holy Grail from an Antarctic cave, while in *Ice Reich* (1998) by William Dietrich, an American pilot is hired by Hermann Göring to sail to Antarctica.

Ecoterrorists try to blow up a Russian whaling factory ship in John Gordon Davis' *Leviathan* (1976), and an oil cartel–backed group seizes control of Antarctica in DC Poyer's *White Continent* (1980). In David Smith's *Freeze Frame* (1992), French adventurers develop a secret uranium mine at Dumont d'Urville. In Kim Stanley Robinson's *Antarctica* (1998), Marxist 'ecoteurs' blow up Antarctic stations established by corporations to exploit the continent's resources. The British, French and Americans are involved in a high-tech battle in Matthew Reilly's *Ice Station* (1998). *Icefire* (1998) by Judith and Garfield Reeves-Stevens, has rogue Chinese generals setting off nuclear weapons beneath the Ross Ice Shelf.

Paralee Sweeten Sutton's *White City* (1949) describes a young couple lost in a small plane, who discover an Antarctic civilization whose members communicate by thought transference. In David Burke's *Monday at McMurdo* (1967), a plane carrying a US congressman crashes on a glacier. John Gordon Davis' *Seize the Wind* (1985) has an Australian DC-10 filled with sightseers crashing on the Beardmore Glacier, while Charles Neider's *Overflight* (1986) slams a DC-10 tourist flight into Mt Erebus.

An American plane is looking for a missing yacht in Clive Cussler's *Treasure* (1988). A yacht crew searches for a 19th-century sailing ship in Hammond Innes' *Isvik* (1991), while the vessel in Charles McCarry's *The Better Angels* (1979) is simply carrying its owner on a vacation. In *158 Vuorokautto* (158 Days; 1983), by Alpo Ruuth, a Finnish yacht sails into a blizzard near the Antarctic Peninsula during a round-the-world race, while a chilling regatta ends near the South Sandwich Islands in Robert Stone's *Outerbridge Reach* (1998).

In Edwin Woodard and Heather Woodard Bischoff's *Storehouses of the Snow* (1980), a cruise ship gets trapped in the Lemaire Channel after a sudden tilt of the earth's axis, while another tour vessel runs aground in Wilbur Smith's *Hungry as the Sea* (1978). A tourist gets stranded on an iceberg in Madeleine L'Engle's *Troubling a Star* (1994). Another is abandoned on Seymour Island in Clive Cussler's *Shock Wave* (1996).

Agatha Christie weaves a good yarn about a geophysicist who returns from the Antarctic to discover that he was the alibi for a late murder suspect, in the mystery *Ordeal by Innocence* (1958). Thomas Keneally tells an eerie tale about the killing of a newsman during the dark Antarctic winter in *Victim of the Aurora* (1977). An Antarctic murder is solved by a policeman working as a research assistant for his son in Emmy Lou Schenk's 'Ice Cave' (in *Alfred Hitchcock Mystery Magazine*, August 1987). In Bob Reiss' *Purgatory Road* (1996), members of an Antarctic station are plagued by madness and murder.

An East Hollywood chef builds a summer home on Ross Island in Crispin Kitto's *The Antarctica Cookbook* (1984). Nikki Gemmell's *Shiver* (1997) sends a young woman journalist to the Antarctic, where she falls in love, while Liane Shavian's *Surfing Antarctica* (1999) promises 'a wild roller-coaster ride of ecoheroics and hot lust.'

Music *Valmar Kurol*

Valmar Kurol is president of the Montreal Antarctic Society.

Antarctica has inspired many musicians from around the world. Individual songs titled 'Antarctica' or about The Ice have appeared on some 90 commercially issued discs in styles ranging from heavy metal to novelty. Below is a discography of CDs currently available about Antarctica.

Antarctic Arrival: A Tribute to a Frozen Land (Valmar Kurol and Marc-André Bourbonnais; 1999; available from the Montreal Antarctic Society, 63 Courtney Drive, Montreal West, Quebec, Canada H4X 1M7) New Age/light rock/classical compositions about the wonders of Antarctica.

Antarctic Symphony (Sir Peter Maxwell Davies' Symphony No 8) Commissioned by the British Antarctic Survey and the London Philharmonia Orchestra and premiered in 2001; not yet issued on CD but to become available by download on the composer's website at www.maxopus.com.

Antarctica (Vangelis; 1983; Polygram 815732-2) Synthesizer music from Koreyoshi Kurahara's film of the same name; the title track is the definitive Antarctic mood music.

Antarctica (Richie Beirach; 1994; ECD 22086-2) Jazz piano solos; titles include 'The Ice Shelf,' 'Deception Island' and 'Neptunes Bellows.'

Antarctica (Ian Tamblyn; 1994; North Track NTCD3; in the US, NorthSound NSCD 29532) New Age/folk-rock/jazz supplemented by Adélie penguin brays and Weddell seal trills.

Antarctica (Douglas Quin; 1998; Miramar 09006-23113-2) Natural recordings of Weddell and leopard seals, orcas, emperor and Adélie penguins, and the creaks and groans of the Canada Glacier.

Antarctica: Suite for Guitar and Orchestra (Nigel Westlake; 1992; Sony Classical SK53361) Westlake wrote the score for the IMAX film *Antarctica*, then reworked it into this; guitar playing by John Williams.

Antarctica Suite for Solo Piano (Wendy Mae Chambers; 1999) A piano tribute to the sights and sounds of Antarctica by this avant-garde American composer.

Antarctica: The Last Wilderness (Medwyn Goodall; 1993; Mar 3812) Dreamy, peaceful instrumental pieces about eternity and emptiness.

Antartida (John Cale; 1995; Les Disques du Crépuscule TWI1008) Soundtrack from the Manuel Huerga film of the same name. Cale is a former member of the Velvet Underground, and the theme song is *Antarctica Starts Here*, from his 1973 solo album *Paris 1919* (Reprise/Warner Bros 2131-2).

Music for the Scotia Centenary (2002; RSCDS CD032) Music to celebrate the centenary of Robert Bruce's Scottish National Antarctic Expedition includes traditional country dance tunes now with Antarctic titles and the longer orchestral suite, *South*, by Gordon McPherson.

On the Last Frontier (Einojuhani Rautavaara; 1999; Ondine ODE 921-2) Spawned by this Finnish classical composer's lifelong interest in author Edgar Allan Poe's *The Narrative of Arthur Gordon Pym*.

Polar Shift: A Benefit for Antarctica (various artists; 1991; Private Music BMG2083-2-P) Compilation of New Age instrumental and vocal music by Vangelis, Yanni, Enya, Kitaro, John Tesh et al.

Shackleton's Antarctic Adventure (Sam Cardon; 2001; WGBH Music/White Mountain Films Music (BMI) JR74222) Soundtrack for the IMAX film of Shackleton's *Endurance* expedition.

Sinfonia Antarctica (Ralph Vaughan Williams' Symphony No 7) The mother of all Antarctic music, originated as the soundtrack for the film *Scott of the Antarctic* (1949); many versions exist, recorded between 1953 and 1996.

The Songs of the 'Morning': A Musical Sketch (2002; Reardon Publishing) Music composed by GS Doorly and lyrics by officers on board *Morning* in 1902 during its relief of Scott's ship *Discovery*; sung by Doorly's descendants and other New Zealanders.

Voyage of Discovery – Dedicated to the Memory of Robert F Scott (DE Farmer; 2000; mp3.com 39391) Instrumental synthesizer music with themes related to Scott's *Discovery* expedition.

White Out (Johannes Schmoelling; 2000; Victoriapark VP00-1) A synthesizer impression of Antarctica's white by a former member of Germany's Tangerine Dream.

FOOD & DRINK

Food on Antarctic cruises varies from ship to ship, in some proportion to the price of the cruise (and the skill of the chefs). Vegans and vegetarians should make their dietary needs known to their tour companies when they book their trip. Shipboard chefs are able to accommodate nearly any diet with advance notice.

At least once during the cruise, you'll probably experience the de rigueur 'Antarctic barbecue,' in which grills are set up out on deck or even down on the fast ice and everyone bundles up for chicken, hamburgers, sausages and the like. It's a bit clichéd, but fun nevertheless, and makes a change from the dining room.

'Many Antarcticans enjoy sipping their Scotch on very old rocks!'

If you have your own favorite 'national' foods – peanut butter, Vegemite, Marmite, Promite, orange marmalade, miso soup – you might want to bring them with you.

Tap water is fine to drink aboard all Antarctic tour ships.

It's fair to say that alcohol is available almost everywhere on the continent you find people, with the possible exception of a remote field camp or two. Champagne is a popular tourist drink, especially in Antarctic-cruise set pieces such as 'Champagne on the Ross Ice Shelf' and 'Champagne on the Sea Ice.' You should also have little trouble finding some glacier ice for your whiskey; many Antarcticans enjoy sipping their Scotch on very old rocks!

One of the very few 'native' Antarctic drinks is a concoction called the Antarctic Old Fashion, invented by the crew at the US Little America V base from 1956 to 1958, and perfected at Camp Michigan on the Ross Ice Shelf. Here's the recipe, as described by James 'Gentleman Jim' Zumberge in the *Antarctican Society* newsletter (reprinted by permission):

> This is a long way around to telling the recipe (formula is a better word) for an Antarctic Old Fashion. It is impossible to make a simple Antarctic Old Fashion. All the research at Little America V was based on a batch quantity. Here are the ingredients: one fifth of Old Methusala (100 proof Navy 'bourbon') and seven packages of multiflavored Life Savers. Pour the Old Methusala into another container and fill the empty bottle half full with freshly melted

EDIBLE ANTARCTICA

Intrepid gourmets may no longer sample the wild foods of Antarctica, because the Antarctic Treaty's Protocol on Environmental Protection signed in 1991 prohibits even 'disturbing' wildlife except in a life-threatening emergency. Until relatively recently, however, visitors to Antarctica and the peri-Antarctic islands regularly ate the animals and plants they found.

Profit-hungry owners of sealing and whaling vessels expected their crews to secure a large part of their rations themselves, so sealers and whalers supplemented their often meager and monotonous diets by hunting. Shipwrecked mariners survived only by foraging, but even well-organized Antarctic expeditions counted on obtaining fresh food in the field. Douglas Mawson wrote in *The Home of the Blizzard* (1915) that his expedition's 100 tons of food was calculated 'based on the supposition that unlimited quantities of seal and penguin meat can be had on the spot.' Eating fresh meat also helped ward off scurvy.

Antarctic 'country foods' held a prominent place on the table during local holidays, especially Midwinter's Day, when nearly every expedition held an elaborate feast accompanied by speeches, toasts and hand-decorated menus. The Scottish National Antarctic Expedition of 1902–04 enjoyed a Christmas dinner of *Penguin à la Scotia*, named for the expedition's ship, while the 1912 Midwinter's Day dinner on the Australasian Antarctic Expedition featured *Noisettes de Phoque* [seal] and *Pinguoin à la Terre Adélie* [penguin].

Seal, penguin and whale meat were often consumed on the first Byrd Antarctic expedition (1928–30), says Colonel Norman D Vaughan, the expedition's last-surviving member: 'They all taste quite alike. It is all heavy, black meat, but as long as it's fresh, it's great.' Dr Phillip G Law, leader of the Australian National Antarctic Research Expeditions from 1949 to 1966, says: 'I have tasted a variety of meats from Antarctic species – seals, penguins, skuas. There is one basic rule of greatest importance when preparing them: get rid of every last remnant of blubber, otherwise the food will have an abominable fishy taste.'

As recently as the IGY [International Geophysical Year], living off the land was a regular part of Antarctic life. A cook at a British base, Gerald T Cutland, even wrote an Antarctic cookbook, c 1957, titled *Fit for a FID, or, How to Keep a Fat Explorer in Prime Condition*.

The animals most often eaten were seals. 'The taste,' wrote Erich von Drygalski in *The Southern Ice Continent* (1904), 'is hardly similar to any of our familiar kinds of meat; it might be thought to resemble something between beef and pork, but it is really like neither, because of its fine dark colour.' In *The Voyage of the Discovery* (1905), Captain Robert Scott confided: 'It is almost impossible to describe the taste of seal; it has a distinctive flavour in a similar degree to beef and mutton, but it cannot be called 'fishy,' or like anything else that is generally known.'

Despite its very dark color even when cooked, seal meat was very popular. William Lashly on Scott's *Discovery* expedition called it 'better than beef.' On the same expedition, Scott himself reported that 'the consumption is so great that we have all our work to keep up the supply, and appetites seem to be increasing rather than lessening.'

Seal organs were eaten as often as the meat, with liver especially favored. Scott wrote in *The Voyage of the Discovery*, 'Everyone partakes of this excellent dish and wishes heartily that the seal was possessed of more than one liver.' Several expeditions also singled out seal brain as a special treat.

Crabeater seals were considered tastier than Weddell seals, perhaps as a result of their different prey. Leopard seal 'is very good eating and wholesome,' wrote Captain Joseph J Fuller,

snow. Then force the Life Savers, one by one, into the mouth of the Methusala bottle and shake until all are dissolved. (Here it should be noted that painstaking research on the formula by the originators revealed that the final product was vastly improved if only two of the red Life Savers were used. All of our Camp Michigan Antarctic Old Fashions were made accordingly.) The final step in the process is to pour the Old Methusala, stir well, and serve over Antarctic glacier ice. No fruit or other garbage is needed since those flavors are all embodied in the mixture.

a 19th-century sealer who made 12 voyages to Kerguelen. 'Large ships coming to these parts consider the leopard seal quite a delicacy.' Elephant seal meat, especially from young animals, was greatly enjoyed; the tongues were pickled as a luxury. Perhaps the most unusual food item in the Antarctic larder was the trunk of bull elephant seals – these were boiled in salt water for hours, then stuffed and roasted, to create a dish called 'snotters.'

Naturally the bird most identified with Antarctica did not escape uneaten. 'If they became too impertinent,' one of Roald Amundsen's men wrote of the little Adélie penguins, 'we did not hesitate to take them, for their flesh, especially the liver, was excellent.' Similarly, Albert Armitage, second-in-command on Scott's *Discovery* expedition, wrote in 1905, 'Numbers of Adélie penguins visited us, and not a few of them found their way into our cooking pots, for they were exceedingly good eating.'

'Because of the powerful pectoral muscles developed for swimming, the meatiest part of a penguin is its breast,' says Law. 'The dense muscle meat resembles ox heart. My favorite recipe is to thinly slice the breast and fry it with a coating of egg and bread crumbs in the fashion of a wiener schnitzel.'

Frederick A Cook, surgeon on the *Belgica* expedition, is often quoted for his memorable description of the taste of penguin in *Through the First Antarctic Night* (1900): 'It is rather difficult to describe its taste and appearance; we have absolutely no meat with which to compare it. The penguin, as an animal, seems to be made up of an equal proportion of mammal, fish, and fowl. If it is possible to imagine a piece of beef, an odoriferous codfish, and a canvas-back duck, roasted in a pot, with blood and cod-liver oil for sauce, the illustration will be complete.' Picturesque, no doubt, but Cook and his men actually liked penguin. 'We have begun to eat penguin meat,' he wrote in the passage immediately preceding the one above. 'The doubtful recommendation it has received from other explorers has caused us to shun it; but now, for variety, we would gladly take to anything...We have tried the meat several times, and it seems to improve upon acquaintance.'

Penguin eggs were also an important part of many Antarctic diets, especially since they keep for up to a year in the natural refrigeration. They are different from hen's eggs, to be sure: the 'white' never sets, even when well-cooked, and the yolk in some species is a bright orange or red. 'A couple of fried penguin eggs on a white dinner plate look like two bloodshot eyes,' wrote Wally Herbert in his book *A World of Men* (1969).

Albatross – especially young chick – was a favorite dish from the time of Captain Cook, and was most famously eaten by the crew of Ernest Shackleton's *James Caird* after their epic crossing from Elephant Island to South Georgia.

Shags were popular with Gerald Cutland, who wrote, 'To those people who have shags in their vicinity and have not included this bird in their diet I would say they are missing one of the luxuries of the Antarctic and my advice is that if you see any around, take a .22 rifle and knock a few off.'

Skua is 'not unlike duck,' according to Alan Gilchrist, who wintered on Heard Island in 1948. Of sheathbills, Thomas Orde-Lees wrote in his *Endurance* expedition diary: 'Notwithstanding that they are carrion feeders we consider that they taste delicious.'

Two similar plants found on sub-Antarctic islands – Macquarie Island cabbage and especially, as its taxonomic name implies, Kerguelen cabbage *(Pringlea antiscorbutica)* – are excellent sources of vitamin C, and were sought after by everyone visiting the islands.

Excerpted from 'Train Oil and Snotters: Eating Antarctic Wild Foods,' in Gastronomica: The Journal of Food and Culture, *Winter 2003; ©Jeff Rubin*

Zumberge also recalled the utility of 60ml bottles of Navy brandy in coping with the cold:

> Our usual practice was to drink half before getting into our sleeping bags and the other half the next morning when rising. Because we slept in unheated tents, an ounce of brandy gave one the feeling of warmth before crawling into a cold sack, and in the morning it gave you the courage to get out.

Environment

THE LAND

Viewed on a map, Antarctica resembles a giant stingray with its tail snaking up toward South America's Tierra del Fuego and its head swimming into the Indian Ocean. Without the 'tail,' the continent is roughly circular, with a diameter of about 4500km and an area of about 14.2 million sq km. If Antarctica were a country, it would be the world's second largest after Russia. It is also the most arid and – with an average elevation of 2250m – the highest continent. Surrounded by the Southern Ocean, it's the most isolated continent as well.

DID YOU KNOW?

Antarctica's ice sheets contain 90% of the world's ice – 30 million cu km – which holds nearly 70% of the world's fresh water.

Antarctica is divided by the 2900km-long Transantarctic Mountains into East Antarctica (sometimes referred to as 'Greater Antarctica') and West Antarctica (or 'Lesser Antarctica'), with the directions deriving from 0° longitude. The continent's highest point is Vinson Massif, recently re-measured to the precise height of 4900.3m.

The Antarctic Peninsula separates the two great embayments into the continent, the Weddell and Ross Seas. Each of these seas has its own ice shelf – the Ronne Ice Shelf and the Ross Ice Shelf, respectively – which are extensions of the great Antarctic ice sheet. The Ross Ice Shelf, which is roughly the size of France, is the world's largest ice shelf.

Satellite images of the continent show that ice covers 99.6% of Antarctica. This ice is up to 4775m thick, and in some places its enormous weight has depressed the underlying landmass by nearly 1600m. Antarctica's

SNOW ACCUMULATION & EXTENTS OF SEA ICE

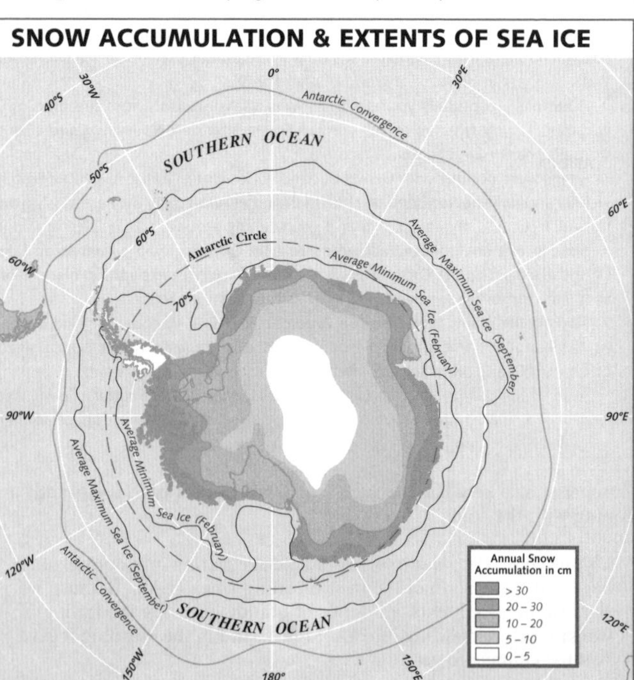

DID YOU KNOW?

Antarctica's coastline measures 30,500km, of which as little as 500km is ice free.

SIZE OF ANTARCTICA IN COMPARISON TO OTHER CONTINENTS

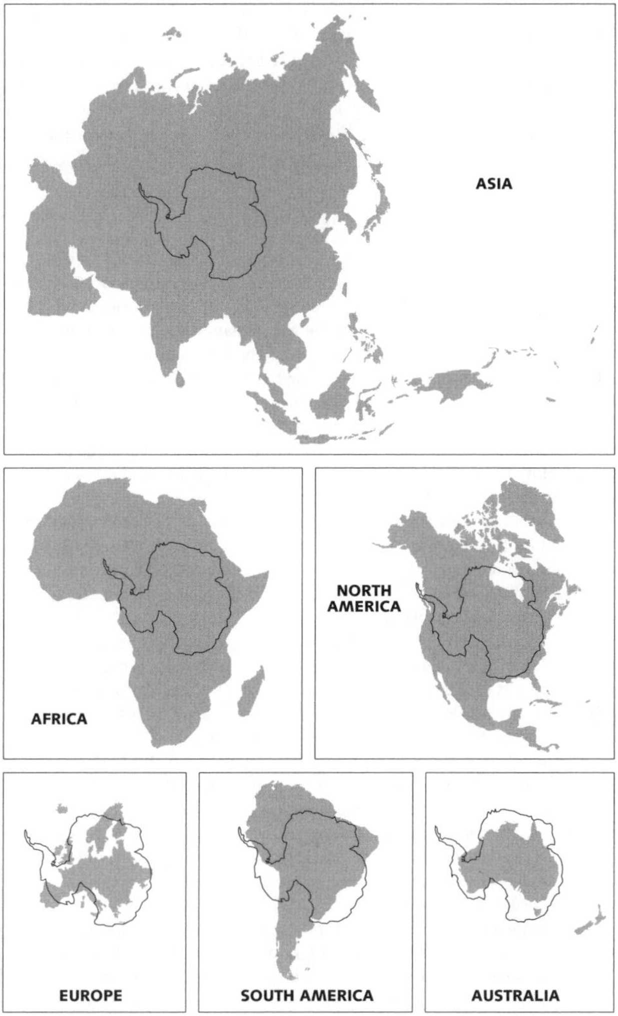

continental shelf is about three times deeper than that of any other continent. In the event of the Antarctic ice sheet melting, the world's oceans would rise by up to 70m. West Antarctica would become an archipelago of small, mountainous islands (much like Indonesia), while East Antarctica would be a continental landmass about the same size as Australia.

In September, Antarctica's late winter, the size of the continent effectively doubles with the freezing of the sea ice, which can extend more than 1000km from the coast.

DID YOU KNOW?

The largest glacier in the world is the Lambert Glacier, which flows onto the Amery Ice Shelf in East Antarctica.

As the captain of any vessel cruising in Antarctic waters will tell you, the coastline of Antarctica is still far from being perfectly charted. As recently as 2001, a US oceanographic expedition working on the western side of the Antarctic Peninsula found that the coastline was drawn on the charts as much as 32km away from where they actually found it.

The rocks of East Antarctica are at least three billion years old, among the oldest on earth. In fact, some of the oldest terrestrial rock yet discovered was found in Enderby Land (roughly between 40°E and 60°E) by Australian geologist Lance Black in 1986 – the rock is estimated to

GLACIOLOGY *Dr Jo Jacka*

The Antarctic Ice Sheet

The Antarctic ice sheet has an area of about 13.3 million sq km (1.7 times the size of Australia, 1.4 times the size of the US or 1.3 times the size of Europe). It is thicker than 4km in some locations and on average is about 2.7km thick – giving it a total ice volume of about 32.4 million cu km.

This enormous amount of ice has formed through the accumulation of snow over millions of years. The amount of snow deposited in any one year is relatively very low – Antarctica is a desert and the driest continent on earth. Because the snow has been deposited over so many years without melting, the ice sheet provides a natural archive that glaciologists and climatologists study for evidence of past environments and of climatic changes.

As snow is deposited year after year in the interior of the ice sheet, it consolidates to form ice. Due to pressure created by its own weight, the ice flows from the high interior toward the Antarctic coast, where large slabs break off to form icebergs.

Glaciologists from several countries measure the amount of snow falling on the ice sheet and compare this with the amount of ice flowing toward the coast, and ultimately with the amount of ice breaking off as icebergs or melting in the warmer coastal margins of the continent. These quantities would be the same if there had been no change in the climate during the thousands of years since the ice in the icebergs was falling as snow.

The mass of the ice sheet is balanced only when the amount of ice coming in is equal to the amount flowing out, a condition called 'steady state.' A positive mass budget – meaning more snow is falling than is flowing out to the coast – suggests that there has been a climate change in which more snow is falling now than did at some time in the past (maybe thousands of years). A negative mass budget suggests that less snow is falling now than in the past.

To calculate the mass budget of a particular section of the Antarctic ice sheet, glaciologists make measurements of ice surface height and thickness, then determine the rate of snow accumulation and the speed of the ice as it moves toward the coast. By flying over the ice sheet, or by traversing it with over-snow tractor trains, glaciologists are able to use satellite surveying techniques to measure the ice's surface height. Ice thickness is measured using downward-looking radars. Global positioning satellites accurately measure the positions of markers in the ice sheet, which over time reveal the speed of the ice flow.

Although such measurements have been made over much of the Antarctic ice sheet, it is not feasible to measure the whole ice sheet directly. But remote sensing from satellites is used to provide observations of large areas and long time intervals, and computer modeling studies are carried out to estimate the mass budget of different areas of the ice sheet and of the whole ice sheet.

Drilling into the Past

As snow is deposited on the surface of the Antarctic ice sheet, different chemicals and gases that have dissolved and mixed in the snow and in the atmosphere become trapped in the ice. By drilling through the ice sheet and analyzing the ice and air trapped in the bubbles, glaciologists access an archive of past climate change.

The oxygen isotope ratio (or 'delta value') of melted ice samples is related to the temperature when the ice was deposited as snow. Thus, a climate history can be built up by measuring delta

be 3.84 billion years old. West Antarctica is relatively new: only 700 million years old.

Iron ore, coal and other minerals have all been found in the Antarctic, but their quantities – and qualities – are still unknown. At present, exploiting any of these mineral deposits would be highly uneconomical; the equivalent, in one scientist's words, of 'mining on the moon.' Although it is theorized that oil and natural gas exist beneath Antarctica's continental shelf, no commercial-size deposits have ever been found. The Protocol on Environmental Protection, signed in Madrid in 1991 by all

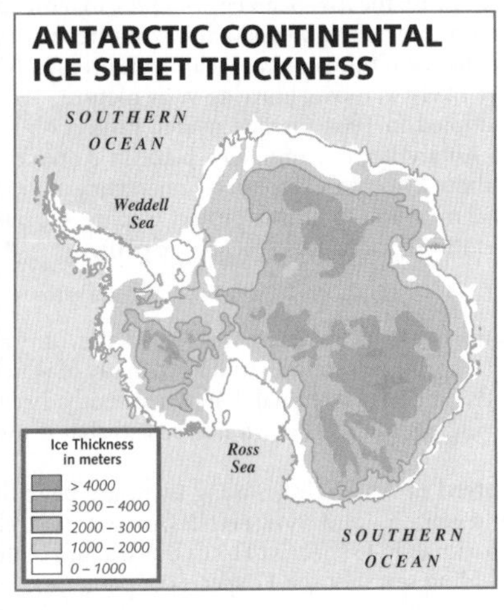

value from the surface of the ice sheet down. At Russia's Vostok station, an ice core has been drilled to a depth of 3348m. The ice at the bottom of this core is about 426,000 years old, and the delta values show several glacial cycles; that is, several ice ages and warmer interglacial periods.

Air pockets between snow grains on the surface of the ice sheet become bubbles under high pressure deep down in the ice. These bubbles contain tiny samples of the atmosphere from earlier times. Analysis of the air trapped in the bubbles allows glaciologists to examine how the concentrations of different gases in the atmosphere have changed over time.

While some ice cores (such as the one drilled at Vostok) can give us a climate history extending back hundreds of thousands of years, they cannot be dated accurately. Others, however, drilled at locations where the snow accumulation is relatively high, can provide very precise dating if the annual snow layer is thick enough, because several samples can be analyzed for each year of snow. However, these ice cores do not extend back in time as far as the deeper, low accumulation cores, so the shallower, high-snow-accumulation ice cores provide very accurately dated climate and environmental data, but only for the past few thousand years.

Because the delta value is related to temperature when the snow was deposited, it has an annual cycle: it is colder in winter, warmer in summer. The chemical compound hydrogen peroxide, which is dissolved in the ice, also shows an annual cycle. Hydrogen peroxide is formed in the atmosphere naturally by a chemical reaction that requires ultraviolet light. In Antarctica, where the sun is above the horizon for 24 hours per day at midsummer yet below the horizon at midwinter, there is a large variation in ultraviolet light throughout the year, and thus a marked annual cycle of hydrogen peroxide in the ice cores. Once the annual cycles in an ice core have been detected, the core is dated very easily by counting the number of cycles.

There is a third technique (completely independent of the above-described annual cycles) for dating an ice core. Sulfate is a chemical that is blasted into the atmosphere from time to time by erupting volcanoes. It is then distributed around the globe in the atmosphere, and dissolved in rain and snow. By measuring sulfate concentration in the ice cores, glaciologists can 'see' past volcanic eruptions. By collaborating with volcanologists, they can then determine which sulfate signals in the ice correspond with which volcanic eruption and, more importantly, when that eruption occurred.

Dr Jo Jacka, retired from the Australian Antarctic Division and the Antarctic Climate and Ecosystems Cooperative Research Centre, is now Chief Scientific Editor of the Journal of Glaciology

26 consultative parties to the Antarctic Treaty, prohibits all mining in Antarctica.

WILDLIFE

When viewing Antarctic wildlife, it is important to keep your distance. For one thing, the *Guidance for Visitors to the Antarctic* (see the boxed text on p90) requires it – and it's important for your personal safety. Your presence changes the animals' behavior, so the further back you keep, the more natural the animal will act. While wildlife may not seem to be concerned about your presence you may in fact be causing it considerable stress. A single thoughtless gesture can cause the loss of an egg or chick to a predator, or the crushing of a seal pup by a frightened adult. Another reason to keep back is that your photos won't turn out as well if you press in too close – the animals are more likely to move, blurring your picture.

DID YOU KNOW?

The Antarctic Circumpolar Current is the world's biggest current, flowing eastward at the rate of 153 million cu meters per second – about 1000 times the Amazon's flow.

International measures adopted in 1964 provide overall protection for animal and plant species in Antarctica. No animal or plant in Antarctica may be collected or killed without a license, except in an emergency as food. For details about international measures to further protect wildlife, see p94, and for information on the status of individual species, see p105.

Animals

Antarctica's native land animals are all invertebrates – and they are all small. They include mites, lice, springtails, midges and fleas, many of which are parasites of seals and birds. The largest animal that permanently dwells on land in Antarctica is a wingless midge *(Belgica antarctica)* that grows to just over 1cm long.

Only a few bird species breed in Antarctica, among them are penguin species – emperor, Adélie and gentoo – and snow petrels, Antarctic petrels and South Polar skuas. Approximately 45 species of birds breed south of the Antarctic Convergence, including seven of the 17 species of penguins.

Compared to Antarctica's relative barrenness, the Southern Ocean teems with life. With krill as the basis of its food web, the Southern Ocean supports a wealth of fish, seal, whale and seabird species.

Dogs were once widely used in Antarctica to pull sledges, but they were banned from the continent by the Antarctic Treaty's Protocol on Environmental Protection and the last were removed in 1994.

For more on Antarctic animals, see the Wildlife Guide (p105).

DID YOU KNOW?

Elephant seals are prolific divers. They have huge reservoirs of blood (22% of their body mass) and can slow their hearts to less than five beats per minute.

Plants

Plant species are actually more numerous than first impressions of Antarctica would lead one to believe, but they are far smaller and less conspicuous than plants in other latitudes. Antarctica is home to some 350 species of lichen, 100 species of moss and hundreds of species of algae – including 20 species of snow algae (p220), which form colorful patches of pink, red, yellow or green on areas of permanent snow. Some remarkable lichens and algae can even live inside rocks, inhabiting the spaces between individual grains of the rock. There are no trees or shrubs in Antarctica and just two species of indigenous vascular plants: Antarctic hair grass *(Deschampsia antarctica)* and Antarctic pearlwort *(Colobanthus quitensis)*. The sub-Antarctic islands, of course, have much more diverse flora, with South Georgia alone boasting at least 50 species of vascular plants.

Commercial Exploitation

Antarctica's exploration was tied directly to the exploitation of its marine mammals, specifically seals and whales. Throughout the 19th century, the

ICEBERGS *Dr Jo Jacka*

The Antarctic ice sheet is the 'iceberg factory' of the Southern Ocean. The total volume of ice calved from the ice sheet each year is about 2300 cu km, and it has been estimated that there are about 300,000 icebergs in the Southern Ocean at any one time. Individual icebergs range in dimension from a few meters (these are often called 'growlers') to about 5m ('bergy bits') to kilometers.

From time to time, particularly large icebergs break off the ice sheet. These can be tens of kilometers to even 100km long. At any one time there might be four or five gigantic icebergs in excess of 50km in length in the Southern Ocean, usually close to the Antarctic coast. It has been estimated that as much as 70% of the total volume of ice discharged from the Antarctic ice sheet is accounted for by icebergs of greater than a kilometer in length.

These larger icebergs are tabular in shape and form by calving from the large Antarctic ice shelves (eg the Ross, Filchner or Amery ice shelves). Typically, these icebergs are about 30m to 40m high (above sea level) and as much as 300m deep. After erosion from wind and waves, and melting from the warmer sea temperatures away from the Antarctic coast, the tabular icebergs become unstable and roll over to form jagged irregular icebergs, sometimes with spikes towering up to 60m into the air and with even greater protrusions deep under the ocean surface. Ultimately, icebergs melt completely as they drift to more northerly, warmer water.

Dr Jo Jacka, retired from the Australian Antarctic Division and the Antarctic Climate and Ecosystems Cooperative Research Centre, is now Chief Scientific Editor of the Journal of Glaciology

discovery of new sealing grounds on sub-Antarctic islands was in each case immediately followed by the near-extinction of the local population.

Whale oil was used for lighting, lubrication and tanning. Until 1870, when Norwegian Svend Foyn patented the exploding harpoon, whaling had been practiced from small boats, as Herman Melville famously depicted in *Moby Dick*. With Foyn's invention, the harpoon, once embedded in the whale's flesh, exploded and killed it – no more being pulled along in a tiny whaleboat by an angry leviathan on a 'Nantucket sleigh ride.'

For more information on human exploitation of Antarctica, see p94.

The Antarctic whaling boom soon followed. South Georgia was one catching ground, important in the early years. The South Shetlands were the other early whaling area, with the first modern floating factory ship, *Admiralen*, operating in Admiralty Bay on King George Island in 1906.

The market for whale oil expanded greatly when a process was invented to turn it into margarine and soap. By the 1920s, advancing technology – particularly the stern slipway, which allowed the entire whale to be winched aboard a floating factory ship for processing – shifted predominance to pelagic, or open-ocean, whaling. Pelagic factory ships had another advantage: by operating on the high seas, they avoided government limits on whale-hunting. In later years, the industry shifted from being a mainly Norwegian and British business to one dominated by the Japanese and Soviets.

To give some idea of the numbers of whales that were caught, it is useful to look at the records from South Georgia, the main site of land-based operations. From 1904 to 1965, when whaling at South Georgia ceased, a total of 41,515 blue whales were caught, along with 87,555 fins, 26,754 humpbacks, 15,128 seis and 3716 sperm whales. The total slaughter: an astounding 175,250 animals. Little wonder that so few whales exist today! Some species, such as the mighty blue whale, are so diminished in number that individuals may have a hard time even finding another of their species to mate with.

About 400 minke whales (out of some 760,000 minkes that the International Whaling Commission estimates live in Antarctic waters) are now

GUIDANCE FOR VISITORS TO THE ANTARCTIC

Activities in the Antarctic are governed by the Antarctic Treaty of 1959 and its associated agreements, referred to collectively as the Antarctic Treaty system. The Treaty established Antarctica as a zone of peace and science.

In 1991 the Antarctic Treaty Consultative Parties adopted the Protocol on Environmental Protection to the Antarctic Treaty, which designates the Antarctic as a natural reserve. The Protocol sets out environmental principles, procedures and obligations for the comprehensive protection of the Antarctic environment and its dependent and associated ecosystems.

The Environmental Protocol applies to tourism and nongovernmental activities, as well as governmental activities in the Antarctic Treaty area. It is intended to ensure that these activities do not have adverse impacts on the Antarctic environment or on its scientific and aesthetic values.

This *Guidance for Visitors to the Antarctic* is intended to make visitors aware of, and therefore able to comply with, the Treaty and the Protocol. Visitors are, of course, bound by national laws and regulations applicable to activities in the Antarctic.

Respect Protected Areas

A variety of areas in the Antarctic have been afforded special protection because of their particular ecological, scientific, historic or other values. Entry into certain areas may be prohibited except in accordance with a permit issued by an appropriate national authority. Activities in or near designated historic sites and monuments and certain other areas may be subject to special restrictions.

- Know the locations of areas that have been afforded special protection, and any restrictions on entry or on activities that can be carried out in and near them.
- Observe applicable restrictions.
- Do not damage, remove or destroy historic sites or monuments, or any artifacts associated with them.

Respect Scientific Research

- Do not interfere with scientific research, facilities or equipment.
- Obtain permission before visiting Antarctic science and logistic support facilities; confirm arrangements 24 to 72 hours before arriving, and comply strictly with the rules regarding such visits.
- Do not interfere with or remove scientific equipment or marker posts, and do not disturb experimental study sites, field camps or supplies.

Be Safe

- Be prepared for severe and changeable weather. Be sure that your equipment and clothing meet Antarctic standards. Remember that the Antarctic environment is inhospitable, unpredictable and potentially dangerous.

killed each year by Japan. To help fund its research, which includes data collected on age, calves and gestation, Japan's Institute of Cetacean Research sells the approximately 2000 tonnes of meat taken from the minkes, mainly to canned-food processors. These sales earn more than US$30 million each year, more than half the cost of running the research program. The retail price of prime-quality red whale meat was set by the government at just under $US100 per kg for the 1997 season. The choicest whale meat – *onomi*, from the fat-marbled tail – can cost up to $US875 per kg. The meat is also used in school-lunch programs and served in *kujira-ya*, or 'whale restaurants,' 22 of which throughout Japan

- Know your capabilities and the dangers posed by the Antarctic environment, and act accordingly. Plan activities with safety in mind at all times.
- Keep a safe distance from all wildlife, both on land and at sea.
- Take note of, and act on, advice and instructions from your leaders; do not stray from your group.
- Do not walk onto glaciers or large snowfields without proper equipment and experience; there is a real danger of falling into hidden crevasses.
- Do not expect a rescue service; self-sufficiency is increased and risks reduced by sound planning, quality equipment and trained personnel.
- Do not enter emergency refuges (except in emergencies). If you use equipment or food from a refuge, inform the nearest research station or national authority once the emergency is over.
- Respect any smoking restrictions, particularly around buildings, and take great care to safeguard against the danger of fire. This is a real hazard in Antarctica's dry environment.

Protect Antarctic Wildlife

- Taking or harmfully interfering with Antarctic wildlife is prohibited except in accordance with a permit issued by a national authority.
- Do not feed, touch or handle birds or seals, or approach or photograph them in ways that cause them to alter their behavior. Take special care when animals are breeding or molting.
- Do not harm plants; damage can be caused by walking, driving or landing on extensive moss beds or lichen-covered scree slopes.
- Do not use guns or explosives. Keep noise to a minimum to avoid frightening wildlife.
- Do not bring non-native plants or animals (including house plants, pet dogs and cats) into the Antarctic.
- Do not use aircraft, vessels, small boats or other means of transportation in ways that disturb wildlife, either at sea or on land.

Keep Antarctica Pristine

Antarctica remains relatively pristine, and has not yet been subjected to large-scale human perturbations. It is the largest wilderness area on earth. Please do your part to keep it that way.

- Do not dispose of litter or garbage on land. Open burning is prohibited.
- Do not disturb or pollute lakes or streams. Any materials discarded at sea must be disposed of properly.
- Do not paint or engrave names or graffiti on rocks or buildings.
- Do not collect or take away biological or geological specimens or artifacts as souvenirs, including rocks, bones, eggs, fossils or parts or contents of buildings.
- Do not deface or vandalize buildings or emergency refuges, whether occupied, unoccupied or abandoned.

have joined together to form the National Association to Continue the Tradition of Whale Cuisine.

Krill have been fished commercially since 1972; the catch reached its peak in 1985–86, when 425,870 tons were caught. Japan is now the primary harvester. In the 1998–99 season, Japan took about 69% of the 103,000-ton catch of the pink, 5cm-long crustaceans, followed by Poland (18% of the catch), Argentina (6%), Ukraine (5.5%) and Korea (1%). Nearly half of the annual catch is canned or frozen and sold as 'Antarctic shrimp.' Brochures marketing krill suggest masking its strong taste by using a pungent flavoring such as soy sauce or garlic. Even in the former

ANTARCTIC SITE INVENTORY *Ron Naveen*

The 1991 Protocol on Environmental Protection to the Antarctic Treaty (the 'Protocol') is an exciting development. The Treaty parties have long grappled with Antarctic environmental issues, and this regime of assessments and monitoring is aimed at protecting Antarctica's environmental riches over time. But assessments and monitoring will have little use unless they are supported by data that allows a fair analysis of whether environmental changes are occurring at visitor sites. Unfortunately, sufficient information is presently unavailable. Such analysis is complicated, as visitors' impact depends on many variables, including the physical and biological features of the sites visited, the frequency and timing of visits, the number of visitors and what visitors do while on site.

The Antarctic Site Inventory project, which began field work in 1994, intends to fill this void. The inventory has begun assembling a database to assist the Treaty parties in determining how best to minimize any potential adverse impacts from tourism or other activities. At key times during the course of the Antarctic spring and summer field season, the project places two-person field teams aboard ships to collect three kinds of information.

The first, Basic Site Information, includes descriptions of key physical and topographical characteristics; latitude and longitude; locations of floral assemblages (lichens, mosses and grasses); haul-out sites and wallow areas of Antarctic seals; discrete groups of breeding penguins and flying birds; penguin molting areas and guano-melt streams; glacial-melt streams; and how the site is accessed and exited.

The second category, Variable Site Information, includes specific data on weather and other environmental conditions (sea ice extent, cloud cover, snow cover, temperature, wind direction and speed); biological variables relating to penguins and flying birds (numbers of adults or individual animals, active nests, numbers and ages of chicks); and the nature and extent of any

Soviet Union – a major krill harvester – where food's palatability was not always the prime consideration for cost-conscious consumers, the 'ocean paste' made from krill tended to remain on store shelves, unsold. Krill is also used as cattle and fish feed.

Fish and squid are caught in large numbers, and around South Georgia, crabs are taken, too. An unfortunate – and completely unnecessary – 'bycatch' of the longline fishermen looking for tuna in the Southern Ocean are some 40,000 albatrosses (including 8000 female wandering albatrosses, which feed at a more northerly latitude than do the males), which are drowned when they are hooked while stealing bait, which gets dragged down to enormous depths. More recently, one fishery has focused on taking *Dissostichus eleginoides*, better known as Patagonian toothfish or Chilean sea bass. Because most Patagonian toothfish is caught illegally, the slow-growing species is in immediate danger of being fished to commercial extinction. Environmentally conscious consumers should avoid it.

PROTECTED AREAS

Since no country indisputably owns any part of Antarctica, there are no national parks. But the Antarctic Treaty System does offer protected areas. Antarctic Specially Protected Areas (ASPAs) are designed to preserve unique ecological systems, natural features or areas where research is either underway or planned.

No one is allowed to enter an ASPA without a specific permit. While many of these areas are not marked by any signs or markers, tour leaders should know where they are and it is their responsibility to ensure that their passengers do not stray into them. It is important to pay attention to your cruise staff so that you are aware of any ASPAs on your visits ashore.

visitor impacts observed (footprints or paths through moss beds, cigarette butts, film canisters and other litter). It is important for the field teams to visit sites during the peak of penguin egg-laying, when the best nest counts are obtained, and then five to six weeks later, when chick numbers are at their peak, because the numbers of chicks produced per active nest indicates a colony's productivity.

At each site, investigators attempt to select and establish control colonies (those that are seldom visited) and experimental colonies (frequently visited) to count. The intent is to repeat censuses regularly, both near and far from landing beaches, to allow for comparisons over time between frequently and infrequently visited areas.

The third information category is Maps & Photodocumentation. The project has produced accurate, up-to-date maps of each site, showing the major physical features of the site, locations of the principal colonies and assemblages of fauna and flora, and points that offer clear vantage for photographing penguin colonies, seal haul-out sites, floral associations and other features.

The locations on the Antarctic Peninsula most frequently visited by tourists are the ones likely to generate the most attention – and possibly concern about potential adverse environmental effects – under the Protocol on Environmental Protection. Since 1994, in ten seasons of data collection, the Inventory has made 503 visits to 82 Peninsula sites, and identified 22 sites with high/medium species diversity, and 16 sites with high/moderate sensitivity to potential disruptions by visitors. In 2004, the Inventory began a five-season monitoring study at Petermann Island.

The Antarctic Site Inventory's database is already assisting the Treaty parties as they discuss the adoption of site guidelines at key locations and, over time, should also lead to a better understanding of the Antarctic Peninsula ecosystem.

Ron Naveen is principal investigator of the Antarctic Site Inventory project

RESPONSIBLE TRAVEL

Antarctica has a sensitive ecology. Visitors must ensure that no damage is done – penalties include fines of up to US$10,000 (for US citizens) or even imprisonment (for British citizens)! The Antarctic Treaty system's Protocol on Environmental Protection is legally binding on all visitors to Antarctica who are nationals of its signatory countries, whether they are on governmental or private visits; for more information see p94.

Although tourism to Antarctica is sometimes criticized as being harmful to the Antarctic environment, in actual fact the impact made by tourists is absolutely minimal when compared to scientific activities on the continent. Using the unit of a 'person-day' (that is, one person spending 24 hours on the Antarctic continent or a peri-Antarctic island), tourists accounted for about 0.5% of all person-days logged in Antarctica during the 1995–96 season. Ship-based tourists leave behind almost no trace of their stay (hopefully!), and those few who do spend the night on the continent are not supposed to leave behind any evidence of having done so.

Some scientists like to raise the point that cumulative visits to the same place (by tourists, for example) may have long-term effects that are not yet understood. In fact, there are several places on Antarctica that do get remarkably high tourist traffic. Many of these locations, however, are being studied (p92). Scientific stations – permanent facilities – represent the largest possible number of cumulative visits to a single site. As any visitor to a station can attest, it's clear that by far the most serious environmental impacts in Antarctica occur at scientific stations, where personnel eat, sleep, work, drive, fly and eliminate onshore every day for years on end.

By the time their ship reaches the continent, many tourists are better versed in environmental concerns in Antarctica than some members of national Antarctic programs.

Environmental Issues

Dr Maj De Poorter

Dr Maj De Poorter worked with Greenpeace as an Antarctic campaigner from 1984 to 1996, participated in five Greenpeace expeditions, and has personally carried out inspections on more than 35 Antarctic bases checking environmental performance. For more on Dr De Poorter, see p17.

Antarctica is often called the 'last paradise on earth.' That may be a cliché description, but it's also a good one. Where else can snow glow with s much deep, pink warmth? Where else can silence be so pervasive, accentu ated only by a distant penguin squawk? Where else will a penguin be s curious as to waddle up to pick at your shoelace, or a seal be so unafrai that it barely even lifts its head to look at you before snoozing on?

As in that other paradise, it was the human species that brough discord. Antarctica has a history of human folly to rival its history c intrepid endeavor.

The contemporary era has brought more modern and enlightene views about environmental protection, including an appreciation of Ant arctica's intrinsic value as 'wilderness.' However, this modern outlook ha not been achieved without significant pressure from the public.

Modern technology has also brought with it new problems and ne threats to the Antarctic environment, such as fishing, tourism and th potential for deep-sea mining. Some of these developments still awai satisfactory resolutions.

Antarctica is also impacted by human activities and pollution from often distant parts of the globe. Radioactive fallout from atmospheric nuclea tests has been traced in snow cores, and birds and seals have been found t have pesticides and other toxins in their tissues. However, with the excep tion of the effects of global warming and the 'ozone hole,' which also hav their root causes half a world away, this chapter focuses on impacts create within the Antarctic itself.

Impacts result not just from activities – but also from attitudes! On of the biggest risks to everything that makes Antarctica special may wel come from a growing trend in some quarters to see it as 'just another place rather than as a unique area that warrants special standards of behavior.

EXPLOITATION OF MARINE LIFE

The Past

Sealers were the first to follow the explorers – and in many cases actu ally preceded them. For example, the South Shetlands were discovere in 1819, and by 1823–24, fur sealing there was over, owing to the virtua extinction of the seals. Look at the present-day fur-seal colony at Bir Island, South Georgia where there are hundreds of thousands of seals and then imagine the level of butchery it must have taken to wipe ou such teeming life in a mere four summers. The sad pattern started wit seals, and repeated itself with whales and then fish.

The first whaling station in Antarctica was established in 1904 by a Argentine-Norwegian company, which took 183 whales in its first season An exploitation explosion followed. In 1912–13 six land stations, 21 factor ships and 62 catcher boats killed and processed 10,760 whales. By 1930–3 the kill had increased to 40,000. With the exception of the years durin WWII, the killing continued at this level for the next 20 years. Targete species had to be switched, as one after another they were driven to nea extinction. Of the large whales, only the minke is still abundant. The othe species, including the humpbacks seen frolicking in the Gerlache Strait have been reduced to just a small percentage of their original number.

After whales, the next species to be exploited, in the 1970s, were fish (fin fish, as they are called, to distinguish them from shellfish). Commerciall interesting species (Antarctic cods and ice fish) in the South Georgia area were 'vacuumed up' with great enthusiasm, mostly by the Soviet Union's fishing fleet. Commercial extinction (a condition in which there are so few individuals of a species remaining that it is no longer economically worthwhile to continue catching or hunting them) followed, from which these species have never recovered.

At the same time, world interest turned to krill. It was postulated that millions of tonnes might be harvested each year, solving the world's famines. Unfortunately, the optimistic estimates of huge sustainable catches were based on a lack of knowledge. For example, the small-sized krill present in wintertime were not juveniles (which would have pointed toward high productivity) but adults shrinking to reduce their need for food. Krill-fishing took off before this was discovered, and krill would probably have been added to the infamous list of mismanagement but for the natural restriction on its use as human food. Fluoride from the krill's carapace starts to move into its meat after the catch, making it unsuitable for human consumption unless it is processed very quickly, which is technologically difficult. The bulk of the annual catch is therefore used as fertilizer or food for fish or cattle.

The Present

SEALS

Seals are officially protected on land and ice shelves, where they can only be killed for scientific purposes, provided a permit has been obtained. The Convention for the Conservation of Antarctic Seals extends this protection to the sea, the sea ice and the pack ice. It prohibits the commercial culling of fur, elephant and Ross seals and establishes closed areas and closed seasons for the other species.

As recently as the 1986–87 season, a total of 4804 seals, mostly crabeaters, were killed by a Soviet expedition near the Balleny Islands. A certain amount of research was done on teeth from these catches, but environmental groups questioned what kind of 'science' could be the motivation for the kill. One of Russia's official explanations was that many schools wanted to have a seal specimen for educational purposes. The fact that no significant catches have taken place since then could indeed be due to the mind-boggling possibility that every school that wanted one now has its own stuffed seal. More likely, however, the decision to refrain from further seal hunting is thanks to the large scars from orca or leopard seal attacks on many crabeater seals. The crabeater skins fall apart along these scars, making them commercially worthless. Talk about being saved by the enemy!

For more information about the commercial exploitation of marine animals in the Antarctic, see p88.

In theory, commercial sealing could occur at any time – the Convention still maintains catch limits for crabeater (175,000), leopard (12,000) and Weddell seals (5000) – but the public outcry it would generate makes this unlikely.

WHALES

The International Whaling Commission (IWC) was established in 1946 to regulate the 'orderly development of the whaling industry' worldwide. It agreed to a moratorium, which came into force in 1986, on all commercial catches, but that agreement has lately come under pressure from whaling nations. Additionally, in 1994 the IWC established the Southern Ocean Whaling Sanctuary to protect the primary feeding grounds of the majority of great whales and to provide an opportunity for depleted species to recover. The sanctuary does not allow commercial whaling, even if the worldwide moratorium were to be lifted again. However, 'science' is

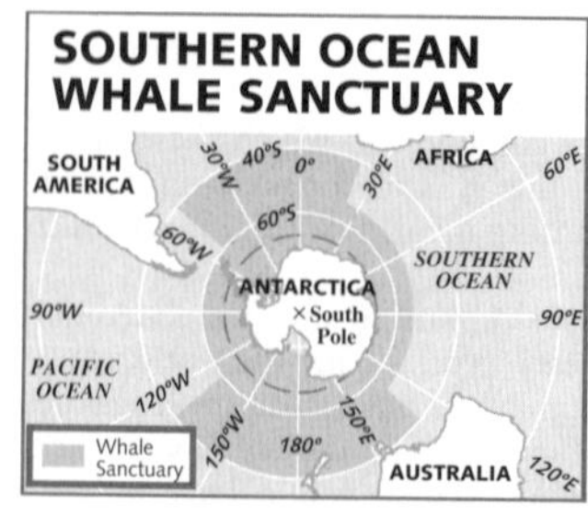

used as a loophole; Japan kills 400 minke whales a year in the Southern Ocean and calls it 'research,' even though the program has not been endorsed by the IWC Scientific Committee and the meat ends up in restaurants.

FINFISH, KRILL & SQUID

The Convention for the Conservation of Antarctic Marine Living Resources (CCAMLR) went into effect in 1982. CCAMLR represents a major breakthrough in marine conservation because, instead of considering each species separately, decisions on harvesting also take into account the effects on other species (ie predators). Its area of application is south of the Antarctic Convergence, a zone much larger than the Antarctic Treaty area, and this makes more sense ecologically.

The principles of CCAMLR are:

- prevention of a decrease in the size of any harvested population to levels below those that ensure stable recruitment (a fisheries term referring to the new animals born each year)
- maintenance of ecological relationships between harvested, dependent and related species, and the restoration of depleted species to the level at which recruitment is stable
- prevention of changes or minimization of the risks of changes in the marine ecosystem that are not potentially reversible over two or four decades.

CCAMLR is one of the most ecologically enlightened international fisheries agreements to date.

Unfortunately, CCAMLR came too late to save many finfish species that had already gone into commercial extinction during the 1970s. Initially, too, CCAMLR could not make much headway toward establishing its innovative principles at all: consensus decision-making was used by fishing nations to block any regulations they didn't like. Moreover, the fishing nations tended not to provide sufficient fishing data, and then insisted that in the absence of such data, there was no scientific basis to the catch limits.

Then, however, it looked like the tide had turned – fishing became limited unless there was scientific data to show that catches could be increased. Inspection and scientific-observer schemes were put in place. This evolution was due in part to the pressure of environmental nongovernmental organizations (NGOs) and in part to increased environmental awareness worldwide. It was also facilitated by the collapse of the former Soviet Union: its change from a communist economy to one where the fleets have to pay market prices for fuel meant that pressure to keep chasing uneconomical catches dropped dramatically.

However, the new 'gold rush' for Patagonian toothfish has set the Southern Ocean fisheries, once again, on a course to disaster. Illegal, unreported, or unregulated (IUU) catches of this valuable fish are thought to be at least double those of the legal catches. CCAMLR reacted with a Catch Certification Scheme (CCS) and Dissostichus Catch Documentation (DCD) requirements, but the massive illegal catches are continuing. So far, CCAMLR has not been able to adequately address this issue and the future looks bleak for the species, despite the success of a consumer boycott on Patagonian toothfish called for by environmentalists around the world.

Another current environmental issue is the killing of albatrosses and petrels in the longline fisheries in the region regulated by CCAMLR – especially in the illegal fisheries for Patagonian toothfish. The wandering albatross has been declining in number for decades. True to their name, wandering albatrosses roam the oceans of the world, and birds banded at South Georgia have been killed as far away as the Brazilian fishing grounds. The birds drown after they get hooked on the longlines when diving for the bait on them. CCAMLR has acted to address this problem in its own area by using streamers to scare the birds away from the bait and by taking measures to ensure that the baited hooks sink faster. In addition, CCAMLR has prohibited longlining during daylight hours, shifting mortality away from albatrosses. However, this has increased the risk for the more nocturnal petrels. While the bird-mortality rate from legal CCAMLR-regulated catches has been reduced considerably, illegal fisheries are not likely to have in place any preventative measures at all, and estimates of bycatch since the late 1990s are of a *yearly* kill of 21,000 to 68,000 albatrosses, 5,000 to 11,000 giant petrels and 79,000 to 178,000 smaller petrels.

The Antarctica Project (www.asoc.org) is the only environmental organization in the world devoted exclusively to protecting Antarctica. It also cofounded the Antarctic and Southern Ocean Coalition (ASOC) and has more than 240 member conservation organizations in 40 countries.

EXPLOITATION OF MINERALS

Throughout the 1980s, Antarctic Treaty nations held a number of closed-door negotiations for an Antarctic minerals regime. According to some, a regime would provide at least some protection when the 'inevitable' mining of Antarctica began. But to environmentalists, the wrong question was being asked. Rather than asking 'How should we mine?' they felt the question needed to be 'Should we touch Antarctic minerals at all?' Convinced that global opinion would answer that question with a resounding 'No,' the NGO community set out to make sure that the world at large knew about the negotiations and about the threat of mining to the Antarctic's environment, peace and science. Petitions were circulated (and millions of signatures collected) and secret documents from the governmental meetings were leaked and distributed to the public. The public movement against mineral exploitation in Antarctica built up and gained momentum. Despite this, governments still signed the Convention for the Regulation of Antarctic Mineral Resources Activities (CRAMRA) in 1988.

CRAMRA was never ratified, though. The *Exxon Valdez* spill in Alaska, and the resulting images of oiled birds, sea otters and beaches on TV every night, followed in 1989 by the sinking of *Bahía Paraíso*, which spilled fuel in the Antarctic itself, brought home to decision makers what environmentalists had been stressing all along: accidents would happen and the results would be devastating.

Shortly after, the Belgian parliament, against its government's position, passed a law prohibiting Belgian nationals from ever taking part in Antarctic minerals activities. Then the French and Australian governments decided not to ratify CRAMRA, stopping it from ever coming into force. As a result, the Protocol on Environmental Protection, including a ban on mining, was negotiated and signed instead. The ban will continue indefinitely. In 50 years' time, the criteria required to lift it becomes less stringent, but if no action is taken, the ban goes on. The Protocol came into force in 1991, a clear example of people-power overturning government plans.

GLOBAL CHANGES AFFECTING ANTARCTICA

Possibly the most spectacular discoveries in Antarctica have been those regarding the global effects of pollution, and the dramatic and disastrous effects that may follow. The issues of ozone depletion and global climate change are of relevance to everyone.

Ozone Depletion

Since its discovery in 1985, the spring ozone 'hole' over the Antarctic continent has continued to grow. This stratospheric ozone depletion is caused by various artificial chemicals such as chlorofluorocarbons (CFCs) and halons, mostly created in the northern hemisphere. This depletion is significant because stratospheric ozone restricts the amount of ultraviolet-B (UV-B) radiation reaching the earth's surface. The hole allows substantially higher levels of UV-B to reach Antarctica and the Southern Ocean in spring and early summer, the peak period of biological activity. These increased UV levels threaten plankton at the base of the Antarctic marine ecosystem, upon which all life – from fish to seabirds, penguins, seals and great whales – ultimately depends. Researchers have found a 6% to 12% reduction in marine primary productivity during the period of the 'hole,' and there are indications that the composition of planktonic communities may also be altered. In addition, Antarctic animals and the continent's sparse vegetation may become directly damaged by increased UV-B, or the even more worrying appearance of a band of shorter wavelength UV-C, by far the most damaging form of this radiation. Nobody knows yet to what degree Antarctic life can adapt to withstand this increasing stress.

Global Climate Change

The world's top climate scientists (members of the Intergovernmental Panel on Climate Change, or IPCC) suggest that global warming, resulting from the production of 'greenhouse gases' such as carbon dioxide will be greatest in the polar regions. Recent British data shows a sustained atmospheric temperature increase of around 2.5°C in the Peninsula region since the 1940s. This rate is a tenfold increase over the last century in the global warming average.

Also consistent with the predictions of global climate change is the rapid disintegration of vast areas of ice shelves, and the breaking off of large icebergs.

Some researchers suspect that winter sea ice is contracting. It is postulated that this will result in fewer associated sea algae. The extent of sea ice is known to influence penguin-breeding success; contracting of the sea ice cover is thought by some to have negatively affected Adélies in the Peninsula because it affects krill reproduction and recruitment, and hence influences the amount of food available to penguins on the Antarctic Peninsula. On the other hand, retreating sea ice is thought to have increased breeding success in Adélie penguins in the Ross Sea, because in that more southern environment, energy expenditure is the critical factor. Less sea ice makes for shorter trips between nest and water, hence less energy use. The different effects in different geographical areas illustrate how complex the ecological ramifications of human impact can be.

Ozone depletion over the Antarctic might exacerbate climate change even further by allowing greenhouse gases to persist longer in the troposphere and by killing off plants and phytoplankton, which remove carbon dioxide from the atmosphere. Disturbances caused by ozone depletion and/or global warming may therefore have major disruptive effects on the Southern Ocean ecosystems. Due to human disturbance, Antarctica, although set aside for its environmental and scientific value, could still be lost.

What effect would the warming of Antarctica have on the rest of the world? It is thought that warming in Antarctica would melt ice sheets and contribute to a rise in sea level. A rise of 30cm or 50cm, for instance, would spell the disappearance of entire Polynesian island-states. An alarming possibility is that the additional loss of West Antarctica's ice sheet, grounded ice that is thought to be unstable, could contribute to a sea level rise of up to 6m.

ENVIRONMENTAL IMPACT OF SCIENCE

There is no doubt that much Antarctic science is of global importance, while other subjects are more local in focus but nevertheless of intense interest. One doesn't have to be a scientist to be intrigued by polar summers with 24 hours of daylight; by ice cores several thousands of meters deep revealing the earth's past climate; by fish with antifreezing agents in their blood; or by emperor penguins fasting for several months in winter while incubating a single egg on their feet.

Most humans on the Antarctic continent and its surrounding islands are involved in some scientific endeavor, either in research or a related logistical operation. However, political motivations have always played a role in a nation's decision to establish scientific stations in Antarctica. Seven nations have territorial claims and the US established a station at the South Pole itself. During the 1980s, there was a rush of Antarctic scientific bases established, coinciding with the negotiations for mineral exploitation.

The website http://southpolestation.com is an absolute gold mine of information about the Amundsen-Scott South Pole station. Produced by 1977 winterover station manager Bill Spindler, the website includes fascinating local lore and an authoritative history.

The apparent lack of environmental awareness at some scientific bases has been criticized. This is not an argument against science, but one proposing that scientific research – as well as all other Antarctic activities – be carried out in such a way that the ecological, wilderness and aesthetic values are protected, along with the continent's value for future science. A clean Antarctic has great scientific value; a contaminated one does not.

Stations and some field activities have undoubtedly had a negative impact on the environment. Hallett, for example, was established in 1956–57 as a joint US–New Zealand station. The site, on the edge of the Ross Sea, was in the middle of a penguin rookery. To make room for it, more than 6000 birds were 'relocated.' Penguins that tried to return to their former nesting site were kept out by barricades of fuel drums.

The US's McMurdo station on Ross Island installed a nuclear reactor in 1961. It was shut down in 1972 and shipped back to the US – along with 101 large drums of earth made radioactive by the 'normal discharge of effluent.' Later, another 11,000 cu meters of soil were removed, and the site – still visible as the 'bite' taken out of Observation Hill – was not released for unrestricted use again until May 1979. The seafloor offshore from McMurdo station, meanwhile, holds the most extraordinary collection of rubbish, and toxic waste (including PCBs) pollutes its sediments.

Meanwhile, the Fildes Peninsula on King George Island, recommended as a Specially Protected Area (SPA) by the 1966 Antarctic Treaty meeting because of the biological value of its melt lakes, was largely turned into a construction site by the Soviet Union and Chile in 1968 and 1969, respectively, when they built stations there. The area's protected status had to be abandoned because its biological value was so diminished. China and Uruguay added bases later, within walking distance of each other. The once-protected melt lakes have been used both for drinking water and, ironically, for rubbish dumps. Today, only a very small area remains protected on the Fildes Peninsula – protecting fossils, not lakes.

Other scientist-imposed damage on the Antarctic environment includes that of Argentina's Marambio station. For decades Marambio threw thousands of empty, full or partially filled barrels containing fuel, chemical waste and ordinary rubbish over a vast slope, which subsequently leaked toxins into soil and streams. At Australia's Casey station, a visiting scientist in 1986 found that a protected area had been partially bulldozed, and that cement from nearby construction was killing mosses and lichens. More famously, in 1982–83, France started the construction of a hard-rock airstrip at its Dumont d'Urville station, destroying the habitat of thousands of birds, including cape pigeons, snow petrels, Wilson's storm petrels and Adélie penguins, in the process. Explosives used to construct the airstrip killed many birds with rock shrapnel.

Improbable Eden: The Dry Valleys of Antarctica (2004), a beautiful book of photographs by Craig Potton, with a long essay by Antarctic writer Bill Green, gives an unprecedented look at these protected areas, to which access is extremely restricted.

Even into the 1980s, many practices that were standard in the rest of the world had not yet caught on in Antarctica. Environmental-impact assessments, for example, were commonplace in many parts of the world, but not in Antarctica, the most pristine place on earth.

Two common methods of waste disposal – open burning and discarding large pieces of equipment on the sea ice until it melted – would not have been acceptable at home in many Antarctic Treaty countries, 'So why in Antarctica?' NGOs asked. Military personnel, logistical restraints and financial considerations had all contributed to the situation in the past, but one of the main reasons for the careless behavior was that there were no independent eyes and ears to see 'down there.'

This situation changed in the 1980s. Tourists on ships were the first independent visitors – they also were the first to comment. Abandoned Hallett station, for instance, was cleaned up after tourists complained about the mess. Then came expeditions by NGOs, such as Greenpeace, who took pictures, wrote reports, brought independent journalists and generally poked their noses where no one had done so before. The results showed. Station personnel, after initial suspiciousness, actually welcomed these environmental 'inspections' from Greenpeace, because they created pressure on the politicians at home to provide bases with the resources to operate in a more environmentally sound manner. The personnel on The Ice quite often had wanted to do the right thing, but hadn't been able to convince headquarters of the need.

What are the results? Hallett station (abandoned after two decades) has been cleaned up, and the penguins have reclaimed their territory. McMurdo (p240) is now running in a much more environmentally acceptable way. It recycles materials, returns wastes to the US and no longer burns, incinerates or 'ice stages' rubbish (although NGOs still question the need for the base to be so big). Bases on the Fildes Peninsula have emptied the lakes of rubbish (although it appears that some merely bulldozed the rubbish under soil and loose rock). They are also collecting and storing wastes for return to their country of origin. Marambio has undergone vast cleanups and regular environmental audits. Australia had a big cleanup of its stations and old rubbish dumps, and initiated the stringent training of personnel. The French airstrip created so much controversy that 'mitigative measures' were put in place, at least preventing birds from being blown up during the dynamiting, and artificial breeding burrows for petrels were established. In spite of widespread protest, the construction continued until January 1994, when a tidal wave caused by a calving iceberg resulted in such destruction that the runway was abandoned (a case of natural justice, according to some).

Many governments now have environmental officers and waste management programs with environmental-awareness training for all staff. The programs have cleaned up several old sites and abandoned buildings and, in some cases, have begun to audit the environmental impact of their activities.

The major international change in attitude, though, was the abandonment of CRAMRA and the 1991 signing of the Protocol on Environmental Protection instead. The Protocol designates Antarctica as a special conservation area. Its main principle states that the protection of the Antarctic environment and dependent and associated ecosystems, and the intrinsic values of Antarctica (including wilderness, aesthetic and scientific values) shall be fundamental considerations in the planning and conduct of all activities in the Antarctic Treaty area. The Protocol also contains provisions for environmental-impact assessments (EIAs), the monitoring of environmental impacts, protection of flora and fauna, waste disposal, avoidance of marine pollution, and protected areas. The Protocol and four Annexes came into force in 1998, with the final Annex following a few years later.

While attitudes toward the environment have changed dramatically in the last decade, not all problems have been solved. To minimize cumulative impact, joint regional planning will be necessary. A first step would be the production of joint EIAs in a cooperative effort by all nations and tour operators active in a particular area, for example, the Dry Valleys.

Increased efforts to avoid the introduction of non-native species, including pathogens, to Antarctica are also urgently required. This urgency was highlighted in 1998 by Australian research, which indicated that some penguin colonies had been in contact with potentially lethal poultry-disease pathogens, presumably transported by human visitors.

Both environmental groups and the Scientific Committee on Antarctic Research are concerned about the increased interest in 'bioprospecting' of organisms by the pharmaceutical industry. The Protocol may not be well equipped to deal with this issue, since it doesn't specifically include microorganisms in its protection. Nor are deep-sea organisms, such as sponges, adequately protected, as CCAMLR does not apply to them, and the Protocol only covers the area south of 60°S.

Another worrying global trend is the increased commercialization of ownership of scientific data. This trend eventually results in the restricted availability of knowledge – limited to those who can pay for it. Antarctic research (including the history of global climate change, ozone depletion, monsoon research and biodiversity) is of great value to all, and if this global trend were to reach the Antarctic, both science and the human race as a whole would suffer. Fortunately, freedom of access to scientific data and results is enshrined in the Antarctic Treaty. The challenge will be to safeguard this.

ENVIRONMENTAL IMPACT OF TOURISM

Antarctica is an increasingly popular tourist destination. In fact, tourists visiting Antarctica greatly outnumber scientists and support personnel working on the continent. While the number of person-days (a 'person-day' is one person spending one day in Antarctica) is higher for scientists than tourists, tourists mainly visit areas where wildlife is concentrated, increasing the risk to plants and animals. Large numbers of people making frequent visits to a few popular sites intensifies cumulative long-term effects.

Some damage from tourism is obvious. Graffiti certainly does not benefit the historic relics on Deception Island, for instance. A more serious possibility is the introduction of non-native organisms to Antarctica. Cockroaches and houseplants have been found aboard tourist ships. Especially on the sub-Antarctic islands these species could create ecological havoc if they were to 'escape' into the environment. In East Antarctica's Larsemann Hills, non-native grasses have been found surviving after their inadvertent introduction by scientific personnel. Incidents of such accidental introduction, reported more and more frequently, are a growing concern.

An older example of environmental impact is Cape Royds, the southernmost Adélie rookery and home of Shackleton's Hut. Between 1956 and 1975, the number of penguins at Cape Royds declined sharply because of the many helicopter flights to and from the area. The site has since been protected, access to the actual breeding colony restricted and penguin numbers have recovered.

On the other hand, recent results from a long-term study near Palmer station, which compared changes in the population sizes of Adélie penguins at Torgerson Island (visited regularly) and Litchfield Island (a protected area) suggest that environmental variability or climate change rather than human disturbance was the key factor in changes to the penguin populations studied. Some saw this as a sign that there's no need to worry about the impact of tourism on wildlife, but this is too simplistic a conclusion. First of all, if wildlife is under pressure from climate change – a manmade impact – isn't that a reason to be even more careful in not adding any further stress? More importantly, one or two studies cannot – and should not – be extrapolated to other sites, other populations, other species or other local circumstances. Many more long-term studies are needed.

'If wildlife is under pressure from climate change – a manmade impact – isn't that a reason to be even more careful in not adding any further stress?'

In general, the absence of data does not equal the absence of deleterious effect. Even if no damage is obvious, it does not mean that there's no impact. It could simply mean that the damage has gone unnoticed, that only in certain conditions is there no damage present, or that not enough research has been done yet. Tourism in particular, with its many repeated visits to breeding colonies, carries numerous questions about its impact.

We know about specific cases in which human presence in the Antarctic has an impact. The classic example is a footprint in a moss bed, still visible a decade or two after it was made. Less obvious is the impact on 'invisible' wildlife, such as an algae species living inside rocks or flora underneath snow that may get trampled, or the damage done to ancient geological formations simply by walking over them (in the Dry Valleys, for example). Animals, too, can be affected even when they don't show it in their behavior, or at least not in a way that humans can easily notice. German researchers, for instance, found that heart rates of incubating Adélies increased markedly when they were approached by a human still 30m away, even though the birds showed no visible response.

Other effects of human presence can be very unexpected. The same German researchers found that a single human being, standing at a 20m distance from penguins 'commuting' on a well-used pathway to the sea, caused the birds to deviate from their path by 70m, even hours after the person had gone. In one case, the single observer caused an estimated 11,934 birds to deviate during 10 hours (resulting in an extra 835 penguin kilometers walked). Not surprisingly, the disturbance from helicopters was even more pronounced.

Does it matter? The assumption has to be that it does. Energy expenditure can be a crucial factor in breeding success. While one disturbance may not matter much, the combined effect of several disturbances could very well be detrimental.

The above research concluded with a recommendation that nesting penguins should not be approached closer than 30m unless absolutely necessary; that penguins walking between the colony and the sea should not be approached closer than 100m by humans on foot; that aircraft should use the same paths each time; and that very noisy aircraft (eg Puma helicopters) should not approach colonies closer than 1000m horizontally or 200m vertically.

Penguins are not the only species likely to be affected by visitors – many researchers are concerned about the effect on skuas, terns, shags and, especially, giant petrels. Many think that giant petrels on the nest should not be approached closer than 50m or even 100m.

One problem specific to the tourist industry is the number of different operators involved, all with their own commercial interests to protect. While most individual International Association of Antarctica Tour Operators (IAATO) members produce reasonable EIAs, this does not properly deal with the overall impact. Instead, operators should produce joint, long-term EIAs, sitting down with each other prior to each season to work out how their activities are going to affect each other and the environment, and how they can limit the combined impact. One shore visit by one vessel to a particular colony may have a negligible impact, but what about several ships a day, several days in row? In practice, this will almost certainly require limits on where to visit, and on the number of ships or people allowed into a particular region or site during a season.

Land-based infrastructure for tourism, including hotels and hard-rock airstrips, is opposed by all environmental NGOs because the environmental impact cannot be justified. Some groups are opposed to all tourism in Antarctica, but many environmental NGOs, including Greenpeace, the Worldwide Fund for Nature (WWF) and the Antarctic and Southern Ocean Coalition (ASOC), are not opposed to most ship-based or yacht-based tourism groups per se, provided their environmental management is, as a minimum, in accordance with the Protocol.

However, the continued growth of tourism, the lack of sufficient knowledge about the environmental impact of visitors and the desire of some to go to new places has led these environmental groups to ask for limits on the number of tourists visiting Antarctica and the number of sites they visit.

The recent appearance of very large tourist ships (carrying more than 400 passengers) with their associated increased risks – and without a discussion on the philosophical or ethical desirability of such developments in Antarctica – has raised the level of concern. If these issues are not satisfactorily addressed, it wouldn't be surprising if environmental concerns focus increasingly on all commercial tourism as a problem activity. The tour industry's attitude toward the Antarctic environment will determine its own fate.

YOUR OWN PRESENCE

Before undertaking a trip to the Antarctic, you should ask yourself: would I be just as happy going somewhere else or watching a documentary? Or is visiting Antarctica truly a dream come true? And what can I do for the Antarctic in return?

When you return from The Ice, you can be a true 'ambassador' – if you're willing to give something back to Antarctica and act on its behalf. For instance, you could write to your government representative about creating large marine parks in the Southern Ocean, or about funding for environmental monitoring or environmental-impact research. You could decide to become a member of an NGO that has an interest in the Antarctic. You could find out more about consumer actions in relation to Southern Ocean fisheries, or you could take some steps in your own life to contribute less to global climate change. You could simply make sure that when you talk about your experience you also point out that Antarctica is still facing threats from human activities. There's always *something* you can do.

While you're on The Ice, there are further aspects to consider. As a minimum, stick to the guidelines that you are given to you by your operator – but don't hesitate to apply your own more stringent rules. Don't be afraid to speak up if there are aspects that you particularly like or dislike about the tour operator, ship or voyage, or about your fellow passengers' environmental attitudes – do it at the time, not later. If you have comments, tell the captain, the expedition leader, the organizing company, IAATO, environmental-watchdog organizations and your department or ministry of foreign affairs. Remember, your comments don't have to be limited to the tour you were on. If you feel positive or negative about anything you witnessed, whether by commercial or government programs, tell people about it. Antarctica is still a remote place, and its native inhabitants cannot speak for themselves. You can – and must – do it for them.

For further guidance about minimizing the risk to wildlife, see the 'Code of Conduct' on the Australian Antarctic Division website at www.antdiv.gov.au.

It's difficult to give absolute guidance on approach distances for wildlife-viewing. In the past, Antarctic Treaty regulations included 'safe' distances when approaching wildlife, but the 1991 Special Consultative Meeting decided to abandon these because they were probably too liberal and because it was very hard to reach an agreement on what they should be.

The recommended distances set by tour companies tend to be based on the former regulations and usually allow far closer approaches than the distances suggested by some researchers such as the German scientist mentioned on p102. Of course, that study was only performed on one species (Adélies) and on a limited number of birds. But who should carry the responsibilities caused by our ignorance about the exact effects of human beings on wildlife? Should we risk disturbing the animals, or should people be unduly restricted at the risk of missing a particular photo opportunity? The precautionary approach, and the fact that we are only visitors in the Antarctic, while for wildlife it is 'home,' demands the latter option.

Going to 'new' places, possibly never visited before, is sometimes one of the attractions highlighted in tourism brochures. But once visited, a location can never again be 'unvisited,' so how about leaving the Antarctic as pristine and 'untouched' as possible?

Antarctica is a continent of beauty and nature, a place to be in awe of – not an amusement park. Just as bungee jumping would be inappropriate in a cathedral, it and similar activities are inappropriate in Antarctica. Jetskis have a role to play on some beaches – but not in the Antarctic.

Every human presence in the Antarctic has an environmental impact. Depending on the activity, the impact will be small or large, direct, secondary or cumulative. There are cases where the impact can be justified and cases where it cannot. If you're visiting Antarctica, you have a responsibility to treat this subject seriously. Attitude plays an important role in safeguarding this special continent for future generations as well as for its own sake.

Wildlife Guide John Cooper

John Cooper has undertaken research on seabirds over more than 30 years at the University of Cape Town. He is a coeditor of *Marine Ornithology*, an international journal of seabird science and conservation. For more on Mr Cooper, see p17.

BLUE WHALES

The blue whale *(Balaenoptera musculus)* is the largest animal that has ever lived on our planet. A female landed at Grytviken, South Georgia, reached 33.5m in length. A 27.6m female caught by a Soviet whaling fleet in 1947 weighed 178 tonnes. Aside from the animal's size, characteristics include its habit of showing its flukes when diving (the other rorqual whales do not). A pygmy blue whale *(brevicauda)* has been described as sub-specifically distinct and may even warrant specific status, according to some.

Blue whales can be found in all oceans. In the southern summer they frequent the fringes of the ice shelf, moving to subtropical waters in winter. The larger individuals occur the farthest south. Blues are usually solitary or travel in pairs. Females reach sexual maturity at about five years of age. In southern waters, blues prey predominantly on Antarctic krill. A single blue whale can eat as much as 4.5 tonnes of krill in one day, filtering the tiny crustaceans from the water with its 250 to 400 pairs of baleen plates.

It is thought that the blue whale population of the southern hemisphere once numbered 200,000 animals. Commercial whaling (360,000 were killed in the 20th century) severely reduced the species' numbers and it became fully protected in 1965 (although illegal catches of pygmy blues by the Soviets continued in the 1960s). Nevertheless, recovery has been slow, and the current population is thought to be just 1% of original numbers. One estimate suggests there are only a 'few hundred' in Antarctic waters.

FIN WHALES

Female fin whales *(Balaenoptera physalus)* attain 27m in length in the southern hemisphere, with males reaching 25m. They are the second-largest members of the whale family, after the blue whale. Unusually, the anterior part of the animal is asymmetrically colored: the left mandible is bluish-grey, the right is white. The reason for this peculiar patterning is unclear but may be related to the species feeding in a tilted position. Fin whales can reach a maximum speed of about 37km/h.

Fin whales occur in all oceans. In Antarctic waters, they have a circumpolar distribution in summer, moving to lower latitudes in winter. Calves are born at about 6.5m in length in temperate or subtropical waters. While their principal food in southern seas is euphausiid crustaceans, fin whales may not feed at all in winter, relying on their accumulated blubber for energy, as do the other baleen whales.

Fins formed the largest part of the whalers' catch after WWII, when a total of 28,761 were taken in 1960–61. Nearly 750,000 were taken in the 20th century in the southern hemisphere alone! The species has been totally protected since 1976. Like all baleen whales, protection only came after the fin had become commercially extinct. Recovery rates are thought to be slow in this species, whose longevity was exemplified when the identifying mark of one whaling company was recovered from an individual after 37 years.

HUMPBACK WHALES

Humpback whales *(Megaptera novaeangliae)* can be recognized by their enormous flippers, which can reach one-third of their total body length. They are normally black, but the undersides of their flippers and flukes have varying amounts of white and can be used as aids for recognizing individual whales. Males have been recorded at a maximum length of 17.5m, with females at 19m. Adult humpbacks can reach 40 tonnes in weight. Young can weigh 680kg at birth: a big baby by any view!

Humpbacks are found in all oceans. They migrate seasonally from their Southern Ocean summer feeding grounds toward the equator, where they breed during the southern winter, generally in shallow waters close to land. Humpbacks are highly vocal on their breeding grounds. Their songs, which last up to 20 minutes, are thought to be mainly produced by adult males to advertise their presence. They eat primarily Antarctic krill – more than a tonne a day may be taken. Humpbacks were grossly overexploited by whalers in the past, but have been fully protected in the southern hemisphere since 1963, although illegal catches continued later than this. A recent estimate puts the Southern Ocean population at 17,000.

For more information about Antarctic krill, see p126.

KILLER WHALES

Killer whales *(Orcinus orca)* are the largest members of the dolphin family. Also known as orcas, their black-and-white markings and tall dorsal fins (especially in the adult male) are distinctive. Males reach 9m, females nearly 8m. Large specimens can weigh 6 tonnes or more. There may be two (or even three) species of killer whales, a smaller one *(O. glacialis)* being restricted to the Antarctic pack ice, but more studies are needed.

Orcas occur in all seas, but are more abundant in colder waters. They travel in schools or pods of up to 50 individuals. Pods have their own 'dialect' of discrete calls and are presumably made up of closely related animals. Maturity is reached from 12 years of age in females and 14 years in males. They feed on squid, fish, birds and marine mammals. Resident killer whales have been seen at sub-Antarctic Marion Island swallowing king penguins whole. Orcas will also tip up small ice floes to get to resting seals.

There are still many killer whales in the Southern Ocean; one estimate puts the summer population at 80,000. They have not been caught commercially since 1979–80, when Soviet whalers killed 916 in that season alone. Catching orcas for display in captivity is an emotive issue, but based on the small numbers taken cannot be said to be of conservation significance. There is no reason to believe that this splendid animal will not continue to grace the southern seas.

MINKE WHALES

Minke whales are now thought to be two separate species following genetic studies: the larger Antarctic minke whale *(Balaenoptera bonaerensis)* and the smaller dwarf minke whale *(B. acutorostrata)*. Minke whales are the second-smallest of the baleen whales, although with a maximum length of 10.7m and a mass of up to 9 tonnes, they are still very large animals. Minkes are fast swimmers and will approach slow-moving and stationary vessels.

In summer minkes are circumpolar in distribution, with the highest densities seen at the pack-ice edge. In winter, most animals move to lower latitudes. Sexes and age classes are often segregated, with the largest animals (usually females) occurring further south. Pairing and calving take place in the southern winter. Their diet consists mainly of krill and copepods.

Minkes are by far the most abundant baleen whales in the Southern Ocean, with a population of possibly half a million. Not originally targeted by whalers because of their relatively small size, they escaped slaughter in the first half of the 20th century. However, a few hundred each year are currently (and controversially) killed by Japanese whalers, ostensibly for scientific purposes, although their meat is sold for human consumption in Japan to 'allay costs.' Both species occur in the Southern Ocean with similar ranges. Telling the two species apart from a tourist ship is tricky, however – it's best to consult an expert or a specialized guide.

SEI WHALES

The sei *(Balaenoptera borealis)* is the third-largest whale in the Southern Ocean. Females may reach 19.5m and 45 tonnes; males are slightly shorter and lighter. One 16.4m female was weighed at 37.75 tonnes. The blow is similar to that of the fin whale but it doesn't reach as high. Seis can achieve speeds up to 55km/h over short distances.

The species can be found in all oceans, but only larger individuals have been recorded south of the Antarctic Convergence. Sei whales occur in small schools of three to eight animals. Some sexual segregation seems to occur, based on records kept by harpooners. The calf is 4.5m long at birth and is weaned after six months, when it has grown to 8m. In the southern hemisphere, sei whales feed on copepods and euphausiids (tiny crustaceans), with the former thought to be the more important. Their finely fringed baleen plates help them to feed on such small prey.

Like humpback, blue and fin whales, seis were grossly overexploited to the point of commercial extinction. Over 20,000 were harpooned in the 1964–65 season alone, immediately after which the population collapsed. They've been completely protected since 1979 but the Southern Ocean population remains sadly depleted: it's currently estimated at under 10,000.

> **'Southern right whales are lucky not to be extinct; they were overexploited to commercial extinction as early as the mid-19th century'**

SOUTHERN RIGHT WHALES

Whalers named the slow-moving, inshore-visiting southern right whale *(Eubalaena glacialis)* 'right' because it was relatively easy to row down and harpoon – and then it obligingly stayed afloat to yield its long baleen plates and lots of oil. Southern rights grow up to 17m in length and can weigh up to 90 tonnes. The whitish callosities on the jaw and forehead can be used to identify individuals.

Southern right whales occur in the southern oceans between 20°S and 50°S, and have been recorded around the more northerly of the southern islands. They are seasonally common (May to September) and can be easily seen from the shore in bays on the southern coast of South Africa, where calving and mating occur. Southern right whales are lucky not to be extinct; they were overexploited to 'commercial extinction' as early as the mid-19th century, although full protection came only in 1935. However, illegal catches in the 1950s and 1960s came to light after the collapse of the Soviet Union. Numbers are now slowly recovering at a rate of 7% a year, based on South African long-term studies. Watching southern rights court within 100m of the shore is an experience not to be forgotten.

SPERM WHALES

The sperm whale *(Physeter macrocephalus)*, of *Moby Dick* fame, is an unmistakable species with its enormous head and narrow, tooth-filled lower jaw. At sea, the low 'bushy' forward-directed blow and small fleshy dorsal fin are important identifying features. Males can reach over 18m in length, females 11m, with males weighing as much as 57 tonnes.

Sperm whales occur in all of the world's oceans, but rarely in shallow seas. Most sperm whales south of 40°S are adult males. Schools, of 20 to 25 individuals, are made up of females and their young, joined by males during the breeding season from October to December. A 4m, 1-tonne calf is born after a gestation period of 15 to 16 months. They eat mid- to deep-water squid, some of which reach 200kg: veritable krakens of the deep, caught by the sperm whale in absolute darkness at depths of nearly 3km.

Sperm whales were much exploited in the past for their oil, ambergris and teeth. Now they are fully protected in the Southern Ocean. It can only be hoped that their numbers will return to pre-exploitation levels.

ANTARCTIC & SUB-ANTARCTIC FUR SEALS

Fur seals can be found on most of the circumpolar southern islands – in very large numbers at some of them. Vagrants have reached the southern continents. The Antarctic fur seal *(Arctocephalus gazella)* occurs further south than its slightly smaller relative, the sub-Antarctic fur seal *(A. tropicalis)*, with which it sometimes hybridizes. Female Antarctic fur seals are grey to brownish in color, with creamy throats and chests. Adult males are silvery-grey with a mane of longer hair. Sub-Antarctic females are greyish with orange throats and chests. The males are buff to black with cream-to-orange throats and chests, and have a 'topknot' that helps distinguish them from male Antarctics. About one in 800 fur seals are of the 'blonde' variety, with markedly yellow- or cream-colored fur. Males, at over 200kg, far outweigh females, which weigh up to 50kg.

> **'Fur seal males can be formidable opponents to rivals and human visitors alike – quite a few scientists bear the scars of injudicious approach'**

Fur seals breed in harems, and males can be formidable opponents to rivals and human visitors alike. Quite a few scientists bear the scars of injudicious approach. Pupping takes place in December. The fur seal diet consists of squid, fish and crustaceans, such as krill. Some Antarctic males kill penguins as well.

Fur seals are now showing a remarkable recovery in numbers since being overexploited for their coats early in the 19th century – so much so that at some localities, they are displacing breeding albatrosses and killing vegetation, leading to conservation dilemmas. Nearly two million Antarctic fur seals crowd the coastline of Bird Island off South Georgia. But if hunting is ever allowed to resume, it is certain to be controversial.

CRABEATER SEALS

Crabeaters *(Lobodon carcinophaga)* are misnamed, since they actually eat krill, not crabs. They are slim seals reaching about 2.5m in length. Their distribution is circumpolar, although they prefer pack ice to open sea. Although considered to be the world's most abundant seal (a recent estimate is 10 to 15 million), the species' habit of occurring in small family groups suggests smaller numbers when compared with the teeming breeding beaches occupied by fur seals.

Not much is known about crabeaters' breeding, which occurs among the pack ice during the austral spring. Like southern elephant seal pups, crabeater pups grow very quickly and are weaned within two to three weeks. Crabeaters have peculiarly shaped teeth that form a sieve to strain out Antarctic krill, their almost-exclusive diet.

Very little is known about this animal, as pack ice is a difficult place for scientists to work. It seems to be under no conservation threat at present and is formally protected by the international Convention for the Conservation of Antarctic Seals – as are all the southern seals.

LEOPARD SEALS

Adult male leopard seals *(Hydrurga leptonyx)* reach a length of 3.4m and weigh up to 450kg. Females are larger, at 3.6m and 590kg. Leopard seals have a large head with a huge gape, making them fearsome predators. They're found among the pack ice in summer and hauled-out on the more southerly sub-Antarctic islands in winter.

Little is known about their breeding behavior. Pups are born on the ice during summer. They are solitary animals, except during the breeding season. Their diet includes penguins and other seals (especially pups), as well as fish, squid and krill.

There is much debate about the dangers of leopard seals. Given their size and formidable jaws, caution is recommended, especially since the first-known human fatality from a leopard seal attack occurred in 2003. There are perhaps 200,000 leopard seals throughout Antarctica, so the species is not considered to be at any risk.

ROSS SEALS

The Ross seal *(Ommatophoca rossii)* is the least-often seen of all Antarctic seals. Until the 1970s, it had been observed by fewer than 100 people, because although it has a circumpolar distribution, the Ross seal lives only in heavy pack ice. A solitary animal, it is usually found hauled-out onto large floes, alone or in pairs.

Ross seals have dark-grey to chestnut backs and lighter undersides. They have very large eyes, a short snout and a wide, short head. The characteristic broad dark streaks on the lighter-colored throat and chest are clearly visible when the animal is disturbed, for then it rears back almost vertically, with its mouth open and its throat inflated. The seal is also known for its distinctive vocalizations: trilling, warbling or 'chugging.' Females reach 2.4m and 200kg; males are slightly smaller.

For futher information about the exploitation of wildlife, see p94.

Ross seals eat mainly deep-water squid and fish. Pups are rarely observed. Much remains to be learned about this species, which is named for its discoverer James Clark Ross (leader of the British Antarctic Expedition of 1839–43), but it is becoming better studied as icebreakers more frequently penetrate the densest regions of pack ice.

SOUTHERN ELEPHANT SEALS

The southern elephant seal *(Mirounga leonina)* is the world's largest seal. Males grow to 3.5 tonnes and 5m in length, females 900kg and 3m. They have a circumpolar distribution, and are found on most of the southern islands and on the Antarctic Peninsula.

Breeding follows a seasonal pattern. Males spend the winter at sea and first haul out in August, followed by the females. Fighting then follows among the males to see who will be 'beachmaster,' with mating rights to a harem of females. Pups grow incredibly quickly on their mothers' rich, 50%-fat milk. By the time they're weaned at 22 days, the pups have quadrupled their mass. Elephant seals feed predominantly on squid, caught during very deep (up to 1.5km) and long (up to two hours!) dives, when they lower their heart rate to as little as a single beat per minute, separated by remarkably short periods at the surface.

Elephant seals were heavily exploited onshore for their blubber oil during the 19th and early 20th centuries by sealers, who called the animals 'sea elephants.' Although this fortunately no longer occurs, numbers have decreased at some of the southern Indian Ocean islands in recent decades, although the total population may still be 750,000. The species is being comprehensively studied in an attempt to explain this alarming trend, which may be linked to climatic changes affecting their food supply.

WEDDELL SEALS

Weddell seals *(Leptonychotes weddellii)* are rotund animals, and not as streamlined as crabeater and leopard seals. They reach 3.3m in length and a weight of 550kg and may live for 20 years. Females are a little larger than males. Weddell seals have a circumpolar distribution, living further south than any other mammal (other than Antarctic scientists!).

Fast-shelf ice is their main home year-round, but sightings have also been recorded in pack ice.

Pups are born in colonies in September and October, on fast ice near cracks and holes that give their mothers access to the water. Extensive tooth wear occurs as the animals use their incisors and canines to scrape away the ice to keep their breathing holes open. Weddells are the best studied of the Antarctic seals, because they can be more easily approached over fast ice than can the pack-ice species. Studies have shown Weddells can dive to 600m and stay underwater for more than an hour. They eat fish, squid and crustaceans. Weddells have been observed blowing air bubbles into cracks under the sea ice to flush out prey. They are the archetypical Antarctic seal, and along with the Adélie penguin are fixed in the public consciousness as animals of the far south. There may well be one million Weddell seals, which are well protected by their remote habitat and the seal convention.

ADÉLIE PENGUINS

Adélies *(Pygoscelis adeliae)*, the archetypical Antarctic penguin, were named after French explorer Dumont d'Urville's wife. They're purely black and white, with a distinctive white eye ring. Like all penguins, the sexes are similarly marked, although Adélie females are smaller. The downy chick is uniformly brown. Breeding occurs all around the Antarctic continent and Peninsula and at some of the more southerly sub-Antarctic islands. There are about 2.5 million breeding pairs known at 177 localities, although there are very likely new colonies yet to be discovered in little-explored sections of the Antarctic coast.

'Comical chases of adults by chicks ensure that meals are not fed to weak or unhealthy chicks'

Breeding occurs during summer in large colonies. Comical chases of adults by chicks ensure that meals are not fed to weak or unhealthy chicks. Diet is mainly Antarctic and ice krill *(Euphausia superba* and *E. crystallarophias*, respectively). Deep dives for prey (reaching depths of nearly 150m) may be undertaken, but usually dives are much shallower. In winter, Adélies stay at sea, resting on pack ice and icebergs in groups.

Adélie penguins are well studied. Their breeding success, numbers and diets are monitored as part of international studies conducted under the auspices of the Convention for the Conservation of Antarctic Marine Living Resources (CCAMLR). Some colonies near Antarctic stations have decreased in size, a change thought to be due to human disturbance. Elsewhere, however, colonies have grown, so the species is not currently in any danger.

CHINSTRAP PENGUINS

Chinstraps *(Pygoscelis antarctica)* are superficially similar to Adélies, being black and white, but they have a distinctive black line connecting the black cap to below the chin – hence their name. Breeding occurs around the Peninsula and on islands south of the Antarctic Convergence. With an estimated four million pairs, the chinstrap is the second-most abundant Antarctic and sub-Antarctic penguin, after the macaroni. On the little-visited South Sandwich Islands, 1.5 million pairs of chinstraps have been reported breeding.

Two eggs are laid in November or December and chicks fledge in late February and early March. Pursuit dives for prey – almost entirely krill – are usually less then 100m deep. Chinstraps forage among the pack ice, although vagrants may be seen in the open sea.

Although population changes have been detected among colonies on the Peninsula studied by a number of nations, the chinstraps' overall population seems stable and the species is not considered threatened.

EMPEROR PENGUINS

The emperor penguin *(Aptenodytes forsteri)* is the world's largest penguin, although fossils have been found of penguins that were larger still. It stands more than 1m tall and can weigh 40kg. The emperor can only be confused with its close relative, the sub-Antarctic king penguin, which is smaller and more brightly marked. Emperor chicks are silvery-grey with a white face mask and blackish head.

About 45 breeding localities are known, concentrated in the Weddell Sea and Dronning Maud Land, Enderby and Princess Elizabeth Lands, and the Ross Sea. The emperors' at-sea distribution does not extend north of the Antarctic Convergence, except for vagrants. The known population is a little under 200,000 breeding pairs.

The emperor is the only Antarctic bird that breeds in winter. A single egg is incubated on the feet of the males, which huddle in the extreme winter cold to reduce heat loss. Incubation averages 66 days, and chicks become independent during November to January. Emperors eat fish such as the Antarctic silver fish *(Pleurogramma antarcticum)*, krill and squid. Breeding birds may travel long distances across the ice to find polynyas in which to feed. Prey is captured by pursuit-diving, often to amazing depths and durations: as much as 535m and 22 minutes, by far the deepest and longest dives known for any bird.

Emperors are not globally threatened, although human disturbance has been implicated at the Pointe Géologie colony in Terre Adélie, which decreased from 6000 pairs to 2000 pairs between 1952 and 1987.

GENTOO PENGUINS

An orange bill and a white flash above and behind its eye distinguish the black-and-white gentoos *(Pygoscelis papua)* from the slightly smaller Adélies and chinstraps. Breeding distribution is circumpolar on the sub-Antarctic islands and on the Antarctic Peninsula. There are an estimated 300,000 breeding pairs. Large populations occur at South Georgia (100,000 pairs), the Falkland Islands (70,000 pairs) and Îles Kerguelen (30,000 pairs).

At the more northerly sub-Antarctic islands, gentoos breed in winter, laying two eggs as early as July. On the more southerly islands and the Peninsula, laying occurs from October to December. Pursuit dives for prey can go deeper than 100m, reaching the bottom in inshore waters, but most dives are probably shallower. Diet includes crustaceans (mainly euphausiids), fish (mainly lantern fish – *Myctophidae)* and squid.

Gentoo populations are showing alarming decreases at some of their sub-Antarctic breeding localities, probably as a result of climate change which is affecting prey abundance, although other populations on the Peninsula are increasing in size. The species has been categorized as 'near-threatened' by the World Conservation Union.

KING PENGUINS

The king penguin *(Aptenodytes patagonicus)* is the world's second-largest penguin, standing 20cm shorter than the closely related emperor. It is also much lighter at 9kg to 15kg. The downy chick is uniformly dark brown – and was once described as the 'woolly penguin,' a species of its own! Kings breed on seven sub-Antarctic island groups, with a breeding population estimated at between one and 1.5 million pairs.

Breeding occurs in often very large colonies, close to the shore on rocky terrain. A single egg is incubated during summer on the feet of both parents, who take turns. It takes 55 days for the egg to hatch. Incubating birds can shuffle along slowly with their eggs – to avoid lumbering southern elephant seals, for instance. Chicks are reared right through the winter (huddling in crèches to keep warm) and only fledge the following summer, making annual breeding impossible. Scientists have worked hard to unravel the species' breeding interval: is it every second year, or two years in three? Diet includes fish and squid, caught by deep (more than 300m maximum) dives lasting as long as 15 minutes.

Kings have been exploited in the past, but thankfully their numbers have subsequently increased at several breeding localities. Their conservation status seems secure at present.

MACARONI PENGUINS

Orange tassels meeting between the eyes distinguish the macaroni *(Eudyptes chrysolophus)* from the slightly smaller (and lighter billed) rockhopper. 'Maccies' breed on sub-Antarctic islands near the Antarctic Convergence from South America eastwards to Heard Island and off the Peninsula. The macaroni is the most abundant of the sub-Antarctic and Antarctic penguins, with a minimum breeding population of 11.8 million pairs. Major concentrations are at South Georgia (5.4 million pairs), Îles Crozet (2.2 million), Îles Kerguelen (1.8 million) and Heard and McDonald Islands (one million).

'Macaronis have decreased at some sub-Antarctic breeding localities recently, arousing conservation concern'

Macaronis breed in summer. Breeding colonies, which can be immense, are deserted in winter. Two eggs are laid, the first smaller than the second (extremely unusual for birds). The first-laid ('A') egg is usually kicked out of the nest soon after the 'B' egg is laid and only one egg ever hatches. This odd system has prompted many studies. Macaronis eat lantern fish and euphausiid crustaceans, caught by pursuit-diving.

Like the pygoscelid penguins, 'maccies' are monitored for CCAMLR purposes. They have decreased at some sub-Antarctic breeding localities recently, arousing conservation concern, as witnessed by their World Conservation Union 'vulnerable' category. More accurate censuses are required at the major breeding localities – easier said than done in a million-strong colony.

ROCKHOPPER PENGUINS

'Rockies' *(Eudyptes chrysocome)* are smaller than macaronis and have yellow tassels that do not meet between the eyes. Three subspecies are recognized, with a suggestion that they be awarded specific status. Rockhoppers are sub-Antarctic and southern, cool, temperate island breeders, found as far north as Tristan da Cunha. There are an estimated 3.7 million pairs. The largest population (one million pairs) is found on the Falklands.

Rockies breed in summer, laying two dimorphic eggs. The smaller, first-laid 'A' egg is often lost during incubation and even if retained, does not always hatch. Rockhopper colonies are smaller than those of macaronis, and rockhoppers are able to breed among tumbled boulders on exposed shores, where their hopping and swimming abilities are required to enter and emerge from the sea and to reach their nest sites. Rockhoppers prey upon lantern fish and small euphausiid crustaceans.

Rockhoppers have decreased alarmingly at islands south of New Zealand and in the southern Indian Ocean. Disease and introduced rats, as well as sea temperature rises due to climate change affecting the availability of prey, have all been implicated. With a well-scattered population in the millions, the rockhopper is not currently at risk of extinction, but the continuing downward population trends are indeed worrying, earning the bird a World Conservation Union 'vulnerable' status.

ROYAL PENGUINS

Royals *(Eudyptes schlegeli)* are found only at sub-Antarctic Macquarie Island. Essentially, they look like white-faced macaronis, although some dark-faces do occur. The most recent census, in 1984–85, found 848,700 breeding pairs, which is now regarded as an underestimate.

Two eggs are laid in often-huge coastal colonies in October. As usual in *Eudyptes* penguins, the smaller, first-laid 'A' egg is ejected from the nest and usually does not hatch; the reason for this is still unclear, despite a number of studies. Chicks fledge in late January or early February. Colonies are deserted by May, after adults complete their molt ashore. Royals eat mainly small euphausiid crustaceans and lantern fish, caught by pursuit-diving.

Royals have been well studied in recent years, and much is now known about their foraging ecology and breeding biology. There appear to be no serious imminent conservation threats to the species although it has a 'vulnerable' status, due to its single breeding locality. Years ago, molting birds, called 'fats,' were exploited for their oil, but protest against this led to Macquarie Island being made the first sub-Antarctic island nature reserve.

AMSTERDAM ALBATROSSES

Confined to Île Amsterdam in the southern Indian Ocean, with a tiny population of fewer than 100 birds and only 13 pairs breeding in 1995, the Amsterdam albatross *(Diomedea amsterdamensis)* was described as a separate species only in 1983. It's the rarest Southern Ocean seabird – indeed, one of the world's rarest birds. Looking for one at sea is thus likely to be a forlorn task. Removal in 1992 of feral cattle from its breeding habitat 600m up on the island's central plateau has helped protect it, but there are now concerns over diseases. Its rarity and single breeding site earns it World Conservation Union 'critical' status.

'The Amsterdam albatross is one of the world's rarest birds'

BLACK-BROWED ALBATROSSES

The black-browed albatross *(Thalassarche melanophrys)* is one of the smaller mollymawks, but with a 2.5m wingspan and a mass up to 5kg, it's still a big bird. It can be identified at a distance by its underwing pattern featuring a wide, dark leading edge. At close range, the adult bird's yellow bill with orange-red tip and dark line through the eye make identification easy. Recent genetic studies have split it into two species, but they are considered as one here, since genetic studies may split the group even further.

Black-brows are widespread in southern seas, and birds may be seen accompanying fishing trawlers off Australasia, southern Africa and South America. Breeding occurs at nine island groups, spread from South Georgia to the Antipodes Islands, as well as Cape Horn. An annual breeder, the bird builds its nest out of mud and vegetation and lays a single egg. It can breed in vast numbers: Beauchêne Island, supports a colony that was estimated in 1991 to contain 135,000 pairs (but now, alas, substantially fewer).

Black-brows eat squid, fish and crustaceans, caught at the sea surface or by shallow dives. Interactions with southern fisheries, both longliners and trawlers, are a major concern. Although the species is abundant, dramatic declines at a number of localities (especially in the Falklands) have led to its successive and rapid re-classification by the World Conservation Union from 'near-threatened' to 'vulnerable,' and then to 'endangered' in 2003.

DARK-MANTLED & LIGHT-MANTLED SOOTY ALBATROSSES

With care, it is possible to distinguish between the two species of sooty albatrosses at sea. The dark-mantled *(Phoebetria fusca)*, often called the sooty, is uniformly chocolate brown, whereas the light-mantled *(P. palpebrata)* has a contrasting pale back. When viewed close-up (impossible at sea unless the bird flies right alongside your vessel), the dark-mantled sooty has a yellow stripe 'sulcus' along its lower mandible, whereas the light-mantled has a blue one. Their long, pointed tails and narrow wings make these two species easily distinguishable at sea from giant petrels, which have broader, shorter wings. The flight of the sooty albatross is most graceful, and many a happy hour can be spent watching them fly behind and alongside vessels traversing the Southern Ocean.

Both species have circumpolar at-sea distributions, but the light-mantled tends to occur further south, reaching the edge of the pack ice. This is mirrored by their breeding distribution, with the dark-mantled generally breeding further to the north, such as in the Tristan group. In contrast, only light-mantleds breed at South Georgia. Both species occur on sub-Antarctic islands in the Indian Ocean, making for interesting comparative studies of their breeding biology and feeding ecology. Both nest in small colonies on cliffs. Their paired courtship flights and haunting calls around misty cliffs make up one of the quintessential experiences for visitors to Southern Ocean islands.

'Dark-mantleds are called 'Peeoos' in the Tristan group because of their haunting call'

Annual breeding populations are about 16,000 pairs for dark-mantleds and 23,000 pairs for light-mantleds. They eat squid, fish, crustaceans and small seabirds, such as prions and diving petrels. Exactly how these seabirds are caught remains unknown, but the species' agile flight and dark coloration suggests predation at night. Dark-mantleds were once exploited in the Tristan group by the inhabitants (where they are called 'Peeoos' because of their haunting call), but fortunately are now fully protected there. *Phoebetria* albatrosses do not seem to get caught as often on longlines as do the great albatrosses and mollymawks, although population decreases in the dark-mantleds in the southern Indian Ocean has led to their 'endangered' status. The two sooty albatrosses are very special birds, admired by all fortunate enough to see them, but like all the world's albatrosses, they now need our concerted efforts to keep them on the wing.

GREY-HEADED ALBATROSSES

The grey-headed *(Thalassarche chrysostoma)* is identifiable by its greyish head, broad, dark leading edge to the underwing and orange stripes on both upper and lower mandibles. A more southerly breeding species than the two yellow-nosed albatrosses, with colonies on South Georgia, the Prince Edwards, Îles Crozet and Kerguelen, Campbell and Macquarie, the grey-head has a circumpolar breeding distribution. A recent population estimate is 106,000 breeding pairs, which can be doubled since the bird normally breeds only every second year.

Grey-heads breed in colonies on cliff ledges, sometimes alongside black-browed or yellow-nosed albatrosses. Like all albatrosses, they lay only one egg. Both parents share incubation and chick-feeding.

The grey-heads' diet consists of fish, cephalopods and crustaceans, including Antarctic krill off South Georgia. Interactions with longline-fishing vessels remain its most serious conservation problem, giving it its 'vulnerable' status.

ROYAL ALBATROSSES

The royal albatrosses (Northern, *Diomedea epomophora*, and Southern *D. sanfordi)* belong to the 'great' albatrosses of the Southern Ocean. They are primarily recognized at sea by their huge size and their all-white tail with mostly black upper wings and a dark edge to the upper mandible which occur at adulthood. You will need to consult a detailed field guide to separate the two species at sea.

They breed on islands off New Zealand (Chathams, Campbell and Aucklands), with a small population on Taiaroa Head near Dunedin on New Zealand's South Island. This is the most accessible breeding locality of a southern albatross and is a famous tourist attraction. Total annual breeding population for the two species combined is about 11,000 pairs, but biennial breeding means there are twice this number of breeders. As with the wandering and Amsterdam albatrosses, the long breeding season means royals can only breed every second year. Interbreeding between the Northern and Southern royal albatrosses has occurred at Taiaroa Head.

Royals eat squid, fish and crustaceans caught at the sea surface. Like wanderers, they are accidentally caught by longlines. It is hoped that the international Agreement on the Conservation of Albatrosses and Petrels, which came into force in February 2004, and enforced mitigation measures, such as only setting lines at night and using bird-scaring lines with attached streamers, will protect these splendid birds (and their relatives).

SHY ALBATROSSES

Shy albatrosses *(Thalassarche cauta)* are the largest of the southern mollymawks, with a wingspan of up to 2.6m. Distinguishing features are a hump-backed appearance in flight, dark upperwings that are not as black as other mollymawks' and a narrow dark leading edge to the underwing in both adults and juveniles. The shy albatross is misnamed, since it will approach and follow ships. It breeds on islands south of New Zealand and around Tasmania, with a tiny population of only four pairs recently found breeding on Îles Crozet. However, the bird (now considered to form three or four species) has a widespread at-sea distribution and can be seen anywhere in the Southern Ocean in the Roaring Forties and Furious Fifties. The total estimated population is one million birds, including juveniles. The largest breeding colonies are on the Bounty and Auckland island groups.

'The shy albatross is misnamed, since it will approach and follow ships'

Shy albatrosses lay a single egg in mud and vegetation nests in colonies on cliffs. They eat fish, squid and crustaceans. Interactions with longline-fishing vessels are a serious concern, leading to the species' 'threatened' categorization. However, during this century some colonies have increased in size as exploitation of the birds' feathers and eggs has halted.

WANDERING ALBATROSSES

The wandering albatross *(Diomedea exulans)* is a bird of superlatives – for many travelers, it is *the* bird of the Southern Ocean. To see one glide past your vantage place on a ship, just a few meters away as it watches you with its soft brown eyes, is to experience a thrill not for 'lesser mortals.' The species is distinguished from the smaller mollymawk albatrosses by its huge size (it has a wing span of up to 3.5m), but telling it at sea from the closely related (but less widespread) royal and Amsterdam albatrosses is not easy and requires recourse to a specialized field guide or friendly marine ornithologist. Recent genetic studies have resulted in splitting the wanderer into four species: the southerly wanderer itself, the Tristan *(dabbenena)* of Gough Island, and the antipodean *(antipodensis)* and Gibson's *(gibsoni)* albatrosses of New Zealand's southern islands.

The latest population estimates are 21,000 annual breeding pairs at 10 island groups in the Southern Ocean for the four 'wanderer' species combined. But the bird's more-than-year-long breeding season means it breeds (if successful) only every second year, so the total breeding population is nearly twice this figure. At several localities, populations have decreased because the bird is at serious risk from being caught by longline vessels fishing for tuna and toothfish – an ignoble death by drowning for such a splendid animal. Much research is currently being done into ways of reducing this mortality, and some populations have stabilized, perhaps as a result.

This albatross group feeds mainly on squid and fish caught, it is thought, by predation at night and scavenging by day. Satellite-tracking and geo-location loggers have revealed that wanderers can cover vast tracts of the Southern Ocean, flying up to several thousand kilometers on a single foraging trip, so they are aptly named. Indeed, young birds may not return to land for five years or more, staying at sea the whole time. The World Conservation Union considers the Tristan albatross 'endangered,' the others in the group 'vulnerable.'

YELLOW-NOSED ALBATROSSES

'Albatrosses, in general, are in a bad way!'

The similar-looking Atlantic *(Thalassarche chlororhynchos)* and Indian *(T. carteri)* yellow-nosed albatrosses are the smallest of the southern mollymawks, weighing up to 3kg. Viewed up close, the black bill with its striking orange streak on the upper mandible is a distinguishing feature. They breed on the northerly islands of the Southern Ocean: Tristan da Cunha, the French sub-Antarctic islands and Prince Edward Island. The Atlantic birds have noticeably greyer heads.

The combined population is about 100,000 breeding pairs. At sea, they can be seen in the South Atlantic and Indian, but not Pacific, Oceans. They breed annually, laying a single egg in summer in mud and vegetation nests. At some localities, such as Tristan da Cunha, they nest in a widely scattered pattern among dense fern vegetation. At Prince Edward Island, they nest on cliff ledges in a mixed colony with grey-headed albatrosses.

Their diet is similar to that of the other mollymawks. Among the yellow-nosed albatrosses nesting at Îles Crozet, fish forms the bulk of the diet. Off southern Africa, yellow-noses scavenge from trawler discards. They were once exploited for their eggs and flesh by the Tristan Islanders, but are now fully protected. Interaction with fishing boats is a great concern. Significant population decreases have led to a World Conservation Union 'endangered' status for both species. Albatrosses, in general, are in a bad way!

ANTARCTIC FULMARS

A medium-sized petrel (800g, 1.2m wingspan), the Antarctic fulmar *(Fulmarus glacialoides)* is readily identified by its pale-grey plumage with white head and black flight feathers. The bill is pink with a dark tip and the dark eye is a distinguishing feature. Antarctic fulmars are a southerly species with a circumpolar distribution at sea and are commonly found on pack-ice fringes. They breed in large colonies on the islands off the Peninsula, the South Orkneys and South Sandwiches, and along the Antarctic coastline and on Bouvetøya. There are no good population estimates yet, but the bird is very abundant and not considered threatened.

They breed from December to April on rock ledges on coastal cliffs, often in large and dense colonies. They feed on Antarctic krill and other crustaceans, fish and squid, as well as carrion. Food is caught by surface-seizing and occasionally by shallow dives.

ANTARCTIC PETRELS

The Antarctic petrel *(Thalassoica antarctica)* is a boldly marked dark-brown-and-white petrel, a little smaller than the Antarctic fulmar. It is bigger but less speckled than the cape petrel, which is also dark brown and white. This species breeds only on the Antarctic continent, but not many olonies are known, and more may still be found. The largest-known olony, Svarthamaren in Dronning Maud Land, supports about 250,000 airs. Thirty-five colonies are known, supporting an estimated 500,000 reeding pairs, but at-sea surveys suggest that there are 10 to 20 million irds, so it is assumed that further colonies await discovery.

Antarctics breed in dense colonies on cliffs and steep rocky slopes, some f them 100km or more from the open sea, on inland nunataks and mounain ranges. Eggs are laid in November after the adults arrive at their nest ites the previous month. Chicks fledge in March. The rest of the year, the olonies are deserted while the birds stay at sea among and just north of the ack ice. They eat Antarctic krill, fish such as *Pleuragramma antarcticum* nd small squid taken by surface-seizing, dipping and shallow diving.

TLANTIC PETRELS

he Atlantic petrel *(Pterodroma incerta)* is one of the largest gadfly etrels, recognized by its white breast and belly, which are clearly demarated from the rest of its uniformly brown plumage. It breeds only on he Tristan da Cunha and Gough island groups. Their at-sea distribution ardly extends out of the Atlantic Ocean.

Practically nothing is known of the Atlantic petrel's population size, but t must be in the low tens of thousands at least. They breed in excavated urrows in winter, with chicks on Gough Island being fed in October. heir diet appears to be mainly squid, with fish a minor component.

In the past, Atlantic petrels – like other burrowing petrels – were xploited for meat and eggs by the Tristan Islanders, but are now legally rotected. Nevertheless, the species is classified as 'vulnerable' and is t risk from introduced house mice at Gough Island, which have been eported to kill chicks.

LUE PETRELS

he small (65cm wing span) blue petrel *(Halobaena caerulea)* supericially resembles a prion, but look for the white – not black – terminal and to the tail. Blue petrels have a prominent dark 'M' shape on their pper wings and back. They breed at the Diego Ramirez Islands off Cape Iorn, South Georgia, the Prince Edwards, Îles Crozet, Kerguelen, Heard nd Macquarie Island. Their at-sea distribution is circumpolar, from far outh to the southern parts of the South American, African and Australan continents (where irregular irruptions following bad weather may ring large numbers to be 'wrecked' on shorelines).

> **'The removal of feral cats from Marion and Macquarie Islands has led to improved breeding success of blue petrels'**

Blue petrels are abundant and breed in large, dense colonies in thick ussock. One rough estimate puts the total population at 'several milon.' No information is available on population trends, except that the emoval of feral cats from Marion and Macquarie Islands has led to mproved breeding success and a return of breeding birds. These eradiation programs are probably the greatest conservation successes at any ub-Antarctic island since the halt of the exploitation of royal penguins or their oil at Macquarie Island many years ago. Blue petrels primarily at small crustaceans, such as krill and amphipods.

APE PETRELS

he cape petrel *(Daption capense)* is a dark brownish–black-and-white etrel smaller than the Antarctic petrel. Its speckled appearance gives it its ther common name, 'pintado,' meaning 'painted' in Spanish. Interestingly s generic name *Daption* is an anagram of pintado, having no meaning therwise. Some ornithologists think 'pintado' a far better name than the dull 'cape.' It was once known as the 'cape pigeon,' which is unhelpful an has gone out of use: no pigeon can fly the oceans the way a petrel can!

Cape petrels have a circumpolar at-sea distribution, which extends muc further north than the Antarctic petrel. In fact, they can be quite commo off southern Africa, South America and Australia, especially in winter. The also have a wide breeding range: from the Antarctic continent to the mor southerly sub-Antarctic islands, where they breed on cliff ledges – about 25 colonies are known. As an assiduous ship-follower, the cape petrel eats jus about anything edible thrown overboard. In the days of whaling, it was see in vast noisy numbers around South Georgia's whaling stations. There i no good information on population size and trends yet, and there current seems to be no conservation problem of note.

'No pigeon can fly the oceans the way a petrel can!'

DIVING PETRELS

Diving petrels are small seabirds with stubby wings that seem to whi like wind-up toys as they fly fast and low over the sea. Two species, th South Georgian *(Pelecanoides georgicus)* and the common *(P. urinatrix* are difficult to tell apart, even in the hand. Most ornithologists do no even attempt to distinguish between them at sea.

Diving petrels are not seen at great distances from their breeding site South Georgians breed at South Georgia, and on islands in the souther Indian Ocean and off New Zealand. Commons breed at a number c southern islands, from South Georgia to Tristan da Cunha and south c New Zealand. Populations are estimated in the millions.

Both species breed during the summer in burrows dug in bare groun or in vegetated peat. They eat planktonic crustaceans, such as krill, cope-pods and amphipods, as well as small fish and squid. Prey is caught un-derwater by pursuit-diving, the birds using their half-open wings to 'fly through the water like the diminutive auks of the Northern Hemispher

As with practically all burrowing petrels, introduced cats and roden have severely reduced some populations of diving petrels. Both specie appear to be extinct at South Africa's Marion Island, for example, mos likely because of predation by the now-eliminated feral cat population.

GIANT PETRELS

Giant petrels are the largest of the petrel family, which goes to make u the order of tubenose or *procellariiform* seabirds, along with albatrosse storm petrels and diving petrels. The crucial feature used to distinguish th northern giant petrel *(Macronectes halli)* from the closely related souther giant petrel *(M. giganteus)* is the color of its bill tip: greenish in northern reddish-brown in southerns. This characteristic is not easy to spot at se Some southerns are all white, except for the odd dark feather. This colo phase does not occur in northerns, helping with species identificatio White-phase southerns are more common at southerly breeding sites, an largely absent at the northerly ones, such as Gough and Marion Islands

Giant petrels can be seen in all parts of the Southern Ocean, with south-erns occurring further south – indeed, some breed on the Peninsula an in Terre Adélie. On New Zealand's southern islands, only northerns occu whereas the birds that breed at the most northerly island, Gough, a southerns – not northerns, as might be expected. Genetic studies shoul lead to a clearer understanding of these patterns. There are an estimate 12,000 breeding pairs of northerns and 36,000 pairs of southerns.

Southerns breed in colonies, whereas northerns breed singly or i scattered groups. Genetic isolation is helped by the fact that northern commence breeding earlier. Both species are annual breeders.

Unlike albatrosses, giant petrels forage on both land and sea. On land, they kill birds as large as king penguins and scavenge in seal colonies. At sea, they eat fish, squid and crustaceans, and scavenge dead cetaceans and seabirds. Watching bloodstained giant petrels (nicknamed 'nellies' or 'stinkers') squalling and fighting over a seal carcass is not for the faint-hearted. Indeed, old-time whalers used to call them 'breakbones.' But the birds have a raffish manner that appeals to some, and they are undeniably magnificent fliers.

Giant petrels are caught by tuna and toothfish longline-fishing vessels in the Southern Ocean. Several populations of the 'vulnerable' southern species are decreasing, probably as a result. Northerns ('near-threatened') are faring better, with some increases recorded, perhaps due to increasing seal populations offering them more opportunity for scavenging.

GREAT-WINGED PETRELS

The great-winged petrel *(Pterodroma macroptera)* is a dark-brown gadfly petrel found in the Roaring Forties. Separating it from the slightly smaller Kerguelen petrel can be tricky and requires guidance from an expert or a good field guide. In New Zealand, a clearly differentiated subspecies is known as the grey-faced petrel. Great-wings breed on the sub-Antarctic islands of the southern Indian Ocean, and also on islands around southern Australia and New Zealand.

'Watching bloodstained giant petrels squalling and fighting over a seal carcass is not for the faint-hearted'

They breed in winter and lay a single egg in May to July in burrows excavated in vegetated peat slopes. Chicks fledge in November and December, just when the summer-breeding burrowing petrels are getting started. Great-wings arrive at their burrows after dark, to reduce their chances of being caught by predatory sub-Antarctic skuas. Breeding in winter may thus be an advantage, since most skuas leave the islands to winter at sea.

Great-wings eat primarily squid, which is caught at night. They are numerous and not globally threatened. At some islands, however, introduced cats have reduced populations and caused nearly complete breeding failure, as at Marion Island in the 1970s and '80s. Happily, Marion Island is now cat-free after a long and expensive eradication program, and the great-wings are breeding successfully again.

GREY PETRELS

Grey petrels *(Procellaria cinerea)* breed at the Tristan and Gough Islands, the South Indian sub-Antarctic islands, Campbell Island and the Antipodes. Their at-sea distribution is circumpolar, extending south past 60°S and north to continental coasts. Little is known of their numbers, because like all burrowing petrels they're incredibly difficult to count accurately.

Grey petrels breed in winter, laying a single egg in burrows in peat or in rock crevices. Their diet is poorly known, but at Îles Crozet it is mainly squid and fish.

Introduced cats have severely diminished some populations, such as at Marion Island, where the grey petrel is now hopefully recovering, and at Macquarie Island, where following the removal of cats, it has returned to breed after many years' absence. Rats have also taken chicks at Îles Crozet and Campbell Island (the latter now thankfully rat-free following an eradication program). Grey petrels, classified as 'near-threatened,' are also caught on longline hooks, so they face threats both on land and at sea.

KERGUELEN PETRELS

Kerguelen petrels *(Aphadroma brevirostris)* are uniformly dark brown, except for their silvery underwings. Their smaller size and proportionally large head distinguishes them from the great-winged petrel. Their distinctive and fast soaring flight is also helpful in identification at sea.

Kerguelen petrels breed on the Tristan and Gough island groups in the south Atlantic, the Prince Edward Islands, and Îles Crozet and Kerguelen. At-sea distribution is circumpolar, with irregular irruptions, linked to adverse weather conditions, bringing sometimes large numbers of birds to the waters off southern Africa and Australasia. Such birds are often then 'wrecked,' and their dead bodies may be found washed up on beaches.

Kerguelens eat mainly squid, fish and crustaceans caught by surface-seizing at night. They breed in burrows in summer. There are probably several hundred thousand birds, so the species is in no danger of extinction, but the eradication of introduced cats and rodents at its breeding islands will help its conservation status.

SNOW PETRELS

'Snow petrels are truly creatures of the ice'

Snow petrels *(Pagodroma nivea)* are unmistakable. With their all-white plumage, black bill and small black eyes, they are truly creatures of the ice. Their flight is more fluttering than most petrels. They breed on the Antarctic continent and Peninsula, and also at Bouvetøya, on rocky slopes and in crevices among boulders on nunataks and sea cliffs. No fewer than 298 breeding sites are known. The birds' at-sea distribution does not extend far north; they are very much denizens of the pack-ice zone, where they roost on icebergs.

They lay a single egg in late November or early December, and chicks fledge in March or April. Snow petrels are nervous at the nest and will desert their eggs if overly disturbed. This is in contrast to most of the petrel family, which are not too concerned about the presence of humans.

Snow petrels eat primarily krill, fish and squid, caught mainly by surface-dipping while on the wing. They can regurgitate their stomach oil as a defense mechanism. Deposits of this substance, called 'mumiyo,' have built up around nest sites over thousands of years and can be radiocarbon dated. The oldest-known colony dates back an astounding 34,000 years. No immediate conservation problems are known for the snow petrel.

SOFT-PLUMAGED PETRELS

The soft-plumaged petrel *(Pterodroma mollis)* is a dark-brown-and-white, medium-sized gadfly petrel. In flight, the back and upperwings carry a dark 'M' shape.

Soft-plumes occur at sea from South American waters east to New Zealand, mainly in sub-Antarctic latitudes, but they are absent from the South Pacific. They breed on the Tristan and Gough islands, the Prince Edwards, Îles Crozet, Kerguelen and the Antipodes. There are no good estimates of total population, since burrowing petrels are notoriously difficult to count, but they are abundant at many breeding localities and are commonly seen at sea within their normal range.

They eat primarily squid, caught by surface-seizing thought to occur mostly at night. Exploitation of the soft-plumaged petrel at Tristan da Cunha has halted, and the removal of feral cats from Marion Island should lead the species to a recovery there. Cat abatement on other islands where they occur (such as Îles Crozet and Kerguelen) would further improve the soft-plumes' conservation status.

WHITE-CHINNED PETRELS

The white-chinned petrel *(Procellaria aequinoctialis)* is the largest burrowing petrel, with a wingspan reaching nearly 1.5m. The clearly marked

RALPH LEE HOPKINS

Fur seal and pup (p108)

JONATHAN CHESTER

Weddell seal (p109)

Crabeater seal (p108)

RALPH LEE HOPKINS

Humpback whales (p105)

DAVE LEVITT

Overleaf:
King penguins (p111),
Macquarie Island

GRANT DIXON

SCOTT DARSNEY

Adélie penguins (p110)

JONATHAN CHESTER

Gentoo parent and chick (p111)

GRANT DIXON

Rockhopper penguin (p112)

Emperor penguins and chicks (p111)

DAVID TIPLING

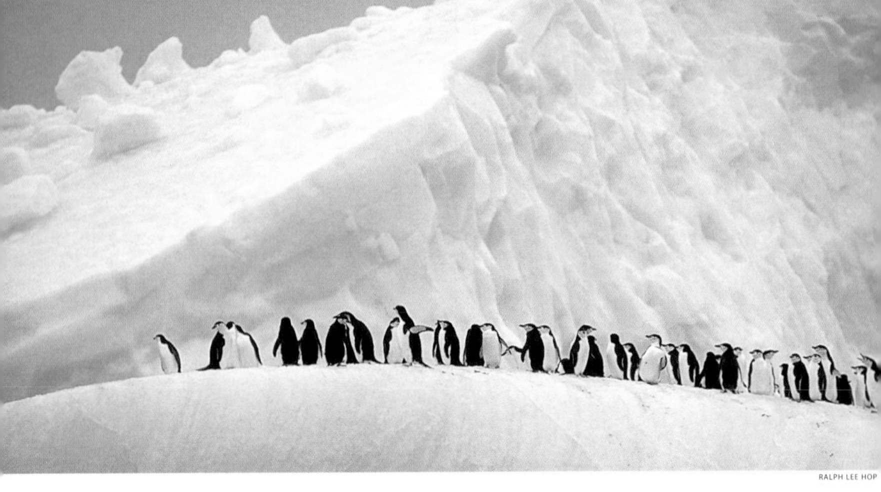

RALPH LEE HOP

Chinstrap penguins (p110)

RALPH LEE HOPKINS

Southern giant petrel (p118)

Cormorant (p123)

CHRIS BAR

CHRIS BARTON

Skua (p125)

spectacled petrel (*P. conspicillata*), of Inaccessible Island in the Tristan group, is now regarded as a distinct species. In the past, white-chinned petrels have been called 'cape hens' and also 'shoemakers,' the latter based on their call, which resembles that of a cobbler hammering shoes. White-chins are bigger than the all-dark gadfly petrel species, such as the great-winged and the Kerguelen, and their wings are held unbent in a 'stiff' manner, making them look like small giant petrels as they follow ships.

They breed in summer at the Falkland Islands, South Georgia, Prince Edwards, Îles Crozet, Kerguelen and on New Zealand's sub-Antarctic islands. At-sea distribution is circumpolar, with a wide latitudinal range. Their burrows are easily recognizable by their large size and the presence of a pool of muddy water at the entrance.

White-chins eat fish, squid and crustaceans, with the proportions of each varying at different localities. On the fishing grounds off South Africa's west coast, they often scavenge for discards left by trawlers. Introduced cats have reduced breeding success on some islands. The white-chinned petrel is killed on longline hooks in large numbers throughout its at-sea range, giving it its 'vulnerable' status.

PRIONS

Prions or whalebirds *(Pachyptila* spp.) are small grey-blue-and-white birds. They can be distinguished from blue petrels by their black terminal band to the upper tail. All have a vague 'M' shape visible on their upperparts in flight. Their taxonomy is still a matter for debate – there may be as many as six species, which vary subtly in their markings and also by the width of their bills. Broadbilled prions *(P. vittata)*, affectionately known as 'Donald Ducks' in some quarters, have the broadest bills, with lamellae for straining out small crustaceans, analogous to the baleen plates of the great whales. The fairy prion *(P. turtur)* and thin-billed prion *(P. belcheri)* have narrow bills. At-sea identification of species can stump the very best experts in all but excellent (and close-up) viewing conditions.

'Broadbilled prions are affectionately known as 'Donald Ducks' in some quarters'

Breeding takes place at many southern islands, with one or two species occurring together. Prions may burrow, or they may breed in crevices among boulders and at the base of cliffs in scree slopes. They can be seen in all areas of the Southern Ocean north of the pack ice and in continental waters, often in very large flocks.

Their diet varies with each species and bill width, as does their method of foraging, but small crustaceans, especially amphipods, taken by filtering or surface-seizing, are their main prey. Like most burrowing petrels of the southern islands, prions have suffered from predation by introduced cats and rats. Removal of these should eventually lead to population recoveries.

GREAT SHEARWATERS

The great shearwater *(Puffinus gravis)* is handsomely marked. Its dark cap and white band at the base of the upper tail are very noticeable. It breeds only in the Tristan and Gough group of islands and is not seen to any great extent outside the Atlantic (except off the east coast of South Africa). The species is a trans-equatorial migrant and is better known from its winter quarters in the North Atlantic than at its southern hemisphere breeding grounds, where it awaits detailed study.

The Tristan and Gough population is huge, and could number more than five million breeding pairs. The population appears stable, although numbers are low because of past exploitation and habitat loss on the main island of Tristan da Cunha. Tristan Islanders on nearby Nightingale Island still legally take eggs and chicks (for their fat, used as cooking oil).

Great shearwaters breed in summer and lay a single large egg in short burrows among tussock and under trees. They often forage by plunge-diving and so can exploit more of the ocean than the surface-seizing gadfly petrels. Conservation threats include ingestion of plastic particles and pesticides. Introduced house mice on Gough Island have been reported to kill chicks: further study is needed to assess this threat.

The Complete Guide to Antarctic Wildlife (2003), by Hadoram Shirihai, is the most authoritative book on Antarctica's wildlife. With more than 500 color photos, each species is well illustrated and described. It's heavy – but essential.

LITTLE SHEARWATERS

The black-and-white little shearwater *(Puffinus assimilis)* is recognizable by its low flight, which alternates glides with a few rapid wing beats. It is often seen in groups of two or three, usually close to breeding localities. It has a circumpolar at-sea distribution in the Southern Ocean.

The birds breed in summer, nesting in burrows, among tussock and in rock crevices on the more northerly islands of the Tristan and Gough group, on Île St Paul and on islands around Australia and New Zealand. They eat fish and squid, caught by pursuit-diving and surface-diving.

Studies are needed of this little-known bird, and the effects of introduced cats and rodents at breeding localities need assessing.

SOOTY SHEARWATERS

The sooty shearwater *(Puffinus griseus)* is all brown, apart from its silvery underwings obvious in flight. Three characteristics distinguish it from the noticeably larger white-chinned petrel and the more solitary gadfly petrels: its distinctive, swift flight; its long, narrow wings; and its habit of occurring in large-to-huge flocks.

Sooty shearwaters have a circumpolar at-sea distribution. Their range crosses the equator in both the Atlantic and Pacific Oceans, and extends south to the pack-ice fringe. They breed in often-vast colonies on islands off New Zealand and Cape Horn, and lay a single egg in burrows in November. Chicks depart in April or May. They eat fish such as anchovies, squid and crustaceans (the proportions of which vary depending on the place and time) by undertaking sometimes-deep dives.

Sooty shearwaters face several pressures. Exploitation continues in New Zealand as part of traditional customs, with perhaps 250,000 chicks taken annually by Maoris, who call them 'titi' or 'mutton birds.' The birds are also drowned by gill nets and longlines in the North Pacific, and on some islands predatory species have been introduced. The huge Snares' population has been estimated to have declined from 2.75 million to one million breeding pairs over 30 years, so there is now reason to be concerned for this admittedly still abundant species.

BLACK-BELLIED & WHITE-BELLIED STORM PETRELS

Black-bellied *(Fregetta tropica)* and white-bellied *(F. grallaria)* storm petrels are medium-sized storm petrels. Closely related, they are separated by the presence or absence of a black line down the center of an otherwise white underbody.

White-bellies breed on the more northerly islands of the Southern Ocean, such as Tristan and Gough. Black-bellies breed on South Georgia, Îles Crozet and Kerguelen, and on islands along the Peninsula.

Both species breed in summer and nest in burrows in loose colonies. Diet, based on a study of black-bellies at Îles Crozet, includes free-living barnacle larvae, amphipods and small euphausiids, with fish also eaten occasionally. Foraging is by pattering and dipping.

GREY-BACKED STORM PETRELS

The small grey-backed storm petrel *(Garrodia nereis)* is distinctively marked with white underparts, a dark-brown head and back and a grey rump. Grey-backs have a discontinuous distribution in the Southern Ocean, with three centers near breeding localities in the South Atlantic Ocean, southern Indian Ocean and south of Australasia.

There are no accurate censuses, but the species probably numbers in the tens of thousands of pairs. They breed in summer and lay eggs in December, nesting in coastal grassland among tussocks and in hollows among rocks. Their diet has been little studied, but at Îles Crozet it consists almost exclusively of immature and planktonic *Lepas* barnacle larvae. They feed by pattering over the sea surface, and by dipping and shallow-diving.

WHITE-FACED STORM PETRELS

The white-faced storm petrel *(Pelagodroma marina)* has a distinctively marked head with a white line above its eyes (the supercilium). The projecting feet on very long legs have yellow webs. They breed on islands around Australia and New Zealand, at the Tristan and Gough group in the South Atlantic, and across the equator in the North Atlantic. The birds must number in the low millions.

White-faces breed in summer, lay eggs in burrows in colonies in November and fledge in February. They eat planktonic crustaceans and small fish and squid, which they catch by pattering and dipping, probably at night. They sometimes get their legs entangled with free-living trematode larvae, which later can cause them to become snared in vegetation at their nest sites. An estimated 200,000 were found dead from this unusual cause in the Chatham Islands off New Zealand in 1970.

WILSON'S STORM PETRELS

Storm petrels are the smallest and lightest seabirds in the world. The Wilson's storm petrel *(Oceanites oceanicus)* weighs only 35g to 45g. 'Willies' have a circumpolar distribution and cross into the Northern Hemisphere in the Atlantic, Indian and Pacific Oceans. They breed on the more southerly sub-Antarctic islands, such as South Georgia, and on the Peninsula and continent, as well as on islands near Cape Horn and in the Falklands. They have been regarded as the world's most abundant seabird; there are certainly several million of them. They are regular ship followers and associate with whales.

'Wilson's storm petrels are regular ship followers and associate with whales'

Wilson's storm petrels lay a single egg in December in burrows and rock crevices in cliffs, rocky slopes and scree banks. They eat mainly planktonic crustaceans, including copepods, krill and amphipods, as well as small squid and fish, feeding while on the wing, skimming and pattering with their feet over the sea surface. Indeed, this behavior earned them their name, for 'petrel' means 'little Peter,' the Apostle who walked on the water with Christ on the Sea of Galilee.

Superstitious sealers and whalers called Wilson's storm petrels 'Mother Carey's chickens,' corrupted from 'Mater Cara,' the Virgin Mary, because they believed that the birds came to collect the souls of dead sailors: possibly too heavy a burden for such diminutive creatures?

CORMORANTS

There is not yet agreement on how many species of cormorants *(Phalacrocorax* spp., or shags, to give them their other commonly used name) inhabit the southern islands and the Peninsula. There could be as many as seven or as few as two, depending on what taxonomic levels are used. All are reasonably similar, with a distinctive fast-flapping flight.

Cormorants are inshore-feeding birds and are not normally seen out of sight of land. Their presence alongside a ship in the mist is a sure sign of approaching land, which must have been a comfort (or a wake-up call!) to sailors of the past.

Cormorants breed on the Peninsula, on all the sub-Antarctic islands and on the islands south of New Zealand. Interestingly, the more northerly islands of Tristan da Cunha, Gough, St Paul and Amsterdam do not have resident cormorant populations. They breed in summer. Nests in colonies are made of seaweed and terrestrial vegetation on cliff tops and ledges directly above the sea. Up to three eggs are laid, and the young hatch naked, unique for a southern seabird. They eat mainly benthic fish, caught by deep and long dives from the surface.

Some island populations have been declining, perhaps as a result of a change in the birds' food supply brought on by global warming.

KELP GULLS

The kelp, or Dominican gull *(Larus dominicanus)* is the only gull of the Southern Ocean. It lives on the Peninsula and at most sub-Antarctic islands, where it is resident year-round, generally in small numbers.

Like most southern seabirds, kelp gulls breed in summer. They lay up to three (although usually only two) mottled eggs in an open nest lined with vegetation. Chicks can leave the nest soon after hatching, but are still fed by their parents until after they can fly. Diet includes scraps scavenged from giant petrel kills, and in penguin colonies, terrestrial invertebrates such as earthworms and moth larvae, and intertidal shellfish such as limpets.

No conservation problems are known for this species, which also breeds in southern Africa, Australasia and South America.

SHEATHBILLS

Sheathbills are odd birds in a number of ways. They're not seabirds (for example, their feet are not webbed) but are in their own family, allied to waders or shorebirds. They cannot be mistaken for anything else as they strut and squabble around penguin colonies. The greater sheathbill (*Chionis alba*)– also known by the names American, snowy or pink-faced sheathbill – is found at South Georgia, the South Shetlands, South Orkneys and on the Peninsula. It migrates north to South America and the Falklands in winter. Lesser or black-faced sheathbills *(C. minor)* are somewhat smaller, with noticeably shorter wings. They are strict residents of the four sub-Antarctic island groups of the southern Indian Ocean, each with its own subspecies.

Under Antarctic Ice (2004), featuring the underwater photographs of Norbert Wu with text by Jim Mastro, offers a fascinating and beautiful look beneath these icy waters.

Sealers called sheathbills 'paddies' because of their so-called thieving nature (really just honest scavenging) – undoubtedly a slur on both the birds and the Irish. They also called them 'sore-eyed pigeons,' a name which seems quite apt when one sees them up close.

Sheathbills nest in crevices in summer, usually near penguin colonies, where they scavenge eggs, spilled food being fed to chicks, and carcasses killed by giant petrels. They also feed on intertidal life and on invertebrates in the peat.

At Marion Island, the lesser sheathbill population has decreased in the last two decades. This may be due to competition for terrestrial invertebrates from an increasing (due to global warming) house mouse population. Further research is needed to see if the species is at risk. Elsewhere, no conservation problems have been described.

SKUAS

Skuas are large, heavily built gull-like birds, mainly brown but with conspicuous white flashes in their wings. South Polar skuas *(Catharacta maccormicki)* are marginally smaller than sub-Antarctic or brown skuas (*C. antarctica*) and have a paler plumage. Their flight is heavy, with relatively little gliding and much flapping.

Sub-Antarctic skuas breed on most of the southern islands, whereas South Polars are found on the Antarctic continent. On the Peninsula, both species occur, and hybrid pairs are regularly recorded. The South Polar skua has the distinction of being the world's most southerly bird: several have turned up (lost?) at the South Pole.

In winter, both species leave their breeding localities and spend time at sea, occasionally even reaching the northern hemisphere. Both breed in summer, generally laying two mottled eggs in open nests on the ground. Breeding birds are strictly territorial and will quickly chase off intruders, not hesitating to fly – claws outstretched – right at the head of an unwelcome human who comes too close to the nest.

South Polar skuas prey upon the eggs and chicks of penguins and other colonial seabirds (including adults of the smaller species), but also clean up any carrion. They also feed on Antarctic krill, squid and fish. At sea, they chase smaller seabirds to force them to regurgitate or drop their prey (an act known as kleptoparasitism), often retrieving it spectacularly before it reaches the water.

Skuas number in the thousands and seem to be at no particular conservation risk, although it has been postulated that decreases in burrowing petrel numbers (important prey) could have led to decreases in sub-Antarctic skua populations at islands with cats. Because of the lack of pre-cat censuses, this is hard to prove.

'Skuas will quickly chase off intruders, not hesitating to fly right at the head of an unwelcome human who comes too close to the nest'

TERNS

Several species of tern *(Sterna* spp.*)* may be seen in the Southern Ocean. The Antarctic *(S. vittata)* and the rarer Kerguelen *(S. virgata)* terns breed at a number of southern islands, the former being more widespread and occurring on the Peninsula as well. Away from land, terns seen at sea are most likely to be Arctic terns (*S. paradisaea*), long-distance migrants from the northern hemisphere.

All three species are slender, long-winged grey-and-white birds, similar in size. Arctic terns in nonbreeding plumage have white foreheads and dark bills. The two breeding species are red-billed and have conspicuous black caps. Distinguishing Antarctic from Kerguelen terns, however, sometimes confounds even the experts. Kerguelens are resident on the few islands where they occur, whereas Antarctic terns migrate, several thousand reaching South African waters to spend the winter.

Antarctic and Kerguelen terns breed in summer, laying mottled eggs in open nests on the ground in loose colonies. They eat mainly small fish caught at the surface or by shallow dives within sight of land, often within the kelp-bed zone. The rare Kerguelen tern is considered 'near-threatened' and both breeding species are at risk from feral cats on islands where the felines still occur.

SOUTHERN OCEAN FISH

The Southern Ocean supports more than 270 species of fish. Several are interesting because of their ability to survive in subzero waters without freezing. They actually have 'anti-freeze' glycopeptides in their blood. Members of the family Channichthyidae, ice fishes of which the mackerel ice fish *(Champsocephalus gunnari)* is a member, have no hemoglobi and are 'white-blooded.'

Some southern finfish are now the target of commercial fisheries. As consequence of initially uncontrolled fishing, several species, such as th marbled notothon *(Notothenia rossii)* and the mackerel ice fish *(Champsocephalus gunnari)*, are now commercially extinct. Fisheries have targete new species, which in turn have been overexploited. CCAMLR attempts t control these fisheries with a system of annual quotas and inspections.

'People should avoid buying toothfish at the market or ordering it in restaurants'

One recently opened fishery is longlining for Patagonian toothfis *(Dissostichus eleginoides)*. This continues to kill seabirds that becom hooked as lines are set around the islands and seamounts of the Souther Ocean. This problem has led to the adoption by CCAMLR of a numbe of measures (such as only setting lines when it is dark) in an attemp to reduce such mortality. However, many fishing vessels operate unlicensed and unchecked in the vastness of the Southern Ocean, making enforcement difficult, although several nations have had success arresting miscreant ships after high-seas chases.

Toothfish is known as 'Chilean sea bass' or 'black hake' in the US 'Antarctic sea bass,' 'Australian sea bass' or 'Antarctic icefish' in the UK '*bacalao de profundidad*' ('cod of the deep') in Spain, '*austro merluza negra*' in Chile and Argentina, '*légine australe*' in France, '*mero*' in Japan and '*patagonsky klykach*' in Russia. Unregulated fishing for and trade in toothfish makes this a decidedly seabird-unfriendly product. Conservation-minde people should avoid buying it at the market or ordering it in restaurants Concerted efforts to control this latter-day goldrush are trying to avoi the fish's commercial extinction, as well as the associated extinction of th affected albatrosses and petrels of the Southern Ocean.

ANTARCTIC KRILL

Antarctic krill *(Euphausia superba)* is a 6cm-long planktonic crustacean that is found in sometimes-enormous swarms south of the Antarctic Convergence. There is also a smaller species, the ice krill *(E. crystallarophias)* Krill is sifted out of the water by baleen whales, and eaten by many species of southern seabirds (especially penguins), squid, fish and crabeater seals, which have specially adapted teeth for this purpose. Without krill the ecosystem of the Southern Ocean would collapse.

Antarctic krill has been the target of fisheries for a number of years although krill is difficult to process for human consumption. Catches peaked in the early 1980s at over 400,000 tonnes per summer season but have subsequently dropped to much lower levels. Quotas are now set by CCAMLR, which also encourages research on krill and its predators.

TERRESTRIAL INVERTEBRATES

The sub-Antarctic islands and the Antarctic continent are populated with specialized terrestrial invertebrates. On the islands, the often-strong winds make flight maladaptive (it's too risky to be blown out to sea), so some flies and moths have become flightless. On the continent, tiny free-living mites inhabit the exposed soil and somehow survive the extreme cold and also the dryness, since liquid water is at a premium.

For more details about Kerguelen cabbage as food, see the boxed text on p82.

Introduced invertebrates can become a problem on the islands. Slugs, snails, earthworms, spiders and aphids have all arrived, some changing the ecosystem balance in subtle ways. The cabbage moth *(Plutella xylostella)*, for example, has attacked the Kerguelen cabbage on Marion Island.

On the Antarctic continent, which supports no native terrestrial vertebrate life, studies have concentrated on the microbiota: ciliates, rotifers, tardigrades – also charmingly called 'water bears' – and free-living nematodes (see p239). Most of these are only visible under a microscope, but their unseen presence does bring life to the continent's seemingly sterile nunataks and mountains.

TERRESTRIAL PLANTS

Antarctica's plants differ greatly from those found on the sub-Antarctic islands. The high rainfall and long hours of summer sunshine allow the islands to support an at-times lush vegetation, epitomized by tussock grassland, which is fertilized by thousands of burrowing petrels. The continent, by contrast, supports only mosses, lichens and algae, along with two flowering plants, a grass *(Deschampsia antarctica)*, and a cushion plant *(Colobanthus quitensis)*, which have footholds on the comparatively milder Peninsula. Interestingly, global warming is believed to be the cause for the observed spread of this grass.

For details about snow algae, see the boxed text on p220.

The true sub-Antarctic islands have many vascular ('higher') plants, but no woody species, so trees are absent. The more northerly cool temperate islands, such as Tristan da Cunha and Gough, support a few native tree species. One of the most intriguing plants of the southern Indian Ocean islands is Kerguelen cabbage *(Pringlea antiscorbutica)*. As its scientific name suggests, it was used by shipwrecked 19th-century sealers to ward off scurvy. The early accounts differed in their opinion of its tastiness (and how to cook it), but it can be imagined that necessity came before flavor.

MARINE PLANTS

The intertidal and subtidal areas of the southern islands support giant seaweeds such as the bull kelp *(Durvillea antarctica)*, which forms thick bands around many of the islands and protects their shores from rough seas. These kelp 'forests' offer an environment that supports fish, shellfish, octopus and crustaceans, which in turn provide food for inshore-foraging birds, such as cormorants and terns.

Kelps have a phenomenal rate of growth and constantly replace fronds as they are worn away by waves. Some plants break free during storms and wash ashore, where they contribute to a new environment by fertilizing shore vegetation and providing soft 'beds' for resting elephant seals.

Other types of marine plants make up the phytoplankton group, which are tiny single-celled plants at the bottom of the pelagic food chain. There are even ice algae, which stain pack ice pink or brown, and snow algae, which grow atop certain areas of snow (see the boxed text on p220). During algal blooms at sea, the sheer density of phytoplankton is so great that they actually color the ocean.

Antarctic Science

Professor David Walton

Professor Walton is the author of more than 80 scientific papers and the editor-in-chief of the international journal *Antarctic Science*. He spent 20 years as a research scientist for the British Antarctic Survey. For more on Professor Walton, see p18.

FROM EXPLORATION TO SCIENCE

Captain James Cook was not impressed by Antarctica in 1775. He had been looking for a fabled continent rich in resources that he could claim for the British Empire. Instead, he found foul weather and endless ice. Cook, who qualified his failure to reach the continent of Antarctica by stating that the world would not 'be profited' by the discovery, would have been surprised to see just how important Antarctica has become for science.

But how could Cook have known about the importance of the Antarctic ice sheet to world climate and sea level? Or the special features of the high atmosphere that produce the southern lights? Or about the remarkable food chains in the Southern Ocean? Or Antarctica's key role in the origin of all the southern continents? Over the last 50 years, Antarctica has come to play a central part in many scientific disciplines, and has turned out to be fundamental in our attempts to understand how the earth functions.

WHY DO SCIENCE IN ANTARCTICA?

Antarctic science is expensive science, probably second only to space research – so why do science in Antarctica? The answers are slightly different for each discipline, but all have three principles in common: Antarctic science should be the kind that cannot be done as successfully anywhere else in the world; it should be the highest-quality science; and whenever possible it should contribute to solving a global problem. Surprisingly, despite the remoteness of Antarctica, much of the research done there is immediately relevant to the more populated areas of the world. The most obvious example is the study of the increase in ultraviolet radiation – but there are others, such as research on the world's sea level, on the circulation patterns in the world's oceans, on southern hemisphere weather and on satellite communications.

Two important features of all science in Antarctica are that the research findings are freely available to everyone and that many of the projects are internationally coordinated and supported. This coordination has been arranged since 1957 through the Scientific Committee on Antarctic Research (SCAR), a nongovernmental organization. Each year, every country active in Antarctic science reports on its projects to SCAR, and every two years SCAR organizes a two-week international meeting to report on progress and plan for the future.

The extent and quality of science undertaken by any nation in Antarctica depends not only on the excellence of the scientists themselves but also on the logistics and the facilities provided. In many fields, state-of-the-art science can now be carried out in Antarctica. The installation, within the last 20 years, of research aquariums at Jubany, McMurdo, Palmer, Rothera and Mario Zucchelli (formerly Terra Nova Bay) stations has been as important to marine biologists as has the expansion of automatic weather stations on the polar plateau to climatologists.

When visiting scientific stations or field camps in Antarctica, you will only be able to catch a glimpse of the complex facilities required to support modern science. Many of the most exciting developments are too remote to be easily accessible to tourists, yet you should see and hear enough from the scientists you meet to capture something of the excitement and importance of Antarctic science.

LIVING ON A SCIENTIFIC STATION

There is a wide range of sophistication among the various stations. Some are little more than storage containers or primitive huts, providing only the most basic protection for short visits. Others are the height of modern convenience, with private rooms, showers and a range of sports facilities. In its own way, each one reflects the culture of the nation that established it – visiting Antarctic research stations is like seeing a distillation of national characteristics.

Many of the scientists and support staff stay only for the summer, or part of it. They come from a wide range of backgrounds, and there are major differences in the way each country organizes its programs. The UK, Germany, Russia and Japan all have major polar research institutes, which provide most of the scientists and the support staff for their stations. Other countries, such as the US, Italy, New Zealand, Sweden, Argentina, Chile and Brazil, draw most of their scientists from universities, contracting support systems either from civilian or military operators. Australia and Norway have a hybrid system, with a research institute that runs the logistics and provides a limited number of scientists; the balance of researchers come from universities. Two countries, the Netherlands and Belgium, possess neither stations nor ships, but instead buy places for their scientists on expeditions organized by other countries.

In December 1990 Germany's Georg von Neumayer station was staffed by the first all-women group to winter in Antarctica.

Some scientists using an air link into stations, such as McMurdo or Rothera, may spend as little as a month in Antarctica, but there are personnel at British and Russian stations who may spend up to two years on the continent without a break. Wintering in a small community, completely cut off from the rest of the world, can be a profound experience and often produces lifelong friendships.

For a long time, Antarctic stations were seen as a male preserve, a historical hangover from the days of Amundsen, Scott and Byrd. All that has changed, with women assuming important roles at all levels in a station's organization, including base commander and the leadership of scientific teams. Most stations are still predominantly staffed by men, especially where the support personnel are supplied by the military, but women have comprised nearly half the population at McMurdo in recent years.

For those who are in Antarctica for a long period, especially over winter, a variety of activities occupies their time. Apart from the work programs, there are quite separate opportunities to develop hobbies, acquire new skills, and learn to ski and travel over snow. Midwinter is a special time for all overwintering staff, when social life and parties take precedence over work. The sun is below the horizon for many stations and all of the encampments have been cut off from the rest of the world for months. Some stations even continue the tradition started by Scott and Shackleton of preparing a 'Midwinter Book,' with poems, paintings and photographs contributed by station members.

For many science and support staff, going to Antarctica is an opportunity to visit perhaps the least-disturbed part of the world, to take part in their own adventure and to go where few have gone before. Others are motivated by their interest in science and by the unique features of Antarctica and its surrounding seas. And some are attracted by the extra pay that they get while in Antarctica. Regardless of their reasons, they all experience the same magic.

THE SOUTHERN OCEAN

The stormy waters of the Southern Ocean encircle Antarctica in a continuous ring of mainly eastward-flowing water. This water comprises 10%

of the world's oceans, and as well as connecting the Atlantic, Pacific and Indian Oceans, it also isolates the continent from warmer waters. The Antarctic Circumpolar Current is the world's largest current, with an average rate of flow four times greater than the Gulf Stream.

One of our major interests in the Southern Ocean arises from its influence on the global climate. The region where the cold Antarctic water meets the warmer waters of the northern oceans is called the Antarctic Convergence, or Polar Front. The seas south of this contain the coldest and densest water in the world. This water, called Antarctic Bottom Water, is formed as seawater sinks to the ocean floor when ice shelves melt. It then moves along the ocean floor into the northern hemisphere, where it adds oxygen and reduces the deep-water temperature of these seas to less than 2°C. This cooling effect on tropical and temperate seas is an important feature of the world's heat balance. Any major changes in the energy transferred by these currents could have dramatic effects on the climates of countries in the northern hemisphere that are warmed by the Gulf Stream.

Several countries have put current meters on the seafloor around Antarctica to provide data on these deep-water movements. This is part of the World Ocean Current Experiment, which is attempting to measure current patterns for all the oceans in order to improve existing computer models for predicting climate change.

Tides are another focus of oceanographic research. In the late 19th century, oceanographers realized that tides were different in different oceans. It has always been more difficult to measure tides in icy waters because the ice destroys the gauges. However, a network of robust gauges, which often report their data via satellite, has been installed at various Antarctic stations. This provides information on how the ocean level is changing, which is of great interest to those living in coastal communities all over the world.

Existing data suggests that the average world sea level has risen by 10cm in the last century due to the thermal expansion of seawater as it warms up, and to the melting of valley glaciers and the edge of the Greenland ice sheet. During that time, the Antarctic ice sheet is believed to have remained roughly stable. It appears that sea level will continue rising by 1mm to 2mm per year, without any extra contribution from the Antarctic. Even minor melting of the Antarctic ice cap will significantly increase the rate of rise in sea level.

ANTARCTIC MARINE LIFE

The very cold water of the Southern Ocean allows more oxygen to dissolve in the sea, which is advantageous for marine life. This – with the upwelling of currents that bring nutrients from the seabed to feed microscopic algae at the surface, and the seasonal formation of sea ice – is the key factor controlling life in the Southern Ocean.

For more information about marine animals in the Antarctic, see p105.

In this marine food chain, the microscopic algae (or plankton) provide food for krill, which in turn are eaten by fish, whales, seals and birds. There are some other diet preferences – eg leopard seals eat penguins, sperm whales eat squid and seals eat fish – but despite this, the food web is remarkably simple when compared with other oceans. Although a tremendous diversity of organisms lives on the Southern Ocean seabed (benthic species), only a limited range of fish inhabits the water column (pelagic species).

A great deal of research is being carried out on seals, birds and terrestrial plants, but the major focus of current studies is the marine ecosystem. To undertake such research requires expensive infrastructure: icebreaking research vessels, scuba-diving facilities, laboratories at research stations and access to satellite data. This high cost has helped to promote international research cruises, such as those by the German vessel *Polarstern*, in which expenses are shared between several countries.

The importance of being able to work anywhere in the Southern Ocean has prompted several countries to make huge investments in modern research vessels capable of operating in sea ice. Some examples that you might see around the Antarctic (besides *Polarstern*) include the US's *Nathaniel B Palmer*, Britain's *James Clark Ross*, Australia's *Aurora Australis*, Japan's *Shirase* and Argentina's *Irizar*.

Birds

Antarctic birds are spectacular – in size, number and habit. Many are very tame, making them excellent research subjects. Their total dependence on the sea for food, the bizarre breeding habits of some species and their unusual ecological adaptations are of great interest to ornithologists. Among the birds, penguins and albatrosses are favorite research subjects.

The initial requirements for studying penguins and albatrosses are to record their breeding behavior, rates of growth and diet. All the species return to the same nesting sites each year, so it's easy to mark individual birds with numbered leg rings when they are chicks and follow them through their lives. Analysis of stomach contents of adults when they return to feed their chicks gives information on diet, while daily weighing of the chicks provides growth rates.

More complex questions – Where are the adults getting their food? When do they find it? How much energy do they use searching for it? – can be answered with the help of modern technology in the form of electronic devices attached to the birds. A tiny satellite transmitter on a bird's back can report on its position, while a small tube on its leg can collect data on the depth and timing of its dives for food. Even the oxygen consumption required for swimming or flying can be measured automatically. Back at the albatross colony, the chick sits on an electronic-replica nest, which weighs the little bird automatically every 10 minutes, avoiding the disturbance caused by handling. From this data, the weight of each meal and the growth of the chick can be calculated very accurately. The latest artificial nests are so sensitive that they even detect rain by the increase in the wet chick's weight!

'The latest artificial nests are so sensitive that they even detect rain by the increase in the wet chick's weight!'

The increasing number of banded birds has resulted in being able to calculate when birds first breed and the success of individuals in raising chicks, as well as pinpointing the origins of birds found dead. Annual monitoring of the breeding success of penguins is undertaken at a number of sites to measure the effects of fishing on the marine ecosystem. If too many fish or krill are caught, there won't be enough to feed the chicks. This monitoring program is a key contribution to the work of the Convention for the Conservation of Antarctic Marine Living Resources (CCAMLR), which sets limits on catches of fish, squid and krill for the Southern Ocean to ensure that fishing doesn't damage bird and seal populations.

Seals

Six species of seals are found in the Antarctic, and another three inhabit the sub-Antarctic islands. Probably no other group of animals hasattracted such a wide and detailed range of legislation. There is the special international Convention for the Conservation of Antarctic Seals, and three species – the fur seal, southern elephant seal and the Ross seal – are the only animals given special protection under the Antarctic Treaty. Such large animals at the top of the marine food chain pose exciting research questions.

Until recently, for example, very little was known about the life of elephant seals at sea, although their mating behavior on land is well understood. Again, the use of satellite transmitters and other electronic equipment has provided remarkable data: while at sea, elephant seals spend almost 90% of the time submerged, making dives of up to two hours' duration and reaching depths of more than 975m. How they manage this is the subject of wide-ranging physiological research, mainly by British scientists at South Georgia and US scientists (working on Weddell seals) at McMurdo.

> **'Seals' blubber and milk has shown an accumulation of pesticides and other organic poisons, transported from the northern hemisphere'**

Harder to determine is the diet of each seal. The latest research analyzes seal feces to identify its prey from hard parts, such as fish bones, or uses unique biochemical markers associated with particular prey types.

Long-term studies by Australian, British, French and US scientists aim to determine if seal populations are increasing or declining. For those species that breed on land, pups can be counted, and for some studies individual animals have been marked with flipper tags. For those that breed on ice, such as crabeaters, even pup-counting is difficult. Efforts continue using helicopters and icebreakers, to allow scientists to penetrate the pack ice when the maximum number of animals is likely to be visible.

Sampling of seals' blubber and milk has shown a slow but steady accumulation of pesticides and other organic poisons, transported south from the industries and agriculture of the northern hemisphere. As yet their long-term effects on seals are unknown.

Whales

The most productive research period on whales coincided with commercial whaling, and the data collected was used by the International Whaling Commission to set quotas. Since the banning of commercial whaling, almost all whale research in the Antarctic has ceased. While there are still occasional attempts to survey areas in order to estimate population numbers, most whale research is now undertaken in more congenial areas, such as Baja California. The Japanese and the Norwegians continue to hunt a few whales, usually minkes, each year under a rule that allows the limited collection of whales for scientific purposes, although many countries object to this.

Fish

The first fish from Antarctica were collected in 1840 during Ross' expedition. Since then, a great deal of research has been undertaken to establish the diversity, life histories and extent of the fish stocks. Commercial fishing began in the Southern Ocean when the first Soviet vessels arrived in the mid-1960s. Fisheries are now regulated by CCAMLR.

About 200 species of fish have been recorded south of the Antarctic Convergence. The main deepwater species are not restricted to the Antarctic, but the coastal species are. Although this latter group has representatives from 15 families, over 60% of the species and over 90% of the individuals belong to just four families, making Antarctic fish very different from those of other oceans.

Most research has concentrated on the two most abundant groups: the Antarctic cod *(Nototheniidae)* and the ice fish *(Channichthyidae)*. Initial interest focused on the evolution of the groups, their ability to survive in icy waters, their reproduction and growth rates and their population age structure. These last areas of research naturally also interest commercial fishermen.

These fish resist freezing, thanks to protein-based antifreezes in their blood that prevent ice crystals from forming in their tissues. The studies analyzing this freezing resistance, which were pioneered largely by US scientists, are of great commercial interest, relating to the way in which freezing changes the texture of food – ice-cream manufacturers, in particular, have taken notice.

The unusual physiology of the ice fish, which have no hemoglobin in their blood to carry oxygen, has spurred scientists from France, Italy, New Zealand and the US to try to learn what mechanisms evolved to take the hemoglobin's place. We now know that oxygen is carried in the ice fish's blood plasma, but this has only 10% of the oxygen-carrying capacity of fish blood containing hemoglobin. To make up for their lack of hemoglobin, ice fish have more blood, a larger heart, larger blood vessels and more gill surface area, and can even exchange oxygen through their tails.

All Antarctic fish grow slowly, with most coastal species requiring five to seven years before they can breed. This is of great importance when deciding sustainable catch limits. Unfortunately, when fishing started in the Southern Ocean, this was not recognized and too many fish were caught, endangering some species. Most of the current research is concerned with making more accurate estimates of growth and population size.

Squid

Little is known about the biology of most species of squid. They seem to grow much faster than Antarctic fish and vary greatly in their adult size (ranging from only 2cm in length up to 20m) and most appear to be cannibals. They have several defense mechanisms, the best known being the black 'ink' squirted out to blind or confuse predators.

'Squid have several defense mechanisms, the best known being the black 'ink' squirted out to blind or confuse predators'

Because they can move very quickly in the water and have excellent vision, squid are difficult to catch. Therefore, much of our knowledge of them has come from those found in the stomachs of fish, birds, seals and whales. Several researchers are now attempting to collect basic data on squid by fishing for them. Questions of particular interest are when and where squid breed, what they eat and the population size of each species.

Squid are also being caught commercially, mainly by boats from Japan and Taiwan. Unfortunately, many squid species have only a one-year life cycle, making them sensitive to overfishing. Although most studies so far have been on the squid stocks around the Falkland Islands, there is every reason to suppose that there are significant populations further south.

Krill

Zooplankton are the tiny sea animals that graze on algae, or phytoplankton. In Antarctic waters, zooplankton are dominated by krill, the single most important food of whales, seals and birds – especially penguins.

Hundreds of research papers have reported on every aspect of krill's life cycle and biology. Many of these papers have obvious commercial uses, describing how to find krill, how to estimate the size of a krill swarm using acoustics and how best to process krill for various uses. Although relatively easy to catch once a swarm has been identified, krill have proved costly to process and difficult to market.

Krill possess some of the most powerful protein-digesting enzymes ever found, so they must be processed very rapidly after catching or their tissues begin to break down, turning black and mushy. They become unfit for human consumption after three hours on deck and unfit for cattle feed after 10 hours. Krill also have high levels of fluorine in their outer shell, making them toxic unless the shell is completely removed. Japan and Russia have perfected equipment for peeling and processing krill rapidly: frozen blocks of krill meat are made for human consumption, while krill paste is a high-protein additive for pig or cattle feed.

The original estimates of the available stock of krill were very large, and some hoped it would provide a cheap, protein-rich food for the world's famine-plagued regions. But catching and processing costs have made krill a first-world food rather than a third-world food so far. However, a growing demand for fish food for aquaculture systems worldwide may change this and bring new pressure on krill stocks.

Interest in krill research continues, with projects being conducted by Australia, Brazil, Chile, Germany, Korea, South Africa, the UK and the US. We still need to know more about krill populations within the winter pack ice, such as how much of the Southern Ocean algae is eaten by krill, how long krill live (they're difficult to age) and the krill population of the Southern Ocean. Even krill behavior is inadequately described, although there has been some success recently using video cameras lowered off the side of a ship into a krill swarm.

Algae

The productivity of all Antarctic ecosystems rests on the photosynthesis of the microscopic algae floating in the upper layers of the Southern Ocean. The upwelling of cold, nutrient-rich water provides ideal conditions for the growth of plankton, which numbers more than 100 species in the Southern Ocean. When a ship is breaking its way through sea ice, the floes often turn over and show brownish bands or discoloration underneath. This is a film of ice algae, grazed during the winter by krill.

'Some scientists have even suggested that iron is in such short supply that we should consider stimulating carbon uptake by dumping iron in the ocean'

Phytoplankton contain chlorophyll, which can be detected by satellite. Recent research shows that the highest concentrations of phytoplankton coincide with high concentrations of nutrients, especially iron. The plankton takes up carbon from carbon dioxide dissolved in the water, and, when it dies, takes the carbon down into the sediments. It can therefore be seen as a 'sink' for carbon. Given the present interest in increasing levels of carbon dioxide and global warming, this finding has prompted considerable research on how much carbon can be taken out of the atmosphere by the phytoplankton and what, if anything, can be done to increase the rate. Some scientists have even suggested that iron is in such short supply that we should consider stimulating carbon uptake by dumping iron in the ocean. So far, experiments have not demonstrated that this would work.

Of equal concern for global warming is the production by phytoplankton of a compound called dimethyl sulfide (DMS). This compound is believed to form aerosols when it leaves the sea, and these aerosol droplets promote cloud formation. The subsequent increase in cloudiness increases the amount of radiation reflected back into space and this in turn leads to atmospheric cooling. This mechanism would therefore act to slow down global warming. We know too little about the whole DMS cycle, but what we do know suggests that the Southern Ocean may play a very important role in DMS production.

The annual increase in springtime ultraviolet levels has stimulated research on its effects on phytoplankton. Historical data derived from the analysis of sediments suggests that overall there has been no significant change, yet experiments have shown that some species are very sensitive to UV, while others, such as diatoms, are able to protect themselves by producing protective pigments.

Many inshore areas of Antarctica have a good covering of seaweeds (macroalgae) below the depth at which the scouring effects of winter ice would remove them. Surprisingly little research has been done on seaweeds, with most of the recent work being done by Dutch and German scientists. Even less is known about giant kelp, a seaweed found around sub-Antarctic islands and the Falkland Islands. The large, brown, straplike fronds of the biggest kelp *(Macrocystis pyrifera)* are known to grow at a rate of 30cm per day during the summer, despite the low water temperature.

Seafloor Communities

Very little is yet known about the species that inhabit the seafloor around Antarctica. These communities are called the benthos, and are as rich in plants and animals as a tropical coral reef. They comprise Antarctica's true indigenous flora and fauna, adapted to life in a cold ocean over tens of millions of years. Many species may be limited to the cold waters south of the Antarctic Convergence but some scientists have suggested that species throughout the world's deep oceans may have come from the Antarctic in the Antarctic Bottom Water. Nearly every time a deep-sea sample is brought up, it includes some species new to science, or one that has been collected only once before.

'Nearly every time a deep-sea sample is brought up, it includes some species new to science'

The annual formation of sea ice has a strong effect on much of the benthos, whose food supply consists mainly of algal cells falling to the bottom of the seafloor as they die. In winter, there is only ice at the surface, so seafloor organisms must live for long periods with little food – or use a much wider range of foods than benthos in other oceans. Not surprisingly, this means that they grow slowly and usually reproduce slowly.

Current marine research increasingly takes place onboard ships or in aquariums at stations. This involves US scientists at Palmer and McMurdo, German and Argentine scientists at Jubany, British scientists at Rothera, Korean scientists at King Sejong and Italian scientists at Mario Zucchelli, with ship-based contributions from China and Spain. Video cameras and diving observations are providing details of the structure of the communities on both rocky and muddy bottoms. The greatest potential for research probably lies in studies of the biochemistry and physiology of benthos. Some species, such as sponges, may have the same sorts of antimicrobial defense chemicals that warm-water sponges do, and these could possibly be of pharmaceutical interest. A better understanding of all these fields might also help in biotechnology developments.

ANTARCTIC TERRESTRIAL LIFE

Plants & Microbes

With only 0.4% of Antarctica free of permanent snow and ice, there is not much habitat for plant communities. In addition, any new species spreading to Antarctica must not only cross the Southern Ocean but also hit one of the snow-free patches in order to survive. Under these circumstances, it is surprising that Antarctica is home to at least 200 species of lichens, over 100 species of mosses and liverworts, more than 30 species of macrofungi, two species of flowering plants and many species of algae. The relationships between these plants and those on the surrounding continents have interested botanists for almost 150 years, and it is only now that the relationships are finally becoming clear.

Definitive guides to both lichens and mosses are being published within the next few years, based on work by British, Norwegian and Polish botanists. These will not only show the distribution of species in and around the Antarctic, but will also provide data on whether all the species spread to the continent after the last glaciation or whether some survived on isolated mountain peaks. Meanwhile, research continues on how these lichens and mosses survive the extreme cold and desiccation of the Antarctic winter. Scientists from Australia, Britain, Germany, the Netherlands, New Zealand and Spain all have ongoing studies.

One of the most unusual plant habitats on earth is in Antarctica. In areas formed from large-grained sandstone, most obviously in Victoria Land, the outer skin of the rocks themselves has been colonized by plants. These plants live within the rock, growing between the sand grains and forming separate layers of algae, fungus and lichen. Just enough light penetrates the rock for photosynthesis to occur for a short period each year when meltwater is available. Acids excreted by the plants eventually dissolve the rock and the outer skin breaks off, leaving an obvious dark mark where the algal cells remain. The growth rate of these plants is so slow that some may well be many thousands of years old.

Very large specimens of lichens and banks of moss more than a meter deep can be seen in some parts of Antarctica, especially in the Antarctic Peninsula region. Because they grow quite slowly, some of the lichens have been estimated at more than 500 years old, while radiocarbon dating shows the base of the large moss banks to be as much as 7000 years old. Both are extremely vulnerable to disturbance.

It has been obvious for a long time that microbial communities are important in Antarctica, and there is increasing interest in how they survive in such inhospitable habitats. In several places, glacier margins are retreating, revealing bare rock and soil. This is what happened at the end of the last ice age in temperate regions, yet we know little about the initial colonization by microbes that eventually developed into the grasslands and forests of today. Using new technologies, it is possible to investigate the earliest stages of the colonization of these areas and to develop a better understanding of how complex communities develop.

A joint program among several countries (Argentina, Australia, Italy, New Zealand, South Africa, the UK and the US) is now studying what is being carried to Antarctica and the sub-Antarctic islands by wind, how these new species establish themselves and what the effects of increased ultraviolet radiation are on survival in terrestrial communities.

Invertebrates

You'll have to look hard to find any insects in Antarctica, but you might see a springtail jumping among vegetation or find a group of tiny mites under a stone. Despite their size, these insects, and the slightly larger ones on the sub-Antarctic islands, are the subject of much research by US, British, French, Italian and South African scientists.

'Many insects are able to make antifreezes, which allows them to survive temperatures as low as -28°C'

How do insects survive extreme cold, a lack of water and oxygen, and high salt levels in the soil? Many are able to make antifreezes, which allows them to survive temperatures as low as -28°C. When frozen into ice, some can put their metabolism into a special state to survive the lack of oxygen. They also show a remarkable ability to survive desiccation without long-term damage to their cells. The lack of species diversity makes these invertebrate communities among the simplest anywhere, so they provide ideal models for understanding how ecosystems work.

LAKES & STREAMS

Most people do not expect to see lakes and streams in Antarctica. Yet there are many ponds and lakes scattered around the ice-free areas, ranging from Don Juan Pond, which contains the saltiest solution on earth (and does not freeze even at -55°C), to small lakes that have almost no nutrients in them. The lakes are ice-covered for most or all of the year and have very limited flora and fauna. The most developed animal is a small shrimp and the most complex plant is an aquatic moss. Many of the lakes are dominated by microbial communities.

It is the simplicity of the systems that attracted scientists, especially since they could choose a lake with just the right chemical characteristics to study. Alot of work has concentrated on the lakes in the Taylor and Wright Valleys (mainly by US, Japanese and New Zealand scientists), at the Vestfold Hills (Australian), at the Bunger Hills (Russian) and at Signy Island (British). Some of the saline water bodies are effectively sterile, with just a few bacteria living in them. In other cases, nutrients from the surrounding catchment have allowed the steady development of the aquatic ecosystem.

For more information about subglacial lakes in Antarctica, see the boxed text on p268.

Lake Vanda in Wright Valley has been intensively investigated for many years. It consists of two ecosystems: the top 45cm (beneath 4m-thick ice) is nutrient-poor freshwater; below that is saline water four times as salty as seawater, with a lake-bottom temperature of 25°C. The two layers support quite different microbial communities.

In more nutrient-rich lakes and in those where there is significant meltwater running in from the surrounding area, there are new research opportunities. The sediment at the bottom of a lake contains a record of how the lake has changed over a period as long as 10,000 years. These lake sediments are valuable in determining the history of Antarctica's recent climate.

GEOLOGY, GEOMORPHOLOGY & PALEONTOLOGY

Even though less than 1% of Antarctica's rock is accessible for direct examination, geologists are very interested in the continent. It forms one of the earth's seven major rock plates, and its margins are constantly changing, making it one of the best places in the world to study the movements of the earth's crust. Indeed, understanding the connections between all the southern continents, how they broke apart and why, continues to fascinate many geoscientists. It also contains one of the best climatic archives of the past, with terrestrial sediments covering the last 200,000 years and marine sediments covering millions of years, as well as even older areas of ancient continental rocks.

Minerals

Are there vast deposits of precious metals and ores beneath the Antarctic ice sheet? Are there huge basins of gas and oil under the Weddell and Ross Seas? Such ideas were the focus of a great deal of diplomatic activity in the 1980s, as governments struggled to agree how the exploitation of the Antarctic could be controlled. Now, the Antarctic Treaty's Protocol on Environmental Protection prohibits any mining or drilling for at least 50 years.

In fact, there are no good data to show that hydrocarbon-rich basins exist in the Antarctic. The geological maps that indicate mineral outcrops merely show where mineral deposits have been identified. None of the minerals are of economic value, since the expense of mining and transporting them to markets would be prohibitive. But Antarctic minerals are still being investigated by geologists, who are not looking for economic value but rather are working to determine how the minerals were formed and what they can tell us about geological processes.

Fossils

Coal beds and plant fossils in the Transantarctic Mountains were reported by both Shackleton and Scott, clearly indicating that the Antarctic was not always covered with ice. Since Shackleton and Scott's time, much more fossil evidence of preglacial periods has been uncovered. Paleontology has been undertaken by geologists of many countries, with those from Argentina, Australia, Chile, New Zealand, Poland, the UK and the US making especially important contributions.

Fossils provide evidence of the connections between the parts of the ancient supercontinent Gondwana, give indirect information about the changes in Antarctic climate over millions of years and offer an insight into the evolution of present Antarctic species.

Petrified wood is widely distributed in Antarctica, sometimes in pieces as long as 20m. The trunks and leaf impressions show that about 80 million years ago the climate was temperate, and distinct annual growth rings show that it was also seasonal. In some places, ferns and other woodland species are also preserved in great detail.

Many deposits contain fossil plants and fossil pollen, but fossils of land animals are much less common. Material that appears to be from carnivorous dinosaurs about 200 million years old has been found in the Transantarctic Mountains, and parts of Cretaceous plant-eating dinosaurs about 75 million years old have been unearthed on James Ross Island off the northern tip of the Antarctic Peninsula, but no complete fossils have been recovered. Marine deposits containing fish, mollusks and many other types of marine invertebrates provide a great deal of information on the evolution of these groups in the Southern Ocean.

In fossil sequences in various parts of the world, there are sudden, major changes in the species recorded at what is called the Cretaceous/Tertiary boundary (about 65 million years ago). Many theories have been put forward to explain this event, since it appears that it caused mass extinctions. The current theory is that a huge meteorite collided with earth, producing such massive climate changes that many species couldn't survive. The evidence cited for this is a high concentration of the rare element iridium, which can be found associated with particular layers in sedimentary rocks. Seymour Island, off the east coast of the Antarctic Peninsula, is one of the best sites in the world for studying the Cretaceous/Tertiary boundary.

Antarctic Landforms

The study of landforms is called geomorphology. In the Antarctic, geomorphologists have mainly been concerned with the effects of the ice sheet on the underlying rock, as well as the study of glacial deposits, the remains of old beaches left when the sea level fell and the formation of patterned ground.

Glaciers have an important effect on the rock beneath them. As the ice flows slowly toward the sea, it grinds up the rock and produces a suspension of fine yellowish or white particles that flow out of the glacier front with the meltwater. This 'glacial flour' runs off into the sea to form sediments. On their way down the valleys, the glaciers may also pick up boulders and weathered rock from the valley sides or outcrops. These, together with glacial flour, are often deposited at the end of the glacier as it melts and retreats, forming mounds called moraines. Where there is a seasonal cycle of melt and retreat of the glacier snout, a series of annual moraines may form, providing clear evidence of the rate of retreat.

Global sea level rises and falls with changes in ice cover. There are relics of previous sea levels all around Antarctica: old beaches of shingle, sand and shells that mark the height of previous wave action. Some of these shells have been dated and mark the timing of major changes in the extent of the ice sheet over the last 5000 years.

Patterned ground is found in polar and mountain regions all over the world. These are the polygons, circles, stripes and sometimes even hummocks that can be seen throughout the Antarctic. They are formed by alternate freezing and thawing of water in the soil, which produces lateral sorting of coarse and fine particles. A stone polygon, with its border of large rocks and center of fine particles, is believed to result from the process of frost heave. This usually happens at night when ice crystals form in the soil and push up the large rocks. When the sun melts the crystals the following morning, the rocks roll down to one side. This, repeated many times over many years, produces the polygons. In extremely dry areas such as the Dry Valleys, a related process called ice wedging produces similar features.

Soils

With less than 1% of Antarctica free of snow and ice, and with very little vegetation, how can there be any soils (mixtures of weathered rock particles, salts and organic matter) on the continent? Antarctic soils are almost without organic matter, are very dry and have a high salt content. They are primitive soils, and as such have been the subject of detailed research, mainly by New Zealand scientists in Victoria Land, by British scientists on Signy Island and by researchers from several countries working on the sub-Antarctic islands.

On the continent, all soils contain permafrost, which means they're permanently frozen just below the surface. The breakdown of the rocks into soil particles is due to damage caused by ice crystals, and to chemical changes caused by high salt concentrations. Scientists working on soils in the Dry Valleys have been able to show that some of them are at least five million years old, giving a possible date for the retreat of ice from these valleys.

There are other unusual soils on some of the islands around the Antarctic Peninsula. These are made from accumulations of dead moss and in some places may be nearly 1.5m thick. Because of the permafrost, the dead moss cannot decay, so these peat banks simply keep getting thicker. Radiocarbon analyses of these banks give ages of up to 7000 years. On the sub-Antarctic islands, with their much warmer climate, the soils have no permafrost and are better developed, resembling those found in more temperate mountain areas.

Meteorites

Meteorites are a major source of information about the early history of our solar system. Most of our knowledge about meteorites comes from analysis of those found in Antarctica, which acts as a huge meteorite collector and preserver. The first Antarctic meteorite was found by Australians in 1912, but serious collecting did not begin until 1969. Since then, more than 10,000 have been discovered, mainly by Japanese and US scientists. The meteorites are generally found in the 'blue-ice' areas of Antarctica, which are expanses of old ice held back by mountains and kept free of snow by constant winds. These areas of sublimating ice allow the meteorites to gradually 'rise' to the surface. The Allan Hills region and the Yamato Mountains have been the most prolific areas so far.

See the boxed text on p258 for more information about meteorite recovery in Antarctica.

ICE ON LAND & SEA

The Ice Sheet

Antarctica's large mass of snow and ice contains about 85% of the world's fresh water and acts as a cold sink for the entire southern hemisphere. The Antarctic ice sheet is constantly changing, with snow falling and icebergs breaking off. Small changes in the ice sheet's volume could cause a catastrophic rise of global sea level. We need to be able to detect small changes in order to provide adequate warning of any such rise.

Many years of effort have gone into trying to determine the volume of the ice sheet. The principal method is to record the top and bottom of the ice sheet using airborne radar. There are now maps showing the topography of the underlying rocks, which allow a rough calculation of total volume. The errors, however, are still considerable and are a result of difficulties in deciding the exact thickness of the ice from radar echoes and in mapping the changes in thickness frequently enough at a continental level. This will change when new satellite instruments come into use, allowing the surface to be measured to an accuracy of a few centimeters.

Researching the History of Our Climate

Snow is a treasure trove of information to a glaciologist. When a snowflake falls, it brings with it valuable details about the state of the atmosphere at the time it was formed. As it is slowly compressed and recrystallized under the snow of later years, it forms a historical record. The present interest in global change makes any information about the earth's past climates valuable for modeling purposes, so a great effort has been made to collect ice cores from some of the oldest and deepest parts of the ice sheet.

Drilling is a difficult and highly skilled activity, extending over several years. The ice sheet is always moving, so the drill hole is continually being bent and squeezed shut. Major cores have been obtained by Russia, France and the US. The deepest core so far has come from the joint French-Italian Concordia station and is 3200m deep – with an estimated age of at least 950,000 years at the bottom.

Ice cores can reveal patterns of mean air temperature, evidence of major volcanic eruptions and, by analysis of the air trapped in ice bubbles, data on the composition of the atmosphere. To make these useful, the levels in the ice core must be dated. No single method works, so glaciologists count annual layers, date the decay rates of natural isotopes and model the changes in ice flow with age.

Since there is still disagreement about the effects of the present increase in carbon dioxide on climate change, the historical record from ice cores is of considerable importance. The data so far indicate that concentrations of carbon dioxide were reduced throughout the last ice age and increased sharply as the ice melted, with a 30% increase in just a few thousand years. The carbon-dioxide concentration remained stable for the next 10,000 years before beginning to increase again about 200 years ago.

Analysis of the ice cores' microparticles will reveal if they come from dust storms associated with more arid conditions or from volcanic eruptions. Analysis of the salt types and concentrations can even indicate which volcano erupted.

The Record of Global Pollution

Since industrial development began, increasing amounts of pollutants have been escaping into the atmosphere. Over the last 200 years, emissions of toxic heavy metals have increased dramatically. Nuclear tests and accidents have released radioactive fallout that has also spread worldwide. Antarctica is remote from all of these sources, but all of the pollutants can be found in snow and ice cores. The continent thus provides a global baseline against which we can measure the damage inflicted on the rest of the planet.

Research has shown that while lead levels in Greenland's snow have increased 100-fold in the last 200 years, there has been little change in Antarctica. Data for other toxic metals, such as cadmium, zinc and mercury, are not yet complete enough to indicate any trends. Nuclear fallout shows up clearly in the ice cores, and is linked to datable events. There is, however, no evidence of high sulfur dioxide, which, as 'acid rain,' has caused so much damage in the northern hemisphere.

Floating Ice Shelves

Satellite data allows glaciologists to monitor not only when a giant iceberg breaks off one of Antarctica's ice shelves, but also to measure its slow progress away from the continent. Other research on the ice shelves concentrates on determining flow rates to see how quickly ice is moving off the continent, and how rapidly the shelf ice thins from the melting of its underside. The long-term objective is to provide researchers with a computer model that will allow the loss of ice to the Southern Ocean to be accurately predicted.

Sea Ice

Antarctic sea-ice cover varies from a minimum of 4 million sq km in February to a maximum of 20 million sq km in September. This huge seasonal change has enormous repercussions, since the ice alters the exchange of heat, moisture and momentum between the sea and the air, and the marine ecosystem has to adapt to lower temperatures and a lack of light under the ice. Developing models of the way sea ice affects energy transfers between the sea and air is a major concern for several countries, including Finland, the UK and the US.

The ice cover, even in September at the height of Antarctica's winter, is not complete, however. Satellite pictures show that areas of open water, called polynyas, occur in the same places deep in the pack ice each year. We know little about these polynyas, as only the strongest icebreakers can penetrate them, but what data we do have suggests that they are very important in energy transfers between the sea and the atmosphere. It seems likely that they play an important role for seals and whales in the winter, providing a breathing space hundreds of kilometers from the open sea.

'Polynyas an important role for seals and whales in the winter, providing a breathing space hundreds of kilometers from the open sea'

The sea ice is considered one of the most important research areas, for several reasons. The big General Circulation Models, which attempt to predict the magnitude of global warming, show important discrepancies in their predictions for the Antarctic. To improve the predictions, we need much better data on sea ice, and much of this is now being obtained by special instruments aboard satellites. These also allow us to determine ice movement and ice type deep within the pack ice, and help provide more accurate estimates of the area covered by the ice.

To make sure the satellite data are verified, however, research needs to be undertaken inside the pack ice. In 1992 a very successful drifting ice camp was established in the eastern Weddell Sea to study features of the summer sea ice. Several countries are showing an increased interest in drifting buoys, which will give more information about ice movement within the pack ice, as well as meteorological and oceanographic data, without requiring a ship to enter the pack ice, where it could be crushed and sunk.

Sea ice was also the focus of a major research program called Coastal and Shelf Ecology of the Antarctic Sea Ice Zone. This project brought together biologists, physicists, chemists and oceanographers in an attempt to understand this rapidly changing and fragile habitat. This was a big program, concluded in 2004, with contributions from most Antarctic countries. The scientists looked at six key questions: What role does ice play in the coastal marine ecosystem? How do Antarctic communities differ from those in other oceans? What factors determine the patterns of production and nutrient cycling in these ecosystems? How are the organisms adapted to low temperatures? What is the interaction between land and sea in the coastal zone? And, how are these coastal communities impacted by human activities?

WEATHER FORECASTING

The countries surrounding the Southern Ocean have great interest in the meteorology of Antarctica. The weather systems that constantly circle the continent drive storms across the Southern Ocean and beyond, while the seasonal formation and melting of sea ice has a major effect on southern-hemisphere weather. Since before the International Geophysical Year of 1957–58, all Antarctic stations have tried to collect daily meteorological observations and broadcast them to surrounding countries to help in weather forecasting. At most stations, you will see a small white meteorological screen housing standard instruments.

But stations were not located on the basis of where it would be useful to collect meteorological data, and for a long time there were huge holes in the data maps for Antarctic weather. Now those holes are being filled, as more and more automatic weather stations are carefully positioned. The majority of these stations belong to the US, but they are sited and maintained by the cooperative efforts of several other nations.

ATMOSPHERIC SCIENCE

Atmospheric science is an expensive and active field of Antarctic research. Global warming and ozone destruction have made the study of atmospheric gases a major discipline, and the Antarctic has an important role in this research. There are also unique features of the invisible magnetic fields that surround the earth that can be most easily investigated in Antarctica.

'A paper published in 1985 provided such alarming evidence of the increasing rate of ozone destruction that it resulted in a worldwide agreement to ban chlorofluorocarbons'

Atmospheric Chemistry & Ozone Depletion

Probably the most famous science project ever undertaken in Antarctica is the monitoring of stratospheric ozone at Britain's Halley station in the Weddell Sea. A paper published in the international scientific journal *Nature* in 1985 provided such alarming evidence of the increasing rate of ozone destruction that it resulted in a worldwide agreement to ban the principal culprits, chlorofluorocarbons (CFCs). It also stimulated a massive increase in research on polar chemistry.

One of the direct results of this research was the discovery that CFCs are not the only chemicals involved in ozone destruction. The destruction was found to be localized in stratospheric clouds formed from nitric acid and water. Discovering other chemical reactions involved has been a major concern of many countries, both in the Antarctic and in laboratories elsewhere. While the chemicals concerned are now fairly well agreed upon, there is still further work necessary to understand the reactions involved. This is especially important to ensure that the chemicals taking the place of CFCs in air-conditioning systems and refrigerators do not produce further ozone destruction.

A variety of approaches is now being used to make sure ozone data are as accurate as possible. Satellites stare down on the continent, reporting the concentrations of ozone as seen from above. Looking up from the ground, many countries use Dobson or Brewer spectrophotometers to monitor stratospheric ozone. Upward-pointing laser systems can also detect the formation of the stratospheric clouds in which ozone destruction occurs. There are even direct measurements of ozone obtained by launching hydrogen- or helium-filled balloons with detectors aboard.

For quite some time, the way in which ozone destruction took place was unknown, as the detailed structure of the cloud particles carrying the nitric acid remained only theoretical. Then balloons were sent up, carrying samplers that could not only catch the microscopic particles but also photograph them and transmit the images back to a ground station.

Now we have a much clearer picture of the whole complex cycle. During the Antarctic winter, a strong westerly circulation is established, which acts as a vortex, cutting the Antarctic stratosphere off from the rest of the atmosphere. Inside this vortex, the atmosphere cools to temperatures as low as -79°C and thin clouds are formed from aerosols, altering the chemical balance between the chlorine derived from the breakdown of the CFCs and other gases in the stratosphere. During this period it is dark, and it is not until the sun returns in spring that enough energy comes back to the atmosphere to begin the chemical reactions in which the chlorine, together with other chemicals, destroys the ozone. Although ozone destruction occurs mainly in the Antarctic, there is increasing evidence for intermittent destruction now in the Arctic.

Greenhouse Gases & Global Warming

Carbon dioxide is produced by all animals when they breathe and is taken up by plants during photosynthesis. It has the important property of absorbing heat from the surface of the earth, thus preventing it from being lost to space and causing the planet to cool. For this reason, carbon dioxide is called a 'greenhouse gas.' Both carbon dioxide and water vapor in the earth's atmosphere make the planet warm enough for life. Of course, too much of these greenhouse gases can cause too much heating of the atmosphere, which equates to what's been labeled 'global warming.' Burning fossil fuels produces a mixture of gases – and the principal one is carbon dioxide.

Agriculture, especially cattle raising and rice growing, produces another greenhouse gas called methane. Because of this, if you want to measure changes in greenhouse gases at a global level, you need a site as far away from industry and with as few animals and plants as possible. For this reason, the US chose the South Pole for global carbon-dioxide measurements in 1956. This series of measurements is still running and is perhaps one of the most important monitoring activities in the world.

Concentrations of other gases that may also be involved in global warming are also rising, and these have been added to the analyses at the South Pole. The measurements from the Pole provide the baseline for global changes in greenhouse gases and are extremely important in deciding what needs to be done to reduce global warming. Decisions on the continued unrestricted use of cars, the burning of coal and gas, and the production of waste gases by factories worldwide will all be influenced largely by projections based on this data. The sampling has now been extended to numerous other sites all over the world, providing independent checks on the rate of change.

GEOMAGNETISM

For physicists interested in what happens to earth's magnetic field, Antarctica is a special place. The magnetic field is invisible, but of considerable importance. The sun produces a continuous stream of electrically charged, high-energy particles. This flow is termed the 'solar wind,' and when it comes into contact with other particles or enters a magnetic field, its energy becomes channeled and discharged. The only visible signs of this discharge are the spectacular displays of aurora that can be seen at both poles as the particles from the sun collide with gas molecules in the ionosphere.

For a more detailed account of the aurora australis, see the boxed text on p236.

A less visible – but much more important – sign of the solar wind is interference with communications. Radio, TV, telephones and a variety of navigation systems are all dependent either on bouncing radio waves off charged particles in the atmosphere or on relaying messages via satellites. The crackling, fading or even complete failure of these signals means that there have been changes in the atmosphere – caused by the solar wind – that block the signals.

The peculiar structure of the magnetic field over Antarctica makes it the best place in the world to investigate how the sun's activities affect the ionosphere and to try and model these effects so that they can be predicted. To do this, the UK, Japan, France, Australia and South Africa have set up three radar systems looking toward the South Pole. The radars are similar to military systems used to look over the horizon to detect incoming missiles. They will utilize the overlap between the beams to create a 3-D picture of the ionosphere above the Pole.

The magnetic field around the earth has changed its polarity several times over geological periods. Measurements show that an area northwest of South Georgia has the world's most rapidly declining magnetic strength but nobody yet knows why – or what it means.

ASTRONOMY

In many parts of the world, air and light pollution makes studying the stars a problem, so astronomers have taken their telescopes to the tops of mountains on remote islands. Still, water vapor in the atmosphere makes it difficult to see certain types of stars. Telescopes mounted on satellites do not have this problem, but they are horrifyingly expensive. Antarctica provides the next best thing – at a much lower cost.

Some stars produce only infrared radiation, which we usually think of as invisible warmth. The amount of this radiation that reaches earth is infinitesimally small and, since water vapor absorbs it, even more is lost as it passes through the atmosphere. Antarctica's thin, dry, cold atmosphere makes it the best place on earth to detect infrared stars.

Another branch of astronomy has also been enthusiastically developed in the Antarctic. Research on the way in which the sun affects the earth has been going on for centuries. For a long time, it has been known that the sun pulsates, producing plumes of gas that shoot out into space. These events are obviously related to what is occurring inside the sun, but it has been difficult to find a way of discovering exactly what happens. A new branch of astronomy called helioseismography is making some progress. Using a special telescope, astronomers monitor the fluctuations in the size of the sun and its relationship to surface changes. Eventually, there will be enough data to extract the frequencies of various types of pulsing, but this is a difficult job since the frequencies produce about 10 million resonations! One scientist has likened the work to 'Trying to record the New York Philharmonic from the other side of a concrete wall, while a guy is using a jackhammer on the wall and someone is playing with the volume control; from an analysis of the measured frequencies, you then attempt to determine which instruments are being played!'

Searching for the Origins of the Universe

For more information about the IceCube project, see p283.

Antarctica is also playing its part in unraveling the mysteries of where the universe came from. It turns out to be the perfect place to study cosmic microwave background radiation, which is believed to be the remaining echo of the big bang. The very dry, cold conditions are ideal for scientists (mainly from Sweden and the US) to make measurements that should show whether there is a spatial structure to the background radiation, as predicted by some theories. IceCube is a large neutrino telescope being constructed in the Antarctic ice sheet near the South Pole. The IceCube detector will search for neutrinos from sources such as active galaxies and gamma-ray bursts from elsewhere in the solar system.

MEDICAL RESEARCH

Many people expect medical research in Antarctica to be about human resistance to low temperatures, but while there is continuing interest in this topic, it's not as important as others. After all, everyone tries hard to stay either in heated buildings or dressed in special clothing to ensure that they keep warm. The real opportunities in Antarctic medical research are the seasonal changes in the climate and the isolation experienced by station personnel during winter, which are similar to conditions on a space station.

Health Care

The length of time that people spend working in Antarctica varies greatly, from just a few months to over two years. All Antarctic station members must undergo stringent health checks before they're allowed to go south. Each country undertakes the checks in a different way, largely influenced by cultural attitudes toward health care. Some countries undertake psychological testing (Australia, New Zealand and France), while others require a wide range of chemical and physiological tests (Italy). India is investigating the value of yoga in promoting good health at its Antarctic stations. With the increasing movement of scientists between national programs, and the formation of large international teams, this could lead to considerable confusion, so the national programs are trying to agree on a standard minimum health check acceptable to all.

Endocrinology

The hormone melatonin is closely associated with regulating body rhythms. Shift workers and long-distance air travelers have difficulty in re-synchronizing their sleeping patterns because their pattern of melatonin secretion becomes disturbed. Obviously, a method for correcting jet lag or sleep disturbance is of great social and industrial importance.

See the boxed text on p306 for more details on Antarctic medicine.

The long Antarctic night removes the normal melatonin-secretion trigger – bright sunlight. Research has therefore concentrated on using bright-light treatment at specific times to bring the body rhythms back to a normal 24-hour clock. So far, results have been mixed, with some people showing a rapid response to these treatments and others showing none at all, but recent work has also shown a link to the timing of meals and the secretion of insulin. There has also been increasing interest in looking at hormones produced by the thyroid gland, and the relationship of these hormones to the immune responses produced by white blood cells.

Epidemiology

With such a carefully selected workforce, it's not surprising that statistics show Antarctica to be quite a healthy place to live. However, living far from sources of infection appears to lower natural immunity. Colds or flu often spread rapidly among a station's overwintering population when people on the first ship or aircraft arrive at the end of winter, bringing their germs.

This isolation can be turned to scientific advantage, however. In normal societies, it's difficult to study how a disease spreads among people. To do this scientifically, it is essential to reduce the opportunities for new sources of infection to enter the experimental group. Apart from hermits and members of closed religious orders, there are few people who are willing to live completely cut off from society for long periods to ensure this. Antarctic stations during winter, however, provide this opportunity. Using the latest molecular-biology techniques, it is possible, on a small station, to characterize every strain of a particular microbe. At the start of the winter, every person has a personal profile made of his or her microbe strains. By monitoring these, it is possible to see which strains become dominant, which are passed on and to whom, and which disappear completely. The most recent development of this research has been to use the rate of evolution of Antarctic microbe strains as a baseline against which to assess natural change in microbial populations.

The Psychology of Small Groups

Remote groups hold a particular fascination for psychologists. Add to this both a hostile environment and an opportunity to assess changes by testing people before and after their Antarctic experience, and you have an ideal opportunity to study personality characteristics and human interactions. The most detailed and longest-running studies in this field have been done by US, French and New Zealand scientists. In general, psychologists are trying to assess three features of behavior: how well a person performs his or her job, how emotionally stable a person remains through the stresses and isolation of the winter, and how well a person integrates into a group. A wide range of tests has been used, and in many countries the conclusions have been incorporated into the screening programs for selecting recruits.

Until recently, however, there has been no attempt to standardize the testing to see how the culture of various nations affects the response of individuals. The experiences of different cultures can now be compared scientifically, with a Canadian-run project using a questionnaire translated into several languages to assess individuals.

THE FUTURE OF ANTARCTIC SCIENCE

The increasing interest in developing global models to try and predict the future of the world has shown very clearly how important Antarctica is. The emphasis these days is on Earth System Science, a holistic approach, and Antarctic science is proving to be far more crucial than many people expected. With scientists from over 30 countries now active in Antarctica there is increasing emphasis on big problems that can only be tackled on a coordinated international scale. Coordinated ice-drilling programs are providing an Antarctica-wide data set on the history of global change. Geophysicists are pooling data to provide a more inclusive picture of the geology of the ocean floor, while oceanographers are sharing data for mapping currents and the formation of deep Antarctic Bottom Water. Seal biologists are counting all the seals in the Antarctic, while glaciologists are cooperating to determine the fate of the ice sheet. In the future, international programs will even investigate the lakes buried deep beneath the ice.

'Antarctic science may be a long way from your backyard, but it is relevant science – now and for the future'

In all these efforts, there is a genuine attempt to utilize the special features of Antarctica to answer scientific questions. Using the latest tools, we can map the Antarctic more accurately than ever before to assess the changing continent. With geographical information systems, we can synthesize widely differing types of data to gain better understanding of how glaciology interacts with meteorology and geology.

At the same time, scientists are working to protect the continent for the future. Antarctic science is conducted under the rigorous requirements of the Antarctic Treaty's Protocol on Environmental Protection. Great efforts are made to ensure that as little ecological damage as possible is done and that all wastes are removed.

When you see an Antarctic station, remember that its impact is local, its inhabitants are trying hard to be more responsible than most of us are back home, and that the research being done there is likely to benefit not only us but all future generations. Antarctic science may be a long way from your backyard, but it is relevant science – now and for the future.

Southern Ocean & Peri-Antarctic Islands

CONTENTS

Antarctica is isolated by the southern portions of the Atlantic, Indian and Pacific Oceans. These are separated from the Southern Ocean (the name for the seas surrounding the continent) by a surface oceanographic phenomenon called the Antarctic Convergence.

For many people, crossing the Southern Ocean is the least interesting – and also least comfortable – part of their trip to Antarctica. But the Southern Ocean is important to the biology and the climate of the continent in particular, and of the earth in general.

There's a psychological benefit to sailing over the Southern Ocean to reach Antarctica: it makes clear the continent's remoteness and immensity. The Southern Ocean gives one time to prepare for Antarctica, to anticipate it. Antarctica is unveiled to the sea traveler slowly, just as it was to human knowledge – the first astonishing iceberg, then many icebergs, then an island, and finally, the continent itself ahead on the horizon.

The peri-Antarctic islands are in many ways much more interesting than large sections of the Antarctic continental coast. For one thing, most of the peri-Antarctic islands have more wildlife than Antarctica itself. Antarctic tour operators make every effort to land passengers on the continent (for some reason, many people seem to believe that they haven't really been to Antarctica unless they set foot on the actual continent). But most of these islands are properly thought of as part of the Antarctic as well.

HIGHLIGHTS

- Catching sight of the collapsed Arched Rock at **Îles Kerguelen** (p163) silhouetted against the dawn
- Strolling the boardwalk through **Campbell Island's** (p177) 'megaherb meadows'
- Transiting the narrow gap of Neptunes Bellows to reach **Deception Island's** (p187) secret inner harbor
- Cruising among the **South Shetlands** (p180), where wildlife abounds among scattered traces of the sealing era
- Landing at **South Georgia's** (p193) tiny Cave Cove, Shackleton's first landfall after his ocean crossing in *James Caird*

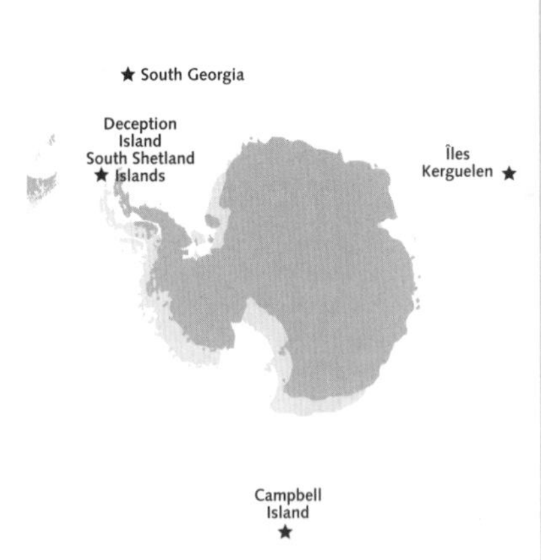

SOUTHERN OCEAN

Most visitors to Antarctica cross the Drake Passage, the narrow stretch of water that separates South America from the Antarctic Peninsula. You may hear about the 'Roaring Forties,' but Tierra del Fuego is located at about 55°S, so in fact you'll be passing through only half of the 'Furious Fifties' and part of the so-called 'Screaming Sixties.' Generally, the passage is quick, and if you're fortunate, you'll experience the quiet waters known as the 'Drake Lake.' Otherwise, prepare yourself for the 'Drake Shake,' which is also known as 'paying the Drake Tax.'

Sailing to Antarctica from Australia, New Zealand or South Africa requires a longer voyage. While there's a greater chance of encountering heavy weather on a longer voyage, there's also more time for bird-watching, stargazing and (perhaps) observing the aurora australis. For more details on sailing to Antarctica, see p296.

At some point you will pass over the **Antarctic Convergence**, which is also known as the Polar Front. The ocean south of the Convergence differs greatly from northern waters in salinity, density and temperature. A great mixing occurs where northern and southern waters meet, with nutrients from the seafloor being brought to the surface of the ocean, making the Convergence a highly productive area for algae, krill and the other small creatures at the base of the Antarctic food web.

The exact location of the Antarctic Convergence varies slightly throughout the year, and also from year to year. Despite what you may hear, there's very little sign that you are actually crossing the Convergence. The sea does not get rougher, and there is usually no change in its appearance. The primary indicator is a dip in the water temperature – a change that the ship's instruments will detect, although you almost certainly will not.

North of this seasonally and longitudinally varying line, the summer surface seawater

A VISIT TO CAPE HORN *Annie Dillard*

This is the headland that sailors shun. We landed on a tiny beach covered with boulders in a cove filled with comb jellies and I wanted to put up a huge sign: IF YOU CAN READ THIS, YOU'RE TOO CLOSE.

Three oceans meet here at basalt cliffs where Magellanic penguins breed. Topsides, you wander the saddles among mounds of tussock grass higher than your head.

We humans are stunned, agape. You'd think we had never seen vegetation before. A hundred flowers bloom on the hillsides – white composites – and green leaves sprout and hang from every crevice in every cliff. Underfoot the wild geraniums and celery, the red berries, the white berries, the succulents that pack every rock, and the heaths whose lives mingle with ours.

All over the rocks, leaves with unique shapes pulse. What is this soft stuff made of sunlight and rainwater? You can even eat it. Songbirds live here, too, and insects – a dragonfly, on Cape Horn! And a white moth drowned in a pond.

Two Chileans man a base here, and a cat, a dog and a puppy, who show and return the tenderness a succession of desolate men must have lavished on them. The only other pets I've seen as deeply loved as these lived in a monastery.

There is a tiny church here, too, double-walled in bark-sided lumber. There is a stone-slab altar, a wooden cross, six or eight short benches, a few garish saint pictures and a few candles. By the door, in a vestibule smaller than a phone booth, hang four pegs for coats.

The sun is out, here where so many men have died, and there's no wind. An old Inuit poem repeats:

Let me see,
Is it real,
This life I am living?

Annie Dillard is a member of the American Academy of Arts and Letters (elected in 1998)

USHUAIA

Nearly 90% of all Antarctic tourists depart from Ushuaia in Argentina, thanks to the city's fortunate location, which is almost directly across the 1000km-wide Drake Passage from the Antarctic Peninsula.

The southernmost city in the world, Ushuaia is located in a dramatic setting beneath the jagged peaks of the Montes Martial, which rise from sea level to more than 1300m and are topped by Monte Olivia (1318m), an easily recognized sharp pinnacle to the east of town.

Over the past 25 years, Ushuaia (the name is pronounced 'oosh-wya' and means 'bay penetrating to the west') has expanded rapidly from a small village into a city of almost 50,000 people. Growth has been spurred only partly by the massive influx of tourists to the Antarctic: this region of Tierra del Fuego attracts visitors on its own, too.

For more than three centuries, this area's climate and terrain discouraged European settlement, yet indigenous people considered it a land of plenty. The Yahgan Indians, now few in number, built the fires that inspired Europeans to call the region Tierra del Fuego, or Land of Fire. In 1520 when Magellan passed through the strait that now bears his name, neither he nor any other European explorer had much interest in the land or its people. Consequently, the Ona (or Selknam), Haush, Yahgan (or Yamana) and Alacaluf peoples who lived in the area faced no immediate competition for their lands and resources.

Beginning in the 1850s Europeans attempted to catechize the Fuegians. Thomas Bridges, who learned to speak Yahgan, became one of the first settlers at Ushuaia. His son, Lucas Bridges, born at Ushuaia in 1874, left a fascinating memoir of his experiences among the Yahgans and Onas titled *The Uttermost Part of the Earth*.

By 1885 Argentina had installed a territorial governor, and in 1904 Ushuaia became Tierra del Fuego's capital. Despite minor gold and lumber booms, the town was for many years primarily a penal settlement for both political prisoners and common criminals. Sheep farming brought great

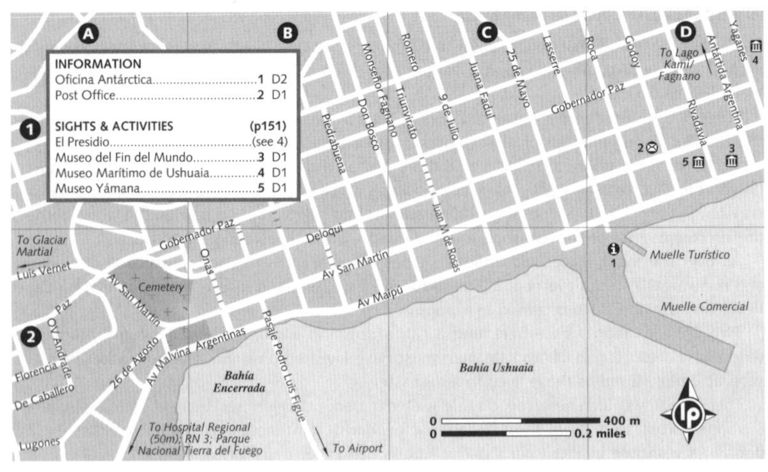

temperature is about 7.8°C, while south of it the temperature drops to 3.9°C. During winter, the temperature drops to approximately 2.8°C north of the Antarctic Convergence and to just 1.1°C south of it. The engine-room crew generally detects the change in the temperature before the officers on the bridge – and changes the flow of coolin[g] water appropriately.

CAPE HORN

Most Antarctic tour ships sail to and fro[m] Ushuaia, which means that passengers ma[y] catch sight of the fabled Cape Horn (Cab[o]

wealth to some individuals and families, and is still Tierra del Fuego's economic backbone. Since 1950 Ushuaia has been an important naval base, supporting Argentine claims to Antarctica.

Orientation

Ushuaia has no central plaza. Most hotels and visitor services are on or within a few blocks of Av San Martín, the principal commercial street, one block north of Av Maipú, which runs along the waterfront. North of Av San Martín, streets rise very steeply, giving good views of the Beagle Channel.

Information

Instituto Fuegino de Turismo (Infuetur; the Tierra del Fuego government tourist office) runs the **Oficina Antárctica** (Muelle Comercial), on the main pier entered across from Av Maipú 505. The friendly staff sells postcards and provides information on Antarctic trips. There's also a modest display of artifacts from the Hope Bay party of Nordenskjöld's ill-fated Swedish South Polar Expedition of 1901. The *oficina* is open daily when Antarctic tour ships are in port.

Most shops and restaurants accept US dollars, although it's wise to confirm this first. Several banks on Avs Maipú and San Martín have ATMs. Ushuaia's **post office** (9am-7pm Mon-Fri, 9am-1pm Sat) is on Av San Martín at the corner of Godoy.

Sights

On the waterfront, the **Museo del Fin del Mundo** (☎ 42-1863; Av Maipú 175-79; 10am-1pm & 3-7:30pm) offers exhibits on Fuegian natural history, aboriginal life, the early penal colonies (complete with a photographic rogues' gallery), replicas of an early general store and bank – and a rare opportunity to see Andean condors, though unfortunately stuffed, not live.

The **Museo Yámana** (☎ 42-2874; Rivadavia 56; 10am-8pm) is a small museum with meticulously crafted and well-labeled exhibits (in English) on the Fuegian peoples who lived in the area before European settlement. It's wonderful.

The **Museo Marítimo de Ushuaia** (☎ 43-7841; 9am-8pm) is within the military base, El Presidio, at the eastern end of town. Use the entrance at Yaganes and Gobernador Paz rather than the base entrance at Yaganes and San Martín.

Closed as a penal institution in 1947, the building at one time held as many as 800 inmates in 380 cells designed to hold just one prisoner each. Some of the displays, which highlight local history and convict life, are in the former cells; this grim jail section is fairly depressing.

Antarctic exhibits include stuffed penguins, a fur-seal pelt you can touch, and photos of Antarctic historical interest. Some artifacts from the Nordenskjöld expedition's huts on Snow Hill Island and at Hope Bay are on display in several of the prison cells. Antarctic fossils from Snow Hill and Seymour Islands are also on view.

Perhaps the best collection of Antarctic ship models anywhere in the world is displayed in various parts of the museum. Among the dozens of examples are Amundsen's *Fram*; Scott's *Discovery*; Shackleton's *Endurance*; DeGerlache's *Belgica*; Charcot's *Le Français* and *Pourquoi-Pas*; Nordenskjöld's *Antarctic*; Argentina's *Uruguay* (which rescued Nordenskjöld in 1903 and also relieved Bruce in 1904); Argentina's *Bahía Paraíso* (wrecked in Antarctica in 1989, causing a massive fuel spill); and the Argentine icebreaker *Almirante Irizar* (the actual ship often reprovisions in Ushuaia).

On the 2nd floor is an extensive exhibit of stamps and postcards from Antarctica, Tierra del Fuego and Ushuaia, along with a 'relax zone' and a gift shop.

de Hornos) – and, rarely, land there. Cape Horn is a synonym for adventure and the romance of the old days of sail – although for most of the poor sailors aboard ships attempting to double the Horn, there was no romance on a cold winter ocean with a gale blowing.

Cape Horn was discovered in January 1616 by two Dutchmen, Jakob Le Maire and Willem Schouten, sailing in the ship *Unity*. They named the cape after their ship *Hoorn*, which had accidentally burned down at Puerto Deseado located on the Patagonian coast.

Horn Island, where the famous cape forms its southernmost headland, is just 8km long. The cape itself rises to 424m, with striking black cliffs on its upper parts.

Although you may be one of hundreds each year who land at Cape Horn and receive a certificate stating that you have done so, be aware of the difference between 'rounding' Cape Horn and merely going ashore for a photo. 'I like to draw a distinction for visitors I take down there,' writes Skip Novak, skipper of *Pelagic*, a charter yacht that often visits the Peninsula. 'I bring people to 'see' the Horn, not to round it. My advice to them is that if they want to 'round' the Horn, they had better start from somewhere like New Zealand.'

It's also worth keeping in mind tha weather plays a large part in one's experienc of Cape Horn, as Ross recognized after h sailed past in *Erebus* in September 1842:

> The poetical descriptions that former navigators have given of this celebrated and dreaded promontory, occasioned us to feel a degree of disappointment when we first saw it; for, although it stands prominently forward, a bold, almost perpendicular headland, in whose outline it requires but little imaginative power to detect the resemblance of a 'sleeping lion, facing and braving the southern tempests,' yet it is part only of a small island, and its elevation,

> not exceeding five or six hundred feet, conveys to the mind nothing of grandeur. But the day was beautifully fine, so that it is probable we saw this cape of terror and tempests under some disadvantage.

Landings at Cape Horn are very infrequent. They are expensive to attempt, since ships must have a Chilean pilot for navigation in the shoal-filled offshore waters and the weather seldom cooperates. In any case, the Chilean authorities routinely refuse requests for permission to make landings – or even to approach closely. When permission is granted, landings are usually made in the westward of the two bays located east of the cape. A steep wooden stairway of about 110 steps leads to high ground above the beach.

Cabo de Hornos Light is a white fiberglass-reinforced plastic tower 4m high with a red band running around it. It's automated, but a nearby Chilean naval observation station, consisting of two huts with a conspicuous radio antenna about 1600m northeast of the light, is home to a few lonesome officers. There is also a small wooden chapel called **Stella Maris**, or 'Star of the Sea.'

A **stone monument** on a plinth surrounded by heavy iron chains honors the ancient mariners who rounded Cape Horn.

Another monument, in the form of a large **abstract sculpture**, depicts – in the negative space formed by four steel plates – an albatross in flight. It commemorates those lost in the treacherous seas off this headland.

The great Andean condors can be seen here, as well as Magellanic penguins, which nest in burrows in the moss and tussock grass.

PERI-ANTARCTIC ISLANDS

These tiny specks of land include the most remote islands on earth. Ecologically, they are extremely important – out of proportion to their size – for a large number of seabird, penguin and seal species, because they are often the only breeding places for thousands of kilometers in the vast ocean surrounding Antarctica.

No Antarctic voyage, even a circumnavigation of the continent, will be able to visit all the peri-Antarctic islands – there are simply too many. But nearly every cruise will visit at least one of the following island groups, and there are even trips that visit *only* islands. Cruises from South America or the Falklands stop at the South Shetlands, while voyages sailing from Australia, New Zealand or South Africa will often stop at, respectively, Macquarie Island or Heard Island; New Zealand's sub-Antarctic islands; or the Prince Edward Islands. Resupply vessels visiting the three French islands take tourists. Tristan da Cunha and Gough Island are usually visited on 'repositioning' cruises, when Antarctic ships sail to or from the northern hemisphere, where they ply Arctic waters during the austral winter. The most rarely visited islands are Bouvetøya, Peter I Øy and Scott Island. For information on booking cruises to the peri-Antarctic islands, see p296.

ISLAS DIEGO RAMIREZ

These Chilean islands, located 100km southwest of Cape Horn, became the most southerly known land in the world when they were discovered on February 12, 1619 by two brothers, Bartolomé and Gonzálo de Nodal, sailing in *Nuestra Señora de Achoa* and *Nuestra Señora de Buen Succeso*, on a Portuguese expedition. The brothers named the archipelago for their expedition's cosmographer, and the islands held their 'southernmost' distinction for more than 150 years, until Cook discovered the South Sandwich Islands in 1775.

Islas Diego Ramirez comprises two small groups of islands: northerly Isla Norte and four smaller islands; and the southerly pair, 93-hectare Isla Bartolomé (maximum elevation, 190m) and Isla Gonzálo (38 hectares and 139m), separated by a narrow channel, along with a dozen other smaller islands and rocks.

During a visit to Diego Ramirez in 1874, William Henry Appleman, master of the American sealer *Thomas Hunt*, wrote about discovering two graves on one of the islands, as described in Briton Cooper Busch's *The War Against the Seals* (1985). One grave belonged to a 19-year-old seaman from Maine buried in 1832; the other was unmarked. Although ship log entries are normally terse and factual, the scene moved Appleman to meditate:

> Such is life and such is Death. How little it matters them whether buried in a quiet New England church yard or here amidst the ceaseless roar of South Atlantic and Pacific waves with timultuous [sic] cry of legions of Birds and the quiet tread of Seals.

A Chilean lighthouse and meteorological station on the islands is resupplied by navy ships several times a year. Macaroni, rockhopper and Magellanics breed here, and king and chinstraps occasionally visit.

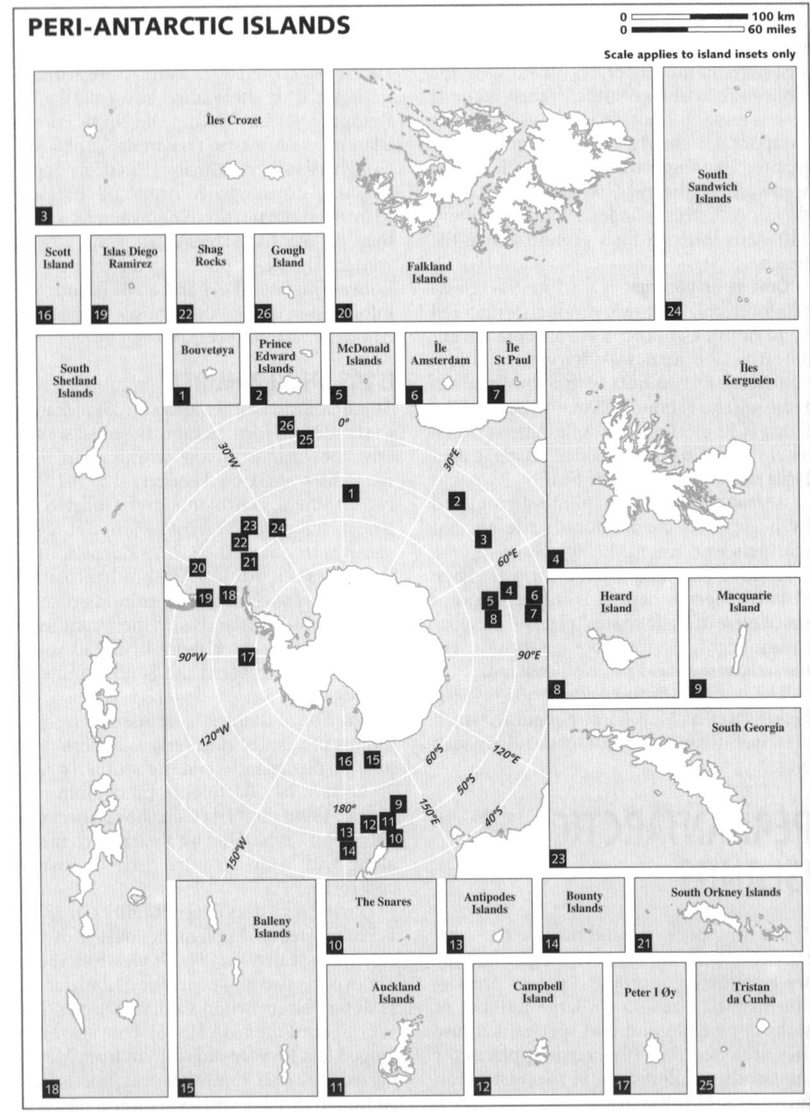

BOUVETØYA

Bouvetøya is the most isolated island on earth. Not counting its tiny neighbor to the southwest, Larsøya, the nearest land (Antarctica) is more than 1600km away.

Bouvetøya is the tip of a volcano that rises out of the Southern Ocean, and although the volcano is dormant, there's still geothermal activity on the island. Another island, Thompson Island, was first sighted by 19th-century sealers northeast of Bouvetøya. It is believed to have been destroyed during a volcanic explosion in 1895 or 1896. Sometime between 1955 and 1958, a low-lying shelf of lava appeared on Bouvetøya's western coast, creating the island's only bird-nesting site of any size. Norwegian discoverers named it Nyrøysa ('New Rubble'); it's also known as Westwind Beach. Scientists landed on Bouvetøya in 1978 and measured a below-ground temperature of 25°C.

Bouvetøya covers about 54 sq km. The highest point is 780m Olavtoppen (Olav Peak). It and another high peak surround the ice-filled crater of an inactive volcano known as the Wilhelm II plateau. Glaciers cover 93% of the island and prevent landings on the southern and eastern coasts, while steep cliffs as high as 490m block access to the north, west and southwest. Landings can be made in only a few places, and numerous offshore rocks make navigation hazardous. Bouvetøya's weather is nearly always cloudy or foggy. The mean temperature is -1°C; in summer, the average high is 2.2°C.

The island is named for French navigator Jean-Baptiste-Charles Bouvet de Lozier, who, sailing in *Aigle*, first sighted it on January 1, 1739, but was unable to get a good fix to determine its position. It was not until 1808 that British whaling captains James Lindsay and Thomas Hopper, sailing in *Swan* and *Otter*, resighted it and proved that it was indeed an island. Bouvetøya's precise position, however, was only pinned down 90 years later by the German Deep Sea Exploration Expedition in 1898 sailing in *Valdivia*, which did not succeed in landing.

The first landing was made by an American sealing expedition led by Benjamin Morrell in *Wasp*, who came ashore on December 8, 1822, and took 172 fur-seal skins, thus encouraging other sealers, who visited sporadically during the 19th century. Two British sealing ships, *Sprightly* and *Lively*, rediscovered Bouvetøya on December 10, 1825, and named it Liverpool Island, taking possession for the British crown.

Science, in the form of a Norwegian oceanographic expedition, first visited Bouvetøya in 1927. The island was claimed for Norway on December 1, and on January 23, 1928, it was formally annexed by Norwegian royal proclamation. (The British Parliament declined to get upset about such an unpromising dot of territory and renounced all claim to Bouvetøya later in 1928.) In 1971 the Norwegian government made the island a nature reserve.

The island has only rarely been visited, so its history is brief. Two events, however, are rather mysterious. First, a sunken lifeboat and assorted supplies were discovered at Nyrøysa in 1964, but their origin could not be determined. Second, a thermonuclear bomb test seems to have occurred to the west of Bouvetøya in 1979. Although no country ever admitted setting off a bomb there, an orbiting satellite detected a brief, intense burst of light on September 22, 1979. Magnetic, seismographic and ionospheric evidence all pointed to a nuclear blast. Personnel at Australian Antarctic stations later detected radiation and radioactive debris.

Another island mystery surfaced in 1986 when a newspaper in the Norwegian capital of Oslo reported that US census records showed that, since 1959, 60 women and 26 men had emigrated from the uninhabited Bouvetøya to the US!

Three huts were set up by a Norwegian research expedition that spent four months on the island in 1978. They're now gone, but in 1997 a shipping container brought to Nyrøysa was converted to a small **Norwegian research station**. It was last used during the 2001–02 season.

PRINCE EDWARD ISLANDS

Bleak and barren in winter, lush and green in summer, the Prince Edward Islands consist of protected Prince Edward Island and the larger Marion Island, 22km to the southwest. They cover 316 sq km and are part of South Africa's Province of Cape of Good Hope.

Dome-like **Marion Island** is dotted by many small lakes and more than 100 small hills; as the 1961 edition of *The Antarctic Pilot* picturesquely notes, the island 'appears from northward as a cluster of rugged nipples.'

Rugged, indeed: a sealing captain who visited in 1842 noted that Marion's volcanic cinders 'will thoroughly demoralize a new pair of boots in one day's time.' **Prince Edward Island** is more vertical than its larger neighbor, with dramatic cliffs towering to 490m high on the southwestern coast. At Cave Bay is a large cave that has sheltered two groups of castaways as well as an incongruous Champagne toast, made by a secret South African naval expedition in January 1948 (see p157).

The islands' highest point, on Marion, is State President Swart Peak (1230m), which has a small icecap. The weather is depressingly constant: low temperatures throughout the year, extremely strong westerly winds, abundant snow and rain, and skies that are usually at least three-quarters covered by clouds.

The South African government declared the islands Special Nature Reserves in 1995. Even research on Prince Edward Island is severely restricted. A group of not more than four people is permitted to land only once every three to five years, staying no more than two or three days.

The islands were first sighted by Dutchman Barent Barentszoon Lam (or possibly Ham) sailing in *Maerseveen* on March 4, 1663, who named the northerly island Dina and the more southerly Maerseveen. But a subsequent Dutch expedition couldn't find the islands in the latitude reported (41°S), and they were all but forgotten.

Frenchman Marc Macé Marion du Fresne, sailing in *Mascarin*, rediscovered them on January 13, 1772. Not realizing at first that they were islands, he called the larger one Terre de l'Espérance, but then changed it to Île de l'Espérance. He called the smaller one Île de la Caverne because of a large cave he saw while circumnavigating it. He also saw tiny white spots dotting Île de la Caverne, which he mistook for sheep (they were albatrosses), but a collision with his accompanying ship *Marquis de Castries* prevented him from landing to investigate. Further east, he discovered Îles Crozet.

The ubiquitous Captain Cook searched for Île de l'Espérance and Île de la Caverne early in 1775, but couldn't find them. Meeting one of the few returning survivors of

NONEXISTENT ANTARCTIC ISLANDS *Robert Headland*

Along with the groups of isolated oceanic islands surrounding Antarctica, there are reports of a curious assortment of 18 nonexistent, but putatively similar, far-southern islands: Aurora Islands, Burdwood's Island, The Chimneys, Dougherty's Island (also called Keats Island), Elizabethides, Emerald Island, Isla Grande, Macey's Island, Middle Island, New South Greenland, Nimrod Island, Pagoda Rock, Royal Company Island, Strathfillan Rock, Swain's Island, Thompson Island, Undine Rock and Trulsklippen. These have all been recorded in the Southern Ocean or the extreme southern limits of the adjoining oceans, and all have appeared on official charts. Several have been seen more than once, and three may once have existed but become submerged following volcanic explosions.

Besides volcanoes, there are several reasons why people may have supposed these islands existed. Many might be explained as sightings in bad weather of icebergs that were carrying rocks and moraine. A captain, rightly erring on the side of safety, would report these (dirty ice can look convincingly like an island). Some sightings, however, were more likely the result of too much rum. A few may have been deliberate hoaxes: sealers always tried to keep secret the locations of good sealing discoveries, especially new islands, in order to reduce the competition. Some of the sealers may well have deliberately led others on wild goose chases. One island, New South Greenland, was probably invented to embellish a book by an author who was known as 'the greatest liar in the Pacific.'

The problem with all these nonexistent islands has been getting rid of them. If there was a possibility of a supposedly sighted island being a hazard to navigation, the British Admiralty and other maritime authorities were very reluctant to expunge it from the charts. It usually took a substantial hydrographic survey before this was done (although the satellite age has now simplified this). The persistence of nonexistent islands is phenomenal: Swain's Island, ordered to be deleted from the charts in 1920, could still be found in a 1995 comprehensive world atlas produced by a well-known publisher. Some nonexistent islands have even appeared in novels – there is a lot of writing that can be done with such a theme.

Robert Headland is the archivist and curator at the Scott Polar Research Institute, Cambridge, England

Marion du Fresne's expedition (which had been attacked by Maoris in New Zealand) in Cape Town, Cook obtained a chart showing the islands' location. On December 12, 1776, Cook spotted the islands – and noting that the chart gave them no name, called them the Prince Edward Islands after the fourth son of the reigning British monarch. Unknowingly causing considerable confusion for latter-day scholars, Cook gave the name Marion and Crozet Islands to the islands that Marion du Fresne had found later on his voyage, the present-day Îles Crozet. Nineteenth-century sealers further confused the issue by transferring the appellation Marion back to the island now known by that name.

French sealers may have made the first landing in about 1799; sealing continued throughout the 19th century and into the 20th. Several wrecks are known on Prince Edward Island. In 1849 the 11 survivors from *Richard Dart*'s complement of 63 were rescued after 2½ months, while *Maria*'s (1857) survivors waited seven months before rescue, and those of *Seabird* (1912) spent nearly six months castaway. On Marion, the only recorded shipwreck is of the Norwegian sealing vessel *Solglimt* (1908), whose crew was stranded for a month.

Despite the islands' discovery by the Dutch (and the French), in 1908 the British government granted one William Newton a 21-year lease to exploit guano deposits believed to lie on the islands, but he never used the concession. In 1926 the islands, along with the Heard and McDonald Islands, were leased by the British government for 10 years to the Kerguelen Sealing and Whaling Co Ltd of Cape Town, which was granted exclusive rights to seals, whales, guano and minerals. The company worked in the islands until 1930.

If the French had any inclination to challenge these tacit British claims of sovereignty, their opportunity vanished in 1947, when a secret South African naval expedition code-named 'Operation Snoektown' raised the Union of South Africa's flag at Marion Island on December 29, 1947, and at Prince Edward Island on January 4, 1948. After the latter flag-raising, the uniformed

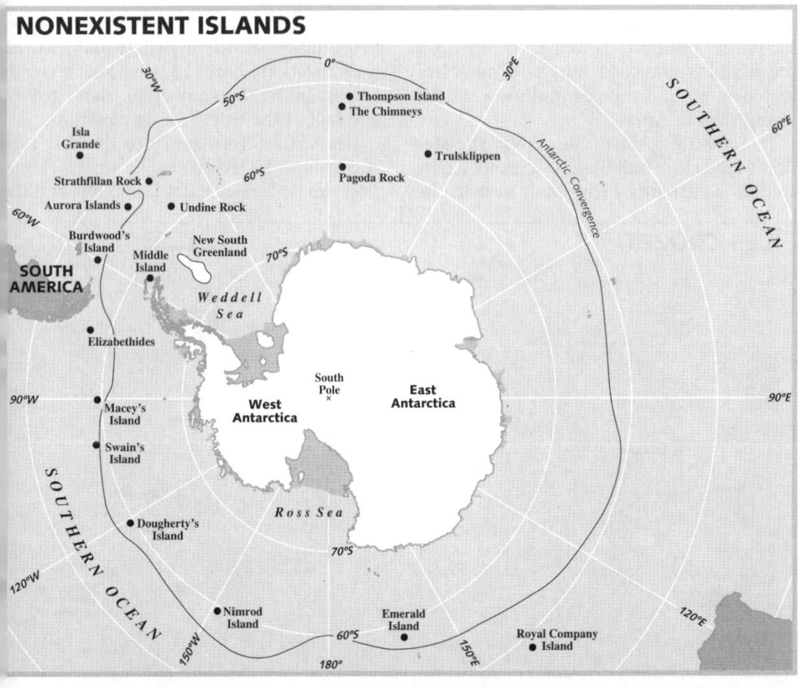

participants raised glasses of bubbly outside the cave that had once sheltered desperate castaways – quite a contrast!

A permanent meteorological station was established at **Transvaal Cove** on Marion Island's northeastern coast. On January 12, 1948, the South African government issued the proclamation that the British Crown's rights over the islands would henceforth be controlled by His Majesty's Government in South Africa.

The **met station**, operated continuously on Marion Island since 1947 despite a fire that destroyed the main living quarters and communications facilities in 1966, has gradually expanded its scientific program to include biology. Boardwalks connect the station buildings to prevent damaging the boggy ground underneath. As many as 15 people winter there and the base can accommodate 64. A volcanic eruption occurred in December 1980 but did not damage the station.

The possibility of constructing a landing strip was investigated in 1987, but was not built for environmental reasons. Nevertheless, air support is crucial to station operations, since the island has just two cobblestone beaches. Helicopters are used for station resupply, as well as to provision the island's nine field huts and move researchers around the island during station changeover in April.

In 1999 a big storm blew away the station's food store building. As a result, a new station is currently being built next to the old one. Construction began in 2003 and should be completed by about 2008.

Introduced species have wreaked havoc on Marion's indigenous flora and fauna. The diamond-backed moth *(Plutella xylostella)* introduced itself to the island in 1986 (researchers think that the moths were blown in on storm clouds) and has badly damaged the Kerguelen cabbage. Mice, inadvertently brought by early-19th-century sealers, have also damaged plant and insect life. Far more damage, however, has been done by the descendants of the five house cats brought to the met station in 1949 to control rodents. By 1977 they had multiplied to about 3400 animals and were eating an estimated 600,000 birds annually. The cats were exterminated by 1991. As a result, the breeding success of burrowing petrels has increased rapidly.

Fur seals (two species) and elephant seals breed on the islands, as do hundreds of thousands of penguins (kings, gentoos, rockhoppers and macaronis), hundreds of thousands of petrels and thousands of albatrosses (four species).

ÎLES CROZET

Boasting one of the highest concentrations of breeding seabirds anywhere in the world the Crozets are home to seven species of albatross (more than any other island group) and half of the world's king penguins.

Îles Crozet (cro-zay) are divided into two groups, L'Occidental (Île aux Cochons, Îlots des Apôtres, Île des Pingouins and the

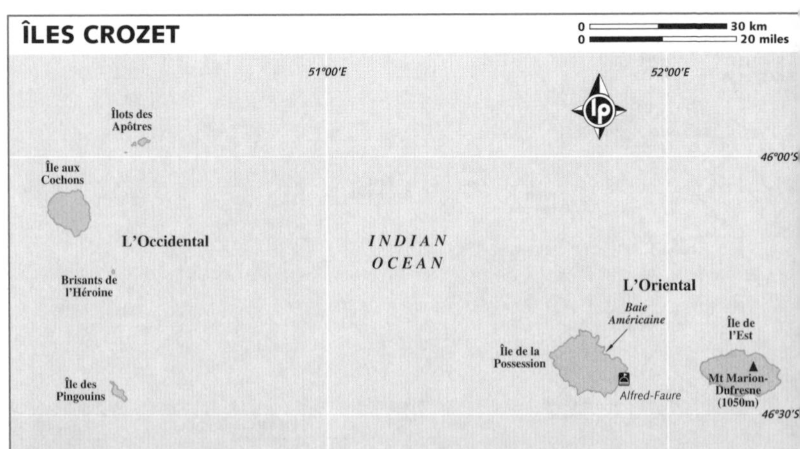

reefs known as Brisants de l'Héroine) and L'Oriental (Île de l'Est and Île de la Possession, the largest of the Crozets), about 100km east. The islands cover 325 sq km. The highest point is Mt Marion-Dufresne at 1050m on Île de l'Est. There are no glaciers. The islands are part of France's Terres Australes et Antarctiques Françaises and have been a national park since 1938. The only island that can be visited is Île de la Possession.

Crozet weather is usually cold, wet, windy and cloudy, but the winters aren't severe.

Frenchman Marc Macé Marion du Fresne, sailing in *Mascarin*, discovered the islands on January 23, 1772. He went ashore the next day and took possession for France (on Île de la Possession), naming them for his second-in-command, Julien Marie Crozet.

Sealers arrived in 1804, taking fur-seal skins and sailing directly to Canton for sale and processing. Just two years later, a group of 14 wretched, stranded sealers was rescued from the Crozets by *Eliza*, sailing from Nantucket. Relentless slaughter soon took its toll on the once-teeming beaches, however, and by 1835 the American sealer *Tampico* reported that fur seals were rare here.

Îles Crozet have a history of shipwrecks. The islands' first-recorded shipwreck was the British sealer *Princess of Wales*, which came to grief in 1821; the crew was rescued 21 months later. After their ship wrecked on Île de l'Est in 1825, the company of the French sealer *Aventure* spent 17 months as castaways. The American sealing brig *Uxor*, on her third voyage to the Crozets, was lost in 1841. The crew of the French ship *Tamaris*, which sank off Île aux Cochons in 1887, were the most inventive of the stranded seamen – during their seven-month stay on the island, they attached a message to a giant petrel, which was recovered seven months later near Fremantle in Western Australia, some 6500km away. According to the message they sent, *Tamaris*' crew planned to set out for Île de la Possession, but they vanished without a trace. Survivors of the shipwreck of the Norwegian schooner *Catherine* actually published an 'illustrated weekly,' *The Crozetta*, during their forced stay in 1906.

Whaling soon replaced sealing as the islands' primary economic activity, and in 1841, 12 whaling expeditions from the US alone operated around Îles Crozet. During the 1843–44 season, the fleet grew to 18: *Aeronaut, Arab, Cicero, Dragon, Fenelon, France, Halcyon, Herald, John & Elizabeth, Majestic, Milwood, Neptune, Popmunnet, Romulus, Roscoe, Stonington, Superior* and *Tenedos.*

In the 20th century, after several visits to the Crozets to reassert its sovereignty, France consolidated its hold over its sub-Antarctic islands. In 1955 French law established the Terres Australes et Antarctiques Françaises, which includes Île St Paul, Île Amsterdam, Îles Kerguelen, Îles Crozet and Terre Adélie in Antarctica. In 1978 France declared a 370km exclusive economic zone around each of the four archipelagos, patrolled by French naval vessels that arrest foreign ships for illegal fishing.

At **Baie Américaine** on Île de la Possession, which was used by early-19th-century American sealers, orcas hunt elephant seal pups by surfing right onto the beach to take them from the shore.

Alien animal species, including cats, rats, rabbits and mice, have damaged some of the islands' fragile ecosystems. Introduced pigs gave Île aux Cochons its name, but caused so much damage that they destroyed their food supply and became extinct, as did goats on Île de la Possession.

Alfred-Faure Station

France set up a temporary scientific camp on Île de la Possession in 1961, and during the 1963–64 summer established a station at Port-Alfred on the island's northeast coast with a (now-disused) aerial cableway running from the beach to the station. Named Alfred-Faure station for its first leader, it houses 35 people over the winter.

On the beach below the base at **Baie du Marin** (Sailors Bay) are 50,000 king penguins. A 1.6km road winds up the hill from the pier to the base – right through the rookery. It's strange to see penguins behind the fences used (fairly successfully) to keep them off the road. On your way up, look for the penguin tracks preserved in the concrete.

Skeletal remains of the **téléférique** (cableway) atop the slope, with a French tricolor sign attached, are vaguely reminiscent of the Eiffel Tower.

Station buildings are striking, each painted in several colors – pink, blue, green – some with murals of orcas or albatrosses. Many offer a good view of neighboring Île de l'Est, although it's often shrouded in fog.

A small **museum case** in the dining room displays historic artifacts, and an elephant seal-hunting lance is mounted on a wall. Two bathtub-sized iron *marmites* (French for try-pots) now rust on the station grounds.

Tiny **Notre Dame des Oiseaux** (Our Lady of the Birds), a white-stucco building with a red corrugated-iron roof, offers a quiet sanctuary for no more than three people at once. The exterior shows the Virgin Mary among penguins; silhouettes of other birds found on Crozet adorn the doorway.

The pride of the base is in the **greenhouse**: an old apple tree, which doesn't bear fruit since there are no bees to pollinate it.

ÎLES KERGUELEN

Îles Kerguelen (*ker*-ga-len) consists of one major island, Grande Terre (sometimes called Île Kerguelen), and about 300 tiny islets and rocks. Formerly administered as a dependency of Madagascar, Îles Kerguelen were incorporated into the Terres Australes and Antarctiques Françaises in 1955.

The archipelago covers 7215 sq km, extending 195km from Îlot du Rendez-Vous in the north to Rochers du Salamanca in the south, and 145km from Îles de la Fortune in the west to the eastern tip of Péninsule Courbet on Grand Terre. A submarine shelf at a depth of 200m extends for many kilometers off Grand Terre's northern coast, evidence that Kerguelen was once a larger land mass.

Grand Terre is heavily serrated by fjords along its northeastern and southeastern coasts, providing excellent anchorages. No point on the island is further than 21km from the coast, which measures an amazing 2800km in length. Many of Kerguelen's isthmuses are so narrow that early sealers sometimes carried their boats across them rather than sail around the large peninsulas they connected; they named these places 'haul-overs.'

Kerguelen is sculpted by glacier action, with deep valleys and lakes carved out of its high mountains and plateaus. The impressive **Calotte Glaciaire Cook icecap**, in the island's west, covers 10% of the island and is the remnant of the ice sheet that once covered the whole of Grande Terre. The island's highest point is **Grand Ross** (1850m), which was first climbed in 1975.

The weather is typically sub-Antarctic: rainy, cloudy, cold and windy, with the prevailing westerlies frequently rising to gale force. 'Fogs and snow squalls alternate with great frequency,' wrote a medical doctor, Nathaniel William Taylor, who accompanied a whaling and elephant-sealing voyage to Kerguelen in 1851–53. 'The gusts often occur so suddenly that one is obliged to prostrate himself on the ground or be driven along without the power to resist, when walking on shore.' France briefly considered setting up a penal colony here – with the idea that the harsh climate would encourage inmates to work!

The archipelago was first sighted on February 12, 1772 by French Captain Yves Joseph de Kerguélen-Trémarec, sailing in *Fortune*. He called his discovery 'La France Australe' because he didn't realize he was looking at islands. Two days later, François Alesno, Comte de Saint-Allouarn, commander of the accompanying *Gros-Ventre*, sent a boat ashore to claim the territory for King Louis XV. The two ships then separated, and Alesno died soon after his arrival in Mauritius.

With no one to challenge him upon his return to France, Kerguélen told wildly optimistic tales – indeed, outright lies – about his discovery. The lands, he boasted, 'appear to form the central mass of the Antarctic continent,' adding that they were perfectly suited to agriculture and promised abundant minerals and even precious gems. 'If men of a different species are not discovered,' he

WINDY KERGUELEN

Wind is so prevalent at Kerguelen that it deserves special mention. 'Usually when there is no breeze there is a gale,' wrote the Reverend AE Eaton, a British naturalist who visited the island for four months in 1874–75. 'A calm day is an exceptional event.' The island's day-in, day-out average wind speed is 35km/h. Gusts have been measured at more than 200km/h. Storms with winds in excess of 85km/h blow for 150 days a year, and on 41 days of the year, the winds exceed 120km/h. In recognition of the island's powerful breezes, the church at Port-aux-Français is named Notre Dame du Vent – 'Our Lady of the Wind' (p163).

said, 'at least there will be people living in a state of nature.'

Suitably impressed, the French monarch dispatched Kerguélen on a second voyage in 1773, with three ships, *Rolland, Oiseau* and *Dauphine*, and 700 men to colonize 'La France Australe.' A second landing was made, in January 1774, and this time there was no hiding the fact that Kerguélen's discovery was far from a southern motherland. Upon his second homecoming, a French court martial sentenced Kerguélen to 20 years in prison (later reduced to six) and dismissed him from the navy.

When Cook landed on Christmas Eve 1776, one of his men found a bottle containing a parchment inscribed in Latin telling of Kerguélen's visits. Cook, however, was much more sanguine about the islands, calling them the 'Isles of Desolation.'

The first sealers, from the US, arrived in 1791, remaining for 15 months. The first-known Kerguelen shipwreck occurred just two years later, stranding *Eleanora*'s crew for seven months. Other shipwrecks include the sloop *Shaw Perkins*, with all hands, in 1847; the schooner *Garland* in 1848, and *Somerset* in 1864.

By 1804–05 eight British sealing ships were landing on the islands. Repeating the pattern of slaughter practised elsewhere, the sealers soon wiped out the colonies. By 1817 the British ship *Eagle* was able to find just four seals – which, naturally, they killed.

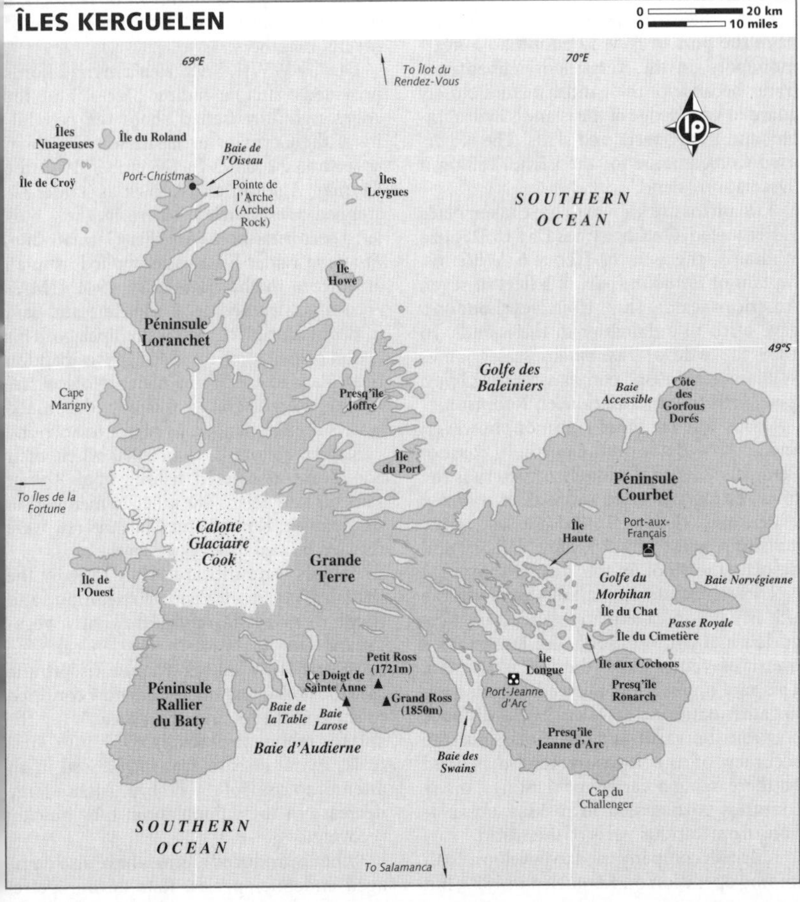

With the fur seals gone (to another island, the sealers always seemed to believe; the thought of extinction appeared never to cross their minds), the sealers turned to elephant seals, whose blubber they rendered into a valuable oil. These 'elephanters' avoided the island's dangerous windward western coast because of the high probability of being blown ashore during the frequent gales. One bold captain of a 100-ton schooner that did work the western coast found it prudent to carry an anchor and cable of the same size as that employed by a 1420-ton vessel.

In a long voyage lasting from 1835 to 1840, the British elephanter *George Howe* visited Kerguelen, taking 3000 barrels of elephant-seal oil, while the American *Columbia* took 3700 barrels in 1838–40.

From 1845 to 1875, Connecticut sealers from the port of New London had a near-monopoly on the Kerguelen elephant-seal trade, because of their intimate and closely guarded knowledge of the island's hydrography and their specialized skills. The sealers used Cook's name for the island, calling it 'Desolation Island.'

Two births are known to have taken place at Kerguelen. On Christmas Day 1852, Eliza Williams, the wife of Henry S Williams, captain of *Franklin* (part of a fleet of seven American sealing ships from New London), gave birth to a daughter in the islands. In 1859 the wife of Tasmanian sealer James William Robinson, commander of *Offley*, gave birth to James Kerguelen Robinson.

Death was far more common, however, and at Anse Betsy on the northern coast of Péninsule Courbet a lonely cemetery is the final resting place for more than a dozen sealers and whalers. 'I need not say,' wrote a visiting sailor in 1874, 'how solitary and desolate they look in this dismal spot.'

Three separate expeditions, sent by the US, Britain and Germany, landed on Kerguelen in 1874 to observe the December 9 transit of Venus across the face of the sun. This rare opportunity allowed astronomers to gather data used to calculate the distance between the earth and the sun. Since the accuracy of the measurement depended on there being a variety of sightings, many countries participated in making observations from various parts of the world.

A British company tried to develop a coal-mining operation on Kerguelen in 1877, but the coal was of poor quality and the attempt was abandoned.

In 1893 France formally annexed Îles Kerguelen. That same year, the French government granted an exclusive 50-year lease to the Frères Bossière, who in 1909 established **Port-Jeanne d'Arc**, a sealing and whaling station on Grand Terre's southeastern coast named to honor France (see p163).

Another sealing and whaling station ran on the island from 1951 to 1956, and the French re-established elephant sealing at Port-aux-Français from 1956 to 1960.

German Erich von Drygalski's *Gauss* expedition landed a scientific research party on Grande Terre from 1902 to 1903. The group did extensive biological and survey work, although an outbreak of beriberi, a disease caused by lack of thiamine, killed several members.

During WWII, Kerguelen's myriad fjords provided valuable hiding places, and the Allies rightfully fretted about the possibility of the Germans or Japanese using them as a strategic base. In December 1940 the German *Atlantis*, also known as 'raider C,' stopped at Kerguelen, where its crew buried a seaman ashore. Another German ship, *Pinguin* ('raider F'), was resupplied from an anchorage in the islands. In 1941 HMAS *Australia* steamed to Kerguelen and laid mines at four places in the archipelago. This action helped force the Germans to abandon their plans to establish a meteorological station on Kerguelen. To this day, the mined waters remain dangerous places to anchor.

Sixteen sailors died in 2000 when their São Tomé–registered fishing boat *Aamor* sank off Kerguelen. The other 26 members of the Spanish, Korean and Chilean crew were rescued by two other boats in the area.

Rabbits were introduced in 1874 by the British Transit of Venus Expedition, and they have ravaged Grand Terre's native vegetation. The namesake Kerguelen cabbage, once prized by sailors as an antiscorbutic (see the boxed text on p82), is now confined to sheer cliff sites and other areas too difficult for rabbits to reach. In 1955, myxomatosis, a viral disease, was introduced in an attempt to control the rabbits. After a large decrease in their population, they quickly recovered.

Other introduced animals have also damaged endemic species. Rats devour petrel eggs and chicks. Cats were introduced by sailors in the early 19th century and again in the 1950s. Today the island's estimated 15,000 feral cats kill nearly five million seabirds annually. An eradication program was begun in 1972, but has not eliminated them. Trout were introduced to the island in 1958. Dogs, mink, mules, ponies, pigs and cattle have all also lived on Grand Terre at some time.

Several introduced species provide fresh meat. More than 2000 sheep live on **Île Longue**, along with a summer-only shepherd, who returns to base on weekends. Some 500 lambs are born each year, and 500 sheep are killed at the Port-aux-Français abattoir. About 35 of Kerguelen's 2000 wide-ranging reindeer are shot annually, as are about 150 of the 500 mouflon (wild sheep from Corsica) on **Île Haute**. The local meat is traded for the beef of Île Amsterdam.

Besides Port-aux-Français and Porte-Jeanne d'Arc (below) three other sites on Kerguelen attract visitors:

The **Arched Rock**, at Baie de l'Oiseau, was a landmark for mariners from the time of Captain Cook, who called the bay 'Christmas Harbour.' One of the best books about Kerguelen available in English is Jean-Paul Kauffmann's evocative *The Arch of Kerguelen: Voyage to the Islands of Desolation* (translated from the French in 2000), which describes his unrealized quest to see this famous landmark – it collapsed sometime between 1908 and 1913.

Le Doigt de Sainte Anne (St Anne's Finger) is a striking 235m monolith sticking up out of the beach at Baie Larose amid a king penguin rookery.

On the northern coast of the **Péninsule Courbet**, king and macaroni penguins breed in large numbers.

Port-aux-Français

France set up Port-aux-Français on Golfe du Morbihan on the island's eastern coast in 1949–50. Known by its acronym PAF (pronounced pahf), the station has been permanently occupied since 1951, and can accommodate 80 expeditioners in winter and 120 in summer. Since 1994 the French National Center for Space Studies has operated a ground station for satellite tracking – identifiable by its two prominent white, spherical radomes to the right of the station.

Kerguelen's most visible introduced species, the dandelion, grows throughout the station grounds. Also keep an eye out for the 'elephant seal crossing' sign on the road to the pier, named Rue de Boisguehenneuc in honor of the officer of *Gros-Ventre* who took possession of the islands with Kerguélen.

The white chapel **Notre Dame du Vent** (Our Lady of the Wind; see the boxed text on p160) was hand-built by station personnel from native stone. After Marc Pechenart and Martine Raulin were married at Port-aux-Français on December 16, 1957, the bride laid the first stone. Beautiful blue-and-red stained-glass windows line the tops of the walls.

La Résidence is the office of the station leader, formally called the 'chef de district' but familiarly known as the 'disker' (*dee*-skay). The station motto '*Vert en Tout Temps*' on the front of La Résidence translates roughly as 'Green in all weather.' There's also a *marmite* (French for try-pot) in front.

The Bureau de Poste sells stamps and phone cards to make international calls at the payphone. Among the books, clothing and other souvenirs available at the station shop, some of the most unique items are the Opinel folding knives prized by French outdoorspeople.

When PAF residents get tired of station surrounds, there are 40 huts and cabins (and a cave or two) for overnight stays. On clear days, the paired snowcapped peaks of Grand Ross (1850m) and Petit Ross (1721m) stand out clearly on the southern horizon.

Port-Jeanne d'Arc

Port-Jeanne d'Arc whaling station (known as PJDA; pronounced payzhidah) operated from 1909 to 1925, with interruptions, and once employed 140 workers. Today, it's abandoned and all but destroyed by Kerguelen's ceaseless winds. The skeletons of the whale-oil tanks are collapsing, and the ground is strewn with rusting drums and the wreckage of the small-gauge railway that once ran out on a pier to waiting ships. A giant propeller projects halfway from the sand, a huge chain lies on the beach, and gentoo penguins wander among the ruins. Only the **piggery** and one other building have been restored; they house summer research parties.

Many artifacts have been 'souvenired,' and much graffiti left behind; some in

German was scrawled by the crew of the WWII German raider *Komet*, also known as *Hilfskreuzer 45*, which visited in 1941 to change its camouflage. Its crew took away cables, paint and other supplies, including 150 tonnes of coal. In February 1941 *Komet* cruised the Antarctic coast seeking whaling vessels for capture.

On the hill overlooking PJDA is a small **cemetery**. While there are many graves here, most have lost their markers and just four crosses remain. Another cross is down near the beach. An unmarked cross is on the hill near the stream that supplied PJDA with its most important resource besides whales: fresh water for trying out the blubber.

HEARD & MCDONALD ISLANDS

Uncharitably – and unfairly – a scientist from HMS *Challenger*, which visited Heard Island in 1874, called it 'so far as I am aware, the most desolate spot on God's earth.'

Heard and McDonald Islands, an external territory of Australia, consists of the main volcanic island of Heard, the tiny Shag Islands lying 11km north and the McDonald Islands (see the boxed text on p166) 43km west. Heard Island is Australia's only active volcano. It's roughly circular in shape, with the 10km-long **Laurens Peninsula** extending northwest and the 7km **Elephant Spit** extending east. The island covers 390 sq km and is 80% glaciated, although many of the glaciers are retreating dramatically. On the northeastern coast, the Brown Glacier is melting at the rate of 2m each year, compared with just half a meter annually during the years 1950–2000.

Big Ben erupted in 1910, 1950, 1985 and again in 1992. Its summit, the island's highest point, is Mawson Peak (2745m), first climbed in 1965 by a private Australian expedition (only two other successful attempts have been made since). The volcano constantly emits steam and occasionally spews lava and ash; its upper slopes are usually shrouded in low cloud.

The climate, as on most of the other sub-Antarctic islands, is cold, wet and windy. In fact, winds blow almost continuously, with frequent gales. The mean annual temperature is 1.4°C.

The date of the islands' first sighting is unknown. Cook noted 'signs of land' near their position in February 1773. Heard was possibly sighted in 1833 by Briton Peter Kemp, sailing in *Magnet*, and again, possibly, in 1848 by American Thomas Long, master of *Charles Carroll*.

American John J Heard, captain of *Oriental*, definitely discovered the island that bears his name on November 25, 1853. Two months later, Briton William McDonald, sailing in *Samarang*, rediscovered Heard and discovered the McDonalds.

The islands were rediscovered three times during the month of December 1854, by three British ships, *Earl of Eglinton, Herald of the Morning* and *Lincluden Castle*. Each ship's crew thought it was the first to see the islands, and each renamed them. In 1857 German Captain Johann Meyer, in *La Rochelle*, named them yet again, this time König Max-Inseln for the King of Bavaria.

American Erasmus Darwin Rogers, sailing in *Corinthian*, made the first recorded landing on Heard in January 1855. He and the crews of six accompanying vessels collected full loads of fur-seal skins and 3000 barrels of elephant-seal oil. There is questionable evidence that fur sealers had been working on the island before this. If the sealers were in fact there, they may have been reluctant to give competing companies any knowledge of their discovery, and may simply have left it out of their logbooks.

Later, 'elephanters' also worked at the Heard Island beaches, shaking iron buckets filled with stones to frighten the elephant seals back up the beach and prevent their escape into the sea. On other beaches, where it was too dangerous to land boats, men were stationed to drive the animals back into the sea – sometimes with whips made of the hide of other elephant seals – so they could be killed on more accessible beaches. One early scientific observer noted that the seals 'are sometimes treated with horrible brutality.'

Since there was no safe anchorage for ships, however, many of the elephanters did not perform the laborious rendering of the blubber down to oil on Heard Island itself. Instead, they sailed down from Kerguelen and, after the seals were flensed, the blubber was minced, put in barrels and taken back to Kerguelen for boiling. The cold air kept it from going rancid en route.

Probably nothing kept the elephanting gangs themselves from becoming rancid-smelling, however, given their smoky, sooty work of rendering the blubber and their low standard of personal hygiene. Captain James Robinson, master of the barque *Offley* from Hobart, left a sealing gang of 17 men to winter at Heard in 1858. 'No one,' he wrote in his log, 'is ever guilty of washing here.'

Sealer's Corner, at the northwestern end of the beach at Corinthian Bay, was first used by elephant-seal hunters in about 1850. The **ruins** of a stone hut, originally built half-buried in the sand for protection from the wind, are clearly visible. Not as easily discerned are several **graves** with thin wooden boards for markers and piles of rocks in the shape of bodies.

Elephant Spit's low sand-and-shingle beach, which rises less than 3m above sea level, is named for its abundance of elephant seals, with around 40,000 coming ashore at the eastern end of the island each year for breeding – more than 15,000 pups are born annually. Little wonder that the Spit was Heard's prime hunting ground during the sealing era. At its peak in 1858, more than 15 vessels worked this area, putting hundreds of men ashore to kill and skin the seals and render the blubber in large iron try-pots. If you're fortunate enough to get ashore at **Spit Bay**, you may see fur seals, gentoo and king penguins, along with evidence of the early elephanters. However, rough surf in this area very often precludes landing.

The first wintering party was landed in 1856 by the American sealer *Zoe*, and in the same year, the American vessel *Alfred* became the first Heard shipwreck. Many others followed: *Frank*, *Mary Powell*, and *RB Coleman* (all 1859), *Exile* (1860), *Pacific* (1863), *ER Sawyer* (1866) and *Trinity* (1880).

Two exceptional artifacts from the sealing era have been found on Heard. A blubber press, one of the few surviving examples, was excavated and is now on loan to the Queen Victoria Museum and Art Gallery in Launceston, Tasmania. A carved basalt rock, the only one ever discovered in the sub-Antarctic or Antarctic, was found on Heard during the 1985–86 summer field season. It depicts the face of a bearded man, and it was carved by an unknown 19th-century sealer, possibly shipwrecked on the island. It is now displayed at the headquarters of the

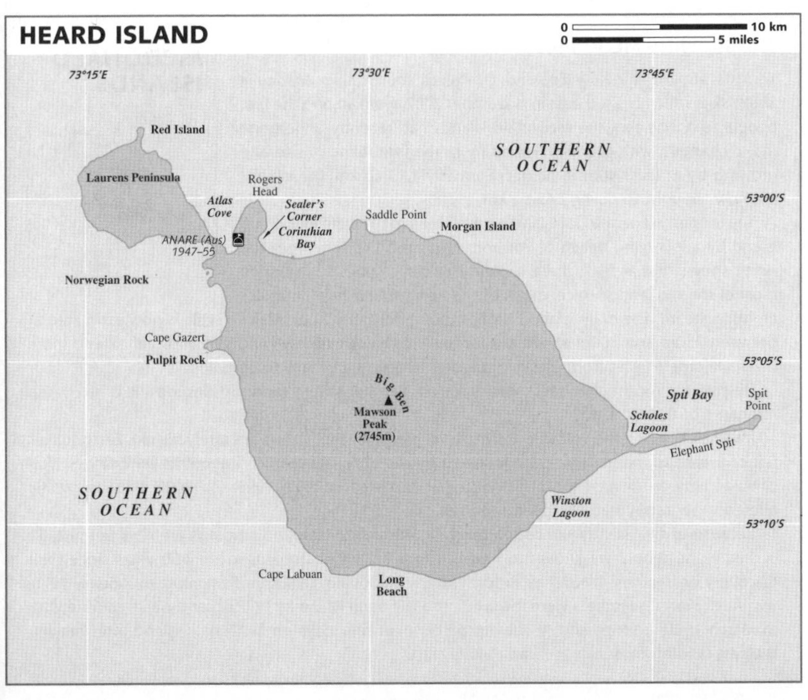

Australian Antarctic Division in Kingston, Tasmania.

In 1908 Heard and McDonald Islands were annexed by Britain. On December 26, 1947, this sovereignty was transferred to Australia. Also on this date, the first of the Australian National Antarctic Research Expeditions (ANARE) established a base at **Atlas Cove** on Heard's northwestern coast, using a WWII naval landing craft driven onto the beach and unloaded through bow doors. Soon after, an aircraft used for aerial surveying was destroyed by a storm after making a single flight. The first wintering party's experiences are chronicled in Arthur Scholes' *Fourteen Men: The Story of the Antarctic Expedition to Heard Island* (1952).

A group from the ANARE station completed the first journey on foot around the island in 1951. The station closed in 1955, transferring personnel and material to Mawson station on Antarctica. Today, the collapsed ANARE station has been largely removed from Atlas Cove, and little remains besides the **cross** commemorating Alistair 'Jock' Forbes and Richard Hoseason, who died in 1952 while returning from an ill-fated journey down island. While walking along the beach beneath the icecliff fronting the Baudissin Glacier, a wave swept them into the sea. Hoseason drowned, and Forbes died of exposure while trying to return to the station over the glacier. The cross is off-limits to tourists and expeditioners alike as it's located in the midst of protected plant life.

Remnants of the **Admiralty Hut**, built by the British in 1929 as a refuge for shipwrecked mariners, also still stand at Atlas Cove.

Summer research programs have operated occasionally on Heard since 1955, and two parties have wintered at Spit Bay since the Atlas Cove station closed: an American satellite-survey team in 1969, as well as an Australian expedition in 1992. An automatic weather station was established in 1990 at Atlas Cove, and another is now located at Spit Bay. The Australian Antarctic Division conducts tri-annual summer scientific expeditions to Heard, the most recent being over the 2003–04 summer.

Over a million pairs of macaroni penguins breed on Heard, but recent volcanic eruptions

THE GROWING MCDONALDS

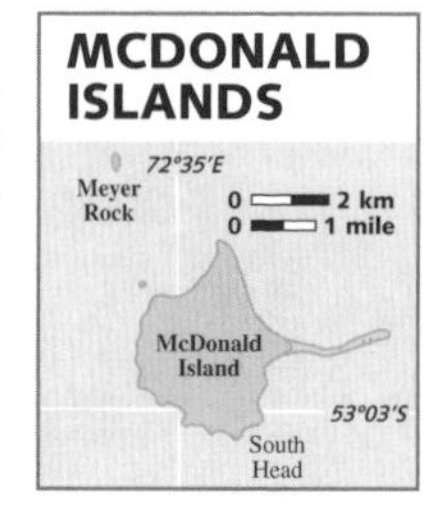

Tourists aboard the New Zealand–chartered tourist ship *Akademik Shokalskiy*, which cruised past in November 2002, were among the first people to notice that the McDonald Islands had recently undergone major changes, with the main island more than doubling in size and growing by at least 40m in height. Formerly 1.13 sq km, the islands are now thought to cover 2.45 sq km.

The formerly separate Flat Island is now joined to the main McDonald Island by a low-lying beach of volcanic sand, and the view from the north shows that at least three separate volcanic cones have buried most of the old land surface; much of the new ground has fumaroles emitting steam. The main island's highest point, formerly 212m Maxwell Hill, is now estimated at between 250m and 300m above sea level. A newly formed low-lying spit and reef extend more than a kilometer east from McDonald Island, creating a hazard to shipping.

Despite the recent changes, some macaroni penguins were seen roosting on the ash-covered remnants of the old land.

It's unclear when the volcanic activity took place, for the islands are rarely visited. Earthquakes felt on Heard Island in 1992 were followed by the arrival of pumice fragments on beaches. Volcanic activity on or near the McDonalds was reported in 1997, 1999 and 2001, but the greatly altered topography had not been reported.

Because of the islands' almost completely untouched state, no landings are now permitted.

Just eight people are known to have set foot on the McDonalds in the 150 years since their discovery on January 4, 1854 by Briton William McDonald, sailing in *Samarang*. In January 1970, two Australian researchers were lowered onto the main island by helicopter for a 20-minute visit. In March 1980, a six-person Australian party spent four days on McDonald Island after making the first landing by sea in an amphibious craft.

on the McDonalds appear to have displaced the thousands that had been present there. Long Beach on Heard's south coast may have the world's largest colony of macaronis. There are also approximately 1000 Heard Island sheathbills (a subspecies) in the islands, and less than 1000 pairs of the endemic Heard shag *(Phalacrocorax nivalis)*.

No known human-introduced species are present on Heard and McDonald Islands, which makes them highly unusual. For this reason, extensive quarantine restrictions apply to all visitors and anyone going ashore must wear clean footwear and clothing.

Heard and the McDonald Islands are included on the World Heritage List. Tourist visits to Heard are rare, thanks to its bad weather and the hazards of landing. All landings require a permit from the **Australian Antarctic Division** (☎ 61-3-6232-3209; information@aad.gov.au; Channel Hwy, Kingston, Tasmania 7050, Australia).

ÎLE AMSTERDAM

Ovoid volcanic Île Amsterdam is part of France's Terres Australes et Antarctiques Françaises, like its neighbor Île St Paul, which is visible 89km to the south on a clear day. All of Amsterdam's 85 sq km are unglaciated. The two highest points, **Mont de la Dives** (881m) and **La Grande Marmite** (742m), are part of the now-collapsed rim of the volcano that formed the island. The volcano's floor now forms a plateau about 600m high. Lava flows radiate from this plateau, spilling down to the sea where they end in cliffs above narrow shingle beaches. These headlands are generally less than 30m high, except on the western coast, where they tower to 700m.

Nicknamed the 'Riviera' of the French peri-Antarctic islands, Île Amsterdam's climate is comparatively warm, windy, wet and humid. June, the coolest month, averages 10°C, while January and February, the warmest, average 15°C.

Juan Sebastián de Elcano, the Basque who completed the voyage of the great Portuguese navigator Fernão de Magalhães (Ferdinand Magellan) after Magellan was killed, discovered the island on March 18, 1522, during the first-ever circumnavigation of the earth. But Elcano did not give the island a name, a task left for Dutchman Anthonie van Diemen, sailing in *Nieuw Amsterdam* in 1633. The first landing was made by a three-ship Dutch survey expedition in 1696.

Oddly, sealers did not arrive on the island until almost three centuries after its discovery. *Nootka*, a British ship, started Amsterdam's fur rush, landing parties on Îles Amsterdam and St Paul for 17 months in 1791–92 and taking 15,000 fur-seal skins. An American sealer, *Flora*, took 13,415 seals in 1792, while another American ship, *Mary*, took 44,517 in 1800.

Shipwrecks occurred on a fairly regular basis throughout the 19th century: *Lady Munro* (1833), *George* (1839), *Meridian* (1853), *Tuscany* (1855), *Vellore* (1865) and *Fernand* (1876). One group of castaways found a unique way to cook: several freshwater mineral springs in the neighborhood of the crater were continually boiling, and they lowered their food into these.

In 1870–71, a Frenchman, with his family and four employees, inhabited the island for seven months in an abortive attempt to raise cattle. Three years later, Captain Coffin of the ship *Annie Battles* and two of his crew were rescued from Île Amsterdam after being abandoned there during a mutiny.

France has operated a permanent scientific station on the island's northern coast since 1949, when 10 men led by Paul Martin de Viviès wintered here. Now called **Martin-de-Viviès station**, it accommodates 30 people in winter and more in summer. The station boasts a swimming pool and tennis court, and as at the stations on the other two inhabited French peri-Antarctic islands, there's a small chapel, **Notre Dame des Anges** (Our Lady of the Angels). **La Mosquée** (The Mosque) is the nickname for a building used to prepare balloons for atmospheric studies. Extensive gardens, including fruit trees, are planted behind La Mosquée in collapsed lava tubes, which provide shelter from the wind.

Île Amsterdam is one of the few peri-Antarctic islands with trees – *Phylica nitida*, which is a close relative of the *Phylica arborea* found on Tristan, Gough, Inaccessible and Nightingale Islands. Records from an East India Company vessel visiting Île Amsterdam in 1770 describe its heavy tree cover, and a French naval expedition in 1792 noted a forest fire. In 1825–26 two Tasmanian sealers started a fire that lasted several months, and in 1833 the survivors of the wreck of the American ship *Lady*

Munro caused another conflagration that destroyed much of the island's forest. The last remaining large stand of *Phylica*, known as the **'Grand Bois'** (Large Forest), covers about 10 hectares. It is fenced and bordered by wind-breaking cypresses (an introduced species). A few isolated *Phylica* grow outside this area, and a replanting program is underway.

One of the rarest birds in the world, the Amsterdam albatross *(Diomedea amsterdamensis)*, breeds only on the island. Although the birds' nesting sites at the top of the island cannot be visited, to avoid disturbing them, sharp-eyed – and lucky – observers may catch a glimpse of one in flight.

The unusual long-crested rockhopper penguin also breeds here (as well as on Île St Paul), as do 70% of the world's population of yellow-nosed albatrosses. Rock lobsters have been commercially harvested on Île Amsterdam since 1948.

The island's wild cattle are descended from five animals left by the 1871 settlers. The herd numbers about 700 and provides beef for an occasional station barbecue.

ÎLE ST PAUL

Île St Paul is a volcanic cone, the easter third of which has either been blown awa by an eruption or eroded by wave action What's left is an unglaciated island shape like a right triangle with the coast runnin from northwest to southeast at its lon side.

The volcanic crater has been breache by the sea, which enters to form the cir cular **Bassin du Cratère**, less than 60m dee and 1200m wide. At the entrance, betwee the two long extending arms of rock, th depth is just a bit over 2m at the highes tides. Interestingly, the earliest visitors t St Paul reported that the crater wall was *no* breached by the sea. Today, the souther arm has been severed by the surging surf.

Even on the inside of the crater, the wall slope steeply into the sea, and there's almos no level ground anywhere except at the sta tion site. The crater's inner walls and th island's eastern coast are cliffs up to 200m high. The west and southern slopes of th volcano are much less steep and end in 30m sea cliffs. These are generally unclimbable

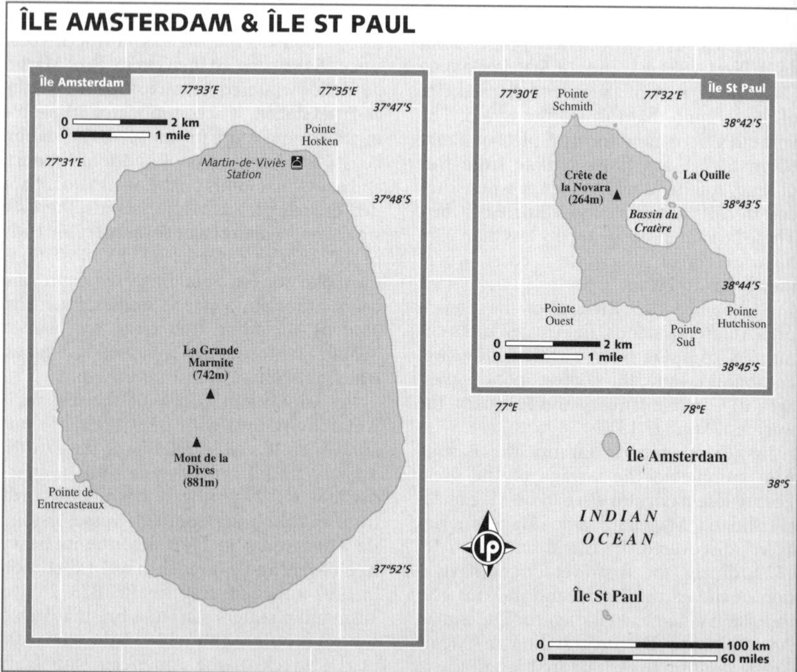

RALPH LEE HC

Paradise Harbor (p223)

JONATHAN CHESTER

Icicles

RALPH LEE HOPKINS

Glacial ice patterns (p86)

Sastrugi, Wilkes Land

DAVID ETHE

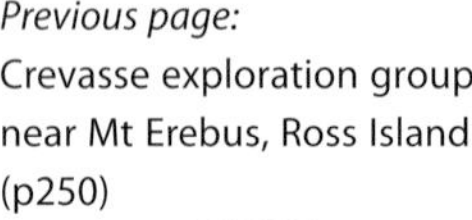

Previous page:
Crevasse exploration group near Mt Erebus, Ross Island (p250)

SCOTT DARSNEY

making landings on the island from these approaches difficult. Île St Paul covers 7 sq km. Its highest point at 264m is **Crête de la Novara**.

Dutchman Haevik Klaaszoon van Hillegom, sailing in *Zeewolf*, discovered Île St Paul on April 19, 1618, but the island was later found marked as 'S Paulo' on an earlier Portuguese chart from 1559. The first landing was made by the Dutch in 1696.

Sealers first arrived in 1789, from Britain, and the usual wholesale slaughter ensued. A group of five French fur sealers were stuck on the island for three years beginning in 1792 when their support ship *Émilie* was captured by the British at Macao; they were rescued by the British ship *Ceres* in 1795.

There have been at least three recorded shipwrecks: *Fox* (1810), *Napoléon III* (1853) and *Holt Hill* (1889).

A Polish settler, Józef Kosciuszko, lived on St Paul between 1819 and 1830. For several years of that time, he was apparently all alone. Fishermen from Réunion lived here periodically in the mid-19th century; their settlement reached a peak population of 45 in 1845. In 1871 after the British troop transport ship HMS *Megaera* sprang a leak and beached at Île St Paul, 500 men were forced to live in a tent camp for three months. In 1874, on December 9, a French expedition observed the transit of Venus from the island.

Rock lobsters thrive in Île St Paul's waters. From 1928 to 1931 a French fishing company, La Langouste Française, operated a lobster fishing enterprise on the island. As many as 100 men spent the summers ashore, fishing and canning. Four of the seven winterers died in 1930, and the next year, 30 more men died of beriberi, so the settlement was abandoned. Today, a ship-based lobster fishery operates around Île Amsterdam and Île St Paul.

In 1955 the island was formally incorporated with Île Amsterdam, Îles Kerguelen, Îles Crozet and Terre Adélie in Antarctica as the Terres Australes et Antarctiques Françaises.

Among Île St Paul's bird species is the unusual long-crested rockhopper penguin, also found on Île Amsterdam. A rat- and rabbit-eradication program completed in 1997 by a team of New Zealanders was successful, and ground-nesting birds have begun returning.

MACQUARIE ISLAND

Commonly known as 'Macca' to its human residents, Macquarie Island has long divided opinions. Mawson, who first visited in 1911, called it 'one of the wonder spots of the world.' Captain James Douglass, master of *Mariner*, which came from Sydney in company with three other sealers in 1822, disagreed, describing it as 'the most wretched place of involuntary and slavish exilium that can possibly be conceived – nothing could warrant any civilized creature living on such a spot.'

Present-day visitors and residents of the ANARE station will be interested to learn that despite the brutal treatment the administrators of Tasmania's colonial penal system happily gave their inmates, they declined to send them to Macquarie: 'the remote and stormy region in which Macquarie Island is placed,' opined the *Hobart Town Gazette* in 1826, 'is a strong reason against the adoption of that place as a penal settlement.'

Halfway between Tasmania (1467km to the northwest) and the Antarctic continent (1296km to the south), Macquarie's leading attractions are its residents: 100,000 seals, mainly elephant seals; and four million penguins, including about 850,000 breeding pairs of royals, which breed nowhere else.

Rising in steep cliffs to a plateau 240m to 345m high, Macquarie is 34km long and between 2.5km and 5km wide, and covers 128 sq km. The highest point, 433m Mt Hamilton, is named for Harold Hamilton, biologist on Mawson's 1911–13 expedition. Numerous small lakes dot the plateau. The Judge and Clerk Rocks lie 16km north and the Bishop and Clerk Rocks lie 28km south.

The climate is one of the most equable (least-changing) on earth. Mean annual temperatures range from 3.3°C to 7.2°C. Strong westerlies blow nearly every day. There is no permanent snow or ice cover. The yearly precipitation (91cm) is spread out over more than 300 days and in a variety of forms: snow, rain, hail, sleet, mist and fog – sometimes all in the same day.

Vegetation at low altitude is dominated by tussock grass, with short grasslands and feldmark communities higher up. There are no trees or shrubs, but there are two species of 'megaherb' on the island, one of which can grow up to a meter high. Among Macquarie's unusual features are the 'featherbeds,' waterlogged areas on the coastal terraces, where sub-surface drainage is poor, and which only just support a person's weight. Also known as 'quaking mires,' they are actually floating patches of vegetation covering lenses of water, which can be more than 6m deep. Crossing them is like stepping on a giant waterbed.

Geologically the island is very interesting, for it's the only place on earth where rocks from the earth's mantle, 6km below the ocean floor, are actively exposed above sea level by the gradual but continuing upthrust of the plate. With all of this seismic activity, large earthquakes occur often. Macquarie was granted World Heritage status in 1997, primarily because of its geological values.

The first-recorded sighting of Macquarie was on July 11, 1810, by Captain Frederick Hasselborough of Sydney on the sealing brig *Perseverance*. But sealers most probably visited Macquarie earlier – for Hasselborough reported finding a shipwreck. He named the island after Lachlan Macquarie, governor of the Australian colony of New South Wales (of which Tasmania was then a part) and collected 80,000 fur-seal skins.

He may also have tried to keep Macquarie Island a secret, but if so he failed badly: just five months later, the island's location was printed in the *Sydney Gazette*. In 1812 a single ship recorded taking 14,000 fur seals, but by 1830 it was no longer worthwhile for sealers to stop here, even for elephant seals. During the boom years of Macquarie's seal trade, dozens of ships came annually, but between 1830 and 1874, fewer than half a dozen visited. One of them, *Lord Nelson*, was wrecked at Hasselborough Bay in 1838, its survivors stranded for two years.

Ships began calling at Macquarie again in the mid- to late 1870s, when king and royal penguins were killed and boiled for their oil. Each bird yielded about half a liter. The royals were preferred, because their oil was not as highly saturated with blood, which tended to ferment and ruin the oil. At the penguin-oil industry's peak, in 1905, the factory at Nuggets Point could process up to 2000 birds at once. But the trade eventually became uneconomical – and conservation rules were applied to the island. Today, seals and penguins breed amid the rusting remains of the cast-iron boilers used in the trade that nearly exterminated their ancestors.

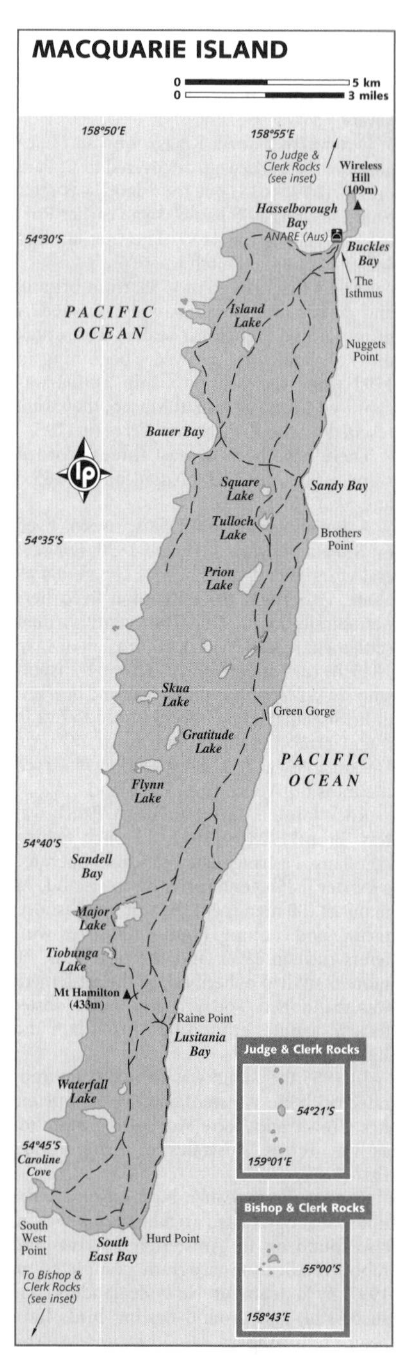

At least nine ships have wrecked on the rocky coast, the oldest being the aptly named *Campbell Macquarie*, which was wrecked at Caroline Cove on June 10, 1812, less than two years after Macquarie Island was discovered. Henry Whalley, a member of the crew of the sealing schooner *Bencleugh* wrecked on the island in 1877, died the day after the wreck. One of his shipmates scratched an inscription on the vessel's folding log-slate, a poetic epitaph appropriate for any of the thousands of mariners buried on the gale-lashed islands of the Southern Ocean:

> There calmly let him sleep.
> Not all the winds that blow
> Can shake his bed, and he shall keep
> A quiet watch below.

The most recent shipwreck occurred on December 3, 1987, when the Danish ship *Nella Dan*, chartered by ANARE for 26 years, ran aground at Buckles Bay. It was scuttled in deep water off the coast on Christmas Eve 1987, following unsuccessful salvage attempts.

Notable among the island's plants is the yellow-flowering Macquarie Island cabbage once eaten by sealers to prevent scurvy (see the boxed text on p82).

Whalers and sealers brought horses, donkeys, dogs, goats, pigs, cattle, ducks, chickens and sheep to Macquarie, although none survive today. Rats, mice, cats, rabbits and wekas (a flightless bird from New Zealand) did thrive – and in recent years have heavily impacted the island's ecology. Although wekas were eradicated in 1988, the rats, mice and rabbits are still numerous.

Feral cats, which killed approximately 60,000 prions and petrels annually, were more difficult to get rid of. Licensed rangers shot, trapped and gassed the felines, and the Australian government spent US$6500 per cat to rid the island of its last 100 wily animals, which weighed up to 6kg and were all muscle. Success was achieved in June 2000, when the last cat, a female tabby, number 2450, was shot. Burrow-nesting seabirds should begin making a comeback, although rats remain a problem as they prey on the eggs of burrow-nesting birds.

When Mawson landed a scientific party on the island during his Australasian Antarctic Expedition of 1911–14, he was met by the crew of *Clyde*, shipwrecked a month earlier and prepared to defend their sealing rights against what they initially thought were rival sealers. Once the mix-up was straightened out, the research party Mawson left on the island used a wireless relay station set up on Wireless Hill in the first two-way communication with the Antarctic continent. The transmissions were a grim exchange of information: news of the death of Mawson's sledging companions was sent from Commonwealth Bay to Macquarie, while word of Scott's death was sent from Macquarie to Antarctica.

Other expedition leaders who stopped at Macquarie include Bellingshausen (who traded one of the sealers three bottles of rum for two live albatrosses, 20 dead ones and one live parrot), Wilkes, Scott and Shackleton.

In 1948 a scientific station was established by ANARE at the isthmus on the site occupied by Mawson's men in 1911. About 15 to 20 people winter at the **ANARE station**; this number climbs to 40 during the summer months. The first woman to winter at an ANARE station, Zoe Gardner, was the station doctor in 1976.

Although it's hard to imagine when looking at the station today, the narrow isthmus it occupies once resembled an abattoir, as AL McLean, a visitor on an expedition, wrote in 1919:

> The rough shingle of the upper part of the beach and boggy tussocks were everywhere covered with the bones, bleached skeletons and putrid carcases of sea-elephants which had been killed, stripped of their blubber and left to rot where they lay. The whole of the foreshore of this narrow neck of land was a charnel of decay and noisome smells.

The island's first tourists were four men carried by the New Zealand sealing ship *Gratitude* in 1891. Today, Macquarie is a Tasmanian State Reserve, and permits to land must be obtained in advance from the **Tasmanian Parks and Wildlife Service** (☎ 61-3-6233-6203; fax 61-3-6233-3477; 134 Macquarie St, Hobart). Ships that arrive unannounced are not allowed to put people ashore. There is a landing fee of not less than A$150 per person (plus GST), although most visitors are unaware of it, since it is included in the price of their cruise. Part of this fee pays for a handsome color booklet distributed to visitors.

Parks rangers oversee visits to the island. Boardwalks have been constructed in several places to prevent erosion, and regulations govern how many people can come ashore at once. For instance, at Sandy Bay, site of a royal penguin rookery, for instance, no more than 60 people may be landed simultaneously. At Lusitania Bay, home of a massive king penguin colony, no visitors are permitted on the beach, and Zodiacs must remain 200m offshore. All visitors to the island must leave by 7pm, and no food or drink can be brought ashore. Just as in Antarctica, nothing – not even a pebble – may be removed.

BALLENY ISLANDS

Straddling the Antarctic Circle and 95% covered in ice, these islands are the tops of volcanoes, which rise from depths of 3km. Rarely visited by anyone, the Ballenys are the northernmost territory of New Zealand's Antarctic claim, the Ross Dependency. Row, Young, Borradaile, Buckle and Sabrina Islands, and the Monolith and Sturge Island stretch some 195km from north to south. Brown Peak (1524m) on Sturge Island is the group's highest point.

The Ballenys are largely unlandable because of their steep basaltic cliffs, and so have been visited only a handful of times. Without large beaches to attract seals, they were ignored by sealers, who regarded them merely as hazards to navigation. English whaling

DEADLY DEBRIS

Despite Antarctica's remoteness, its surrounding seas are becoming as polluted as waters in more populated regions – with tragic consequences for wildlife. Every year, thousands of Antarctic seabirds and marine mammals are killed or injured by marine debris.

Dumping any trash overboard south of 60°S is prohibited by the agreements of the Antarctic Treaty. This includes all plastics, ropes, nets, paper, rags, glass, metal, bottles, crockery and even incineration ash – in short, anything. But many vessels ignore these regulations.

Fishing is the main cause of Southern Ocean debris. Fishing boats either toss or lose overboard many types of litter: plastic packaging bands from bait boxes; fishing net panels; buoys; ropes; and fishing lines – often with hooks still attached.

One researcher estimates that debris in the Southern Ocean has increased one hundredfold between 1992 and 2002.

Fur seals often become entangled in plastic debris, particularly in net fragments, packaging bands and six-pack rings. Because the plastic doesn't stretch, these items become deadly nooses for fur seals, slowly strangling them as they grow.

Albatrosses, penguins, gulls and shags can likewise be killed or injured when they eat plastic and other debris that can cause intestinal blockages or starvation. When used as a nesting material, the same debris can fatally entangle birds. Among South Georgia's wandering albatrosses, an estimated 20% of all chicks may have swallowed the large steel hooks used in longline fishing.

Even debris left over from worthwhile scientific work, such as weather balloons used in atmospheric research, may be harmful. Antarctic stations launch 10,000 balloons every year. Within hours of their ascent, they burst and fall, often into the sea. Others are blown into the water. Most weather balloons are made from highly durable polythene, and could last for decades in the chilly Southern Ocean. One researcher has calculated that every whale has a 7% chance of encountering a spent balloon during the course of a single year. Although no one is certain what effects might be suffered by a whale ingesting a balloon, whales have been found dead with plastic bags in their stomachs, and it's possible that they choked to death on them.

People are not immune from the threat posed by marine debris. In 1984 a fishing boat's propellers became fouled by the very nets it had earlier discarded overboard, putting both the vessel and her crew in peril.

Marine debris, particularly plastic, poses another danger. Alien species such as worms, larvae and barnacles often hitch a ride aboard, allowing them to colonize areas they would otherwise be unable to reach. Such stowaways can wreak chaos by displacing native species. Human rubbish is now the largest carrier of invasive species, which were once restricted to driftwood.

captains John Balleny, in the schooner *Eliza Scott*, and Thomas Freeman, in the cutter *Sabrina*, were the first to visit. Freeman went ashore – or at least stepped into waist-deep water and collected some pebbles – probably on Sabrina Island, on February 9, 1839. This 'landing' was the first ever south of the Antarctic Circle. Unfortunately, *Sabrina* later became separated from *Eliza Scott* and was never heard from again, which helps to explain how the islands came to be called the Ballenys and not the Freemans.

Sabrina Island was designated in 1969 as a protected area under the Antarctic Treaty, because of the islands' isolation. No landings can be made without special permission. About 500 Adélies nest here each year, as well as the occasional chinstrap or macaroni penguin, and numerous species of seabirds.

The first tourist landing was made in 1968. An automatic weather station set up by the US on Brown Peak is checked annually by helicopter, but the mountain remains unclimbed.

An enormous earthquake – 8.1 on the Richter scale – occurred just offshore in March 1998, one of the biggest to occur anywhere that year. In comparison, the 1995 earthquake in Kobe, Japan that killed 6000 people measured 7.2 on the Richter scale.

Australian physicist Louis Bernacchi, who sailed past in 1899 on Borchgrevink's *Southern Cross* expedition, was moved by the Ballenys' bleakness to quote Tennyson's 1833 poem *Mariana in the South*:

> I can imagine no greater punishment than to be 'left alone to live forgotten and die forlorn' on that desolate shore.

NEW ZEALAND'S SUB-ANTARCTIC ISLANDS

New Zealand maintains five sub-Antarctic island groups as National Nature Reserves: the Antipodes, Auckland, Bounty, Campbell and Snares groups. These islands teem with wildlife, particularly seabirds, which nest by the millions on these oases. Ten species of penguin have been recorded on the islands, and four species breed regularly on them.

All of the island groups are managed by the **New Zealand Department of Conservation** (☎ 64-3-214-4589; PO Box 743, Invercargill). Entry is by permit, issued only if the group is accompanied by a Department of Conservation representative. Just 550 visitors each calendar year are permitted to visit the islands.

To prevent the accidental introduction of non-native species such as rats, which could wipe out local bird and insect populations, no landings are allowed in the Antipodes, Bounty or Snares groups, or on pristine islands of the Aucklands and Campbell Island groups. A NZ$200 per person fee is charged for landing, good for all of the islands on the same trip. The fee includes a copy of Neville Peat's handsome full-color, 96-page guidebook, *Sub-Antarctic New Zealand: A Rare Heritage*, published by the Department of Conservation in 2003.

Antipodes Islands

Named 'Isle Penantipode' on March 26, 1800, by Captain Henry Waterhouse of the HMS *Reliance*, for being almost directly opposite London on the globe, the Antipodes group totals 21 sq km. The group consists of the eponymous, 20-sq-km main island,

with the two tiny **Windward Islands** lying appropriately to the west, the equally small **Leeward Island** to the east, and 50-hectare **Bollons Island** and its attendant **Archway Island** to the northeast.

Sealing in the islands began in February 1805, when the first gangs were landed by the American schooner *Independence*. Later that year more sealers were landed from *Independence* and three other vessels, and by the year's end over 80 sealers were living on the Antipodes. These castaways made profitable use of their time, and by February 1806 well over 100,000 fur-seal skins had been shipped from the island to Sydney and London. Such was the slaughter, that the Antipodes fur-seal trade peaked during the next 12 months when a further 165,000 skins were exported. In total, about 350,000 fur seals were killed at the Antipodes and the species became extinct there by 1828. Seals did not visit the islands again until 1950. Even today, very few breed here, although numbers visiting from the Bounty Islands, and elsewhere, build up to about 5000 each March.

The Antipodes, too, saw their share of shipwrecks. The survivors of the British ship *Spirit of the Dawn*'s wreck in 1893 spent nearly three months living in a cave, and without fire, before being rescued. The 22-member crew of *President Félix Fauré*, wrecked while sailing from New Caledonia to France in 1908, had more luck and survived two months in a castaway depot before aid arrived.

No tourist landings are allowed in the Antipodes, but Zodiac cruising offers superb scenery and wildlife-viewing. Along with the Bounty Islands, the Antipodes are the only home of the world's estimated 70,000 pairs of erect-crested penguins. Also endemic to the islands is the brilliant-green Antipodes parakeet *(Cyanoramphus unicolor)*, which is found with, but does not breed with, the islands' red-crowned parakeet (similar to the New Zealand species of this parakeet). Over 5000 pairs of Antipodean wandering albatross nest among tussock grass on top of the main island. The Antipodes' only introduced animals are mice.

Auckland Islands

At 626 sq km, the Aucklands are the largest of New Zealand's sub-Antarctic island groups. The group consists of four main islands. Southernmost **Adams Island**, which has no introduced species, was declared a nature reserve in 1910 in recognition of its pristine state. Between Adams and the main island, **Auckland Island**, lies the superb three-armed natural anchorage of Carnley Harbour. The islands' highest point is Mt Dick (705m) on Adams Island.

Deep fjords serrate Auckland Island's eastern coast, while the western coast features steep cliffs up to 300m high. At times the powerful westerlies striking the cliffs turn cascades there into 'reversible' waterfalls, actually blowing the water that has fallen part of the way down the cliffs back up onto the plateau, where the process is repeated as long as the wind keeps up. **Disappointment Island**, also without any introduced species, lies to the west of Auckland Island, while **Enderby Island**, with its striking cliffs of columnar basalt, lies to its northeast.

Maori people from New Zealand may have visited Enderby Island more than 600 years ago, as shown by carbon-dating charcoal that they left behind at Sandy Bay, although this is still being debated.

The group was first visited by Europeans on August 18, 1806, by British Captain Abraham Bristow of the whaler *Ocean*, who named them for his friend Lord Auckland.

An odd near meeting occurred in 1840 in a natural harbor on Auckland Island's northeastern tip: Wilkes' US Exploring Expedition ship *Porpoise* landed on March 10 and set up a sign for anyone who might follow. Incredibly, Frenchman Dumont d'Urville came ashore just two days later and added to the sign a message of his own. Both communiqués were found eight months later by Ross, for whom Port Ross (the protected expanse of water between Auckland and Enderby Islands) is named.

Sealers also worked the Auckland Islands, and one of them, J Inches Thomson, noted c 1912 the contrast between the elegance of the final product and the brutality and danger required to obtain it:

> Ladies in the cosy seal-skin jackets seldom think of the perils endured in obtaining them. In some localities at the Auckland Islands, the sealers are lowered over cliffs hundreds of feet high, and then have to carry the skins on

their backs for miles. It is seldom that a season passes without loss of life.

A group of Maoris, with a group of Moriori slaves, moved to Port Ross in 1842, after finding it convenient to leave the Chatham Islands (770km east of Christchurch). The Maoris were there to greet Charles Enderby, of the famous London whaling firm Samuel Enderby & Son, when he arrived in 1849 to set up a colony he called Hardwicke, hoping to duplicate the success of the Falkland Islands colony, which thrived on whaling and ship refitting. Perhaps he should have called it 'Hardworke' instead. Although its peak population of nearly 300 people struggled mightily, the colony survived just three years. The crops failed, whale catches were minimal and few ships called in needing overhaul. The little community did record, however, five marriages, 16 births and four deaths.

By 1852 the last colonists had departed, leaving behind a forlorn ghost town at Erebus Cove on Port Ross' northern shore. Two buildings stand there today, though neither is contemporary with the colony. One is a former **castaway depot**, the other a boatshed now rather grandiosely called the **Erebus Cove Museum**, containing relics. From just south of Erebus Stream, 10 minutes' walk up from the beach brings you to Hardwicke's **cemetery**, where half of the graves are of shipwrecked sailors. Further east lie

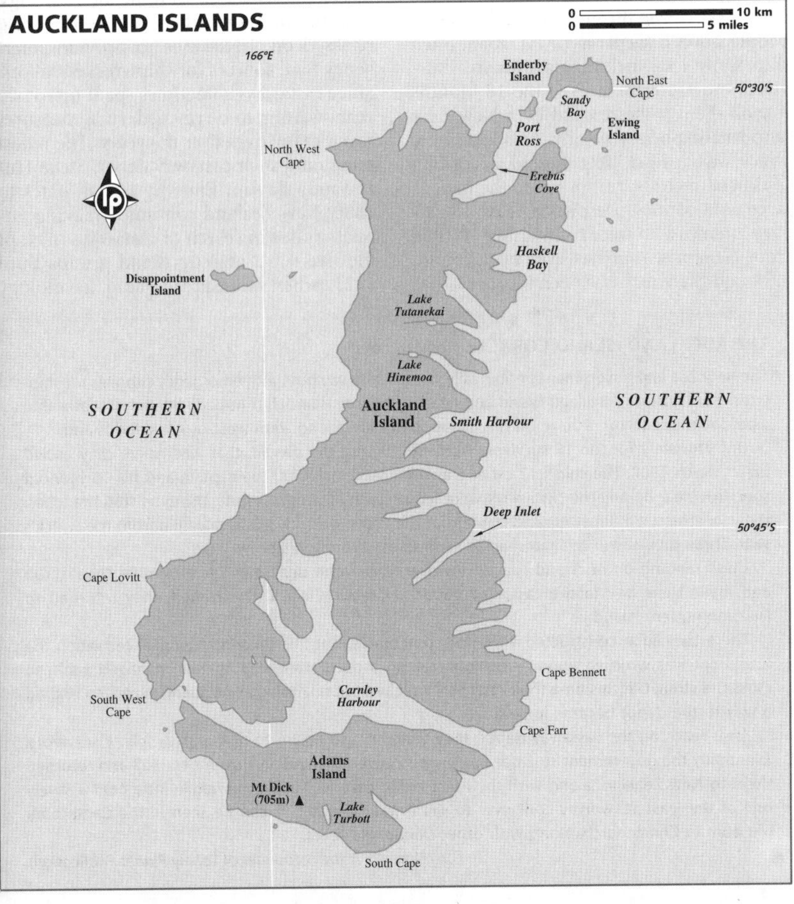

the settlement's overgrown cobblestone paths, and at Davis Bay (directly south of Davis Island) are glass-strewn **ruins** of the colony's house sites. Taking anything is forbidden.

The Maoris left soon after the Hardwickers did. By 1856 the islands were uninhabited once more.

At least nine ships have wrecked on the Auckland Islands, including, most famously, *General Grant* in 1866. London-bound from Melbourne and the Australian goldfields, the American-flagged treasure ship was driven into a huge cavern on Auckland Island's western coast, ironically, not by a storm, but by very light winds which prevented her from steering away. When a rising tide and the cavern's roof forced the mainmast down through the hull, the 83 people aboard *General Grant* abandoned ship. Only 15 – including a woman – survived, but 10 of them lived the 18 months it took them to be rescued by a New Zealand whaling brig, *Amherst*. Also lost in the wreck was at least 70kg of gold, according to official records; rumor made the haul as large as 8 tonnes. Despite at least 18 salvage attempts, no trace of anything of value from *General Grant* has ever been found, although the wreck has been located.

Wake of the Invercauld (1997) is a fascinating memoir by Madelene Ferguson Allen, a descendent of one of the survivors of another Aucklands wreck (*Invercauld*; 1864) who made her own trip to the island in the early 1990s.

Many other ships were lost during the years when the Great Circle Route – the shortest distance between any two points on the earth's surface – was used to sail from Australia to Cape Horn. So great was the danger of a ship wrecking here that the New Zealand government set up castaway huts containing food, clothing, blankets and weapons (for procuring food) at prominent sites. 'Finger posts' – poles supporting wooden hands with pointing fingers – were placed on headlands to show the way. Pigs, rabbits, goats and other animals were also released on the islands to provide emergency food sources for shipwrecked sailors. Since castaways sometimes spent up to two years waiting to be rescued, such measures saved many lives over the years. The oldest remaining such castaway depot, Stella Hut at Sandy Bay on Enderby Island, dates to 1880. New Zealand continued making annual cruises in search of castaways in all of the five sub-Antarctic island groups until 1923, when widespread radio technology

THE AUCKLAND ISLAND CORACLE *Tony Wheeler*

The New Zealand government periodically set up castaway huts with emergency supplies for shipwreck survivors on Auckland Island and nearby Enderby Island, but nobody imagined that a ship would manage to run ashore on tiny Disappointment Island, 7km west of Auckland Island.

Unfortunately for the 15 survivors from the barque *Dundonald*, that was where they ended up in March 1907. The ship's 12 other crewmembers, including the captain and his 16-year-old son, drowned. By July the castaways were fed up with life in grass huts. Using twisted branches, they constructed a flimsy coracle frame that they covered with fabric salvaged from the wreck's sails. Three men sailed this ramshackle craft across the often-stormy strait.

Upon landing on Auckland Island, however, they were unable to penetrate the thick scrub and make their way to the castaway depot at Erebus Cove. Disheartened, they returned to Disappointment Island.

There they soon constructed a four-person coracle, but this second attempt failed when the little boat was wrecked upon launching. Making a third attempt, the crew managed again to cross the strait, but this time their craft was wrecked upon landing at Auckland Island, so finding a way to the depot became imperative.

After reaching the castaway depot, they were able to return to rescue their fellow survivors. Eventually the government steamer *Hinemoa* collected them all in November 1907 and returned them to New Zealand, along with their first crude coracle. Today, the fragile little boat – surely one of the least seaworthy craft ever to sail Antarctic waters – can be seen in the Canterbury Museum in Christchurch, along with other *Dundonald* relics.

Tony Wheeler is the cofounder of Lonely Planet Publications

endered the searches unnecessary, as had he 1914 opening of the Panama Canal, which eliminated the need for ships to use he Great Circle Route.

Pastoral leases were set up in the Aucklands in 1894, but the 2020 sheep that were mported did not thrive, and the last lease vas forfeited in 1910. In the mid-1990s wild horthorn cattle, descendants of an early ancher's herd, which survived by eating eaweed, were exterminated from Enderby by shooting. Fifty Agente de Champagne, or French blue, rabbits, the last of their ype left in the world, were also removed and taken to New Zealand for breeding. ntroduced goats have been eliminated rom Auckland Island, and wild pigs and ats – both of which eat seabird chicks – are now on the hit list.

During WWII, the secret Cape Expeditions set up coast-watching stations for he Allies on the islands to watch Ross and Carnley harbors, and ensure that enemy hips weren't using the islands as a staging post for an invasion. Despite their daily observations, the coast watchers never saw an enemy vessel. One of them, Alan W Eden, wrote a book about his experiences with the evealing title *Islands of Despair* (1955).

Among the twisted trunks of Enderby sland's red-flowering southern rata tree (*Metrosideros umbellata)* hides the elusive and solitary nesting yellow-eyed penguin. One of the rarest penguins, the yellow-eyed penguin numbers only about 5000 animals and prefers not to congregate in large colonies like most other penguins. More breed on Enderby than anywhere else.

Ninety-five percent of the global population of the Hooker's sea lion *(Phocarctos hookeri)* – one of the world's rarest sea ions, with about 12,000 animals – breeds in the Auckland Islands. But Enderby's Sandy Bay – one of only three places in the world where it breeds – has illustrated the sea lions' fragility: rabbit burrows behind the beach once killed one of every 10 pups born each year after the baby sea lions crawled in and got stuck. Unfortunately, 70 to 100 adults are still killed each year in squid trawlers' nets, but New Zealand has instituted strict limits on the number of accidental net deaths that it will allow each year before closing the squid season. A large population of southern right whales *(Eubalaena australis)* come to breed and calve in Port Ross in winter.

The Auckland Islands are also home to the world's largest breeding population of wandering albatrosses, as well as 65,000 white-capped mollymawks. The islands' plant life is especially rich: of the 233 vascular plants, 84% are indigenous.

Bounty Islands

The rarely visited Bountys, covering just 1.4 sq km, are a sprinkling of some 22 islets, the largest of which is not more than 1km across. Barely rising above sea level, with the highest point just 73m, they are all but barren of vegetation. Discovered on September 19, 1788, by the infamous Captain William Bligh of mutiny fame, they were named for his ship *Bounty*.

Here, as at many of the other islands in the region, an onslaught of sealers arrived soon after the islands' discovery. By 1831 when British whaler-explorer John Biscoe visited, the Bountys' fur seals had very nearly been exterminated.

British Captain George Palmer, in HMS *Rosario*, landed and took formal possession of the islands for Queen Victoria in 1870. A quarter-century later, the New Zealand government advertised the availability of the islands for sheep farming, but – unsurprisingly, given the near-complete lack of plant life – got no takers.

The erect-crested penguin *(Eudyptes sclateri)* breeds only here and on the Antipodes Islands. The Bountys are also home to 25,000 pairs of Salvin's albatrosses. Amazingly, there's a small community of invertebrates: a flightless beetle, two moth species and two species of spider.

Campbell Island

Most southerly of the five New Zealand sub-Antarctic island groups, Campbell Island covers 113 sq km. Of volcanic origin, the group consists of a large main isle and two tiny islets: Dent to the west and Jacquemart to the south. The highest point is 569m Mt Honey.

The island's climate is typical of the sub-Antarctic: cold, wet and windy. It rains, on average, 325 days a year.

New Zealand is so proud of Campbell Island that it is featured on the back of the country's five-dollar notes, which have

Everest conqueror Sir Edmund Hillary on the front. The Campbell Island scene shows the yellow-eyed penguin (known to New Zealanders as the 'Hoiho'), the sub-Antarctic lily and the giant Campbell Island daisy.

Campbell was discovered by Captain Frederick Hasselborough in the ship *Perseverance* (for which Perseverence Harbour is named) on January 4, 1810. The island was named for the owner of Hasselborough's sealing company. Sadly, Hasselborough drowned in Perseverence Harbour exactly 10 months later – along with a woman and a young boy – when their boat capsized. In a twist of fate, *Perseverance* was wrecked in the same place 18 years later. Hasselborough was able to keep his discovery a secret for nearly a year, profiting from the island's seal-rich beaches. But as on all the other sub-Antarctic islands, the sealing 'gold rush' eventually swept over Campbell, and by the 1820s the seal population had effectively been exterminated.

In 1839 a fur-sealing party of three men and a woman were rescued after being marooned for 27 months when their ship, *New Zealand*, wrecked after dropping them o there. The seals had been so depleted b then that the castaways were able to fin only 170 in all their time stranded on th island.

Two 19th-century expeditions stoppe at Campbell. Ross conducted the firs plant and animal surveys of the island i 1840–42, while the French government' 1873–75 expedition to observe the transi of Venus visited Campbell twice on the frig ate *Vire*. Clouds prevented any observatio of the celestial phenomenon, and the ship' engineer, Duris, died of typhoid and wa buried opposite Venus Cove. In 1993 hi grave was discovered under 30cm of peat having last been seen in 1931. With a strik ing iron cross as its headstone, the grave i now fenced to keep out seals.

Pastoral enterprises fared better on Camp bell than they did on Auckland. A lease wa set up in 1895, and a rancher built a home stead at Tucker Cove on Perseverance Har bour. Wool-raising continued until 1931 when the island was abandoned to the 400 remaining sheep. After the island became

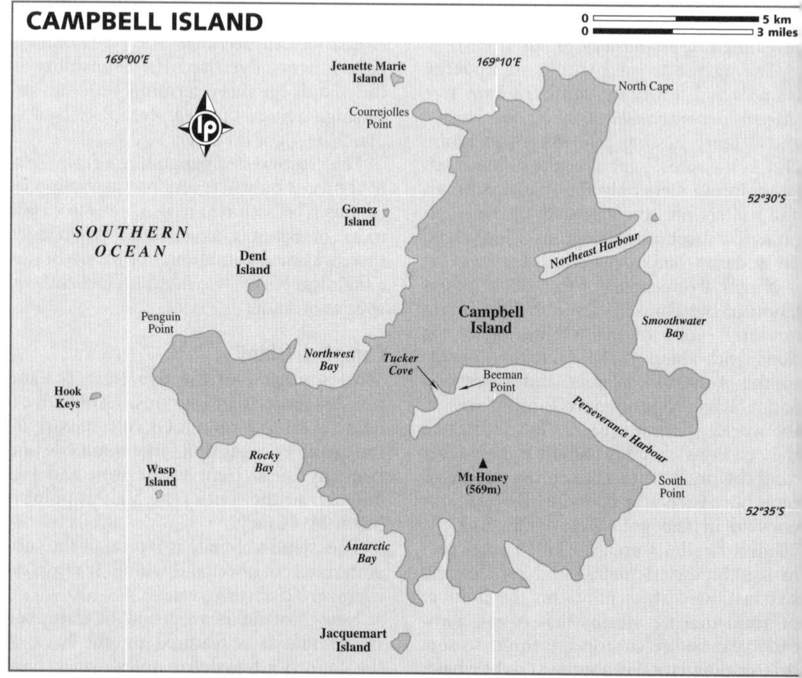

nature reserve in 1954, a control program was begun to limit destruction of native vegetation. The site of the Tucker Cove home is still visible; the last sheep were shot in 1990.

The secret wartime Cape Expeditions set up a coast-watching station in 1941 to keep Perseverance Harbour under surveillance. Although no unauthorized vessel was ever spotted, the coast watchers performed valuable surveys on the island and maintained meteorological records. After the war, this work was continued; but because the coast-watching station was built 800m inland to avoid detection, the scientific station was moved in 1957 to Beeman Point on Perseverance Harbour. In 1992 the station's five members were on a snorkeling trip at Northwest Bay when a shark attacked, tearing off one man's arm. The station closed in October 1995, replaced, after 54 years of service, by automatic instrumentation.

From the landing dock at the station, a boardwalk leads about 5km up to the **Col-Lyall Saddle**, where a large colony of royal albatrosses nest. The meadows on both sides of the walk are filled with 'megaherbs.' These flowering perennials with oversized blossoms and leaves include: white alpine daisy *(Damnamenia vernicosa)*, violet and white Campbell Island daisy *(Pleurophyllum speciosum)*, yellow sub-Antarctic lily *(Bulbinella rossii)*, pink broccoli-like Campbell Island carrot *(Anisotome latifolia)* and brown button daisy *(Pleurophyllum hookerii)*. Smaller, but still striking, flowers include the deep blue-purple *Hebe benthamii* and the purple *Myosotis capitata*.

The brief flowering season for all of these plants is usually in January.

Campbell Island is also the home of the **world's loneliest tree**. A single 6m Sitka spruce, planted in 1902 by New Zealand's governor, is the only tree for hundreds of kilometers around.

An ambitious NZ$2 million program undertaken in 2000 to eradicate rats was successful, providing ground-nesting seabirds with the opportunity to eventually repopulate the island. Campbell is the largest island in the world that has been cleared of rats so far.

Unfortunately, other species on Campbell have not fared as well. Rockhoppers have declined by about 90% in the past half-century here, perhaps due to changes in sea temperature that affect their food sources.

The Snares

Named to warn mariners about their unpleasant ship-'snaring' potential, this group covers just 3.3 sq km. The Snares consist of the Western Chain – Rima, Wha, Toru, Rua and Tahi – and Northeast Island and its adjuncts, Alert Stack, Broughton Island and Daption Rocks. (The Traps, an even smaller and more dangerous group of rocks to the northeast, were discovered by Cook in 1770 and so named 'because they lay as such to catch unwary strangers,' as he wrote in his journal.)

A stone adze (cutting tool), found in 1961 and estimated to be several hundred years old, provides evidence that Maoris from New Zealand visited the Snares before Europeans did.

In a rare coincidence, the Snares were 'discovered' independently – on the very same day, November 23, 1791 – by two different shipmasters, Captain George Vancouver of *Discovery*, and Lieutenant Broughton of *Chatham*. Vancouver called the islands the Snares, while Broughton called them Knight's Islands.

Little more than a year later, in December 1792, Captain William Raven, sailing in *Britannia*, independently sighted the Snares and named them the Sunday Islands.

Four men were marooned on the Snares between 1810 and 1817, having been forcibly put ashore from the ship *Adventure* by its master, Captain Keith. One man, who became disturbed by their ordeal, was shoved off a cliff by the other three, who were later rescued by the American ship *Enterprise* in 1817.

Literally millions of seabirds breed in the Snares group. Nearly three million pairs of sooty shearwaters alone breed in burrows, where they hide from predators. Taking off at dawn on foraging flights and returning home before sundown, the great clouds of birds are an awesome sight.

The Snares are the only home of the Snares crested penguin *(Eudyptes robustus)*, probably the only penguin that regularly climbs trees. It is also one of the five species of crested penguins, the world's only bird species to first lay a smaller, rarely hatched egg before producing a larger white egg whose chick usually survives. Although scientists have made several studies of crested penguins, no solid explanation has yet been offered for their unusual breeding.

Because of their abundant wildlife, no landings are permitted on any of the Snares.

SCOTT ISLAND

Remote, barren and rarely visited, Scott Island is the remains of a volcanic crater. It includes an isolated offshore stack, the 63m **Haggit's Pillar**, about 800m west of the island. Covering less than one hectare, Scott Island is just 370m long and 180m wide, with its long axis running north–south. The northern coast ends in cliffs 50m high, while the southern coast is barely above sea level. The island is entirely covered in snow and ice during the winter, but in summer large areas of bare rock are exposed.

Evading detection until 1902, thanks to its location and extremely tiny size, Scott Island was found by British Captain William Colbeck, sailing in *Morning*, on Christmas Day. Colbeck, carrying stores to Scott's *Discovery* expedition in McMurdo Sound, sent a party ashore and claimed the island for Britain, calling it Markham Island after Sir Clements Markham, President of the Royal Geographical Society and the architect of the expedition. (The name was later changed to memorialize Scott.)

Tourists first landed in 1982.

PETER I ØY

Inaccessible nearly all year-round thanks to the heavy surrounding pack ice, Peter I Øy covers 158 sq km and is 95% glaciated. The highest point, 1640m **Lars Christensentoppen** (Lars Christensen Peak), is an extinct volcano. Glaciers extend tongues into the sea nearly all around the island, but in a few places narrow, rocky beaches are exposed. To the east of the island lie two flat-topped, ice-free columns, the Tvistein Pillars.

Peter I Øy was discovered on January 21, 1821, by the Russian Fabian von Bellingshausen, who named it for czar Peter the Great, founder of the Russian navy. 'Words cannot describe the delight which appeared on all our faces at the cry of 'Land! Land!',' Bellingshausen wrote. 'Our joy was not surprising, after our long monotonous voyage, amidst unceasing dangers from ice, snow, rain, sleet and fog.' It was the first land discovered south of the Antarctic Circle and thus the most southerly land known at the time.

The first landing took place more than a century after Peter I Øy's discovery, when Norwegian Ola Olstad, leading the *Norvegia* expedition, went ashore February 2, 1929, and claimed it for Norway. It was formally annexed by Norway in 1933.

A very narrow (less than 4m wide) beach at Norvegia Bay is entered via a natural arch, Tsars Porten. Peter I is home to small rookeries of both Adélies and chinstraps, as well as several hundred pairs of southern fulmars.

Beginning in 1980 a few tourist ships have succeeded in landing passengers on the island, but it is still estimated that fewer than 600 people have ever stood on Peter I Øy.

SOUTH SHETLAND ISLANDS

This major group of islands at the northern end of the Antarctic Peninsula is one of the continent's most visited areas, thanks to its spectacular scenery, abundant wildlife and proximity to Tierra del Fuego. The 540km-long chain consists of four main island groups. From northeast to southwest, they are Clarence and Elephant Islands; King George and Nelson Islands; Robert, Greenwich, Livingston, Snow and Deception Islands; and Smith and Low Islands.

There are also 150-odd islets and rocks, many with picturesque names: Potmess Island, Hole Rock, Stump Rock, Sea Leopard Patch, Square End Island, The Watchkeeper, Desolation Island, Pig Rock, Salient Rock, Cone Rock, Conical Rock, The Pointers and Sewing-Machine Needles. The South Shetlands are about 80% glaciated and cover 3688 sq km. The archipelago's highest point is Smith Island's **Mt Foster** (2105m), first climbed in 1996 by a group from the Canadian yacht *Northanger*.

William Smith, sailing in the British ship *Williams*, was blown off course while rounding Cape Horn for Valparaiso, Chile, and discovered the islands on February 19, 1819, but made no landing. Sailing eastward on his return from Chile he headed south again, but this time was too far west and missed the islands. He returned later in the year and landed on King George Island on October 16, claiming the islands for King George III.

On Christmas Day that same year, the first British sealing ship arrived – with Joseph Herring, who had been the mate of *Williams* when the islands were discovered. (He obviously saw his chance to make a fortune – and acted quickly.) This vessel was the advance party for a veritable navy that proceeded to descend upon the seal-rich islands the next year.

During the summer of 1819–20, the senior British naval officer for the western coast of South America, William Henry Shirreff, chartered *Williams* from Captain Smith and placed Edward Bransfield aboard as senior naval officer. Smith and Bransfield surveyed the island group and today the strait between the South Shetlands and the northwestern coast of the Antarctic Peninsula (which he discovered) bears Bransfield's name. Bransfield landed on both King George Island (January 22, 1820) and Clarence Island (February 4) to claim them for the new sovereign, King George IV.

Smith returned to the South Shetlands for a fifth time during the summer season of 1820–21, this time on a sealing voyage designed to reap a rich harvest from his discovery – a goal he certainly achieved. His two vessels alone took an extraordinary 60,000 fur-seal skins.

An incredible 91 sealing ships operated in the South Shetlands during that season, most of them British or American. The predictable result: the fur seals were almost completely gone by the end of 1821. It was half a century before sealers visited the islands again in great numbers. From 1871–74 a handful of American sealing ships returned to kill anew, taking another 33,000 fur seals from the slowly recovering populations. By 1888–89 the American sealer *Sarah W Hunt* reported taking just 39 skins in a season of South Shetland sealing, and two years later, found just 41.

As they sought unexploited new islands, the sealers must have ranged throughout the Bransfield Strait area. They probably 'discovered' the Antarctic Peninsula several times over, but because the finding of untouched sealing grounds was always a secret, no such discoveries were reported.

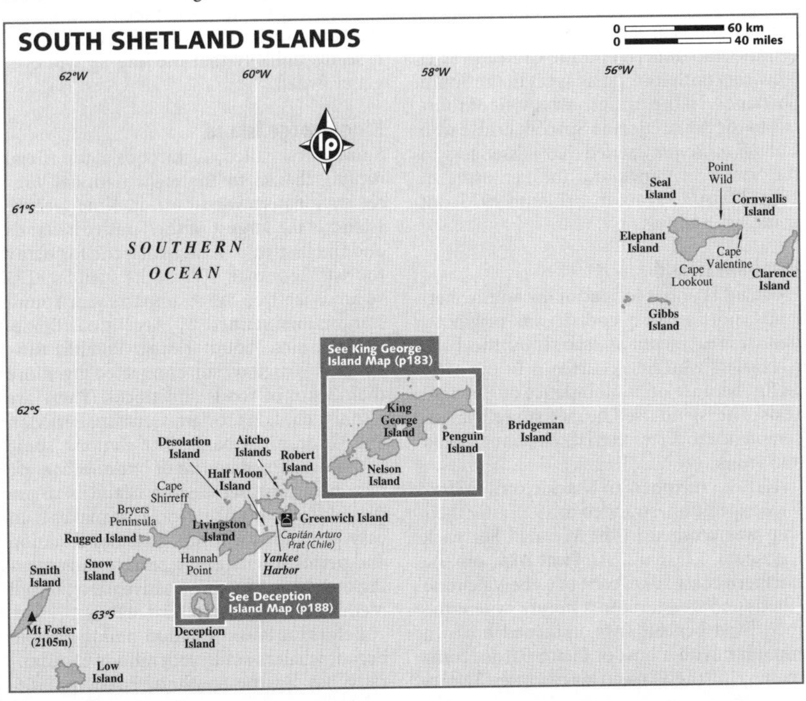

Death visited the sealers as well as the seals: with so many vessels operating in such treacherous waters, there were many wrecks. Six ships – *San Telmo, Ann, Clothier, Lady Troubridge, Cora* and *Venus* – all foundered within just three years, 1819–21. Over the succeeding decades, there were more wrecks: *Richard Henry* (1845), *Catherine* (1847), *Lion* (1854), *Graham* (1924) and *Professor Gruvel* (1927).

In 1944, despite having its hands full with war in Europe, the British government took steps in the islands to detect enemy raiders and to underscore its sovereignty. It established permanent stations and issued postage stamps for the South Shetlands, South Orkneys, South Georgia and Graham Land, or the Antarctic Peninsula. Argentina and Chile naturally protested, since they had rival territorial claims.

Some of the first Antarctic tourism took place in the South Shetlands. The first Antarctic tourist flight, by LAN Chile in 1956, flew over the South Shetlands and the Antarctic Peninsula. Two of the earliest cruises to Antarctica, by the Argentine ship *Les Eclaireurs*, reached the South Shetlands in January and February 1958. In 1959 the Argentine ship *Yapeyú* and the Chilean vessel *Navarino* both took passengers to the South Shetlands. In the earliest mass visit of tourists to the Antarctic, the Spanish cruise ship *Cabo San Roque* carried 900 passengers to the South Shetlands and the Peninsula in 1973. It visited again in 1974 and 1975, but made no landings.

Elephant Island

Elephant Island is located at the South Shetlands' northeastern end. It was originally named 'Sea Elephant Island' by the British sealers who first charted it in the early 1820s, because of its abundance of elephant seals. The island itself bears a superficial resemblance to a (terrestrial) elephant's head and trunk.

Here 22 members of Shackleton's *Endurance* expedition, stranded in 1915 after their ship was crushed in the Weddell Sea pack ice, spent 135 days. At **Point Wild**, on the northern coast 10km west of Cape Valentine (the island's easternmost point), where the men lived beneath two upturned boats, a monolith with a bust of Pilato Pardo, commander of the Chilean navy cutter *Yelcho*, commemorates the rescue on August 30, 1916. Landings are difficult – heavy surf often prevents even Zodiac tours, and if it is calm, the beach may be too crowded with fur seals and chinstraps to go ashore.

At **Cape Lookout**, a 240m-high bluff on the southern coast charted in 1822 by Powell, there are chinstrap, gentoo and macaroni penguins.

Elephant Island is also home to some very old moss colonies, dated at more than 2000 years old – with peat nearly 3m deep.

Wreckage of a wooden sailing vessel found on the southwestern coast was examined in 1999, raising hopes that it was from Nordenskjöld's *Antarctic*, or even Shackleton's *Endurance*. Subsequent tests suggest that it was the remains of a Connecticut sealing ship, *Charles Shearer*, lost en route to the South Shetlands in 1877.

A group of surfers from the US and elsewhere surfed here in February 2000 while visiting on a passenger yacht. They wore fleece-lined neoprene undersuits, oversuits and drysuits with specially fitted hoods. They later reported that 'there's good surf in Antarctica' – the best they found was at the southwestern tip of Low Island – but it seems unlikely that the line-up will ever get crowded.

King George Island

Sometimes called Antarctica's unofficial capital, thanks to the eight national winter stations crowded onto it, King George Island is the largest of the South Shetlands and the first stop in the Antarctic for many tourists. Less than 10% of the island's 1295 sq km is ice-free, yet it supports year-round stations maintained by Argentina, Brazil, Chile, China, South Korea, Poland, Russia and Uruguay, all connected by more than 20km of roads and tracks. There are also Dutch, Ecuadorian, German, Peruvian and US summer bases. The stations, some within walking distance of one another, are here because King George Island is so accessible to South America. This makes it an easy place for a country to build a station and perform scientific research, thus earning the status of a consultative party, or full member, of the Antarctic Treaty.

Before the island's station-building boom began, whalers set up operations at Admiralty Bay on the southern coast in 1906.

Two years later the whaling supply vessel *Telefon* ran aground on Telefon Rocks at the entrance to the bay and was abandoned. In 1909 it was salvaged and towed to Tele fon Bay at Deception Island, where it was repaired.

The British were first to build a base on King George Island, in 1946–47, on Admiralty Bay, but it was closed in 1961. Base G, as it was known, was removed by members of Brazil's nearby Comandante Ferraz station in 1995–96.

Argentina built **Teniente Jubany station** at Potter Cove in 1953. It has been a year-round facility since 1984. It accommodates 80 people; 20 people normally winter here. Prominent above the station is Three Brothers Hill (210m). The summer-only **Dallman Laboratory**, opened in 1994 by Argentina, the Netherlands and Germany, is the first research facility in Antarctica designed as a multinational laboratory.

Russia set up its **Bellingshausen station** in 1968 on the nearly ice-free Fildes Peninsula at the island's southwestern tip. After a fuel-tank farm was established, the station became a major fuel depot for the Soviet Antarctic fishing fleet. Bellingshausen has a normal population of only 25, despite its maximum capacity of 50. Unfortunately, due to Russia's ongoing economic troubles, the station has not been well maintained. Waste and large amounts of scrap metal are in piles outdoors, awaiting return to Russia, so the station has a somewhat dumpy look, although efforts are being made to clean it up. **St Trinity**, the first Orthodox church in Antarctica, was pre-assembled of cedar and larch in Siberia and sanctified in February 2004. The church can accommodate 30 worshippers.

Chile constructed **Presidente Eduardo Frei Montalva** station, known as 'Frei,' in 1969, adjacent to Bellingshausen and separated from it by a small stream (although in places the two stations' buildings are intermixed). Ten years later, Chile built **Teniente Rodolfo Marsh Martin** station less than 1km across the Fildes Peninsula from Frei station, which Frei has incorporated. (Thus, the station's name appears either as Frei or Marsh on various charts.) Together with the Escudeoro base (described later in this section),

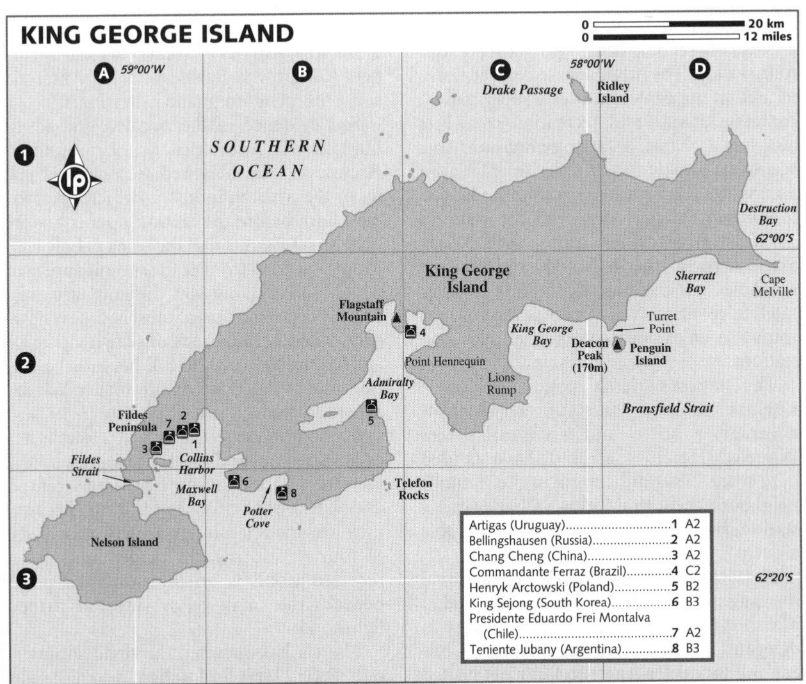

Frei/Marsh is one of the Peninsula region's largest and most complex stations.

As part of Chile's policy of trying to incorporate its claimed Territorio Chileno Antártico into the rest of the country, the government has encouraged families to live at Frei station. The first of several children was born there in 1984. Families are housed in an apartment complex around Villa Las Estrellas (Village of the Stars), built in 1984. Today, the station accommodates as many as 170 people in an emergency, but normally only 110 (mostly military personnel and their dependents) live here. Among the few civilians are air-traffic controllers and teachers for the children, who make up nearly 25% of the population. Parties of station kids sometimes greet tourists upon arrival. One woman who lived here recently with her family recalled nostalgically: 'I started crying about a week before we left. You get so attached to the rustic environment, the house, the scenery, the fauna.'

When seen from afar, Frei looks like a small village with more than 40 buildings, including 15 chalets painted in bright colors on the hillside. In the station center, buildings are painted red-orange and include a hospital, school, bank, post office and a tourist shop. The original base complex, also located in the center, houses a supermarket, canteen, kitchen and recreation area. Frei also has a chapel, a large gymnasium (the scene of a weekly soccer tournament played among the local stations), accommodations for unmarried personnel and the station's administrative center, along with nearly 5km of gravel roads. Among the unusual amenities (for an Antarctic station): 24-hour satellite coverage, which allows station personnel to enjoy four commercial television stations.

The station's Marsh section includes a 1300m compacted-gravel runway, a hangar, a garage, a hostel and a control tower. Wheeled Hercules aircraft have landed here since 1980, and several of the station's neighbors, including China's Chang Cheng station, have flown in personnel using this airstrip.

In 1982 Chile held the first international meeting in Antarctica, a conference held at Marsh on Antarctic resources policy, with delegates from 12 countries attending. Chilean military ruler Augusto Pinochet visited the station in 1984 and officially opened its quarters for married couples.

In what was certainly one of the first public concerts in Antarctica, Japanese pop singer Yasunori Sugawara held a concert at the station in 1993 for about 100 people from Frei and the neighboring Uruguayan and Russian stations.

Not until 1995, rather revealingly, was a scientific annex added to Frei's sprawl. The five attractive, blue-roofed white buildings of the separate, summer-only **Professor Julio Escudeoro base** are located along the bottom of a steep hill southeast of Frei. The base accommodates 16 people.

Poland's **Henryk Arctowski station**, opened in 1977 and named for Henryk Arctowski, geologist on De Gerlache's *Belgica* expedition, accommodates as many as 50 people. A handsome and well-illustrated color brochure (in English) sold at the station provides a brief history, proudly declaring that 'visitors are honored at Arctowski.' Women visitors were once presented with small bouquets of flowers that had been grown in the station greenhouse, but this has been discontinued because growing of nonfood plants now requires special permission under the Antarctic Treaty. Station members still grow vegetables – using Antarctic soil, with penguin guano as fertilizer.

Sad evidence of the negative impact of humans on Antarctica can be found at Arctowski. Sun-bleached whalebones, relics of the whaling industry (which operated here long before the station opened), were once so numerous that the black pebble Half Moon Beach in front of the station appeared white, and walking was difficult in places. The bones are noticeably absent today, however, taken by hundreds of selfish visitors.

The **iron cross** on the hill behind the station marks the grave of filmmaker Wladzimierz Puchalski, who died here in 1979.

To help manage tourists, Arctowski has established several walking routes in the vicinity of the station. The large gentoo and Adélie rookeries are off limits because they are encircled by protected moss beds. A tourist information center built from recycled wood is on the unnamed point beneath the small yellow-and-red striped lighthouse.

The US has operated the small summer-only **Peter J Lenie field station**, near Poland's

Arctowski station, since 1985. It's also called 'Copacabana.'

Brazil's **Commandante Ferraz station**, on Admiralty Bay, opened in 1984. It is located between an old whaling station and the site of the abandoned British **Base G**, which was removed in 1996. Ferraz's distinctive orange-roofed, pine-green buildings accommodate 60 people. Mount Cross lies behind the station, and a small cemetery contains several graves and memorials. The boundaries of a nearby sensitive bed of lichens are marked in stone. A composite whale 'skeleton' on a moss bed near the station contains, as researcher Ron Naveen has pointed out, the bones of no fewer than nine species of whales.

Uruguay's **Artigas station**, which was established in 1984, accommodates 14 in winter and 60 in summer. The station is named for Uruguay's national hero, José Gervasio Artigas, a progressive early leader who redistributed land and abolished slavery. About 200m south of the station is the wreck of a wooden sailing ship.

China's **Chang Cheng station** (Great Wall of China), established in 1985, accommodates 45 people, but recent winter crews have been less than one-third that number. A white two-story addition was built in 1998. One of Antarctica's oddest ceremonies was performed at the red-and-orange station during the 1987–88 season, when hundreds of domestic pigeons were freed in a 'Dove of Peace' ritual. Nearly all froze the same day.

South Korea set up its **King Sejong station**, named after a 15th-century Korean king who was also a scientist and inventor, at Marian Cove close to Maxwell Bay in 1987–88. The collection of orange buildings accommodates 45 people.

Peru established its summer-only **Machu Picchu station** on Admiralty Bay in 1989. Its white-and-red buildings accommodate 28 people. In 1977 Italy also set up a small hut on King George Island, which was later removed unilaterally by Argentina. Ecuador established its summer-only **Point Hennequin station** in 1987–88.

Tourism to King George Island, as to anywhere else in the region, is not without its hazards. In 1972, *Lindblad Explorer*, the first passenger ship built specifically for polar cruising, ran aground in Admiralty Bay. The 90 passengers were rescued by a Chilean naval vessel, and a German tugboat towed the ship off the rocks 18 days later.

Among the most popular landing sites on King George Island today is **Turret Point**, at the eastern end of King George Bay on the island's southern coast. The point takes its name from a group of prominent high rock stacks above the beach, a nesting area for Antarctic terns. You'll also find chinstraps, Adélies, blue-eyed shags and southern giant petrels. Beaches in the area have yielded evidence of 20th-century whaling, including harpoon heads.

Penguin Island

Just offshore from Turret Point is Penguin Island. While there are many Penguin Islands scattered throughout the Antarctic, this one's pedigree is longer than most – it was named by Bransfield in 1820. Its highest point, 170m **Deacon Peak**, with its red cone, is easily identifiable; an extensive crater is at the summit. It's easy to climb, and so many people do that a path is worn into the ground early each season – even with the best of care, people *do* leave their mark on Antarctica. There's also a meltwater lake in a former volcanic crater. You may see chinstrap penguins here, and Adélies also nest on an out-of-the-way beach.

Bridgeman Island

Steep-sided and nearly circular, volcanic Bridgeman Island is about 800m long. Its snow-covered summit (240m) is inclined toward the south, and its reddish-brown sides are nearly vertical on the northern coast. Bridgeman was discovered by Bransfield on January 22, 1820, and named after Captain Charles O Bridgeman of the British Royal Navy. Volcanic activity was observed on the island by Powell in 1821, by Weddell in 1821 and by Wilkes in 1839. Charcot made the first landing, in 1909, and found proof of 'comparatively recent (volcanic) activity.'

Aitcho Islands

Cleverly named for the British Admiralty's Hydrographic Office ('HO'), the Aitchos are covered with extensive beds of moss and lichens and are home to gentoos and chinstraps.

Greenwich Island

Sealers stalked the beaches of this island, as they did nearly all the South Shetlands, during the early 1800s. A British captain working here in 1821–22 reported finding a cave on Greenwich with the eerie inscription 'J Macey 1820–21 & 22 but never more' along with several other names.

As early as 1820, circular **Yankee Harbor**, on the island's southwestern side, was an important anchorage for sealers, who knew it as Hospital Cove. Somewhat confusingly, the harbor at Deception Island was also once known as Yankee Harbor. A stone and gravel spit extends nearly 1km in a wide curve, protecting Yankee Harbor and making it a favorite yacht anchorage. The spit is an ideal place for walking; look for an old sealer's try-pot on this strand. Further up the beach, by the Argentine *refugio* (refuge) built in the 1950s, several thousand pairs of gentoos nest. A small plaque commemorates Robert McFarlane, a British sealer who operated in the region in 1820 in his brigantine *Dragon*.

Chile's **Capitán Arturo Prat station**, a collection of orange buildings on Discovery Bay on Greenwich's northern coast, was opened in 1947 as Soberania station, and later renamed to honor the Chilean naval hero. The first head of state to visit Antarctica, Chile's Presidente Gabriel González Videla, stopped here in 1948 – with an entourage of 140. The station accommodates 15 personnel and has a small museum displaying photos, early expedition equipment and whaling artifacts. A bust of Prat stands outside, and nearby is a cross and shelter commemorating the 1960 station leader, who died while in charge. A cross and shrine to the Virgin of Carmen, erected in 1947, is also in the vicinity.

Ecuador's **Pedro Vicente Maldonado station**, completed in 1998, operates in summer only, and accommodates 18 people.

Half Moon Island

Crescent-shaped Half Moon, just 2km long, lies in the entrance of Moon Bay on the eastern side of Livingston Island. Here the Argentine navy operates the summer-only **Teniente Cámara station**, built in 1953. Landings are usually made on the wide sweeping beach east of the station. A handsome wooden boat lies derelict on the shore below the chinstrap colony. In 1961 21 tourists were stranded here for three days when the landing craft from their chartered vessel *Lapataia* was damaged.

Livingston Island

Livingston Island's prominent, 1790m central peak, **Mt Friesland**, is often obscured by cloud; it was first climbed in 1992 by a pair of Spaniards.

The island was a major early-19th-century sealing center, and the remains of primitive shelters and assorted artifacts have been found on many of its beaches. In fact, the entire **Byers Peninsula** on the island's western end is protected, because it contains the greatest concentration of 19th-century historical sites in Antarctica.

British Captain Robert Fildes, who survived the wrecks of two ships (*Cora* and *Robert*) while sealing in the South Shetlands in the early 1820s, wrote about the superabundance of fur seals on Livingston's northern coast during that period:

> ...in many places it was impossible to haul a boat up without first killing your way, and it was useless to try to walk through them if you had not a club in your hand to clear your way and then twas better to go two or three together to avoid being run over by them...

Fildes added that English sealers had taken more than 95,000 fur-seal skins from that stretch of coast alone.

Hannah Point, on Livingston's south coast, is an extremely popular stop, with its large chinstrap and gentoo rookeries and the occasional macaroni pair nesting among them. The point is named after the British sealer *Hannah* of Liverpool, wrecked in the South Shetlands on Christmas Day, 1820. Be careful of southern giant petrels nesting in the area – they are skittish and will abandon eggs or chicks if nervous.

On a hill above the Hannah Point landing beach, a prominent red vein of jasper runs through the rock. From this lookout, you can survey a sheltered beach on the opposite side of the point where elephant seals bask and young male fur seals spar. But if there are elephant seals in the wallow on this lookout, do not walk up to them. They might be intimidated and retreat – over the cliff, to their deaths onto the rocks below. Tourists have done this in the past, which accounts for the place's nickname, Suicide Wallow.

Walker Bay is occasionally used as a landing site instead of the overvisited Hannah Point to its east. On Walker's broad beach is a fascinating collection of fossils left by researchers on a table-like rock among a group of boulders. There are also seal jaws and teeth and penguin skulls and skeletons. This open-air museum is right below the squarish outcrop on top of the ridge above.

Just east of Hannah Point lies Spain's **Juan Carlos Primero station**, a summer-only base established in 1987–88, which accommodates up to 19 people. It has one of the few alternative-energy systems at an Antarctic station, using both solar power and wind generators, which can provide as much as 20% of the station's power needs. Fire destroyed part of the station in 1994.

Bulgaria's **St Kliment Ohridski station** is less than 2km northeast of Juan Carlos Primero. A summer-only station, it was built in 1988, operated for only a year, then reopened in 1993. The station accommodates 20 people; it's named for St Kliment of Ohrid (840–916), a scholar and bishop who helped introduce the Cyrillic alphabet to Bulgaria.

Antarctica's worst loss of life occurred in September 1819 near **Cape Shirreff** on Livingston's northern coast. The 74-gun *San Telmo*, a Spanish man-of-war sailing from Cadiz to Lima, encountered severe weather while crossing the Drake Passage and lost her rudder and topmasts. Although taken in tow by an accompanying ship, the hawsers parted and the ship was lost – along with 650 officers, soldiers and seamen. Circumstantial evidence points to *San Telmo*'s destruction on Livingston: an anchor stock and spars were found by sealers in 1820, and in the same year Weddell found evidence that survivors of a shipwreck had lived for a period on the island. A cairn on Livingston's northern coast at Half Moon Beach, named by sealers in 1820, commemorates those lost in *San Telmo*, perhaps the first people to die in Antarctica.

Deception Island

Easily recognized on any map by its broken-ring shape, Deception Island's collapsed volcanic cone provides one of the safest natural harbors in the world – even despite periodic eruptions.

To attain this secret haven, however, vessels must navigate a tricky 230m-wide break in the volcano's walls – known since the early-19th-century sealing days as **Neptunes Bellows** for the strong winds that blow through this strait. Even veteran captains navigate carefully through the Bellows, for hull-piercing Ravn Rock lies just 2.5m beneath the surface in the center of the channel – and foul ground lies between Ravn Rock (named by Charcot in 1908 for the whale-catcher *Ravn* then based at Deception) and the southern headland, called Entrance Point. The 'deceptive' entrance to the island has been known since the early 19th century, when it was called Hell's Gates or Dragon's Mouth (perhaps after the British sealing vessel *Dragon*, reported to have landed on the mainland coast of Antarctica in 1820–21).

Sharp-eyed observers may spy, on the northern coast of Entrance Point, evidence of how dangerous the narrow channel can be: the wreck of the British whale-catcher *Southern Hunter*, which ran aground on New Year's Eve 1957 while avoiding an Argentine naval vessel steaming in through the Bellows.

As you enter the harbor, notice the striking colors of the rock faces on either side. One of Deception's earliest visitors, surgeon William HB Webster (who arrived in 1829 aboard the British *Chanticleer*), wrote that these cliffs 'present a curious and not unpleasing appearance.' It's true.

Upon reaching this interior sea, visitors land at **Whalers Bay** on a black-sand beach cloaked in mysterious white clouds of sulfur-scented steam. Those with cold feet need only dig their boots into the sand to warm them from the heat escaping from subterranean volcanic vents. The island's sloping, snow-covered walls, which reach 580m, tower above the beach.

Early sealers used Deception's 12km-wide harbor as a base. Palmer, who first explored the island and discovered its inner harbor, is thought to have seen the Antarctic Peninsula in 1820 from the break in the caldera wall at **Neptunes Window**, known to sealers as 'the Gap.'

Chanticleer, commanded by Captain Henry Foster, entered the 190m deep harbor now known as **Port Foster** in 1829. The ship anchored at Pendulum Cove and magnetic experiments were performed there for two months. Besides Webster, the first scientist to visit the Antarctic, *Chanticleer* also carried Lieutenant Edward Kendall, who made the first survey of the island and some of the first paintings of Antarctica.

WHALING AT DECEPTION

In 1906 a joint Norwegian–Chilean whaling company established by Captain Adolfus Amandus Andresen, a Norwegian-born immigrant to Chile, began using an area on the northern side of the caldera at Whalers Bay as a base for *Gobernador Bories,* his floating factory ship. (Floating factory ships were large vessels that processed whales brought to them by 'catcher' ships. The development of floating factories, which could operate at sea, heralded the decline of shore-based whaling stations.) Andresen was accompanied by his wife, family and pets: a parrot and an Angora cat. His company, the Sociedad Ballenera de Magallanes, was based in Punta Arenas and used Whalers Bay for 10 years. In 1907 the company's factory ship was joined by two more Norwegian whaling companies and another from Newfoundland, all of which operated factory ships at Deception Island.

Britain, which had formally claimed the island in 1908 as part of the Falkland Islands Dependencies, gave a 21-year lease to Hvalfangerselskabet Hektor A/S, a Norwegian whaling company based in Tønsberg, in 1911. One of the reasons for granting the license was to utilize the estimated 3000 whale carcasses that littered the shores of Port Foster. They had been abandoned by ships that had stripped them of their blubber but were unable to process the meat and bones, which contain 60% of a whale's oil. British authorities hoped to end this terrible waste. Hektor established a shore station at Whalers Bay in 1912, although it was not fully operational until 1919.

In the 1912–13 season, 12 floating factories, 27 catcher boats and the shore station operated at Whalers Bay, processing more than 5000 whales. The whalers called the station **New Sandefjord** after the Norwegian whaling town. Unlike many other whaling

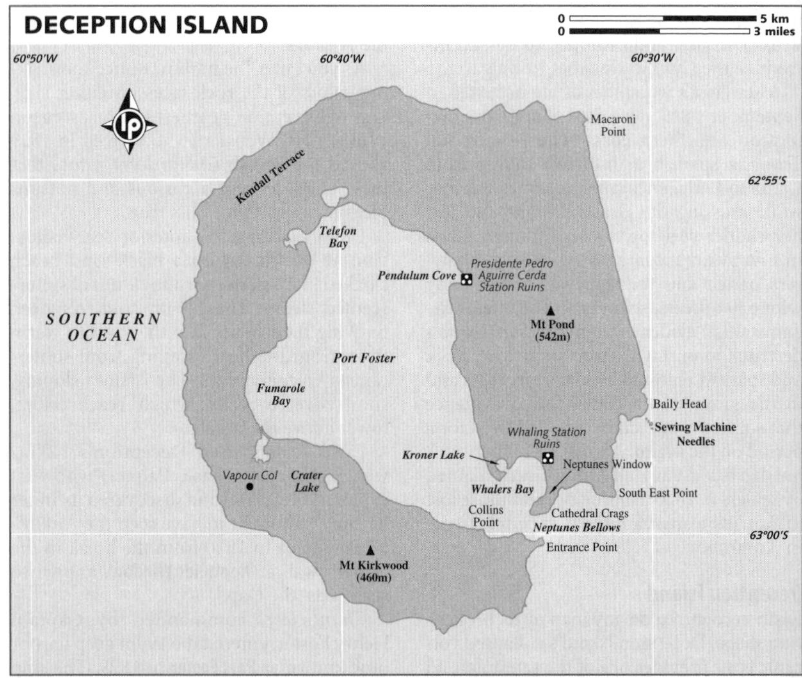

stations, however, New Sandefjord only processed whale carcasses that had already been stripped of blubber, which was processed by the floating factories anchored offshore. Instead of rendering blubber into oil, the shore station boiled down meat and bones to get the oil.

Charcot, who visited in 1908, described the bustling station in operation:

> We find two three-masters and two steam vessels, surrounded by several little steam-whalers, this fleet belonging to three different companies. Pieces of whale float about on all sides, and bodies in the process of being cut up or waiting their turn lie alongside the various boats. The smell is unbearable.

The shore station closed in 1931, partly because of a slump in whale oil prices and partly because technology had advanced. Floating factories could efficiently process a whale at sea, especially once the stern slipway was invented, allowing the whole carcass to be hauled aboard.

Today at Whalers Bay, where the beach is more than 300m wide in places, several wooden huts (well houses) stand disintegrating. Flensing boats and water barges lie buried to their gunwales in black volcanic sand. Huge boilers and tanks that once processed and held the whale oil now stand rusting under the southern sky.

A **whalers' cemetery** once held the graves of 45 men (38 Norwegians, three Swedes, one Chilean, one Russian, one Briton and one of unknown origin) who died lonely deaths half a world away from their loved ones. The cemetery is now buried under several meters of sand from a *lahar*, or mudslide, released in 1969 when a volcanic eruption melted the glacier above. Sharp-eyed visitors wandering in the area behind the station may find one of the cemetery's simple wooden coffins (empty), which was tossed about by the massive wave of mud and water. Nearby is a wooden **cross**. It had been set up behind the Argentine station until 2002, when it was recognized to belong to this cemetery. It had been found washed up on the beach in 1992; the Argentines, out of respect, had raised it behind their station.

A **cross** that commemorates Tømmerman (carpenter) Hans A Gulliksen, who died in 1928, is far down the beach toward the 17m by 22m corrugated-steel **aircraft hangar** built in 1961–62. There was once a north–south runway alongside this hangar. Today the orange fuselage of a British Otter survey aircraft, stripped of its wings, stands derelict outside.

FIRST FLIGHT BY WILKINS

Australian Hubert Wilkins made the first powered flight in Antarctica on November 16, 1928, taking off from this runway in his Lockheed Vega monoplane *Los Angeles* and flying for 20 minutes. A month later, on December 20, Wilkins and his pilot, Carl Ben Eielson, took off in his other Vega, *San Francisco*, and flew 2100km to about 71°20'S along the Peninsula.

After his flight, Wilkins accepted the hospitality of the Norwegian whalers who had been so helpful to him. New Years' Day at the station, as recounted in Lowell Thomas's biography of Wilkins, was celebrated with games, songs, eating, drinking – and much gunfire. Two drunk whalers climbed atop a pair of big sperm whales on the flensing plan awaiting processing; the whales had been cooking themselves from the heat of the blood fermenting inside their bodies and were swollen with gas. One whaler thrust his

DORMANT, NOT DEAD

Because Deception Island is one of Antarctica's most popular visitor sites, it's thought-provoking to learn that volcanologists consider the volcano dormant, not dead. *Geology and Geomorphology of Deception Island, 2003,* a British Antarctic Survey publication, concludes that it is 'likely that it will erupt again in the future.' A sudden collapse of the caldera could cause a major eruption, 'with potentially devastating effects on anyone on the island at the time and a low probability of escape.' The likelihood of the caldera collapsing, however, is 'very low' and would probably be preceded by earthquakes for several days or weeks prior to an eruption. The report offers this helpful suggestion: 'If ships are present within Port Foster when an eruption occurs, they should depart the island immediately, ideally after uplifting all people ashore.' Ideally indeed.

long knife into this veritable whale-balloon. It promptly exploded, hurling both men into the harbor, where they had to be rescued by some of the few sober observers.

Meanwhile, two other whalers decided to ignite an explosives barge moored to the beach. It contained 65 tonnes of black powder, as well as other combustibles. Taking a 22kg keg of powder, they began laying a trail to the barge. One of the pair got impatient and lit the powder trail, which burned up to the half-empty keg, which had wisely been dropped by the other man. The keg exploded, blowing both whalers some distance and burning off all their hair. Flames had ignited in the other direction, too, and were still burning steadily toward the barge. Fortunately, the powder trail stopped on the gangplank to the barge – not aboard it.

Just west of the old hangar, toward the point and **Kroner Lake**, is an area protected by the Antarctic Treaty. Entry is forbidden. No boundaries are marked, but to be safe, don't wander past the hangar toward the point. Go up the hill behind the hangar instead, to get a view into a small volcanic cone.

VOLCANIC DECEPTION

The volcano that formed Deception is only dormant. In 1923 water in Port Foster boiled and removed the paint from ships' hulls, and in 1930 the floor of the harbor dropped 3m during an earthquake. Two 1967 eruptions forced the evacuation of the Argentine, British and Chilean research stations, and the Chilean station was destroyed. More eruptions occurred in 1969, forcing another round of evacuations and damaging the British station. There were further eruptions in 1970. In 1991–92, with increased seismic activity at the island, some ships thought it prudent not to enter Port Foster that summer.

There is a positive side to all this volcanic activity. **Pendulum Cove**, which takes its name from the experiments performed there by Captain Foster aboard *Chanticleer*, is a popular tourist site. Doff your parka and go 'bathing' in the thermally heated waters. But be warned: moving even a meter from the warm water can lead to a real shock – you may either scald yourself or else hit a patch of unheated (frigid) water.

Also at Pendulum Cove, which was once a much deeper inlet but has been much altered by volcanic activity, are the ruins of Chile's **Presidente Pedro Aguirre Cerda station**, which was destroyed by the 1967 eruption. A protected area lies 300m south of the ruins. Although no boundaries are marked, entry is forbidden to protect the abundant mosses.

Telefon Bay is named for the whaling supply vessel *Telefon*, which ran aground in 1908 at the entrance to Admiralty Bay on King George Island. It was repaired here in 1909. Although there is no wildlife at Telefon Bay, it's a spectacular place to view the results of some recent volcanic activity.

TERRITORIAL DISPUTES

Deception's strategic location and superb harbor have made it a contested piece of real estate. A British naval operation, mounted in 1941 to thwart German raiders, destroyed coal and oil-fuel depots at the whaling station. In 1942 Argentina sent its naval vessel *Primero de Mayo* to the island to take formal possession of all territory south of 60°S between 25°W and 68°34'W. The ship repeated the possession ceremony at two other island groups and left behind copper cylinders containing official documents claiming the islands for Argentina.

In January 1943 Britain dispatched HMS *Carnarvon Castle* to Deception, where it removed evidence of the Argentine visit, hoisted the Union Jack and returned the copper cylinder and its contents to Argentina through the British ambassador in Buenos Aires. Two months later, *Primero de Mayo* was back, removing the British emblems and repainting the Argentine flag. At the end of 1943 the British once again removed Argentina's marks. In February 1944, Britain established a permanent meteorological station, **Base B**, in former whaling-station barracks, first in 'Bleak House,' then, after a fire, in 'Biscoe House.'

Today, the ruins of the base's surviving main timber building (30.6m by 10.4m), **Biscoe House**, can be seen to the west of the whaling station at Whalers Bay. Biscoe was badly damaged by the 1969 mudslide, which carried away several sections of its walls.

Another structure – mostly intact – the **FIDASE building** (19.3m by 6.3m), housed the Falkland Islands and Dependencies Aerial Survey Expedition (FIDASE), which spent two seasons (1955–56 and 1956–57) taking aerial photographs of the South Shetlands and northern Peninsula for mapping purposes. Using Canso flying boat aircraft, FIDASE photographed nearly 90,000 sq km of territory.

Predictably, the bickering between Argentina and Britain continued after the establishment of Base B, and the Argentines built their own base Decepción in 1948. In 1952 the Argentines and Chileans both built refuge huts on Britain's airstrip (formerly Wilkins'). The British navy removed the huts the next year and deported two Argentines to South Georgia. In 1953–54 a detachment of Britain's Royal Marines arrived to 'keep the peace' and spent four months on Deception. In 1955 Chile formalized its presence on Deception, building its station at Pendulum Cove. In 1961 Argentina sent President Arturo Frondizi to show the country's official interest in the island. Today, all three countries claim the island, but official posturing aside, they get along pretty well.

Today, Deception's only regularly open stations are both summer-only facilities. Spain's **Gabriel de Castilla station**, on the southern side of Fumarole Bay, accommodates 12, but is open only occasionally. About 1000m west is Argentina's **Decepción station**, occupation of which is becoming sporadic.

WILDLIFE

Few marine animals venture into Port Foster, since numerous volcanic vents heat the water inside, making it several degrees warmer than the sea outside. Chinstraps are Deception's most common penguins, with several rookeries exceeding 50,000 pairs each. Rookeries are on the southwestern coast at **Vapour Col** and on the eastern coast at **Macaroni Point** and at **Baily Head** (also called Rancho Point), a natural amphitheater with a melt stream running through it. Visiting Baily Head can be difficult due to heavy surf. Just south of Baily Head, the picturesquely named seastacks, the **Sewing Machine Needles**, once included a natural rock arch; it collapsed in 1924 after an earthquake.

SOUTH ORKNEY ISLANDS

Usually visited en route to the Antarctic Peninsula from South Georgia, or vice-versa, the South Orkneys consist of four major islands (Coronation, the largest, and Signy, Powell and Laurie), along with several minor islands and rocks, as well as the Inaccessible Islands 29km to the west.

Covering 622 sq km, the group is 85% glaciated. The highest point, 1265m Mt Nivea, was first scaled in 1955–56; it takes its name from the snow petrel *(Pagodroma nivea)*, which breeds in the area.

South Orkney weather is cold, windy (westerlies) and overcast. On average the sun shines fewer than two hours a day.

The islands were discovered jointly, by American sealer Nathaniel Palmer sailing in *James Monroe* and British sealer George Powell in *Dove*, on December 6, 1821. Powell named the islands Powell's Group and took possession for the British crown the next day on Coronation Island. On December 12, British sealer Michael McLeod, sailing in *Beaufoy*, independently discovered the group. Weddell, who visited in *Jane* in February 1822, gave the islands their present name in recognition of their position at the same latitude in the south that Britain's Orkney Islands occupy in the north.

Sealing took its usual course – until nearly every last animal had been killed. As late as 1936, a visitor found just one solitary fur seal.

Britain declared the South Orkneys part of its Falkland Islands Dependencies in 1908, a territorial claim later challenged by Argentina in 1925.

In 1933 the South Orkneys became one of the first Antarctic regions to receive tourists, when an Argentine naval voyage to relieve the Laurie Island meteorological station brought visitors.

Besides Laurie and Signy Islands, **Shingle Cove** on Coronation Island is often visited, offering excellent wildlife-viewing.

Laurie Island

In 1903 Bruce wintered on mountainous Laurie Island, where he helped set up a meteorological station, which opened on April 1. The ruins of the stone hut where the expedition spent the winter, **Omond House**, are still visible at the end of the beach. When Bruce departed in February 1904, the station was turned over to Argentina's Oficina Meteorologica, which has operated it ever since, making it the oldest continuously run research facility in Antarctica.

Renamed **Orcadas station** in 1951, it accommodates 45 people in the summer; the average winter population is 14. A three-room **museum** in the Casa Moneta (built in 1905) features a replica of an early hut interior, as well as an array of artifacts, some from Bruce's expedition. Chinstraps, Adélies and gentoos nest nearby.

On Jessie Beach, north of the station, is a small **cemetery** containing 10 graves. The oldest belongs to Scotsman Allan Ramsay, chief engineer on Bruce's *Scotia*, who died of heart disease August 6, 1903. Other graves mark the final resting places of men from Argentina, Germany, Norway, Scotland and Sweden, but only seven are filled. Three are memorials to Argentines who disappeared from the station together in 1998.

Almost a century to the day after Ramsay's death, on August 4, 2003, Orcadas experienced an earthquake centered 70km to the northeast at a depth of 10km. It measured 7.5 on the Richter scale, but caused no damage other than some broken windows. By comparison, a 1970 quake in northern Peru of similar magnitude triggered avalanches and landslides that killed as many as 70,000 people – the western hemisphere's worst earthquake.

Signy Island

Whaling in the South Orkneys began in January 1912, when the Norwegian company Aktieselskabet Rethval of Oslo deployed the factory ship *Falkland* at Powell Island. The captain who took the first whale, Petter Sørlle, master of the whale-catcher *Paal*, surveyed the South Orkneys in 1912–13 and named low-lying Signy Island after his wife.

A Norwegian–Chilean enterprise, Sociedad Ballenera de Magallanes, sent a factory ship to Signy in 1911–12, and floating factory ships visited the archipelago until 1914–15. *Tioga*, the first ship to undertake open-ocean whaling in Antarctica, was wrecked at Signy in 1913. Whaling reopened in the South Orkneys in 1920–21, when a Norwegian company operated a shore station on Signy, and floating factories operated here from 1920 to 1930. About 3500 whales were caught in that decade.

The shore station at Signy took the *skrotts*, or stripped carcasses, cast off by the floating factories and from them extracted the remaining oil – 60% of a whale's oil is in its meat and bones. The station also made 'guano,' or meat and bone meal, from the remains after oil extraction.

Britain established a meteorological station in 1946–47, **Base H**, at Factory Cove, site of the old whaling station. Over the years, its successor, **Signy station**, expanded its program to include biological studies. The station is located on a site with particularly rich plant life, including steep moss-covered terraces rising behind it. In the station's wooden Tønsberg House is a marine biology aquarium. Until 1995 Signy was operated as a permanently staffed – although small – research base. Since 1996 it has operated as a summer-only program, and is now open from November to April with a maximum population of 10. To continue the half-century data record collected when the station was open year-round, an automatic camera records the sea-ice conditions in Factory Cove throughout the year. **Cemetery Flats** is the site of five graves from the whaling days.

Signy's fur seals, nearly exterminated by hunting, have rebounded dramatically. In 1965 there were practically none; in 1995 researchers estimated that 22,000 lived on the island, which is just 6.5km by 5km. In fact, Signy's seal population is 75% greater than its highest previous level, according to a report in *Nature* in 1997. A British researcher who counted seal hairs in sediment cores from Signy going back at least

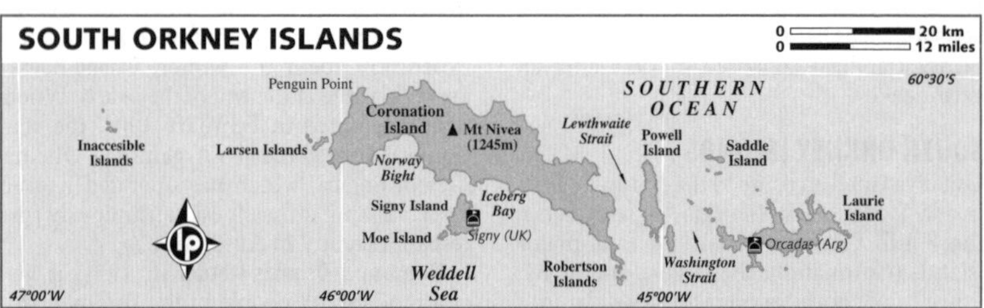

6000 years speculated that the precipitous decline in baleen whales has created a virtually limitless food supply for the seals, since krill is a primary prey of both species.

SHAG ROCKS

Six isolated, guano-covered rocks, along with Black Rock and another low-lying rock 20km to the southeast, make up the group known as Shag Rocks, the smallest of the sub-Antarctic islands.

Rising straight out of the sea, reaching a peak elevation of 71m, they cover just 20 hectares and are part of Britain's South Georgia and South Sandwich Islands territory. Landings are nearly impossible, although the islands are frequently passed en route to South Georgia.

Mislocated by their discoverer, the Spaniard Joseph de la Llana sailing in *Aurora* in 1762, the rocks were originally named the Aurora Islands. In 1819, American sealer James Sheffield in *Hersilia*, searching for the Auroras, found Shag Rocks. The first landing was not made until 1956, when an Argentine geologist was lowered by helicopter to spend a few hours collecting samples. The first tourists landed in 1991. Wildlife includes prions, wandering albatrosses and the eponymous shags.

SOUTH GEORGIA

Crescent-shaped South Georgia, 170km long and 40km wide at its broadest, was one of the first gateways to Antarctica and the center for the huge Southern Ocean whaling industry from 1904 to 1966. Several important expeditions to Antarctica called at the whaling stations en route to or from Antarctica, notably those of Shackleton (see the boxed text on p199).

With its sharp, heavily glaciated peaks, South Georgia presents a rugged appearance. The Allardyce Range forms the island's spine. The highest point is **Mt Paget** (2934m), first ascended in 1964. Glaciers cover 57% of the island, which covers 3755 sq km. The northeastern coast, with many fjords, is protected by mountains from the prevailing westerlies; this is where all of the whaling stations were built. Bird Island and the Willis Islands lie off South Georgia's northwestern tip, Annenkov Island lies off the southwestern coast, and Cooper Island off the eastern coast. The outlying Clerke Rocks are 72km southeast.

South Georgia's weather is cold, cloudy and windy, with little variation between summer and winter.

London-born merchant Antoine de la Roche probably was the first to sight the island. In April 1675 while sailing from Lima to England, his ship was blown south as he rounded Cape Horn and he caught a glimpse of South Georgia's ice-covered mountains. The island was seen again in 1756 by Spaniard Gregorio Jerez, sailing in *Léon*, who called it 'Isla de San Pedro.'

Captain James Cook made the first landing on January 17, 1775, when he named it the Isle of Georgia after King George III and claimed it for His Majesty. Cook called it:

> savage and horrible...the wild rocks raised their lofty summits until they were lost in the clouds, and the valleys lay covered with everlasting snow. Not a tree was to be seen nor a shrub even big enough to make a tooth-pick.

Sealing at South Georgia

When Cook's account of South Georgia was published in 1777, his descriptions of fur seals there set off a stampede of British sealers, who began arriving in 1786. American sealers followed shortly after, and within five years there were more than 100 ships in the Southern Ocean taking fur-seal skins and elephant-seal oil. The British sealer *Ann*, for example, took 3000 barrels of elephant-seal oil and 50,000 fur-seal skins from South Georgia in 1792–93.

In that same season, an American sealer hit upon the idea of taking fur-seal skins from the Southern Ocean to the market in China, circumnavigating the globe in the process. During the next season, eight British sealing ships worked in South Georgian waters. Just one, *Mary*, took 5000 fur seals, which we can reasonably assume was an average harvest.

South Georgia's rock-filled waters have proven treacherous, with more than four dozen wrecks or sinkings near the island. The first recorded was the British sealing vessel *Sally* in 1796; the most recent were two fishing vessels, *Lyn* and *Moresko 1*, driven ashore in Cumberland Bay by high winds in 2003.

An amazing 57,000 fur-seal skins were taken in 1800–02 by the American sealer

Edmund Fanning, in what was probably the most profitable sealing voyage ever made to South Georgia. Sixteen other British and US sealers worked at South Georgia that season. By 1831, the American ship *Pacific*, landing a sealing gang for eight months, found fur seals scarce. As late as 1909, when the American ship *Daisy* stayed for five months in what was probably the last fur-sealing visit to South Georgia, only 170 fur seals could be found.

Elephant seals likewise were slaughtered by the thousands for their oil. A large elephant seal yielded one 170L barrel of oil (although a big bull could produce double that amount), so the 15,000 barrels taken in 1877–78 by the American sealer *Trinity* show the huge number of seals that could be exterminated in a single year by just one ship. By 1885–86 the crew of *American Express* secured just two elephant seals and 123 'sea leopards' (probably Weddell seals), which all together produced only 60 barrels of oil.

Science intruded on this slaughter briefly in 1882–83, when the German International Polar Year Expedition, part of a 12-country effort to make scientific observations in the polar regions, set up a station at Royal Bay on the southeastern coast. They worked for 13 months, and ruins of their hut remain today.

So complete was the slaughter of South Georgia's fur seals that by the 1930s, the local population of *Arctocephalus gazella* was probably at its lowest extreme, with only about 100 individuals left. In the seven decades that followed, the species made an astounding recovery. Today there are more than 3,000,000 fur seals at South Georgia, and in certain seaways, particularly on the western end of the island, they swim in large herds.

Antarctica's Whaling Capital

South Georgia whaling began in 1904, when the Compañía Argentina de Pesca, a Norwegian company based in Buenos Aires, established the first Antarctic whaling station at Grytviken. Using only one whale-catching ship, the Compañía took 183 whales in its first year. This modest

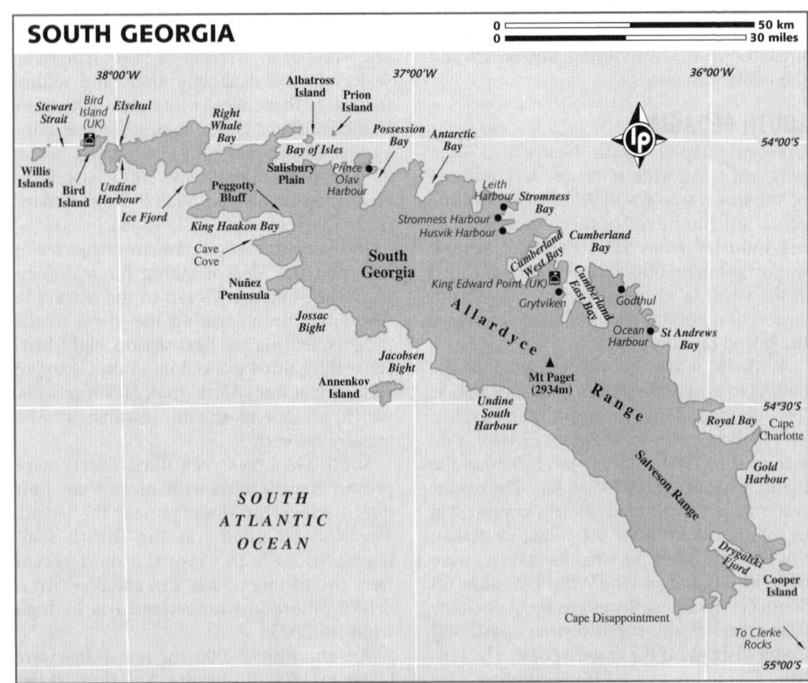

start quickly became an enormous industry that generated millions of kroner for its primarily Norwegian owners. It also marked the beginning of South Georgia's permanent occupation.

Eventually six shore stations were built – at Grytviken, Ocean Harbour, Leith Harbour, Husvik Harbour, Stromness Harbour and Prince Olav Harbour – plus an anchorage for floating factory ships at Godthul. **Grytviken** was the first and longest-running station, operating until 1965. Godthul ran from 1908 to 1917 and from 1922 to 1929. **Ocean Harbour**, which opened in 1909, closed in 1920. **Leith Harbour** opened in 1909, closed for a year in 1933 and again during WWII, and closed for good in 1965. **Husvik Harbour** operated from 1910 to 1931 and again from 1945 to 1960, missing the 1957–58 season. **Stromness Harbour** operated from 1912 to 1931, and then became a repair yard until it closed fully in 1961. **Prince Olav Harbour** operated from 1917 to 1931.

Considering the whaling catch during just two of South Georgia's peak seasons, it's easy to understand why whales are so scarce today. In the 1925–26 season, there were five shore stations, one factory ship and 23 whale-catching ships. In that season, 1855 blue whales, 5709 fin whales, 236 humpbacks, 13 sei whales and 12 sperm whales were caught. The total catch made it a record year: 7825 whales, which produced 404,457 barrels of whale oil. During the 1926–27 season, the same number of catcher ships took 3689 blue whales (a record), 1144 fin whales, no humpbacks, 365 sei whales and 17 sperm whales. The total catch was 'only' 5215 whales, but they produced a record at the time of 417,292 barrels of oil.

The Great Depression beginning in 1929, although it caused severe economic hardship in many parts of the world, proved fortuitous for the whales of Antarctica. Combined with a barely nascent realization that controls were needed, it put the brakes on the booming business of whale-hunting. By the 1931–32 season, the economic crisis, as well as severe overproduction the season before, forced Prince Olav and Stromness stations to close for good. Husvik Harbour also closed, but it reopened in 1945. Leith closed only for the 1932–33 season, and Grytviken operated continuously.

By 1961–62 the Norwegian companies that once dominated the trade – a 1909 census at Grytviken found that 93% of the 720 whalers were Scandinavian – could no longer make a satisfactory profit. Hoping to make money on frozen whale meat, Japanese investors took over the South Georgia whaling operations the next season, but soon also found it unprofitable and closed the last shore station, Grytviken, in 1965.

South Georgia's total whale catch from 1904 to 1966 included 41,515 blue whales, 87,555 fin whales, 26,754 humpbacks, 15,128 sei whales and 3716 sperm whales: a total of 175,250 animals. Land stations, however, accounted for *just 10%* of the total Antarctic whale catch.

A female blue whale, which was caught at Grytviken in the 1911–12 season, measured just over 33.5m – the largest animal ever recorded.

Elephant seals were also killed again during the whaling era. Their oil was mixed with inferior-quality whale oil to improve it. Grytviken was able to remain open longer than the other South Georgia stations in part because it processed elephant seals. From 1905 to 1964, another 498,870 seals (most of them elephant seals) were killed at South Georgia for their oil.

Grytviken

The Grytviken whaling station operated from 1904 to 1965.

Although a whole whale could be butchered in as little as 20 minutes, it was sometimes hard to keep pace with the catcher boats! As many as four dozen whales might be brought in at once, with the whole of Grytviken Bay covered by carcasses, which were inflated with compressed air to make them float. Handling that many whales sometimes necessitated night shifts, but the workers didn't complain, because overtime meant double pay.

Alcohol was banned, but illicit stills produced home-made aquavit. Crime was not a big problem at Grytviken – the jail was used mainly to house expeditions visiting the island.

Be sure to look up when entering the wonderful **South Georgia Museum**. Otherwise, you'll miss – as many do – the mounted wandering albatross soaring overhead. Unless you're a scientist, this is the closest you'll

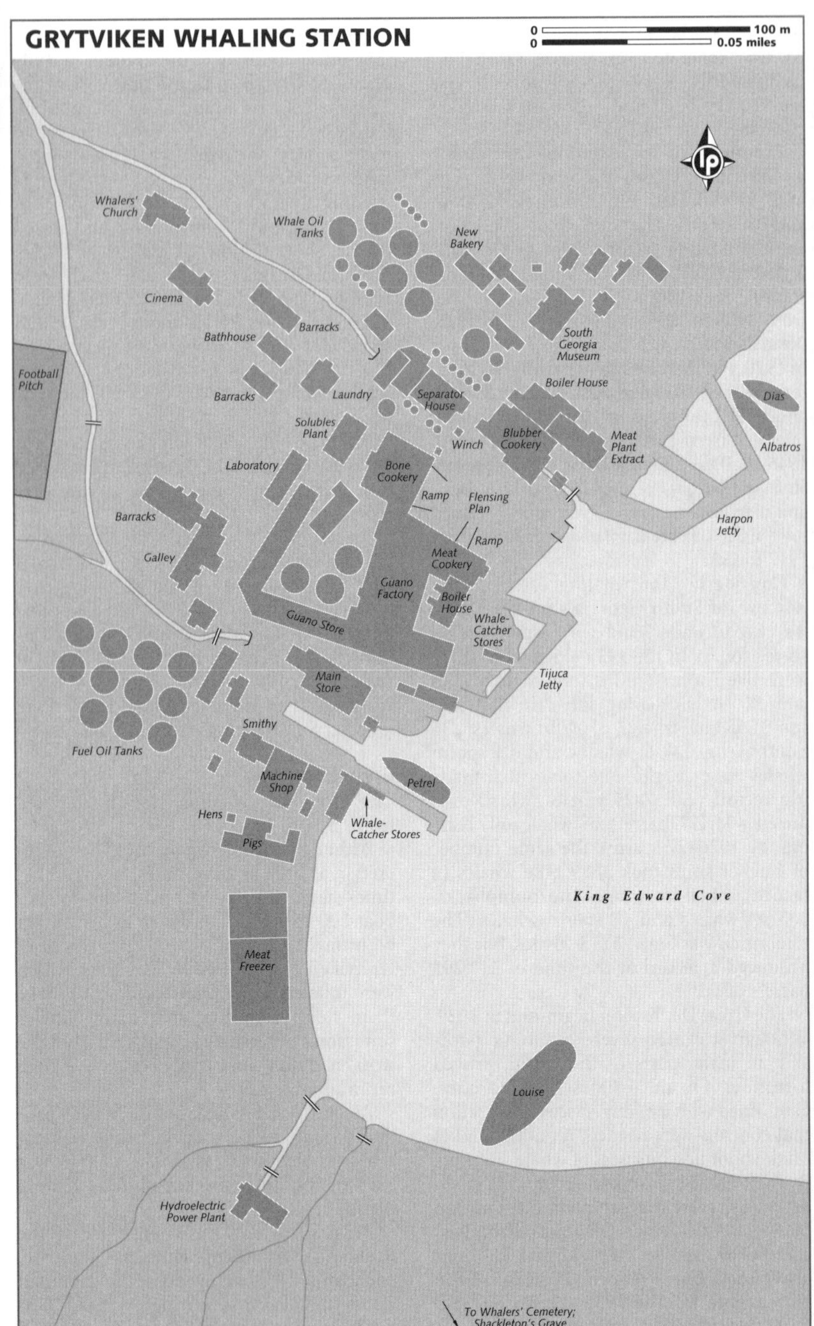
GRYTVIKEN WHALING STATION
0
100 m
0
0.05 miles
Whalers' Church
Whale Oil Tanks
New Bakery
Cinema
Barracks
Bathhouse
South Georgia Museum
Football Pitch
Barracks
Laundry
Separator House
Boiler House
Dias
Solubles Plant
Winch
Blubber Cookery
Meat Plant Extract
Albatros
Laboratory
Bone Cookery
Ramp
Flensing Plan
Harpon Jetty
Barracks
Ramp
Galley
Meat Cookery
Guano Factory
Boiler House
Guano Store
Whale-Catcher Stores
Main Store
Tijuca Jetty
Smithy
Fuel Oil Tanks
Machine Shop
Petrel
Hens
Whale-Catcher Stores
Pigs
King Edward Cove
Meat Freezer
Louise
Hydroelectric Power Plant
To Whalers' Cemetery; Shackleton's Grave

GRYTVIKEN WHALING STATION OPERATIONS *Robert Burton*

Grytviken means 'Pot Cove' and is named for the sealers' try-pots that were discovered there. As a 'bay within a bay,' it is the best harbor in South Georgia and was chosen by the Norwegian Captain Carl Anton Larsen as the site of the first whaling station in Antarctic waters. On November 16, 1904 Larsen arrived with a small fleet of ships to build a factory, and whaling started five weeks later. Although the company was Argentine-owned, the whalers were mostly Norwegians. Huge profits were made at first, but Grytviken was eventually forced to close because whales had become so rare.

During Grytviken's first years, only the blubber from the whale was utilized. Later meat, bones and viscera were cooked to extract the oil, leaving bone and meat-meal as important by-products.

Life for the station workers was arduous. The 'season' ran from October to March, and the workers put in 12-hour days. As many as 300 worked here during the industry's heyday. A few stayed over winter to maintain the boats and factory. Transportation ships brought down coal, fuel oil, stores and food for the workers and took away the oil and other products.

Attitudes toward whaling were very different a generation ago, and whaling was a highly respectable profession among Norwegians. Through the development of its whaling industry, Norway became a leading industrialized nation known for its shipbuilding and oil technology.

The flensing plan is the large open space between the two main jetties. Whale carcasses were brought to the iron-plated whale slip at the base of the plan and hauled onto the plan by the whale winch. (The 40,815kg electric winch has been removed from the top of the plan.) The blubber was slit by flensers armed with hockey stick–shaped flensing knives. Strips of blubber were then ripped off the carcass, like the skin from a banana, by cables attached to steam winches, which you can still see.

The blubber was minced and fed into the blubber cookery, the large building on the right of the plan. Each cooker held about 24 tonnes of blubber, which was cooked for approximately five hours to drive out the oil. The oil was piped to the separator house for purification by centrifuging. The separator house, and the generator house behind it, were destroyed by fire but you can still see the separators in the ruins. Finally, the oil was pumped into tanks behind the station. If there was a good supply of whales, about 25 fin whales, each 18m long, could be processed in 24 hours. They would yield 1000 barrels (160 tonnes) of oil.

When the whale had been flensed, the meat, tongue and guts were cut off by the lemmers, drawn up the steep ramp on the left of the plan to the meat cookery and dropped into rotating cookers. The head and backbone were dragged up another ramp at the back of the plan to the bone cookery, where they were cut up with large steam saws and also cooked.

After oil extraction, the remains of the meat and bone were dried and turned into guano for animal feed and fertilizer. In later years meat extract was made by treatment with sulfuric acid in a plant next to the blubber cookery. Meat extract was used in dried soups and other prepared foods.

Along the shore, past the boiler house and guano store, is the slipway where *Petrel* lies. Built in 1928, she was used for whaling until 1956 and then converted for sealing. The catwalk connecting the bridge to the gun platform has been removed and the present gun is a recent addition. In this area of the station are the engineering shops, foundry and smithy, all of which enabled the whalers to repair their boats. Further along is the piggery, the meat freezer and, on the hillside, the hydroelectric power plant. On the shore is the burnt-out remains of the wooden barque *Louise*, a sailing ship built in 1869 at Freeport, Maine. She came to Grytviken in 1904 as a supply ship and remained as a coaling hulk, until she was burned as a training exercise by the UK's garrison at King Edward Point in 1987.

Robert Burton is a past director of the South Georgia Museum

come to one of these magnificent birds, and their size is startling.

The museum, opened in 1992, is housed in the former station manager's house, built in 1916 by the Norwegians. It's filled with fascinating exhibits on South Georgia's history and wildlife; nearly all visitors wish they could spend more time here. The shop sells an amazing array of clothing, patches, souvenirs, postcards, slide sets and books. Euros,

US dollars and British pounds are accepted, as are Visa and MasterCard credit cards. Proceeds assist museum improvements.

The restored **Whalers' Church**, consecrated on Christmas Day 1913, is a typical Norwegian church. Inside are memorials to Grytviken's founder Carl Anton Larsen and to Shackleton, whose funeral was held here. Visitors are invited to go upstairs to ring the two bells. Grytviken's first pastor, Kristen Löken, lamented that 'religious life among the whalers left much to be desired.' The church has been used for a few baptisms (13 births have been registered on the island) and four marriages (the most recent was in 1999), but it has been used more often for funerals.

Shackleton's grave is the highlight of the attractive **whalers' cemetery** at Grytviken. 'The Boss' is buried at the left rear of the graveyard. On the back of the granite headstone (engraved with the nine-pointed star that Shackleton used as a personal emblem) is one of his favorite quotations, from the poet Robert Browning: 'I hold that a man should strive to the uttermost for his life's set prize.'

There are 64 other graves here, several of which may belong to 19th-century sealers. Most belong to Norwegian whalers, including nine who died in a 1912 typhus epidemic. One grave holds the remains of an Argentine soldier killed during the Falklands War. The cemetery's abundant dandelions come from seeds in the soil, some of which was imported from Norway to allow the dead whalers to be buried in a bit of home. The cemetery is surrounded by a fence to keep molting elephant seals from scratching against the gravestones – and thereby destroying them.

The cross on the hillside above commemorates Walter Slossarczyk, third officer on Filchner's *Deutschland* expedition, who committed suicide at Grytviken in 1911; he rowed off in a ship's dinghy one night and never returned, although the boat was found three days later. The cross higher up the hill commemorates 17 men who died when their fishing vessel *Sudurhavid* sank off the island in 1998. The hillside is a good place to take panoramic photos of the station, but it's quite steep.

Recent History

In 1908 the British government consolidated earlier claims of sovereignty into a territory called Dependencies of the Falkland Islands, which includes South Georgia, the South Orkneys, the South Shetlands, the South Sandwich Islands and Graham Land on the Antarctic Peninsula. A magistrate has resided at Grytviken continuously from 1909, except briefly during the Falklands War in 1982.

In 1949–50 the Falkland Islands Dependencies Survey established a new base at **King Edward Point** on South Georgia's northeastern coast. This station assumed responsibility for meteorological observations, which had been made since 1905 and continued throughout the whaling era. In the 1962–63 season, a large hospital and residential building, called 'Shackleton House,' was built at King Edward Point, but today no scientists work at the station; they're all out in field camps.

War intruded on South Georgia in 1982. On March 25, the Argentine naval vessel *Bahía Paraíso*, later to become infamous for spilling fuel at Anvers Island along the Antarctic Peninsula, arrived at Leith Harbour and set up a garrison in a clear challenge to Britain's sovereignty over South Georgia. On April 3, *Bahía Paraíso*, *Guerrico* and their accompanying helicopters landed 200 Argentine forces at King Edward Point, which was defended by just 22 Royal Marines. After a two-hour battle in which several Argentine soldiers were killed and two Argentine helicopters were shot down, the Argentines captured the station and took the Marines and scientists to Argentina as prisoners. The Royal Navy later relieved 15 British researchers at four field stations. For more information, pick up a copy of Roger Perkins' fascinating book *Operation Paraquat* (1986), the definitive account of the war at South Georgia.

In response to the Argentine aggression, London dispatched six Royal Navy ships, including the nuclear submarine HMS *Conqueror* for reconnaissance. This force retook King Edward Point on April 25, and the Argentine garrison at Leith Harbour the next day. An Argentine submarine, *Santa Fé*, was sunk; 185 Argentines were taken prisoner and later released in Uruguay. During the Falklands War, the Royal Navy used South Georgia as a base. The last 15 British troops remaining at King Edward Point departed in March 2001.

SHACKLETON AT SOUTH GEORGIA

Ernest Shackleton's name is inextricably linked with South Georgia, and visits to the island often include landings at places associated with his expeditions.

Grytviken is the most important – and most visited. Shackleton first stopped here in November 1914 on his way south with *Endurance*. From the whalers, he learned that it was a bad ice year in the Weddell Sea. Although he delayed his departure by several weeks, the ice got his ship nevertheless.

Another eight years and one month passed before Shackleton returned. This time southbound on *Quest*, he died of a heart attack aboard his ship, moored at Grytviken, early on the morning of January 5, 1922. A few hours before, he wrote his final diary entry, ending on a poetic note: 'In the darkening twilight I saw a lone star hover, Gem like above the bay.' Even as his body was en route home to Britain, his widow Emily decided he should be buried at South Georgia. Today, his grave in the Grytviken whalers cemetery is one of South Georgia's highlights for many visitors.

At tiny Cave Cove, at dusk on May 10, 1916, Shackleton and his five companions made landfall after their amazing 16-day, 1300km crossing from Elephant Island in the lifeboat *James Caird*. It had been 522 days since they left South Georgia. The men immediately fell to their knees at a freshwater stream, 'drinking the pure, ice-cold water in long draughts that put new life into us,' Shackleton wrote in *South* (1919). The cave, at the left side of the head of the cove, is in fact just an overhang of the cliff. When Shackleton and his men stayed here, 5m-long icicles hung down in front of the cave mouth. The men supplemented this cover with *James Caird*'s sail, and spread tussock grass on the floor to lay their sleeping bags on. They also feasted on albatross chicks (albatrosses still nest on the slopes opposite the cave). Frank Worsley later recalled: 'By jove, they were good, damn good!' At Cave Cove, too, occurred one of the several miracles of the *Endurance* saga: *James Caird*'s rudder, which had been lost just as they arrived at South Georgia, came floating back into the cove on the returning tide. Today, a discreet plaque commemorating Shackleton and his men, left by the Irish 'South Aris' expedition of 1997, is bolted to the cliff wall to the left of the cave.

After five days at Cave Cove, Shackleton and his crew sailed *James Caird* deeper into King Haakon Bay, making camp on the northern shore by overturning the boat on the sand at a place they named Peggotty Bluff, after the family in Dickens' *David Copperfield* whose home was made from a boat. Hundreds of elephant seals lay on the beach, and Shackleton wrote, 'our anxieties with regard to food disappeared.' Before dawn on May 19th, Shackleton, Worsley and Tom Crean began their crossing of the island by walking along the jetsam-strewn beach. Shackleton reflected soberly on 'the many tragedies written in the wave-worn fragments of lost vessels.' Even now, the beach is littered with wood, ropes, buoys and other debris swept into the bay by the westerlies.

Shackleton and his two companions reached Stromness at 4pm on May 20, 1916, after crossing the island's 1800m range – the first time it had been done. The whaling station manager, Thoralf Sørlle, gave them food, shocking news of the progress of WWI – and a bath. 'I don't think I have ever appreciated anything so much as that hot bath,' Worsley wrote in his book *Endurance* (1931). 'It was really wonderful and worth all that we had been through to get it.' The manager's villa still stands at the station's southern end.

Vildlife

iouth Georgia's wildlife is varied and .bundant, despite the incredible slaughter hat took place just a century ago. During he 1960s and '70s, the Antarctic fur-seal opulation increased about 15% annually. Today, the South Georgia population is nore than three million. Found mainly n the northwestern coast, the seals are o numerous that during breeding season they present a hazard to Zodiacs trying to land.

More than five million pairs of macaroni penguins nest on the island. King penguins breed on the beach at **St Andrews Bay** where a melt stream from the Ross Glacier runs through the rookery of 100,000 birds, South Georgia's largest king rookery. Kings also nest at **Salisbury Plain** in the Bay of Isles on the northwestern coast.

Albatross Island and **Prion Island** in the Bay of Isles are home to the magnificent wandering albatrosses. Thousands of burrowing seabirds also thrive, since there are no rats on the islands. Three other rat-free islands (on which tourist landings are prohibited) – **Cooper Island** off the southeastern coast, **Annenkov Island** off the southern coast and **Bird Island** at the northwestern end of the island – are also home to enormous seabird populations.

Two fascinating birds also reside on the island. The South Georgia pipit is the only songbird in Antarctica, while the South Georgia pintail is the world's only known carnivorous duck.

South Georgia's 2000 reindeer were introduced by whalers in 1911 and are confined by glaciers to two regions.

Visiting South Georgia

Visitors to the island are charged a landing fee of £55 (set to rise to £75 for the 2005–06 season, and £100 for the 2006–07 season), and without exception visits must be approved in advance. Tour companies take care of the paperwork for their passengers, but yachts must apply to the **Commissioner for South Georgia and the South Sandwich Islands** (☎ 500-27433; gov.house@horizon.co.fk; Government House, Stanley, Falkland Islands via UK).

Three excellent books offer more information: Tim and Pauline Carr's *Antarctic Oasis: Under the Spell of South Georgia* (1998) is a well-written photographic book by a couple who lived on their yacht *Curlew* at Grytviken for many years. Robert Headland's *The Island of South Georgia* (1984) is a definitive study of the island, its history and geography. Sally Poncet's *Antarctic Encounter: Destination South Georgia* (1995) describes the island's wildlife and history through the eyes of three boys who explore it with their parents by yacht.

For an amazing look at South Georgia's wildlife, watch the BBC Natural History Unit's video *The Living Edens: Paradise of Ice, South Georgia Island*. Shot during eight months on the island spread over two years, the hour-long film will have you asking, 'How did they get that spectacular footage?'

SOUTH SANDWICH ISLANDS

The 11 volcanic islands of the South Sandwich group are spread over a rough 250km-long arc running north to south: Zavodovski Leskov (the archipelago's smallest), Visokoi Candlemas, Vindication, Saunders, Montagu (the largest), Bristol, Bellingshausen Cook and Thule. Five of the islands (Thule Cook, Bristol, Montagu and Visokoi) are mostly ice covered, while two (Saunders and Candlemas) are more than half covered with ice. The remaining four islands have almost no ice caps.

Together the South Sandwiches cover 31[illegible] sq km. On the archipelago's convex eastern side is a deep-sea trench with a depth of 8265m. The highest point in the islands is 1375m Mt Belinda on Montagu Island.

Although they're more northerly than either the South Shetlands or the South Orkneys, the South Sandwiches have a much colder climate, thanks to a cold ocean current originating in the Weddell Sea. The sky is almost constantly cloud-covered.

The eight most southerly islands in the group were discovered on January 30, 177[illegible] by Cook, sailing in HMS *Resolution*. He named the islands 'Sandwich Land' after the 4th Earl of Sandwich, then the First Lord of the Admiralty. Ironically, Cook was killed in the Sandwich Islands, now called the Hawaiian Islands.

Vividly describing one of the islands Johann Reinhold Forster, who sailed with Cook, wrote:

> Wrapt in almost continual fogs, we could only now and then have a sight of it, and that only of its lowest part, an immense volume of clouds constantly resting on the summits of the mountains, as though the sight of all its horrors would be too tremendous for mortal eyes to behold. The mind indeed, still shudders at the idea, and eagerly turns from so disgusting an object.

Sealers made the first landing in 1818.

The three northernmost islands were first sighted in 1819, by Bellingshausen who landed on Zavodovski and named [illegible] for Lieutenant Ivan Zavodovski, captain of his flagship *Vostok*, on Christmas Eve 1819.

Volcanoes formed all of the islands [illegible] relatively short time ago. Volcanic activity has been recorded in the past century

RALPH LEE HOPKINS

Glacier face (p86)

Tabular iceberg (p89)

DAVID ETHERIDGE

RALPH LEE HOPKINS

Icebergs at sunset

Pack ice, Southern Ocean (p141)

GRANT DIXON

RALPH LEE HO

Snow algae (p220)

RALPH LEE HOPKINS

The ice at sunset

JULIET COOMBE

Lichens growing on rock surface (p135)

Raised sea-stacks and mire, Macquarie Island (p169)

GRANT D

on all the South Sandwiches except Cook, Montagu and Vindication. In 1908, Larsen was almost asphyxiated by volcanic fumes on Zavodovski. He also noted many places from which pure liquid sulfur oozed from the ground. Filchner, visiting in 1911, reported that both his landing party and those who remained aboard *Deutschland* were 'severely troubled...by the sulphur gases blowing from the land.'

In a dramatic demonstration of the islands' continuing volcanism, in January 1956 a group of Argentines at the Teniente Esquivel refuge hut on Thule witnessed an extraordinary sight: three jets of glowing material shot 300m into the air for 48 hours. Understandably, the men evacuated as soon as possible.

In 1962 the South African research ship *RSA*, beset by ice, was freed by shock waves believed to be caused by a volcanic eruption in the South Sandwiches. In March of that year, rafts of pumice were sighted offshore of the islands. About 35km off the northwestern end of the chain at Protector Shoal, there's a submarine volcanic cone just 25m underwater – which could someday grow to become the newest island in the chain.

In recognition of its underworld-like landscape, the British Antarctic Survey has named the features of **Candlemas Island** evocatively: Cauldron Pool, Demon Point, Chimaera Flats, Gorgon Pool, Lucifer Hill and Sarcophagus Point. Surveyors of **Zavodovski Island**, meanwhile, have named salient features in accordance with how they smell: Reek Point, Pungent Point, Fume Point, Stench Point, Acrid Point, Noxious Bluff and Mt Asphyxia.

The islands are part of Britain's territory of South Georgia and South Sandwich Islands. Argentina, which claims the islands as part of its Islas del Atlántico Sur, established a 50-member naval station on Thule in 1976 and occupied it for the summer without authorization from Britain. The next season the naval station, Corbeta Uruguay, opened for the winter. It remained active until June 20, 1982, when its 10 remaining personnel were removed by the British navy because of its role as a staging point in the attack on South Georgia. The following January, the station (except for a refuge hut) was destroyed by British forces after they discovered an Argentine flag flying. What's left is a mess; there was no clean-up after the charges were exploded.

Tourists first landed on the South Sandwiches in 1982. Among the islands' attractions are 1.5 million breeding pairs of chinstraps. Some Antarctic tour brochures once claimed that more than 12 million chinstraps breed on Zavodovski Island alone, but this very rough estimate has been superseded by recent surveys. Biologists say there are in fact about one million breeding pairs on Zavodovski – or about two million birds – which still makes it one of the world's largest penguin colonies.

Visitors to the South Sandwiches are charged a landing fee of £55 (set to rise to £75 for the 2005–06 season, and £100 for the 2006–07 season), and without exception visits must be approved in advance. Tour companies take care of the paperwork for their passengers, but yachts must apply to the **Commissioner for South Georgia and the South Sandwich Islands** (☎ 500-27433; gov.house@horizon.co.fk; Government House, Stanley, Falkland Islands via UK).

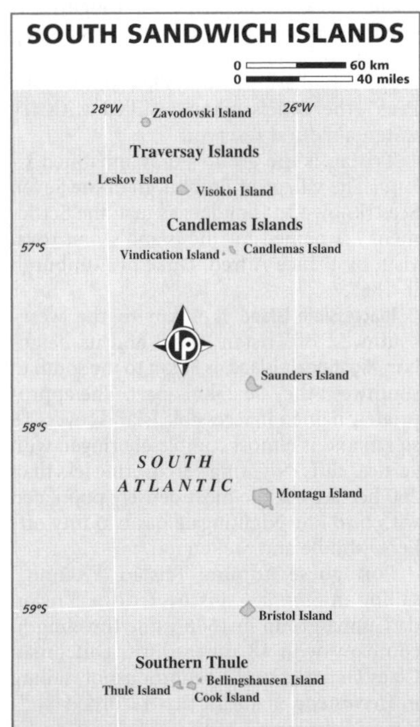

TRISTAN DA CUNHA GROUP

You can call Tristan da Cunha 'the middle of nowhere,' for it is the world's most isolated inhabited island. Indeed, a large sign welcomes visitors to 'The Remotest Island.' Only a handful of vessels call here each year – a fishing boat every couple of months, and a tourist ship perhaps two or three times a year. Satellite TV arrived only in 2001.

The island used to be even more isolated. During one three-year period, not a single ship visited, and the islanders once went 10 years without mail. Unmarried Tristanian women used to pray for shipwrecks as a source of potential bridegrooms, and islanders themselves used to refer to 'the outside world.'

Midway between South Africa and Brazil, these volcanic islands stand astride the border between the sub-Antarctic and subtropical climatic zones. Tristan is often included on the 'repositioning voyages' at the end of the Antarctic tour season, in part because of its millions of nesting seabirds.

The northernmost of the group, **Tristan Island**, is also the largest, being roughly circular and covering 98 sq km. It has a steep extinct volcanic cone rising to 2060m, the group's highest point. Called simply 'the Peak,' the cone's crater is filled with icy water, a natural reservoir.

Tristan is the group's only inhabited island. The village of Edinburgh of the Seven Seas (known to islanders as just 'the Settlement') is named for the island's first royal visit, by Prince Alfred, Duke of Edinburgh in 1867.

Inaccessible Island is 40km to the west-southwest of Tristan Island and its neighbor, **Nightingale Island**, is 38km to the south to southwest; they lie 23km apart. The appropriately named Inaccessible Island covers 18 sq km and is almost completely ringed with vertical cliffs. Nightingale, covering less than 260 hectares, is the most densely populated with bird life. Nightingale has two tiny offliers, Middle and Stoltenhoff.

Portuguese Admiral Tristão d'Acunha, sailing in *Santiago*, discovered the Tristan da Cunha group in 1506 while traveling in company with 13 other ships. Dutchman Claes Gerritszoon Bierenbroodspot, sailing in *Heemstede*, made the first-recorded landing on February 7, 1643.

Austrian Guilleme Bolts, sailing in *Joseph et Thérèse*, landed on Tristan da Cunha in 1775 and took possession for the Emperor of Austria, Joseph II.

The usual sad sequence of discovery, exploitation, and extinction was repeated on Tristan. The first sealers, Americans sailing in *Industry*, visited for eight months in 1790–91, industriously taking 5600 fur seal skins. By 1801–02 sealers sailing in *Phiamingi* from the Cape Colony were able to take fewer than 10 skins.

Three Americans landed by the sealing ship *Baltic* in 1810–12 established the first settlement on Tristan. One of them, Jonathan Lambert from Salem, Massachusetts, declared himself emperor and proclaimed that Tristan should henceforth be called 'the Islands of Refreshment.' He hoped the name would inspire passing ships to call in for provisions. A copy of Lambert's personal flag can be seen in Tristan's museum. The three men began killing fur seals, hoping to sell the skins to passing vessels.

After two of the men drowned in 1812, the lone survivor, Thomas Curry, continued working. When a British naval vessel stopped in March 1813, two new settlers joined him. According to the history notes at **Tristan's official website** (http://website.lineone.net/~sthelena/tristaninfo.htm), Curry 'aroused their interest with stories of buried treasure but never revealed its whereabouts. He died of drink, plied to him by the members of the garrison seeking the treasure!' It has never been found.

During the 1812–15 war between Britain and the US, the islands were used by American ships as a base for raids on British vessels. In one offshore gunbattle, USS *Hornet* sank HMS *Penguin*. Partly to prevent a rescue of Napoleon – exiled on St Helena in 1815 – Britain set up a garrison and took possession of Tristan in 1816. After the garrison was withdrawn in 1817, three men, a woman and two children, all British, remained along with horses and cattle. One of them, Corporal William Glass of Scotland, is recognized as Edinburgh's founder.

British artist Augustus Earle was stranded on Tristan in 1824 when en route to India his ship, *Duke of Gloucester*, was forced by a storm to shelter offshore. Anxious to see an island that, as he said, was 'hitherto unvisited by any artist,' Earle went ashore with his dog and a crewmember for what they thought would be a day visit. Instead, the ship left without them when the weather worsened. Earle spent eight months on the island. The population was then six adults and several children, whom he tutored until a passing ship took him to Hobart. Earle was later briefly attached to Darwin's *Beagle* expedition as its official artist before illness forced him to resign. Sixteen works from his Tristan exile are now at the National Library of Australia.

Shipwrecked sailors added to Tristan's tiny community, and by 1826 the island's population was 14: Glass, his wife, their seven children and five other men. The population began to rise fairly quickly after the bachelors asked a ship captain to procure wives from the British colony of St Helena 2100km northeast. In addition, by the time Glass died in 1853, he had fathered a total of eight sons and eight daughters.

For a time in the 19th century, Edinburgh thrived as a convenient mid-ocean filling station – ships stopped for water, vegetables and meat from the islanders' sheep and cattle. The surrounding seas were a favored hunting ground for American whalers – and as many as 70 ships stood offshore of the island simultaneously. Crews of passing ships often remarked upon the islanders' abstemiousness – they neither smoked nor drank, perhaps not surprising given their isolation. But Tristan's ship traffic dwindled as Atlantic and Pacific whaling came to an end and the Suez Canal opened in 1869, eliminating the need to sail around Africa to reach India and the Far East.

Shipwreck Saviors

Residents of the settlement rescued dozens of mariners whose ships had foundered or burned offshore. The first recorded wreck came in 1817, when HMS *Julia*, dispatched to the island to withdraw the garrison, came ashore on the northwestern coast; 55 men died. Over the years, many more vessels have been wrecked on or near Tristan. These include *Sarah* (1820), *Blendon Hall* (1821), *Nassau* (1825), *Emily* (1836), *Joseph Comes* (1850), *Lark* (1864), *Sir Ralph Abercrombie* (1868), *Bogota* (1869), *Beacon Light* (1871), *Czarina* (1872), *Olympia* (1872), *Mabel Clark* (1878), *Edward Vittery* (1881), *Henry B Paul* (1882), *Shakespeare* (1883), *Italia* (1892), *Allanshaw* (1893), *Helen S Lea* (1897), *Glen Huntley* (1898), *Köbenhavn* (1929) and *Coimbra* (1953).

So many times did the islanders aid shipwrecked sailors that as thanks the British government sent provisions in 1858 and a new lifeboat and other equipment in 1884. In 1879–80, a British naval voyage dropped off presents sent by US President Rutherford B Hayes in gratitude for the Tristanians' role in saving *Mabel Clark*'s crew – and sheltering them for six months.

One of the island's most intriguing wrecks occurred in 1864 when the American ship *Lark* was caught in a hurricane. The crew managed to get ashore with £35,000 in gold and currency, then a considerable fortune. The loot was left on the island after the survivors were rescued, and although *Lark*'s captain died of smallpox on the voyage home, the first mate later returned for the stash.

Shipwrecks' greatest gift to the islanders – aside from the occasional crewmember who decided to join the small community – was building materials. Because the island is extremely short of big trees, Tristanians have incorporated wreckage from the numerous shipwrecks in their home construction. The 5m evergreen 'island tree' *Phylica arborea* is used for firewood.

To prevent overpopulation, in 1857 a British naval expedition removed 45 of Edinburgh's settlers, leaving 28 people. Ironically, fate took its own cruel measure 27 years later, when 15 men drowned while rowing out in a small boat to try to hail a passing ship for provisions after the potato crop failed. The tragedy left only four adult men on Tristan, which became known as 'the island of widows.'

At least two of the ships that called in at Tristan had connections with Antarctic exploration. In 1893 Henrik Bull's *Antarctic* visited before heading south to the Ross Sea. In 1922 *Quest* landed at Tristan after Shackleton's death.

Annual voyages to bring mail and provisions were begun by Britain in 1927, and in 1938 British Letters Patent defined the Tristan da Cunha group and Gough Island as Dependencies of St Helena.

During WWII, the British navy established a meteorological and radio station on the island to prevent Nazi ships from using Tristan as a watering place. The detachment was withdrawn in 1946 and the South African Weather Bureau took over responsibility for the station.

The 'Volcano Years'

A volcanic eruption in 1961 followed more than two months of seismic activity, including nearly 100 small earthquakes. A small volcanic cone, 3m high, appeared overnight – and later grew at the rate of nearly 2m each hour. The eruption destroyed the island's crayfish-processing plant, but added 35 hectares of land. The eruption forced Edinburgh's evacuation on October 10. Two fishing boats took the entire population (290 people) to Nightingale Island. The next day they sailed for Cape Town, and later to England, where they remained until November 1963, when nearly all returned to the island. Many Tristanians found England too cold and too noisy. Visitors can now hike up the **cinder cone** at the edge of the settlement.

Tristan Today

Edinburgh's population today is just under 300, with 80 families sharing eight surnames. Homes are surrounded by low stone walls sheltering handsome gardens. The Prince Philip Hall is the island's social center, with a weekly dance, a pub and indoor sports. There's an outdoor swimming pool and a café, as well as two churches, a school with about four-dozen students, a supermarket, a gym, a public library, a museum and a golf course. There's one public satellite telephone, and mail arrives every three months. The Internet arrived in 1998.

Elections are held every three years for the eight positions on the Island Council, which also has three appointed members. The Administrator, appointed by the governor of St Helena, is the head of government and must act in accordance with advice from the Island Council. At least one councilor must be female. The councilor who receives the most votes is named Chief Islander.

Employment consists of either a government job or working for the plant that processes the local catch of rock lobster (crayfish), exported to France, Japan and the US. Other exports include handicrafts and postage stamps, which are prized by collectors. The island is almost completely self-supporting.

Edinburgh, says one of Tristan's recent Administrators, Brian Baldwin, 'is a very small community with the characteristics of small communities all over the world. But the isolation factor has required Tristanians to work at solving interpersonal relations in a realistic way.' Equality of opportunity, he adds, is important. 'No one islander will try to outdo another. This attitude derives from a very egalitarian declaration made by William Glass and the original settlers, the original of which is in the British Museum.' There is no serious crime.

A study of the Tristanians' DNA in 1997 found the cause of asthma (known locally as 'ashmere') suffered by about 30% of the population: a mutated gene, apparently passed down by an early settler.

A devastating hurricane struck Tristan in May 2001, damaging many buildings and homes and leaving the islanders without electricity for six days.

Tristanians' distinctive speech shows influences of Dutch/Afrikaans, American English and British English. Islanders greet each other with 'How you is?' and reply 'I's fine.' Other local words include *cappie* (hood) and *gansey* (pullover); the island's potato-growing section is called Patches.

Anyone interested in learning more about the island's recent history should read the invaluable *Tristan da Cunha: History, Way of Life, Language* (2003), written by Daniel Schreier and islander Karen Lavarello-Schreier. For current events, check out the **Tristan Times** (www.tristantimes.com).

GOUGH ISLAND

Rising steeply out of the sea, oblong Gough Island covers 65 sq km, with several pillars and rocks lying offshore. Its coasts are nearly all cliffs, especially on the windward western side, where they stand nearly 460m high. Many steep-walled canyons known as 'glens' cut the eastern side of the island. **Edinburgh Peak** (910m) is the island's highest point. There are no glaciers.

Because the island receives more than 3m of rainfall each year, and has an average annual temperature of 11.7°C, a lush green tangle of mosses, tussock grasses and ferns covers its lower elevations during the summer. As the cool weather arrives in April, these turn brilliant autumn colors. Gough boasts two tree species: the Sophora tree (*Sophora microphylla*), confined to one valley on the eastern side of the island called Sophora Glen, and the Phylica tree (*Phylica arborea*), most numerous on the island's protected eastern side.

Gough was probably first sighted in 1505 by the Portuguese Gonçalo Alvarez when he was blown south while rounding the Cape of Good Hope. For this reason, the island is occasionally referred to as Gonzalo Alvarez. The Dutchman January Jakobszoon van Amsterdam examined Gough and the Tristan da Cunha group in 1655–56.

The first landing on Gough was probably made when Antoine de la Roche, a London-born merchant, came ashore in May 1675, a month after he discovered South Georgia. Such mid-ocean discoveries were not always shared, however, especially among rival seafaring nations. British Captain Charles Gough, sailing in *Richmond*, rediscovered the island on March 3, 1732, naming it for himself, although he made no landing.

Sealers arrived in 1804, and the island's resources were exploited throughout the 19th century. The island's only known shipwreck is *Philena Winslow*, an American collier that ran ashore in 1878, although all hands were saved. In 1881 parties from Cape Town reported taking 8 tonnes of guano, 4000 penguin eggs and 151 fur-seal skins.

George Comer, a Connecticut sealer who arrived in 1888 aboard *Frances Alleyn*, spent five months on the island. In addition to collecting fur-seal skins and elephant-seal oil, he made important natural history observations, including the first sightings of the island's two endemic bird species: the secretive, flightless Gough moor hen (*Gallinula comeri*) and the straw-colored Gough bunting (*Rowettia goughensis*), which is relatively unafraid of people.

In 1919 a group from Cape Town spent four months prospecting on the island for diamonds – unsuccessfully.

Shortly after Britain defined Gough Island as a dependency of St Helena in 1938, a formal territorial claim was made during a British naval visit by HMS *Milford*.

During WWII, Germany sent *Stier*, also known as 'Raider J,' to investigate Gough as a potential base of operations and prison camp. Britain quickly dispatched HMS *Hawkins* to ensure that the Germans would not be able establish a beachhead.

In 1955–56 a comprehensive examination of Gough was made by British scientists, who built a small station on the northeastern coast. In May 1956 the British scientific station was transferred to the South African Weather Bureau, which continues meteorological observations today, although the station was moved to the southeastern coast of the island in 1963.

The first tourist landing was made in 1970, and Gough was declared a Wildlife Reserve in 1976. In late 1995, after a comprehensive management plan was adopted, it was declared a World Heritage Site, the first Southern Ocean or sub-Antarctic island so designated. Today, no tourist landings are permitted at Gough, but Zodiac cruising along the shore give a glimpse of this truly amazing seabird paradise.

Half of the world's population of northern rockhopper penguin (*Eudyptes chrysocome moseleyi*) breed at Gough. The island is a major breeding site of the great shearwater, with up to three million pairs nesting on the island, and the wandering albatross, with up to 2000 breeding pairs. Gough is also one of the most northerly habitats of the southern elephant seal.

FALKLAND ISLANDS

The Falkland Islands are a popular addition to many Antarctic voyages. Surrounded by the South Atlantic and by centuries of controversy, the islands lie 490km to the east of Patagonia.

Consisting of two main islands, East and West Falkland, and about 700 smaller ones, they cover 12,173 sq km, about the same area as Northern Ireland or Connecticut. Except for the low-lying southern half of East Falkland, known as Lafonia, the terrain is generally hilly to mountainous. East Falkland's highest point is 705m **Mt Usborne**, West Falkland's is 700m **Mt Adam**. Among the most interesting geological features are the 'stone runs' of quartzite boulders that descend from many of the ridges and peaks on both East and West Falkland.

The climate is temperate, with frequent high winds. Maximum temperatures rarely reach 24°C, while even on the coldest winter days the temperature usually rises above freezing. Average annual rainfall at Stanley, one of the islands' most humid areas, is only 600mm.

Grasslands and shrubs dominate the flora. There are no native trees. At the time of European discovery, extensive stands of the native tussock grass *(Parodiochloa flabellata)* dominated the coastline, but very little remains today, although some offshore islands have preserved significant areas of it. Among the 13 endemic plants are several unusual species, including: snake plant *(Nassauvia serpens)*, with its phallic-looking stalks and tiny leaves; Felton's flower *(Calandrinia feltonii)*, a caramel-scented, magenta-blossomed annual until recently thought to be extinct in the wild; and vanilla daisy *(Leuceria suaveolens)*, which, while not endemic, is still very interesting – its flowers smell remarkably like chocolate.

Besides the five types of penguin (Magellanic, rockhopper, macaroni, gentoo and king) that breed here, there are many other birds, equally interesting and uncommon. There are no native land animals.

There are about 2913 Falklanders (sometimes called 'Kelpers') living on the islands, with about 2000 residing in Stanley, as well as another 2000 British military personnel. The rest live in 'Camp,' the name given to all of the Falklands outside Stanley. Only a few of the numerous smaller offshore islands are inhabited. About 60% of Falklanders are native born, some tracing their ancestry back six or more generations. Most of the remainder are immigrants or temporary residents from the UK.

The islands are laced with 400km of roads, but there's not a single traffic light.

Since the advent of large sheep stations in the late 19th century, rural settlement in the Falklands has consisted of tiny hamlets (really company towns) built near sheltered harbors where coastal shipping could collect the wool clip. On nearly all of them, shepherds lived in 'outside houses,' which still dot the countryside.

Although there's evidence that Patagonian Indians may have reached the Falklands in canoes, the islands were officially discovered on August 14, 1592 by John Davis, master of HMS *Desire*, during an English naval expedition, although a 1522 Portuguese chart indicates knowledge of the islands. The Falklands' Spanish name, Islas Malvinas, derives from early French navigators from St Malo, who called the islands 'Les Malouines' after their home port.

No European power established a settlement until 1764, when the French built a garrison at Port Louis on East Falkland, disregarding Spanish claims under the papal Treaty of Tordesillas that divided the New World between Spain and Portugal. Unbeknown to either France or Spain, Britain set up a West Falkland outpost at Port Egmont on Saunders Island, in 1765. Spain, meanwhile, discovered and then supplanted the French colony after an amicable settlement. Spanish forces then detected and expelled the British in 1767. Under threat of war Spain restored Port Egmont to the British, who only a few years later abandoned the area – without, however, renouncing their territorial claims.

For the rest of the 18th century, Spain maintained the islands as one of the world's most secure penal colonies. After it abandoned the colonies in the early 1800s, only maverick whalers and sealers visited, until the United Provinces of the Rio de la Plata (as Argentina was formerly known) sent a military governor in the early 1820s to assert its claim as successor to Spain. Later, a naturalized Buenos Aires entrepreneur named Louis Vernet initiated a project to monitor uncontrolled sealers and exploit local fur-seal populations in a sustainable manner.

Vernet's seizure of three American sealing vessels, *Harriet*, *Superior* and *Breakwater*, in Berkeley Sound triggered reprisals from a hotheaded US naval officer, Captain Silas Duncan, commanding the corvette USS *Lexington*, who vandalized the Port Louis settlement beyond restoration in 1831. After Vernet's departure, Buenos Aires kept a token force there until early 1833, when it was expelled by Britain. Vernet pursued his claims for property damages in British courts for nearly 30 years, without success.

Under the British, the Falklands languished until the mid-19th century, when sheep began to replace cattle and wool became an important export. Founded by Samuel Lafone, an Englishman from Montevideo, the Falkland Islands Company became the islands' largest landholder. Other immigrant entrepreneurs occupied all other available pastoral lands in extensive holdings by the 1870s.

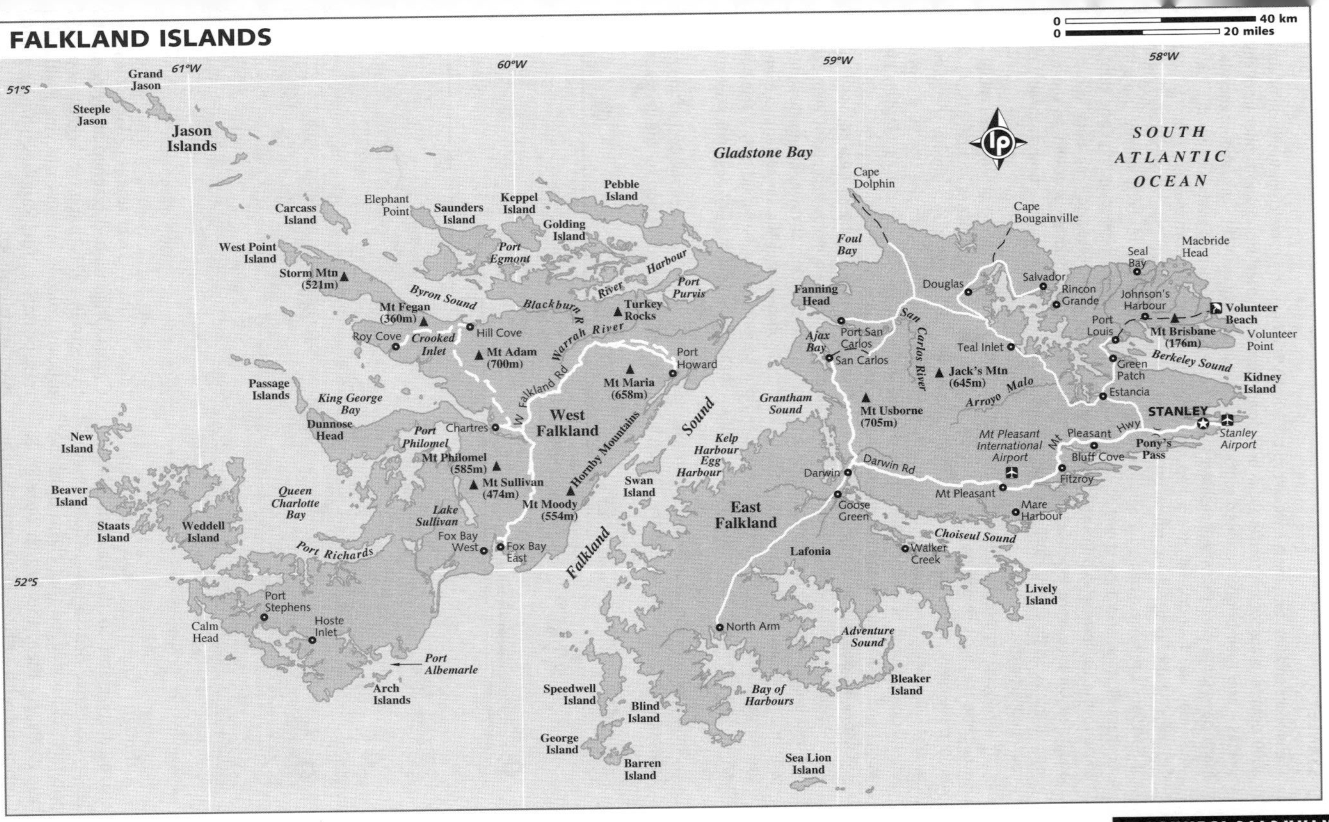
FALKLAND ISLANDS
0 40 km
0 20 miles
SOUTH ATLANTIC OCEAN
51°S
52°S
61°W
60°W
59°W
58°W
Grand Jason
Steeple Jason
Jason Islands
Carcass Island
Elephant Point
Saunders Island
Keppel Island
Pebble Island
Golding Island
Gladstone Bay
Cape Dolphin
Cape Bougainville
Macbride Head
Seal Bay
West Point Island
Storm Mtn (521m)
Port Egmont
Harbour
River
Port Purvis
Foul Bay
Douglas
Salvador
Rincon Grande
Johnson's Harbour
Volunteer Beach
Volunteer Point
Byron Sound
Blackburn R
Turkey Rocks
Mt Fegan (360m)
Hill Cove
Roy Cove
Crooked Inlet
Mt Adam (700m)
Warrah River
Port Howard
Fanning Head
Port San Carlos
Ajax Bay
San Carlos
San Carlos River
Teal Inlet
Port Louis
Mt Brisbane (176m)
Green Patch
Berkeley Sound
Kidney Island
Jack's Mtn (645m)
Arroyo Malo
Estancia
Passage Islands
King George Bay
Mt Maria (658m)
W Falkland Rd
West Falkland
Grantham Sound
Mt Usborne (705m)
STANLEY
Stanley Airport
Mt Pleasant Hwy
Pony's Pass
New Island
Dunnose Head
Port Philomel
Chartres
Sound
Kelp Harbour
Egg Harbour
Mt Pleasant International Airport
Bluff Cove
Darwin Rd
Darwin
Fitzroy
Mt Philomel (585m)
Mt Sullivan (474m)
Hornby Mountains
Swan Island
Mt Pleasant
Beaver Island
Queen Charlotte Bay
Mt Moody (554m)
East Falkland
Goose Green
Mare Harbour
Lake Sullivan
Staats Island
Weddell Island
Choiseul Sound
Fox Bay West
Fox Bay East
Port Richards
Lafonia
Walker Creek
Falkland
Lively Island
Port Stephens
Hoste Inlet
Calm Head
North Arm
Adventure Sound
Port Albemarle
Arch Islands
Bleaker Island
Speedwell Island
Bay of Harbours
Blind Island
George Island
Barren Island
Sea Lion Island

STANLEY

The world's smallest and most remote capital, Stanley is a handsome, welcoming village of about 2000 people. Many of its houses were built from locally quarried stone and timber from shipwrecks – and their brightly painted roofs contrast dramatically with the surrounding moorland. Many have large gardens where residents grow flowers and much of their own food.

Stanley was founded in 1844, when the British Colonial Office ordered the removal of the Falklands' seat of government from Port Louis on Berkeley Sound to the more sheltered harbor of Port Jackson, since renamed Stanley Harbour. The town is named for Lord Stanley, the British secretary of state, and grew slowly as a supply and repair port for ships rounding Cape Horn en route to the California Gold Rush. Some damaged vessels were forced to limp back into port, and their cargoes were legitimately condemned and sold, but Stanley acquired an unsavory reputation as ships were scuttled under questionable circumstances, which undoubtedly discouraged growth.

When sheep replaced cattle in the late 19th century, Stanley began to grow more rapidly, as it became the trans-shipment point for wool between the outlying ranches and the UK. As the wool trade grew, so did the influence of the Falkland Islands Company (FIC), already the islands' largest landowner. FIC soon became the town's biggest employer. From the late 19th century on, its political and economic dominance was uncontested, and the company's relatively high wages and good housing provided a paternalistic security.

Despite its occupation by thousands of Argentine troops from April 2 to June 14, 1982, during the Falklands War, Stanley escaped almost unscathed. The two major exceptions were both sad and ironic: a British mortar round hit a house on the outskirts of town, killing three local women, while Argentine conscripts rioted against their officers after the surrender and burned the historic Globe Store, a business whose Anglo-Argentine owner had died only a few years earlier. The minefields that still infest many of the beaches around Stanley have not prevented the return of penguins, which are too light to set off the charges.

Stanley remains the service center for the islands' wool industry, but since the declaration of a fisheries protection zone around the Islands, it has become an important port for the deepwater

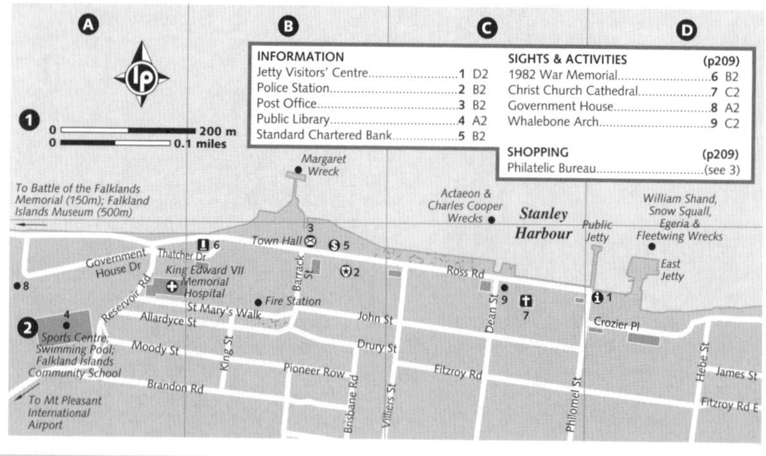

Although Argentina had persistently affirmed its claim to the Falklands since 1833, successive British governments never publicly acknowledged that claim until the late 1960s. By then, the British Foreign & Commonwealth Office (FCO) and Argentina's military government of General Juan Carlos Onganía had reached an agreement, to begin in 1971, that gave Argentina a significant voice in matters affecting Falklands transportation, fuel supplies, shipping and even immigration.

fishing industry, and many Asian and European fishing companies have offices here. The potential oil boom promises further changes.

Orientation

Stanley is located on a steep hillside on the southern shore of Stanley Harbour, Port William's sheltered inner harbor. The town is surrounded by water and low hills. For protection from the prevailing southwest winds, Stanley has grown east and west along the harbor rather than onto the exposed ridge of Stanley Common to the south. Ross Rd, running along the harborfront, is the main street. Most government offices, businesses and houses are within a few blocks of each other in the compact town center.

Information

You'll almost certainly arrive at the **Jetty Visitors' Centre** (Cnr Philomel St & Ross Rd), a red-roofed white building, open whenever tour ships are in port. It has public toilets, provides information about the islands, and sells postcards, stamps, souvenirs and telephone cards for use in the public phones.

There's no ATM. **Standard Chartered Bank** (Ross Rd; 8:30am-3pm Mon-Fri), between Barrack and Villiers Sts, is only open weekdays, but most Stanley businesses readily accept cash or travelers checks in British pounds, US dollars or euros. Visa and MasterCard are generally accepted. Falklands currency is valueless outside the islands, so change or spend it before you depart.

Sights

Stanley's most distinguished landmark, **Christ Church Cathedral**, completed in 1892, is a massive brick-and-stone construction with attractive stained-glass windows. It reminds many people of a small parish church in rural England. On the adjacent square, the **Whalebone Arch** commemorates the 1933 centenary of British rule in the Falklands.

Probably Stanley's most photographed landmark, rambling **Government House** (Ross Rd West) has been home to London-appointed governors since the mid-19th century. Once a very minor post within the UK's Foreign & Commonwealth Office, the governorship is more significant now.

The **Battle of the Falklands Memorial** (Ross Rd West), a 1914 obelisk just past Government House, commemorates a naval engagement between British and German forces in WWI. Nine British ships, refueling in Stanley, quickly responded to sink four of five German cruisers that had earlier surprised them in southern Chile.

Just west of the Secretariat on Ross Rd, the **1982 War Memorial** is a wall honoring the victims of the Falklands War. Designed by a Falkland Islander living overseas, it was paid for by public subscription and built with volunteer labor. Somber ceremonies take place here every June 14.

The **Falkland Islands Museum** (Holdfast Rd) is south of Ross Rd West, just beyond the 1914 Battle Memorial. It contains natural history specimens and artifacts from everyday life in the islands, and includes a fascinating section on the Falklands War, with many items collected from the battlefields. It is open whenever tour ships are in port.

Shopping

Most Falklands souvenirs come from the UK, but some exceptions include locally spun and knitted woolens, Falklands books and wildlife prints by local artists. Postage stamps are popular with collectors and the **Philatelic Bureau** (Ross St) also sells stamps from South Georgia and the British Antarctic Territory.

Islanders and their supporters in Britain saw the Argentine presence as ominous. Only a few years earlier, right-wing guerrillas had hijacked an Aerolíneas Argentinas jetliner, which had crash-landed on the Stanley racecourse (the islands had no airport then). Afterward, the guerrillas briefly occupied parts of town. Concerned about Argentina's chronic political instability, Falklanders suspected the FCO of secretly arranging transfer of the islands to Argentina. They may have been correct.

This process dragged on for more than a decade, during which Argentina's brutal Dirty War after 1976 gave Falklanders good reason to fear increasing Argentine presence. What was too fast for the Islanders was too slow for Argentina, especially the military government of General Leopoldo Galtieri, which invaded the nearly undefended Falklands on April 2, 1982. The seizure briefly united Argentina and made Galtieri a hero, but he never anticipated British prime minister Margaret Thatcher's decisive response.

The fight was one-sided, despite Britain's substantial naval losses. Experienced British troops landed at San Carlos Bay, routing ill-trained and poorly supplied Argentine conscripts. The most serious battle took place at Goose Green on East Falkland, but the Argentine army's surrender at Stanley averted the capital's destruction. A total of 635 Argentines and 255 Britons died in the war, along with three Falkland Island women killed by a stray British mortar round. Today, Britain spends about US$1 billion annually to maintain a 2000-troop garrison.

Since the war, most Falklanders want little or nothing to do with Argentina, which continues to send mixed messages to the islands. Argentine politicians brag that the Falklands will soon be Argentine once again.

The Falklands remain a colonial anachronism, administered by a governor appointed by the FCO in London. In local affairs, the eight-member elected Legislative Council (Legco) exercises power over most internal matters. Four of the eight members come from Stanley, with the remainder representing Camp. Britain has control over defense and international relations.

From the mid-19th century until 1986, the Falklands' economy depended almost exclusively on wool exports. However, fishing has eclipsed agriculture as a revenue producer. Asian and European fleets seeking squid and finfish have brought as much as £25 million per year into the islands. Most of this money has paid for improvements in public services. Also, local government began permitting offshore seismic surveys for oil in 1993 and is also considering issuing licenses for offshore petroleum exploration.

Most of Stanley's population works for the local government (FIG) or for the Falkland Islands Company (FIC), the major landowner and economic power in the islands for more than a century. The FIC continues to provide shipping and other services, but it has sold all its pastoral property to the government for subdivision and sale to local people. In Camp, nearly everyone lives on relatively small, widely dispersed family-owned units and is involved in wool growing.

Many books have been written since the 1982 war, but the most readily available general account is the third edition of Ian Strange's *The Falkland Islands* (1983), which covers the islands' geography, history and natural history. To get the most out of your visit, pick up *A Visitor's Guide to the Falkland Islands* (2001), by Debbie Summers, a native Falklander. Published by **Falklands Conservation** (www.falklandsconservation.com), it's filled with color photos, excellent maps and interesting facts.

East Falkland

East Falkland has the islands' most extensive road network, consisting of a good highway to Mt Pleasant international airport and Goose Green. **Port Louis** is the Falklands' oldest settlement, dating from the French foundation of the colony by Louis de Bougainville in 1764. One of the oldest buildings is the ivy-covered 19th-century farmhouse, still occupied by farm employees. Scattered nearby are ruins of the French governor's house and fortress and Louis Vernet's settlement. Visit the grave of Matthew Brisbane, Vernet's lieutenant, murdered by gauchos and Indians after British naval officer JJ Onslow left him in charge of Port Louis in August, 1833. Brisbane, who twice survived being shipwrecked, was also the master of *Beaufoy*, which accompanied James Weddell's *Jane* on his furthest south of 74°15'S in February 1823, when Weddell discovered his namesake sea. Sir James Clark Ross in 1842 dug up Brisbane's body from the rough grave in which the Indians had buried it and reinterred it, giving it a wooden marker. The grave marker, now in the Falkland Islands Museum, was replaced in 1933 by a marble stone.

SEA LION ISLAND

The most southerly inhabited island in the Falklands is little more than 1km across at its widest, but has more wildlife in a smaller area than almost anywhere in the islands: all five species of Falklands penguins, enormous colonies of cormorants, giant petrels and the 'Johnny Rook' (more properly the striated caracara *Phalcoboenus australis*), one of the world's rarest birds of prey.

For most of its history, Sea Lion's isolation – and the fact that it has no introduced rodents and cats – has undoubtedly contributed to the continuing abundance of wildlife, but much credit must go to Terry and Doreen Clifton, who farmed the island from the mid-1970s to the early 1990s, when they sold it. The Cliftons developed their 905-hectare farm with the idea that wildlife, habitat and livestock were compatible.

The island's small inn markets itself as 'the most southerly British hotel in the world.'

BLEAKER ISLAND

The northern part of Bleaker is a wildlife sanctuary; the rest is a sheep farm. Rockhopper, gentoo and Magellanic penguins are resident, along with king cormorants, elephant seals and sea lions.

West Falkland

West Falkland's only proper road runs from Port Howard on Falkland Sound to Chartres on King George Bay, but there's also a system of rough tracks. **Port Howard** is West Falkland's oldest farm and one of very few large sheep stations to survive the major agrarian reform of the past decade. About 40 people live on the 81,000-hectare station, which has 42,000 sheep and 800 cattle. The most scenic part of the Falklands, **Port Stephens'** rugged headlands are open to the blustery South Atlantic. Thousands of rockhopper penguins, cormorants and other seabirds breed on the exposed coast.

PEBBLE ISLAND

Elongated Pebble, off the northern coast of West Falkland, has varied topography, a good sampling of wildlife and extensive wetlands. There are also about 13,000 purebred Corriedale sheep.

KEPPEL ISLAND

The South American Missionary Society established an outpost on Keppel Island in 1853 to catechize Yahgan Indians from Tierra del Fuego and teach them to become potato farmers instead of hunter-gatherers. The mission was controversial because the government suspected that Indians had been brought against their will, but it lasted until 1898, despite the Indians' susceptibility to disease. One Falklands governor attributed numerous Yahgan deaths from tuberculosis to their:

> delicacy of constitution...developed owing to the warm clothing which they are for the sake of decency required to adopt after having been for 15 or 20 years roaming about in their canoes in a very cold climate without clothing of any kind.

It's likely that hard physical labor, change of diet, European-introduced diseases and harsh living conditions in their small, damp stone houses played a greater role in the Yahgans' demise than any inherent 'delicacy of constitution.' The mission was undoubtedly prosperous, however, and by 1877 it was bringing in an annual income of nearly £1,000 from its cattle, sheep and gardens. Although Keppel is now exclusively a sheep farm, several interesting ruins remain. The former chapel is now a wool shed, while the stone walls of the Yahgan dwellings remain in fairly good condition. The mission bailiff's house stands intact, though in poor repair. Keppel is also a good place to see penguins.

SAUNDERS ISLAND

Port Egmont was the site of the first British garrison on the Falklands, built in 1765. In 1767, after France ceded its colony to Spain, Spanish forces dislodged the British from Saunders and nearly precipitated a war between the two countries. After the British left voluntarily in 1774, the Spaniards razed the settlement, including its impressive blockhouse. Remaining are jetties, extensive foundations and some of the buildings' walls, plus garden terraces built by British marines. Saunders continued to be controversial in the late 1980s, when the property was passed by inheritance into the hands of Argentine descendants of the Scottish pioneer sheep farmer John Hamilton. For years Falklanders agitated for the farm's expropriation, but the owners sold the island to its local managers in 1987. The numerous rockhoppers breeding on the island have actually clawed scratch marks into rocks as they clamber out of the surf; gentoo, king and Magellanic penguins also breed here.

CARCASS ISLAND

Despite its name, Carcass is a small, scenic island with a good variety of wildlife, including a large gentoo rookery.

The island takes its name from HMS *Carcass*, which, along with HMS *Jason*, established Port Egmont on Saunders Island in 1765–67. HMS *Carcass*, a bomb vessel, was strongly built and designed for use in the bombardment of forts and harbors. The two ships also surveyed the Falklands, and when *Carcass* sounded the harbor on this island, it gave it its name.

WEST POINT ISLAND

A 2.5km walk past the main house of the settlement on this island brings you to rockhopper penguins and black-browed albatrosses in a natural amphitheater with the sea as its stage.

JASON ISLANDS

Stretching 65km off the west coast of West Falkland, this chain is among the westernmost in the Falklands. The Jasons take their name from HMS *Jason*, dispatched to survey the Falklands in 1766. The archipelago's largest islands are **Grand Jason**, 11km long and about 3km across, and, to the west, **Steeple Jason**, 10km long and 1.5km wide at its broadest. Both are uninhabited nature reserves owned by the Wildlife Conservation Society in New York City. Steeple Jason is home to the largest colony of black-browed albatrosses in the world: 157,000 pairs nest in a vast colony that continues for 5km along the island's windward western coast. There are also 90,000 pairs of rockhoppers.

NEW ISLAND

The Falklands' most westerly inhabited island is also a unique wildlife area, with large colonies of penguins, albatrosses, petrels and seals.

The island comprises two properties but is effectively run as a wildlife reserve. **New Island South** is cared for by the New Island South Conservation Trust, which promotes the study of ecology and conservation and ensures that the reserve retains its status in perpetuity. Several long-term research projects are underway on New Island South. Privately owned **New Island North** is also run as a nature reserve.

In the late 18th century, New Island's excellent harbors and rich wildlife resources turned it into an important base for North American whalers and sealers. The island's name originated from the voyagers' New England home ports: New York, New Bedford, New London and others.

American sealer Captain Charles H Barnard, master of *Nanina*, was marooned here after a disastrous encounter with the crew of a shipwrecked British vessel, *Isabella*, in April 1813, soon after the beginning of the 1812–15 war between Britain and the US. To thank him for rescuing them, all but two of the shipwreck survivors took over Barnard's ship, leaving him and four other men stranded for almost two years. But just as *Nanina* was being sailed away by the castaways-cum-pirates, the British gun-brig *Nancy* arrived and took her as a prize of war. Barnard and his fellows, meanwhile, were left behind and not rescued until December 1814 by two British sealing ships, *Indispensable* and *Asp*.

Barnard published a book in 1829 about his ordeals, descriptively titled *A Narrative of the Sufferings and Adventures of Captain Charles H Barnard, In A Voyage Round The World, During The Years 1812, 1813, 1814, 1815 & 1816; Embracing An Account of the Seizure of His Vessel at the Falkland Islands, By An English Crew Whom He Had Rescued From The Horrors Of A Shipwreck; And Of Their Abandoning Him On An Uninhabited Island, Where He Resided Nearly Two Years.* It was reprinted with an introduction by Bertha Dodge under the much more succinct title *Marooned* (1979).

A Norwegian whaling company, based in Sandefjord, sent *Admiralen*, the first modern floating factory ship to reach the southern regions, and began whaling at New Island on Christmas Eve, 1905. The ship went to Admiralty Bay on King George Island in the South Shetlands in early 1906, returning to New Island in February.

A **shore-based whaling station** was operated on New Island by the whaling firm Salvesen's of Leith (in Scotland) from 1908 to 1916.

The venture didn't last long because there weren't enough whales nearby; the company subsequently operated on South Georgia. A few **ruins** of the station – building foundations and some machinery – remain about 3km south of the settlement on the eastern coast.

Beached in Settlement Harbour lies *Protector*, built in Nova Scotia in the late 1930s/early 1940s as a minesweeper for the Canadian navy. She was brought down to the Falklands for a local sealing venture, eventually discontinued for lack of seals. The then-owner of New Island, a shareholder in the sealing venture, sailed *Protector* around the islands and eventually ran her onto the beach here.

A rough **stone hut** assembled from the original structure built by Captain Barnard is just off the beach opposite *Protector*. It's being restored as a museum.

On the island's precipitous western coast are large colonies of rockhoppers, king cormorants and black-browed albatrosses, as well as a large rookery of southern fur seals. Gentoo and Magellanic penguins also breed on New Island.

WEDDELL ISLAND

Scot John Hamilton, also a major landholder in Argentine Patagonia, acquired this western offshore island – named for Antarctic pioneer James Weddell – and others nearby to experiment with various agricultural improvement projects, including replanting of tussock grass, establishing forest plantations and importing Highland cattle and Shetland ponies. Hamilton, well-meaning but perhaps misguided, also introduced exotic wildlife such as guanacos (still present on Staats Island), Patagonian foxes (common on Weddell proper) and otters (apparently extinct).

Antarctic Peninsula & Weddell Sea

CONTENTS

With its hundreds of tiny offshore islands, the Antarctic Peninsula is one of Antarctica's richest breeding grounds for seabirds, seals and penguins. During the 19th century, it was extensively explored, primarily by sealers from Britain and the US. In the early 20th century, scientific expeditions began visiting the Peninsula.

Although there appears to be a wide variety of places in the Peninsula region for Antarctic tour operators to choose from when deciding where to take passengers, they all visit nearly the same places. More than 10,000 people now come to Antarctica each year, and almost half visit the same handful of landing sites because they offer easy access to wildlife, a station or a museum. The cumulative impact of all these tramping feet, unfortunately, is starting to become apparent.

The Weddell Sea is less frequently visited, since extremely heavy pack ice usually does not allow ships to penetrate the sea to any great distance. This is where Shackleton's *Endurance* was trapped, and where at least four other ships have been crushed and sunk by pack ice. The Weddell Sea's primary attractions are its emperor penguin rookeries and the Ronne and Filchner Ice Shelves.

HIGHLIGHTS

- Squeezing through the tight passage of the steep-sided **Lemaire Channel** (p222), known as 'Kodak Gap'
- Cruising among the icebergs and the reflections of mountains in the water at **Paradise Harbor** (p223)
- Seeing how mid-20th-century British scientists lived at the old base-turned-museum, **Port Lockroy** (p221)
- Listening to the incessant squawking of the estimated 100,000 Adélie penguins nesting on **Paulet Island** (p217)
- Searching for fossils on **Seymour Island** (p228) – but remember, you can't take anything from Antarctica

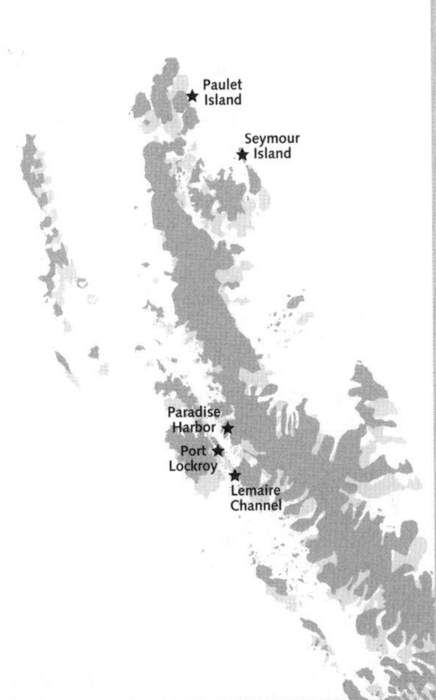

ANTARCTIC PENINSULA

ASTROLABE ISLAND

Discovered by Dumont d'Urville's 1837–40 expedition and named for his chief ship, this infrequently visited, 5km-long island is home to several thousand pairs of chinstraps.

Visitors can take Zodiacs (motorized dinghies) to view the **Dragon's Teeth**, a small group of huge rocks off the island's northeast coast; cruising between them is known, naturally, as 'flossing.'

CAPE LEGOUPIL

One of the oldest stations on the Peninsula, Chile's **General Bernardo O'Higgins station**, stands on this ice-cliffed cape – or more precisely, 80m offshore on a small island. The station was established in 1948 and inaugurated by Chilean president Gabriel González Videla, the first head of state to visit Antarctica. A jetty provides easy access, and a wooden plank and wire suspension **bridge** for pedestrians links the island to the mainland. The station, which accommodates 50, is operated by the Chilean army; only meteorological and sea-temperature data are collected here. There is a small **museum** in the stores building.

Gentoos breed successfully among the station buildings.

The separate **German Receiving Station** on the island was built by Germany in 1988–89. It accommodates nine people. Operated only periodically, it acquires data from European Remote Sensing satellites via a large, white, 9m parabolic dish.

HOPE BAY

On the northernmost tip of the Peninsula, Hope Bay is home to one of Antarctica's largest **Adélie rookeries** – 125,000 pairs, along with a few gentoo penguins. The entrance to Hope Bay, reached via the Antarctic Sound, is often filled with tabular icebergs calved from the bay's glaciers.

Argentina built **Esperanza station** in 1951, then expanded it significantly in 1978 and began sending women and children to live there year-round as part of its efforts to establish 'sovereignty' over the Antarctic territory. One of these women was Silvia Morello de Palma, the wife of Army Captain Jorge de Palma, Esperanza's station leader. Flown in from Argentina when she was seven months pregnant, Silvia gave birth to Emilio Marcos de Palma, the first native-born Antarctican, on January 7, 1978. Over the next five years, four more boys and three girls were born at Esperanza.

Today, usually about a dozen children live with their families year-round at the station, which can accommodate up to 79 people. Most personnel are military, and about 35% of Esperanza's population is made up of spouses and children. These families help make Esperanza feel like a small village. With a school, chapel, post office, infirmary; a graveyard with a stele in memory of Argentine expedition members who died in the area; 1.5km of gravel roads; and 13 chalets housing families, it *is* more a village than a scientific station, as there are only two modest laboratories.

An Adélie penguin rookery with more than 100,000 pairs adjoins the station, but much of it is off-limits.

Close to the jetty and behind ropes are the ruins of a **stone hut** where three members of Nordenskjöld's Swedish Antarctic expedition spent a desperate winter in 1903, surviving on seal meat. Nordenskjöld named the bay in honor of these three men. Esperanza staff rebuilt the hut in 1966–67, and a small **museum** of historic relics is in one of the station's central buildings. Other historic equipment, including sledges and an old Sno-Cat, is kept outside near the stone hut.

On the hill about 500m from Esperanza is **Trinity House**, a hut remaining from Base D, built by the UK's Operation Tabarin in 1944–45 and closed in 1963. The building was transferred to Uruguay in 1997 and is now named **Ruperto Elichiribehety station** after the captain of the Uruguayan steam trawler *Instituto de Pesca No 1*, which Shackleton used in his second of three unsuccessful attempts to reach the castaways stranded on Elephant Island. The summer-only facility accommodates 12 people.

Crosses in the nearby **cemetery** commemorate two men lost in a 1948 fire.

BROWN BLUFF

Brown Bluff is an ice-capped, flat-topped 745m extinct volcano on the Peninsula's northeastern tip. The original diameter of the volcano has been calculated at 12km to

15km; it's approximately one million years old. The bluff takes its name from a striking cliff of reddish-brown rock on its north face. Several hundred gentoos and 20,000 Adélies nest here; rock slides on to the 3km-long beach sometimes wipe out groups of them.

PAULET ISLAND

About 100,000 Adélies nest on this circular volcanic island – an attraction that makes it one of Antarctica's most visited sites. There are also blue-eyed shags and southern giant petrels. Paulet is just 2km in diameter but 353m high.

Paulet Island was discovered by Briton James Clark Ross' expedition of 1839–43 and named for the Right Honorable Lord George Paulet, a captain in the Royal Navy.

On February 12, 1903 Nordenskjöld's ship *Antarctic*, which had been crushed by the

DON'T COLLECT, PLEASE! *Dr Ralph P Harvey*

One of the most difficult things in life is learning not to covet and collect things. Let's face it, the whole world is infected with capitalism, and few people are immune to the disease of acquiring things based on desire rather than need. At the same time, most of us recognize the innate goodness of those who manage to control feelings of temptation. As the Zen sages put it, 'desire is suffering.'

But the desire to collect little souvenirs of your trip to Antarctica can have a profound impact on the white continent.

The Antarctic Treaty encourages everyone who visits Antarctica to protect all its living creatures and to forgo any exploitation of minerals or other resources (see p291). The Treaty has been uniquely successful, more so than almost any other. Scientists, tourists, politicians, environmentalists, businesspeople, historians – all their interests converge on maintaining the beauty and untrammeled nature of Antarctica.

And there we find a deep irony. No place on this planet is more awe-inspiring than Antarctica – how could you *not* want to bring a piece of it home with you? Exposure to Antarctica will profoundly affect you for the rest of your life. It's perfectly natural to want that embrace to be represented by something tangible. The Treaty, however, is clear on this point: scientific study is the only reason samples of any kind may be removed from Antarctica. How can we reconcile the strong global mandate to protect Antarctica's pristine state with our powerful desire for a souvenir?

The key is to recognize that the physical things you bring home are nothing more than symbols or icons. The real value of your trip lies in simply having been to Antarctica. The most valuable things you can bring home are the changes that Antarctica has wrought upon you.

Don't try to fool yourself by rationalizing. It's easy to convince yourself that taking a pebble off a beach to give to a child may inspire the youngster, who may in fact want to be a scientist. That soggy little penguin feather, you may say, can educate someone about science. But this is false altruism. If you pick up that Antarctic stone 'just for the grandchildren,' you're setting a poor example for them. Show your respect for the special, unique nature of the Antarctic environment by resisting that temptation. Leave the rock, feather, bone, egg, fossil or artifact where you saw it.

Why should scientists get all the goodies? First of all, it's not as though scientists are allowed to take home anything they wish from Antarctica. In fact, without the deeply felt respect for the continent every Antarctic researcher has, Antarctic science would have ground to a halt long ago under the burden of permits, restricted procedures and off-limits areas imposed by the Treaty. But these restrictions ensure an undisturbed Antarctica where our grandchildren can make new discoveries without having to deal with the impact of past generations. Future tourists and scientists benefit when we restrain our 'collective' desires.

Instead of the rocks you trod upon, give your grandchild the hat or gloves you wore in Antarctica. Rather than a feather, give your friends a photo of the penguin that came right up to you. Or, just to satisfy the capitalist system, go ahead and buy a T-shirt from a station or aboard ship. Do your part to preserve the irony.

Dr Ralph P Harvey has spent 14 summers in Antarctica as the principal investigator of the Antarctic Search for Meteorites program (http://geology.cwru.edu/~ansmet/)

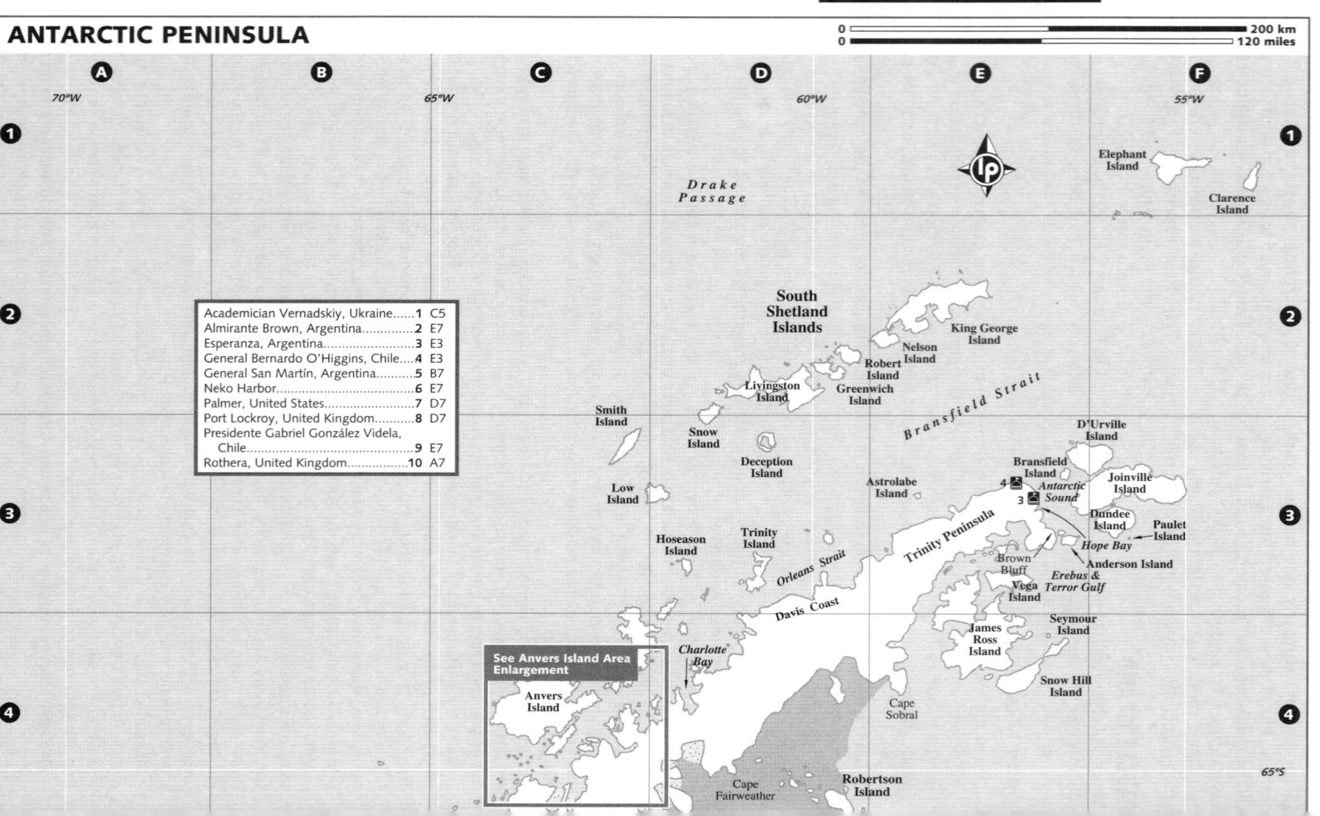
ANTARCTIC PENINSULA
Academician Vernadskiy, Ukraine......1 C5
Almirante Brown, Argentina..............2 E7
Esperanza, Argentina.........................3 E3
General Bernardo O'Higgins, Chile....4 E3
General San Martín, Argentina..........5 B7
Neko Harbor......................................6 E7
Palmer, United States.......................7 D7
Port Lockroy, United Kingdom...........8 D7
Presidente Gabriel González Videla, Chile.........9 E7
Rothera, United Kingdom................10 A7
0 200 km
0 120 miles
70°W
65°W
60°W
55°W
65°S
Drake Passage
South Shetland Islands
Elephant Island
Clarence Island
King George Island
Nelson Island
Robert Island
Greenwich Island
Livingston Island
Deception Island
Snow Island
Smith Island
Low Island
Bransfield Strait
D'Urville Island
Joinville Island
Dundee Island
Paulet Island
Hope Bay
Anderson Island
Bransfield Island
Antarctic Sound
Erebus & Terror Gulf
Brown Bluff
Vega Island
Seymour Island
Snow Hill Island
James Ross Island
Trinity Peninsula
Astrolabe Island
Cape Sobral
Robertson Island
Trinity Island
Orleans Strait
Davis Coast
Hoseason Island
Charlotte Bay
Cape Fairweather
See Anvers Island Area Enlargement
Anvers Island

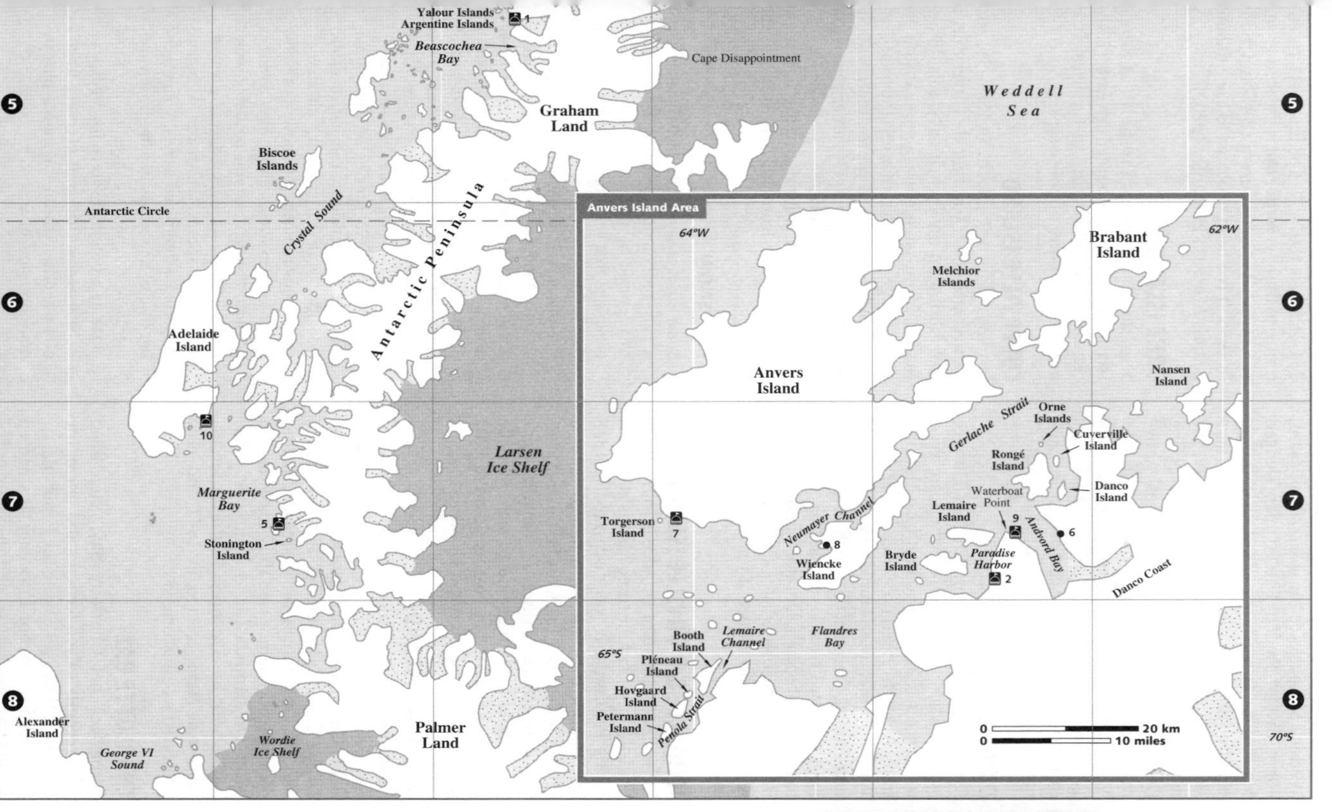

ANTARCTIC PENINSULA & WEDDELL SEA

Weddell Sea pack ice for weeks, finally sank 40km east of Paulet. The 20 men sledged for 14 days to reach the island, then built a 10m by 7m hut on the northeast coast, where all but one survived the winter. Today, the **ruins** – just a pile of stones and some roofing timbers – are populated by Adélies. Above the ruins is a 100m-long, ovoid melt lake. Marked by a cross, the **grave** of Ole Christian Wennersgaard, a seaman on Nordenskjöld's expedition who died of heart disease in 1903, lies along the shore 300m east of the hut.

DUNDEE ISLAND

Lying 5km northwest of Paulet is Dundee Island, where millionaire American aviator Lincoln Ellsworth took off on the first trans-Antarctic flight on November 22, 1935. With his quiet, pipe-smoking copilot, Herbert Hollick-Kenyon, Ellsworth flew – in five hops over two weeks – across the continent to the Ross Ice Shelf. Dundee was discovered in 1893 by British whaler Captain Thomas Robertson, who named it for his home port in Scotland.

JOINVILLE & D'URVILLE ISLANDS

Immediately north of Dundee is Joinville Island, the largest of the three islands at the end of the Peninsula. It was discovered in 1838 by Dumont d'Urville, who named it for a French nobleman, François Ferdinand Phillipe Louis Marie, Prince de Joinville. Joinville Island's northerly neighbor, D'Urville Island, was charted by Nordenskjöld in 1902 and named for Dumont d'Urville.

MELCHIOR ISLANDS

Sixteen of the Melchior Islands are named for letters of the Greek alphabet: Alpha, Beta, Gamma, Delta, Epsilon, Eta, Theta, Kappa, Lambda, Omicron, Pi, Rho, Sigma, Tau, Psi and Omega; for more information on Antarctic names, see the boxed text on p230. On Lambda Island is the first lighthouse built by Argentina in the Antarctic, **Primero de Mayo**, erected in 1942 and now protected as a historic site.

CHARLOTTE BAY

Some feel that Charlotte Bay, often filled with recently calved icebergs and one of the most beautiful spots along the Peninsula, rivals Paradise Harbor in beauty. It's named for the fiancée of the second-in-command of de Gerlache's 1897–99 expedition. At the entrance to the bay, **Portal Point** is the former site of a British Antarctic Survey (BAS) hut, built in 1956. It has been relocated to the Falkland Islands Museum in Stanley (p209).

ORNE ISLANDS

This small archipelago just north of Rongé Island was probably named by early-20th-century whalers working in the area. It is home to a colony of chinstraps.

CUVERVILLE ISLAND

Discovered by de Gerlache in 1897–99, and named after JMA Cavalier de Cuverville, a vice admiral in the French navy, this dome-shaped, 250m-tall island is a popular stop. Its several large gentoo rookeries (the total gentoo population here is approximately 4000) comprise one of the largest gatherings of this penguin in Antarctica.

University of Cambridge researchers spent three years here from 1992–95 studying the

PINK SNOW

Snow is not always white. Sometimes it has a pink, red, orange, green, yellow or gray cast, caused by snow algae, single-celled organisms that live atop snowfields around the world.

Snow algae have been remarked upon for at least 2000 years, since Aristotle wrote about snow that was 'reddish in color' in his *History of Animals*. In alpine areas of North America, snow algae's color and fruity scent create what hikers call 'watermelon snow' (although wise people avoid tasting it). In Scandinavia, it's known as 'blood snow.'

Somehow 350 species of snow algae manage to survive in the harsh, acidic, freezing, nutrient-starved, ultraviolet-seared environment of snow. But snow algae tend to live in either high altitudes or high latitudes, so you probably won't find it in your yard. It reproduces by remarkably hardy spores, which can withstand very cold winters and very dry summers. Because of its success in extreme environments, researchers are investigating snow algae as a potential source for medicines.

Near penguin rookeries, of course, there's often another reason for snow's pinkish-orangish tinge: guano!

impact of their presence and the presence of tourists on the penguins. After monitoring the gentoos' heart rates and observing skuas and other species, they concluded that well-conducted groups, with tourists observing the *Guidance for Visitors to the Antarctic* (p90), had no detectable effects on the penguin's breeding behavior or success.

The slopes above the landing beach shelter extensive and deep beds of moss, which shouldn't be stepped on, and snow algae stain the hillsides (see the boxed text on p220).

RONGÉ ISLAND

De Gerlache named this island for Madame de Rongé, a wealthy contributor to his expedition. It is home to several large colonies of gentoos and chinstraps. The cave on the hillside may have sheltered early sealers.

DANCO ISLAND

Danco Island, 1.5km long, has a wide, sloping cobblestone beach. It was charted by de Gerlache in 1897–99 and later named for the expedition's geophysicist, Émile Danco, who died in the Antarctic. A hut, built as **Base O** by the British in 1955–56, is now maintained as a refuge. Researchers still occasionally use it for short visits. There's a large anthracite dump in front. Gentoos nest right up to the summit of the island's 180m peak.

PALMER STATION

Mountainous **Anvers Island**, 70km in length, was discovered by de Gerlache in 1898 and named for the Belgian province of the same name. It is home to the US Palmer station, which was built in 1968 on the island's southwest coast to honor American sealer Nathaniel B Palmer, who in 1820 was one of the first to see Antarctica. The new station replaced the prefabricated wood huts of 'Old Palmer,' established in 1964 about a kilometer across Arthur Harbor from the present station. Old Palmer itself superseded Britain's **Base N**, which was occupied from 1955 to 1958. In 1963 the hut was loaned to the US, which converted it to a biology lab. Fire destroyed the building in 1971 when it was being renovated, and the debris were removed from Antarctica in 1991.

Palmer station accommodates 44 people. During summer it's usually full, but only about 20 people winter at the station because there's little research going on then. The station is accessible by sea year-round and is resupplied by ship every six weeks.

Palmer comprises two main buildings, as well as a boathouse, a dive locker, workshops, a clean-air laboratory, a sauna and storage buildings all placed close together. The three-story **BioLab** includes a newly renovated laboratory facility, a dining area, offices, communications facilities, storage and sleeping facilities. The two-story **GWR** (garage, warehouse and recreation) building also houses generators, sleeping facilities, a small medical facility and the station store.

Research at Palmer focuses on the long-term monitoring of the marine ecosystem (with an emphasis on seabirds and krill), atmospheric studies, and the effects of increased ultraviolet radiation (caused by the ozone hole) on marine and terrestrial communities. Climate-change research is a major focus because the average local wintertime temperature has risen more than 6°C over the past 50 years. This has resulted in a decrease in winter sea-ice extent and caused glaciers to recede, changing the local landscape around Palmer dramatically: ice bridges have collapsed and what were formerly 'points' are being revealed as 'islands.' Meanwhile, the 'warm-weather' chinstrap and gentoo penguins are increasing in numbers, while the more cold-loving Adélies are decreasing.

Only 12 ship visits are permitted annually, to avoid disruption to research. Tourists get a station walking tour, including an interesting peek into two **aquariums** filled with anemones, mollusks, sea urchins, krill and fish. You may also shop at the station **store** (which accepts credit cards and US dollars) and taste the locally famous 'Palmer brownies' in the dining room.

The **Adélie rookery** at Torgerson Island is often visited in conjunction with the nearby Palmer station. Since 1974, however, the population of Adélie penguins has dropped by 60% to fewer than 3300 pairs today, due to climate-induced changes in sea-ice conditions and snowfall. Researcher Bill Fraser now predicts that Adélies will disappear from this island by 2014.

PORT LOCKROY

De Gerlache named **Wiencke Island** in 1897–99 for Carl August Wiencke, a young seaman who fell overboard and drowned while trying to clear *Belgica*'s scuppers.

An 800m-long harbor on the west coast of Wiencke, Port Lockroy is one of the most popular tourist stops in Antarctica, thanks to **Base A**, the former British station-turned-museum on tiny **Goudier Island**, operated by BAS under the guidance of the UK Antarctic Heritage Trust. During the 2003–04 season, 9621 people visited the museum.

Visits are usually made in conjunction with landings at the gentoo rookery at **Jougla Point**, where other highlights include blue-eyed shags and a composite whale skeleton reconstructed on the shore.

Port Lockroy was discovered by de Gerlache in 1899, but remained unnamed and uncharted until Charcot arrived in February 1904. It's named after Edouard Lockroy, vice president of France's Chamber of Deputies, who helped Charcot secure funding for his expedition. Until about 1931 Port Lockroy was a major harbor for whalers. Around the landing site, chains and eyebolts and the date '1921' inscribed in the rock can be seen; these were moorings for *Solstreif*, one of 11 factory ships that anchored and processed whales here.

After the Argentine navy ship *Primero de Mayo* left a cylinder at Port Lockroy in 1943 claiming the harbor and all territory between 25°W and 68°34′W south of 60°S, Britain moved to uphold its rival claim. In 1943–44 Britain's secret naval Operation Tabarin (named for a bawdy Parisian nightclub) removed the Argentine emblems and established Base A. Some of the timber used in its construction was salvaged from platforms and rafts left nearby by the whalers, and also from the abandoned whaling station at Deception Island.

Base A was staffed almost continuously until 1962 – normal occupancy was four to nine people, with the usual tour of duty lasting about 2½ years! – but then it fell into disrepair.

BAS beautifully restored the original station building, Bransfield House, in 1996. Don't miss the full-length portrait of Marilyn Monroe painted on the back of the generator-shed door, a memory aid to lonely winterers during Antarctica's all-male era. Displays on the station's history hang inside Bransfield House. Artifacts shown include clothing from Operation Tabarin, a clandestine 1944 radio transmitter, an HMV gramophone and wooden skis purchased from the Grytviken Whaling Station Stores on South Georgia in 1957. A scientific highlight: a restored 'Beastie' (an early apparatus for upper-atmospheric research).

Three BAS staff members live at Port Lockroy in the summer to maintain the historic site and act as wardens. They also run a busy, well-stocked post office (during the 2003–04 season, 40,000 hand-canceled items were sent to 116 countries!) and a souvenir shop, with the proceeds funding operation of the base. Port Lockroy is self-financing; surplus profits from the shop also help pay for the conservation of other British historic sites on the Peninsula.

To manage the growing number of visitors to Base A, BAS has set some limits: up to 350 people may visit Goudier Island in any one day, but no more than 60 persons are allowed ashore at once.

The hut is the BAS staff members' temporary home ('camp' is more like it, since there is no heat or electricity), so please respect their personal areas. For safety reasons, the staff are not allowed to have a boat. One good-humored worker joked recently about the claustrophobia this can induce, insisting that he always took his walks at low tide – so he could cover the maximum possible distance!

Goudier Island is home to 800 pairs of gentoos. Monitoring of their breeding success since 1995 has found no discernible impact from tourists, who tramp past their nests by the thousands each year. Breeding success seems more closely linked to local environmental conditions, such as snow cover or the availability of krill. Indeed, the gentoos seem to care little about Bransfield House; in the beginning of the summer, the snow can be as high as the building's eaves – and the penguins attempt to nest on the roof.

LEMAIRE CHANNEL

This steep-sided channel – just 1600m wide – runs for 11km between the mountains of Booth Island and the Peninsula. It is so photogenic that its nickname is 'Kodak Gap.' The passageway is only visible once you're nearly inside.

The channel was discovered by a German expedition in 1873–74, but wasn't navigated until December 1898, when de Gerlache's *Belgica* sailed through. In a decidedly odd choice, de Gerlache named the channel for

Belgian adventurer Charles Lemaire, who explored the Congo. Unfortunately, ice sometimes blocks the way, so ships may be forced to retreat and sail around Booth Island. At the northern end of the channel are two tall, rounded, and often snowcapped peaks at **Cape Renard**.

PLÉNEAU ISLAND

Almost 1km long, this island is home to thousands of gentoos. It was named for Paul Pléneau, the expedition's photographer, by Charcot during his 1903–05 expedition. When Charcot changed his plans at the last minute (he had originally intended going to Greenland) Pléneau replied by telegram, as described in William J Mill's book *Exploring Polar Frontiers* (2003), in a way that would gratify any leader: 'Where you like. When you like. For as long as you like!'.

NEKO HARBOR

Many people are glad to land at Neko Harbor, if only because it's on Antarctica itself, so they can officially 'bag' the continent. The glacier across from the landing site often calves with a thunderous roar, offering dramatic video footage for those lucky enough.

Deep inside Andvord Bay, Neko Harbor was discovered by de Gerlache, but takes its name from the Norwegian whaling ship, *Neko*, which operated in the area between 1911 and 1924.

The small orange hut with the Argentine flag on the side is a *refugio* (refuge hut), built in 1949 and named 'Captain Fleiss.' Gentoos nest on the hillside, while sheathbills often hide in the rubbish outside the *refugio*.

As you gaze out over Neko's iceberg-filled waters, consider how American long-distance swimmer Lynne Cox must have felt in December 2002, when she swam nearly 2km (in 25 minutes) in the 0.5°C waters here – a fatal stunt for almost anyone else. Cox has spent many years training in super-chilled waters, but doctors say that she is also physiologically unique, with an evenly distributed layer of body fat and the ability to re-route her blood flow to her body's core. Read her fascinating autobiography, *Swimming to Antarctica* (2004).

PARADISE HARBOR

Paradise Harbor is described in Antarctic tour brochures as 'the most aptly named place in the world.' That may be overstating

BAHÍA PARAÍSO

Antarctica's worst environmental disaster occurred on January 28, 1989, when the 131m Argentine navy supply ship *Bahía Paraíso*, with 234 passengers and crew (including 81 tourists), ran into a submerged rock pinnacle off DeLaca Island, 3km from Palmer station. The pinnacle ripped a 10m gash in the ship's hull, spilling 645,000L of diesel fuel and other petroleum products and creating a slick that covered 30 sq km. Fortunately, no one was injured, and Palmer residents towed the *Bahía*'s unmotorized lifeboats to shore and fed the passengers and crew. Two nearby cruise ships and an Argentine vessel carried the tourists out of Antarctica.

The spill severely harmed seabirds and the marine environment. Skua chicks and blue-eyed shag chicks each experienced a mortality rate of nearly 100%. Adélie numbers dropped 16% that season. Mollusks and macroalgae were also immediately damaged. Perhaps worst of all, the spill disrupted or destroyed research that in some cases went back two decades.

In 1992 a joint Argentine-Dutch operation recovered most of the remaining 148,500L of fuel and some hazardous lubricants from the submerged tanks (although some still leaks out from the wreck today). The spill had already caused great damage, however, and if it had been crude oil rather than diesel and jet fuel, the effect would have been far worse.

In the course of the 1990s most local marine communities recovered, with the exception of the blue-eyed shags, which have not been able to regain their former numbers.

Today, *Bahía Paraíso*'s nearly submerged hulk is still visible. From the station as well as from approaching vessels, its rusty hull can be seen between DeLaca and Janus Islands, in front of and slightly closer to DeLaca. Vessels enter Arthur Harbor between Bonaparte Point and Janus Island. Sharp-eyed observers can spot a 3m-long section of *Bahía*'s hull at high tide. At low tide, the section above the waterline is 10m long and 50cm high – a reminder of the dangers of operating in Antarctica, and of our responsibility to take care of it.

it – more people would probably say paradise is a sunny tropical isle. Still, with its majestic icebergs and reflections in the water of the surrounding mountains, Paradise Harbor is undeniably beautiful. Even the early-20th-century whalers operating here recognized its extreme beauty, for they named it.

This is a favorite place for Zodiac cruising around the ice calved from the glacier at the head of the bay. You may pass beneath blue-eyed shags nesting on cliffs, which can be colored blue-green by copper deposits, emerald green by moss and orange or yellow by lichens.

The original portions of the Argentine station **Almirante Brown** were destroyed on April 12, 1984 by a fire set by the station's physician/leader, who didn't want to stay another winter. Station personnel were rescued by the US ship *Hero*. Gentoo penguins nest among the ruins.

Climb the hill behind the station for a great view of glaciers. The memorial stone commemorates Jostein Helgestad, who died in 1993 on Monica Kristensen's expedition (p69) when his snowmobile plunged down a crevasse en route to the South Pole.

WATERBOAT POINT

Although it appears to be an island, Waterboat Point is separated from the Peninsula mainland only at high tide. At low water, it's possible to walk across a stretch of low rocks to the Peninsula.

British researchers Thomas W Bagshawe and Maxime C Lester spent a year here from January 1921 to January 1922 recording meteorological, tidal and zoological data. They supplemented their insufficient stores with penguin and seal meat, living in a rough shelter partially constructed from an upturned water boat left by the Norwegian factory ship *Neko* about eight years before.

The pair was part of the smallest British Antarctic expedition ever mounted, a four-man effort led by John Cope; the other member was Hubert Wilkins. The expedition was supposed to be much larger, but funds were tight. The **ruin** of Bagshawe and Lester's hut is a protected historic site.

The Chilean air force operates summer-only **Presidente Gabriel González Videla station** amid a gentoo rookery. It's named for the Chilean president who in 1948 became the first head of state to visit Antarctica – with an entourage of 140! The station members used to keep pigs, sheep and chickens, all of which roamed freely, 'an incongruous scene in the Antarctic,' as one visitor in 1964 later recalled.

PETERMANN ISLAND

Home to the world's southernmost gentoo colony, 135m-high Petermann Island is one of Antarctica's most visited spots. At 65°10'S, it's one of the most southerly landings most cruises make. Just under 2km long, the island was discovered by an 1873–74 German whaling and sealing expedition in the steamship *Grönland*, led by Eduard Dallman, who named the island for German geographer August Petermann. Adélies, gentoos and blue-eyed shags nest here, and snow algae (p220) is abundant.

Charcot's expedition of 1908–10 wintered aboard *Pourquoi Pas?* at Port Circumcision, a cove on the island's southeast coast. It was discovered by Charcot on New Year's Day 1909 and named for the holy day of the Feast of the Circumcision, January 1, when tradition says Christ was circumcised. While today none of the small huts constructed for scientific purposes by the expedition remain, a **cairn** it built on Megalestris Hill (named after an obsolete species name for the South Polar skua) can still be seen, as can an Argentine **refuge hut** built in 1955. Near the hut is a **cross** commemorating three BAS men who died in 1982 while attempting to cross the sea ice back to Faraday station from Petermann.

YALOUR ISLANDS

This group of islands, about 2.5km in extent, was named by Charcot for Lieutenant Jorge Yalour, an officer of the Argentine navy ship *Uruguay*, which rescued the Swedish Antarctic expedition in 1903. About 8000 pairs of Adélies nest here. There are often beautiful examples of orange lichens and green mosses, as well as small clumps of Antarctic hairgrass.

ARGENTINE ISLANDS

Discovered by Charcot on his *Français* expedition and named after the Argentine Republic in thanks for its help, the islands offer several sheltered yacht anchorages.

Ukraine's **Academician Vernadskiy station**, which accommodates 24 people, is located on Galindez Island in the archipelago. Transferred from the UK in 1996 for £1 (look for the actual coin embedded in wood at the station bar), it was previously called Faraday (after Michael Faraday, the English discoverer of electromagnetism). The station now commemorates Vladimir Vernadsky, first president of the Ukrainian Academy of Sciences. Currently it is the most senior station open continuously in Antarctica.

A popular remnant from its British era is the pub, with a dartboard, billiards table and a magnificent carved wooden bar – built by station carpenters who were supposed to be working on something else. One oddity is the pub's large collection of bras, periodically added to by visitors. Sample the *gorilka*, a tongue-burning pepper vodka made locally. One upgrade to the station was made soon after the transfer: the Ukrainians added a sauna.

Long-running weather records kept at the station show that mean annual temperatures along the Peninsula's west coast have risen by about 2.5°C since 1947. Local ice cover has declined, and the number of plants – such as Antarctic hairgrass and Antarctic pearlwort – in the vicinity has increased, possibly as a result of the warming.

Wordie House, built in 1947 as the first part of what would later become Faraday, is located about 1km from the station. It's a protected historic site, restored in the late 1990s by BAS. The rooms have been returned to their early-1950s appearance and contain period artifacts and furniture. Signs describing the building's history line the walls.

MARGUERITE BAY

Few Antarctic tour ships make it as far south as this extensive bay on the west side of the Peninsula. Well below the Antarctic Circle, it was discovered by Charcot on his 1909 expedition and named for his wife.

The **Dion Islands** at the northern end of Marguerite Bay are home to the only emperor penguin rookery in the Antarctic Peninsula region.

Argentina's **General San Martín station**, the most southerly Peninsula station, was established in 1951 on Barry Island in the Debenham Islands, between Adelaide and Alexander islands. Closed between 1960 and 1975, it now accommodates 20 people.

ROTHERA STATION

The UK's Rothera station, built in 1975, occupies a small rocky peninsula on **Adelaide Island**. The 900m gravel airstrip and hangar were added in 1990–91, making Rothera a regional logistics center for British Antarctic operations using Twin Otter aircraft. The station is also resupplied by ships, using a 60m wharf built in 1990–91. Rothera accommodates up to 130 people in the summer and an average of 22 in winter.

The **Bonner Laboratory**, named for eminent polar biologist Nigel Bonner and completed in 1997, was destroyed by fire on September 28, 2001. Some of the station's 21 winterers used a snow-blowing machine and a small fire engine to put out the fire – but darkness, snowdrifts and 140km/h wind gusts made the efforts fruitless. A huge explosion rocked the building during the fire as oxygen cylinders in the scuba-dive store exploded.

The station was rebuilt at a cost of £3 million and reopened in January 2004. It includes an emergency compression chamber in case of diving accidents, and a cold-water aquarium in which researchers have noted the dramatic effects that even slight warming can have on key species in the Antarctic marine environment. Just a 2°C rise in the water temperature rendered three species unable to defend themselves from predators.

Large new sleeping quarters for 88 people were completed in 2002. The 95m by 11m single-story building boasts triple-glazed windows and Swedish pine furniture.

Those at Rothera were stunned by the death of a young British marine biologist, Kirsty Brown, who was killed by a leopard seal while snorkeling offshore in July 2003.

STONINGTON ISLAND

Named for the home port of Connecticut sealer Nathaniel Palmer, Stonington Island is an Antarctic ghost town. Two abandoned stations, separated by about 200m, are rarely seen by tourists, being too far south of the Antarctic cruise routes, but they do get occasional visitors from Rothera and San Martín stations.

The UK's **Base E**, established in 1945–46 and used until 1975, consists of two wooden huts and some steel-mesh dog pens. The larger, two-story hut served as sleeping quarters, while the smaller was a generator shed. A **cross** on the point commemorates two Britons who died while waiting out a bad storm in a snow-hole during a field trip in 1966.

East Base was built during Richard Byrd's third Antarctic expedition, the US Antarctic Service Expedition of 1939–41. It was also used in 1947–48 by the private Ronne Antarctic Research Expedition, which included the first women to winter in Antarctica, Edith Ronne and Jennie Darlington, who accompanied their husbands. Unfortunately, their husbands quarreled, so, out of loyalty, they also did not speak to one another! After the Ronne expedition departed, the UK used East Base until 1975.

The US government funded a historic preservation program at East Base in 1990–91. A small display of artifacts has been set up in one of the three base buildings, marked as a museum.

WEDDELL SEA

British sealer James Weddell, sailing in the brig *Jane*, discovered the sea in February 1823 and named it 'King George IV Sea' for the British sovereign. German Antarctic historian Karl Fricker proposed the name Weddell Sea in 1900.

The Weddell Sea side of the Peninsula is surprisingly different from its west coast, where the mountains often drop straight into the sea. On this side, the mountains are at a greater distance from the sea, and there are large areas of snow-free gravel. It reminds many people of the deserts of Australia or the American Southwest, although without vegetation, naturally.

See p295 for information on visiting the Weddell Sea region.

VEGA ISLAND

Vega is 27km long and 10km wide. Nordenskjöld named it for the ship *Vega*, used by his uncle Baron AE Nordenskjöld, who made the first crossing of the Northeast Passage in the Arctic in 1878–79.

On October 12, 1903, Nordenskjöld encountered the three missing members of his party, who had wintered at Hope Bay, at a place they renamed Cape Well-Met on Vega's north coast.

The first discoveries of Antarctic dinosaurs were made here and on nearby James Ross I; for more details, see the boxed text on p246.

Along Vega's north coast in the summer time, snowmelt waterfalls stream down the steep cliff face to the scree slopes below – a beautiful sight.

DEVIL ISLAND

This narrow island, just under 2km long, was named by Nordenskjöld for its low summits at each end. It lies just off the north coast of Vega Island, over which it gives good views, and is home to 8000 Adélies.

SNOW HILL ISLAND

This descriptively named 395m-high island was discovered by Ross in 1843, who called it simply 'Snow Hill' because he was uncertain of its connection with the mainland. Nordenskjöld, who set up a winter base in February 1902, determined its insular nature.

Today the Nordenskjöld expedition's prefabricated black-walled **hut**, in which three Swedish and one Argentine scientist spent two years, is a protected historic site. The group's second year was unplanned, forced upon them by the crushing and sinking about 100km away of Nordenskjöld's ship *Antarctic*. The 6m by 8m hut contains three double bunks, a kitchen and a central living room. Two large metal signs in Spanish describe the site's history, as do leaflets in English inside the hut. Two angled wooden planks, original to the design, support the northeast wall. The Argentine government, whose Vicecomodoro Marambio station on Seymour Island is 21km northeast of the hut, does a good job of maintaining the hut.

No wildlife breeds on the island.

JAMES ROSS ISLAND

Until 1995 an ice shelf permanently connected this 65km-long island to the Antarctic mainland before the ice shelf collapsed. The Greenpeace vessel *Arctic Sunrise* made the first circumnavigation of the island in February 1997.

Nordenskjöld named this island for its discoverer, Ross, who sighted it in 1843 but thought it was part of the Antarctic Peninsula because of the connecting ice shelf. The 'James' in the island's name distinguishes it from Ross Island in the Ross Sea, but all are named for the wide-ranging explorer.

Marine fossils and fossilized wood can be found on the island's west coast. At nearby **Botany Bay** on the Trinity Peninsula, which

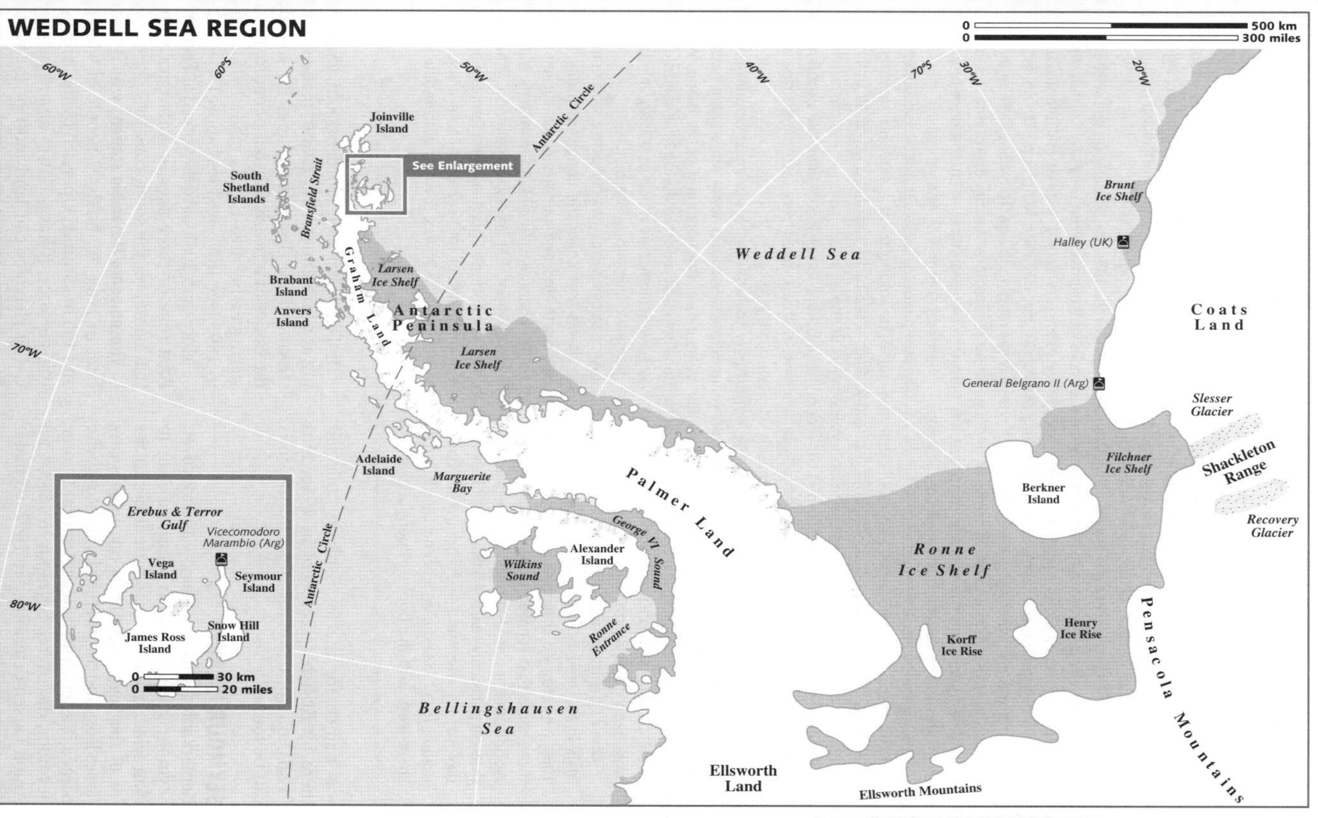

ANTARCTIC PENINSULA & WEDDELL SEA

SEYMOUR ISLAND: ANTARCTICA'S ROSETTA STONE *Dr William J Zinsmeister*

Little did I know, when I landed on the runway at Marambio station on Seymour Island in January 1975, that I would spend the rest of my life working on the treasures of this unique island.

The landscape of this small, ice-free island off the northeast tip of the Antarctic Peninsula looks much like the badlands of the southwestern US. In fact, when you're working here, the only signs that you're actually in Antarctica are the large tabular icebergs slowly drifting northward past the island and the occasional group of Adélie penguins walking along the beach.

Seymour Island is truly remarkable. The slopes of many of the hills, particularly on the western side, are literally paved with fossils. Not only are the rocks well exposed, but they also contain rich and well-preserved assemblages of marine invertebrates and terrestrial animals and plants. The problem of working on Seymour is not finding the fossils, but deciding which ones to collect.

Seymour is also the only place in Antarctica where rocks ranging in age from about 120 million to 40 million years are known. In terms of understanding the geologic history of Antarctica's last 100 million years and the role the continent has played in the evolutions of the modern faunas and floras of the southern hemisphere, Seymour is the Rosetta Stone of Antarctica.

Among the 800 fossils found here so far are 2m-tall giant penguins (now extinct, unfortunately), starfish, crabs, crinoids, corals and nearly 200 new mollusks, among them a 4m-long ammonite (related to the pearly nautilus). Another interesting find: a sea turtle that lived 40 to 45 million years ago and was the size and shape of a Volkswagen Beetle.

When we arrived in 1975, we planned to work on neighboring James Ross Island, but problems with the Argentine helicopters prevented our reaching it. That proved very fortunate, since we were forced to spend the entire field season on Seymour Island.

We were the first geologists to have the opportunity to look for fossils on Seymour since Swedish explorer Otto Nordenskjöld visited 75 years before. We found some remarkable fossils from the marine Eocene deposits (about 35 million years old) at the north end of the island. We also found the bones of the giant penguins that Nordenskjöld first reported during his expedition. These penguins stood nearly 2m in height and may have weighed as much as 135kg. It must have been quite a sight to see thousands of these giants walking along the beach.

One of the major paleontological questions about Antarctica's history was whether land mammals lived there before the development of the ice sheets that cover the continent today. In 1981 we returned to continue our work at Seymour's north end and to carry out a survey of those rocks that seemed to have the greatest potential for containing fossil land mammals. Mike Woodburne, a noted vertebrate paleontologist, and his assistant, Bill Dailey, came along. While they meticulously searched the most likely localities, I worked on the Eocene marine faunas. Each day was an adventure and ended with backpacks full of fossils. In mid-season I came across a unique fossil locality: an Eocene beach, exposed by erosion, which was covered with mollusks, shark teeth and the bones of penguins and whales.

was named for the fossil plants collected there by British researchers in 1946, fern fossils and other plant-stem impressions can be found.

SEYMOUR ISLAND

Remarkable for its lack of snow and ice cover, Seymour Island is 20km long and 3km to 9km wide. It's ice-free because it lies in the lee of the high mountains on neighboring James Ross and Snow Hill islands. Ross, who named it after British Rear Admiral George Seymour, discovered Seymour in 1843. Carl Anton Larsen determined in 1892–93 that it was in fact an island.

In December 1902 Nordenskjöld, wintering at nearby Snow Hill Island, made some striking fossil discoveries here. He found the bones of a nearly 2m-tall penguin, bolstering earlier fossil finds made by Larsen in 1893 (see the boxed text above).

More than 20,000 Adélies breed at **Penguin Point** (one of three sites in Antarctica with that name) on the south coast.

Vicecomodoro Marambio station, which was built in 1969–70, holds 22 people in winter and 150 in summer. Operated by the Argentine air force, it has a 1200m airstrip where C-130 Hercules can land most of the year. In summer, Twin Otters and helicopters

Although Mike and Bill spent the entire season crawling on their hands and knees looking for mammal bones, they found only a few scattered fish bones. Two days before the end of the season, I suggested that they join me in collecting the abundant penguin bones at the Eocene beach deposit. After 1½ hours of walking into the wind, we reached the site and Mike sat down to rest. Looking at the surface, he immediately saw a tooth of the small primitive marsupial *Polydolops*.

This was the first discovery of a fossil land mammal in Antarctica. It also answered a question concerning the origin of Australian marsupials that had puzzled scientists since the 19th century: how did marsupials get to Australia? The oldest marsupials known were from rocks in Wyoming about 100 million years old, while Australia's oldest marsupials were only about 30 million years old. Mike's discovery helped prove that early marsupials migrated from North America through South America, then across Antarctica to Australia.

Seymour also contains one of the most important records of the circumstances surrounding the worldwide 'extinction event' 65 million years ago that wiped out 70% of the world's species, including the dinosaurs. Most scientists now generally accept that the mass extinction was related to a major meteorite impact in Central America. Today, the debate has shifted to whether it was the sole cause – or whether a conjunction of events, including the impact, led to the dinosaurs' extinction. Conditions portrayed by supporters of the impact hypothesis were so extreme that I asked: How did any life survive? And why don't we see a layer of burnt and twisted dinosaur bones?

During the 1994–95 season, we found on Seymour the first documented victims of the mass extinction. We made a detailed map of the layer of iridium-rich sediments dating from the impact – known to geologists as the KT boundary. Nearly everywhere along the KT boundary, there were scattered bones of fish, killed by the impact 65 million years ago.

But the decline in the number of species of marine life on Seymour began about eight million years *before* the impact, clearly showing that the earth's climate was cooling. Species of marine life that lived for millions of years before the impact disappeared first in the high southern latitudes, then in the temperate and middle latitudes. Approaching the KT boundary on Seymour, more and more species disappear. Just below the boundary, 55% of the remaining species vanish. And the fish bones above the KT boundary are in scattered concentrations over about 3m of section, suggesting that they represent not a single mass kill, but a number of mass kills due to unstable conditions that may have lasted for thousands of years after the impact.

So I believe that the Cretaceous-Tertiary extinction was not related to a single event, but was the result of a conjunction of events. The impact was only the final straw for an already stressed environment. You could almost use this as a model for the present: how long can we stress the biosphere before something small pushes things over the edge?

Dr William J Zinsmeister, a paleontologist at Purdue University in West Lafayette, IN, has spent eight field seasons on Seymour Island

ANTARCTIC PENINSULA & WEDDELL SEA

ansport supplies and personnel to outlying stations and camps. North of Marambio ation are barren-looking landscapes rich in vertebrate fossils.

ONNE ICE SHELF

ogether with its eastern neighbor, the Filcher Ice Shelf, the Ronne Ice Shelf forms the Veddell Sea's southern coast. It was discovred by American naval commander Finn onne, leader of the private Ronne Antarctic esearch Expedition in 1947–48, and named or his wife, Edith, who accompanied the xpedition at the last minute and spent a difcult year at Stonington Island (p225).

Germany's summer-only **Filchner station**, established on the Ronne Ice Shelf in 1982, accommodated 12 people. But the calving of an enormous iceberg that took the station with it was observed via satellite on October 13, 1998. Fortunately the station was unstaffed at the time. A 10-day recovery operation in February 1999 removed the sleeping facilities, laboratories and 170 tonnes of equipment, using the research vessel *Polarstern*; they are now in storage.

FILCHNER ICE SHELF

When Filchner discovered this ice shelf in January 1912, he named it after his emperor,

Kaiser Wilhelm, who decided that the honor should return to Filchner. **Berkner Island**, separating Filchner from the Ronne Ice Shelf, is often the start of 'trans-Antarctic' ski trips.

Argentina's **General Belgrano II station**, built in 1979 on a 50m nunatak 120km from the coast, fits 18 people year-round. Its predecessor, General Belgrano station, was built on the Filchner Ice Shelf as a meteorological center by the Argentine army in 1954–55 and became a scientific station in 1969–70. The original Belgrano station was abandoned in January 1980, having been nearly destroyed by snow buildup; it subsequently floated out to sea when the ice shelf calved.

HALLEY STATION

British scientists first measured the ozone depletion of the Antarctic stratosphere at Halley station in 1985. Their discovery that this critical protection from ultraviolet radiation had been decreasing from 1975 to 1985 made headlines around the world and spurred the international agreement on bannin chlorofluorocarbons (CFCs).

Named after the astronomer Edmond Hal ley, this is the most southerly British Antarc tic station. Halley was established in 1956 o the floating Brunt Ice Shelf and requires re newal every decade or so as it approaches th ice edge. To date, two stations (built in 196 and 1972) have calved off, one (1982) is abou to, and one (1989) is buried and closed.

Halley V was built in 1994 and is currentl about 10km from the ice edge. With a sum mer population of 65 and 15 in winter, it built on stilts above the ice surface, whic moves about 2m a day! The stilts are jacke up annually so the station can be maintaine 2m above the snow surface. Because the ex pensive jacking process takes a week, Britai is considering using sled-based, mobile build ings as the station's eventual replacemen Already an accommodations building and garage weighing 50 tonnes are mounted o skis and towed each year to new positions.

WHAT'S IN A NAME?

Antarctica has no native inhabitants and because it was discovered relatively recently, large swaths of territory were often mapped and named all at once. In some cases, groups of associated geographic features were given associated names.

British expeditions in particular used associated place names freely. The UK's Antarctic gazetteer lists 45 name groups comprising a total of 998 names, 23% of all official place names in Britain's Antarctic claim.

Place names in the South Shetlands, appropriately enough, include 112 commemorating 19th-century sealers and their ships, while 16 of the Melchior Islands are named for letters of the Greek alphabet and nine names on the Wilkins and Bowman Coasts commemorate gods in Greek mythology. Fifty-one names on southeastern Alexander Island commemorate planets, their satellites and discoverers, and 23 on Rymill Coast are named after stars and constellations. Another six on northeastern Alexander Island commemorate Saxon kings of England.

Composers and their works lend their names to 67 features on Alexander Island. Literature is also well represented, with Chaucer's *Canterbury Tales* providing appellations for 10 features in the Wauwermans Islands, Dickens' *Pickwick Papers* giving 18 in the Pitt Islands, Homer's *Iliad* inspiring 15 on Anvers Island, Kipling's *The White Seal* supplying five on James Ross Island, Melville's *Moby Dick* furnishing 26 along Oscar II Coast, and Verne's *20, Leagues under the Sea* accounting for five on Pourquoi Pas Island.

Professions associated with Antarctic research get their due in the name game, including glaciologists (103 names), geologists (29), Antarctic historians, bibliographers and cartographers (23), Antarctic oceanographers and marine biologists (22), Antarctic meteorologists and atmospheric physicists (19) and glacial geologists (16), not to mention biochemists and designers of sledging rations (12) and continental-drift scientists (eight).

Other name groups commemorate pioneers: of medicine (Brabant Island), of aviation (Davis Coast and Danco Coast), of photography (Danco Coast), of vitamin research (Graham Coast), of navigation (Bowman Coast and Falliéres Coast) and of ski-mountaineering (Graham Coast). Even pioneers of prevention of snow blindness (Graham Coast and Loubet Coast) and pioneer designers of over-snow vehicles (Trinity Peninsula and Nordenskjöld Coast) are not left out.

Ross Sea

CONTENTS

As the watery but ice-choked path by which explorers of the 'Heroic Era' penetrated to the continent's interior, the Ross Sea region is sometimes called the 'Gateway to the South Pole.' James Clark Ross, for whom the sea is named, pushed through the Ross Sea pack ice in February 1842, becoming the first to reach the mind-bogglingly large Ross Ice Shelf.

Despite its fascinating icescapes and well-preserved history, the Ross Sea has been visited infrequently by tourists until the last decade or so. Even now, just a couple of voyages go to the Ross Sea each year, compared with the more than 100 trips to the Antarctic Peninsula annually.

The volcano Mt Erebus, the mysterious and otherworldly Dry Valleys and the awe-inspiring Ross Ice Shelf are only three of the rewards earned by travelers determined and persistent enough to reach this relatively inaccessible part of Antarctica.

Nowhere else in Antarctica is there a richer 'Heroic Era' heritage. On Ross Island at the Ross Sea's southernmost reach, the wooden houses left behind by Scott and Shackleton stir the imagination and make the explorers' diaries come to life. If the Ross Ice Shelf didn't calve icebergs, there would be even more history to see – Amundsen's base at Framheim in the Bay of Whales, plus all five of Richard E Byrd's Little America stations covered by drifting snow, have long since gone to sea inside giant tabular bergs

HIGHLIGHTS

- Stepping into **Scott's hut** (p246) at Cape Evans on Ross Island and feeling the chill of the ghosts of the polar party, who never returned to their base
- Wondering at the fantastic wind-sculpted ventifacts in the **Dry Valleys** (p238)
- Cruising along the front of the magnificent **Ross Ice Shelf** (p252) – and perhaps even landing on top via helicopter
- Climbing **Observation Hill** (p247) and pausing at the memorial cross raised to Scott and his men
- Peering into the **marine aquariums** (p245) at McMurdo's Crary Lab to see local sealife up close

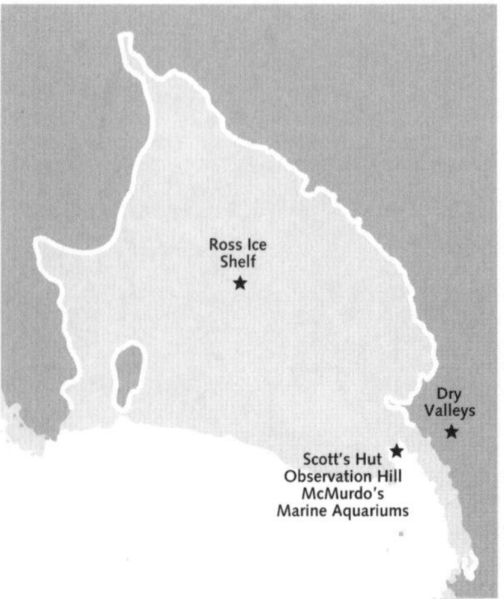

CAPE ADARE

This northernmost headland at the entrance to the Ross Sea was named for Britain's Viscount Adare, Member of Parliament for Glamorganshire, by his friend James Clark Ross, who discovered the cape in 1841. Here is Antarctica's largest **Adélie rookery** – 250,000 nesting pairs – as well as two sets of historic huts. Unfortunately, Cape Adare is an extremely difficult landing, with heavy surf and strong offshore winds usual. Because of the penguin rookery, helicopters cannot be used except very late in the season. Between 200 and 500 people land at Cape Adare annually; the exact number varies with the weather.

One of the first landings on the Antarctic continent – approximately the fifth, in fact (see the boxed text on p24) – occurred here on January 24, 1895, when Captain Leonard Kristensen of the whaling ship *Antarctic* landed a party including expedition leader HJ Bull and Carsten Borchgrevink.

Borchgrevink's Huts

Four years after Kristensen's landing, Borchgrevink was back at Cape Adare as the leader of the *Southern Cross* expedition, which landed in 1899. Two weeks later, two prefabricated huts had been erected, the remains of which can be seen today on Ridley Beach, which Borchgrevink named for his mother. These are the oldest buildings in Antarctica.

Here, a party of 10 spent one of the loneliest Antarctic winters ever, being the only humans on the continent, although they had the company of 90 dogs.

When they were occupied, the huts must have felt something like rustic fishing or hunting cabins. In *First on the Antarctic Continent*, Borchgrevink wrote:

> On the ceiling were hanging guns, fishing tackle, knives, mittens, chains, and odds and ends. The bunks were closed after the plan followed by sailors on board whaling vessels, with a small opening, leaving yourself in an enclosure which can hold its own with our modern coffin; and, like this, it is private; for some minds it is absolutely necessary to be alone, out of sight and entirely undisturbed by others. It was by special recommendation from the doctor that I made this arrangement and found that it answered well.

Borchgrevink's huts have outlasted the 'Northern Party' huts (see p235), even though they are 12 years older, because they were built from sturdier materials – interlocking boards of Norwegian spruce.

The accommodations hut, which housed all 10 men, was 5.5m by 6.5m. Upon entering the hut, an office/storeroom is to your left and a darkroom to your right. Both were once lined with furs for insulation. Continuing inside, a stove stands to the left, a table and chairs are on the left past the stove, and five of the double-tiered coffinlike bunks

THE HISTORIC HUTS

Only by entering the historic explorers' huts can one truly sense what it must have been like on early expeditions. In the black-and-white photos of the era, explorers crowd around a table or pack together in groups of bunks. When you step inside Scott's hut at Cape Evans, you suddenly realize that those men didn't crowd together just for the photographer – this was how they lived every day. Note also the rough construction of the huts' interiors – the buildings were only expected to be in use for two or three years, so they were built in a hurry, without having their corners squared off or rough edges sanded.

Today, the huts are all locked. A representative of New Zealand's Antarctic Heritage Trust (AHT), which maintains and conserves the huts, will monitor your visit. AHT representatives are not policemen, but caretakers. They're also very good guides, familiar with the huts through their restoration and conservation work, and they can point out things visitors would otherwise miss. One good suggestion, which the guides may share with you, is to keep backpacks, life jackets, fire extinguishers and other gear at least 10m from all huts so their modern look doesn't spoil your photos.

David Harrowfield's handsome book *Icy Heritage: Historic Sites of the Ross Sea Region*, available from AHT, is fascinating reading. It gives details on 34 sites and includes dozens of photographs, many in color and many published for the first time. The AHT representative on your ship will also distribute brochures about each hut.

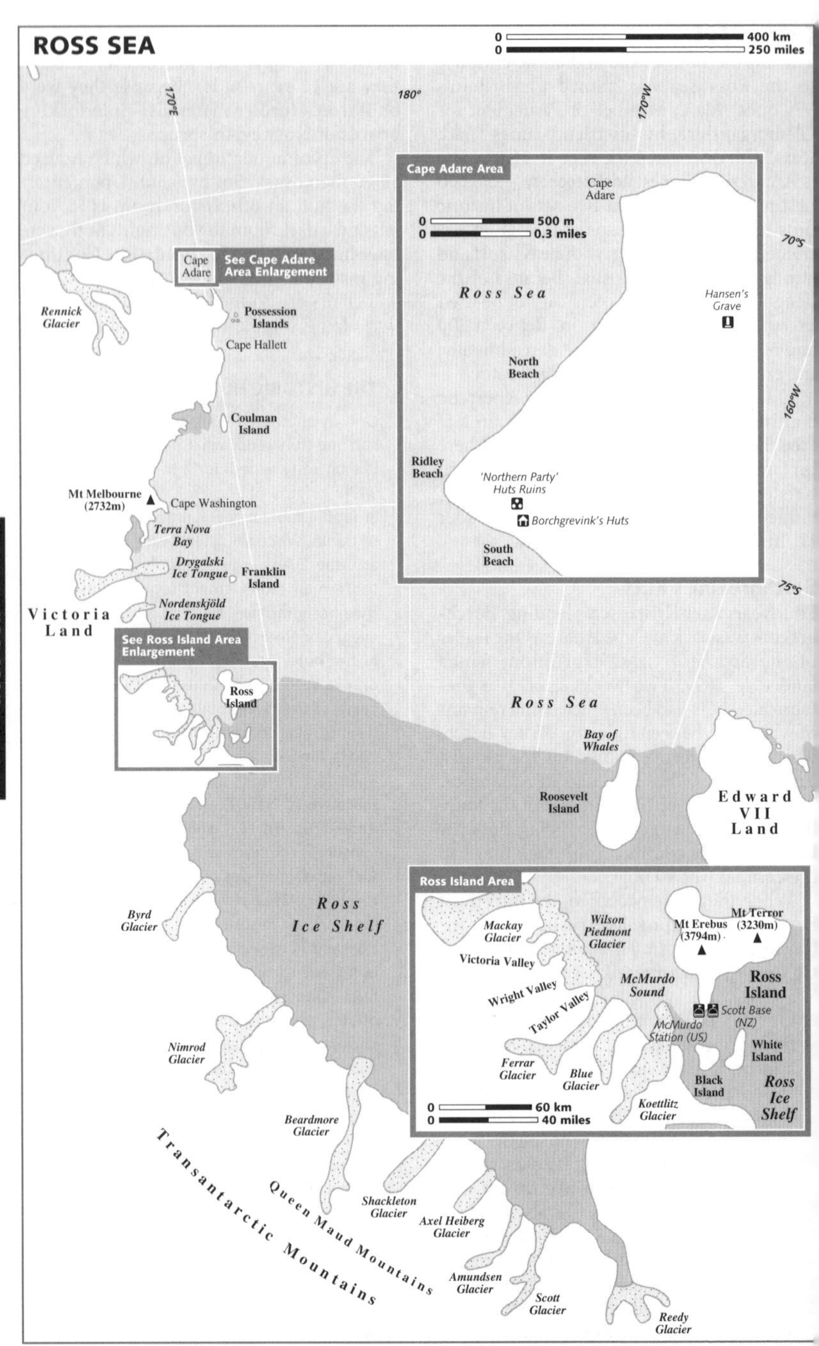
ROSS SEA
0 400 km
0 250 miles
170°E
180°
170°W
160°W
70°S
75°S
Cape Adare Area
Cape Adare
0 500 m
0 0.3 miles
Ross Sea
Hansen's Grave
North Beach
Ridley Beach
'Northern Party' Huts Ruins
Borchgrevink's Huts
South Beach
Cape Adare
See Cape Adare Area Enlargement
Rennick Glacier
Possession Islands
Cape Hallett
Coulman Island
Mt Melbourne (2732m)
Cape Washington
Terra Nova Bay
Drygalski Ice Tongue
Franklin Island
Nordenskjöld Ice Tongue
Victoria Land
See Ross Island Area Enlargement
Ross Island
Ross Sea
Bay of Whales
Roosevelt Island
Edward VII Land
Ross Ice Shelf
Byrd Glacier
Nimrod Glacier
Beardmore Glacier
Transantarctic Mountains
Queen Maud Mountains
Shackleton Glacier
Axel Heiberg Glacier
Amundsen Glacier
Scott Glacier
Reedy Glacier
Ross Island Area
Mackay Glacier
Wilson Piedmont Glacier
Mt Erebus (3794m)
Mt Terror (3230m)
Victoria Valley
Wright Valley
Taylor Valley
McMurdo Sound
Ross Island
Scott Base (NZ)
McMurdo Station (US)
White Island
Ferrar Glacier
Blue Glacier
Black Island
Ross Ice Shelf
Koettlitz Glacier
0 60 km
0 40 miles

line the remaining wall space. Borchgrevink's bunk was in the back left corner, on the top. The hut had papier-mâché insulation and a single double-paned window. Be sure to look out for the fine pencil drawing of a young Scandinavian woman on the ceiling above one of the bunks. Despite Borchgrevink's careful planning, the huts were not, apparently, comfortable homes. Australian physicist Louis Bernacchi wrote of leaving Cape Adare: 'May I never pass such another 12 months in similar surroundings and conditions.'

The stores hut, to the west, is now roofless. It contains boxes of ammunition that Borchgrevink brought in case the expedition encountered large predators such as polar bears. (He was the first to winter on the continent.) Coal briquettes and stores barrels litter the ground outside this hut.

Today, the huts are completely surrounded by an Adélie penguin colony, and care must be taken to avoid disturbing the penguins. The Antarctic Heritage Trust (AHT), which is working to conserve the huts, re-roofed the accommodation hut and installed support braces during the 1989–90 season.

To limit the possibility of damage, only four people (including the AHT representative, who will accompany your cruise or come over from Scott Base) are permitted inside the Cape Adare huts at one time. In any case, there's not much room inside. Only 40 people are allowed in the area of the huts at one time.

Hansen's Grave

The *Southern Cross* expedition's biologist, Norwegian Nicolai Hansen, died on October 14, 1899, probably of an intestinal disorder. On his deathbed Hansen's wish was to be buried on the ridge above Ridley Beach, so his expedition mates built a coffin and dynamited a grave up on the stone ridge for the first-known human burial on the continent. Dragging Hansen's heavy coffin up the steep incline was a major effort.

When *Southern Cross* returned, a graveside memorial was held and an iron cross and brass plaque were attached to a boulder on the site. Later, when Victor Campbell's men used the ridge as a lookout for *Terra Nova*, one of them spelled out Hansen's name with white quartz pebbles. Visitors to the site in 1982 restored the inscriptions.

Unfortunately, the safest route up the 350m ridge is blocked by an Adélie penguin colony, so the gravesite is effectively off-limits.

'Northern Party' Huts

Almost nothing remains of the hut built by Victor Campbell, a member of Scott's *Terra Nova* expedition of 1911–14. Cape Adare's raging winds have pretty well wrecked it. Its ruin lies east of Borchgrevink's huts. The

CODE OF CONDUCT FOR VISITING HISTORIC ANTARCTIC HUTS

These guidelines have been established by the Antarctic Heritage Trust to minimize the adverse effects of visitors. Please observe this code at all times.

- Reduce floor abrasion. Thoroughly clean grit and scoria, ice and snow, from boots before entering.
- Salt particles accelerate the corrosion of metal objects. Remove any clothing made wet by seawater, and any sea-ice crystals from boots.
- Many areas are cramped and artifacts can be accidentally bumped. Do not wear packs inside.
- Handling artifacts causes damage. Do not touch, move or sit on any items or furniture in the huts.
- When moving around the sites, take great care not to tread on any items. Many may be partially covered by snow. Do not disturb or remove anything from around the huts.
- Fire is a major risk. You are strictly forbidden to smoke or use combustion-style lanterns or naked flames in or around the huts.
- As a visitor, you should record your name in the book.
- Flash photography *is* permitted inside the huts.

prefabricated building, originally standing 6.4m by 6.1m, once housed six men.

POSSESSION ISLANDS

Ross discovered the group's two main islands, Foyn and Possession, together known as the Possession Islands. After pushing *Erebus* and *Terror* through the Ross Sea pack ice to open water, he was surprised to sight land on January 10, 1841. To Ross, this was quite unexpected, because he hoped to sail west from the Ross Sea to the area where the South Magnetic Pole was calculated to lie. In that era, the pole was in fact well inland.

Despite his disappointment, Ross landed a boat two days later on Possession Island and claimed it for Queen Victoria. It was, declared the expedition's 24-year-old naturalist Joseph Dalton Hooker, 'surely the whitest if not the brightest jewel in her crown.' An engraving of the event shows penguins lined up even on the highest ridge of the island. Indeed the thousands of Adélies that nest on both islands today climb right to the to of the small hill on Possession.

In 1895 Borchgrevink found a lichen here the first plant discovered in Antarctica.

A century later, in February 1995, a smal modern wreck of unknown origin was dis covered on the western side of Possessio Island: a mystery.

CAPE HALLETT

Cape Hallett was discovered by Ross in 184 and named for Thomas Hallett, *Erebus* purser. When a scientific station jointly ru by the US and New Zealand was built in Jan uary 1957 as part of the International Geo physical Year, 8000 Adélie penguins wer moved to another part of the cape to mak way for the base. It accommodated 11 Ameri cans and three New Zealanders for the win ter. It was operated year-round until 1964 when it became a summer-only facility afte fire destroyed the main science building. Th station was closed in 1973, and since the lat

AURORA AUSTRALIS *Dr Gary Burns & Dr Ray Morris*

> Mysterious, beautiful, wonderful – colored profusion in visual chaos – ribbons of light snake across the night sky – batteries of celestial searchlights zero in on the magnetic zenith, waltzing to the music of the celestial spheres, forming an ever-changing crown in the heavens. Successive bands of increased light intensity move upwards, highlighting the display and flaming heavenwards – patches of light pulsate rhythmically; in another region of the night sky, other patches of light pulsate, out of phase – such is the aurora australis or southern lights at the height of a display.
>
> *FR Bond, 'Background to Aurora Australis'*

The aurora is the collective name (taken from the Roman goddess of the dawn) given to photons (light) emitted by atoms, molecules and ions that have been excited by energetically charged particles traveling along magnetic field lines into the earth's upper atmosphere. The aurora results from the interaction of the solar wind with the earth's magnetic field.

The colors in the aurora result from photons of specific energy-level transitions in the excited atoms, molecules and ions of the upper atmosphere returning to their lowest energy state. There are hundreds of individual color mixture of the major green, red and purple emissions may combine to give an aurora a general whitish appearance.

Most commonly, auroral glows form a band aligned in a magnetic east–west direction. If sufficient numbers of energetic electrons are impacting the upper atmosphere, bands may have shimmering rays extending upward from them. These rays define magnetic field atmosphere. The twisting of auroral rays and bands results from the dynamic interaction of electric currents and magnetic fields in the upper atmosphere.

In active displays, you may be able to see multiple bands, which may break into small arcs. If you can see rapid horizontal motion of the auroral form, it may appear more purplish on its leading edge and greenish on its trailing edge. This results from a small delay (less than a second) between the peak intensity of the nitrogen molecular-ion emission and the green oxygen-atom emission. The active phase of an auroral display will last in the order of 15 to 40 minutes and may recur in two to three hours. Auroral band features may persist much longer. A red-dominated

1970s the disused buildings have gradually been removed to allow the Adélies to return. A stained, white, domed refuge building is all that remains. Cape Hallett can usually only be visited by Zodiac (motorized dinghy); helicopter landings are not permitted while the penguins occupy their rookery.

MT MELBOURNE

This 2732m cone is one of the very few volcanoes on the Antarctic continent itself. Almost all the others – including Mt Erebus, Mt Siple and Deception Island – are on off-lying islands. Like the Australian city of the same name, the volcano commemorates Lord Melbourne, British Prime Minister in the 1830s and '40s. Like so many other features in the Ross Sea region, Ross discovered it in 1841.

TERRA NOVA BAY

This 65km-long bay was discovered by Scott's *Discovery* expedition and named after the relief ship *Terra Nova*. Italy operates **Mario Zucchelli station**, which accommodates approximately 80 people during the summer months. The station was known as Baia Terra Nova station until January 2004, when it was renamed to honor the longtime director of the Italian Antarctic program. The station, a collection of blue buildings with orange trim, was established in 1986–87. A sea-ice runway, opened in 1990, is used by about 10 Hercules flights per season. The original building is known as the 'Pinguinattollo,' an imaginative conjunction of *pinguino* (penguin) and *scoiattolo* (squirrel). It's a kind of inhabitable diary, the interior walls entirely covered with inscriptions, drawings and signatures of dozens of visitors and staff over the years. The new Pinguinattollo is a large wooden chalet, with a granite fireplace fueled – somewhat surprisingly, given the extreme danger of fire in the dry Antarctic air – by scraps of wood.

auroral glow will be very diffuse. It will fluctuate slowly in location and intensity (on timescales of half a minute or so). This results from a significant time delay in the emission of light by the atomic oxygen state, which smoothes out any rapid variation in which the auroral electrons are impacting on the atmosphere.

If an auroral band has an easily discernible lower border, this will generally be at around 100km to 110km in altitude. Auroral rays may extend above the lower border for hundreds of kilometers. If the lower border has a pinkish edge (resulting from an emission of molecular nitrogen), the altitude may be around 90km to 100km. A diffuse red aurora occurs above 250km.

During an active auroral display, the intensity variations will be rapid and spectacular. A most dramatic variation is an increase in brightness moving up the auroral display. Faster electrons reach the atmosphere first and deposit their energy low in the atmosphere. These are followed by lower-energy electrons, which are stopped at progressively higher altitudes giving an enhanced brightness moving upwards from the lower border. These variations may occur in rapid succession.

The global distribution of auroral activity is an oval around the magnetic poles in both the southern and northern hemispheres. As the level of disturbance of the earth's magnetic field increases, the oval of auroral activity expands equatorward. The auroral oval in the southern hemisphere, the aurora australis, is linked by magnetic field lines to the auroral oval in the northern hemisphere, the aurora borealis.

Auroral electrons are often accelerated along magnetic field lines toward the opposite hemispheres from a region near the magnetic equator. The aurora australis and aurora borealis thus develop simultaneously, as near mirror images of each other. Aurora in the two hemispheres, if directly linked by the earth's magnetic field, are said to be 'conjugate.'

Auroral displays are seen more often equatorward of their normal locations at times of high sunspot activity. Auroral occurrence in these regions has a broad two- to three-year maximum around the peak in the 11-year sunspot cycle. The next aurora is expected in the middle of 2011.

Dr Gary Burns is a Principal Research Scientist, Australian Antarctic Division
Dr Ray Morris is with Atmospheric and Space Sciences, Australian Antarctic Division

DRYGALSKI ICE TONGUE

Discovered by Scott in 1902 and named for German explorer Drygalski, this ice tongue is the seaward extension of the David Glacier. It ranges from 14km to 24km wide and is nearly 50km long.

FRANKLIN ISLAND

The ubiquitous Ross landed on this 11km-long island on January 27, 1841, claiming the Victoria Land coast for Queen Victoria. He named the island itself for John Franklin, Governor of Van Diemen's Land (Tasmania), who had shown the expedition considerable hospitality when it called in at Hobart in 1840 on the way south. Affixed to only this tiny island in the Antarctic, Franklin's name is writ much larger in the history of the Arctic, where major discoveries were made by explorers searching for his missing ships, *Erebus* and *Terror*, the same vessels Ross used to explore this area. Franklin Island is home to a large Adélie rookery.

NORDENSKJÖLD ICE TONGUE

Discovered by Scott's National Antarctic Expedition of 1901–04, this ice tongue is named for Swedish explorer Otto Nordenskjöld. It is the seaward extension of the Mawson Glacier.

DRY VALLEYS

The Dry Valleys are some of the most unusual places on earth. They are magnificent spaces: huge, desolate, and beautiful. As with other parts of Antarctica, it can be hard to comprehend the Dry Valleys' scale. What appears to be a nearby mountainside or glacier could in fact be several hours' walking distance. Despite the oft-quoted statement that no rain has fallen there for at least two million years, it has indeed rained in the Dry Valleys recently; several times, in fact, including in 1959, 1968, 1970 and 1974.

From north to south, the three main Dry Valleys are **Victoria**, **Wright** and **Taylor**. The air is so dry in the Dry Valleys, which cover 3000 sq km, that they have no snow or ice. Such ice-free areas in Antarctica are called 'oases.' The conditions required for an oasis are a retreating or thinning ice sheet, and a large area of exposed rock from which snow becomes ablated due to solar radiation absorbed by the rock. Although these valleys are the most prominent Antarctic oases, there are at least 20 others, including the Bunger, Larsemann and Vestfold Hills of East Antarctica. The Dry Valleys were formed when the terrain uplifted at a faster rate than glaciers could cut their way down through them. Eventually, high necks at the head of each valley stopped the glaciers.

Robert Scott accidentally discovered the first of the Dry Valleys in December 1903 and named it for geologist Griffith Taylor. Scott and two others had sledged up the Ferrar Glacier to the East Antarctic Ice Sheet. On their return, they became lost in thick cloud and descended the wrong valley. Because they were equipped for sledging, not hiking, they were forced to turn back after a brief exploration. In *The Voyage of the Discovery*, Scott wrote:

> I cannot but think that this valley is a very wonderful place. We have seen today all the indications of colossal ice action and considerable water action, and yet neither of these agents is now at work. It is worthy of record, too, that we have seen no living thing, not even a moss or a lichen; all that we did find, far inland amongst the moraine heaps, was the skeleton of a Weddell seal, and how that came there is beyond guessing. It is certainly a valley of the dead; even the great glacier which once pushed through it has withered away.

Although the valleys appear lifeless, they harbor some of the most remarkable organisms on earth. In 1976 American biologists discovered algae, bacteria and fungi growing *inside* Dry Valley rocks. This 'endolithic' vegetation grows in the air spaces in porous rocks. Light, carbon dioxide and moisture penetrate the rock, and the rock protects the organisms against excessive drying and harmful radiation. Some of these plants are believed to be 200,000 years old.

A collection of unusual ponds and lakes within the Dry Valleys also harbors life (at least, some of them do). Although Taylor Valley's **Lake Hoare** is permanently covered by 5.5m-thick ice, dense mats of blue-green algae carpet its bottom. **Lake Bonney**, also in Taylor Valley, is freshwater at its surface and at its bottom is 12 times more saline than the sea. Saltwater **Lake Fryxell** is the third lake in Taylor Valley. Wright Valley's **Lake Vanda**, named for a sled dog, is 60m deep and 25°C at its bottom. Antarctica's longest river, the 30km meltwater stream called the **Onyx River**, flows into Lake Vanda from the glacier at the end of the valley; it's one of very few rivers in the world to flow inland from the coast. **Don Juan Pond**, also in Wright Valley, is only 10cm deep. It is the most saline body of water on earth – 14 times saltier than seawater – and so salty that it never freezes, even at -55°C. It takes its name not, alas, from the legendary lover, but from two US Navy aviators named Don and John who helped the first field party studying the pond. White crusts of calcium salt crystals and of a rare mineral called antarcticite precipitate on Don Juan Pond's shores.

Another reason the Dry Valleys appear so otherworldly is the bizarre, sculpted form of the rocks. These ventifacts are highly polished on their windward surfaces. Some have been carved by the wind into pocked boulders or thin, delicate wafers; others fit into your hand so well that they resemble smoothly ground primitive tools. Although they feel good to pick up, the ventifacts should not be removed. As one scientist familiar with the Dry Valleys puts it: 'You either understand the ethics of such a place, or you don't.'

Mummified seals such as those seen by Scott are not uncommon in the Dry Valleys,

THE LIONS OF THE DRY VALLEYS *Dr Diana Wall & Dr Andy Parsons*

Although the Dry Valleys appear to be a completely lifeless void, there is abundant microfauna in the soils, primarily bacteria, yeasts, protozoa and nematodes. Picture an ecosystem teeming with as much life as Africa's Serengeti Plain, with its vast migrating herds, except invisible to the naked eye.

Nematodes are tiny, elongated, cylindrical worms measuring only about a millimeter long. They are the most numerous creatures on earth – four out of five animals is a nematode – living in many different environments, including ocean sediments. In most Dry Valley soils, just two or three nematode species occupy the top of a very simple food chain, leading some people to describe them as the 'lions of the Dry Valleys.' In stark contrast, most soils in temperate regions contain more than 100 species of nematodes and thousands of other organisms in a complex food web.

One nematode species, *Scottnema lindsayae*, has the highest population densities in the Dry Valleys in some of the most extreme soils – those containing virtually no water and high levels of salt. Nematodes need water to move, feed and reproduce, but *Scottnema* survives the winter in dry saline soils by coiling up into a state of reversible dormancy called anhydrobiosis (literally 'life without water'). Individuals can remain dormant for years – and then become active within minutes of getting wet. Although *Scottnema*'s longevity is not known, some species of nematodes have been in anhydrobiosis for as long as 60 years and have then become active again.

'Life without water' offers another advantage for this nematode: dispersal. Even in optimum conditions, nematodes travel in soil only centimeters per year. By drying out like a tiny speck of dust, *Scottnema* can be carried many kilometers by the wind. It may be particularly well adapted to this form of dispersal, as it is smaller and lighter than the other species of nematodes in the Dry Valleys. Genetic analyses of the different populations throughout the region suggest that *Scottnema* can also adapt to 'local scale' variations in soils and environmental conditions.

These nematodes and their habitats are extremely vulnerable to human influence. Their numbers are reduced by one-third in soil on paths that are moderately trampled by people. Human activities – and disturbance to soils – in the Antarctic will undoubtedly increase. As more people enter the Dry Valleys, the fragile soil ecosystem will experience species loss, erosion and compaction. Additionally, as global changes affect the Dry Valley environment, species introduced by winds and soil from other continents may be able to survive, with unknown consequences to this fragile soil community.

Dr Diana Wall, professor and director of the Natural Resource Ecology Laboratory (NREL) at Colorado State University, has spent 14 field seasons in the Dry Valleys studying nematodes

Dr Andy Parsons, research associate at NREL, has spent seven seasons in the Dry Valleys

although most appear to be crabeaters, not Weddells. They have been found as far as 40km inland, a remarkable journey for an animal that is as awkward on land as a seal. Given the number of seals, it's not difficult to believe that one or two per year might wander into the valleys and get lost. The occasional carcass of a disoriented Adélie has also been found in the Dry Valleys, as far as 50km from the sea. The remains of both seals and penguins become freeze-dried by the extreme aridity of the valleys, and then eroded by the scouring wind, just like the ventifacts.

Scientists believe the Dry Valleys are the nearest equivalent on earth to the terrain of Mars. NASA performed extensive research here from 1974 to 1976 before sending the Viking Lander spacecraft to Mars.

In addition to Victoria, Wright and Taylor Valleys, several smaller valleys are also part of the region. Interestingly, the Americans call them the 'McMurdo Dry Valleys,' while the British prefer the 'Victoria Land Dry Valleys.' Most people just call them the 'Dry Valleys.' Tourists generally fly by helicopter into Taylor Valley, the most accessible from the Ross Sea. Large sections of the others are protected areas under the Antarctic Treaty, and access is restricted or forbidden, even to scientists.

ROSS ISLAND

Both New Zealand and the US have their principal Antarctic stations on Ross Island. As part of NZ's Ross Dependency territorial claim, Ross Island is – as the joke goes – the only island in New Zealand without sheep. It's also the location of the three most famous historic huts.

Scott Base

An attractive collection of lime-green buildings, New Zealand's Scott base is located at Pram Point, on the southeast side of Hut Point Peninsula. Pram Point was named by Scott's *Discovery* expedition because getting from there to the Ross Ice Shelf in summer requires a pram, or small boat.

Scott base was established in 1957 by Edmund Hillary as part of Fuchs' Commonwealth Trans-Antarctic Expedition (TAE). The TAE building now houses a small museum, while the base accommodates 11 winterers and up to 90 people in summer. Compared to McMurdo's 'urban sprawl,' Scott base looks trim and tidy.

Tourists can easily overwhelm a smaller Antarctic station such as Scott base, where the staff must dedicate itself to accommodating a ship visit. Still, the New Zealanders are very friendly. Several hundred people visit annually. Once a week, Scott base hosts 'American night,' a way to ensure that its more populous neighbor doesn't overwhelm its hospitality. The relatively few Kiwis have an open invitation to events at McMurdo, just 4km away by gravel road.

Although there are no mail facilities at Scott base, phone calls can be made using the two public telephones in the foyer of the Command Centre. You can use phone cards purchased in the base shop, call collect (reverse charges) or use a credit card. The shop accepts NZ and US currencies, Visa, MasterCard and American Express.

McMurdo Station

Antarctica's largest station, McMurdo is home to about 1100 people during the summer – one-third of them women – and 250 in winter. More than 100 buildings sprawl over nearly 4 sq km between Hut Point and Observation Hill; the structures are built on short stilts, and water, sewer, telephone and power lines all run aboveground.

The industrial-looking station can be an overwhelming sight after Antarctica's clean white icebergs and scarce signs of human life. In early summer when the dusty ground mixes with meltwater, the station resembles a mining town of the Old West, and some residents refer to it as 'McMudhole.'

Established in 1956, McMurdo takes its name from McMurdo Sound, which Ross named in 1841 after Lieutenant Archibald McMurdo of the ship *Terror*. The settlement was big right from the start: 93 men wintered the first year.

Today, McMurdo is both a logistics center and Antarctica's premier scientific base. Researchers are flown to nearby field camps via helicopter and to remote field camps and the South Pole via ski-equipped LC-130 Hercules and Twin Otter aircraft.

'You will find,' says a handbook issued to new residents, 'that McMurdo station resembles an urban center in its population diversity and hectic pace.' Called MacTown (or just 'Town') by its residents, the station

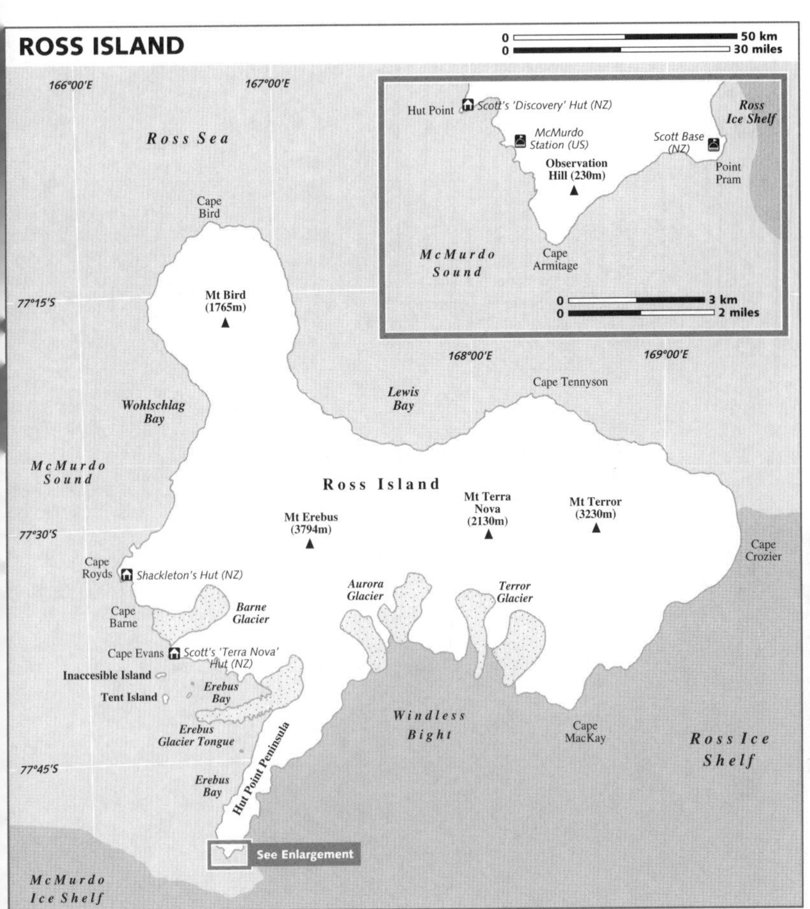

does have the feel of a bustling town. Nearly 80 vehicles (excluding heavy equipment) roll through its streets, although not very quickly: the station speed limit is 30km/h. (Although New Zealand time is used in the Scott base/McMurdo station area, driving is American-style, on the right.)

McMurdo has its own hospital, a church, a post office, library, 42-member fire department with two separate stations, barbershop, video store and ATMs. There's a coffeehouse and two clubs: the Southern Exposure, and Gallagher's (commemorating a McMurdo resident who died in 1997). The station has a 24-hour shuttle bus to its various districts, as well as to Scott base. There are video-teleconferencing facilities, a diving recompression chamber, a 220m-long Ice Pier, a fuel-tank farm with a total capacity of 30 million liters and a seawater reverse-osmosis desalination plant. In 2003, the US opened a sewage-treatment facility; before that, raw sewage was discharged into the sea after being ground and diluted. Now, the solid residue left after wastewater treatment goes back to North America with the rest of McMurdo's waste.

The US Antarctic program has worked hard to minimize McMurdo's impact on the environment. Before 1990 the station's accumulated trash – including junked vehicles, empty fuel barrels and scrap metal – was hauled out onto the sea ice each spring before the annual breakup. Today, the station's

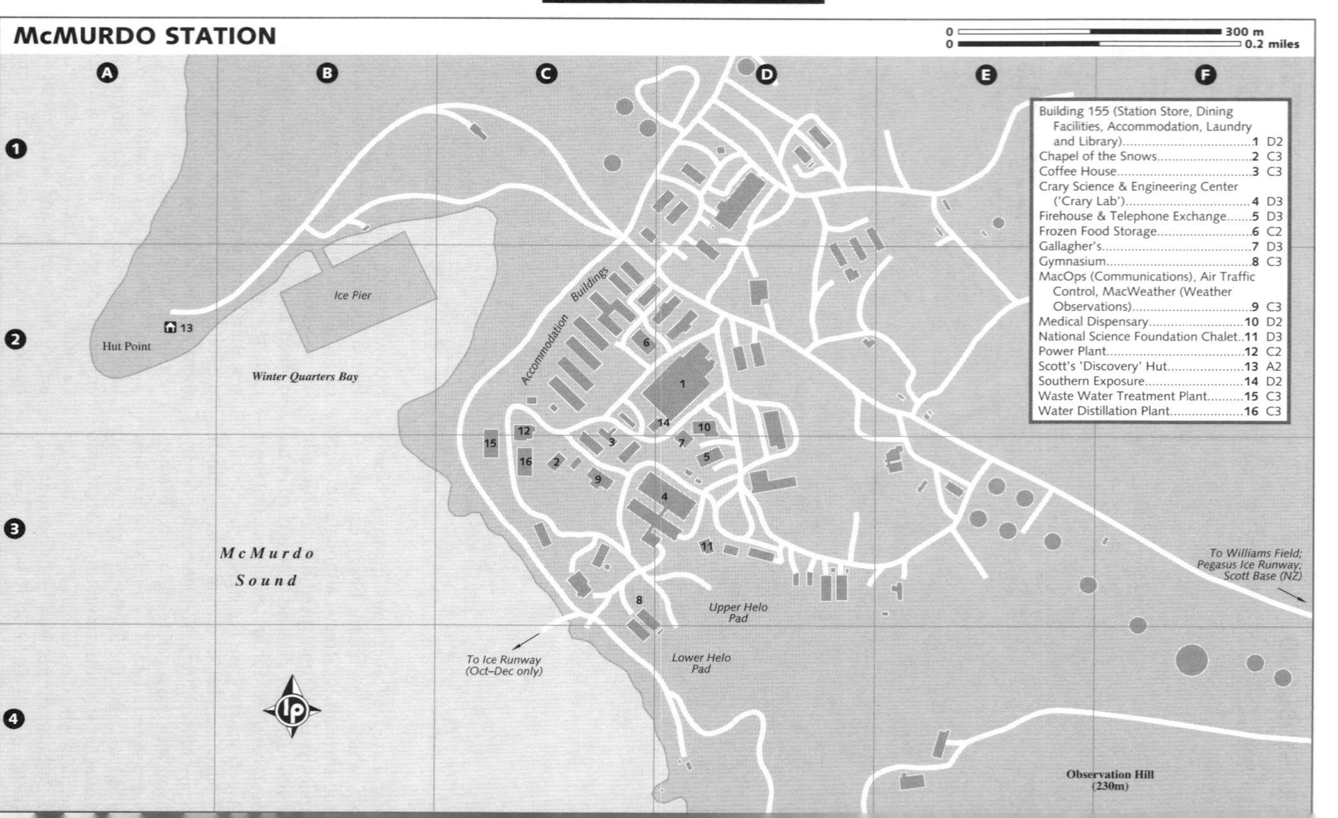
McMURDO STATION
0 300 m
0 0.2 miles
Building 155 (Station Store, Dining Facilities, Accommodation, Laundry and Library) 1 D2
Chapel of the Snows 2 C3
Coffee House 3 C3
Crary Science & Engineering Center ('Crary Lab') 4 D3
Firehouse & Telephone Exchange 5 D3
Frozen Food Storage 6 C2
Gallagher's 7 D3
Gymnasium 8 C3
MacOps (Communications), Air Traffic Control, MacWeather (Weather Observations) 9 C3
Medical Dispensary 10 D2
National Science Foundation Chalet 11 D3
Power Plant 12 C2
Scott's 'Discovery' Hut 13 A2
Southern Exposure 14 D2
Waste Water Treatment Plant 15 C3
Water Distillation Plant 16 C3
Hut Point
Winter Quarters Bay
Ice Pier
McMurdo Sound
Accommodation Buildings
Upper Helo Pad
Lower Helo Pad
To Ice Runway (Oct–Dec only)
To Williams Field; Pegasus Ice Runway; Scott Base (NZ)
Observation Hill (230m)

recycling program is almost bewilderingly complex: aluminum, clothing, construction debris, food waste, glass, hazardous waste, heavy metals, light metals, magazines, newspapers, packaging, plastics, white paper and wood – among other materials – are now all recycled. During a typical year, as much as 75% of the station's solid waste (which totals more than 2000 tonnes annually) is recycled, three times the rate achieved by the average US city.

McMurdo's greenhouse uses hand pollinating, since there are no insects – and none can be imported, due to environmental restrictions. Nevertheless, using thousands of watts of artificial light and hydroponic techniques, the local 'farmers' manage to produce 1600kg of lettuce, herbs, tomatoes and cucumbers annually.

The continent's only large nuclear-power plant, a 1.8-megawatt experimental reactor, known colloquially as 'Nukey Poo,' was deployed on Observation Hill in December 1961 and went online in March 1962. Unfortunately, the reactor experienced numerous problems, and in 1972, faced with a large repair bill, the US shut it down. Eventually, some 10,000 tonnes of radioactively contaminated soil and rock were removed from the site, although some scientists believe that the rock in that area was naturally radioactive.

McMurdo housing is allocated through a points system, in which position and previous months on the continent determine your berth. Scientists and others moving frequently between the field and town will probably bunk in one of the large dorms overlooking the helicopter pad. Two of these dorms are picturesquely named the 'Hotel California' and the 'Mammoth Mountain Inn.' There are newer dorms that overlook the Ice Pier.

The station's newspaper, the *Antarctic Sun*, is published weekly during the summer (and is available online all year at www.polar.org/antsun). There's also 'The Scroll,' a televised list of the day's activities, announcements, weather information, movie schedules and other station news, which can be viewed on one of the station's several hundred TVs. Other media include Radio McMurdo (104.5 on your FM dial), two TV broadcast channels, 8 and 13, plus two channels of cable TV, 24 hours a day. Direct-dial, in-room phone service is available from many rooms in McMurdo.

Recreation opportunities for the station personnel abound: aerobics, basketball, bingo, bowling, chili cook-offs, country dancing, cross-country skiing, darts, hiking, jogging, soccer, softball, table tennis, tae kwon do, volleyball and weight-lifting. Residents can even borrow bicycles to cruise around town. For golfers, there is the McMurdo Open tournament. For runners, there are the 5km Run Across Ross Island, the McMurdo Midsummer Midnight Mile and the 7.25km Scott's Hut race.

Sunday science lectures, computer classes, cardiopulmonary resuscitation (CPR) training, Alcoholics Anonymous meetings, Town Choir rehearsals, the Ross Island Drama Festival, the Ross Island Art Show, the Icestock music festival with local talent, meetings of the McMurdo Historical Society and even occasional tours of Scott's *Discovery* Hut are also offered.

Outings can be also organized to beautiful ice caves, which are made accessible by the winter sea ice. These are formed during the summer by wave action eroding part of the Erebus Glacier Tongue. Station residents may also win a special lottery to go on a very special day trip from McMurdo to the South Pole station, by taking a space-available flight – a unique reward known locally as a 'sleigh ride.'

Three different airfields serve McMurdo, each operating at different times of the year. In the spring, a **sea-ice landing field** is laid out on McMurdo Sound for use by wheeled aircraft flights in October, November and early December. There's one local hazard found at almost no other airfield in the world: penguins and seals occasionally wander across the runway, requiring an official, trained 'escort' off the field to ensure their safety – and that of the plane! Later in December, as summer temperatures weaken the sea ice, flight operations shift to **Williams Field**, a 3000m skiway on the Ross Ice Shelf. Also known as Willy Field or just plain 'Willy,' it was named for Richard T Williams, who died during Operation Deep Freeze I (1955–56) when his 30-tonne tractor broke through sea ice off Cape Royds. Williams Field is 16km from the station. This being McMurdo, there's an airport shuttle: a huge TerraBus vehicle (nicknamed 'Ivan') carries passengers over

DIVING IN MCMURDO SOUND *Jim Mastro*

I'm finning slowly over the bottom, nearly 40m down. It's early spring and far overhead the sea surface is a solid, 2m-thick sheet of ice. In the distance, I can clearly see our safety line with its flashing strobe lights. It marks the manmade hole that is our only access to the surface.

Ahead of me, my dive partner is a shadow in the darkness. The sea ice permits only 1% of the sunlight that falls upon it to penetrate to the water below. Yet this water is so clear that even in the dim light the visibility is astounding – perhaps 245m. Strange, irregular shapes project upward from the dull, blue-brown seafloor. When I snap on my underwater light, the colors leap out – bright reds, vibrant greens, luminescent yellows, glaring whites.

The bottom is literally covered with a garden of life. Most of the conspicuous animals are sponges, in a multitude of shapes and colors. A yellow rope sponge thrusts its slim fingers toward the sky. A white volcano sponge the size of an armchair sits at a curious angle, its single giant osculum gaping like an open mouth. A large colony of pink staghorn sponge resembles a pile of discarded elk antlers.

I'm diving in the frigid waters of McMurdo Sound as part of a team of scientists trying to unravel the mysteries of this little-understood environment. The richness and diversity of the seafloor community we've found is mind-boggling: the bottom is as thick with living creatures as some tropical reefs.

Getting into the water wasn't easy, though. We used a diesel-powered auger to drill a 1.25m diameter hole through the ice, then positioned a mobile hut over it to protect us from blizzards and bitter cold while we prepared to dive.

Scuba diving in Antarctica presents other dangers, too. Unprotected exposure to the water will cause severe hypothermia in minutes, so even a minor equipment malfunction can become life-threatening. If a regulator freezes up or a dry-suit zipper fails, a diver may have only a few moments to get to the dive hole. For this reason, our dives are limited to 40m or less. Deeper dives frequently require decompression stops. In case of an equipment failure, that could force us to choose between hypothermia and the bends.

One reason for the density and diversity of the creatures here is the remarkable stability of the marine environment, thanks to two main factors. First, the massive Ross Ice Shelf keeps the temperature in McMurdo Sound from fluctuating more than 0.2°C. Second, every year with unerring predictability, the seafloor here is bathed with a rich rain of food. By mid-December, the height of the Antarctic summer, the midnight sun has fueled a stupendous growth of plankton in the nutrient-rich ocean. A southerly current carries this plankton under the ice, where it drifts down to nourish the hundreds of species of sponges and other suspension feeders that live on the sea bottom.

a snow road to the station. A third airfield, the **Pegasus ice runway** (named for Pegasus, a US Navy C-121 Super Constellation that crashed nearby during the 1970–71 season; everyone aboard survived the crash, and the wrecked plane is still there today), is about 45 minutes' drive from McMurdo. It was inaugurated in 1993.

Since 2002 a new compacted-snow runway at the Pegasus site has allowed large wheeled aircraft to land at McMurdo. About a hundred flights from Christchurch arrive each year: C-130 Hercules, C-5 Galaxies, C-141 Starlifters, C-17 Globemasters and LC-130 ski-equipped Hercules. While most arrive between early October and late February, some land in late August during the latter part of the winter, in an operation called 'Winfly,' or Winter Fly-In.

VISITING MCMURDO

In addition to those places listed here, tourists will catch only glimpses of the station's busy life, through a guided walking tour of **MacWeather** (the weather-observations center) and the **communications center**, which are in the same building, and a hospitality stop at the coffeehouse.

The **Chapel of the Snows**, a 64-seat house of worship with a pretty, unique penguin-motif stained-glass window and the station's only organ, is the third chapel raised at McMurdo; the first two were destroyed by fire.

We often see Weddell seals – they swim slowly by, studying us from a safe distance and perhaps wondering what we odd, bubbling creatures are. Leopard seals, fortunately for me, cannot survive under the fast ice. They're very aggressive, fear only orcas, and have been known to harass – and, in one instance, even kill – divers.

I peer down the steeply sloping bottom into the depths. Between my position here at the 40m diving limit and about 80m, where the dim light disappears and everything fades to black, I see an endless forest of sponges. Some look big even from this distance, and so must be huge. Remotely operated vehicles (ROVs) sent into these depths of more than 200m have brought back videos of an incredible kingdom. Giant, knobby vase sponges litter the stygian depths like the trunks of an ancient forest. Strange creatures abound, some of which have not yet even been named: 2m-long white stalks, strange purple mollusks, orange blobs on sticks.

The seafloor around Ross Island is separated into three distinct zones. Sponges and accompanying organisms rule the depths below 30m. At 30m, the sponge community abruptly gives way to bare rock and beds of frilly soft corals and orange sea anemones. Above 15m, I find only motile animals such as common red sea stars, science fiction–ugly crustaceans called giant isopods, and slimy, meter-long nemertean worms.

Most benthic ecologists believe that the cause of this zonation is the formation each spring of anchor ice, which, if anything, gives this environment an otherworldly aspect. The water in McMurdo Sound is the coldest liquid water on earth. At -1.8°C, it cannot get much colder and remain liquid. In the spring, however, the pattern of currents occasionally shifts to allow supercooled water to flow north from deep under the Ross Ice Shelf. This water is -1.9°C and, amazingly, that mere 0.1°C has a profound effect on the surrounding water. Tiny ice crystals begin to form, shimmering like a million diamonds in the faint light. On the sea bottom, ice begins to crystallize on rocks, and even on some unfortunate animals. This ice quickly grows into a maze of interlocking plates 20cm to 25cm across. Soon it covers the seafloor in the shallows, forming a glittering, brittle blanket.

On occasion, the mass of ice will grow so large that the item to which it is attached is no longer heavy enough to keep it down. Like a hot-air balloon, the ice and its cargo float up and stick to the underside of the sea ice, ultimately freezing in. When this happens to either an urchin or sea star, the animal often does not survive. It's easy to see why sponges and soft corals cannot grow in the shallow water: the anchor ice scours off any settling larvae.

I fin over this surreal coating of ice on my way back to the dive hole. For a moment it feels as though I'm in an underwater crystal cave, sandwiched top and bottom by glittering ice. It's a sight every bit as wonderful and mysterious as the sponge garden I left behind in the depths.

Jim Mastro, author of Antarctica: A Year at the Bottom of the World *(2002), has made 250 dives in Antarctic waters*

ROSS SEA

The **Crary Science and Engineering Center**, usually just called the 'Crary Lab,' is named for Albert P Crary, a geophysicist and glaciologist who was the first to visit both the North and South Poles. The 4320-sq-meter building, completed in 1991, houses work space for biological studies, earth science and atmospheric science. The equipment is state-of-the-art, with facilities as good as or better than those found at major research universities. It's a bit disconcerting to go straight from a penguin rookery to a place where scientists have digital-card keys to their offices, but then again, this is the Big City! The Crary Lab also has a darkroom, freezers for processing ice cores, an electronics workshop, a seismic observatory that monitors Mt Erebus (it's a volcano, after all), a library, and three large **aquariums** filled with local marine life. These aquariums offer the rare chance to see Antarctic undersea life without having to undergo the suffering and danger of scuba diving under the sea ice. Depending on what the biologists have collected recently, you might get to look at Antarctic krill, starfish, isopods, sea spiders or even some of the big Antarctic cod, with their unique 'anti-freeze' blood.

The Station Store, located in **Building 155**, along with dining facilities, the laundry, accommodations and the library, sells postcards, T-shirts and other souvenirs and accepts credit cards as well as US dollars. Liquor and cigarette prices are quite reasonable, at least compared to those aboard your ship, but the clerks won't sell these items to you, as that would deplete the station stock. The US Antarctic Program doesn't carry tourist mail on its ships or aircraft, so you can't send letters or postcards from McMurdo. Also, tourists may not use the station's ATMs or payphones.

Scott's *Discovery* Hut

Scott's National Antarctic Expedition built this hut in February 1902. The prefabricated building, purchased in Australia, is of a type still found in rural Australia, with a wide overhanging veranda on three sides. It was originally painted a terra-cotta color, but wind has scoured it bare. Despite the building's expense and the effort required to erect it, Scott's men never used it for accommodations, since it was difficult to heat efficiently. Instead it was used for storage, repair work and as an entertainment center, when it was called 'The Royal Terror Theatre.'

In fact, the *Discovery* Hut was used more heavily by several expeditions that followed *Discovery*. Shackleton's *Nimrod* expedition, based at Cape Royds, found it a convenient en route shelter during sledge trips to and from the Ross Ice Shelf in 1908. Scott's *Terra Nova* expedition also used it in 1911 for the same purpose.

The Ross Sea party of Shackleton's ill-fated Imperial Trans-Antarctic Expedition benefited most from the hut. Their arduous task was to lay depots for the party crossing the continent from the Weddell Sea side to use on the second half of their journey. Unfortunately, *Endurance* was crushed and sunk by the Weddell Sea ice, so the depots were never used. The Ross Sea party, meanwhile, holed up in the hut in 1915 and again in 1916. Unfortunately, the men were unaware of vast quantities of stores buried in the ice that had accumulated in the hut, and nearly starved – despite the hidden bounty lying literally underfoot. But they did find some food, cigars, Crème de Menthe, sleeping bags

ANTARCTICA DURING THE 'AGE OF REPTILES' *Dr William R Hammer*

The first Antarctic terrestrial vertebrate fossil was discovered in 1967. Since the finding of that single jaw fragment in Early Triassic age sediments (245 million years old) near the Beardmore Glacier, four different Mesozoic terrestrial vertebrate assemblages – including several species each – have been collected from Antarctica.

The Early Triassic assemblage is dominated by synapsids, an extinct group of animals that link primitive reptiles to mammals. Perhaps the best-known member of this assemblage is *Lystrosaurus*, a small herbivore also found on most of the other southern continents and in China and Russia. Its discovery in Antarctica in the early 1970s added strong support to the theory of plate tectonics.

In 1985 a vertebrate community of Middle Triassic age (235 to 240 million years old) was found near the first Early Triassic *Lystrosaurus* site in the central Transantarctic Mountains. This assemblage is dominated by larger synapsids than those from the Early Triassic and includes the wolf-sized carnivore *Cynognathus*. At least two large capitosaurids with skulls nearly a meter long also occurred in the Middle Triassic. Capitosaurs were semi-aquatic and, although they resemble very large crocodiles, are actually amphibians, distant relatives of frogs and salamanders.

The first discoveries of Antarctic dinosaurs were made during the late 1980s in Late Cretaceous (65 to 70 million years old) deposits on James Ross and Vega islands. These remains included partial skeletons of a nodosaurid ankylosaur (armored dinosaur) and a hypsilophodontid (a small herbivorous ornithopod dinosaur). A few small limb pieces have also been referred to the Theropoda (carnivorous dinosaurs). In 1998 a single tooth from a hadrosaur (duck-billed dinosaur) was collected from the same area on James Ross Island. It is the first hadrosaur found in Antarctica; others are known from South America, North America and Eurasia.

A fourth terrestrial vertebrate community was found in 1990, again near the Beardmore Glacier. This Early Jurassic (190 to 200 million years old) assemblage includes the nearly 7m-long bipedal carnivorous dinosaur, *Cryolophosaurus* ('frozen-crested reptile'). Represented by the most complete dinosaur skeleton known from Antarctica, *Cryolophosaurus* is also the only dinosaur known to be unique to the continent (the Cretaceous dinosaurs are too incomplete to determine

and a pair of long underwear. The interior of the hut is soot-blackened from the smoky blubber stove they used to try to stay warm.

Because it is the hut closest to McMurdo station and has received the most visitors (and souveniring) over the years, the *Discovery* Hut is the least interesting of the three Ross Island historic sites. The AHT estimates that 1000 people visit the hut each year. The heavy chain that once surrounded the hut, and the nearby pumping station and fuel tanks – ugly intrusions of modern-day McMurdo – were removed in 1998.

There are few artifacts in the dingy hut, which smells strongly of burnt seal blubber. Stores line the right-hand wall as you enter. The central area is occupied by a stove, piles of provisions and a sleeping platform. Much of the hut feels empty. A square hole in the floor was used for pendulum experiments. A mummified seal lies on the open southern veranda, its back covered in liquefying blubber. The hut sharply conveys the hardships endured by the early explorers.

For conservation purposes, only eight people are permitted inside the hut at a time, and only 40 people are allowed in the area of the hut at any time. Make sure you sign the visitor's book, which helps AHT maintain its records.

Vince's Cross

About 100m from the *Discovery* Hut, an oak cross stands as an enduring memorial to Able Seaman George T Vince, who fell to his death over an ice cliff into McMurdo Sound on March 11, 1902.

Observation Hill

The 3.5m cross surmounting this 230m volcanic cone was raised in memory of the five men who perished on the return from the South Pole: Henry Bowers, Edgar Evans, Laurence Oates, Robert Scott and Edward Wilson. Its fading inscription is the closing line from Tennyson's poem *Ulysses* – 'To strive, to seek, to find, and not to yield.' Erected on January 20, 1913, the cross has

whether or not they represent new genera). The Latin term 'loph' was included in the generic name *Cryolophosaurus* because of a unique bony display crest on the top of the head above the eyes. The Latin 'cryo' was included because although Antarctica wasn't frozen when the dinosaur lived there, we nearly froze to death while collecting it.

Parts of a prosauropod dinosaur were found with the skeleton of *Cryolophosaurus*. In fact, ribs of the prosauropod were in the mouth of the cryolophosaur when it died, leading to the assumption that the carnivore may have choked to death on its last meal. Prosauropods were smaller (7.5m long) predecessors to the well-known large sauropods *(Apatosaurus, Brachiosaurus)* of the later Jurassic.

After the *Cryolophosaurus* died along an Antarctic riverbank 200 million years ago, smaller carnivorous theropods scavenged the skeleton. Gnaw marks were found on some of the bones and small broken theropod teeth were collected nearby. Other members of the Jurassic fauna are represented by single elements, including a tooth from a rodentlike synapsid and the upper arm of a small pterosaur (flying reptile).

During the 2003–04 Antarctic field season, separate teams of paleontologists returned to both the James Ross Island and Mt Kirkpatrick (near the Beardmore Glacier) dinosaur localities. New discoveries were made at both sites. Fragmentary remains of a small (1.8m long) theropod dinosaur were collected on Vega Island and elements of a primitive sauropod were excavated from a new locality on Mt Kirkpatrick. Both of these specimens are currently under study.

These vertebrate assemblages suggest that Antarctic climates were relatively mild during the Mesozoic, and also that connections once existed between Antarctica and the other southern continents. Since Antarctica was part of the supercontinent Gondwana for much of the Mesozoic, it was also further north, which partially explains the milder climate. During the Triassic and Jurassic, however, the paleolatitude of the continent was still fairly high, probably between 65°S and 70°S. Although some of the larger animals may have migrated north during the winter months, the ectothermic (cold-blooded) semiaquatic amphibians would have been restricted to limited watersheds, suggesting that ice-free rivers and lakes existed all year.

Dr William R Hammer, Fritiof Fryxell professor and chair of the department of Geology at Augustana College in Rock Island, IL, discovered Cryolophosaurus with William Hickerson

been blown over by storms at least twice. At the last re-erection, in January 1994, it was placed in a concrete base.

Cape Evans

TERRA NOVA HUT

In stark contrast to the *Discovery* Hut, Scott's Hut from the *Terra Nova* expedition is filled with an incredible feeling of history. Erected in January 1911 at the place Scott named Cape Evans after his second-in-command, Edward Evans, the prefabricated hut is 14.6m long and 7.3m wide. It accommodated 25 men in fairly crowded conditions, although it is the largest of the three historic huts on Ross Island. It must have been chilly inside, despite the insulation of seaweed sewn into jute bags.

This is the real thing, what you came for, the reason you paid thousands of dollars and suffered through long days of seasickness. Here, dog skeletons bleach on the sand in the Antarctic sun and chiding memento mori of Scott's death march from the Pole. Inside the hut, unquiet ghosts glide soundlessly through memories of sledging pennants, the rustle of pony harnesses and a sighing wind. It is an absolutely amazing and also eerie feeling to stand at the head of the wardroom table and recall the famous photo of Scott's final birthday party, with the men gathered around the huge meal spread out before them, and their banners hanging behind. You definitely feel their ghostly presence! Between 700 and 800 visitors land at Cape Evans each year, making it the most frequently visited Ross Sea tourist site.

Located on what Scott called Home Beach, the hut stands close to the shore of McMurdo Sound. A long, narrow building (the latrines, with separate facilities for officers and men) stands in front of the hut.

After Scott's last expedition, 10 members of the Ross Sea party of Shackleton's Imperial Trans-Antarctic Expedition were stranded here in May 1915, when their ship *Aurora* was blown from its moorings. The men passed a very difficult 20 months before *Aurora* was able to return.

Entering the hut, you pass through an outer porch area. To the left are the stables on the hut's beachfront side. Still in the porch today are a box of penguin eggs, big piles of suppurating seal blubber, lots of shovels and implements hanging on the walls, and geologist Griffith Taylor's bicycle.

Inside the hut proper, your eyes will take a while to adjust to the half-light. Stand quietly for a moment and take it all in. You're standing in what the expedition called the mess deck. In keeping with Royal Navy practice, Scott segregated expedition members into officers and men. In the mess deck lived Edgar Evans, Crean, Keohane, Ford, Omelchenko, Gerov, Clissold, Lashly and Hooper. To the right as you enter the hut is the galley with a large stove.

Continuing further into the hut, past what was once a dividing wall made out of packing cases, you'll come to the wardroom. Straight in back is the darkroom and Ponting's bunk. To the right is the laboratory, along with Wright's and Simpson's bunks. To the left of the wardroom table from front to back of their alcove were: Bowers (top bunk) and Cherry-Garrard (bottom bunk); Oates (top bunk, with only floor space beneath); and Mears (top bunk) and Atkinson (bottom bunk). To the right of the wardroom table were (front to back): Gran (top bunk) and Taylor (bottom bunk); a small geology lab; Debenham (top bunk, with nothing beneath); and Nelson (top bunk) and Day (bottom bunk). A special note about Day's bunk: Dick Richards used it during the Ross Sea party's occupation of the hut. Look for the depressing notation he made on his bunk wall after three of the party's members had died:

> RW Richards August 14th, 1916
> Losses to date –
> Hayward
> Mack
> Smith

The back left corner of the hut is the sanctum sanctorum. Scott's bunk, to the left, is separated from the bunks of Wilson and Edward Evans by a work table covered with an open book and a fading stuffed emperor penguin.

Throughout the hut are provisions and photographic supplies. There's a strong, not unpleasant musty smell, like that of dusty old books and pony straw. Boxes hold candles that could be used today without problem. The name brands on many of the supplies

GRANT DIXON

Macquarie Island (p169)

RALPH LEE HOPKINS

Elephant Island (p182), South Shetland Islands

Abandoned Grytviken whaling station (p197), South Georgia

GRANT DIXON

Camp site, Patriot Hills (p285)

DAIVD TIPLING

JULIET COOMBE

Cruising through the Lemaire Channel (p222)

CHRIS BARTON

Ukraine's Academician Vernadskiy station (p224), Argentine Islands

DAVID TIPLING

Adélie penguins, Paulet Island (p110)

Gentoo penguin colony near British Antarctic Survey huts, Port Lockroy (p221)

CHRIS BAR

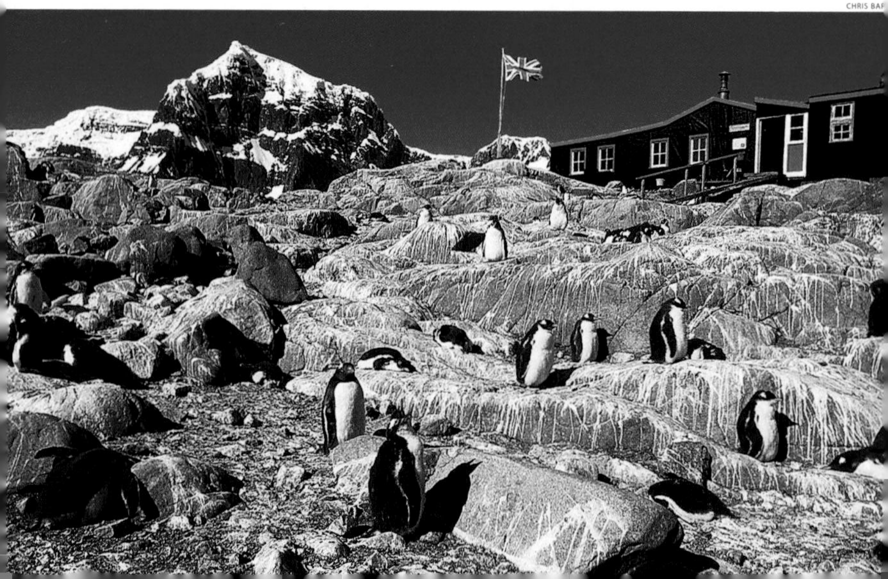

are still familiar, with label designs that are hardly changed even now. Be sure to look for the telephone, which connected this hut with the *Discovery* Hut using bare wire laid across the sea ice.

Only 12 people are permitted inside the Cape Evans hut at one time, and only 40 people are allowed ashore at once.

OTHER SITES AT CAPE EVANS

During the site's occupation by the Ross Sea party of Shackleton's Imperial Trans-Antarctic Expedition, three of the party's members perished while returning from a trip laying depots for the Weddell Sea party, which they were expecting to arrive from across the continent. The Reverend Arnold Spencer-Smith died of scurvy on March 9, 1916, and two others, Aeneas Mackintosh and Victor Hayward, vanished in a blizzard while walking on thin sea ice on May 8, 1916. The cross on **Wind Vane Hill** commemorates them. Two of *Aurora*'s **anchors** remain embedded in the sand on Home Beach, one directly in front of the hut, the other 25m north of it.

The environmental organization Greenpeace had a year-round base at Cape Evans between 1987 and 1982. It was dismantled and removed in 1991–92. A rather-difficult-to-find **Greenpeace Base Plaque** is now all that marks the site. Walk north up the beach to find it.

Cape Royds & Shackleton's Hut

Besides being the home of Shackleton's *Nimrod* expedition, Cape Royds also harbors a rookery of 4000 Adélies. Scott named the cape for *Discovery*'s meteorologist, Charles Royds. The small pond in front of the hut is called Pony Lake, because the expedition kept its ponies tethered nearby.

Shackleton erected his hut here in February 1908. Unlike the class-minded Scott, he imposed no division between officers and men at Cape Royds, although as 'The Boss' he did invoke executive privilege to give himself a private room near the hut's front door. Fifteen men lived in the hut, which is much smaller than Scott's at Cape Evans.

The feeling inside is still very ghostly, although perhaps not as eerie as Cape Evans with its lingering sense of tragedy. All of Shackleton's men, after all, left here alive. Apparently they did so in a hurry – when members of the *Terra Nova* expedition visited in 1911, they found socks hanging to dry and a meal still on the table. Members of Shackleton's Ross Sea party also stopped by, collecting tobacco and soap among other items.

Although the hut has been cleaned up since these long-ago stopovers (snow filled it during one long interval between visits), there is still a strong historical presence about the place. If you're tall, you will need to duck slightly as you step inside so you don't hit your head on the acetylene generator over the entryway. It once powered the hut's lamps.

Cape Royds is the least visited of the Ross Island historic huts. About 700 people land each year.

A freeze-dried buckwheat pancake still lies in a cast-iron skillet on top of the large stove at the back of the hut, beside a tea kettle and a cooking pot. Colored glass medicine bottles still line several shelves. One of the few surviving bunks, to the left toward the back, has its fur sleeping bag laid out on top. Many tins of food with unappetizing names such as Irish brawn (head cheese), boiled mutton, Army Rations, Aberdeen marrow fat, lunch tongue and pea powder lie on the floor next to the walls, along with still-bright red tins of Price's Motor Lubricant. The dining table, which was lifted from the floor every night to create extra space, is gone. It may have been burned by one of successive parties who ran out of fuel. A bench still piled with mitts and shoes stands on the right.

Ask your AHT guide to point out Shackleton's signature – which may or may not be his own – in his tiny bunk room. It's upside down on a packing crate marked 'Not for Voyage' that he made into a headboard for his bunk.

Outside the hut, remnants of the pony stables and the garage built for the Arrol-Johnson motorcar (Antarctica's first car) are tumbling into ruin. Pony oats spill from feed bags onto the ground. One of the car's wheels leans up against a line of provision boxes, its wooden spokes scoured by the wind. Two wooden doghouses are likewise being eroded.

On the hut's south side, the wood has weathered to a handsome bleached grey. Nail heads that were once pounded flush now stick out a centimeter or more. Boxes of rusting food tins stand against the side and back. Although rust has completely destroyed the labels, one wooden carton is literally spilling its beans.

Cables running over the hut lash it to the ground, and the AHT attached rubber sheathing to the roof in 1990 for further protection. For conservation reasons, only eight people are permitted inside at one time, and only 40 people are allowed ashore at once.

Mts Erebus & Terror

Mt Erebus, the world's most southerly active volcano, is 3794m high. Its lazily drifting plume of steam is a familiar sight in the Ross Sea region. It gives a good indication of wind speeds at altitude. Mt Erebus was first climbed in 1908 by a party from Shackleton's *Nimrod* expedition.

Modern-day visitors will understand the awe of Erebus as it was expressed by Joseph Hooker, the young botanist on Ross' expedition, in a letter written to his father in 1841:

> To see the dark cloud of smoke, tinged with flame, rising from the volcano in a perfectly unbroken column, one side jet black, the other giving back the colours of the sun, sometimes turning off at a right angle by some current of wind, and stretching many miles to leeward...was a sight so surpassing everything that can be imagined, and

ANTARCTICA'S HOT SPOTS *Dr Philip Kyle*

Beneath the icy exterior of Antarctica is a dynamic continental geologic plate. Tectonic forces are at work within the Antarctic plate, and in places the continent is slowly being torn apart by rifting, much like East Africa. As the earth's crust is extended and thinned, deep hot mantle rises and partially melts to form basaltic magma, which rises and is often stored within the crust in magma chambers. Where the magma reaches the surface, it is erupted as lava or volcanic ash and volcanoes are formed.

Active volcanoes are found today in three areas of Antarctica: the western Ross Sea, West Antarctica and along the Antarctic Peninsula. There remains a high probability that significant volcanic eruptions could occur at any time in Antarctica.

In the western Ross Sea region, most volcanism occurs on or along the front of the Transantarctic Mountains. Many small volcanic vents have been detected beneath the Ross Sea as magnetic anomalies, but none of these vents are currently active. Among a group of volcanic cones and domes called The Pleiades, high in the Transantarctic Mountains of northern Victoria Land, is a very young-looking dome, which probably erupted less than 1000 years ago. Mt Melbourne near Terra Nova Bay has steaming ground at its summit and an ash layer showing it erupted less than 200 years ago.

In Marie Byrd Land of West Antarctica, only Mt Berlin is considered active. There is also a possibility that an eruption is currently ongoing beneath the ice of the West Antarctic ice sheet. Airborne studies have shown a circular depression consistent with the melting of the ice by a volcanic vent. The presence of a volcano beneath the depression is confirmed by studies that show magnetic rocks typical of volcanoes.

In the Antarctic Peninsula region, volcanic Deception Island lies at the south end of Bransfield Strait.

Antarctica's best-known volcano is Mt Erebus on Ross Island, discovered by Ross in 1841. Ross noted in his journal that Erebus was erupting, '...emitting flame and smoke in great profusion... some of the officers believed they could see streams of lava pouring down its sides until lost beneath the snow.' Erebus is one of the largest volcanoes in the world, ranking among the top 20 in size.

Erebus has many unusual features, the most notable being a permanent convecting lake of molten magma with a temperature of 1000°C. In late 2003 the lake was 50m in diameter. The magma, which is very rich in sodium and potassium, is called phonolite. This name comes from the German and refers to rocks that ring like a bell when hit. Unique to Erebus is the occurrence of large crystals in the magma. They can exceed 10cm in length and take many different forms.

so heightened by the consciousness that we had penetrated into regions far beyond what was ever deemed practicable, that it really caused a feeling of awe to steal over us at the consideration of our own comparative insignificance and helplessness, and at the same time, an indescribable feeling of the greatness of the Creator in the works of His hand.

A geological curiosity, Erebus emits about 80g of metallic gold crystals each day. It is also one of only a handful of volcanoes in the world with a permanent convecting-lava lake; the others include the Erta Ale volcano in Ethiopia and the Nyiragongo volcano in Congo. Researchers recently developed a DNA-testing technique that promises to reduce crime-solving delays by using an enzyme from a microorganism found at a volcanic vent on Erebus.

In the area near Erebus' summit crater, the atmosphere's acrid mix of hydrochloric and hydrofluoric acids and sulfur dioxide caused volcanologists to give it the nickname 'Nausea Knob.'

Mt Erebus is infamous as the site of Antarctica's worst air tragedy. All 257 people aboard Air New Zealand Flight 901 were killed when their DC-10 slammed into Mt Erebus on November 28, 1979. The Antarctic Treaty members have declared the crash site a tomb. One edge of the crash site is marked by a stainless-steel cross, where memorial services are held.

Easily eroded out from the soft glassy matrix of volcanic bombs erupted from the volcano, the crystals litter the upper crater rim like a carpet. They are of a mineral type called feldspar and belong to the anorthoclase variety. The anorthoclase is spectacular, and among the most perfect and largest crystals found in volcanic rocks anywhere on earth.

Small eruptions were common from Erebus' magma lake, occurring six to 10 times daily during the mid-1980s and 1990s. Eruptive activity has declined since 2000 and eruptions are rare. The eruptions are referred to as Strombolian eruptions, after the volcano Stromboli near Sicily. Only rarely since 1984 have bombs been ejected from the 600m-diameter crater.

However, beginning in September 1984, a four-month episode of more violent eruptions showered bombs more than 3km from the vent inside the crater. Scientists had to abandon a small research facility near the crater rim while volcanic bombs – some as big as cars – rained down around the summit crater, forcing the scientists to keep their distance. The bombs whistled as they fell, but the most memorable part of the eruption was the sound of the sharp explosions that threw the bombs from the volcanic vent. (Upon landing, the bombs crackle as they cool. The interior of the bombs can be very hot, and if you break one open, you can pull the plastic hot lava out like taffy candy.)

Today a network of about a dozen seismic stations (which have continuous GPS, microphones and meteorological sensors) monitors Erebus, recording its small explosions and the earthquakes within its bowels. Since 2000 the seismometers have recorded tremor events generated by collisions between huge icebergs that broke from the Ross Ice Shelf. The seismometers should allow scientists to predict the next episode of eruptions. While there's no evidence in the geologic record of huge eruptions of the magnitude of the 1980 eruption at Mt St Helens in the US, the presence of volcanic ash from Erebus in blue ice near the Transantarctic Mountains several hundred kilometers from the volcano attests to its potential for larger eruptions.

Erebus' summit features beautiful fumarolic ice towers. From sea level these can be observed with binoculars on the upper summit plateau of the volcano. The ice towers represent places where heated gases, rich in water, vent to the surface along fractures. When the gas reaches the cold air, the water freezes and forms bizarre shapes of varying size. Beneath the ice towers it is common to find tunnels and caves melted into the underlying snow and ice. These ice caves are warm and steamy and in some cases feel like a sauna. Access to the cave system can be difficult and may require an abseil (a rappel) of more than 20m. During the summer, when the sun dips toward the horizon around midnight, the ice towers look spectacular, as steam slowly ascends through the hollow towers and vents out the top.

Dr Philip Kyle, a professor of geochemistry at the New Mexico Institute of Mining and Technology, has spent 32 field seasons in Antarctica and returns yearly to Mt Erebus to monitor its activity

Mt Terror (3230m) is an extinct volcano, which is separated from Mt Erebus by Mt Terra Nova.

Cape Crozier

Site of the first emperor penguin rookery ever discovered (by Scott in 1902), Cape Crozier is named for Commander Francis Crozier, captain of *Terror*, one of the two ships on Ross' expedition, which first sighted the cape.

Cape Crozier is inextricably linked with the infamous 36-day, 105-km midwinter trek to Cape Crozier made by three members of Scott's *Terra Nova* expedition in the winter of 1911, eloquently chronicled by one of them, Apsley Cherry-Garrard, in his classic *The Worst Journey in the World* (1922). With Edward Wilson and 'Birdie' Bowers, he braved 24-hour darkness and temperatures as low as -59°C – so cold that the men's teeth cracked in their mouths and they began 'to think of death as a friend,' as Cherry-Garrard wrote – all so that they could be the first to collect emperor penguin embryos.

Besides the emperors incubating their eggs on the sea ice, Cape Crozier is home to 300,000 Adélies.

ROSS ICE SHELF

Covering 520,000 sq km – an area roughly the size of France – the Ross Ice Shelf was discovered on January 28, 1841 by Ross, who called it the Victoria Barrier in honor of Queen Victoria. Since then it has been called many things, namely the Barrier, the Great Barrier, the Great Ice Barrier, the Great Southern Barrier, the Ice Barrier, the Icy Barrier, the Ross Barrier, the Ross Ice Barrier and, these days, the Ross Ice Shelf.

Its mean ice thickness is 335m to 700m, but where glaciers and ice streams meet it, the shelf is up to 1000m thick. At the ice front facing the Ross Sea, it's less than 100m thick. It is rather hard to believe, but the whole ice shelf is actually *floating*.

It moves as fast as 1100m per year, and calves an estimated 150 cu km of icebergs annually, out of its total of 23,000 cu km of ice. In 1987, a berg measuring 155km by 35km calved from the eastern side.

Another giant iceberg, code-named B-15, calved from the Ross Ice Shelf in March 2000. Measuring 298km by 37km and covering an area of some 11,000 sq km, it was the largest iceberg ever recorded. Although an iceberg sighted by USS *Glacier* in 1956 was reported to be 335km by 97km and cover nearly 32,500 sq km, researchers now believe these measurements were incorrect and that the berg was far smaller.

Scientists regard the calving of gigantic bergs as part of a normal process in which the ice sheet maintains a balance between constant growth outward from the continent and periodic loss by icebergs breaking off.

The Ross Ice Shelf has inspired many awe-struck responses. The blacksmith aboard *Erebus* in 1841 was uncharacteristically moved to write a couplet:

> Awful and sublime, magnificent and rare
> No other Earthly object with the Barrier can compare.

Ross himself wrote in 1847, six years after discovering it:

> this extraordinary barrier of ice, of probably more than a thousand feet

ICEBERG NAMES

Large icebergs – those at least 10 nautical miles (18.5km) long – are given code names that sound like those used for military aircraft: C-16, B-15A, and so on. The codes derive from the quadrant of Antarctica where the icebergs were originally sighted – often by satellite. 'A' designates the area from 0°–90°W (Bellingshausen/Weddell Seas), 'B' the area from 90°W–180° (Amundsen/eastern Ross Seas), 'C' the area from 180°–90°E (western Ross Sea/Wilkes Land), and 'D' the area from 90°E–0° (Amery Ice Shelf/eastern Weddell Sea).

After an iceberg is sighted, the US National Ice Center assigns a quadrant letter and a number based on its point of origin. C-16, for example, is the 16th iceberg tracked by the center in quadrant C since it began tracking big bergs in 1976. Large icebergs are tracked even after they split, and continue to be watched until the pieces are too small to be seen by satellite. Such pieces get a suffix letter after their original name, so B-15A is the first fragment to calve from iceberg B-15.

> in thickness, crushes the undulations of the waves, and disregards their violence: it is a mighty and wonderful object, far beyond anything we could have thought or conceived.

Roald Amundsen saw it in 1911:

> At 2:30pm we came in sight of the Great Ice Barrier. Slowly it rose up out of the sea until we were face to face with it in all its imposing majesty. It is difficult with the help of the pen to give any idea of the impression this mighty wall of ice makes on the observer who is confronted with it for the first time. It is altogether a thing which can hardly be described...

Louis Bernacchi, the Australian physicist on Borchgrevink's *Southern Cross* expedition, climbed to the top of the shelf in 1900 with William Colbeck, the British surveyor. 'Nothing was visible,' Bernacchi later wrote, 'but the great ice cap stretching away for hundreds of miles to the south and west. Unless one has actually seen it, it is impossible to conceive the stupendous extent of this ice cap, its consistency, utter barrenness, and stillness, which sends an indefinable sense of dread to the heart.'

Borchgrevink himself found the shelf to be much smaller than it appeared when Ross discovered it. In fact, at a place located at about 164°W (Scott later called it 'Discovery Inlet,' after his ship), the ice shelf was only 4.5m above the water. In 1900, Borchgrevink landed stores, sledges and dogs here. With two members of his expedition, William Colbeck and Per Savio, he trekked to 78°50'S, at the time the furthest south ever reached.

Roosevelt Island, 130km long and 65km wide, is completely covered by ice and is identifiable mainly by a central ridge of ice 550m above sea level. The island, of which the northernmost point is just 5km south of the Bay of Whales, was discovered by Byrd in 1934 and named for Franklin D Roosevelt, then president of the US.

East Antarctica

CONTENTS

Sometimes called Antarctica's 'far side' thanks to its isolation and the long voyages required to reach it, East Antarctica has been all but untouched by tourists until recently. Even now, however, no one would call it crowded: at most, one or two tourist ships visit each year!

East Antarctica is the Far South, where you'll see huge tabular icebergs, emperor penguin rookeries – and nobody else. Just a handful of stations are spread out along thousands of kilometers of coastline, and some are now abandoned – heavy pack ice made them too difficult to resupply regularly, even with icebreakers.

A high plateau covered by a vast, thick ice sheet, nearly all of East Antarctica lies in the eastern hemisphere, divided from West Antarctica by the Transantarctic Mountains. Although it's sometimes called Greater Antarctica, since it's the larger half of the continent, the name East Antarctica, coined by Antarctic historian Edwin S Balch in 1904, is preferred.

East Antarctica's interior, although rarely if ever seen by tourists, is home to two important inland research stations: Russia's Vostok, the coldest place on earth, and the new joint French-Italian Concordia station.

HIGHLIGHTS

- Marveling at **emperor penguins** (p264) brooding their chicks in one of the numerous rookeries on this icebound coast
- Wandering through an Antarctic 'ghost town' at one of the abandoned Russian bases, **Leningradskaya** (p257) or **Molodezhnaya** (p261)
- Visiting **Commonwealth Bay** (p265), Mawson's 'Home of the Blizzard' and site of his historic hut
- Seeing the innovative and environmentally responsible **wind turbines** (p261) at Australia's Mawson station
- Cruising past **Scullin Monolith** (p262), home of the continent's highest concentration of breeding Antarctic petrels

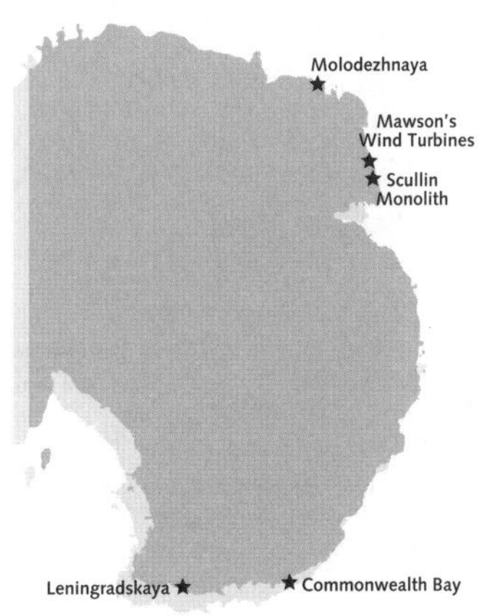

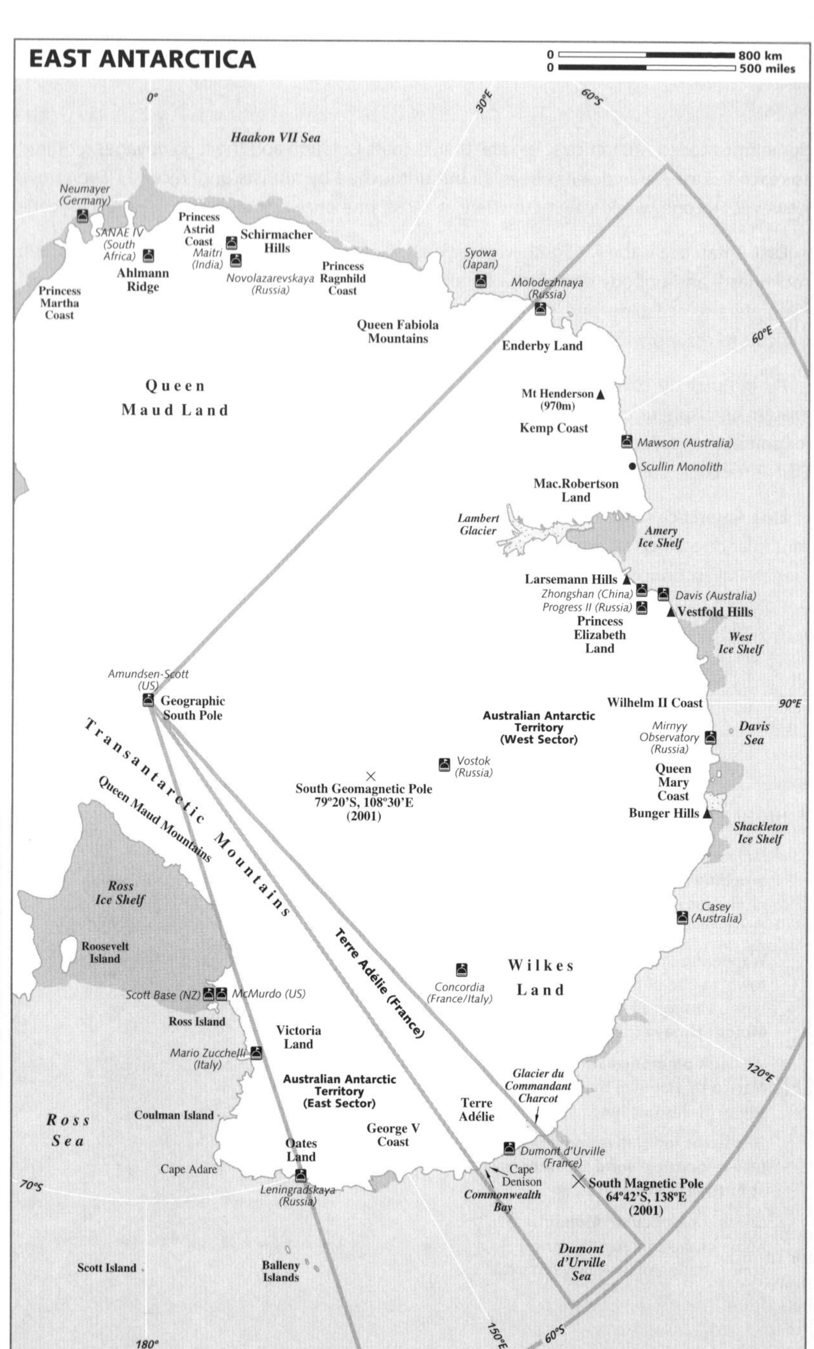
EAST ANTARCTICA
0 800 km
0 500 miles
0°
30°E
60°S
Haakon VII Sea
Neumayer (Germany)
SANAE IV (South Africa)
Princess Astrid Coast
Schirmacher Hills
Maitri (India)
Novolazarevskaya (Russia)
Princess Ragnhild Coast
Ahlmann Ridge
Princess Martha Coast
Syowa (Japan)
Molodezhnaya (Russia)
Queen Fabiola Mountains
Enderby Land
60°E
Queen Maud Land
Mt Henderson (970m)
Kemp Coast
Mawson (Australia)
Scullin Monolith
Mac.Robertson Land
Lambert Glacier
Amery Ice Shelf
Larsemann Hills
Zhongshan (China)
Davis (Australia)
Progress II (Russia)
Vestfold Hills
Princess Elizabeth Land
West Ice Shelf
Amundsen-Scott (US)
Geographic South Pole
Wilhelm II Coast
90°E
Australian Antarctic Territory (West Sector)
Mirnyy Observatory (Russia)
Davis Sea
Vostok (Russia)
South Geomagnetic Pole 79°20'S, 108°30'E (2001)
Queen Mary Coast
Bunger Hills
Shackleton Ice Shelf
Transantarctic Mountains
Queen Maud Mountains
Ross Ice Shelf
Roosevelt Island
Casey (Australia)
Terre Adélie (France)
Wilkes Land
Concordia (France/Italy)
Scott Base (NZ)
McMurdo (US)
Ross Island
Victoria Land
Mario Zucchelli (Italy)
120°E
Glacier du Commandant Charcot
Australian Antarctic Territory (East Sector)
Terre Adélie
Ross Sea
Coulman Island
George V Coast
Oates Land
Dumont d'Urville (France)
Cape Adare
Cape Denison
70°S
Leningradskaya (Russia)
Commonwealth Bay
South Magnetic Pole 64°42'S, 138°E (2001)
Dumont d'Urville Sea
Scott Island
Balleny Islands
180°
150°E
60°S

Orientation

East Antarctica includes regions claimed by Norway, Australia and France. Much of the Norwegian claim (called Dronning Maud Land and extending from 20°W to 45°E) was explored by Norwegian whalers. During the 1930–31 whaling season alone, about 265 whaling ships, most of them Norwegian, worked the Southern Ocean in the area between 20°W to 50°E. Although exploration was only their second line of work, these whalers discovered much of the Dronning (Queen) Maud Land coast, naming sections for members of the Norwegian royal family, including Kronprinsesse Martha Kyst (Crown Princess Martha Coast), Prinsesse Astrid Kyst (Princess Astrid Coast) and Prinsesse Ragnhild Kyst (Princess Ragnhild Coast).

Australia's claim, which is called the Australian Antarctic Territory, or AAT, extends from 45°E to 160°E, apart from the thin slice of France's Terre Adélie. Australians including Douglas Mawson, George Hubert Wilkins and Phillip G Law explored much of this area. Reflecting its numerous other discoverers, the region includes Enderby Land, Kemp Coast, Mac.Robertson Land, Princess Elizabeth Land, Wilhelm II Coast, Queen Mary Coast, Wilkes Land and George V Coast.

Terre Adélie, France's Antarctic claim, extends from 136°E to 142°E and is wholly within Australia's claim. This section of the coast is distinguished by its French names, including Cap Bienvenue, Glacier du Commandant Charcot and Glacier du Français.

Tourists rarely visit East Antarctica because of the difficulty of getting to the region. In some years, it goes entirely unvisited by tourist vessels. For further information on cruise operators, see p296.

LENINGRADSKAYA STATION

Perched atop the 304m Leningradsky nunatak behind a 220m seacliff, Leningradskaya opened its doors in 1971. Resupplying the station was always difficult, however, because of the heavy pack ice off the coast, and even icebreakers were sometimes trapped for months. The station closed in 1992. The first tourists to Leningradskaya visited by helicopter only in February 2002 – perhaps the first people to call in on the station since it closed.

NEUMAYER STATION

With only its wind-powered generators poking above the surface of the snow, ultramodern Neumayer appears at first glance to be a modest station. But buried 3m beneath the snow surface of the 200m-thick Ekström Ice Shelf are two parallel galvanized-steel tubes, each 90m long and 8.4m in diameter, connected by two transverse tubes. Inside are shipping containers outfitted as living quarters, a kitchen, a hospital, labs and workshops. About 22 people can be accommodated in the sub-ice station and another 36 during the summer in above-ice huts. Nine people generally winterover.

The first Georg von Neumayer station was built in 1981 and named after one of the promoters of the First International Polar Year in 1882–83. After it was buried by drifting snow, this replacement was completed about 10km away in 1992.

In December 1990 the first all-female group to winter in Antarctica staffed Neumayer. Two meteorologists, two geophysicists, two engineers, a radio operator, a cook, and a doctor who also served as the station's leader, spent 14 months on The Ice, including nine months in complete isolation.

SANAE IV

SANAE stands for South African National Antarctic Expedition. The first SANAE base was occupied in 1959, when Norway handed it over to South Africa after deciding its work was finished there. Since then, there have also been SANAE II and SANAE III bases. The latter, closed for wintering in 1994, had over the years been buried by 14m of drifting snow on the surface of the Fimbul Ice Shelf, on which it was built. It became unsafe, as the snow was crushing it.

SANAE IV is located on a nunatak at **Vesleskarvet** (Norwegian for 'little barren mountain') on the Ahlmann Ridge, 170km from the coast. Hence the station's nickname of 'Vesles.'

Built from 1993 to 1997 at a cost of R64 million, SANAE IV is one of Antarctica's most modern stations – it includes an enclosed helicopter pad and a handicapped-accessible bathroom. Consisting of three linked double-story units totaling 176m in length, the entire station is built on stilts 4m above the rock surface. Occupied by its first wintering team in 1997, the station

THEY COME FROM OUTTA SPACE *Dr Ralph P Harvey*

One special night in 1969, the world watched with amazement as humanity planted its first steps on the moon, changing forever the point from which we view our planet. I was one of those viewers, and as an eight-year-old, was filled with visions of a future exploring the planets, piloting spacecraft and fighting ferocious aliens.

On a cold summer's day six months later, something nearly as momentous occurred, this time witnessed by only a few Japanese glaciologists. They discovered the first concentration of Antarctic meteorites, nine specimens in all, near the Queen Fabiola Mountains in East Antarctica. They had no idea their discovery would prove as important as the Apollo program in opening doors to the exploration of our solar system. Their discovery evolved into a collection of more than 25,000 specimens – our only current and continuous source of macroscopic extraterrestrial materials. While the Apollo program ended just three years later, the Antarctic search for meteorites continued to grow and thrive. In the end, I did end up exploring other planets – by going to one of the most otherworldly places on earth, searching for rocks from outer space.

There are two principal reasons Antarctica is the world's best place to look for meteorites. First, if you want to find objects that fall from the sky, simply spread out a giant white sheet and see what lands on it. Indeed, almost any rock you find on the East Antarctic ice sheet had to fall there. Second, there's a more subtle and dynamic mechanism concentrating meteorites in Antarctica. Meteorites falling randomly across the ice sheet get buried and travel with it as it flows out toward the Antarctic coast. The vast majority of these imbedded meteorites are lost to the Southern Ocean as the ice sheet calves icebergs. But in a few places, particularly where the ice sheet tries to squeeze through the Transantarctic Mountains, the flow of the ice can be dramatically slowed or stopped. If that happens where the ice is also exposed to the fierce winds of the plateau, massive amounts of ice sublimate, or change directly from solid to vapor. Where sublimation is strong, the loss of ice can be as much as several centimeters per day, producing beautiful deep-blue expanses of old glacial ice. Littered across this ice are meteorites, left behind because they can't evaporate. If we're really lucky, we find a place where this process has gone on for hundreds of thousands of years or more, allowing the meteorites to pile up until there are hundreds in an area the size of a football field.

Who cares? Why recover meteorites from anywhere, let alone Antarctica? Meteorites are rare scientific specimens – and outside of Antarctica, only a few are recovered each year. With the exception of a few lunar specimens, meteorites are the only samples we have of the extraterrestrial materials making up our solar system. Some represent the primitive building blocks from which our solar system formed, and are essentially unchanged since its birth 4.56 billion years ago. Others represent fragments of small planetary bodies broken up by impacts, providing samples from their deep interior. Still others are samples of intermediate planetoids with active and alien geological processes. A very small set of meteorites are pieces of the moon and Mars, knocked loose by giant impacts and sent on a collision course with earth. Among these is the

accommodates about 10 people in winter and 80 in summer.

Tractor trains unloading from ships at the ice shelf's edge resupply SANAE. In 2000 the station lost six large 8.5-tonne fuel tanks after the calving of the section of the ice shelf on which they stood. Fortunately, they were empty at the time.

Controversy over the coloring of SANAE erupted in 2001. The station was blue on the bottom to absorb solar energy and help keep the area beneath it snow free, and the roof was orange for visibility from the air. Because these colors, along with the white sides of the station, were the colors of the apartheid-era South African flag, politicians demanded change. But since the colors were impregnated into the fiberglass panels during their manufacture, only the blue section was covered with red paint (which will require periodic repainting as wind-driven snow scours it away).

SCHIRMACHER HILLS

Much of this narrow strip of land, 17km long and 3km wide, is ice free year-round, earning it the name 'oasis.' Dotted with as many as 180 lakes and ponds, the terrain

now-famous ALH84001 meteorite, a Martian sample within which some NASA researchers have suggested may be traces of ancient biological activity on Mars.

The most consistent Antarctic meteorite recovery program has been ANSMET (Antarctic Search for Meteorites), whose annual expeditions, with support from the US National Science Foundation, have recovered nearly 15,000 specimens since 1976. Other nations, particularly Japan, Italy and China, support the active recovery of Antarctic meteorites. Like all Antarctic specimens, meteorites are collected only for scientific purposes and are protected by the Antarctic Treaty.

The life of a meteorite hunter is scenic, cold and a little lonely. There is no trash at the camp site, no bugs, no rain. We camp near blue ice areas on the margins of the high-altitude polar plateau, sometimes with little to see but ice and snow in all directions. Many of these areas are literally off the map, and we give them colorful, unofficial names such as Footrot Flats and Mare Meteoriticus. We make our homes in double-walled Scott tents and depend on the 24 hours a day of sunshine to keep warm in temperatures as low as -40°C and winds that can blow at 60km/h for weeks. For most volunteers, however, tolerating these conditions is a modest price to pay for the privilege of being the first to see a visitor from space.

If the blue ice we search is far enough out on the ice sheet, terrestrial rock that may camouflage our prey is limited, and we can cruise slowly across the ice on snowmobiles and spot even the smallest speck. At other sites closer to the Transantarctic Mountains, glacial moraines or fierce winds may carry in some earth rocks, so we end up walking or even crawling on hands and knees, sorting out the meteorites from what we call the 'meteorongs' and 'leaveorite' (leave 'er right there) specimens.

The quarries we hunt are rarely as glamorous or beautiful as the meteorites you see in museums. The average find is about 10g and smaller than a golf ball. They range from unweathered specimens still dressed in the formal, glossy-black fusion crust they acquired during their fiery plunge through the earth's atmosphere to crumbling, rusty-grey fragments nearly indistinguishable from road gravel. To the meteorite hunter, of course, all meteorites are beautiful. But it's too hard to stay warm, and there are too many specimens for sentimentality, so they get mundane names such as EET96538. In a typical season we recover between a few hundred and a thousand specimens, each one bagged quickly, cleanly and efficiently with Teflon tongs to avoid human contamination (and frozen fingers).

At the end of a six-week season, we've recovered a suite of meteorites representing the rocky fragments our planet has swept up from space. The specimens are shipped, still frozen, to the Johnson Space Center (JSC) in Houston, Texas, for initial characterization and curation. Scientists knock off a few chips, looking for minerals or textures that help define the kind of meteorite it is, and write up an initial description of the sample. Twice a year, the JSC lab issues the *Antarctic Meteorite* newsletter, detailing recently recovered specimens and offering samples to interested researchers around the globe. Sharing the 'treasure' this way has made ANSMET expeditions a unique example of cooperation in science, worthy of the international spirit shown by so many Antarctic endeavors.

Dr Ralph P Harvey has spent 14 summers in Antarctica as the principal investigator of the Antarctic Search for Meteorites program (http://geology.cwru.edu/~ansmet/)

is hillocky with a maximum elevation of 228m. The hills were discovered by a secret Nazi Antarctic expedition in 1938–39 led by Alfred Ritscher, who was dispatched to claim Antarctic territory for Germany. The hills are named for Richardheinrich Schirmacher, who flew one of the expedition's seaplanes, and are home to two research stations.

NOVOLAZAREVSKAYA STATION

Located at the southeastern tip of the Schirmacher oasis, Russia's Novolazarevskaya station, opened in 1961, is named for Mikhail Petrovich Lazarev, second-in-command of Bellingshausen's expedition and captain of *Mirnyy*.

Soviet/Russian activity in the area dates to the establishment of the Lazarev base in 1958, and the current station replaced the old Novolazarevskaya in 1979. 'Novo' can accommodate about 57 winterers and 60 summer personnel, but far fewer people live here now. A 1200m ice-sheet runway for ski and wheeled aircraft is 15km south of the station. The station is 80km from the Lazarev Sea coast but only 4.5km east of Maitri.

MAITRI STATION

India's first Antarctic base, Dakshin Gangotri, was initially established as a refuge hut in January 1982. In 1984 another Gangotri was constructed further inland, in the Schirmacher Hills, and the first group wintered over there. Maitri (Hindi for 'friendship') was built on adjustable telescopic legs at a site 80km inland in 1989. It replaces Gangotri, which was becoming buried in ice and is now used as a supply base, transit camp and storage area for ice cores. Maitri's winter and summer complement is 26 and 65, respectively. A bust of Mahatma Gandhi was installed in 1997.

SYOWA STATION

A collection of about 50 brightly colored structures, Japan's Syowa station was established in 1956–57, and has been used continuously since then except for a four-year period from 1962–65. It's built on the northern half of East Ongul Island, 4km off the mainland coast.

Syowa's main building, built in 1992, is a four-story structure topped by a domed skylight. With a winter complement of 31 people, Syowa station has adopted the admirable practice of using grey water from dishwashing and showers for the station toilets, making for low water consumption.

The season after Syowa was built, its first wintering crew was flown by small plane to the relief ship *Soya*, which could not approach the station closer than 100km because of heavy pack ice. Helicopters ferried people and equipment to the ship, but when the last plane flew off the station on February 11, 1958, severe weather prevented it from returning to Syowa from the ship with the new wintering crew.

Tragically, the station's 15 sled dogs had been chained up and given a small amount of food while they awaited the arrival of the new station members. Although the ship waited for weeks to try to fly the men ashore, it was impossible to reach the station. Even the US icebreaker *Burton Island*, called in to assist, was unable to help. With winter approaching, the possibility that *Soya* could become beset was a real danger, so the station relief effort was reluctantly abandoned and the dogs left to fend for themselves.

When the next station team returned in January 1959, two dogs – Taro and Jiro – were found alive. Since neither penguins nor seals remain ashore in the Syowa region over the winter, it is unknown how the dogs managed to survive. Even the possibility that they ate some of their dead fellows does not explain the feat, since seven dogs were found still chained up, untouched.

For their amazing feat of survival, Taro and Jiro became famous in Japan. Although Jiro died at Syowa station the following year, Taro was returned to Japan in 1961, where he lived another nine years at the University of Hokkaido and received thousands of visitors each week. A film made about the canine pair, Koreyoshi Kurahara's *Antarctica*, was Japan's biggest movie in 1984 – and probably the most moving of all the Antarctic films. (Thanks to Baden Norris, former curator of Antarctic history at the Canterbury Museum in Christchurch, for this information.)

SELF-APPENDECTOMY

Antarctica's most celebrated surgical feat took place at Novolazarevskaya station in 1961. Leonid I Rogozov, a physician on the Sixth Soviet Antarctic Expedition, successfully removed his own appendix in an operation that lasted one hour and 45 minutes. Dr Rogozov had first noticed the symptoms of acute appendicitis the day before: weakness, nausea, fever and pain in his right lower abdomen. No nearby Antarctic station had an aircraft, and poor weather would have prevented a flight anyway. The next day, his fever increased. 'An immediate operation was necessary to save the patient's life,' he wrote later in *Information Bulletin of the Soviet Antarctic Expedition*. 'The only solution was to operate on myself.' Half-reclining in bed with his weight on his left hip, the doctor anesthetized his abdomen with Novocaine and made a 12cm incision. Using a mirror held by one of his two assistants – and sometimes working entirely by feel, he excised the diseased appendix and placed antibiotics into his abdomen. 'General weakness became severe after 30 to 40 minutes, and vertigo developed, so that short pauses for rest were necessary,' he wrote. Nevertheless, he concluded the surgery at midnight. A week later, the wound had completely healed.

In 1979 from January 28 to February 3, the first live TV transmission from Antarctica was broadcast from Syowa to Tokyo.

One part of the research done at Syowa in recent years is a study of microclimates in Antarctic moss beds. In 1996 Japanese scientists were startled to find a 20cm-high flowering plant growing in a rock fissure about 25km south of Syowa, creating concern that global warming might be behind the plant's ability to thrive. Also nearby is **Yukidori Valley**, named for the large numbers of snow petrels which nest in the area. The valley is protected by the Antarctic Treaty.

MOLODEZHNAYA STATION

Once the summer home to as many as 400 residents, Molodezhnaya is now deserted. Established in 1962 and formerly the premier Russian station in Antarctica, 'Molo' closed in 1999 due to Russia's precarious financial situation. The station gets its name from the *molodezh*, or young people, who helped build it. Two small Adélie penguin rookeries are nearby, and in a lonesome cemetery about 6km east of 'Molo,' the caskets are covered by steel vaults, which are themselves covered with rocks to secure them against the high winds.

MAWSON STATION

The oldest continuously occupied station south of the Antarctic Circle, Australia's Mawson station was established in 1954 on the southeastern shore of Horseshoe Harbour. Named after Douglas Mawson, it is approached through **Iceberg Alley**, a channel lined with huge tabular bergs that have run aground on underwater banks. **Horseshoe Harbour** is the best natural harbor for thousands of kilometers, a 90m-deep anchorage protected by two projecting arms of land.

Mawson accommodates as many as 70 people, but usually there are fewer than 50 during the summer and about 20 in winter.

Visitors to Mawson immediately notice two prominent features of its skyline: the 970m peaks of the nunatak **Mt Henderson** sticking out of the ice sheet 10km southeast and the 34m-tall **wind turbines**. These off-white windmills are by far the most ambitious alternative-energy project anywhere in Antarctica, and Mawson is the perfect place for them, since the average monthly windspeed is 72km/h at the elevation of the turbine hubs, with gusts well above 180km/h. The turbines are designed to withstand 260km/h winds. You may hear a 'whoosh' sound when you're within 150m of the turbines, but if it's windy, the sound of the wind is louder than the turbines. The first two turbines were commissioned in 2003; a third is due to be installed in 2006. When the wind blows, the turbines supply up to 80% of the station's energy needs.

Mawson's high-latitude location makes it a good place for studying cosmic rays. This research is done in an underground vault in solid rock, 20m below the surface. The station was also the principal home of Australia's much-loved Antarctic huskies, before the Antarctic Treaty's Protocol on Environmental Protection forced their removal (see p88). Many of the dogs were transferred to northern Minnesota in the US, while the oldest were taken by expeditioners back to Australia as pets.

As with Australia's other two Antarctic stations, a massive construction program modernized Mawson in the 1990s. Each structure is color-coded and vividly visible against the white Antarctic snow. The large building containing the living quarters at Mawson, like its counterpart at Casey, is known as the 'Red Shed.'

One of the few surviving buildings from 'old' Mawson is the small wooden **Weddell hut**, the second building built at the station. It was originally erected at Heard Island but later moved here. Attached to its ceiling are 92 pinups cut out of American magazines between 1972 and 1988 by station members. The small gallery is irreverently known as 'the Sistine Ceiling.'

The small **cemetery** contains the graves of men who died in 1963, 1972 and 1974.

The longest golf drive on earth (the lunar golf drive record is longer) was made at Mawson in 1956, when Norwegian dogsled driver Nils Lied whacked a black-painted golf ball 4km across new and extremely smooth sea ice. 'For once, I made a good hit,' Lied later told Tim Bowden, author of *Antarctica and Back in Sixty Days* (1991). 'It was a beauty!...So we saddled up Oscar, my lead dog, with a sledge behind him. We knew if any dog could sniff the ball out, Oscar would. And he did.'

COLORED & STRIPED ICEBERGS *Dr Collin Roesler*

Every once in a great while, visitors to Antarctica – particularly East Antarctica – are shown a rare and exceptional wonder: a green iceberg. As many as 10% of all icebergs from this region may be green, but they are only rarely seen.

Pure ice is blue in color because it absorbs red light most efficiently, green light less efficiently and blue light minimally. When sunlight, which is white, shines upon pure ice, only the blue light is reflected back to your eye as the other wavelengths are absorbed. Glacial ice ranges in color from white to milky blue because air bubbles trapped in the ice scatter white light very efficiently. Thus all colors of light are reflected to your eye before they have a chance to be absorbed by the ice. The more bubbles the ice contains, the whiter it appears; the fewer bubbles, the bluer it appears.

Until recently, however, scientists couldn't satisfactorily explain what causes the beautiful jade or bottle-green icebergs. We have now learned that icebergs can be blue or green for the same reason seawater can be blue or green: both contain organic material from the degradation of marine plants and animals. This organic material absorbs blue light very efficiently, green light less so and red light only minimally. When this organic material is frozen into ice, blue light is absorbed by the organic material, red light is absorbed by the ice, and only green wavelengths of light are left over to be reflected to our eyes. The more organic material, the greener the ice or the seawater.

How does this organic material become trapped in the ice? Under very special conditions – found primarily in East Antarctica – the organic material in seawater can become frozen into icebergs. The story begins high on the Antarctic continent where thousands of years worth of snowfall is compressed into ice. This ice flows toward the sea as glaciers. Upon reaching the sea, the glaciers float and are called ice shelves. Because the density of glacial ice, with all of its air bubbles, is less than that of water, approximately 90% of the ice shelf is underwater and only 10% is visible to us.

That nine-to-one ratio of ice underwater to ice above water means that some of the underwater ice is at great depth. In the case of the Amery Ice Shelf – a source of green icebergs – the ice

SCULLIN MONOLITH

Scullin Monolith, 180km east of Mawson, is known for its remarkable bird life, with the continent's highest concentration of breeding Antarctic petrels (157,000 pairs) and an extensive Adélie penguin rookery. Mawson, who discovered it in 1931, named the crescent-shaped monolith for Australian Prime Minister James H Scullin. At about the same time, a group of Norwegian whalers named the feature for Norwegian whaling captain Klarius Mikkelsen. As the result of a later compromise, the highest point measuring 420m on Scullin Monolith is known as Mikkelsen Peak.

AMERY ICE SHELF

The Amery Ice Shelf is the seaward extension of the **Lambert Glacier** (which someday soon will need to be renamed as a glacier tongue, since it was recently found to be afloat for much of its length, and glaciers do not float). Up to 65km wide and 400km long, the Lambert drains about 8% of the Antarctic ice sheet out into Prydz Bay. Named in 1957 for Bruce Lambert, Australia's director of National Mapping, it was originally called Baker Three Glacier for the photo reconnaissance aircrew that discovered it during Operation Highjump in 1946–47. The Amery Ice Shelf is a source of the rare and beautiful jade-green icebergs (see the boxed text above).

LARSEMANN HILLS

The Larsemann Hills, 11 rocky peninsulas discovered by Norwegian Captain Klarius Mikkelsen in 1935, are an ice-free oasis extending 15km from the Dålk Glacier. Mikkelsen named the hills after young Lars Jr, son of expedition organizer Lars Christensen. The Larsemanns, which reach a maximum elevation of 160m, contain about 200 lakes, including some with water that is among the freshest in the world.

China's year-round **Zhongshan station** was founded in 1989 and accommodates about 22 people in winter. A quiet room in Zhongshan features a bust of Sun Yat-sen, first president of the Chinese republic, for whom the station is named. The station's most colorful

shelf's cliffs are approximately 50m above the water, suggesting that the base of the ice shelf is 450m deep. At that depth and pressure, seawater slowly freezes to the underside of the ice shelf, forming 'marine ice.' At its greatest, the accumulation of marine ice can be tens of meters thick.

Icebergs that calve from the edge of the ice shelf are composed of two kinds of ice literally stuck together: glacial ice made of compressed snow that originated from the continent and flowed down to become the ice shelf, and marine ice from the freezing of seawater on the underside of the ice shelf. If an iceberg becomes unstable due to uneven melting, it may list and then turn over, exposing its marine ice underside.

Green icebergs are rarely seen because not all ice shelves have the right conditions for marine ice to form. They are also rare because the icebergs have to turn over and show their verdant bellies before the marine ice underside is melted by the relatively warm waters that circulate around Antarctica.

Marine ice's most striking characteristic – even more than its color – is its unbelievable clarity, caused by the absence of air bubbles. Observers often comment that they can see 'meters and meters' into marine ice. At the depth and pressure that marine ice forms, air is highly soluble in seawater. This is in sharp contrast to sea ice, which is formed by the freezing of seawater at the ocean surface. At the surface, air is not so soluble in seawater and air bubbles are trapped in the forming ice. Thus sea ice contains lots of bubbles and has a milky appearance.

While green icebergs are spectacular in appearance, observers should also look for variations in the color of marine icebergs ranging from deep indigo to jade to yellow-brown, depending upon the amount of organic material that is trapped in the ice. The different colors are due to the changing concentrations of organic material in the seawater that was frozen into the marine ice.

An even rarer phenomenon is the striped iceberg. These form when seawater fills up and freezes in crevasses occurring on the bottom side of ice shelves. The result is a bubbly, milky-blue iceberg with dark blue or green stripes.

Dr Collin Roesler is an oceanographer at Bigelow Laboratory for Ocean Sciences in West Boothbay Harbor, ME

feature: six large fuel tanks, whose ends depict brightly painted masks from the Chinese national opera.

Very close to Zhongshan are two other facilities: Australia's summer-only **Law base**, named for Phillip Law and established in 1986–87, and Russia's **Progress II** base, opened in 1989. Progress II accommodates a maximum of 77 people in summer and 20 in winter. An earlier Progress I base nearby is now abandoned.

DAVIS STATION

Named after Captain John King Davis, master of ships used on expeditions led by Shackleton and Mawson, Australia's Davis station opened in 1957. Located on the edge of the biologically important Vestfold Hills, Davis can accommodate as many as 100 people, but usually there are about 80 during the summer and 20 over the winter.

During its first years, Davis accommodated very small wintering parties: in some cases, just four or five men stayed through the long polar night. In 1965 Davis was closed temporarily to allow Australia to concentrate its efforts on building Casey station. It reopened in 1969 and has been operating continuously since then.

Compared to its two Australian sister stations, Davis' climate is relatively mild, thanks to the moderating influence of the Vestfold Hills, which separate the station from the Antarctic ice sheet. Thus Davis' nickname: 'the Riviera of the South.'

VESTFOLD HILLS

Covering 400 sq km, the Vestfold Hills are an area of ice-free rock. These hills, 25km across with a maximum elevation of 159m, are especially beautiful when viewed from the air, revealing long, black volcanic dikes striping the bare rock. The first woman to set foot in Antarctica, Caroline Mikkelsen, came ashore here on February 20, 1935 with her husband, Klarius Mikkelsen, captain of the Norwegian whaling support ship *Thorshavn*. The Mikkelsens named the Vestfolds for their home county in Norway, the center of the country's whaling industry.

The Vestfolds Hills are biologically unique, dotted with a series of remarkable lakes, both freshwater and saline. Some of the hypersaline lakes are more than 13 times as salty as seawater, and have freezing points as low as -17.5°C. In summer, when the ice on these lakes acts as a lid trapping solar energy absorbed by the saline water, the temperature of the bottom water can reach 35°C. Life in these lakes is highly specialized – and rare. In **Deep Lake**, for instance, only two species have been found, an alga and a bacterium. Because no burrowing organisms disturb the lake-bottom sediment, cores taken here provide an unparalleled record going as far back as 5000 years.

At **Marine Plain**, fossils of whales and dolphins have been found. The area is protected by the Antarctic Treaty.

MIRNYY OBSERVATORY

Russia's first station on the Antarctic continent, Mirnyy Observatory was opened in 1956. It has been visited by tourists only a few times. Mirnyy means 'peaceful,' and it was named after Bellingshausen's ship.

Mirnyy's 200m main street was once officially called Ulitsa Lenina (Lenin St). The original station was replaced in 1970–71 and now lies under 2m of ice. In front of Mirnyy lies Komsomolskaya Hill (35m), named for the Young Communist League; beneath that, fronting the often-frozen sea, is a 25m ice-cliff known as Pravda Shore.

The enormous Kharkovchanka tracked vehicles, used to make the long oversnow traverse to Vostok 1400km inland, can be seen parked here between trips.

Gilbert Dewart, an American scientist, spent the year of 1960 living at Mirnyy, where he was warmly welcomed by the Russians, despite such Cold War flare-ups as the U-2 spyplane incident. Dewart's *Antarctic Comrades* (1989) offers a revealing glimpse into US-Soviet relations in Antarctica. He also describes such unique local phenomena as the 'blue-out,' when the sea and sky are precisely the same hue, causing the horizon line to disappear and icebergs and islands seem to float on a blue background. Dewart also writes feelingly about the horrific fire that killed eight members of the Russian expedition during his year at Mirnyy. Flames fanned by 190km/h gusts destroyed the station's meteorology building, one of the worst disasters in the history of Antarctic expeditions.

One of Mirnyy's major attractions is the large **emperor penguin rookery** among the Haswell Islands just offshore. From this rookery in 1997, Swiss wildlife photographer Bruno Zehnder became lost in a whiteout and died of exposure.

Zehnder's body, along with those of the men killed in the 1960 fire and dozens of others who have died at Mirnyy over the years, now rests in an imposing cemetery on tiny **Buromskiy Island**, just offshore from Mirnyy. Buromskiy is named after hydrographer Nicolay Buromskiy, a member of the 1957 Russian Antarctic Expedition and the first person to die at Mirnyy. A tall, wooden Russian Orthodox cross towers on the island's crest. Marking the graves of Russian, Czechoslovak, German, Austrian, Ukraine and Swiss members of Soviet and Russian Antarctic expeditions, the coffins and memorials are bolted to the exposed rock, because there's no soil in which to bury them. Visiting the graves is complicated by the many Adélie penguins nesting among them.

BUNGER HILLS

When their discovery was announced to the world, the 952-sq-km Bunger Hills caused a sensation. Because they are an area of ice-free rock, newspaper headlines blared 'Antarctic Shangri-La,' helping explain why some science-fiction movies about Antarctica depict a tropical region inhabited by dinosaurs. The largest ice-free oasis on the East Antarctic coast, the hills are named for US Navy pilot David Bunger, who landed a seaplane on an unfrozen lake here in 1947 while on a photographic mission for Operation Highjump. Dotted with numerous meltwater ponds, the Bunger Hills are bisected by the 145m-deep, 14-sq-km **Algae Lake**, which is covered by ice for 10 months of the year. The hills reach a maximum elevation of 180m and are surrounded on all sides by 120m walls of ice.

CASEY STATION

Located in a beautiful area known as the **Windmill Islands**, a group of more than 50 islands teeming with seabirds, Australia's Casey station was established in 1969, but occupation of the area commenced 10 years

SCOTT DARSNEY

Rock climbing on ventifact boulder, Taylor Valley in the Dry Valleys (p238)

SCOTT DARSNEY

Observation Hill (p247), Ross Island

SCOTT DARSNEY

Glacier, Dry Valleys (p238)

Ice climbing, Ross Island (p240)

SCOTT DARSNEY

GRANT DI

Glacier, East Antarctica (p86)

KERRY LORIMER

Mawson's hut (p265), Commonwealth Bay

Hägglunds tracked vehicle, near Davis station (p312)

DAVID ETHER

Icebergs at midnight in summer, near Casey station (p89)

GRANT DIXON

earlier when Australia took over responsibility for the US's Wilkes station.

Wilkes was built in 1957 for the International Geophysical Year and named for Lieutenant Charles Wilkes, leader of the US Exploring Expedition (p29). When its main building was covered over by snow, Australia replaced Wilkes with Casey station, which is 3km to the south across the bay. Casey was a radical innovation in Antarctic design. To avoid Wilkes' problem of inundation with snow, it was built on stilts to allow snow to blow through beneath. It also had a long corrugated-iron tunnel on the windward side connecting all the buildings, which were built separately as a safety measure against fire. Casey was first known as 'Repstat,' or replacement station, but its name was changed to honor Australia's Governor-General Richard (later Lord) Casey, who was a staunch supporter of Australia's fledgling Antarctic program.

Casey itself had to be replaced in the late 1980s when corrosion threatened its metal supports. The new station, also called Casey, was built 1km away and completed in 1988. The old Casey was dismantled from 1991 to 1993 and returned to Australia; today the only signs of it are drill holes in the rock where its supports once stood.

Casey now accommodates 70 people in summer and 17 in winter.

Landings are made at the station landing, linked to the station by a 1.5km road. Among the places visitors are likely to see is the Red Shed, which provides kitchen, dining, recreation and living quarters, as well as a hospital and medical suite. Artifacts from the early days of the station and its predecessor, Wilkes, are on display in the building.

A large emperor penguin colony was sighted in late 1994 among the maze of icebergs grounded on **Petersen Bank**, offshore of Casey. Despite more than 40 years of operations, including helicopter flights over the bank during station resupply visits, the bank is so large that the penguins had remained undiscovered until then.

DUMONT D'URVILLE STATION

Colloquially known as 'Du-d'U' (doo-doo), France's Dumont d'Urville station, named after explorer Dumont d'Urville (p31), is located on Pétrel Island in the Géologie Archipelago. It was built in 1956 to replace Port Martín station, which burned down in 1952 without injuring anyone. The station accommodates 30 winterers and 120 summer personnel.

The station allows only 40 people to come ashore at one time, but ice and strong katabatic winds often prevent landings by Zodiac (motorised dinghy) or helicopter. Indeed, Antarctica's highest wind velocity was recorded here in July, 1972 – 327km/h – but even that isn't the world record. New Hampshire's Mt Washington recorded a gust of 372km/h in 1934.

Dumont d'Urville became the focus of international attention in 1983 when the French government began construction of a 1100m crushed-rock airstrip. Unfortunately, Lion Island and two adjacent islets were dynamited to level them and provide material to fill in the sea separating them. Greenpeace made headlines around the world when it visited the runway construction site during the 1983–84 season and obtained photos of dead penguins killed by rock shrapnel. The airstrip was completed – at a cost of 110 million francs – in early 1993 and was due to be used for test flights the next season. In January 1994, however, the nearby Astrolabe Glacier calved, causing an enormous wave that destroyed an equipment support building. The French government subsequently decided not to utilize the airstrip.

There are major emperor and Adélie rookeries in the area of the station, but they're off-limits to visitors.

COMMONWEALTH BAY

Mawson's Australasian Antarctic Expedition was based here from 1912 to 1914. Mawson (p50) named Commonwealth Bay after the Commonwealth of Australia, while Cape Denison commemorates one of the expedition's main supporters, Hugh Denison.

The same furious katabatics that caused Mawson to call this the 'Home of the Blizzard' often make landing here impossible. Even walking was difficult, as recalled by Charles F Laseron in his 1947 book *South with Mawson*:

> ...with practice we learned the knack of wind-walking, leaning always at an angle, and bracing our feet against every projecting piece of rock and ice. In this way we could walk against a

EXPEDITION ICEBOUND: A YEAR AT COMMONWEALTH BAY *Don & Margie McIntyre*

In the period from 1911 to 1914, Douglas Mawson spent two winters at Cape Denison in Commonwealth Bay, one of the most inhospitable spots on earth. He was well equipped and had a number of companions. Although tragedy struck during his foray onto the Antarctic ice cap, Mawson and the rest of his men fared well in the relative comfort of their hut. Could a privately funded and much smaller expedition winter as successfully?

That was the question in Don's mind after he returned from a voyage to Cape Denison early in 1993. We decided to find out, launching what we called Expedition Ice-Bound in February 1994.

Living for a year at the windiest place on the planet would be more than just a simple camping trip. Among other preparations, it required nearly 10 months of negotiations with the Australian Antarctic Division. We submitted a full report on our proposed activities to the division's policy section, and we sought in every way to meet the same criteria that official government activities must. We assessed all impacts on flora, fauna, ecological processes, ice, air, water and the heritage qualities of Cape Denison, along with the waste-handling methods we would use while living there.

On January 15, 1995 we reached Commonwealth Bay in our 18m expedition support vessel, *Spirit of Sydney*. On board were 4.5 tonnes of equipment, including a two-year supply of food and fuel and a prefab 2.4m by 3.6m box that was to be our home. Before the month was out, the yacht's five-member crew sailed home and we were left alone in the world's last great wilderness.

Only days later, the wind worked itself up into a screaming fury and the first blizzard struck. The roar of the wind would rise to a howling climax in a gust, and there was no way we could escape from the sound. It filled our world, needling us second by second, worrying, tormenting, wearing us down. All we could do was sit and wonder how long the hut, which we called Gadget Hut (after one of Mawson's huskies), could stand the punishment. Battered by winds that exceeded 240km/h and gripped by temperatures as low as -38°C, our tiny hut shook and creaked and grew a lining of frost as thick as that found in any home freezer. At times, the interior temperature dropped to -18°C and our breath froze to our sleeping bags.

We had come in search of adventure. We were alone, together without any possibility of rescue, yet we were able to share our experience daily with thousands of schoolchildren around the world, thanks to our sponsor, Comsat, who provided a satellite-telephone system. (Despite this connection to the outside world, we sometimes found ourselves feeling depressed on Sunday

> seventy-miler, and could stand against eighty, but when the ninety and hundred miles were reached we gave up, and were content to wriggle about like snakes.

Because of these violent winds, conservation of Mawson's huts is much more difficult than it is for the historic buildings on Ross Island.

No more than 20 people are allowed to come ashore here at one time. Visitors to the main hut are asked not to climb on structures and they must not take anything from the site.

The areas where artifacts (building materials, domestic and scientific equipment, food, packaging, clothing and other historic rubbish) are scattered on the ground between the Main Hut and Boat Harbor are off-limits to tourists.

From January 1995 to January 1996, an Australian couple named Don and Margie McIntyre wintered at Cape Denison, the first to do so since Mawson himself. They lived in a 2.4m by 3.6m cabin they built, which has since been removed (see the boxed text above).

Warning: explosives left over from Mawson's expedition lie approximately 50m southwest (or inland) of the Main Hut. Keep away.

Main Hut

Mawson originally intended to have two separate huts, one housing 12 men, the other six. But it was decided instead to join the two, creating an accommodation area and a workshop. The larger building, about 53 sq m, was surrounded on three sides by a veranda, which held stores, food and biological supplies. Mawson's room, a darkroom and

nights when we left the telephone on and no one called!) We also spent time writing, observing wildlife, recording weather data and, in Margie's case, hand-sewing 86 teddy bears to be auctioned for charity.

There were dangers, difficulties and disappointments. On two occasions we were made sick by carbon-monoxide poisoning when our roof ventilators iced up. Whenever we cooked or turned on the heater, the ice on the walls and ceiling melted, creating rain inside the hut. We had to cover the bed every day to catch the meltwater, and pools of water puddled the floor. When we opened what we thought was our last can of potatoes, which we had been hoarding, we were crestfallen to discover (the label had fallen off) that it was in fact asparagus.

As autumn gave way to lifeless winter, the psychological pressure increased. For three months we lived in almost complete darkness, and for 21 days we didn't see the sun at all. Margie suffered bouts of profound despondency, particularly when we were confined indoors for long periods; she cried for six months, from March until October, and felt sorry for Don when she couldn't stop the crying. Once, we were stuck inside for 20 days in a row. We'll never forget the roar of the wind – it will stay with us forever. We had to shout just to talk to each other in bed.

With the arrival of spring came life – killer whales, seals and penguins – and days of never-ending sunshine. Occasionally, we had such brilliant days that the stunning panoramas outside inspired moods close to euphoria. We would sit for hours watching the penguins and seals, which became our friends. At night, we were impressed by the aurora, with its green and yellow 'waterfall' effects. On Christmas, we were visited by a US helicopter – the first people we had seen in 12 months!

Our adventure cost us around A$600,000, including the purchase of *Spirit of Sydney*. You could say that our hut was the most expensive – and smallest – hotel room in the world. But we felt we were privileged to be staying at the most remote and beautiful place in the world.

We found that we are two sides of the same coin; we have our differences, but we make a formidable unit. Today Don is 50 and Margie is 44; we have been married for 21 years. We didn't have a single fight all year – except for what we'd term two 'debates.' That's pretty incredible, considering that we were never more than 100m apart for a whole year. We really had to support each other to survive, which meant that we had to become closer. Yet our differences came to an extraordinary climax at the end of our stay, when Don pleaded with Margie to let him stay on for another year, completely alone. It was another testing time for our relationship, which survived stronger than ever. (Don came home with Margie.)

Don & Margie McIntyre, authors of Two Below Zero: A Year in Antarctica

the cook's table and stove surrounded a central dining table. Bunks were placed along the perimeter.

A door on the northern side of the larger building connected the workshop, covering roughly 30 sq m. Dogs were kenneled on the eastern veranda, while the western veranda contained a meat cellar, a roof door for entrance in winter and a latrine. The entrance to the whole complex was through a 'cold porch' on the western veranda, with the door facing north to avoid the furious winds coming from the south.

Lighting consisted of acetylene lamps and skylights. Winter snowdrifts kept the quarters at a frosty 4°C to 10°C.

Magnetograph House & Magnetic Absolute Hut

Cape Denison's location close to the South Magnetic Pole makes it an ideal place to observe the earth's magnetic field. These huts, northeast of the Main Hut, are where this work was conducted. A stone wall built on its windward side, which helps explain its good condition, protected the magnetograph house, the best-preserved building at Cape Denison.

Transit Hut

East of the Main Hut, this building was used as shelter while taking in the sights from the stars to determine the exact position of Cape Denison.

Memorial Cross

Erected by the expedition in the spring of 1913, this memorial honors Xavier Mertz and Belgrave Ninnis, who perished on the Far Eastern Journey with Mawson, an ordeal from which Mawson himself barely escaped alive.

LAKE VOSTOK & THE SUBGLACIAL LAKES *Martin J Siegert*

Subglacial lakes are bodies of liquid water that exist at the base of large ice sheets. Around 100 subglacial lakes have been identified in Antarctica, most of which are about 3km to 5km in length. They occur due to several factors: geothermal heating from the earth; the insulating effect of the overriding ice; and the enormous pressure – thought to be between 300 and 400 atmospheres – of the ice overburden, which allows the ice to melt at around -3°C. Meltwater flows under gravity, and collects in topographic hollows to form lakes.

Subglacial lakes were discovered in the late 1960s and 1970s by British glaciologists using ice-penetrating radar. Radio waves travel well in cold ice, but reflect off boundaries where there is a contrast in electrical properties. Reflections off the ice and rock interface are very different to those from the ice and water surface of a subglacial lake, which are stronger and flatter.

Lake Vostok, about the size of Lake Ontario, is much larger than any other subglacial lake – in fact, it's one of the 10 largest lakes on earth. Russia's Vostok station sits atop the 3.7km-thick ice covering the lake's southern end. Lake Vostok is 50km wide, and extends in a crescent shape more than 240km north from Vostok station.

Huge scientific and media interest focused on Lake Vostok and subglacial lakes following the discovery 10 years ago that Lake Vostok was deep. The lake's water depth has yet to be evaluated accurately, but data suggests that at the lake's southern end, it is around 510m deep. The volume of water in Lake Vostok is of the order of several thousand cubic kilometers. Interestingly, the lake's surface is thought to be just below sea level.

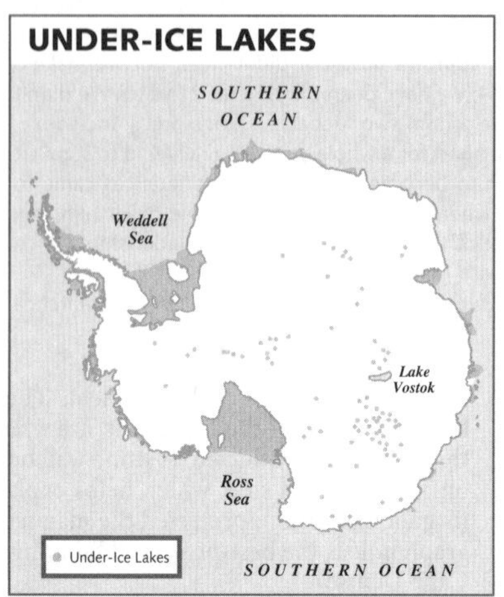

Lake Vostok is at least two or three million years old, and possibly as old as 15 million years. Some scientists now think Lake Vostok's trough formed well before the ice sheets covered Antarctica. This may limit the possibility of hydrothermal activity, which would be beneficial to any organisms that might live in the lake. The lake's water, melted from the underside of the ice sheet, is probably around one million years old, which effectively marks the last time the lake was in contact with atmospheric constituents.

Discussion about whether to make in situ measurements of Lake Vostok has been driven by two scientific hypotheses. The first is that unique microorganisms inhabit the lake. In fact microbes have been found in the Vostok ice core's accreted ice, which may provide a strong indication of what to expect living in the water body. The second hypothesis is

CONCORDIA STATION

Well-named Concordia station is a joint effort by France and Italy, which in 1993 agreed to build a new permanent Antarctic research station at a cost of €31 million. Construction began during the 1998–99 season, and the station is to be inaugurated in 2005.

Concordia is located at **Dome C**, formally known as Dome Charlie, a massive ice dome in the vast snow plateau of Wilkes Land. The station is 1200km south of France's Dumont d'Urville station and 1100km southwest of Italy's Mario Zucchelli station at Terra Nova Bay. Concordia is resupplied by regular flights and a thrice-yearly truck traverse from Dumont d'Urville, a 20-day round trip.

The completed Concordia station will consist of twin cylindrical buildings, each with 36 faces and three stories. The galvanized steel-frame buildings, connected by an enclosed walkway about 10m long, will yield 1500 sq m of living space. Like the new South Pole station, Concordia's buildings will be able to be raised periodically with hydraulic

that a complete record of ice-sheet history is available from the layer of sediments – probably tens of meters deep, possibly hundreds of meters deep – which lie across the lake floor. Future exploration of subglacial lakes will be focused on testing these hypotheses.

No one expects fish or other large creatures to live in Lake Vostok, but biologists do think they will find unique microbes there. Probably only bacteria will be able to survive in the lake's extreme environment.

For life to exist in Lake Vostok it must endure permanent darkness, pressures around 350 atmospheres and temperatures below 0°C. This means that it must use chemicals to power biological processes. Since it is highly likely that nutrients may be sparse in the lake water, so too may be the life. The lake floor, with its sediments, could provide a food source.

What makes the thought of life in Lake Vostok so fascinating is that these organisms must have developed in complete isolation from the outside world for as long as one million years.

To identify this life, sterile equipment is necessary to protect the lake from contamination – and to ensure the experiment is not compromised. This is easier said than done, because the technology currently used to drill down through the ice sheet uses contaminants such as kerosene to keep the drill hole from freezing shut.

NASA is also interested in solving this problem, since its planned exploration of Europa, one of the moons of Jupiter, will present similar technical hurdles. Europa's several-kilometers-thick ice crust covers a liquid ocean which some scientists suspect may harbor life.

One possible method for exploring Lake Vostok would involve hot-water drilling to within about 200m of the lake. A robotic probe – a few meters long and just a fraction of a meter in diameter – would then be lowered into the drill hole. This 'cryobot,' with its package of sampling instruments, would be connected to the surface by a power cable that could also carry data upwards. From its position above the lake, the cryobot would then melt its own way down through the remaining ice.

The cryobot would also need to sterilize itself, perhaps using hydrogen peroxide, after it melted into the ice. (Hydrogen peroxide could be broken down into oxygen and water by electrolysis.) After the clean cryobot reached lake waters, it would begin making measurements. A separate 'hydrobot' could also be released from the main probe into the lake to explore and, perhaps, investigate lake-floor sediments.

Lake Vostok is unlikely to be the first subglacial lake to be penetrated for exploration. Over the next five to 10 years, subglacial lakes in West Antarctica and elsewhere in East Antarctica stand a much better chance of being explored. However, as the drill is presently only a few tens of meters above Lake Vostok, the Russians may enter it (without equipment) soon.

There is strong opinion that Lake Vostok must not be polluted – with some environmentalists demanding that it must not be penetrated at all. Clearly, the means by which Lake Vostok is cleanly accessed will involve a huge technological challenge, which is why exploratory research has yet to be undertaken.

Martin J Siegert is Professor of Physical Geography at the Bristol Glaciology Centre of the University of Bristol's School of Geographical Sciences in the UK

jacks to avoid snow accumulation. Station activities will be separated by building; one will include the kitchen, dining, storage and technical rooms; the other, labs, bedrooms, a library, a hospital and a gym.

Concordia will accommodate an international team of 16 people: nine scientists, five technicians, a cook and a doctor, with double that many Concordians during the month-long annual changeover.

The deepest ice core drilled so far – 3200m deep – has come from Dome C. It is the earth's oldest-known ice, with an estimated age of at least 950,000 years at its bottom layer.

Lake Concordia, 50km long and 30km wide, lies beneath 4150m of ice about 100km north of Dome C; it is Antarctica's second-largest subglacial lake, after Lake Vostok.

VOSTOK STATION

Russia's awe-inspiring Vostok Station – an outpost if ever there was one – is located near the **South Geomagnetic Dipole Pole** (one

VOSTOCHNIKI

Those who winter at Vostok, known as 'Vostochniki,' are respected throughout Antarctica for their ability to endure not only Vostok's extraterrestrial cold, but also the lack of many comforts at the spartan station. In the Antarctic lexicon, Vostok is a synonym for privation. It's a place where, as the BBC once put it, 'science takes second place to survival.'

Newcomers gasp for breath at Vostok, for although the station sits at an elevation of 3448m, the low pressure of the atmosphere makes it feel like 5000m. Vostok's air contains just 60% of the oxygen in the air at sea level.

Because of its elevation, Vostok is colder than the South Pole. In fact, it's so cold at Vostok that if the atmosphere contained 100% carbon dioxide, it would actually snow CO2 ('dry ice'), for it freezes at -78.5°C.

Despite the fearsome low temperatures, Vostochniki sometimes walk between buildings in the summer wearing as little as a T-shirt and jeans! For a minute or so, it's possible to do just that, but any longer, and frostbite awaits. In winter, such an exercise is impossible.

Even cooking is difficult at Vostok. Because of the altitude, water boils at 86°C instead of 100°C, so it takes three hours to boil potatoes, and as long as 14 hours to cook beans and peas. Because yeast and baking powder react differently in the low air pressure, baking is trial and error. On the other hand, crackers never go stale in the extremely dry air.

Vostochniki manage with a remarkable stoicism that borders on the heroic. In April 1982 catastrophe struck when a fire destroyed the station's power plant, killing one person and nearly dooming the rest. Left in the dark with just oil heaters for warmth, the desperate survivors worked for two weeks to restore some power and light, by using an old diesel generator they dug up from the snow.

of four poles defined by geomagneticians), where the flux of the earth's main magnetic field is manifested. Vostok was built in 1957 and named for one of Bellingshausen's two ships, *Vostok* (East). The first wintering crew gave Vostok its enduring nickname: 'the Pole of Cold.'

No tourists (except members of an international expedition in 1989–90) have ever visited Vostok, but it's of interest as the site of the lowest temperature recorded on earth: -89.6°C on July 21, 1983. (Vostok's record *high* temperature, set in 2002, is -12.3°C.)

Although only by chance, the station sits atop the southern end of the enormous subglacial **Lake Vostok** to which it gave its name. Interestingly, the station was built well before the existence of Lake Vostok was even suspected; it was not until the late 1960s and early 1970s that echo sounding through the ice revealed the lakes beneath.

Vostok's most visible landmark is the 10m-tall drilling tower covered in reddish sheet metal. Most of the station's original buildings are nearly completely drifted-over, and some lie buried under as much as 10m of snow. Nevertheless, many remain accessible, including a storeroom holding 1000 16mm movies.

One of the world's most important treasures lies in a chamber 10m below the snow surface. The **Vostok Ice Core Vault**, which remains at a constant -57° C, contains the hundreds of 3m-long, 10cm-diameter ice cores which were painstakingly extracted from the ice sheet beneath the station during the 1990s. They contain data about earth's climate over the past 400,000 years and may prove invaluable to discerning future trends for our climate. Drilling has currently stopped to avoid polluting Lake Vostok, since the drill-hole is filled with kerosene and other contaminants to keep it from freezing shut again.

The ice cores are kept in heavy cardboard tubes that line the walls of the vault, and vary in appearance according to age. In 'younger' cores (those less than 50,000 years old), air bubbles make the ice appear white. The oldest (and therefore deepest) cores, however, have a rare, transparent beauty like pure crystal, or glass without any defects.

Vostok is resupplied by tractor-train expeditions which take a month to travel the 1400km from Mirnyy on the coast, as well as by occasional flights from the US' McMurdo station. But like Russia's other Antarctic stations, Vostok has seen its operations and personnel substantially reduced in recent years.

South Pole

CONTENTS

'Great God! This is an awful place!' British explorer Robert Falcon Scott famously wrote in his diary on the day in 1912 that he reached the South Pole – only to discover that his Norwegian rival, Roald Amundsen, had arrived 35 days earlier. Scott's exclamation reflected not only his anguish over losing the great polar race he had labored for a decade to win, but also his awe of the near-mythical spot itself. He had good reason to marvel. As the 'Polies,' the denizens of the station here, are fond of saying, the South Pole is a 'latitude with attitude.'

Almost nothing lives here. The two exceptions are a species of algae and a species of bacteria, which were probably blown in from somewhere else, as there are no indigenous species at the Pole. Only a handful of other animals have ever visited: humans, sledge dogs, hamsters (experiment subjects), skuas (presumably lost, they may have followed the vapor trails of aircraft resupplying the station), plus a few others that hitched in with shipments of vegetables: a bee, a ladybug, flies, spiders, gnats and worms.

Just a few years ago, the South Pole – known to Polies simply as 'Pole' – was still accessible only to the US government and the small number of other national expeditions that made long traverses from the coast. A handful of adventurers launched private expeditions at a cost of hundreds of thousands of dollars – and their safe return was sometimes doubtful. Now, anyone with a reasonably thick wallet can visit this remote redoubt in the high Antarctic desert. Still, in recent years, no more than 75 tourists annually have reached the Furthest South.

HIGHLIGHTS

- Getting your 'hero picture' at the red-and-white striped **Ceremonial South Pole** (p278)
- Running around the world in just a minute as you circle the earth's southern **Geographic South Pole** (p278)
- Learning about universe-deciphering experiments such as **IceCube** (p283)
- Gazing out across the vast white **polar plateau** (p276) and recalling the pole-seekers' agonizing struggles
- Marveling at the futuristic-looking, US$162 million **Amundsen-Scott South Pole station** (p278)

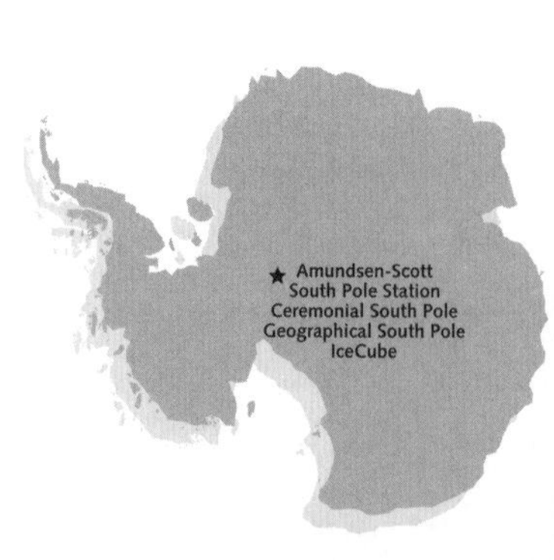

HISTORY

Scott's *Discovery* expedition of 1901–04 was the first to set off with the explicit goal of reaching the Pole – and to have a reasonable chance of doing so. After an initial foray south with a large supporting party, Scott and two fellow Britons, Edward Wilson and Ernest Shackleton, set off on what they hoped would be the final push to the Pole. But the untrained men's attempts at driving their sled dogs were inefficient, and they reached only 82°16′30″S. Although this was a record for furthest south, it was more than 725km from the mark.

Shackleton tried again in 1908. His *Nimrod* expedition was a close scrape with death, part of an emerging pattern for South Polar exploration that by this time was becoming all too familiar (and in hindsight, completely avoidable through better planning). Shackleton and three companions – Eric Marshall, Jameson Adams and Frank Wild – trekked on foot to within 180km of the Pole before they calculated that their dwindling provisions would make suicide the price of reaching it. Making a decision that haunted him for the rest of his life, Shackleton ordered a retreat. The men returned to base in extremely poor condition and with all their supplies exhausted.

It was generally believed that the next expedition to tackle the Pole, strengthened by the knowledge gained from previous attempts, would most likely reach it. Scott, therefore,

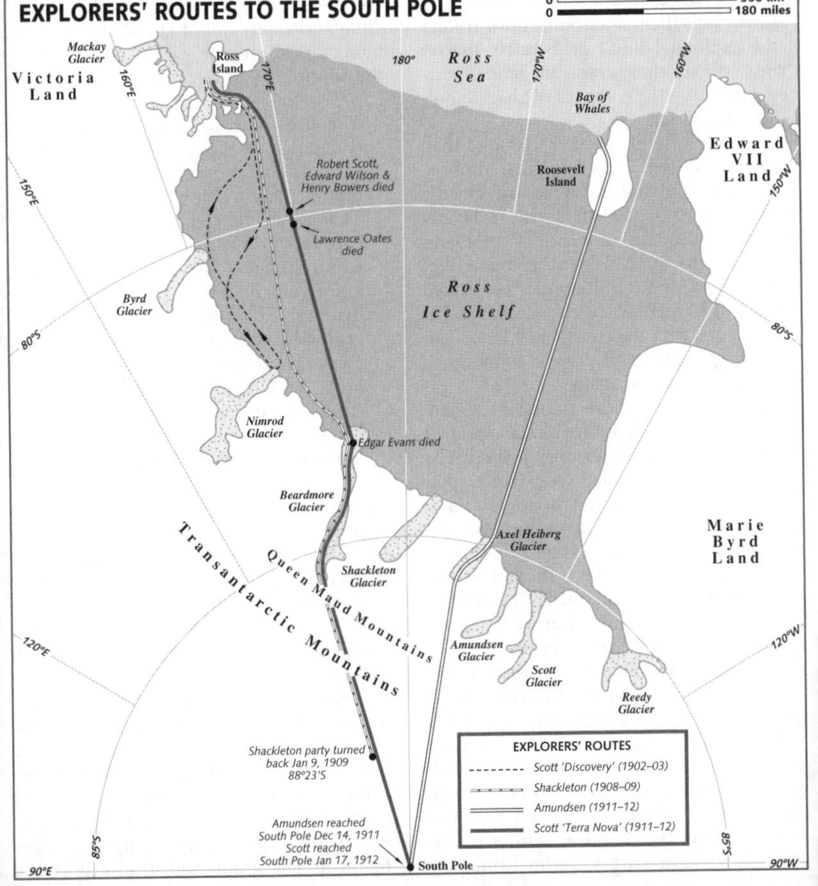

felt justifiably confident when he set sail for the south again in 1910, on his *Terra Nova* expedition. Unfortunately, as had Shackleton, Scott drew the wrong conclusion from his earlier ill-fated attempts at dog sledging. He tried several methods of travel – including motor-sledges, ponies and dogs – but eventually selected manhauling. This brutal exercise – walking or skiing while pulling sledges heavily laden with supplies – is among the most strenuous of human activities.

Once again, it was a race with death. Scott and four companions arrived at the South Pole to find, in his words, that they had done so 'without the reward of priority.' Amundsen's dark-green tent, topped with the Norwegian flag, made that painfully clear. The grim photo Scott's party snapped of themselves tells it all. Hollow-eyed despair darkens their faces. Some now wonder if the explorers didn't deliberately martyr themselves on their desperate return journey, preferring the converse of Shackleton's simple equation.

Certainly one of the men did just that, sacrificing himself in the hope that his three remaining companions might live. On the morning of his 32nd birthday, his feet badly frostbitten, Captain Lawrence 'Titus' Oates hoped not to wake. When he found that he had lived through the night, he walked out into a blizzard, excusing himself to his companions with the courtly exit line: 'I am just going outside and may be some time.' They never saw him again.

Their own fate, meanwhile, was sealed. Just two days later, another blizzard pinned them down – just 18km from a major cache of provisions they called One Ton Depot. They remained in their tent for 10 days, their supplies gradually dwindling to a single sputtering lamp. By its light, Scott, who may or may not have been the last to die, scrawled his immortal words: 'It seems a pity, but I do not think I can write more... For God's sake, look after our people.'

A search party found their bodies the following November. Buried in the tent beneath a snow cairn by the search party, the bodies will reach the Ross Sea in a few hundred years. Because of the accumulated snowfall on the icecap as it advances toward the sea, Scott, Wilson, Bowers and their tent will reach the sea through the *bottom* of the Ross Ice Shelf, making it extremely unlikely that they will be spotted by anyone. All in all, a fitting grave.

Roald Amundsen, Scott's rival, was a polar technician. His approach was slow, methodical and proven (although he made one false start, trying to leave his coastal base too early in the season, and was forced to retreat with severe frostbite). He carried spare food, extra fuel and backups for all essential equipment. Most importantly, he brought dogs to do the heavy pulling, saving the men's strength. He also coldly calculated the worn-out dogs as food for the others.

Amundsen had a different problem than Scott: he actually wanted to reach the North Pole. His expedition left Norway with that stated intention. But after American Robert Peary announced that he had attained the North Pole on April 6, 1909, Amundsen secretly turned his ambition 180°. In his diary, he remarked upon this irony after reaching the South Pole on December 14, 1911:

> The goal was reached, the journey ended. I cannot say – though I know it would sound much more effective – that the object of my life was attained. That would be romancing rather too bare-facedly. I had better be honest and admit straight out that I have never known any man to be placed in such a diametrically opposite position to the goal of his desires as I was at that moment. The regions around the North Pole – well, the North Pole itself – had attracted me from childhood, and here I was at the South Pole. Can anything more topsy-turvy be imagined?

In contrast to the Britons' desperate race against starvation, the Norwegians' return trip from 90°S was little more than a bracing ski outing. After three days spent at the Pole making weather observations and precisely calculating their position, they headed north, reaching their base on the coast 'all hale and hearty.'

Amundsen's polar camp also remains buried under the annual accumulations of snow, and by now should be about 12m below the snow surface. In 1993 a Norwegian group came to the Pole with hopes of recovering the tent, Norwegian flag and sledge for display at the 1994 Winter Olympics in Lillehammer. The group had to give up when

FURTHEST SOUTH *Robert Headland*

Claims of having reached the North Pole were made in 1908 by Frederick Cook and in 1909 by Robert Peary. Although most polar historians doubt both claims today, their presumed authenticity at the time served to divert attention to attaining the South Pole.

The following notes describe successive penetrations leading up to Roald Amundsen's attainment of the Pole in December 1911, as well as subsequent landmark voyages.

1603 Gabriel de Castilla (Spain), aboard *Nuestra Señora de la Merced*, probably penetrated to 64°S in the Southern Ocean south of Drake Passage. Subsequently, several Spanish and other merchant vessels reported being blown south of 60°S rounding Cape Horn in severe weather.

1773 James Cook (United Kingdom), with companies aboard HMS *Resolution* and HMS *Adventure*, crossed the Antarctic Circle (66°33'S) off Enderby Land on January 17, and later reached a furthest south of 71°10'S off Marie Byrd Land on December 30, 1774.

1842 James Clark Ross (United Kingdom), with companies aboard HMS *Erebus* and HMS *Terror*, reached 78°10'S in the Ross Sea on February 23.

1900 Hugh Evans (United Kingdom) and three others from *Southern Cross* sledged to 78°50'S on the Ross Ice Shelf on February 23. This was the first southern penetration by land.

1902 Robert Scott (United Kingdom) and two others sledged to 82°17'S, near the foot of the Beardmore Glacier, on December 30.

1909 Ernest Shackleton (United Kingdom) and three others sledged up the Beardmore Glacier to 88°23'S on January 9. This was approximately 180km from the South Pole – but insufficient supplies necessitated their return.

1911 Roald Amundsen (Norway) and four others dog-sledged to 90°S on December 14.

1912 Robert Scott and four others sledged to 90°S on January 17. They arrived 33 days after the Norwegians had departed and all perished during the return journey.

1929 Richard Byrd (United States), with an aircraft crew, claimed to have flown over the South Pole from the Ross Ice Shelf on November 29, but the navigation has been questioned. On February 15, 1947, he definitely flew over it, with crew aboard two aircraft.

1956 John Torbert (United States) and six others flew across Antarctica via the South Pole (Ross Island to Weddell Sea and back, without landing) on January 13. On October 31, Conrad Shinn (United States), with an aircraft crew, landed at the South Pole. A permanent station was established and sustained by aircraft.

1958 Vivian Fuchs (British Commonwealth), with an expeditionary party, reached the South Pole by motor vehicles and dog sledges on January 20, and continued across Antarctica (from the Weddell Sea to the Ross Sea).

Subsequently, several expeditions have crossed the Antarctic through the South Pole by surface, and many have made one-way surface journeys to the Pole, departing by aircraft. Most adventurers' South Pole journeys during the past decade have used aircraft, and many started well inland, far from any place that a ship could reach.

Robert Headland is the archivist and curator at the Scott Polar Research Institute, Cambridge, England

one of its members fell 40m down a crevasse and was killed. The huts Amundsen left at his camp on the Ross Ice Shelf at the Bay of Whales disappeared long ago as pieces of the ice shelf calved and floated out to sea.

American Richard E Byrd reported flying over the Pole with three other men on November 29, 1929. Byrd pretty well summed up the quixotic quality of all quests, polar and otherwise: 'One gets there, and that is about all there is for the telling. It is the effort to get there that counts.' He dropped a rock wrapped in the American flag out the window of his Ford Trimotor plane and flew back to his camp at Little America. Although the navigation of Byrd's flight has been questioned by some authorities, the point is actually moot, for Byrd himself was among the six men in two aircraft who definitely flew over 90°S on February 15, 1947.

On neither of his flights did Byrd land, however, meaning that after Amundsen and Scott, the Pole lay untouched for another 44 years. During that interval, two world wars raged, and a third at times appeared imminent. On October 31, 1956 an American ski-equipped plane set down on the ice, making it the first aircraft to land at the Pole. Pilot Conrad 'Gus' Shinn landed his Navy R4D (the military version of a DC-3) named *Que Sera Sera*, along with Admiral George Dufek and five other US Navy men who surveyed the area for a permanent scientific base. Construction began the next month, and the first South Pole station was completed by February 1957. It has operated ever since.

Although no one owns the South Pole, the US Amundsen-Scott South Pole station (p278) is, among other things, an ice-and-steel lesson in Antarctic realpolitik. While no certain ownership of Antarctica exists, and the Antarctic Treaty agrees to set aside the territorial claims made by seven countries, the stark reality is that some countries are more equal than others in Antarctic politics. Before its collapse, the Soviet Union, for example, maintained a ring of research bases that encircled the continent, while the Pole station sits astride all the lines of longitude, neatly occupying all time zones – and six of the seven Antarctic claims – at once. (Amundsen-Scott station, by the way, uses New Zealand time since resupply flights to the Pole and McMurdo station originate in Christchurch, and this simplifies logistics.)

Three modified Ferguson farm tractors, outfitted with rubber tracks, were the first motor vehicles to reach the Pole overland, on January 4, 1958, led by New Zealander Edmund Hillary of Mt Everest fame. Hillary's team was laying depots for the first successful crossing of the continent, by British explorer Vivian Fuchs' Commonwealth Trans-Antarctic Expedition.

The first women joined the US Antarctic Program in 1969. The first women to reach the Pole arrived by US Navy aircraft on November 11 that year. The six of them – not wishing for one to later claim she had been first out of the aircraft – linked arms and walked out the back of the plane together. They spent a few hours visiting the station before flying back to McMurdo. Another two years passed before the first woman actually spent a 'night' at the Pole, in December 1971. She was Louise Hutchinson, a reporter for the *Chicago Tribune*, and she only got to stay because weather delayed her flight out. But two years later, two American women, Nan Scott and Donna Muchmore, became the first women to work at the Pole. By 1979, the station had a female physician, Dr Michele Eileen Raney, the first woman to winter at 90°S. On January 6, 1995, Norwegian Liv Arnesen arrived at the Pole after skiing unaccompanied from the edge of the continent in 50 days, the first woman to accomplish the feat. For more information about women in Antarctica, see p58.

Tourists first arrived in 1968, when a chartered Convair flew over both poles from November 22 to December 3. The South Polar leg left Christchurch, landed at McMurdo Sound, then flew over the Pole at a low altitude and on to Argentina. The first tourist flight to land at the Pole was on January 11, 1988, when a pair of DHC-6 Twin Otters operated by Adventure Network International, also known as 'Antarctic Airways,' brought the first 15 paying passengers to 90°S – for a cool US$25,000 or US$35,000 each. The seven tourists who wished to be in the first plane, which landed 15 minutes before the other, paid the higher price.

Three skydivers free-fell 2500m to their deaths over the South Pole in 1997 when they failed to open their parachutes. Because station members had the grisly task of excavating the bodies from the 1.2m-deep craters they made in the snow, such 'adventure tourism' remains a point of controversy. The official US government position on private expeditions is to refuse them any support, although they no longer get the chilly brush-off that once decreed that station members were not even to speak to such arriving 'guests.'

In recent years, a series of medical evacuations of personnel at the Pole have generated media attention. The most dramatic occurred in October 1999, when the station physician, Dr Jerri Nielsen, diagnosed her own breast cancer and was evacuated. Her book *Ice Bound* (2001) gives a fascinating insider's view of living at 90°S.

GEOGRAPHY

Unlike its northern conjugate, which sits in the middle of the Arctic Ocean, the South Pole lies amid a mind-bending wasteland of monotonously flat snow-covered ice called the polar plateau. The Pole itself is among the most isolated spots on earth, surrounded by thousands of square kilometers unrelieved by a single feature to interest the eye. In every direction you look, there is only unbroken horizon. The nearest protrusion through the ice is Mt Howe, a nunatak 290km away, home to a colony of bacteria and yeasts. The nearest settlement is Vostok, 1255km in the distance.

CLIMATE

Temperatures on the polar plateau range from -82°C to -14°C. The mean temperature is -49.4°C. Winter wind chills can plummet to -110°C. The elevation is 2835m, but the cold and polar location makes the average air pressure the equivalent of about 3230m. New arrivals are often exhausted after even gentle exercise until they become acclimated. The average wind speed is just 20km/h, a gentle breeze compared to the 320km/h katabatic winds on the coast. The extreme cold and very low absolute humidity (3%) combine to make this the world's driest desert.

When locals here refer to temperatures, it can be confusing. They simply use numbers like '22,' meaning -22°F, (-30°C) – the minus is *always* implied, since the highest recorded temperature is -13.6°C. Thus, you have the seeming paradox of the temperature at the Pole 'dropping' from 60 to 80. Explains Jerry Macala, a recent winterover: 'Saying minus is rather redundant here and what the heck, it saves two syllables!'

Very little snow falls in Antarctica's interior, thanks to this extreme cold and low humidity. The most common form of precipitation is ice crystals, also called 'diamond dust.' These often fall out of a clear sky, sometimes creating sundogs, sun pillars and other refractions around the sun and the moon.

The sun ends a spectacular sunset lasting weeks and dips below the horizon on about March 22 – although the extreme atmospheric refraction sometimes allows it to be seen for a day or two more, and occasionally causes it to appear to rise again briefly. Twilight lingers for another six or seven weeks. Then the potentially depression-inducing darkness sets in, lightened only by the surreal sky show of the aurora australis (see the boxed text on p236) and the stars. During the six-month polar night, the moon is visible for two weeks, then sets for two weeks before rising again and repeating the cycle. Many people comment on the beauty of its silvery-grey light. Because the moon provides so much light, some winterovers come to think of the moonlit periods as 'daytime.'

On about September 22, winterers rejoice at sunrise, although up to seven weeks of dawn precede the actual arrival of *El Sol*. All year-round, Polies can fall victim to a peculiar form of polar pathology called 'Big Eye,' a period of disorientation and sleeplessness caused by the lack of a regular light-dark cycle.

VISITING THE SOUTH POLE

The Pole's extreme altitude causes many visitors to experience altitude sickness upon arrival (at least, those who do not come on foot or skis). Shortness of breath, lethargy and painful headaches are among the symptoms. The first 24 hours are the worst, it is said, but since most tourists remain at the Pole for only a few hours, that doesn't help much. Some visitors recommend taking

SOUTH POLE WEATHER DATA

The following is derived from Amundsen-Scott South Pole station Meteorology Department records dating from 1957 to 2003.

Average Snow Accumulation (fallen and drifted)	23cm per year
Average Liquid Equivalent	8.6cm per year
High Temperature	-13.6°C (December 1978)
Low Temperature	-82.8°C (June 1982)
Average Annual Temperature	-49.4°C
Highest Pressure	719.0 millibars (August 1996)
Lowest Pressure	641.7 millibars (July 1985)
Average Pressure	681.4 millibars
Average Wind Speed	20km/h
Peak Wind Speed	88.5km/h (August 1989)

three or four aspirin on the flight to the Pole to ease the headache.

At 90°S, you'll probably first visit the Ceremonial Pole and the Geographic Pole to take your 'hero pictures.' You can also expect to be invited inside the Amundsen-Scott South Pole station for a visit to the dining room and possibly a quick look around the station. The station shop sells souvenirs, and you can have letters or postcards stamped with the station's postmark.

CEREMONIAL SOUTH POLE

The flags of the original 12 Antarctic Treaty signatories surround this red-and-white-striped 'barber' pole, capped by a chromium globe, so it offers the perfect photo-op. But it's just for show.

GEOGRAPHIC SOUTH POLE

The ice at the Pole moves about 10m per year in the direction of 43°W (toward Brazil), which means that the Geographic Pole marker has to be moved each summer. The 'new' South Pole is recalculated annually and marked by a 4m steel pole topped by a medallion designed by the previous year's winterover crew; each design is unique. The American flag is planted about a meter from the Pole sign, which is also moved each year to keep up with the moving ice sheet. It reads:

> Geographic South Pole
> Roald Amundsen, December 14, 1911
> 'So we arrived and were able to plant our flag at the geographical South Pole'
> Robert F Scott, January 17, 1912 'The Pole, Yes, but under very different circumstances from those expected'
> Elevation: 9301ft (2835m)

You may also hear about three other Poles while in Antarctica.

The **South Magnetic Pole** (located at 64°42'S, 138°E in 2001), off the coast near Commonwealth Bay, is where a magnetic compass needle will try to point straight down. Its position presently moves 10km to 15km a year in a north to northwesterly direction. Tourist ships frequently sail over it. The South Magnetic Pole, then on land, was first reached by Douglas Mawson, Edgeworth David and Alistair Mackay in 1909.

The **South Geomagnetic Pole** (located at 79°36'S, 108°24'E in 2001) is where the flux in the earth's electromagnetic field is manifested. Russia's Vostok station is nearby.

The **Pole of Maximum Inaccessibility** (located at 84°S, 65°E) is the point furthest from any Antarctic coast.

AMUNDSEN-SCOTT SOUTH POLE STATION

From 1975 onwards, home at the Pole was known familiarly as 'the Dome,' or, affectionately, 'Dome, Sweet Dome.' Built from 1971 to 1975, the silver-grey aluminum geodesic Dome is 50m in diameter at its base and 15m high. It covered three structures, each two stories high, which provided accommodation, dining, laboratory and recreational facilities. Although the Dome protected these buildings and their occupants from the wind, it did nothing about the cold, for it was unheated. It had an opening at the top to let out water vapor and a packed snow floor.

The Elevated Station

The Dome had a hard life under harsh conditions. Parts of the under-ice complex became unsafe. Occasional power brownouts and fuel leaks threatened station security, as did drifting snow, which began to crush the Dome. Because of all these problems, the US government decided to build a new 6129 sq meter aboveground facility to replace it.

The project, which began in 1997, requires 80 construction workers working round-the-clock shifts during summer, with its 24-hour sunlight. The winter population, meanwhile, nearly doubled, with the extra staff devoted to construction. To bring in all the necessary building materials, hundreds of flights to the Pole were made from McMurdo.

The new US$162 million station is due to be completed in early 2007, but because it's being built in phases, the first group of occupants was able to take up residence in January 2003.

The elevated station will stretch 128m, facing the prevailing winds. Two separate blue-grey, horseshoe-shaped modules will be connected by flexible walkways and raised on stilts to prevent the destructive snow buildup. The stilts will be able to be jacked up as snow accumulates underneath and eventually rises to the level of the buildings. Being on the surface, the new station will also prevent the claustrophobic 'cabin fever' sometimes induced by living underground. It will accommodate 154 people.

One module will house living quarters, dining room, bar, hospital, laundry, store, post office and greenhouse (adding to the futuristic, space station–ish feeling of the elevated station, the greenhouse is officially known as the 'food growth chamber'). In the other will be offices, labs, computers, telecommunications, an emergency-power plant, conference rooms, music practice rooms and a gym. Reading rooms and libraries will be scattered throughout both units. The new station has triple-pane windows, 200kg stainless-steel outside doors and a pressurized interior to keep out drafts. At one end, a four-story, aluminum tower, familiarly known as 'the Beer Can,' contains a stairwell, cargo lift and utilities. Photovoltaic panels will take advantage of the summertime's 24 hours of sunlight; wind turbines were considered, but the light winds of the polar plateau would have required a very large windmill farm.

The old Dome will be dismantled and taken back to the US for disposal or, perhaps, re-erection at a museum.

In the summer, the station accommodates as many as 240 people, with up to 190 crowded into the aboveground Summer Camp. From mid-February to late October, there are no scheduled flights, so the winter crew is physically cut off from the rest of the

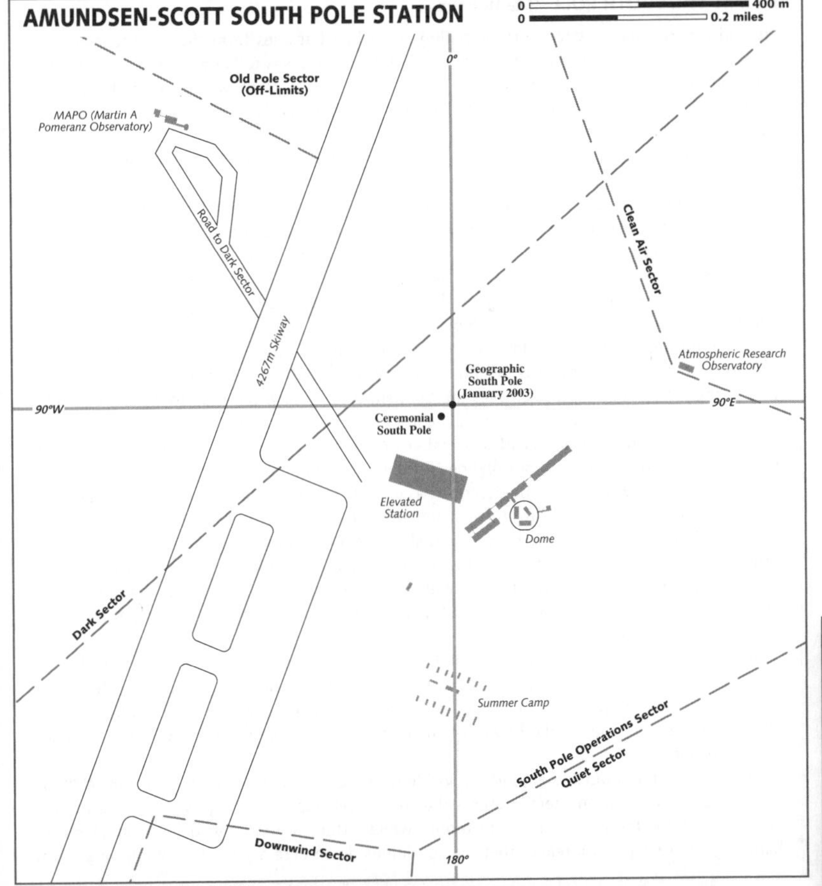

SOUTH POLE

world. From 1957 to 2004, when a record 75 people stayed over the winter, fewer than 1200 people ever have wintered over at the station, according to South Pole historian Bill Spindler. A couple dozen of those winterovers have repeated at least once, and the current record is five consecutive winters at the Pole.

Station Life

Living at the South Pole is difficult. But Polies, clad in their grubby Carhartts (an American brand of clothing popular here for its extreme durability), take a special pride in meeting adversity head-on and actually seem to relish the challenges of working at 90°S.

It takes some people two or three weeks just to adjust to the Pole's oxygen-thin air. Extreme cold limits the time one can spend outdoors, and the darkness and even more extreme cold of the polar winter can be hazardous. (Station members, however, routinely go outside even on the coldest and darkest days. Flag lines – bamboo poles with small flags attached to the top and spaced every 2m – guide the way to outlying buildings.) During the summer, showers are limited to two minutes' running water and can be taken only twice a week. Fire is an omnipresent danger in the dry atmosphere, which can turn wood buildings into tinderboxes. That same dry air cracks skin,

LIFE AT THE SOUTH POLE *Mike Masterman*

Pic and I were walking back from preparing some bad batteries from the emergency-power plant for return to the States. It was a clear night, the moon was full and there was hardly any wind, although it was -70°C. Through the smoke of the power plant, we noticed a slight green glow. We crossed over to the other side of the exhaust plume and saw the sky beginning to come alive with aurora.

The two of us stood there watching the aurora grow until it almost covered half the sky, lighting up with all the colors of the spectrum, colors that can never be reproduced or described. It danced around like a curtain blowing in the wind, continuing to shift and flicker, darting upward and all across the sky from horizon to zenith. After 15 minutes, our boots froze solid. It felt as if we were wearing wooden shoes, but we didn't pay any attention to the cold. The display was so impressive that our gaze remained skyward for 45 minutes. When the aurora died down, we strolled inside the Dome, thinking how unfortunate some people were, since they would never get to experience such a magnificent show.

This is the reason we come down here and endure the winter temperatures and not being able to see the sun for six months. Seeing the aurora or the dust glow from the arms of the Milky Way or the stars in the night sky makes the temperatures – which can drop to -80°C – bearable. It's magical standing out on this barren plateau of ice. The 41 of us here – nine women and 32 men – live from mid-February to early November with no physical contact with the outside world. All that breaks our 8½ months of isolation is the Internet and ham radio.

Winter at the South Pole can be described as one of the world's best-kept secrets. During the long dark night, people must use their imaginations to keep themselves entertained. Brewing beer, watching movies, building models and studying a foreign language are just some of the activities people enjoy here. There is always an abundant amount to do as long as you keep the right attitude. The best way to deal with the isolation and darkness is to stay busy. One favorite activity is sitting around the galley looking at an atlas and discussing travels and home – if a place to call home even exists.

Just arriving on station can take its toll. Every year, some people are sent back to McMurdo with altitude sickness. The actual altitude at Pole is 2835m, but due to atmospheric effects, the air is thinner, so the physiological altitude can vary from 2800m to 3690m. As the physiological altitude increases in the middle of winter, many people find themselves lying in bed at night unable to sleep.

Our food is stored outside around the inside of the geodesic dome that we live in. With no animals to consume it and temperatures that never get above freezing, we have the perfect environment for food storage. Many nights while sitting around the galley, eating either hamburgers or steaks, you realize that the conditions down here are not bad. We have a warm

lips and the inside of nostrils, so petroleum jelly must be used to keep them moist.

The isolation can be overwhelming. Wintering at the Pole is in some ways similar to being an astronaut, albeit one who has a bit more room to walk around and can use email. The accommodation probably doesn't help much, since the rooms – which at least are private for winterovers – are smaller than the average prison cell.

During the summer, ham radiophone patches allow station members to call family and friends at home, but the calls can only be originated at the station – no one can call the Pole this way. During the winter, atmospheric conditions sometimes don't allow for good signal propagation, so the ham radio is unreliable. In any case, as newer technologies have taken over, the ham patch appears to be losing popularity. Now station members can also use high-frequency radio to patch calls via McMurdo. Internet telephone technology produces high-quality calls, and the station also has two Iridium satellite telephones.

A psychologist who has studied Antarctic winterovers and helped in their selection sums up their isolation like this: 'The normal ways we deal with things when we're fed up – either withdrawing and shutting the door or going out to seek other people – are not available.'

place to live and always plenty of good food. We even manage to have a barbecue occasionally, although it can be difficult to get the barbecue lit in this intense cold.

Winterovers are given their own rooms. It's a very small space, but a very big necessity in coping with life here. The rooms are as small as 1.8m by 3m, but that space becomes treasured as the year progresses. Because everything must be shared during the winter, your room is the only place to go that is your own private space.

Holidays are celebrated with great enthusiasm. At Christmas there is a gift exchange and a 'race around the world.' New Year's is kind of a free-for-all party. The main celebrations during the times of isolation are sunrise, sunset and solstice, and since there is only one sunset and one sunrise during the year, both are celebrated. The solstice is the middle of the period of darkness, the point when the sun starts its slow return back up above the horizon. The solstice is very symbolic for the winterover crew, since it means that it will be only another three months until we get to see the sun again. In 1998–99 we celebrated the solstice with a formal dinner. Every year these events are celebrated differently, as determined by the ever-changing crew.

The people here are from all walks of life. They maintain the generators, repair broken equipment, cook, construct new buildings and operate the science experiments. The crew is selected from across the US, with some scientists coming from other countries. Watching the last plane leave for the winter, you realize that these 41 people are your new family, upon which your life depends.

Everyone must work closely together, especially in emergencies. When the fire alarm goes off or when a generator stops working, the entire crew stops its normal day-to-day operations and responds. Fire is one of our biggest dangers – even the smallest fire in the wrong area could produce a life-threatening situation. When the fire alarm goes off or the power goes out, one of the things running through your mind is that we're on our own – there is no way out!

The Pole is an unknown element to most of the world, something that very few people understand. The Pole's conditions are hard to compare to everyday life, as most people cannot imagine what it is like. When companies try to design items for use at the Pole, they have a hard time. Everything from bulldozers to computers, has to be modified or specially treated in order to operate here. The simplest things become extremely difficult because of the altitude, dryness, six months of daylight, then six months of darkness, and the lowest temperatures on earth.

Wintering at the South Pole teaches you a great deal and helps you appreciate things back home that most people overlook: a rainy day, the smell of fresh-cut grass and watching the sun rise and set every day. Most important, it teaches you that getting along with your neighbors can make life so much more enjoyable.

Mike Masterman, winter site manager at Amundsen-Scott South Pole station in 1998–99, has wintered over at the Pole twice

Indeed, on cloudy and moonless winter nights, station residents may feel they're on another planet. One winterover described walking outside on such a night. 'I couldn't see anything...It was so dark I couldn't see my own hand in front of my face,' he said. 'I might as well have been walking with my eyes closed. It took my eyes at least three minutes to adjust enough so that I could see even very faint outlines of nearby buildings.'

That kind of sensory deprivation is also evident in that one of the biggest treats enjoyed by some Pole station members is opening magazines to find the perfume-sample strips included in some advertisements. It's a nice contrast to the pervasive smell of JP-8 (jet fuel), which is used to run the furnaces and machinery because it works better than other fuels at cold temperatures.

On the plus side, of course, there are no bills, traffic jams or biting insects. On clear nights, the stars and aurora australis provide a spectacular show, and the winter-over crew gets treated to the Green Flash (caused by the prismlike effect of the earth's atmosphere on the rays of the setting sun) in March and early April.

Polies eat very well – steak and lobster are often served – even though frozen, dried and canned food obviously form the majority of meals. One chef with a fine sense of humor tried starting up a new custom he called 'Dog Day' by serving hot dogs for lunch on the day that Amundsen had to shoot his remaining dogs on his journey to the Pole. The custom, however, appears not to have taken hold. Through the long dark winter, chocolate is a favorite. One popular dessert is 'buzz bars' – not what some people might guess – brownies with chocolate-covered espresso beans baked into them. 'Slushies' are very fresh snow with Coke or liquor added. Ice cream is also a local favorite, but since it's stored outdoors, it has to be warmed in a microwave before it can be eaten. And yes, despite the thousands of cubic kilometers of ice outside, the galley has an ice machine for drinks.

Despite the effort put into procuring and preparing top-quality food, this is a *very* good place to lose weight. Even with three meals a day plus numerous snacks, many people still manage to lose several kilograms during their stay, with losses of 20kg not uncommon in a 15-week summer!

Interestingly, the station now gets its water from a well, a welcome improvement over the former inefficient system of melting clean snow, which required large amounts of fuel and time. The well, more than 120m deep, is created by using waste heat from the power plant to make a hot-water 'drill.' Below the firn layer, the snow is no longer porous, so adding heat melts the ice, but the water can't seep out into the surrounding ice. As a result, a large pool of water is created that can be pumped out and used. Of course, the water is also very old, since the well is so deep. There's an unusual side benefit: the filtered water has yielded hundreds of thousands of micrometeorites for scientific study.

Recreation opportunities are limited, but inventive Polies have come up with improvisations such as volleybag, a version of volleyball using a beanbag. Radio darts, played against other winter stations around the continent (scores are sent by radio), has been popular despite its heavy dependency on trust – although one station (and frequent winner) was later found not to even have a dartboard! 'Dome sledding' is done on the back side of the Dome. The library houses more than 6000 videos and books. On Christmas Eve, the 4.4km Race Around the World circles the Pole in -23°C temperatures, challenging runners, joggers, walkers, skiers and even snowmobilers. A recent winner (on foot) had an impressive time of 13:55.

One popular hangout is the volunteer-run, small hydroponic greenhouse. As one veteran says, 'The lights, warmth, plants and humidity make it a nice place to get away from the normal reality of daily life at the South Pole.' While the garden's yield is modest – 500g of fresh vegetables a week, enough for winterers to enjoy a monthly salad – tending the plants can be a nice diversion.

Then there's the unique membership known as the 300 Club (see the boxed text opposite). To join, you simply wait until the temperature drops below -100°F (-73°C). After steaming in a 200°F (93°C) sauna, candidates run naked (shoes, however, are highly recommended) out of the station onto the snow. Some people push on even further, going around the Ceremonial Pole. While some claim that the rime of flash-frozen sweat acts as insulation, if you fall, the ice against your reddened skin feels as rough as rock. Induction into the club requires photographic documentation – but with so much steam rising from the hot bodies, most pictures turn out rather foggy.

Science Facilities

Most of the scientific facilities at the Pole are off-limits to visitors, to avoid disrupting research. Other laboratories are off-limits because their instrumentation could be contaminated or decalibrated by unauthorized visitors. Still, it's interesting to know about the cutting-edge science being done at Pole.

Among the most important research is work on the notorious 'ozone hole,' the thinning of the atmosphere's ozone layer, caused by halocarbons and other synthetic chemicals (see p142 for more information). Scientists at the Atmospheric Research Observatory study some of the purest air on earth in the hope of learning about pollution and how it spreads around the globe. Another group in this observatory is using Lidar, or light radar, to study the formation of polar stratospheric clouds, which act as the seeds for the depletion of ozone each spring.

The South Pole is a world center for astronomy, thanks to its high altitude and thin, dry atmosphere. The centrifugal force of the earth's rotation flattens out the atmosphere at both poles, and the extreme cold freezes water vapor out of the air. The astronomical instruments are located about 1km from the station in the so-called Dark Sector, where extraneous light, heat and electromagnetic radiation are prohibited, so as not to disturb the experiments. Noise and other earth-shaking activity, meanwhile, are banned in the Quiet Sector, where seismological studies are done.

A new 8m South Pole Telescope, to be completed in 2007 at a cost of US$17 million, will seek cosmic microwave background (CMB) radiation to investigate the so-called 'dark energy' that appears to be accelerating the expansion of the universe. The telescope will also search for the signature of primordial gravitational waves and test models for the origin of the universe.

IceCube is a US$253 million, kilometer-scale neutrino observatory, a collection of long strings of instruments called photomultipliers lowered into holes drilled deep into the ice with hot water. This device looks for ultra-high-energy subatomic particles called neutrinos that pass through the earth and interact with atoms in the ice – perfectly transparent at that depth – creating blue flashes of light detected by the photomultipliers. Neutrinos may shed light on the power sources of galaxies and the workings of supernovae, the massive explosions of stars. AST/RO, the Antarctic Submillimeter Telescope and Remote Observatory, surveys emissions of carbon atoms from the large clouds of gas and dust that lie between stars. Researchers hope to learn more about how the collapse of these dust clouds gives birth to stars. Finally, SPASE-2 (South Pole Air Shower Experiment, part 2) searches for sources of gamma radiation out in the universe.

All of these instruments detect radiation invisible to the human eye. There are, of course, several telescopes at the Pole in the visible range of light. Taking advantage of the thin atmosphere, they peer far into the Pole's star-filled night sky.

THE 300 CLUB *Ricardo Ramos*

One day, it was announced that the temperature was steadying at around -101°F (-73.9°C). So a group of us – 15 men and four women – gained our exclusive membership in the 300 Club. We crowded into the sauna – cranked up to 200°F (93°C) – and began to work up a sweat. About 15 minutes later, we burst through the door, down the hallway and out of the Dome – a sheer drop of 300°F. I wore nothing but socks, tennis shoes and a neck gaiter over my nose and mouth so my lungs wouldn't get frostbitten while I ran. Someone was taking pictures – I could see the flash going off but not much else, thanks to all the steam coming from our bodies. Once outside, I ran up the slight snow incline to the surface. Some people stopped there, took a few photos and returned to the sauna. A few of us continued. I stopped halfway across the taxiway because I couldn't run any further, but six people made it to the Ceremonial Pole, and one made it all the way to the Geographic Pole. Then it was a mad dash back inside. I'm glad I did it, although I did get a touch of frostbite on my thumbs (of all places) – nothing serious. Better my thumbs than somewhere more important!

Ricardo Ramos was the 1995–96 station science leader at Amundsen-Scott station

Directory

CONTENTS

ACCOMMODATIONS

Nearly all Antarctic tourism involves ship-based visits. Costs range upward from about US$4000, which buys you a bed in a four-person cabin with bathroom facilities down the hall from your cabin, on a small-ship tour with only three or four days of landings in Antarctica. Not all ships offer these 'quad' accommodations, and they may also sell out quickly. Large ships (more than 400 passengers) may offer two-person cabins at similar prices for cruises of the same length of time, but the experiences are very different. (For more details, see the boxed text on p298.) Standard cabins generally have two single beds, two closets, a sofa, a desk and bookcase, and a bathroom with shower. Large ships tend to have larger public areas, not necessarily larger cabins. Obviously, larger cabins cost more, whether on small ships or large ships. Families can purchase suites, although the cost is steep, and solo travelers can pay a premium to occupy a cabin alone. Seasickness is best counteracted by medicine (p307), but the motion is greater on upper decks, so a cabin on a lower deck (ironically, usually cheaper) may be more comfortable.

ACTIVITIES

By and large, tourist activity in Antarctica is limited to shore visits via Zodiac from the ship. Aboard the ship, you can attend educational lectures by Antarctic experts, see wildlife or adventure videos, or watch for whales or seabirds. For further information, see the boxed text on p10.

Companies such as Aurora Expeditions, Heritage Expeditions, Lindblad Expeditions, Mountain Travel-Sobek, Oceanwide Expeditions and Peregrine Expeditions (p296) offer additional activities on selected trips (usually for an extra US$500 or more) such as scuba diving for advanced divers, sea kayaking for experienced paddlers or brief camping and mountain-climbing trips. Ultra-fit adventurers with a certified résumé and US$22,000 or more to spend – as well as at least a month of vacation time – can fly into the continent's interior with Antarctic Logistics & Expeditions (p295) for mountain climbing, skiing, camping and trekking.

CHILDREN

Particularly during the Christmas and New Year holidays, more families are visiting Antarctica, some with children as young as five years old. One recent 96-passenger cruise had 27 passengers younger than 18; ship staff included an 'activity coordinator' to entertain them.

But children are still relatively rare visitors to Antarctica, which is a shame. Antarctica's amazing landscapes and abundant wildlife are especially exciting for young people. But if your kids can't go for more than an hour without playing with their Game Boy, leave them at home; they won't be able to handle the long sea time, which

ELECTRICAL SYSTEMS ON BOARD

Each ship has its own type of electricity, based on its country of origin, so you should check with the tour operator before buying converters. Many ships are Russian, and use 220 volts, 50 hertz, with electrical sockets accommodating the standard European two round-pin plug.

PATRIOT HILLS, ANTARCTICA

Antarctic Logistics & Expeditions' clients generally spend a few days at the company's Patriot Hills base camp to get acclimated to Antarctica's altitude and cold before heading off on flights to their climbing, skiing or photographic destinations. Weather may delay takeoff, but Patriot Hills – just 1100km from the South Pole – is a reasonably comfortable place to wait out a blizzard.

As the only private seasonal camp in Antarctica, it offers accommodations for 60 guests in large insulated tents (bring your own polar-rated sleeping bag). The tents are so well insulated, a resident says, 'we find that most tents are naturally heated by the midnight sun.' This despite the air temperature, which in early October can be around -30°C , rising to a high of -5°C in mid-December, with steady 20km/h to 30km/h winds.

Cooking and kitchen facilities, which turn out such delicate meals as smoked salmon, chocolate mousse and Welsh rarebit, accompanied by fresh fruit, vegetables and wine flown in from Chile, are in one tent, while the staff of 20 sleeps in several others. (The Chilean military posts a small contingent of personnel here each summer as well.) There's even a library tent. Primitive hot-water showers are also available, although most guests prefer sponge baths or even 'snow baths.' A physician is on the camp staff for the entire season.

A wind generator and solar panels produce enough power to operate all the camp equipment on a daily basis, a commendable achievement – and one that doubtless also greatly helps the company's bottom line, given the enormous cost of transporting fuel to Patriot Hills.

There's a strict carry-in carry-out policy at Patriot Hills. All refuse, including human waste, is removed from Antarctica, and no incineration takes place. All fuel drums are inventoried and either reused or removed from Antarctica. Even climbing expeditions on Vinson Massif are expected to pack out all their waste. Only grey water from Patriot Hills' kitchen and showers is disposed of in Antarctica.

can be tedious even for adults. If it is financially possible, try to get a suite so children have enough room to spread out on the floor and play with toys and books. Also, check to see if an in-cabin video player is available, so children can watch their favorite videos as well as educational tapes about Antarctica. You should probably count on there being no other children aboard the ship for your kids to play with.

Unfortunately, you should also be prepared to encounter resentment from other passengers – especially older travelers – until they see that your children can behave in a civilized manner. 'No one talks to you for the first three days,' said a perfectly behaved young girl on one Antarctic voyage. People will even sometimes tell parents later in the trip that they weren't happy to see the children aboard the ship – at first. But often youngsters find themselves becoming the object of grandparentlike attention from other travelers, especially in the dining room, where seating is usually open.

Children traveling to Antarctica (just like adults) will get more out of the experience if they're prepared for it. Watching videos and reading about Antarctica (there are many excellent children's books about the continent) before you set sail can help build excitement and knowledge. Giving children 'assignments' to learn about particular Antarctic topics while on the voyage – and encouraging them to ask the ship's staff to help them with research – can enrich their experience. Remember to bring plenty of materials for arts-and-crafts projects.

CLIMATE

Antarctica is synonymous with cold, thanks to its polar location, its high elevation, its lack of a protective, water-vapor-filled atmosphere and its permanent ice cover, which reflects about 80% of the sun's radiation back into space. Interestingly, the South Pole is not the coldest part of the continent. The lowest temperature ever recorded on earth's surface was -89.6°C at Russia's Vostok station on July 21, 1983. The warmest temperature ever recorded for Antarctica was 15°C on January 5, 1974 at New Zealand's Vanda station.

Mean temperatures in the Antarctic interior range from -40°C to -70°C during the coldest month, and from -15°C to -35°C during the warmest month. On the coast,

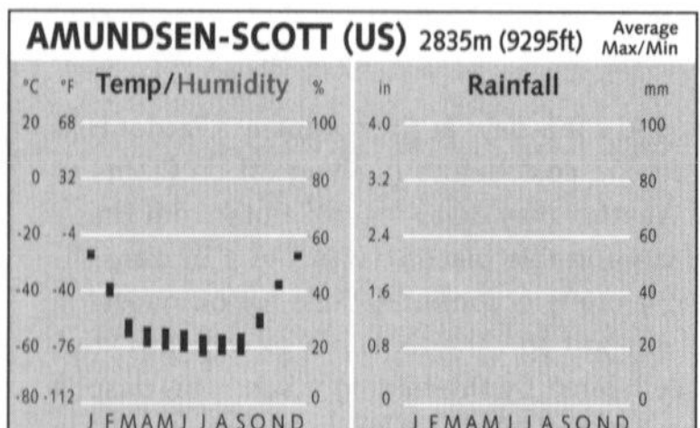

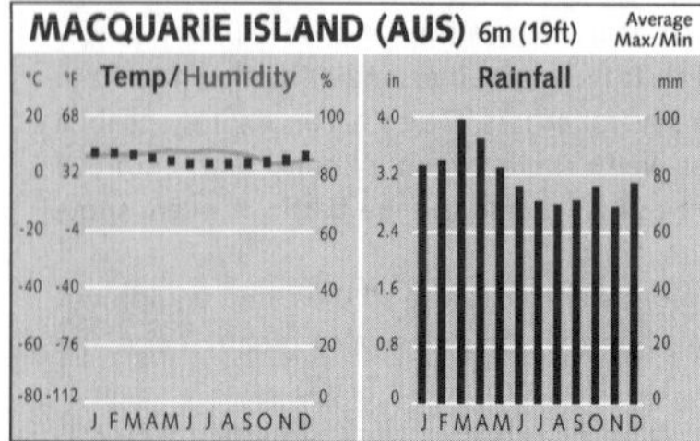

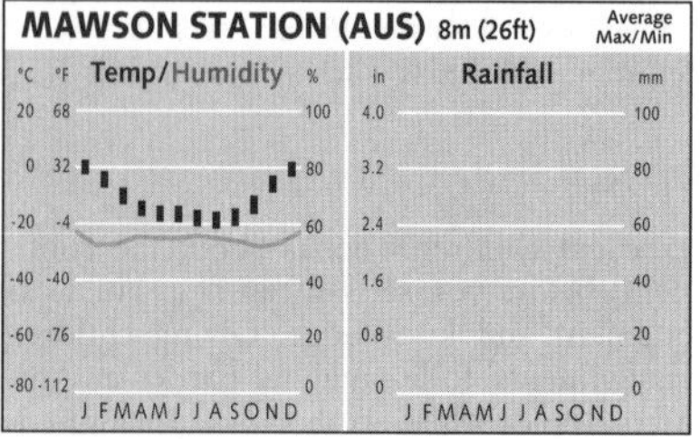

temperatures are considerably warmer: -15°C to -32°C in the winter and from 5°C to -5°C in the summer. The Antarctic Peninsula experiences the highest temperatures year-round.

The interior of Antarctica, despite its ice cap, is the world's driest desert, since the extreme cold freezes water vapor out of the air. Annual snowfall on the polar plateau is equivalent to less than 5cm of rain.

Antarctica experiences the strongest winds on the planet because of the katabatics caused by denser, colder air rushing down off the polar plateau to the coast. These can achieve velocities of up to 320km/h. The winds on the polar plateau, by contrast, are usually very light.

Antarctic blizzards are common. During a typical one very little, if any, snow actually falls. Instead, the snow is picked up and blown along the surface by the wind, resulting in blinding conditions in which objects less than a meter away may be invisible. Obviously such conditions are extremely dangerous, and several people have perished just meters from safety when they couldn't find their way to shelter.

Whiteouts are another peculiar Antarctic condition, during which there are no shadows or contrasts between objects. A uniformly grey or white sky over a snow-covered surface can yield these whiteouts, which cause a loss of depth perception – for both humans and birds.

DANGERS & ANNOYANCES

Tourists are largely shielded from Antarctica's worst dangers such as blizzards and crevasses, but life aboard ship has its own unique hazards. Always keep 'one hand for the ship' in case you suddenly need support as the ship rolls. Take care not just when climbing ladders and stairs, but anywhere that a sudden slam into furniture could result in a fractured limb or skull – yes, it happens nearly every year. A vessel pushing through ice can lurch suddenly, pitching an unaware passenger onto his or her nose. Doors likewise can swing dangerously, so don't curl your fingers around door jambs. Wide-open decks can be slippery with rain, snow or oil, so take it easy when moving about. Beware of raised doorsills, stanchions and other shipboard hardware, which can easily trip you.

Shipboard theft is so unusual that many passengers on Antarctic cruises don't even lock their cabin doors. In fact, a greater annoyance usually is dealing with balky or lost cabin keys.

If you fall overboard, you will die – simple as that. Although this may not be true in every case, it is almost certain, as human survival in the 4°C water of the Southern Ocean is calculated in minutes. Since drowning is thought by some to be preferable to freezing to death, one bit of half-cynical advice for those who fall overboard is to swim as hard as you can to the bottom. In March 2003, within 10km of Cape Horn, a male passenger disappeared from a tourist ship returning to Ushuaia from the Antarctic Peninsula. Because the sea temperature was approximately 11°C, his survival time was calculated at approximately half an hour. But his body was never found, despite an all-day search.

Cold and exposure on land can also be dangerous, so be sure you're properly clad before leaving the ship. The infamous windchill factor is a scientific way of measuring the intensifying effect of moving air upon heat loss. Since Antarctica is the windiest continent on earth, it pays to have a windproof (and waterproof) outer garment. Remember that the intense rays of the sun more easily penetrate the ozone-depleted Antarctic atmosphere, so you should wear sunscreen and sunglasses even on overcast days when the sun doesn't shine.

One often overlooked aspect of shipboard travel is the common feeling of claustrophobia that comes from being stuck in close quarters with people you can't escape from. The best way to keep this in perspective is to remind yourself that it will all be over with shortly – and to consider that your shipmates just might feel the same way about you. Showing a little consideration goes a long way in matters of snoring (bring earplugs for unsuspecting cabinmates), smoking (most tour operators have specific rules about it) and personal hygiene (fastidiousness in this matter is always appreciated).

DISABLED TRAVELERS

The physical challenges of shipboard life, Zodiacs and icy landing sites can make Antarctica difficult for able-bodied, as well as disabled travelers. However, disabled travelers may be able to make special arrangements with a tour operator, especially if an able-bodied traveler accompanies him or her. A ship equipped with helicopters and/or elevators may offer advantages. Check with tour operators to see how flexible they are and how well-equipped the ship is to handle wheelchairs.

FOOD

See p81 for information on food and drink aboard Antarctic ships, as well as the 'local foods' eaten by early explorers.

HOLIDAYS

Antarctica's most important holiday is the winter solstice, or Midwinter's Day (June 21 or 22, depending on the year), when the long polar night – with its darkness and extreme cold – is half over. It's traditionally celebrated in fancy dress with, among other things, feasting, gift-giving, games, barbecuing, karaoke, magazine publishing, wine tasting, songs, showing of old film footage from the station library and theatrical performances. Winter stations exchange radio messages, and national leaders often find it convenient to send congratulatory and encouraging messages to the polar denizens.

The last day of the sun and the return of the sun are also, understandably, very important dates on the Antarctic calendar; they occur on different dates at different latitudes.

Tourists won't get to experience any of these holidays, since they occur during winter, but Christmas and New Year's Eve are celebrated in unique Antarctic style aboard ship, and many families find them a good time to travel together since schools are on vacation.

LEGAL MATTERS

Many countries apply their national laws to their citizens in Antarctica, so despite its extralegal status, the continent is not somewhere you can rob or kill with impunity.

Marriages are among the most common of Antarctica's few legal ceremonies. Spur-of-the-moment newlyweds should check the validity of their Antarctic weddings to be sure that their local authorities legally recognize them.

MAPS

The best general map of the continent is the *Antarctica Satellite Map* (US$11), published by the **National Geographic Society** (☎ 800-437-5521, 717-633-3319; http://shop.nationalgeographic.com; 5022 Hollins Rd, Roanoke, VA 24050 USA). The map is a digital mosaic of 4500 satellite scans showing incredible detail of Antarctica's terrain, along with lots of up-to-date information on the continent.

The very good Ocean Explorer series of maps includes Antarctica, South Georgia and the Falkland Islands (each about US$10 to US$12.) These maps – along with a host of other Antarctic maps and books – can be ordered from either of the following:

Longitude Books (☎ 800 342-2164, 212-904-1144; www.longitudebooks.com; 115 West 30th St, Suite 1206, New York, NY 10001 USA)

The Antarctic Connection (☎ 877-766-9423, 603-383-6282; www.antarcticconnection.com; PO Box 538; Jackson, NH 03846 USA)

MONEY

Each ship runs its onboard economy differently, but in general a chit system is used, whereby you sign for items and pay at the end of the trip. These bills can be settled with cash, traveler's checks or credit cards.

No matter what country is operating them, most bases expect tourists to pay in either the national currency or in US dollars, with the latter preferred almost everywhere, even over the national currency. Tourists will not be able to access any ATMs or banks while in Antarctica or aboard ship, so must have cash or credit cards ready. For a list of exchange-rate conversions to US dollars, see the inside front cover.

Tipping is not included in the cruise fare and so is an additional, although optional, cost. While tipping is always at your discretion, it is considered an appropriate supplement to crew and staff wages for service. Near the end of the voyage most tour operators distribute tipping guidelines (between US$7 to US$10 per day), which are just that: suggestions only and not requirements in any way.

PHOTOGRAPHY & VIDEO

It can't be repeated too many times: bring more film (or storage capacity for digital cameras) than you think you'll need. You can always take it home, or sell or give it to film-starved fellow passengers. But you'll be sorry if you run out before that magnificent sunset or amazing encounter with humpbacks or... whatever! Don't think black-and-white film will do justice to Antarctica's beauty, unless you're aiming for an artistic or historical look. Bring it *in addition to* your supply of color film.

A UV filter on your lens keeps it from being scratched and works better than a lens cap, which may get lost. Polarizing filters cut through glare in the water and darken skies.

Finally, don't forget to bring lots of spare batteries. The ship's shop probably won't have what you need, and if it does, the stock may be outdated.

Photographing Wildlife

Although Antarctic animals may appear unconcerned by humans nearby, they may in fact be under considerable stress. People as far as 30m from a penguin rookery have been shown to increase the birds' heart rates significantly. And penguins may deviate from their usual path when approaching or leaving a colony for as long as three days after people visit.

Always remember to keep the required distances from animals: *at least* 5m from penguins, seabirds and seals – except fur seals, which should not be approached closer than 15m. Never block an animal's path to the sea or its young. When approaching, stay low. Don't move suddenly or speak loudly. When you're finished, back out quietly. If an animal starts to move, you're too close. The further you stay from an animal, the more natural its behavior will be. For this reason, many biologists prefer to view wildlife through binoculars or telephoto lenses even when ashore.

It's much better to get animals to come to you, which they will often do if you merely sit down, stay quiet and be patient.

POST

Send postcards from Antarctica for the novelty of doing so, understanding that service is slow – often as long as two or three months. Many stations send tourist mail back to their program's home country for forwarding to the recipient. You'll get a (sometimes surprising) postmark, and – if you send one to yourself – a happy reminder of your trip.

SHOPPING

Most stations and ship shops have at least a small selection of souvenirs (shirts, caps, postage stamps, trinkets and books). Prices vary.

TELEPHONE & FAX

Ship communications (fax, telephone and, in some cases, email) use the INMARSAT (International Maritime Satellite), which provides reliable if not inexpensive connections. Iridium phones also work well in Antarctica.

TIME

Time is all but irrelevant to most visitors to the Antarctic, since the tourist season occurs during summer, when the sun stays up as long as 20 hours a day. Most Antarctic ships' clocks remain at their port of departure time (if they're returning to the same port). Or they keep 'ship time' day by day, based on the port of disembarkation as they cross the Southern Ocean on the return voyage. Life aboard ship is usually ruled by landing opportunities, with meals delayed or advanced according to the possibilities for getting ashore.

Your main concern with time will be to make sure that when you call someone in the 'civilized world,' you won't be waking him or her up. The ship's radio officers can help you calculate the time difference.

VISAS

No single government controls Antarctica, so visitors do not need visas to go there. But with the ratification of the Antarctic Treaty's Protocol on Environmental Protection in 1998, all visitors who are citizens of countries that are signatories of the Antarctic Treaty must have a permit to visit Antarctica. Cruise ship passengers are covered under the permits applied for by the cruise company. Yacht passengers and crew, and anyone visiting Antarctica by air, should check with their national government to make sure they have their paperwork in order. If you are uncertain about your status, check with your tour operator.

WORK

Unless you're a scientist (and even then), landing a job with one of the national programs in Antarctica is very difficult. Anyone working in Antarctica has to submit to a battery of physical and psychological tests – and most important, must possess advanced skills in one or probably several areas. Length of service varies from three to 24 months. Be prepared for long hours: in the US program, for instance, the working week is six 10-hour days – with no overtime pay.

Scientists are usually sent to Antarctica as the result of specific research proposals approved by peer review, but support personnel are selected by the national programs themselves, or, in the case of the US, Antarctica's largest employer, by a private contractor. National programs usually hire only citizens, or people who have eligibility to live and work in that country. For this reason you should contact your country's national Antarctic program to inquire about employment. The following is a list of some addresses:

Antarctica New Zealand (☎ 64-3-358-0200; www.antarcticanz.govt.nz; International Antarctic Centre, Orchard Rd, Private Bag 4745, Christchurch, New Zealand)

Australian Antarctic Division (☎ 1800 030 755; www.antdiv.gov.au; Human Resources Section, Channel Hwy Kingston, Tasmania 7050, Australia)

British Antarctic Survey (☎ 44-1223-221508/7; www.antarctica.ac.uk/Employment/index.html; Personnel Department, High Cross, Madingley Rd, Cambridge, England CB3 0ET, UK)

French Institute for Polar Research and Technology (Institut Français pour la Recherche et la Technologie Polaires; ☎ 44-1223-361188; Technopôle Brest-Iroise BP 75 – 29280 Plouzané, France)

Japanese National Institute of Polar Research (☎ 81-3-3962-4711; fax 81-3-3962-2529; Kaga 1-9-10, Itabashi-ku, Tokyo 165, Japan)

Raytheon Polar Services Company (☎ 303-306-8822; http://rpsc.raytheon.com; 16800 East CentreTech Pkwy, Mail Stop DN/485/5M86, Aurora, CO 80011-9046 USA) Recruits about 600 people a year to work at US Antarctic stations. Proof of US citizenship or permanent residency is required, and candidates must pass stringent physical and dental examinations after receiving an offer of employment. Positions range from chefs and clerks to hair stylists and physicians, but the hot jobs – those for which openings are most often available – are usually in the trades or construction. A five- to 13-month contract is usual.

South African National Antarctic Programme (☎ 27-12-310-3560; Dept of Environmental Affairs and Tourism, Directorate: Antarctica & Islands, 315 Pretorius St, Private Bag X447, Pretoria 0001, South Africa)

The Antarctic Treaty

The Antarctic Treaty was made on December 1, 1959, and came into force on June 23, 1961.

TEXT OF THE ANTARCTIC TREATY

The Governments of Argentina, Australia, Belgium, Chile, the French Republic, Japan, New Zealand, Norway, the Union of South Africa, the Union of Soviet Socialist Republics, the United Kingdom of Great Britain and Northern Ireland, and the United States of America,

Recognizing that it is in the interest of all mankind that Antarctica shall continue for ever to be used exclusively for peaceful purposes and shall not become the scene or object of international discord;

Acknowledging the substantial contributions to scientific knowledge resulting from international cooperation in scientific investigation in Antarctica;

Convinced that the establishment of a firm foundation for the continuation and development of such cooperation on the basis of freedom of scientific investigation in Antarctica as applied during the International Geophysical Year accords with the interests of science and the progress of all mankind;

Convinced also that a treaty ensuring the use of Antarctica for peaceful purposes only and the continuance of international harmony in Antarctica will further the purposes and principles embodied in the Charter of the United Nations;

Have agreed as follows:

Article I

1 Antarctica shall be used for peaceful purposes only. There shall be prohibited, inter alia, any measure of a military nature, such as the establishment of military bases and fortifications, the carrying out of military maneuvers, as well as the testing of any type of weapon.

2 The present Treaty shall not prevent the use of military personnel or equipment for scientific research or for any other peaceful purpose.

Article II

Freedom of scientific investigation in Antarctica and cooperation toward that end, as applied during the International Geophysical Year, shall continue, subject to the provisions of the present Treaty.

Article III

1 In order to promote international cooperation in scientific investigation in Antarctica, as provided for in Article II of the present Treaty, the Contracting Parties agree that, to the greatest extent feasible and practicable:

(a) information regarding plans for scientific programs in Antarctica shall be exchanged to permit maximum economy of and efficiency of operations;

(b) scientific personnel shall be exchanged in Antarctica between expeditions and stations;

(c) scientific observations and results from Antarctica shall be exchanged and made freely available.

Article IV

1 Nothing contained in the present Treaty shall be interpreted as:

(a) a renunciation by any Contracting Party of previously asserted rights of or claims to territorial sovereignty in Antarctica;

(b) a renunciation or diminution by any Contracting Party of any basis of claim to territorial sovereignty in Antarctica which it may have whether as a result of its activities or those of its nationals in Antarctica, or otherwise;

(c) prejudicing the position of any Contracting Party as regards its recognition or nonrecognition of any other State's rights of or claim or basis of claim to territorial sovereignty in Antarctica.

2 No acts or activities taking place while the present Treaty is in force shall constitute a basis for asserting, supporting or denying a claim to territorial sovereignty in Antarctica or create any rights of sovereignty in Antarctica. No new claim, or enlarge-

ment of an existing claim, to territorial sovereignty in Antarctica shall be asserted while the present Treaty is in force.

Article V

1 Any nuclear explosions in Antarctica and the disposal there of radioactive waste material shall be prohibited.

2 In the event of the conclusion of international agreements concerning the use of nuclear energy, including nuclear explosions and the disposal of radioactive waste material, to which all of the Contracting Parties whose representatives are entitled to participate in the meetings provided for under Article IX are parties, the rules established under such agreements shall apply in Antarctica.

Article VI

The provisions of the present Treaty shall apply to the area south of 60°S Latitude, including all ice shelves, but nothing in the present Treaty shall prejudice or in any way affect the rights, or the exercise of the rights, of any State under international law with regard to the high seas within that area.

Article VII

1 In order to promote the objectives and ensure the observance of the provisions of the present Treaty, each Contracting Party whose representatives are entitled to participate in the meetings referred to in Article IX of the Treaty shall have the right to designate observers to carry out any inspection provided for by the present Article. Observers shall be nationals of the Contracting Parties which designate them. The names of observers shall be communicated to every other Contracting Party having the right to designate observers, and like notice shall be given of the termination of their appointment.

2 Each observer designated in accordance with the provisions of paragraph 1 of this Article shall have complete freedom of access at any time to any or all areas of Antarctica.

3 All areas of Antarctica, including all stations, installations and equipment within those areas, and all ships and aircraft at points of discharging or embarking cargoes or personnel in Antarctica, shall be open at all times to inspection by any observers designated in accordance with paragraph 1 of this Article.

4 Aerial observation may be carried out at any time over any or all areas of Antarctica by any of the Contracting Parties having the right to designate observers.

5 Each Contracting Party shall, at the time when the present Treaty enters into force for it, inform the other Contracting Parties, and thereafter shall give them notice in advance, of

(a) all expeditions to and within Antarctica, on the part of its ships or nationals, and all expeditions to Antarctica organized in or proceeding from its territory;

(b) all stations in Antarctica occupied by its nationals; and

(c) any military personnel or equipment intended to be introduced by it into Antarctica subject to the conditions prescribed in paragraph 2 of Article I of the present Treaty.

Article VIII

1 In order to facilitate the exercise of their functions under the present Treaty, and without prejudice to the respective positions of the Contracting Parties relating to jurisdiction over all other persons in Antarctica, observers designated under paragraph 1 of Article VII and scientific personnel exchanged under sub-paragraph 1(b) of Article III of the Treaty, and members of the staffs accompanying any such persons, shall be subject only to the jurisdiction of the Contracting Party of which they are nationals in respect of all acts or omissions occurring while they are in Antarctica for the purpose of exercising their functions.

2 Without prejudice to the provisions of paragraph 1 of this Article, and pending the adoption of measures in pursuance of subparagraph 1(e) of Article IX, the Contracting Parties concerned in any case of dispute with regard to the exercise of jurisdiction in Antarctica shall immediately consult together with a view to reaching a mutually acceptable solution.

Article IX

1 Representatives of the Contracting Parties named in the preamble to the present

Treaty shall meet at the City of Canberra within two months after the date of entry into force of the Treaty, and thereafter at suitable intervals and places, for the purpose of exchanging information, consulting together on matters of common interest pertaining to Antarctica, and formulating and considering, and recommending to their Governments, measures in furtherance of the principles and objectives of the Treaty, including measures regarding:
(a) use of Antarctica for peaceful purposes only;
(b) facilitation of scientific research in Antarctica;
(c) facilitation of international scientific cooperation in Antarctica;
(d) facilitation of the exercise of the rights of inspection provided for in Article VII of the Treaty;
(e) questions relating to the exercise of jurisdiction in Antarctica;
(f) preservation and conservation of living resources in Antarctica.

2 Each Contracting Party which has become a party to the present Treaty by accession under Article XIII shall be entitled to appoint representatives to participate in the meetings referred to in paragraph 1 of the present Article, during such times as that Contracting Party demonstrates its interest in Antarctica by conducting substantial research activity there, such as the establishment of a scientific station or the despatch of a scientific expedition.

3 Reports from the observers referred to in Article VII of the present Treaty shall be transmitted to the representatives of the Contracting Parties participating in the meetings referred to in paragraph 1 of the present Article.

4 The measures referred to in paragraph 1 of this Article shall become effective when approved by all the Contracting Parties whose representatives were entitled to participate in the meetings held to consider those measures.

5 Any or all of the rights established in the present Treaty may be exercised as from the date of entry into force of the Treaty whether or not any measures facilitating the exercise of such rights have been proposed, considered or approved as provided in this Article.

Article X

Each of the Contracting Parties undertakes to exert appropriate efforts, consistent with the Charter of the United Nations, to the end that no one engages in any activity in Antarctica contrary to the principles or purposes of the present Treaty.

Article XI

1 If any dispute arises between two or more of the Contracting Parties concerning the interpretation or application of the present Treaty, those Contracting Parties shall consult among themselves with a view to having the dispute resolved by negotiation, inquiry, mediation, conciliation, arbitration, judicial settlement or other peaceful means of their own choice.

2 Any dispute of this character not so resolved shall, with the consent, in each case, of all parties to the dispute, be referred to the International Court of Justice for settlement; but failure to reach agreement on reference to the International Court shall not absolve parties to the dispute from the responsibility of continuing to seek to resolve it by any of the various peaceful means referred to in paragraph 1 of this Article.

Article XII

1 **(a)** The present Treaty may be modified or amended at any time by unanimous agreement of the Contracting Parties whose representatives are entitled to participate in the meetings provided for under Article IX. Any such modification or amendment shall enter into force when the depository Government has received notice from all such Contracting Parties that they have ratified it.
(b) Such modification or amendment shall thereafter enter into force as to any other Contracting Party when notice of ratification by it has been received by the depository Government. Any such Contracting Party from which no notice of ratification is received within a period of two years from the date of entry into force of the modification or amendment in accordance with the provision of subparagraph 1(a) of this Article shall be deemed to have withdrawn from the present Treaty on the date of the expiration of such period.

2 **(a)** If after the expiration of 30 years

ANTARCTIC TREATY PARTIES

Country	Date Ratified or Acceded to Treaty	Country	Date Ratified or Acceded to Treat
Argentina	June 23, 1961	India	August 19, 1983
Australia	June 23, 1961	Italy	March 18, 1981
Austria	August 25, 1987	Japan	August 4, 1960
Belgium	July 26, 1960	Netherlands	March 30, 1967
Brazil	May 16, 1975	New Zealand	November 1, 1960
Bulgaria	September 11, 1978	Norway	August 24, 1960
Canada	May 4, 1988	Papua New Guinea	March 16, 1981
Chile	June 23, 1961	Peru	April 10, 1981
China	June 8, 1983	Poland	June 8, 1961
Colombia	January 31, 1989	Republic of Korea	November 28, 1986
Cuba	August 16, 1984	Romania	September 15, 1971
Czech Republic	June 14, 1962 [1]	Russian Federation	November 2, 1960 [3]
Democratic People's Republic of Korea	January 21, 1987	Slovak Republic	June 14, 1962 [1]
Denmark	May 20, 1965	South Africa	June 21, 1960
Ecuador	September 15, 1987	Spain	March 31, 1982
Estonia	May 17, 2001	Sweden	April 24, 1984
Finland	May 15, 1984	Switzerland	November 15, 1990
France	September 16, 1960	Turkey	January 24, 1995
Germany	February 5, 1979 [2]	Ukraine	October 28, 1992 [4]
Greece	January 8, 1987	United Kingdom	May 31, 1960
Guatemala	July 31, 1991	United States	August 18, 1960
Hungary	January 27, 1984	Uruguay	January 11, 1980
		Venezuela	March 24, 1999

Notes

1 The Czech and Slovak Republics inherited Czechoslovakia's obligations; Czechoslovakia ratified the Treaty on June 14, 1962.

2 The German Democratic Republic united with the Federal Republic of Germany on October 2, 1990; the GDR had acceded to the Treaty on November 19, 1974.

3 Following the dissolution of the USSR, Russia assumed the rights and obligations of being a party to the Treaty.

4 Ukraine has asserted that it has succeeded to the Treaty following the dissolution of the USSR.

from the date of entry into force of the present Treaty, any of the Contracting Parties whose representatives are entitled to participate in the meetings provided for under Article IX so requests by a communication addressed to the depository Government, a Conference of all the Contracting Parties shall be held as soon as practicable to review the operation of the Treaty.

(b) Any modification or amendment to the present Treaty which is approved at such a Conference by a majority of the Contracting Parties there represented, including a majority of those whose representatives are entitled to participate in the meetings provided for under Article IX, shall be communicated by the depository Government to all Contracting Parties immediately after the termination of the Conference and shall enter into force in accordance with the provisions of paragraph 1 of the present Article.

(c) If any such modification or amendment has not entered into force in accordance with the provisions of subparagraph 1(a) of this Article within a period of two years after the date of its communication to all the Contracting Parties, any Contracting Party may at any time after the expiration of that period give notice to the depository Government of its withdrawal from the present Treaty; and such withdrawal shall take effect two years after the receipt of the notice by the depository Government.

Article XIII

1 The present Treaty shall be subject to ratification by the signatory States. It shall be open for accession by any State which is a Member of the United Nations, or by any other State which may be invited to accede to the Treaty with the consent of all the Contracting Parties whose representatives are entitled to participate in the meetings provided for under Article IX of the Treaty.

2 Ratification of or accession to the present Treaty shall be effected by each State in accordance with its constitutional processes.

3 Instruments of ratification and instruments of accession shall be deposited with the Government of the United States of America, hereby designated as the depository Government.

4 The depository Government shall inform all signatory and acceding States of the date of each deposit of an instrument of ratification or accession, and the date of entry into force of the Treaty and of any modification or amendment thereto.

5 Upon the deposit of instruments of ratification by all the signatory States, the present Treaty shall enter into force for those States and for States which have deposited instruments of accession. Thereafter the Treaty shall enter into force for any acceding State upon the deposit of its instruments of accession.

6 The present Treaty shall be registered by the depository Government pursuant to Article 102 of the Charter of the United Nations.

Article XIV

The present Treaty, done in the English, French, Russian and Spanish languages, each version being equally authentic, shall be deposited in the archives of the Government of the United States of America, which shall transmit duly certified copies thereof to the Governments of the signatory and acceding States.

In witness thereof, the undersigned Plenipotentiaries, duly authorized, have signed the present Treaty.

Done at Washington this first day of December, one thousand nine hundred and fifty-nine.

Transportation

CONTENTS

AIR

Flights to the Interior

Antarctic Logistics & Expeditions (ALE; www.antarctic-logistics.com; 4376 South, 700 East, Suite 226, Salt Lake City, UT 84107 USA) is the only private company offering flights to the interior of Antarctica. In 2003 ALE acquired the pioneering tour operator, Adventure Network International (ANI), the first company to offer flights to Antarctica's interior, which operated for 18 seasons.

Using Ilyushin IL76 and ski-equipped Twin Otter aircraft, ALE offers expedition support and tours to such destinations as Vinson Massif (see the boxed text on p66 for more details; guided trips US$27,300, unguided US$22,000) and the South Pole. The 'South Pole Fly-In' is US$33,000; a guided 'South Pole – All the Way' trip, skiing 1175km from the edge of the continent to the Pole, 'the most incredible journey you will ever accomplish,' costs US$67,500.

For information about the accommodations and activities of ALE, see the boxed text on p285.

> **THINGS CHANGE**
>
> The information in this chapter is vulnerable to change. Check with the tour operator to make sure you understand the fare and the itinerary you've chosen. Shop carefully. The details given here should be regarded as pointers rather than a substitute for your own research.

Flights to the Peninsula

Chilean regional airline **Aerovías DAP** (☎ 56-61-223-340; www.dap.cl; O'Higgins 891, Punta Arenas, Chile) flies from Punta Arenas to Chile's Frei station on King George Island several times a month during the summer, using twin-engine Beechcraft King Air turboprops (10 passengers) and four-engine de Havilland Dash 7 turboprops (50 passengers). As always, the weather can be very uncooperative, and it may take several days before a flight can be made; sometimes flights must be canceled after five or six weather delays. Aerovías DAP offers one-day programs, and two-day, one-night stays (King Air flights only) at what DAP calls 'our own refuge' at Frei, made from modified shipping containers, with five rooms, a bathroom and a kitchen.

Fly-Cruise

AntarcticaXXI (☎ 56-61-228-783; www.antarcticaxxi.com; Roca 998, office 104, Punta Arenas, Chile) flies to Chile's Frei station on King George Island using 50-passenger, four-engine de Havilland Dash 7 turboprops. Passengers transfer to the 46-passenger ship *Grigoriy Mikheev* for several days of cruising in the South Shetlands and Peninsula region before their return flight to Punta Arenas.

Flightseeing

Day-long flights over the continent on a Boeing 747 are offered several times a year between the months of December and February by Australia's Qantas airlines. **Croydon Travel** (☎ 61-3-9725-8555, in Australia ☎ 800-633-449; www.antarcticaflights.com.au; 34 Main St, Croydon, Vic 3136 Australia) is the primary booking agency. There are five categories for fares: 1st class A$4899; business deluxe, A$3799; economy premium (not over a wing) A$2199; economy standard (over a wing) A$1349; and economy center A$899. All passengers except those in economy center are required to rotate their seating, which is accomplished without too much fuss – after all, the flights spend around three to four hours over The Ice.

For more information, see the boxed text on p296.

THE CONTINENT IN A DAY *Martin Betts*

Overflights are the quickest and least-expensive way to see Antarctica. Although no landings are made, observing the continent from altitude provides a unique perspective – unavailable to those who remain at sea level.

Some preparation hints: checked baggage is not permitted, so limit yourself to a small bag. Wear loose-fitting clothes, a light baggy sweater (this is not a fashion contest) and shoes you can easily kick off during the 13- to 14-hour, 10,000km round trip. Sunglasses are a must, since the glare from the ice can be blinding. If you have small, lightweight binoculars, take them as well. If you smoke, bring some nicotine substitute, as these are strictly nonsmoking flights.

Remember your camera and plenty of film. Your preflight package contains advice on photography, but you should still test your camera well before your trip. A commercial photographer also records the flight on video, and you can buy a copy after the flight.

Interestingly, you'll receive two boarding passes: one for the journey south until midway through the viewing period, the other from then until the flight's conclusion. Don't worry if you're not close to a window. Seats are rotated during the flight and there's a friendly, cooperative spirit on board. Passengers move about the plane more freely than normal, and people like to get the view from several vantage points, including the exit zones. But remember, you get what you pay for: some tickets do not provide you with direct window access at any time in the flight, and you may have to look over someone's shoulder. Make sure to read the fine print when booking your tickets.

Upon boarding, you'll find on your seat a package of information on Antarctica, its history and current research work there, along with maps showing the flight route. In addition to the usual safety video shown at the beginning of all airline flights, a special video gives instructions in the unlikely event that an emergency landing is required in Antarctica.

People with considerable Antarctic field knowledge and expertise will also be aboard, and they'll be keen to answer your questions. During the first few hours of the flight, they wear brightly colored, heavily insulated Antarctic clothing, thus subjecting themselves to the flight's only real danger: heatstroke from the cabin's constant 22°C temperature. The experts provide continuing commentary – and also try to leave some time for silence, so people can absorb what they're seeing.

Food is standard aircraft fare. A meal is served en route south, and another soon after the aircraft commences its northward journey. Plenty of complimentary liquid refreshment, including bar

SEA

Ship Cruises

The number of companies offering cruises to the Antarctic has increased dramatically during the past four years. Below are some of the oldest and most established companies crusing The Ice. For even more choices, contact the **International Association of Antarctica Tour Operators** (IAATO; ☎ 970 704-1047; www.iaato.org; PO Box 2178, Basalt, CO 81621, USA).

Abercrombie & Kent (☎ 630-954-2944, in USA ☎ 800-554-7016; www.abercrombiekent.com; 1520 Kensington Rd, Oak Brook, IL 60523, USA) Charters *Explorer II* (formerly called *Minerva*), an ice-reinforced vessel carrying 198 passengers.

Adventure Associates (☎ 61-2-9389-7466; www.adventureassociates.com; 197 Oxford St Mall or PO Box 612, Bondi Junction, NSW 2022, Australia) Offers trips to a number of parts of Antarctica on several different ships.

Aurora Expeditions (☎ 61-2-9252-1033, in Australia ☎ 1800-637-688; www.auroraexpeditions.com.au; 182A Cumberland St, The Rocks, Sydney, NSW 2000, Australia) Operates the 54-passenger *Polar Pioneer* (formerly called *Akademik Shuleykin)* and the 46-passenger *Akademik Shokalskiy*. Aurora also offers scuba diving, sea kayaking, mountain climbing and camping.

Clipper Cruise Line (☎ 314-655-6700, in USA ☎ 800-325-0010; www.clippercruise.com; 11969 Westline Industrial Dr, St Louis, MO 63146, USA) Operates the 122-passenger *Clipper Adventurer* (formerly called *Alla Tarasova)*.

Expeditions Inc (☎ 541-330-2454, in USA ☎ 888-484-2244; www.antarctica-journeys.com; 20525 SE Dorchester, Bend, OR 97702, USA) Sells a wide variety of Antarctica trips.

Fathom Expeditions (☎ 416-925-3174, 416-925-4219, in USA ☎ 800-621-0176; www.fathomexpeditions.com; 67 Yonge St, Suite 1001, Toronto ONT M5E 1J8, Canada) Offers small-ship voyages to the Peninsula.

Hapag-Lloyd Kreuzfahrten (☎ 49-40-3001-4600; www.hlkf.de in German; Ballindamm 25, 20095 Hamburg, Germany) Operates two luxury ice-strengthened ships: the 184-passenger *Hanseatic* and the 164-passenger *Bremen* (formerly called *Frontier Spirit)*.

service, is also on hand. For New Year's Eve flights, it flows in particular abundance. About four hours into the flight, the first icebergs and sea ice are often spotted, depending on the location and weather conditions. Generally, a maximum of three hours is spent viewing the continent, and another five are spent flying home. When the weather is right, viewing is spectacular, the clear air of Antarctica allowing objects 100km or more away to be seen. Over points of interest, the aircraft flies long figure eights to ensure that both sides of the plane have good views. While enjoying the ice cream that is served while you're warm and snug, the airplane flies over The Ice, with a single glance you can take in entire routes of famous, back-breaking journeys that took many months to complete. Seeing the rugged terrain below inspires many to marvel at the pioneer expeditions, and to realize what formidable difficulties still confront modern operations in Antarctica.

Individual buildings can be seen clearly when stations are overflown. But it is impossible to observe individual animals such as penguins, even with binoculars. Those wanting more detail will need to land on the continent, arriving there by ship or by aircraft.

Several times during the flight, the plane makes radio contact with some of the stations in the region, and the conversations are relayed into the cabin for everyone to hear. These chats with overwintering personnel provide a feel for what it's like to be on The Ice for an extended period.

Although little physical effort is required during the flight, you may start to feel the excitement and length of the day as the plane turns homeward and weariness sets in. Now is the time to eat a leisurely dinner, to watch Antarctic films and to purchase memorabilia such as T-shirts and books.

A few hours before touchdown, an auction is held. Four-figure sums are often paid, the money going to a nominated charity. Those interested in bidding must remember to take with them that modern survival tool: a credit card.

Upon landing, the experts gather at the exit door to wish everyone well. People usually leave with a faraway look in their eyes. This is partly from the long journey, but mostly it is from the experience of seeing Antarctica for the first time. The reaction of those who see the continent this way is the same as those who actually step ashore: wonder – coupled with a desire to return soon.

Martin Betts, the former Senior Policy Officer at the Australian Antarctic Division, has been on four overflights

Heritage Expeditions (☎ 64-3-365-3500, in NZ ☎ 800-262-8873, in Australia 1800-143-585; www.heritage-expeditions.com; 53B Montreal St or PO Box 7218, Christchurch, New Zealand) The only family-operated business in Antarctic tourism, operates the 48-passenger *Spirit of Enderby* (formerly *Professor Kromov*), which carries a helicopter. Heritage offers trips to New Zealand's sub-Antarctic islands, Macquarie Island and the Ross Sea region. It also offers scuba diving.

Lindblad Expeditions (☎ 212-765-7740, in USA ☎ 800-397-3348; www.expeditions.com; 720 Fifth Ave, New York, NY 10019, USA) Operates the 110-passenger *Endeavour* (formerly called *Caledonian Star*). *Endeavour* carries an onboard ROV (remotely operated vehicle), operated by a staff 'underwater specialist,' with video footage shown on monitors in the ship's lounge. Lindblad also offers kayaking.

Mountain Travel-Sobek (☎ 510-594-6000, 888-687-6235; www.mtsobek.com; 1266 66th St, Emeryville, CA 94608, USA) Sells several trips and offers kayaking.

Oceanwide Expeditions The Netherlands (☎ 31-118-410410; www.ocnwide.com; Bellamypark 9, 4381 CG Vlissingen, The Netherlands); United States (☎ 281-987-9600, in USA ☎ 800-453-7245; fax 281-987-1140; 15710 JFK Blvd, Suite 285, Houston, TX 77032, USA) Operates the 46-passenger *Grigoriy Mikheev* and offers scuba diving.

Orient Lines (☎ 954-527-6660, in USA ☎ 800-333-7300; www.orientlines.com; 1510 SE 17 St, Ft Lauderdale, FL 33316, USA) Operates the 826-passenger *Marco Polo*.

Peregrine Expeditions (☎ 61-3-9663-8611; www.peregrine.net.au; 258 Lonsdale St, Melbourne, Vic 3000, Australia) Operates the 110-passenger *Akademik Ioffe* and the 110-passenger *Akademik Sergey Vavilov* and offers camping and kayaking.

Quark Expeditions (www.quark-expeditions.com); United States (☎ 203-656-0499, in USA ☎ 800-356-5699; 1019 Post Rd, Darien, CT 06820, USA); United Kingdom (☎ 44-1494-464-080; Crendon St 19A, High Wycombe, Bucks, HP13 6LJ, England) Offers a variety of ships to the Peninsula and the Ross Sea region aboard the powerful Russian-flagged, helicopter-equipped, 108-passenger icebreaker *Kapitan Khlebnikov*.

SMALL SHIP OR LARGE SHIP? *Dr Peter Carey*

Small ships and large ships both conduct landings in Antarctica using inflatable boats with naturalists as guide, but there are important differences between the two. Small ships offer passengers more adventure and time ashore but are likely to have greater environmental impacts at landing sites. Large ships, on the other hand, give passengers much less time ashore but make the traveling more comfortable with a smoother ride in rough seas, and a wider choice of amenities on board.

Shore Time

On small ships, all passengers are invited to stay ashore for the duration of the landing, usually three to four hours at a site. A small ship will usually make *at least* two landings per day for about seven days, while a large ship will make just one landing per day over four days. Large-ship passengers are divided into groups that must take turns, so an individual is usually ashore just one hour at each landing. Therefore, a small-ship passenger can spend as much as 40 to 50 hours ashore during a cruise, versus a large-ship passenger's four hours for an entire cruise.

Behavioral Controls

Small-ship passengers tend to roam widely and have the opportunity for great independence. At some sites, this can mean passengers are more than a kilometer from the landing beach – and often out of view of staff members. The ability to choose where you go and how you spend your time ashore is one of the things that makes small ships so attractive and popular, and staff are usually very conscientious about environmental issues and passenger needs where possible. However, because of the large areas over which people can be spread, there are often many small-ship passengers who are completely unsupervised.

In contrast, large-ship passengers are extremely restricted in where they can go: usually an area close to the landing beach, with boundaries clearly delineated by a temporary 'fence' made up of the ship's crew and orange traffic cones. The boundaries are set to minimize impact on wildlife, and 'fences' are sometimes moved to accommodate the changing needs of the wildlife. Naturalists are stationed near sites of interest to better provide interpretation, and passengers are always within view of staff members. With just an hour on shore, there is no expectation of roaming widely.

WildWings/WildOceans Travel (☎ 44-117-9658-333; www.wildwings.co.uk; 577 Fishponds Rd, Bristol BS16 3AF, UK) Operates bird- and wildlife-focused tours to Antarctica.

Zegrahm Expeditions (☎ 206-285-4000, in USA ☎ 800-628-8747; www.zeco.com; 192 Nickerson St, Suite 200, Seattle, WA 98109, USA) Offers cruises on several different vessels.

Yacht Cruises

A small but growing handful of visitors reach Antarctica aboard private vessels. All are sailboats (although obviously equipped with auxiliary engines), and some have even wintered in sheltered anchorages such as Yankee Harbor at Greenwich Island or near Palmer station on the Peninsula. In three decades of Antarctic cruising, there have been about 200 yacht voyages to The Ice. For some reason, this type of travel particularly seems to appeal to the French, who have made up the majority of yacht visitors to Antarctica. About 125 fare-paying passengers visit Antarctica by yacht each year.

Although the national Antarctic programs cannot regulate yacht tourism, since Antarctica is open to everyone, research stations are no longer instantly hospitable whenever a yacht turns up on their doorstep. Where once they welcomed the rare visitors from the outside world, these days the traffic is so heavy at most stations that advance notice of several weeks or even months is required for a station tour; there are some exceptions, mainly among the smaller countries operating in Antarctica.

Sailing to Antarctica is not something one undertakes lightly. An old sailor's adage has it that 'Beyond 40°S, there is no law... Beyond 50°S, there is no God.' And, by trad-

Environmental Impact

Tighter control on passenger movements is the key to minimizing environmental impacts during visits ashore, and restricted passengers are usually happy to comply when it's explained to them why their wanderings are limited. Less-restricted, and therefore less-supervised visitors, have more opportunity to interact with wildlife – in both the negative and positive senses – and station personnel, who have watched a variety of ships under a variety of expedition leaders land in their backyards, comment on the reckless visits of some small ships and the subsequent disturbance of seals and nesting birds.

Some people assume that one visit by a 500-passenger vessel has more impact on a landing site than five visits by a 100-passenger vessel, but given the different standards of on-shore behavior they are not easily compared. There is as yet no data to support either side of the argument, but this is an area of research worthy of investigation.

Safety

Larger vessels, with their larger fuel capacities, are apt to cause a bigger mess if they have an accident. However, they are also less likely to run aground, since they tend to stick to the established sea-lanes where soundings are plentiful. Like their passengers, they don't go exploring. Large size also is an advantage in the event that another ship has trouble – a big ship could accommodate all the passengers and crew from a small one, should it need to be abandoned.

Comfort

While no ship can make a millpond out of the sea during a truly nasty storm, large ships really do take a lot of the pain out of the Drake Passage crossing. This is because they have such good stabilizers, and because their deeper draft and sheer size also help to limit the motion. On top of that, they are usually a lot faster, cruising at 18 knots or more in open seas, and this lessens the time of suffering. I once made a crossing in a large ship that took only 22 hours from the shelter of the South Shetlands to the shelter of Cape Horn. Most small ships would take about 36 hours to get across.

In the end, small ships and big ships cater to two different markets with the former fulfilling the desires of adventurous souls who're not too worried about luxury and want to take the biggest bite out of Antarctica, and the latter appealing to those for whom comfort is more important, and who are satisfied with just a taste of The Ice.

Dr Peter Carey has worked for many years as a naturalist and expedition leader on both small and large ships in Antarctica, and as a scientist with various national Antarctic programs

ition, writes Alan Gurney in *Below the Convergence* (1997): 'Those who have rounded Cape Horn under sail can take their after-dinner drink with one foot upon the table; those who have sailed across the polar circles can drink with both feet upon the table.'

It would be unwise to attempt to sail to Antarctica without taking one – or, preferably, both – of the following books: *The Antarctic Pilot*, fifth edition (1997), published by Britain's Hydrographer of the Navy, and *Sailing Directions (Planning Guide & Enroute) for Antarctica*, fourth edition (2002), published by the US National Imagery and Mapping Agency. *The Antarctic Pilot* (US$70) is superior, with more comprehensive entries, as well as a hardcover binding, which *Sailing Directions for Antarctica* (US$26) lacks. Both are available from **New York Nautical** (☎ 212-962-4522; www.newyorknautical.com; 140 West Broadway, New York, NY 10013, USA).

Anyone who is seriously considering a yacht voyage to Antarctica should also try to obtain Sally and Jérôme Poncet's excellent 60-page book, *Southern Ocean Cruising*, which was published privately in 1991 (see also the boxed text on p302 for more information).

For a list of private yachts that take fare-paying passengers, see the boxed text above. A number of other yachts also sail to the Antarctic regularly, mostly from Ushuaia or Stanley. They primarily charter to private expeditions and commercial groups such as film crews.

Alex Foucard (☎ 33-4-7636-5698; afoucard@club-internet.fr) *Croix St Paul II* is an 18m aluminum sloop skippered by Alex Foucard. It accommodates eight participants.

ANTARCTIC YACHTING AGENCIES

For those who don't own a yacht, or prefer to have someone else do the skippering, an increasing number of private yachts take fare-paying passengers, who are generally expected to help with the sailing and watch-keeping. Yacht crew and passengers must follow the same rules when ashore in Antarctica as passengers from cruise ships.

Many yachts work independently, while the following three agencies act as clearing houses for Antarctic yachts:

Croisieres Australes (☎ 33-2-9923-6741; www.nature-sailing.com; 3 allée de l'Oseraie, F 35760 St Grégoire, France)

Ocean Voyages Inc (☎ 415-332-4681, in USA ☎ 800-299-4444; www.oceanvoyages.com; 1709 Bridgeway, Sausalito, CA 94965, USA)

Victory Yacht Cruises (☎ 56-61-621-010; www.victory-cruises.com; PO Box 70, Teniente Munoz 118, Puerto Williams, Tierra del Fuego, Chile)

These agencies each manage a number of yachts including the following:

Name	Type	Skipper	No of participants
Croisieres Australes			
Baltazar	16m schooner	Bertrand Dubois	6
Fernande	21.5m aluminum ketch	Pascal Grinberg	10
Kekilistrion	12m steel sloop	Olivier Pauffin	4
Kotick I	15m steel schooner	Alain Caradec	5
Valhalla	20m steel schooner	Pascal Boimard	8
Ocean Voyages Inc			
Darwin Sound	22m fiberglass ketch	Yvon Fauconnier	10
Fernande	21.5m aluminum ketch	Pascal Grinberg	10
Kotick II	18.7m steel schooner	Oleg Bely	8
Ocean Leopard	24.7m sloop	Mark Tomlinson	8
Victory Yacht Cruises			
Baltazar	16m schooner	Bertrand Dubois	6
Fernande	21.5m aluminum ketch	Pascal Grinberg	8
Kekilistrion	12m steel sloop	Olivier Pauffin	4
Kotick II	18.7m steel schooner	Oleg Bely	8
Le Sourire	20m aluminum sloop	Hugh Delignières	8
Mago Del Sur	16m steel sloop	Alejandro Da Milano	8
Santa Maria	14.7m steel sloop	Wolf Kloss	6
Unicornio	11m fiberglass sloop	Julio Brunet	4

Eef Willems (☎ 31-228-319230; www.tooluka.com; Zuider Havendijk 72, 1601 JD Enkhuizen, The Netherlands) *Tooluka*, a 14.2m steel sloop, accommodates up to six participants.

Eric Barde & Gudule Wyser (☎ 41-79-338-2668; www.philos.us; Hameau de la Poya, F74660 Vallorcine, France) *Philos*, a 14m steel schooner, accommodates five participants.

Expedition Sail (☎ /fax 888-250-4852; www.expeditionsail.com) *Seal*, a 17m aluminum cutter designed for high-latitude voyages, carries six passengers and is skippered by Hamish and Kate Laird.

Frances David (caribcon@candwbvi.net; CC PO Box 3069 Road Town, British Virgin Islands) Frances David is the agent for **Dove** (thedove88@iname.com), a 16.5m sloop, skippered by Larry Tyler, which accommodates four guests.

Henk Boersma or Jacqueline Haas (☎ /fax 54-2901-43-45-43; www.sarahvorwerk.com; PO Box 61, Ushuaia 9410, Argentina) *Sarah W Vorwerk*, a 16m steel sloop, accommodates eight guests.

Jérôme Poncet (☎ /fax 500-42316; goldenfleeceltd@yahoo.com, golden.fleece@horizon.co.fk; Beaver Island, PO Stanley, Falkland Islands via UK) *Golden Fleece* is a

19.5m steel schooner accommodating eight passengers. It's skippered by Jérôme Poncet, who has sailed in Antarctic waters for more than 30 years, making him the world's most experienced Antarctic yachtsman.

Lucas Trihey (☎ 61-2-4784-1029; www.ocean-expeditions.com; 2 Victoria St, Leura, NSW 2780, Australia) Contact Lucas Trihey for information about *Australis*, a 23m steel motor sailor, skippered by Roger Wallis, which carries 10 passengers.

Northanger (www.northanger.org) *Northanger*, a 15.6m steel ketch, owned and operated by Greg Landreth and Keri Pashuk, accommodates five participants.

Skip Novak (☎ 27-21-791-2479; www.pelagic.co.uk; Postnet Suite 279; Private Bag X4, Hout Bay 7872, South Africa) *Pelagic* is a 16.5m six-passenger steel sloop specially built for polar expeditions, as is its newer sister ship *Pelagic Australis*, a 23m 10-passenger aluminum sloop. Both are operated by Pelagic Expeditions Ltd, managed by Skip Novak.

Turismo Sea, Ice & Mountain Adventures (SIM) Ltd (☎ 56-61-621-150; www.simltd.com; PO Box 6, c/o 'Backpacker's Lodge,' Calle Ricardo Maragano 168, Puerto Williams, Tierra del Fuego, Chile) *Santa Maria* is a 14.7m steel sloop owned and skippered by Wolf Kloss. It carries five participants and two crew members.

Waterline Yachts (☎ 64-9-372-3105; www.tiama.com; PO Box 106390, Auckland, New Zealand) *Tiama*, a 15.2m steel cutter owned and skippered by Henk Haazen, accommodates six participants.

Resupply Vessels

The 110-passenger French resupply ship *Marion Dufresne II* visits France's Terres Australes et Antarctiques Françaises to deliver personnel and provisions to the three research stations there. Since 1994 the territory's administration has allowed a number of tourists to travel on the resupply voyages. About 30 people visit the French sub-Antarctic this way each year. The voyages last 21 to 29 days and sail from Réunion in the western Indian Ocean. The amount of time spent at the islands depends on how long is required to load and unload goods and people at the station. To safeguard the islands' environments, guides accompany tourists on landings. At Kerguelen, tourists can stay overnight at Port-aux-Français station and go on hikes of up to several days' duration, staying overnight in small refuges including at Port-Jeanne d'Arc. Bookings are handled by the travel agency **Mer et Voyages** (☎ 33-1-4926-9333/444; www.mer-et-voyages.com in French; 9 rue Notre Dame des Victoires, 75002 Paris, France).

Zodiacs

Without Zodiacs, tourism in the Antarctic would be much more difficult and much less pleasurable. Popularized by the late French oceanographer Jacques Cousteau, Zodiacs are small, inflatable boats powered by outboard engines. Their shallow draft makes them ideal for cruising among icebergs and ice floes and for landing in otherwise inaccessible areas. They are made of a synthetic, rubberlike material forming a pontoon in a roughly wishbone shape, with a wooden transom on the back holding the engine. The deck (floor) is made of sections of aluminum. Zodiacs are very safe and stable in the water and are designed to stay afloat even if one or more of their six separate air-filled compartments are punctured. Zodiacs come in a variety of sizes, but on most trips you can expect to share your boat with nine to 14 other passengers, a driver and one other cruise staff member.

Smoking near Zodiacs is prohibited – and dangerous – since the fuel tanks are exposed. Life jackets must be worn during Zodiac trips. Wet weather jackets and pants are also critical, because even in fine weather the boat's flying spray will give you a good shower. Personal items should be carried in a waterproof backpack (or in a waterproof bag inside the backpack); you can also tuck cameras, binoculars or bags inside your foul-weather jacket or parka to keep them dry. Remember, there are no toilets ashore, so be sure to go before you leave the ship.

To ensure that no one gets left behind in Antarctica, tours maintain a system for keeping track of passengers. On some ships,

EXAGGERATION WARNING

Some tour brochures still get carried away with the 'exploring' theme and exaggerate claims slightly: 'Experience the thrill of treading where no one has gone before as we land our versatile Zodiacs on barren shores....' Not quite! With the large number of ships now visiting the Antarctic Peninsula each season, it's much more probable that another shipload of passengers has just landed on 'your' beach less than 12 hours before.

SOUTHERN OCEAN YACHTING *Sally Poncet*

Yachts have visited the Antarctic since 1966, when Bill Tilman in *Mischief* called in at Deception Island. Since then, hundreds of yacht voyages have been made south to The Ice, in vessels ranging from luxurious 30m motor-sailors, with professional crews and the latest in electronic wizardry, to more modest 10m cruising yachts equally well prepared but crewed by husband-and-wife teams. These yachts and their crews and passengers go to Antarctica primarily to experience the beauty of the white continent. Some are on expeditionary, sporting or scientific missions, while others carry small numbers of tourists. All share a common awe for Antarctica.

In recent years, an average of 15 yachts has visited the Antarctic Peninsula each summer, a remarkably small number, given the popularity of cruising. The widespread use of radar, GPS navigation devices, radio, satellite communications and weather fax – together with the availability of strong, reliable hull materials and improved navigation charts – may tempt some sailors to rely less on experience and skill and increasingly on modern technology. It is far easier to sail to the Antarctic today than it was 35 years ago – but the rules remain the same.

Whatever the size of the yacht and its budget and goals, there are a few essential points to remember when preparing for a cruise to the Antarctic. The first is autonomy: you must make sure to carry enough of everything – food, fuel, clothing and spare parts – to be completely self-sufficient for the duration of your cruise. A reliable engine, a cabin heater, a hull strong enough to withstand collision with ice and rocks, and a generously dimensioned anchor and chain – together with an experienced crew – will increase the odds for a trouble-free cruise. It's also important to be certain you are physically and mentally capable of coping with several weeks of isolation under often-strenuous conditions.

Familiarize yourself and your crew with the latest Antarctic Treaty regulations for visitors; see the boxed text on p90 for more information.

When planning your itinerary, bear in mind that there are a number of protected areas, which may not be entered. Also, most stations maintain long-term scientific research programs on nearby islands or ice-free areas, to which access is restricted. Visits to stations require advance notice so they can be scheduled around the station's work program and its resupplying. Even if you are simply anchoring in the vicinity of a station, courtesy requires that you inform the station manager by VHF radio of your intentions while in the area.

Typically, a voyage to Antarctica commences in Tierra del Fuego. This is the shortest ocean crossing, taking around four days, depending on the weather and the yacht. Chilean Navy personnel, who follow yacht movements with administrative zeal and friendly interest, carry out formal clearance for Antarctica at Puerto Williams, 50km east of Ushuaia along the Beagle Channel.

Actual departure time may depend on the succession of low-pressure systems coming in from the west and funneling through the Drake Passage. A deep front and its usual attendant gale-force winds can transform the crossing from an exhilarating three-day cruise into six days

a staff member checks your name off of a list when you leave the ship, and again when you leave the shore. On others, you are responsible for turning over a colored tag on a noticeboard inside the ship, indicating your departure and return.

Entering and exiting Zodiacs are probably the most hazardous activities a tourist in Antarctica will undertake – but with a little care, there is no need for anyone to get hurt. Passengers descend the ship's gangway to the Zodiac, which is held to the landing at the bottom of the gangway by a crewmember and/or several lines. Since the Zodiac will be rising and falling with the swell, it's important to have both hands free. If you have a camera or a bag, the Zodiac crew will ask you to hand it to them. They will then take hold of your wrist (you should likewise seize theirs) in a hold known as the 'sailor's grip.' This is much safer than a mere handshake grip, since if one party accidentally lets go, the other still has a firm hold. Move slowly: step onto the pontoon of the Zodiac and then down onto the deck or floor, before moving to your seat, a spot along the pontoon. Sit facing the inside of the boat, and hold onto the ropes tied to the pontoon behind you, since the ride can be quite bumpy.

of headwinds, huge seas and much discomfort. Yachts with weather fax facilities plan their departure accordingly, seeking shelter among the islands near Cape Horn while waiting for fronts to pass through.

Once at sea, life on board quickly settles into a routine of watch-keeping, with crew members sharing the cold hours on deck, keeping watch for fishing boats, freighters and icebergs. Although most yachts are equipped with self-steering, which obviates the need for a helmsman, crew and passengers alike benefit from being outside each day. Astern, the wake spins out a voyager's tale to the ocean and its seabirds as the yacht heads south at 6 or 7 knots, covering 300km every 24 hours.

During a four-week voyage to the Antarctic, a yacht will probably experience extremes. Cruising the Southern Ocean is as much a feat of mental strength as of practical physical preparation.

There is nothing quite like an ocean passage in the southern latitudes; it can be cold, uncomfortable and frightening. Yet the miseries of yesterday are quickly forgotten after a few hours of fair winds, sailing along at 8 knots in a white-crested sea, with a cape petrel keeping pace at the stern rail.

On a clear day the white peaks of Brabant and Anvers Islands are visible more than 80km away. Tucked between them are the Melchior Islands, a popular landfall for yachts, with seaward approaches clear of dangers. There's also an excellent anchorage within the island group, which is only a few hours' sail from one of the most beautiful – and most visited – areas of the Antarctic: the Gerlache Strait, with its 100km of sheltered waterways, its bays, coves, islands and glaciers, all dominated by the mainland plateau and mountain peaks, which rise 1800m above the sea.

Exploring this coastline by boat is a constant challenge, but it has daily rewards. Working with incomplete – and in some cases, inaccurate – marine charts means that constant vigilance is required when close inshore; the danger of uncharted rocks is very real.

There is a handful of all-weather anchorages, among them, Dorian Cove at Port Lockroy, the Argentine Islands and Pléneau Island, while Cuverville, Enterprise and Booth Islands and Paradise Harbor offer temporary shelter in certain conditions. Thus, a day's cruising can be planned around reaching safe anchorage by nightfall – and hopefully before the worst of a gale arrives.

Sea ice is rarely a problem in this area during the height of austral summer. There is little risk of becoming beset if extensive fields of sea ice are avoided and a careful eye is kept on the weather. A healthy respect for bergs and pack ice is essential, however, particularly in areas where current and wind could jeopardize a yacht's attempts to reach the safety of open water.

But there will be moments when the sea and the sky could not be more tranquil, when the high plateaus of the Antarctic Peninsula reflect in waters of perfect silence and utter stillness, peaks aglow in evening gold tinged with pink and lilac. From a nearby Adélie colony you may hear the distant clamor of hungry chicks and harassed parents, with the occasional raucous call of a passing skua. To glimpse the Antarctic on such a day is incomparable.

Sally Poncet is the co-author of Southern Ocean Cruising

Only one passenger at a time should stand in a Zodiac. You should never stand while the boat is moving; ask the driver to slow the Zodiac down before you do.

Exiting a Zodiac is as simple as entering one. Most landings are made bow-first, and tour staff will be on hand to help you get out of the boat. Passengers sitting in the bow should swing their legs toward the stern of the Zodiac (naturally taking care not to kick their neighbor), then over the side and down onto the beach. Swinging your legs to the front of the Zodiac would be more difficult, since the pontoon is higher in the bow, and you might well fall back into the Zodiac, presenting a great photo opportunity for all your fellow passengers. If there is a large swell, landings may be made stern-first. In this case, passengers in the stern will be asked to disembark first. Never try to exit over the transom, since a surging wave could knock you over or lift and drop the heavy engine or even the entire Zodiac onto you.

Zodiac landings are either 'wet,' meaning you have to step into a bit of water before getting to the dry beach, or 'dry,' in which case you can step directly onto a rock, jetty, dock or other piece of dry land. *All* landings in Antarctica are 'wet.'

12 QUESTIONS TO ASK YOUR TOUR OPERATOR

How many days will you actually spend in Antarctica?
This may be the most important question. Some tours include several nights in South America as part of a 14-day 'Antarctica' program. Crossing the Southern Ocean takes a couple of days each way, which also significantly reduces your time on the continent. How many days of landings are planned? For a bit more money, you may buy yourself several extra days, which can make a big difference in your experience. When it's time to head home, most people wish they could have 'just a day or two more.'

How much does it cost?
Price should only be one factor in your decision. By paying marginally more, you may have a completely different experience.

What exactly is included in the quoted price of the trip?
For example, are port taxes included in the total price? They can add hundreds to your cost. What about airfare? Some tour operators include this, most don't.

What kind of ship is it?
Is it ice-strengthened? Or an unstrengthened cruise liner just visiting The Ice for a cruise or two? An icebreaker can push through much thicker ice than an ice-strengthened vessel, but an icebreaker's shallower draft means it rolls more in heavy seas.

How many other passengers will be on board?
The smallest ships accommodate fewer than 50 passengers, while the largest carry more than 1000. Travel on a large ship can feel like a Caribbean cruise, with glitzy nightclubs, marble bathtubs and six-course dinners. Smaller ships concentrate on Antarctica itself. On which will you feel most comfortable? See also the boxed text on p298.

What kind of atmosphere prevails on board?
Smaller ships offer a more intimate experience, while on larger ships you can remain more anonymous.

What about rescue in case of an accident?
Rescuing hundreds of passengers and crew would present an enormous challenge in the unlikely event that a large ship ran aground or unexpectedly met an iceberg – this is always a possibility in the Antarctic.

Is the tour operator an International Association of Antarctic Tour Operators (IAATO) member?
IAATO is an industry group that promotes responsible travel to Antarctica.

Who are the other passengers?
Special interest groups such as bird-watchers or alumni groups sometimes buy a large proportion of a ship's cabins. Divergent agendas can cause tensions on a voyage. And although meeting people from other countries can be one of travel's chief joys, language can present challenges.

Who are the lecturers?
The quality and enthusiasm of lecturers varies greatly from ship to ship – and from cruise to cruise. Many eminent scientists can be poor lecturers. Delivering a top-quality talk is a special skill, blending knowledge, entertainment and good humor, with information. Is there a dedicated lecture hall aboard? Are there seats for all passengers, or is it standing-room only for latecomers?

How experienced is the expedition leader?
Antarctic tour companies refer to cruise directors as 'expedition leaders.' Since the expedition leader and the ship's captain make all on-the-spot decisions about landings and itinerary choices, they're an important factor in your cruise. Inexperienced leaders may be overly ambitious in their planning, or may fail to conduct as many landings as might be possible.

Does the ship carry helicopters?
This may be important to your trip as helicopters can be invaluable for getting to places inaccessible by Zodiac.

Health

Dr David Goldberg & Jeff Rubin

CONTENTS

Antarctica is a clean, healthy, disease-free place, but medical resources are limited. Serious health problems will require evacuation to a country with state-of-the-art care. While the ship's doctor stands ready to treat any problems arising *en voyage*, he or she is not available for general consultation. Antarctica's greatest health risks are cold exposure, sun exposure and dehydration.

BEFORE YOU GO

RECOMMENDED VACCINATIONS

No special vaccines are required or recommended for travel to Antarctica. All travelers should be up-to-date on the routine immunizations listed below.

Bring medications in their original containers, clearly labeled. A signed, dated letter from your physician describing all medical conditions and medications, including generic names, is also a good idea. If carrying syringes or needles, be sure to have a physician's letter documenting their medical necessity.

If your health insurance does not cover you for medical expenses abroad, consider organizing supplemental insurance. Check out the Subwwway section of the **Lonely Planet website** (www.lonelyplanet.com/subwwway) for more information about insurance. Find out in advance if your insurance plan will make payments directly to providers or reimburse you later for overseas health expenditures.

INTERNET RESOURCES

There is a wealth of travel health advice on the Internet. For further information, **Lonely Planet** (www.lonelyplanet.com) is a good place to start with loads of general information. The **World Health Organization** (www.who.int/ith/) publishes a superb book, called *International Travel and Health*, which is revised annually and is available online at no cost. Another website of general interest is **MD Travel Health** (www.mdtravelhealth.com), which provides complete travel health recommendations for every country, updated daily, also at no cost.

It's usually a good idea to consult your government's travel health website (if one is available) before departure:

RECOMMENDED VACCINATIONS

Vaccine	Recommended for	Dosage	Side effects
Chickenpox	Travelers who have never had chickenpox	Two doses one month apart	Fever; mild case of chickenpox
Measles	Travelers born after 1956 who've had only one measles vaccination	One dose	Fever; rash; joint pains; allergic reactions
Tetanus-diphtheria	All travelers who haven't had booster within 10 years	One dose lasts 10 years	Soreness at injection site

ANTARCTIC MEDICINE *Des Lugg*

> The chief work of the surgeon of a polar expedition is done before the ship leaves...if it has been properly carried out there should be little to do during the actual journey...casualties are excepted, for...they cannot be foreseen...ordinary sickness can be largely ruled out by careful examination....

Thus wrote Dr AH Macklin at the conclusion of Shackleton's *Quest* expedition, on which the leader died of a heart attack, a pre-existing condition. Macklin's words are still relevant for anyone journeying to Antarctica, where health care services are limited. All persons, whether they be tourists, scientists or support staff, should be physically fit and free of significant disease. National operators as well as tourist groups and private expeditions have varying standards of medical screening and provision of health care services. All, however, must be self sufficient.

Most wintering expeditions have a rigorous screening program, and some include psychological testing. Despite this, doctors selected for Antarctic service must have the skills to cope with any eventuality. Since it's unrealistic to expect any doctor to have all the specialist skills necessary, predeparture training is organized in environmental and occupational medicine, anesthetics, surgery, laboratory techniques, radiography, dentistry, physiotherapy and medical communications so that specialist advice can be obtained from outside Antarctica. As there has been a high rate of appendicitis in Antarctica, some nations require their doctors to undergo a prophylactic appendectomy. Lay personnel are given basic first aid training, and some are trained in anesthetics and sterile operating theater techniques in order to assist a doctor if necessary.

The lack of all-weather airfields or permanently based aircraft in Antarctica and the inability of all but a few nations to make direct intercontinental flights during most of the year mean that many stations and bases remain largely inaccessible. Most wintering groups are accompanied by one doctor (some national expeditions have two doctors; others have paramedics). This doctor works on the principle that he or she must handle any medical, surgical or dental emergency without the assistance of medical evacuation.

There is no Antarctic-specific disease or ailment. Cold injury, snow blindness and other environmental conditions are always a threat, but serious cases occur infrequently. Trauma resulting from accidents is most common, along with resultant lacerations, broken bones, burns or death.

Nearly 1200 people have died in Antarctica since humans first went to the continent (three-quarters of them in the wreck of *San Telmo* and the Air New Zealand crash on Mt Erebus), but the mortality in this relatively young and fit population is still low compared with more densely populated regions. Antarctica travelers are not spared from such conditions as heart attacks, ulcers, intracranial bleeding, psychiatric ailments, carbon-monoxide poisoning and infectious diseases (malaria, sexually transmitted diseases, amoebiasis, polio) brought from the outside world.

Antarctic doctors must be masters of improvization. In 1961 the physician to the Soviet expedition was forced to operate on himself for acute appendicitis (see the boxed text on p260). He was

Australia (www.dfat.gov.au/travel/)
Canada (www.hc-sc.gc.ca/pphb-dgspsp/tmp-pmv/pub_e.html)
United Kingdom (www.doh.gov.uk/traveladvice/index.htm)
United States (www.cdc.gov/travel/)

FURTHER READING

If you're traveling with children, Lonely Planet's *Travel with Children* may be useful. *Medicine for the Outdoors*, by Paul S Auerbach, and The *ABC of Healthy Travel*, by E Walker et al, are other valuable resources.

IN TRANSIT

DEEP VEIN THROMBOSIS

Blood clots may form in the legs (deep vein thrombosis) during plane flights, chiefly because of prolonged immobility. The longer the flight, the greater the risk. Although most blood clots are reabsorbed uneventfully, some may break off and travel through the blood vessels to the lungs, where they could cause life-threatening complications.

assisted by two coworkers, who held the retractors and a mirror. The operation was successful. In the same year, a ruptured intracranial aneurysm was operated on at an Australian station. The doctor had neither previous neurosurgical experience nor sufficient instruments, but a brain cannula and sucker were improvised based on illustrations from a surgical catalog. A neurosurgeon in Melbourne provided advice via radio telegrams for the operation, which also was successful.

The records of most expeditions highlight ingenuity: dentures have been repaired with parts made from a seal's tooth, and intricate equipment has frequently been repaired and fabricated. One scientist lost both glasses and contact lenses, so new ones had to be ground out of Perspex in the station workshop to conform to a prescription provided by an eye specialist outside Antarctica.

Primitive Antarctic medical offices, however, are now being replaced. Modern facilities contain a consulting room, dental and examination room, operating theater, laboratory, medical ward, storeroom and area for treatment of hypothermia. Equipment includes X-ray machines, electrocardiograph monitors and defibrillators, anesthetic machines, pulse oximeters, electrosurgical units, dry chemistry laboratory analyzers, dental equipment, autoclave and gas sterilization and therapeutic ultrasound. The doctor's work includes all the practical tasks of lab tests, radiology, nursing, cleaning the surgery, sterilizing instruments and even bed-making. A wide range of pharmaceuticals is supplied, and as with the equipment, the selection is continually reviewed and upgraded.

Many doctors also perform research. Particular emphasis has been placed on research in the applied areas such as health and behavioral studies, nutrition, epidemiology, thermal adaptation, hormone adaptation, cardiovascular studies, photobiology (especially ultraviolet radiation) and diving medicine. Research into the capacity of winterers to resist infection has indicated that living for long periods in Antarctic isolation causes reduced immunity.

International cooperation has always been excellent in the Antarctic, especially in dealing with operational problems. Although polar human biology research was carried out on early Antarctic expeditions, it was ad hoc and had little continuity or coordination. The advent of the Scientific Committee on Antarctic Research (SCAR), and coordination by subsidiary groups such as the SCAR Working Group on Human Biology and Medicine, have had a great impact on research and Antarctic health care. The International Biomedical Expedition to the Antarctic 1980–81 (IBEA), the first Antarctic expedition solely for human studies, was organized by the SCAR Working Group.

Collaborative research is now taking place between Antarctic and space agencies. Much of the research has relevance beyond Antarctica. The problems faced by personnel in polar regions, including those related to isolation and living and working in confined environments, are also experienced by space crews. Mutual studies have enormous potential to enhance the performance, health and safety of people in both settings.

Des Lugg, MD, Head of Polar Medicine at the Australian Antarctic Division from 1968–2001, is now Chief of Medicine of Extreme Environments at NASA in Washington, DC

The chief symptom of deep vein thrombosis is swelling or pain of the foot, ankle, or calf, usually but not always on just one side. When a blood clot travels to the lungs, it may cause chest pain and difficulty breathing. Travelers with any of these symptoms should seek medical attention immediately.

To prevent the development of deep vein thrombosis on long flights you should walk about the cabin, contract the leg muscles while sitting, drink plenty of fluids, and avoid alcohol and tobacco.

JET LAG

Jet lag is common when crossing more than five time zones, resulting in insomnia, fatigue, malaise or nausea. To avoid jet lag drink plenty of fluids (nonalcoholic) and eat light meals. Upon arrival, get exposure to natural sunlight and readjust your schedule (for meals, sleep etc) as soon as possible.

SEA SICKNESS

The bane of many a traveler, seasickness (or, in French, the more poetic *mal de mer*) can be one of the prices exacted by King

Neptune for passage through his oft-stormy Southern Ocean. Many explorers also suffered. Wilhelm Filchner wrote in 1922, 'I felt miserable, as I almost invariably do at sea.' In fact, seasickness is simply a natural response to the abnormal motion of the sea. If you've never been seasick, sailors say, you just haven't sailed enough. You may not be seasick en route to The Ice; there's a chance the waters will be calm and you'll be just fine.

Eat lightly during your trip to reduce your chances of seasickness. Try to find a cabin that minimizes motion – close to midship can be slightly more comfortable, as can lower-deck cabins. Fresh air and a view of the horizon usually help. Things that definitely won't help you feel better include reading, cigarette smoke, alcohol and diesel fumes.

Over the years, many bizarre methods have been tried to alleviate seasickness. In fact, no single method works for everyone. There are many commercial motion-sickness remedies, and the ship's doctor will dispense at least one or two types. Antihistamines such as dimenhydrinate (Dramamine) and meclizine (Antivert, Bonine) are often the first choice for treating motion sickness. Their main side-effect is drowsiness.

In recent years, however, the drug of choice among many expedition staff has become promethazine (Phenergan) – also the preferred medication for NASA astronauts trying to combat microgravity motion sickness ('space sickness'). Promethazine causes less drowsiness than motion sickness itself, and it also promotes adaptation to motion.

If you're concerned about seasickness, consider bringing several remedies in case one is ineffective. Each must be taken before heavy seas start the ship rolling. By the time you're feeling sick, it's too late.

A herbal alternative is ginger, which can work like a charm for some people – although not many!

Even if you do get sick, once you get to Antarctica you'll be fine. The protected waters of its bays and channels experience almost no wave action, and pack ice dampens the ocean's motion almost completely.

For humorous – and fascinating – reading on the subject, pick up Charles Mazel's wonderful *Heave Ho! My Little Green Book of Seasickness* (1992), a slim volume packed with historical notes, interesting quotes and loony 'remedies,' as well as some serious advice on dealing with 'the liquid laugh.'

IN ANTARCTICA

AVAILABILITY & COST OF HEALTH CARE

There are no public hospitals, pharmacies, or doctor's offices in Antarctica. Ships and research bases have infirmaries, but with usually just a single doctor or nurse, and limited equipment. A life-threatening medical problem will require evacuation to a country with advanced medical care. Since this may cost tens of thousands of dollars, be sure you have insurance to cover this before you depart. You can find a list of medical evacuation and travel insurance companies on the website of the **US State Department** (www.travel.state.gov).

ENVIRONMENTAL HAZARDS

Cold Exposure

Although shore visits are not conducted in severe weather, and most are not long enough to induce hypothermia, prolonged cold exposure *may* lead to either frostbite or hypothermia.

Frostbite is most likely to occur in the nose, cheeks, chin, fingers, and toes. The first sign is numbness and redness, followed by the development of a waxy, white or yellow plaque. Severe frostbite may lead to blisters, gangrene and loss of the affected body part.

Hypothermia occurs when the body loses heat faster than it can produce it, and the core temperature falls. It is surprisingly easy, even if the air temperature is above freezing, to progress from very cold to dangerously cold due to a combination of wind, wet clothing, fatigue and hunger. It is best to dress in layers; silk, wool and some of the new artificial fibers are all good insulating materials. Keeping dry is critical, so a strong, waterproof outer layer is essential. A hat is very important, as a lot of heat is lost through the head.

Symptoms of hypothermia include exhaustion, numb skin (particularly in the fingers and toes), shivering, slurred speech, irrational or violent behavior, lethargy, stumbling, dizzy spells, muscle cramps and violent bursts of energy. Sufferers who become irrational may claim that they are feeling warm and try to take off their clothes. During periods of prolonged cold exposure, be sure to observe your companions closely for the 'umbles' – stumbles, mumbles, fumbles and grumbles – which are important signs of impending hypothermia.

To treat hypothermia, first get the patient out of the wind and rain, remove any wet clothing and replace it with dry items. Give the person hot liquids – not alcohol – and some high-calorie, easily digestible food. This should be enough to treat the early stages of hypothermia, but if it has gone further, consult the ship's doctor. If it is possible, place the sufferer in a warm (not hot) shower.

Dehydration

The extremely dry Antarctic environment can lead to dehydration, so it is a good idea to drink at least 4L of water a day. Signs of dehydration include dark yellow urine and/or a feeling of fatigue. Coffee and tea are diuretics and as such are counterproductive when trying to combat dehydration.

Eye Hazards

Antarctica's reflected sunlight produces a powerful glare, so sunglasses are essential. Be sure to buy UV-filtering glasses and not just untreated dark lenses, which cause your pupils to dilate while offering no protection from UV rays. Your best bet is glacier glasses, which come equipped with leather flaps to block light coming in from the sides. Snow blindness, an extremely painful – although rare – inflammation that causes headaches and temporary loss of sight, is preventable.

Sun Exposure

In Antarctica, it is very easy to get sunburned quickly, even on overcast days, since the sun reflects off snow, ice and the sea. Use sunscreen with SPF 15 or higher! Calamine lotion is good for mild sunburn.

WOMEN'S HEALTH

There are no special health risks for pregnant women in Antarctica, if normal precautions are observed. But be aware that, should you develop a complication such as premature labor, advanced obstetrical care is not available and you'll probably need to be airlifted home, at great expense and with a degree of risk.

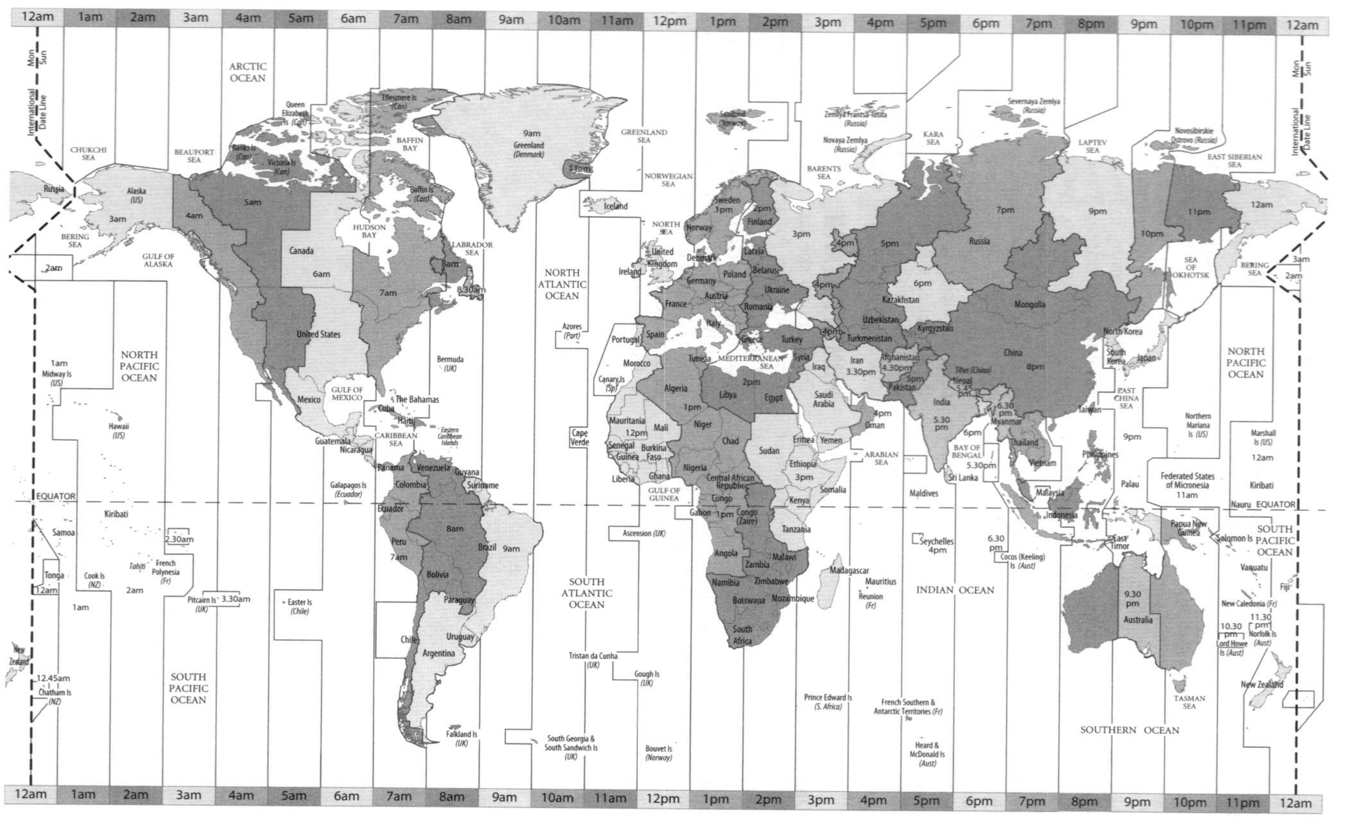
12am 1am 2am 3am 4am 5am 6am 7am 8am 9am 10am 11am 12pm 1pm 2pm 3pm 4pm 5pm 6pm 7pm 8pm 9pm 10pm 11pm 12am
International Date Line
Mon Sun
ARCTIC OCEAN
NORTH PACIFIC OCEAN
SOUTH PACIFIC OCEAN
NORTH ATLANTIC OCEAN
SOUTH ATLANTIC OCEAN
INDIAN OCEAN
SOUTHERN OCEAN
EQUATOR
Alaska (US)
Canada
United States
Mexico
Greenland (Denmark)
Brazil
Argentina
Russia
China
India
Australia
New Zealand

Glossary

Several of these glossary entries are taken from Bernadette Hince's *Antarctic Dictionary* (with permission).

A Factor – the Antarctic Factor; Murphy's Law in Antarctica
ablation – the loss of snow or ice by melting or evaporation
ANARE – Australian National Antarctic Research Expeditions
anchor ice – submerged ice that is attached to the sea bottom
Antarctic Convergence – the region where the colder Antarctic seas meet the warmer waters of the northern oceans; also called the Polar Front
apple – a small, round, red prefabricated hut used in Australian and other government field camps in Antarctica; by adding additional panels to make an apple hut larger, you get 'melons,' 'zucchinis' and 'cucumbers'
ASPA – Antarctic Specially Protected Area

Bag Drag – (American) a designated time before leaving McMurdo station when station members' luggage is put on a pallet and weighed for loading onto departing aircraft
banana belt – warmer part of Antarctica, especially the Antarctic Peninsula
BAS – British Antarctic Survey
beachmaster – large, dominant male seal who guards and breeds with a *harem* on a breeding beach
beaker – (American) slang term for scientist
berg – an iceberg
bergy bit – piece of floating ice rising 1m to 5m out of the water
Big Eye – period of sleeplessness caused most often by the 24-hour daylight of Antarctic summertime, but also by the 24-hour darkness of winter
blizz static – electric charge that builds up because of the dry atmosphere, high winds and blowing snow in a blizzard
blow – a blizzard
boffin – (Australian) slang term for scientist
BOLOW – (Australian) burnt-out left-over winterer
boomerang – (American) to start on a flight to or from Antarctica, only to be forced by inclement weather to return
boondoggle – (American) desirable trip away from station; see also *jolly* and *sleigh ride*
brash ice – the wreckage of larger pieces of ice
bummock – submariner term for a ridgelike ice formation hanging down from beneath pack ice; a *hummock* that is under water
bunk-ride – what many passengers prefer to do in rough seas; to sleep
bunny boots – (American) huge inflatable boots that make their wearer resemble a cartoon character

cairn – pyramid of stones or pieces of ice or cut snow raised as a marker
calve – the breaking off of an iceberg from a glacier or ice shelf
Camp – Falkland Islands term for the countryside; all areas outside of Stanley
CCAMLR – the Convention for the Conservation of Antarctic Marine Living Resources
Chch – (pronounced cheech) Christchurch, gateway to Antarctica for the US, New Zealand and Italian national Antarctic programs
commercial extinction – a condition in which there are so few individuals of a species remaining that it is no longer economically worthwhile to continue catching or hunting them
crack – crevasse
crèche – group of penguin chicks attended by a small group of adults while most of the parents are out at sea hunting for food
crud – flulike illness that strikes the wintering-over crew of an Antarctic station when a new group arrives, caused by the weakening of the winterers' immune systems, which have not been stimulated by any germs for many months

dieso – (Australian) mechanic, usually diesel
DNF – do not freeze; a label for cargo that must not be frozen
dock rock – swaying sensation felt on land after being at sea for a long time
Dome or The Dome – former main building at Amundsen-Scott South Pole Station, a geodesic dome; used in phrases such as 'Dome, Sweet Dome' and 'It's time to go Dome'
Dome slugs – South Pole station members whose jobs do not require them to leave the Dome
donga – (Australian) individual bedroom at an Antarctic station
'doo – (British) skidoo or snowmobile
driftiness – slowed thinking and speech, and an inability to concentrate experienced by some Antarctic station members
DV – (American) distinguished visitor; bureaucratic parlance for politician or bureaucrat visiting *The Ice* through the auspices of a national research program

ECW gear – (American) extreme cold weather gear

fast ice – sea ice attached to the shore or between grounded *bergs*
FID – British Antarctic worker (this term is still in use today, even though the Falkland Islands Dependencies Survey from

which the name derives was replaced by the name British Antarctic Survey in 1962)
firn – see *névé*
flense – to strip of blubber or skin (referring to whales or seals)
FNG – (American) pronounced 'fingie;' stands for (expletive deleted) New Guy; a new member of an Antarctic station
frazil ice – needle-shaped ice crystals forming a slush in the water
freezer suit – windproof insulated jumpsuit
freshies – fresh fruits and vegetables, much-appreciated commodities in Antarctica and rare between resupplies
frost smoke – condensed water vapor that forms a mist over open water in cold weather
Furious Fifties – nickname for the latitudes between 50°S and 60°S, often lashed by gales

gash – (British) rubbish or trash
Geographical South Pole – located at 90°S; the ice at the Pole moves about 10m per year in the direction of 43°W (toward Brazil), which means that the Geographic South Pole marker has to be moved each summer; the 'new' South Pole is recalculated annually
googy – (Australian) fiberglass field hut resembling a spheroid UFO
GPS – global positioning system; a satellite-based system that employs triangulation to determine geographic location to within 10m
grease ice – ice in a later stage of freezing than *frazil ice*; takes its name from the matte appearance it gives to the sea
greenout – shock experienced by Antarctic station members upon returning home and seeing trees and grass
Grid – coordinate system designed to allow navigation at the South Pole, where all 'directions' are north; Grid North is the Prime Meridian, Grid South 180° longitude, and so forth
growler – small (and therefore difficult to see or pick up on radar) piece of ice awash with waves and thus a hazard to shipping
guano – bird excrement; also the remains of whalemeat and bones that were dried and turned into meal after the oil-extraction process

Hägglunds – Swedish-made, tracked vehicle used at many Antarctic stations
ham radio – ham radio telephone patches from Antarctic stations to home
hardwater sailing – slang term for icebreaking
harem – group of female seals jealously guarded on a breeding beach by a *beachmaster*
helo – (American) helicopter (never 'chopper')
herbie – blizzard, especially at McMurdo station
Herc – Hercules C-130 cargo plane, which can be equipped with skis as well as wheels, commonly used for resupplying Antarctic stations
hero picture – (American) photograph taken of oneself standing by the sign marking the Geographic South Pole
Hollywood shower – (American) term of derision for a shower lasting longer than the allotted two minutes at many Antarctic stations; originally a US Navy term
homer – home-brewed beer popular on Australian stations
hoosh – thick hot stew made usually of *pemmican*, crumbled dry *sledging biscuits* and boiled water, eaten on early expeditions
house mouse – the duty, rotated among station members at the US's South Pole and Palmer stations, of cleaning up common areas
hummock – area where ice floes have rafted, or piled atop one another, often reaching heights of several meters

IAATO – International Association of Antarctica Tour Operators, the industry trade association
ice blink – lighter, brighter section on the underside of clouds, caused by light reflected up from ice below; used by early explorers to detect and thus avoid the pack ice
Ice time – amount of Antarctic experience one has; how long one has lived on *The Ice*
ice window – short summer season when the fast ice has broken out, allowing ships to near the Antarctic coast
IGY – International Geophysical Year; it ran from July 1, 1957 to December 31, 1958
INMARSAT – International Maritime Satellite; used to make telephone calls and send faxes aboard ships
IWC – International Whaling Commission; set up in 1946 to regulate the harvesting of whales

jolly – (Australian and British) pleasure or sightseeing trip, often made by helicopter

katabatic – gravity-driven wind caused by colder, heavier air rushing down from the polar plateau
knot – one nautical mile (1.15 statute miles or 1.85km) per hour
Kodachrome poisoning – phenomenon experienced by heavily photographed Antarctic wildlife such as Adélie penguins

LARC – (Lighter Amphibious Resupply Cargo) five-tonne combination boat/truck used by Australia to service ships and bases; the driver is a 'LARCie'
lead – section of open water within pack ice between large floes

manhaul – an archaic term meaning to pull a sledge carrying supplies and food on a South Polar journey, while either skiing or walking
manky – (British) bad or foul (said of weather)
me-pickie – (Australian) photo of oneself
mid-rats – (American) midnight rations, served at McMurdo station for late-shift workers

moon dog – 'false moon,' or paraselena: an optical phenomenon caused by the refraction of moonlight by ice crystals suspended in the air; see also *sun dog*
moraine – rock debris moved and deposited by a glacier; lateral (at the sides), medial (at the center) or terminal (at the foot)

nelly – member of either of the two species of giant petrel
névé – literally, 'last year's snow;' hard granular snow on the upper part of a glacier that hasn't yet turned to ice; also known as *firn*
NGO – nongovernmental organization
nilas – thin crust of floating ice that bends with waves but does not break; the darker its appearance, the thinner the nilas is
NSF – National Science Foundation; the part of the US government in charge of the US Antarctic program
nunatak – mountain or large piece of rock sticking up through an ice sheet

OAE – old Antarctic explorer; used to describe someone who has worked at an Antarctic station
oasis – area of bare rock without ice or snow caused by a retreating or thinning ice sheet and *ablation* of any snow that does fall; examples include the Bunger Hills, Dry Valleys, Larsemann Hills and Vestfold Hills
old ice – sea ice that is more than two years old; up to 3m thick

pancake ice – discs of young ice, formed when waves jostle them against one another, rounding their edges
pax – passengers
pemmican – ground dried meat mixed with lard; this concentrated food was a primary ration on early expeditions
PI – principal investigator; the lead scientist on a project
Pole of Maximum Inaccessibility – located at 84°S, 65°E; the point furthest from any Antarctic coast
polynya – area of open water within the pack ice that remains free of ice throughout the winter
pyramid – double-skinned pyramid-shaped tent used in field work in Antarctica

quad, quike – four-wheeled motorized vehicle

Roaring Forties – nickname for the latitudes between 40°S and 50°S, known for the high winds and heavy seas often experienced there
rotten ice – older ice that has severely weakened prior to melting
RTA – (Australian) return to Australia supplies, materials or specimens

SANAP – South African National Antarctic Programme
sastrugi – furrows or irregularities formed on a snow surface by the wind; they can be more than a meter in height
SCAR – Scientific Committee on Antarctic Research; originally the Special Committee on Antarctic Research
shuga – spongy white ice lumps, formed from *grease ice* or slush
skerry – rocky isle or reef
skijouring – being pulled on skis by one or more dogs in harness; no longer possible in Antarctica since dogs were banned
skua – (American) nickname for frozen chicken, a staple on Antarctic station menus; also to swipe or scavenge – after the skua's propensity to scavenge food from Antarctic stations
sledging biscuits – dry, crackerlike food usually made from wheat
sleigh ride – special day-trip flight from McMurdo to the South Pole, occasionally awarded to a McMurdo resident through a lottery, done on a space-available basis
slot – crevasse
slushy – (Australian) station kitchen hand, a rotating duty
smoko – (Australian and British) tea break
snow blindness – debilitatingly painful inflammation of the eyes, with a resulting (usually temporary) loss of eyesight; caused by the glare of sunlight reflected off ice or snow
snow bridge – crustlike lid that often covers a crevasse; formed when windblown snow builds up on the leeward wall of the crevasse
South Geomagnetic Pole – located at 79°36'S, 108°24'E in 2001; where the flux in the earth's electromagnetic field is manifested
South Magnetic Pole – located at 64°42'S, 138°E in 2001; where a magnetic compass needle will try to point straight down; its position presently moves 10km to 15km a year in a north to northwesterly direction; tourist ships frequently sail over it
souvenir – to remove (steal) artifacts or natural history specimens; the term is usually used to refer to the theft of historic items from an early explorer's hut for a personal collection – an act performed mainly by visitors from nearby scientific stations, as they were the only people who had access to these huts
SPA – Specially Protected Area; outdated term, now called ASPA
SSSI – Site of Special Scientific Interest; outdated term, now called ASPA
sublimate – to pass from the solid state directly to vapor; ice and snow commonly sublimate in dry areas of Antarctica
sun dog – 'false sun,' or more correctly, a parhelion: an optical phenomenon caused by the refraction of sunlight by tiny ice crystals, themselves known as 'diamond dust,' suspended in the air; see also *moon dog*
sun pillar – another solar phenomenon, this one a vertical shaft of light from the rising or setting sun, also caused by ice crystals in the atmosphere

tabular berg – iceberg with vertical sides and a flat top, indicating that it has calved relatively recently
Terres Australes et Antarctiques Françaises (TAAF) – French Southern and Antarctic Lands; France's sub-Antarctic islands and territorial claim in Antarctica, Terre Adélie
The Ice – Antarctica
tide crack – crack separating sea ice from the shore, caused by the rise and fall of the tide; often too wide to cross safely
toasted, toasty – burned out; what many *winterovers* feel before leaving *The Ice*
try-pot or tryworks – cauldron for rendering the blubber of whales, seals or penguins into oil

USAP – US Antarctic Program

ventile – windproof outer clothing

wallow – muddy, noxious-smelling hollow made by seals, especially elephant seals
water sky – dark section on the underside of clouds, indicating open water below; used by early explorers to help penetrate the pack ice
Wellies – calf- or knee-high rubber boots worn by most Antarctic tourists to go ashore
whiteout – condition in which overcast sky descends to the horizon, causing a blurring between ground and sky and eliminating all points of perspective; described by pilots as 'like flying in a bowl of milk'
windscoop – area where high winds have scoured away snow downwind of an obstruction like a building or mountain; these can be more than 100m deep and hundreds of meters long
wind tail – snow deposited downwind of a *windscoop*
Winfly – Winter Fly-In; the first flights following the Antarctic winter darkness, made by the US and New Zealand Antarctic programs in mid-August to bring supplies and new personnel to McMurdo station and Scott base, to help prepare for the summer season, which gets underway in early October
winterovers – station members who remain in Antarctica through the long dark winter; also known as winterers
WYSSA – (Australian) slang for a message sent to or received from home, from code letters used in telex messages meaning 'all my love darling'

Zodiac – inflatable rubber dinghy powered by an outboard engine and used for making shore landings

Behind the Scenes

THIS BOOK

This 3rd edition of *Antarctica* was researched and written by Jeff Rubin, who also wrote the first two editions. John Cooper wrote the Wildlife Guide, Dr Maj De Poorter wrote the Environmental Issues chapter, Colin Monteath wrote the Private Expeditions chapter, Professor David Walton wrote the Antarctic Science chapter, and Dr David Goldberg and Jeff Rubin wrote the Health chapter.

In the Culture chapter, Fauno L Cordes wrote the Literature section and Valmar Kurol wrote the Music section.

As for the boxed texts, Martin Betts wrote 'The Continent in a Day,' Gary Burns & Ray Morris wrote 'Aurora Australis,' Robert Burton wrote 'Grytviken Whaling Station Operations,' Peter Carey wrote 'Small Ship or Large Ship?,' Annie Dillard wrote 'A Visit to Cape Horn,' William R Hammer wrote 'Antarctica During the 'Age of Reptiles',' Ralph P Harvey wrote 'Don't Collect, Please!' and 'They Come from Outta Space,' Robert Headland wrote 'The Earliest Antarctic Landings,' 'Antarctic Museums,' 'Furthest South' and 'Nonexistent Antarctic Islands,' Jo Jacka wrote 'Glaciology' and 'Icebergs,' Andrew Jackson wrote 'The Antarctic Treaty: A Unique Pact for a Unique Place,' Philip Kyle wrote 'Antarctica's Hot Spots,' Phillip G Law wrote 'The Origins of ANARE,' Des Lugg wrote 'Antarctic Medicine,' Mike Masterman wrote 'Life at the South Pole,' Jim Mastro wrote 'Diving in McMurdo Sound,' Don & Margie McIntyre wrote 'Expedition Icebound: A Year at Commonwealth Bay,' Ron Naveen wrote 'Antarctic Site Inventory,' Baden Norris wrote 'A Window on the 'Heroic Era',' Sally Poncet wrote 'Southern Ocean Yachting,' Ricardo Ramos wrote 'The 300 Club,' Collin Roesler wrote 'Colored & Striped Icebergs,' Martin J Siegert wrote 'Lake Vostok & the Subglacial Lakes,' Diana Wall & Andy Parsons wrote 'Lions of the Dry Valleys,' Tony Wheeler wrote 'The Auckland Island Coracle' and William Zinsmeister wrote 'Seymour Island: Antarctica's Rosetta Stone.'

THANKS from the Authors

This book is dedicated to Stephanie, for all she does and is. Without the help of the dozens of experts around the world who contributed their time and knowledge – in the best spirit of the Antarctic Treaty – this book would not be what it is. I am grateful for your assistance and generosity. May all who travel to The Ice appreciate and embrace the international cooperation that operates there, and may that spirit move ever northward.

At Lonely Planet, my thanks go to Erin Corrigan, Hunor Csutoros, Nancy Ianni, Alison Lyall, Wendy Smith, Tony Wheeler and all the many others at LP with whom I did not have direct contact but who helped make this book what it is. Thank you.

CREDITS

Antarctica 3 was commissioned and developed in Lonely Planet's Oakland office by Wendy Smith. Alex Hershey assessed and transmitted. Erin Corrigan helped during the in-between time. Cartography for this guide was developed by Alison Lyall. Coordinating the production of this title were Nancy Ianni (editorial), Hunor Csutoros (cartography), Jim Hsu (layout) and Sally Darmody (color).

Overseeing production were Glenn van der Knijff (project manager), with assistance from Sally Darmody, and Alison Lyall (managing cartographer).

Editorial assistance was provided by Jackie Coyle and Elizabeth Swan.

The index was prepared by Nancy Ianni and the cover was designed by Candice Jacobus.

THANKS from Lonely Planet

Many thanks to the following travelers who used the last edition and wrote to us with helpful hints, useful advice and interesting anecdotes.

B Jacques Belge, Charles Bobbish, Les Bonwell, Dave Burkitt **C** Alain Caradec, Elizabeth Chipman, Max Corry, J Max Creswell, C Cruysberg, **D** Jono David **E** Anne L Erdmann, Susan Erk, Bill Essig **F** Jono Feldman, Kimberly Fisher **G** Daryl Galloway, Chrissen Gemmill, M Gommans, Jerry Gottlick **H** Caroline Hall, Jean M Hayler, Tim Hendley, Mike Hergert, Timo Holkeri, Lina Hornton **J** John Jacobsen **K** Clare Kines, Sandy & Donald Komito, Patrick & Mardelle Kopnicky, Kou Kusunoki **L** Terry Last, HC Lee, Stephen Leong, Gillian M Lindsay, Tommy

& Katie Lorden **M** Bill McAuliffe, JoAnn Moon, David Morton, R J Muirhead **P** Caron Patterson, Stephen Pendleton, Trevor Potts, Ton F J Pronker **R** Andy Redman, F Scott Robert, Karen Rowland, Catherine Rutter **S** Jean Maurice Silagy, Scott F Smith, Tanya Smith, Arne Sorensen, Suzanne Southon, Mary Stripling **T** John R Taylor, Roland Thanner, Stephen G Tirner **W** Anthea Wallhead, Ani Wallis, Michael Ward, Kurth Werner, Katherine Winter **Y** Megan Young **Z** Reidunn Wiencke Zimmer

ACKNOWLEDGMENTS

Many thanks to the following for the use of their content:

Globe on back cover © Mountain High Maps 1993 Digital Wisdom, Inc.; McMurdo Station map (Ross Sea chapter) courtesy of the US National Science Foundation; Amundsen-Scott South Pole Station map (South Pole chapter) courtesy of the US National Science Foundation Office of Polar Programs; Under-Ice Lakes map (Environment chapter) courtesy of Martin J Siegert.

Index

000 Map pages
000 Location of colour photographs

000 Map pages
000 Location of colour photographs

INDEX

THE LONELY PLANET STORY

The story begins with a classic travel adventure: Tony and Maureen Wheeler's 1972 journey across Europe and Asia to Australia. There was no useful information about the overland trail then, so Tony and Maureen published the first Lonely Planet guidebook to meet a growing need.

From a kitchen table, Lonely Planet has grown to become the largest independent travel publisher in the world, with offices in Melbourne (Australia), Oakland (USA), and London (UK).

Today Lonely Planet guidebooks cover the globe. There is an ever-growing list of books and information in a variety of media. Some things haven't changed. The main aim is still to make it possible for adventurous travelers to get out there – to explore and better understand the world. At Lonely Planet we believe travelers can make a positive contribution to the countries they visit – if they respect their host communities and spend their money wisely. Every year 5% of company profit is donated to charities around the world.

SEND US YOUR FEEDBACK

We love to hear from travelers – your comments keep us on our toes and help make our books better. Our well-traveled team reads every word on what you loved or loathed about this book. Although we cannot reply individually to postal submissions, we always guarantee that your feedback goes straight to the appropriate authors, in time for the next edition. Each person who sends us information is thanked in the next edition – and the most useful submissions are rewarded with a free book. See the Behind the Scenes section.

To send us your updates – and find out about Lonely Planet events, newsletters and travel news – visit our award-winning website: **www.lonelyplanet.com/feedback**.

Note: We may edit, reproduce and incorporate your comments in Lonely Planet products such as guidebooks, websites and digital products, so let us know if you don't want your comments reproduced or your name acknowledged. For a copy of our privacy policy, go to www.lonelyplanet.com/privacy.

Published by Lonely Planet Publications Pty Ltd
ABN 36 005 607 983

Cover photographs by Lonely Planet Images: emperor penguins, David Tipling (front); crevasse exploration, near Mt Erebus, Scott Darsney (back). Many of the images in this guide are available for licensing from Lonely Planet Images: www.lonelyplanetimages.com.

Printed by Craft Print International Ltd, Singapore

LONELY PLANET OFFICES

Australia
Head Office
Locked Bag 1, Footscray, Victoria 3011
☎ 03 8379 8000, fax 03 8379 8111
talk2us@lonelyplanet.com.au

USA
150 Linden St, Oakland, CA 94607
☎ 510 893 8555, toll free 800 275 8555
fax 510 893 8572, info@lonelyplanet.com

UK
72–82 Rosebery Ave,
Clerkenwell, London EC1R 4RW
☎ 020 7841 9000, fax 020 7841 9001
go@lonelyplanet.co.uk